Development Across Adulthood

Development Across Adulthood: Multicultural Perspectives on Adult Development and Aging provides a novel and comprehensive understanding of development across adulthood.

Presenting adult development and aging in a way that applies to student's lives, the book prepares them for their role as critical consumers and decision-makers as well as culturally competent individuals inspired to pursue related careers. With an emphasis on aging and the end of the lifespan, as well as middle adulthood, the book provides a more balanced presentation of the life changes that occur from emerging adulthood to the end of life. Through an engaging presentation of ideas, scholarship, and pedagogical features that promote active and self-regulated learning and development, the book presents the most exciting theoretical and scientific discoveries of today and incorporates recent and current global issues to help readers understand the impact of these events on the development of adults from different cultures.

Focusing on diversity in developmental outcomes including age, culture, ethnicity, and gender and sexual identity, and the increasingly interconnected global world and its influences on longevity, health, and quality of life, this textbook is core reading for undergraduate students studying adult development and aging courses, as well as other allied health disciplines.

Leslie D. Frazier is an Associate Professor of Psychology in the Department of Psychology at Florida International University, USA.

Kim Shifren is a Full Professor of Psychology in the Department of Psychology at Towson University, USA.

Development Across Adulthood

Multicultural Perspectives on Adult Development and Aging

Leslie D. Frazier and Kim Shifren

Routledge
Taylor & Francis Group
NEW YORK AND LONDON

Designed cover image: Getty Images

First published 2026
by Routledge
605 Third Avenue, New York, NY 10158

and by Routledge
4 Park Square, Milton Park, Abingdon, Oxon, OX14 4RN

Routledge is an imprint of the Taylor & Francis Group,
an informa business

ISBN: 978-1-032-77572-2 (hbk)
ISBN: 978-1-032-77482-4 (pbk)
ISBN: 978-1-003-48380-9 (ebk)

DOI: 10.4324/9781003483809

Typeset in Optima
by KnowledgeWorks Global Ltd.

Access the Support Material: www.routledge.com/9781032774824

To my grandmother (Shirley), whose experience with Alzheimer's Disease inspired my interest in understanding the challenges of growing old.

Leslie D. Frazier

To my dad, Harvey, who just turned 90, despite many life obstacles, and continues to be an inspiration to me in how to live my life.

In memory of my mother, Norma, whose courage fighting her own heart disease, from age 42 until her death at age 79, showed me that we can overcome exceedingly difficult and life-threatening health issues.

Kim Shifren

Contents

About the Authors

Dr. Leslie D. Frazier is an Associate Professor of Psychology in the Department of Psychology at Florida International University. She has a PhD in Lifespan Developmental Psychology from Syracuse University and held a National Institutes of Health/National Institute on Aging (NIH/NIA) Postdoctoral Fellowship at the University of California San Francisco Medical School.

A developmental psychologist, Dr. Frazier is interested in the intersections among psychosocial factors and identity/sense of self within the contexts of health and chronic illness in emerging adulthood and later life. Dr. Frazier's research program focuses on stress and coping during life transitions to maximize mental and physical health outcomes. Of specific interest is understanding the processes associated with adjustment to living with chronic illness that lead to developing resilience and successful aging. More recently, Dr. Frazier has studied how middle-age and the menopausal transition may be a developmental window of vulnerability that puts women at higher risk for eating disorders. She has also examined the psychosocial and cognitive factors that influence identity and sense of self in individuals with disability. Dr. Frazier is a person with disability.

Dr. Frazier has served as director of graduate studies and as the Faculty Fellow in the Office to Advance Women, Equity and Diversity. She has authored more than 37 articles and book chapters, and her research has appeared in *Psychology and Aging, Journal of Gerontology: Psychological Sciences, The Gerontologist, Experimental Aging Research, Research on Aging, International Journal of Aging and Human Development, Basic and Applied Social Psychology, Eating and Weight Disorders, Journal of Behavioral Health, Eating Behaviors, Journal of Eating Disorders, Menopause*, and *Journal of Applied Social Psychology*. Dr. Frazier was the recipient of a grant from the NIA/NIH and two foundation grants from the Mental Research Institute. Her professional memberships include the American Psychological Association's Division of Adult Development and Aging and the Division of Health Psychology, the Southern Society for Philosophy and Psychology, and the Association for Psychological Science. Dr. Frazier has written two editions of a textbook titled *Health Psychology* published by Macmillan Publishing and a textbook titled *The Psychology of Health and Illness: A Multicultural Perspective* published by Routledge/Taylor & Francis.

When she is not engaged in scholarship, Dr. Frazier spends her time at the pottery studio, doing yoga, reading crime fiction, and in nature. She loves to travel, to scuba dive, and to be with family and friends. Writing this book has brought her back to her roots as a gerontologist and has taught her many new and important things that will help her age successfully.

Dr. Kim Shifren is a Full Professor of Psychology in the Department of Psychology at Towson University. She has a Ph.D. in Lifespan Developmental Psychology from Syracuse University and held a Postdoctoral Fellowship at the University of Michigan Institute of Gerontology and Institute for Social Research.

As a lifespan developmental psychologist, Dr. Shifren is interested in personality characteristics, health-related behaviors, social support, and coping in relation to mental and physical health in individuals from emerging adulthood through later adulthood. Dr. Shifren's research program focuses on individuals living with a chronic illness as they age, and the effects of very early caregiving (under age 18) on adult development and aging.

Dr. Shifren has authored more than 36 articles and book chapters, co-authored a book titled *Medical Information Processing in Aging Patients: Cognitive and Human Factors Perspectives* published by Erlbaum, and was the editor of a book titled *How Caregiving Affects Development: Psychological Implications for Child, Adolescent, and Adult Caregivers* published by the American Psychological Association. Dr. Shifren's research has appeared in *Psychology of Aging, Journal of Gerontology: Psychological Sciences, The Gerontologist, Experimental Aging Research, International Journal of Aging and Human Development, Journal of Adult Development, Psychology, Health and Medicine, Journal of Behavioral Medicine, International Journal of Behavioral Development, Health Care for Women International, Personality and Individual Differences, and Multivariate Behavioral Research*. Dr. Shifren's professional memberships include the American Psychological Association's Division of Adult Development and Aging, the Gerontological Society of America, and the Association for Psychological Science.

When she is not engaged in teaching and scholarship, Dr. Shifren enjoys time with her family, and her hobbies include painting, reading, baking, and travel. Working on this book has helped to strengthen Dr. Shifren's knowledge of multicultural experiences in adult development and aging processes, knowledge beneficial for teaching, scholarship, and life in general.

Preface

We first became interested in adult development and aging specifically when we entered the Lifespan Developmental Psychology doctoral program at Syracuse University. Our passion and commitment to understanding age-related changes and successful aging were a product of the excellent mentorship and learning we received there. We worked hard, enjoyed the challenges of research on aging, and upon completing our dissertations went on to begin our careers. Dr. Frazier began her career as a postdoctoral developmental scientist at University of California, San Francisco, and Dr. Shifren began her career as a visiting assistant professor at the University of Florida, before completing a postdoctoral fellowship. Eventually, we both became tenured professors whose scholarship continued to grow and change but which always focused on finding ways to improve the lives of adults across the lifespan.

Teaching adult development and aging courses at the undergraduate and graduate levels has been inspiring and motivating. We are all aging, and there may be no other psychology course that touches on the lives of so many, including every one of our students. Grounded in the theoretical world view of developmental systems theory, we know first-hand, and we encourage our students to also experience, how they are both the producers and the products of their own unique developmental strivings. It does not matter what age you are, you are facing developmental milestones, and having a solid foundation in developmental science and especially adult development is invaluable for navigating life's challenges, and ultimately, having a life well lived.

Worldwide people are living longer than they ever have before and because of this we are witnessing an acceleration in the pace of population aging. Globally, by 2050, the number of people over age 60 will double from 12% to 22% (WHO, 2023a). Already by 2020 there were more people over age 60 who outnumbered children under five years old. By 2050 the global number of people over age 80 will triple to reach 426 million. These changes differentially influence how people grow and change in later life and understanding the factors that promote quality of life is important for all of us individually and collectively.

Adult development is not just about growing older though. Recent advances from a life course perspective coupled with new data from large-scale multicultural longitudinal studies have identified novel conceptions of different phases of the adult lifespan (i.e., emerging and established adulthood) that shed new light on the biopsychosocial, sociocultural, and diversity of factors that may shape growth and change during adulthood. Twenty-first century advances in developmental psychology, neuropsychology, biology, social genomics, health psychology, public policy, social justice, and medicine have extended the human lifespan and impacted both the lived experience and the social perceptions of growing older. Understanding these changes is critical to promoting evidence-based learning and inspiring people to pursue careers that engage with and promote successful development in adulthood.

Despite greater longevity, health disparities are increasing globally. Awareness of the social determinants and cultural differences that may impact developmental and health outcomes worldwide are critical. Intersecting with adult development are the many public health threats facing the world today, including rising rates of infectious diseases, obesity, substance use and addiction, dementia, and the numbers of people living with disability. Additionally, myriad factors have influenced the shrinking pool of health care professionals, educators, and service providers who are trained in gerontology and understand the challenges faced in adulthood and aging. Therefore, there has never been a more important need to understand the biopsychosocial and sociocultural factors that influence development across the adult years. This textbook provides a contemporary strengths-based and diversity-affirming approach with integrated content that flexibly maps onto varied student career interests, learning styles, different learning platforms, and an array of learning activities to match instructors' pedagogical goals.

The COVID-19 pandemic led to burnout and workforce shortages in health care professions as well as many other professional careers. A goal for higher education should be to excite and encourage students to gravitate toward careers in the health, service, education, technology, and helping professions where they will interact and provide valuable services for adults of all ages. Understanding developmental theory, scientific research, and the evidence-based applications of scholarship to everyday life will help them to be informed about issues of aging in these professional contexts, as well as their own lives and the lives of their loved ones. *Development Across Adulthood: Multicultural Perspectives on Adult Development and Aging* provides a foundation in contemporary developmental science to help students understand how people grow and change within and across mutually influential, reciprocal, and synergistic contexts. In contrast to extant textbooks, the blending of developmental science with a biopsychosocial approach and a focus on global multicultural diversity to study growth and change across adulthood is unique and relevant to multiple levels of the ecology of human development, from the cellular to the global (Baltes, et al., 1977; Bronfenbrenner & Morris, 2006; Lerner, 2012; Greenberg & Tobach, 2014).

About This Text

Development Across Adulthood: Multicultural Perspectives on Adult Development and Aging is a primary textbook for undergraduate courses. It integrates developmental theories, biopsychosocial, and sociocultural perspectives and covers innovative scientific and real-world adult development topics in ways that students can understand. It goes beyond other mainstream textbooks in significant ways, building on traditional topics to aid student understanding, interest, and learning.

First, we take a developmental approach. Regarding adult development and aging, we believe that there is a dynamic and reciprocal relationship between the individual and the contexts in which they live throughout the lifespan. They shape their environments and are in turn shaped by them. This reciprocity applies to all aspects of their lives from intimate partners, families, neighborhoods, and communities to the larger sociopolitical environments in which they live. Both of us have focused on advancing understanding of development across adulthood that can be applied to help adults live richer, fuller, healthier, and more satisfying lives. For example, both of us have studied how older adults cope with age-related transitions, including being diagnosed with a chronic illness or becoming a caregiver for a chronically ill loved one. These topics have special relevance to students, too, no matter where they are in the lifespan. Many students often enter this course with a layperson's knowledge of how development unfolds across adulthood. Particularly with aging, many students may have **misconceptions and biases about aging**. Stereotypes often cast elderly people as frail and doddering and aging as a time of losses. However, what we now know is that there is vitality and room for growth across adulthood, and old people have higher quality of life, more positive emotions, and more life satisfaction than younger adults, despite having chronic health problems.

Students may tend to approach a course in adult development and aging with preconceived notions that are not always grounded in science. Anyone teaching this course knows well the importance of providing strong, credible scientific evidence to help them put those assumptions aside. As professors and now as textbook authors, our most important goal is to emphasize that the psychology of adulthood is a science and that its theories are grounded in science. It is our hope that we have conveyed how a foundation in science helps us understand and make more informed decisions throughout our development as adults.

Second, we also emphasize that adult development and aging are directly relevant to each student's personal experience. Many students may have little background in biology, physiology, or indeed developmental science. The biological and neurological aspects of aging may be challenging for them. Our goal in writing this textbook is to convey this material in ways that are understandable, relatable, and relevant to students' personal lives.

Students need to understand theory and research methods, but they thrive on practical examples and applications. *Development Across Adulthood* illustrates core theories with relevant and timely examples from a variety of perspectives and cultures. These examples will help put students' experiences into a larger global developmental psychological context. We also involve the students directly in these issues through engaging and thought-provoking questions.

Third, we provide a global and multicultural perspective. Many students approach learning developmental psychology with a nationalistic and ethnocentric view. An important goal for this textbook is to introduce global and sociocultural perspectives. It is our job to get students interested and to provide them with a fuller perspective, including how adulthood and later life are experience for people from different social demographics. Many aspects of development are common or universal while for others there are disparities across gender, race/ethnicity, socioeconomic status, and different minoritized identities within the United States and around the world.

Pedagogical Approach

The goal of *Development Across Adulthood: Multicultural Perspectives on Adult Development and Aging* is to capture students' interest and to provide them with a background in scientific principles in the field of adult development psychology. Our aim is to integrate a developmental perspective with sociocultural and biopsychosocial and global perspectives. The textbook is an informative, readable, student-friendly learning aid.

Development Across Adulthood was written with student learning in mind. Topics are presented in an intriguing and engaging way to encourage student interest. Several pedagogical techniques that have been shown empirically to improve learning and understanding are used to that end.

The emphasis of this textbook makes adult development clearly relevant to a student's lived experience. This includes its integration of global, cross-cultural, socioeconomic, multiethnic, and gender and sexual identity issues. Together, they provide the broadest possible context for understanding adult development and aging, using the most current theory, research findings, and applications. We hope to inspire students to think critically and to become involved in developmental science.

Pedagogical Tools

Specific pedagogical tools will help students as well. Their aim is to underscore the text's unique emphases, to engage the student, to promote critical thinking, and to aid in learning.

Within each chapter, thought-provoking issues drawn from developmental science highlight our current understanding of adult development and aging. Chapters open with learning objectives and where appropriate we present personal profiles or vignettes to illustrate concepts in real life.

Learning Outcomes: appear at the beginning of each chapter to help guide students in their learning.
Chapter Summaries: allow students to assess their understanding of the chapter. This feature will reinforce the major points, help students review the content, and allow them to develop a bigger picture.

Key Terms: key terms are boldfaced in the body of the text and listed at the end of each chapter.

Infographics and Other Artwork: we use figures and tables as necessary to illustrate the results of studies and available data or to help students organize material or compare and contrast topics. Of particular value are the frequent infographics. We also include photographs and, where appropriate, cartoons to help illustrate certain important points.

Acknowledgments

This book is an outgrowth of our passion for adult development and our careers as developmental scientists. So much has changed in our understanding of how we age since we were graduate students. Our experiences researching and teaching in the field have also evolved over time and we are excited to share with our students the important things that we learned as we compiled this book.

The final product would not have been possible without the support of many people.

First and foremost, we thank Molly Selby, our Executive Editor, for her encouragement and support for us as authors and for the book as a concept through its completion. We also are grateful to have worked with Shivranjani Singh. The team at Routledge/Taylor & Francis have been terrific.

The many reviewers who shared their insights and knowledge of the field have also helped to shape this book, and it is better because of them. Thanks to the following reviewers:

Leslie D. Frazier: my deepest thanks and gratitude go to my husband, Dr. Bennett Schwartz, and my daughter, Sarina Schwartz, for their love and encouragement throughout the process, and especially when I most needed it. I would also like to thank Georgianna Brown for her meticulous organizational skills and for all her help and feedback on my chapters. I could not have completed this work without her help.

Kim Shifren: my love and thanks go to my husband, Dr. Robert Bauserman, and our children, Alexander and Kayla Bauserman, for their patience, understanding and support while I looked up all of the research and spent many hours preparing the chapters for this book. I appreciate all of the encouragement and support from my family.

1 Framing the Issues of Development Across Adulthood

Learning Outcomes

Describe the distinct periods of development within adulthood (i.e., emerging adult, established adult periods of development).
Explain the different ways we define age (i.e., chronological age, biological age).
Articulate Baltes' principles of lifespan development.
Describe the unique contributions of the biopsychosocial model of development.
Identify the critical features of Bronfenbrenner's ecological systems theory.

Do you want to see your future self?

Many people do, but then they do not like what they see!

In the summer of 2023, there was an interesting viral trend taking over Tik Tok – the aging filter! It was all the rage. You upload a photo of yourself and click the filter and see what you look like as you grow old.

The Tik Tok "aging" filter is generated by artificial intelligence (AI) and designed to give users a realistic and accurate idea of what they will look like as they age. Basically, the AI modifies the image to create the common visible signs of aging (e.g., fine lines, wrinkles, dark spots, loss of firmness, gray hair). Dermatologists report that the representations created by the filter are quite accurate. Over 20 million videos were created with the filter and it led to a lot of public discourse on aging. For some, it was shocking and devastating, for others, humorous. But the interest in it and the response to it clearly draws attention to our anxieties about growing older. It tapped a vein, one that the multibillion-dollar anti-aging industry will no doubt capitalize on.

Interestingly the data on who used the filter shows that it was most widely used by Gen Z, young people (people born between 1996 and 2010), who have grown up in the digital age. Many articles in the popular press summarize people's responses to using the filter. While for many it activated their fears about growing older and capitalized on vulnerabilities to ageist attitudes

DOI: 10.4324/9781003483809-1

and cultural ideals of youth equaling beauty, for others it was motivating and helped them commit to making lifestyle changes to protect their health and age with a more positive attitude. As polarizing as it was, the Tik Tok "aging" filter capitalized on the psychological drive to want to peer into the future. Who are our future selves? What will we look like? What will our lives be like?

Overview of Development Across Adulthood

In this textbook we will take a deep dive into human **development** from **emerging adulthood** through the end of life. Development is the process through which a human being evolves over time, including the progressive changes in their physical, cognitive, neurological, emotional, and social functioning; it encompasses growth and change from conception to death. **Developmental psychology** is the field that studies how people grow, change, and adapt across the lifespan. Specifically, developmental psychologists study the physical, neurological, cognitive, emotional, personality, and social processes and how they are influenced by the passage of time. For decades research on human development was focused on childhood and adolescence, with little interest in what happens once someone enters "adulthood." Then, in part because of the realization of the potentially overwhelming impact of the wave of Baby Boomers (a generation that was born between 1946 and 1964), concern created interest in understanding age-related changes in the last phase of life: old age. But development is a dynamic and lifelong process. Therefore, in this textbook we will be learning about what growth and change occurs as one transitions into adulthood and throughout the adult lifespan from a developmental perspective. Keep in mind that aging is a process that occurs from conception through death. Everyone is aging all the time. Aging also refers to the period of the lifespan that happens in later life. So the term aging is both a process and a life stage.

The Demographics of Adulthood

People around the world are living longer than ever before. Globally, the life expectancy at birth for a child born in 2023 is 73.16 years, compared with just 47.3 years in 1900 (National Center for Health Statistics, 2014). Historically, people in 1900 did not live through middle age. Many women died in childbirth, and diseases like the Black Death and influenza caused many untimely deaths. According to the World Population Review (2023) Monaco, one of the smallest countries in the world, has the highest life expectancy. People born there today have an expected lifespan of 85.17 years if they are male and 88.99 years if they are female.

All over the globe people are living longer and that means they are spending more time living as adults. The demographic shifts happening worldwide highlight the importance of gaining a deeper understanding of the biological, psychological, social, and cultural factors that influence adult development and aging.

What is Adulthood, Anyway?

The Developmental Period of Adulthood

Historically, in the United States the age of 18 has been identified as the age of adulthood. The legal definition of an adult is a person who is fully grown and developed. Age 18 is legally the age of "consent," when individuals are assumed to have the ability to distinguish between right and wrong and therefore to be held legally responsible for their actions as an adult. It is also the age at which a person is considered old enough to vote and to fulfil their civic duties such as serving on juries when called upon to do so. Once a person turns 18 they no longer need parental permission to do many things. So, age 18 has traditionally been the marker of the transition into adulthood. There are cultural variations in who is considered an adult – in many cultures the late teens and early 20s are considered the demarcation of being an adult.

With demographic shifts, such as increased longevity and a rise in the age at which people get married and have children, the nature of development and the timing of developmental benchmarks has changed (Arnett, 2000). While there are many 18-year-olds who are extraordinarily mature and independent, in the United States most 18-year-olds are just beginning college and are therefore afforded the luxury of a hiatus before taking on many of the responsibilities of adulthood. Most 18-year-olds, especially if they are in education, are also not yet financially independent, they have not solidified their career plans, and they are not yet ready to settle down and start a family, which are considered some of the developmental benchmarks of adulthood. In fact, the late teens and early 20s are a kind of transitional period that has come to be known as emerging adulthood. Emerging adulthood is the developmental period between age 18 and 25 (Arnett, 2000), recently extended to 29 (Arnett, 2015; Lowe & Arnett, 2020). According to Arnett, the developmental scientist who coined the term, emerging adulthood exists in cultures that provide a period of role exploration during the late teens and 20s. Emerging adults are moving from the dependency on parents that is characteristic of childhood and the teenage years to the normative responsibilities of adulthood. This is a time of self-exploration in "love, work, and worldviews" (Arnett, 2000, p. 46). Arnett has conducted extensive research to support his theory. As you can see from the figure below, when he asked people in their late teens to late 20s, most did not feel that they had reached "adulthood." Participants in Arnett's research studies said that they would feel like they had reached adulthood when they were able to accept responsibility for themselves, when they were making decisions independently, and when they had become financially independent (Arnett, 1997, 1998, 2000).

Figure 1.1 Young adults.

Emerging adulthood is a relatively new way of thinking about when one becomes an adult, in the eyes of the individual, society, and developmental psychologists.

As more developmental research is carried out, we learn more about the period of life previously known as adulthood. Mehta and her colleagues (2020) have also developed a new conception of what was previously known as "young adulthood." They call this **established adulthood** and it comprises the ages of 30 to 45. Arnett (2015) discovered from his research that many adults in this age range are not still exploring their identities, and they have not yet entered the developmental challenges of midlife. Specifically, established adults are focused on forming and maintaining long-term committed relationships, advancing in their professional careers, and for some who become parents during this time, raising young children. The stressors and concerns of this period are different from those in emerging adulthood and also from those of middle age. This period has been called the "rush hour of life" (Knecht & Freund, 2016; Mehta et al., 2020).

Individuals in **middle adulthood** (i.e., those aged 45 to 64 years old) have more financial stability than those in emerging adulthood and established adulthood, but they are dealing with a balancing act between work, raising their children, and taking on caregiver roles for parents or other adult relatives, which can be extremely stressful (Fingerman et al., 2016; National Alliance for Caregiving & AARP, 2020). **Older adults** (aged 65 or older) may

Figure 1.2 People enjoying the later years.

not be performing the balancing act of those in middle adulthood, but are increasingly likely to have one or more chronic illnesses as they age (Tavares et al., 2023). Older adults may need to find new purpose outside of the workforce upon retirement, and may end up in caregiver roles for spouses or grandchildren late in life (Shifren, 2009). As people live longer, the nature of the later years changes. The key to understanding aging is to consider the aging individual within the biopsychosocial contexts that they exist within. Despite the negative stereotypes of older people, this period of the lifespan is marked by tremendous variability.

We will explore each of these developmental periods in greater detail in the coming chapters. For now, we present them to introduce the overarching developmental periods that fall within adulthood. Just as there has been conceptual ambiguity over these developmental periods, there are also different conceptions of age that are important to think about.

Concepts of Age and Cultural Differences in the Concept of Age

Just like the concept of development itself, the concept of age is complex. If you think about your age, the first thing you may think of is how old you are. That is, how many years you have been alive. This is your **chronological age**. Your chronological age is the bit of data everyone wants to know; when you apply for a job, when they "card" you at a liquor store, when you fill out the census report. It dictates when you can enter a bar (21 in most states in the U.S.), when you can collect social security (62 in the United States), and when you can have your second bar mitzvah if you are a Jewish man. In many societies, chronological age is tied to important benchmarks as we discussed above.

There are some people though who do not "feel" their age, meaning they have a perception of what 50 should feel like and they feel either younger or older than that perception. When someone has a lot of aches and pains that make them feel older than their chronological age, it may be because their **biological age** is older. Biological age is the age of the physiological systems of your body. It is also sometimes called physiological age. We age on a cellular level and if you have had disease or injuries your body can age faster than is typical for a person who has lived the number of years that you have. Our genes interact with our environment to influence the aging of the cells in the body. There are a few tests and assessments that look at biomarkers (such as genes and organ functioning) to determine biological age. Biomarkers of age can provide information about morbidity and mortality risk, and years left to live, so they can have important clinical and research implications (Lohman et al., 2021).

Related to biological age is **functional age**, which is a measure of how well a person is able to perform the basic activities of daily living in order to live independently. Functional age is particularly relevant for older adults and adults with some kinds of disability. Functional age is assessed based upon how able someone is to carry out personal hygiene, meal preparation, medication management, housekeeping. It can be influenced by both physical and cognitive changes. By now you may be thinking how closely connected aging and health are, especially from midlife and beyond. It is important to think about development in adulthood in terms of the lifespan, that is the arc from birth through death, but it is also important to think about the healthspan, which is also an arc from birth through death but integrates the concepts of growing older and the age-related health changes that happen at different points along the lifespan (Lohman et al., 2021).

Another way of assessing age is to consider **social age**. As we go through life we are assuming and shedding and changing our roles. Think of the transition from college graduate, to manager, to CEO; or the transition from daughter, to wife, to mother, to grandmother. Each role has social, cultural, and age-normative expectations. Social age represents the age-normative expectations of society or culture. When people engage in behaviors that are considered nonnormative or inappropriate for "someone their age" they are not "acting" their social age. You can probably see the problematic aspect of social age and how it relates to age-related stereotypes. Finally, there is psychological age. If you are asked "how old do you feel," you will respond with your psychological age. Psychological age is our self-perception of how old we feel based on our thoughts, emotions, and behaviors. It is by nature subjective and takes into account many things that we know about ourselves that we think influence how old we feel.

Growing older, aging, and the later years of life are viewed differently in different cultures. In our appearance and youth driven culture, many women who have passed menopause and show physical signs of aging report feeling "invisible" (Frazier & Bazo Perez, 2024; Frazier & Saunders, 2025). In one mixed methods study of middle-aged women, participants were asked their thoughts and feelings and goals for the future. Their transcripts were rich with descriptive details of the experience of being a woman of this age. Many, though, also mentioned noticing that now when they walk into a room, no one notices. Or for one woman, how annoying it was for her when a young person stepped in to help her with free weights at the gym. "Couldn't he see I had already done 25 curls on 30lbs? Did I look like I needed help?" This study focused on how people's perceptions of aging might influence their quality of life and as you can imagine those who perceive aging in a negative way had lower quality of life (Frazier & Saunders, 2025). These experiences fit with the belief that in the United States, as in other Western cultures, aging is a negative thing and ageist views are common. Whereas in other cultures, especially Eastern cultures, there are more accepting views of aging and older adults. In fact, in cultures with Confucian values, there is great respect for elders, positive views of aging, and an intergenerational transmission of values that flow from older to younger people (Nelson, 2005). Recent research seems to show a trend of increased ageism indicating that views may be changing or are more nuanced than previously thought (Vauclair et al., 2017).

Overarching World Views

In psychological science we are guided by the world views or metatheories that we hold about human nature and human behavior. **Metatheories** are coherent sets of principles or a story or narrative that describes and directs what we believe and how we approach understanding it. A metatheory transcends and influences the specific theories we might examine and the methods we use to examine them. Our study of development is guided by the assumptions and beliefs we have about the nature of human growth and development.

An example of an outdated metatheory is the belief that when people are born they come into the world as a "blank slate" or "tabula rasa." We now know this is not true because we have decades of empirical evidence showing that people are born with a temperament (the biological/physiological disposition to respond to environmental stimuli in a unique and specific way) that may influence their behavior throughout their lifespan.

As developmental scientists we believe that development is a lifelong process and that while some aspects of an individual may be present at birth and continuous throughout their life, there are always opportunities to learn new skills, to abandon approaches that do not lead to adaptive outcomes, and to find meaning in the way they interact with the world and live their lives.

Just think about your hoped-for future selves. What do you want to become in the future? Why is this important to you? What are you doing now to achieve this goal in the future? Through self-reflection and thinking about how the decisions you make in the moment and the behaviors you engage in today will help you or hinder you from reaching your desired self, you are shaping your own development!

Let us take a close look at the metatheory guiding our exploration of adulthood and aging.

The Life-span Developmental Perspective

The life-span developmental perspective, which was developed by Paul Baltes and his colleagues (Baltes et al., 1977; Baltes, 1987), explores the continuity and change in biological, cognitive, and psychosocial processes across the lifespan. It is a theoretical approach that holds several fundamental tenets and shapes how we think about and study human development. As a theoretical perspective, Baltes (1987) believed that there are seven key ideas that are critical for appreciating development. First, development is a continuous process encompassing the entire lifespan, from conception through death. Second, development is multidirectional and multidimensional, meaning that not every individual develops the same way because each has their own unique biological, psychological, and sociocultural characteristics that shape their developmental trajectory. The third key idea is that development encompasses both growth and decline. That is, we gain and lose skills and abilities throughout our lives, and both the gains and losses constitute developmental change. Fourth, there is plasticity in development. The idea of plasticity originally related to how our early life experiences may shape our adult traits. Plasticity can be thought of as our capacity for change (Wettstein & Wahl, 2017). Baltes and his colleagues were forward-thinking for their time; the fifth key idea is the role of **sociocultural factors** on development. Sociocultural factors come from the ethnic, gender, religious, socioeconomic, educational, and other contexts that shape the thoughts, feelings, values, beliefs, behaviors, attitudes, and interactions that people have with those around them. Sixth are the interactions among what Baltes and others have called age-graded, history-graded, and nonnormative historical influences that impact development. These influences interact with one's cohort. Age-graded influences are shared within a cohort, history-graded are different for different cohorts, and nonnormative are unique and idiosyncratic for individuals and do not represent cohort effects. These influences are age-graded if they happen for most people at the same age (e.g., most women in the United States experience menopause or the cessation of menstruation around the age of 51). So, menopause is an age-graded influence. A history-graded influence is something that everyone of a common age experiences at the same time. For example, emerging adults who were in college when COVID-19 happened. They all share experiences of being college students during the pandemic that have shaped their lives in some similar ways. Nonnormative influences are more random events that shape development but do not happen to most people. An example is becoming a widow in early adulthood. Most young adults in a committed relationship expect to have a whole future with their partner, and so when they experience the unexpected, untimely, and unanticipated death of a partner it has a very unique and profound influence on their development. It is considered nonnormative because it does not happen to most people and is not a common aspect of development at that time.

Finally, Baltes, his colleagues, and all those who adopt a developmental perspective appreciate the multidisciplinary nature of development. By that they mean that no one area of science can fully explain development, but a combined biopsychosocial approach can. We will explore each of these key ideas further in this chapter and they will emerge in most chapters that follow. We, as scholars in developmental science, have taken the developmental approach as the world view we bring to understanding development and we strongly believe that it will help you to learn about and understand the theoretical, empirical, and applied aspects of development we discuss in this book.

We have mentioned the concept of generations and cohorts already, and in our discussion of the lifespan developmental model, age-graded and history-graded factors clearly influence development, so it is important to clarify what these concepts mean and how they influence development.

"Okay boomer." This is an internet meme that has been used by Gen X, Millennials, and Gen Z to dismiss or make fun of things said by older people.

Table 1.1 Characteristics of Baltes developmental approach

Baltes (1987) Key Ideas of the Developmental Approach		
Development is:		
1	Continuous across the lifespan	A continuous process encompassing the entire lifespan from conception through death
2	Multidirectional and multidimensional	Multidirectional and multidimensional, meaning that not every individual develops the same way because each has their own unique biological, psychological, and sociocultural characteristics that shape their developmental trajectory.
3	Gains and losses	Encompasses both growth (gains) and decline (losses)
4	Plasticity	Characterized by plasticity or the capacity for change
5	Sociocultural influences	Shaped by sociocultural factors
6	Age-graded, history-graded, and nonnormative influences	Influenced by age-graded, history-graded, and nonnormative effects
7	Multidisciplinary	No one scientific approach can fully explain development, we need a biopsychosocial approach

The underlying message is that there is no point discussing anything with them because they do not know what they are talking about. It is cutting, dismissive, and ageist.

Most people have encountered some information about different generations. But what are **generational cohorts**? A generational cohort is a group of people who were born during the same historical time period and as a result experienced similar sociohistorical events that may have shaped their development in ways that are different from people born before or after their generation.

For developmental scientists the goal is to describe, explain, and optimize growth and change within individuals as well as to understand the individual differences among people (Baltes et al., 1997; Lerner & Lerner, 2019). Several other theoretical approaches will help us to do that.

Table 1.2 Characteristics of generational cohorts over time

Historical Period	*Name*	*Characteristics of Generation/ Shared Experiences*	*Origin of the Name*
Born between 2010 and 2024	Gen Alpha	First generation to never know life without social media. Highly tech savvy. First generation to be born during the COVID-19 pandemic.	The first letter of the Greek alphabet and the first generation to be born into a world with smartphones and social media.
Born between 1996 and 2010	Gen Z	Lived their lives with personal technology at their fingertips. Known to be more racially and ethnically diverse, better educated, and more familiar with non-heteronormative identities. Experienced a rise in mass shootings, dire climate change, the COVID-19 pandemic, and the wars in Ukraine and Gaza. Expresses anxieties about climate change, social justice issues, other socio-political pressures, and has been found to be "the most depressed" generation, though they are also the most engaged in social activism.	Also known as iGen.

(*Continued*)

Table 1.2 (Continued)

Historical Period	*Name*	*Characteristics of Generation/ Shared Experiences*	*Origin of the Name*
Born between 1981 and 1996	Millennials	Came of age during the turn of the century/millennium. Experienced 9/11, the rise of the internet, and the financial impact of the Great Recession.	They became adults at the turn of the millennium. Also called Generation Y.
Born between 1965 and 1980	Gen X	Came of age to see the Berlin Wall fall and the first personal computers. Known for its reactionism, rebellion, self-reliance, large mistrust of institutional authority, and high collective emphasis on education.	X symbolized an unknown variable or a desire not to be defined. Also known as the "baby busters" because of the drop in birth rate after the Baby Boomer generation.
Born between 1946 and 1964	Baby Boomers	Came of age after WWII, experienced the Cold War, Vietnam War, first moon landing, civil rights movement, and the assassinations of Dr. Martin Luther King and President John F. Kennedy. Characterized by their optimism and prosperous consumerism.	The "boom" in population after WWII.
Born between 1926 and 1945	The Silent Generation	Came of age in the post-WWII period. Accepted politics and government rather than speaking out against it.	Their lack of protest and advocacy.
Born between 1901 and 1924	The Greatest Generation (also known as the G.I. "government issue" generation)	Came of age during the Great Depression, many fought in WWII.	Named the greatest generation by Tom Brokaw based on the moralistic attitudes toward conflict.
Born between 1883 and 1900	The Lost Generation	Came of age during WWI and experienced unimaginable loss of life.	Sense of purposelessness and aimlessness, disillusionment and cynicism.

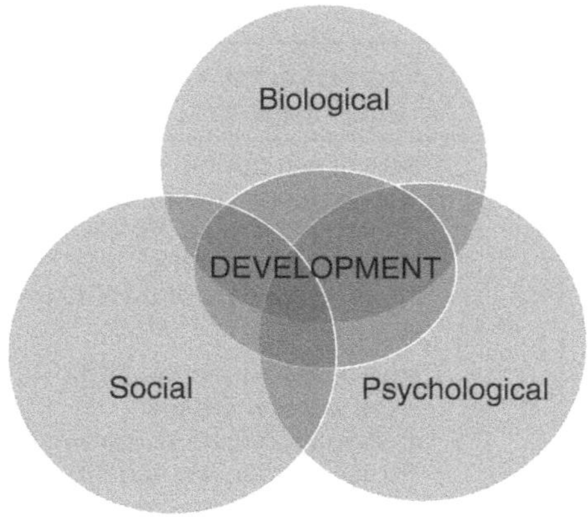

Figure 1.3 Biopsychosocial development

The Biopsychosocial Model

In this textbook we also take a biopsychosocial approach to understanding growth, change, and adaptation across adulthood. The **biopsychosocial model**, as seen in Figure 1.1, highlights the role of biological, psychological, and social processes in development (Brody, 2014; Engel, 1977; Engel, 1980; Lehman et al., 2017). It considers the interactions between these processes, as well as the entire experience of development, and it is an outgrowth of the lifespan developmental perspective.

Biopsychosocial Development

Development is a complex process. At its heart it is a biological process. Our bodies are changing throughout our lifespan. From conception, the maturation of an embryo is shaped by the genes that code for the development of systems and functions of the human body as well as the physiological systems that influence the functioning of our bodies. Many biological factors influence our development. For example, your height is a function of your genes. The risk factors for gray hair, cardiovascular disease, and dementia are also biologically based. But just because a person has a genetic risk for a particular condition does not mean that they will, in fact, develop that condition. For example, a person may have a family history of dementia, they may have done genetic testing and determined that they carry two copies of the *APOE ε4* gene and have a high risk for Alzheimer's disease – however, they may never develop it because of lifestyle choices and behaviors that offset the risk.

From a psychological perspective, there are many personality, cognitive, emotional, and behavioral factors that can influence one's development.

These psychological factors interact with our biological factors. If a person discovers that they have a high risk for Alzheimer's disease they may choose to engage in cognitively stimulating activities, eat a healthier diet, and get regular physical exercise to reduce their risk. Research shows that physical exercise in adulthood can serve as a protective factor against brain atrophy related to the development of Alzheimer's disease (Erickson et al., 2011). Moreover, once a person has symptoms of early Alzheimer's disease, regular physical activity can slow the progression (Rolland et al., 2007; Pitkälä et al., 2013). This example illustrates how a psychological factor such as behavioral choices can offset a biological factor such as genetic risk to determine a developmental outcome. Another example of this interaction is seen in the research on the linkages between depression (a psychological factor) and an increased risk, especially in people with a genetic predisposition, for the development of Alzheimer's disease. Specifically, for people who have a history of depression, the age of onset for Alzheimer's disease is earlier (Barnes et al., 2012; de Oliveira et al., 2015; Steenland et al., 2012).

In the biopsychosocial model, the social domain pertains to all aspects of social influences and contexts. It can include the quality of our intimate relationships, our chosen identity groups (i.e., gender, race/ethnicity, sexual identity, disability status), our socioeconomic status, our faith/religious/political affiliations, our geographic region, or any other kind of sociocultural influence. As an example of how the biological, psychological, and social interact to influence developmental outcomes, let us build on our example above. A person knows that they carry an elevated genetic risk for Alzheimer's disease, but with this knowledge they have chosen to cope with daily stressors in a more healthful way, they have made sure to seek treatment when they felt depressed, they have followed a healthy diet, and engage daily in regular cognitively stimulating and physically engaging activities. Research shows that there are **health disparities** due to **social determinants** that influence the incidence of Alzheimer's disease. Individuals from underrepresented minority groups, particularly Black or Hispanic people, are at nearly two-times the risk for developing Alzheimer's disease than their White, non-Hispanic counterparts (Alzheimer's Association, 2025). Understanding how social determinants create health disparities is critically important to advancing diversity-affirming understanding of health and development. Another example is the role of social isolation and poor social relationships in Alzheimer's disease (National Academies of Sciences, Engineering, and Medicine, 2020). So, in our example, the biological (genetic) risk can be offset by the psychological and behavioral factors, but social factors play an important role too.

What is important to remember is that from a biopsychosocial perspective, each of these three factors can influence development and they interact with each other to shape development as well. In the biopsychosocial model we consider the multidisciplinary, multidirectional, and multidimensional factors that Baltes thought were important to development. Biological, psychological, and social factors make up the fabric of all of our lives. Every one of us is who we are as a function of the contributions and interactions among these three factors. Because the biological, psychological, and social factors are constantly influencing each other it is impossible to understand development without considering them from the biopsychosocial perspective.

Systems Theory

Both the lifespan developmental model and the biopsychosocial model are grounded in **Systems theory**. Systems theory conceptualizes something (the human body, the family, or society, for example) as a *system* governed by many different factors. Fundamental to Systems theory is the belief that a change in any level of the system can ripple outward or inward and influence many other levels of the system. In the same way, developmental psychologists look at how biological, psychological, and social factors come together to shape growth, change, and adaptation across the lifespan.

Systems theory began with the ancient Sumerians, who believed that systems like these are found in nature. It was originally applied in biology by Ludwig Von Bertalanaffy (1968). Examples of systems include the solar system, a family, and the life cycle of cells in the body. The internet, your college, the economy, and society are also all systems. In time, Systems theory caught on and is now an integral part of modern science and economics.

Two Systems theories are particularly relevant for understanding development in adulthood. In 1979 Urie Bronfenbrenner developed the **ecological systems theory** to provide a contextual approach for understanding how

Figure 1.4 Examples of systems: the solar system (a), a family system (b), and a cellular system (c). (*Continued*)

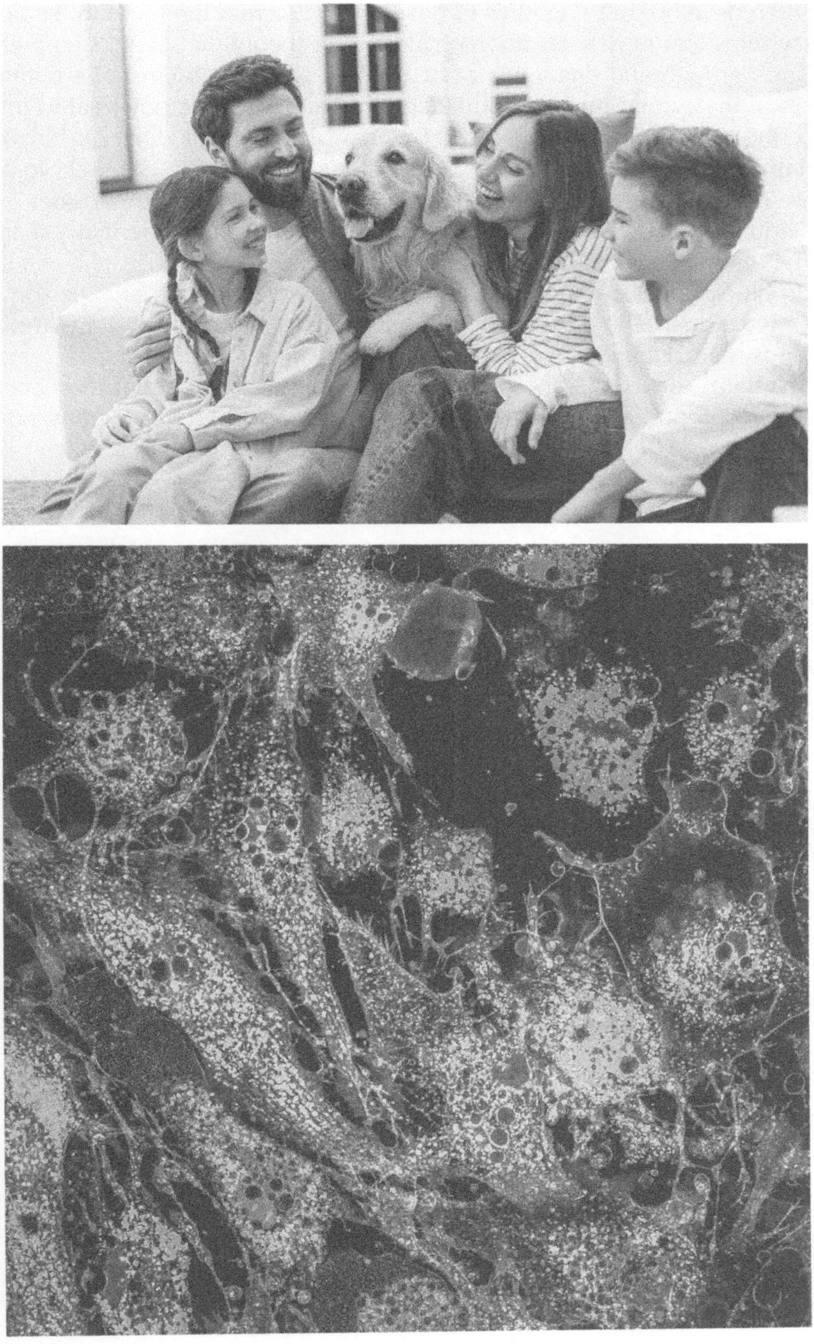

Figure 1.4 (Continued)

children develop, but it applies to development across the lifespan. Ecological systems theory is a developmental systems theory that depicts how each person's growth and change is nested within various systems. The different levels of the system interact with each other and have the potential to influence the person and be influenced by them. The systems differ and involve social, cultural, economic, political, and global factors, not just psychological ones. This systems theory is particularly important when we consider how individuals from diverse and global backgrounds may be differentially shaped by the unique systems that influence their lives.

Bronfenbrenner envisioned that the systems that influence each person are the microsystem, the mesosystem, the exosystem, the macrosystem, and the chronosystem. Figure 1.5 shows examples of what is included in each system. This systems theory is important for identifying the factors that may impact development and adaptation at any time and it also helps to identify points

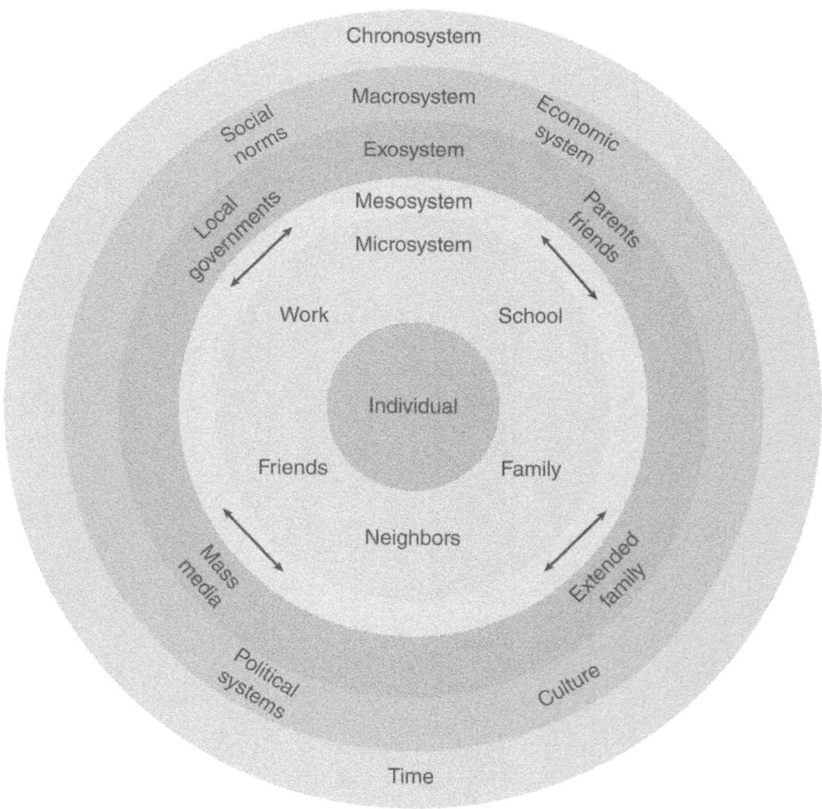

Figure 1.5 Bronfenbrenner's Ecological Systems Theory model.
Source: Simply Psychology.

that contribute to individual differences in experience and development. For example, two students, one who identifies as a lesbian woman, and one who identifies as a heterosexual woman, may have the same sort of family background, and attend the same college, but depending on where they live in the United States, their school, their local government, and the societal and political expectations they encounter will be different. The individual who identifies as a lesbian may suffer from minority stress that creates obstacles to their growth and development and personal relationships that the person who identifies as cisgender does not. Minority stress theory states that people who identify as sexual minorities have unique stressors (e.g., discrimination, coming-out stress, stigmatization, and internalized homophobia) that may be related to elevated mental health symptoms (Meyer, 1995; 2003). The experience of higher levels of stigma-related stress that is directly associated with their minority identity status can influence their health and development (Convertino et al., 2021).

We will talk more about the ecological systems theory and keep it in mind when we are thinking about how systems interact to influence development across adulthood. It will be very important for us to look at how sociocultural factors influence individuals' development and to appreciate the diversity and global differences in how people grow and change worldwide.

Like the ecological systems theory, **relational developmental systems theory** (RSD) is an extension of developmental systems theory (Lerner & Lerner, 2019). It is also a more specific conceptual framework to help understand how individuals develop. Relational developmental systems theory is the leading metatheory in developmental psychology today. This theory posits that it is the interactions among individuals and their environments, reciprocally influencing each other, that cause all aspects of development. In RSD individuals are both the producers and the products of their own developmental efforts (Lerner, 2021). This theory builds upon ecological systems theory to suggest the ways in which individuals influence the contexts that they exist within, and vice versa. Consider this example: an individual decides to wait to get married until late in established adulthood (e.g., age 40) and have children (Martinez & Daniels, 2023), and this leads to the individual being an older parent. The older parent now has a chronic illness such as Alzheimer's disease or Parkinson's disease, and may need assistance with activities of daily living such as dressing and preparing meals from their children who may be in adolescence. The children of this older parent may end up becoming very young caregivers, taking on many responsibilities that are not common for children their age (Siskowski, 2006). There is likely to be a reciprocal relationship between the influences of aging on the older parent and their teenage children. Chronic illnesses tend to increase with age (Tavares et al., 2023) so it is likely that the older parent's needs will continue to increase. While this may be normative for the older adult, the caregiving responsibilities falling on the adolescent child is less normative and may impact that child's normative developmental trajectory. For example, the teenager who may have had aspirations to attend college may have to postpone or choose a college closer to home and balance the responsibilities of being a college student and a caregiver at the same time.

What can we take away from RSD? We can increase the probability of positive development and achieve desired developmental outcomes by capitalizing on our strengths and aligning them with the resources that are present in the contexts that we find ourselves in and that will lead to optimal adaptation and growth. When we select contexts, environments, and social networks that support and challenge us, we grow to meet those challenges. As we change we influence the context, which then expands as a result of our actions within it.

Table 1.3 Characteristics of the generations

	Type of Theory	*Basic Premises*	*Author*
Lifespan Developmental Approach	Metatheory	Development is a lifelong process, with gains, losses, and plasticity. It is multiply determined and multidirectional. Both sociocultural and historical influences shape development.	Baltes
Biopsychosocial Model	Metatheory	Development and health are influenced by interactive biological, psychological, and social factors.	Engel
Systems Theory	Metatheory	A system is a configuration of parts that are connected through relationships, influence each other and create a whole.	Von Bertalanffy
Ecological Systems Theory	Metatheory and type of systems theory	A developing individual is embedded within different contexts that both shape and are shaped by their development.	Bronfenbrenner
Relational Developmental Systems Theory	Metatheory and type of systems theory	Development is influenced by the reciprocal interactions between the individual and the context.	Lerner

Factors that Influence the Study of Adult Development

Diversity in Aging

Aging is not a monolithic process (Shifren, 1996). That means that not all people grow and change in the same way. There is a tremendous amount of variability in the experiences of people as they move through the lifespan. This variability represents **interindividual differences** (or differences among people). People change over time as they develop, and that variability within one person is called **intraindividual change**. Both intraindividual change and interindividual differences create the variability that is seen in adulthood.

Historically, in psychological science and in developmental science too, the conclusions that have been drawn have been based on research conducted with middle-class white males. This is referred to as W.E.I.R.D. science – science based on people from Western, educated, industrialized, rich, and democratic nations. That creates biases in science and leads us to conclusions that do not generalize to people who do not fit into this group. This historical trend has led to research not being representative of people of different ethnic, racial, educational, socioeconomic, geographic, political, and global regions.

Across adulthood identity is a key factor that shapes development. Traditionally, developmental psychology has not been inclusive of the different types of identity. For example, most studies in journals report gender in a binary way and do not survey or consider people who identify outside traditional gender labels. Similarly, heterosexuality has been considered the norm despite the fact that in the U.S. today over 7% of the population identifies as LGBTQ+ (i.e., lesbian, gay, bisexual, transexual, queer, and others). In a global survey, over 3% of the world's population identified as LGBTQ+ (Statista, 2023). Brazil (14%), Spain (13%), the Netherlands (12%), Columbia (11%), and Great Britain (10%) reported higher percentages of people identifying as sexual minorities than the United States. Figure 1.6 shows the frequencies of self-identification and how it is changing in the United States.

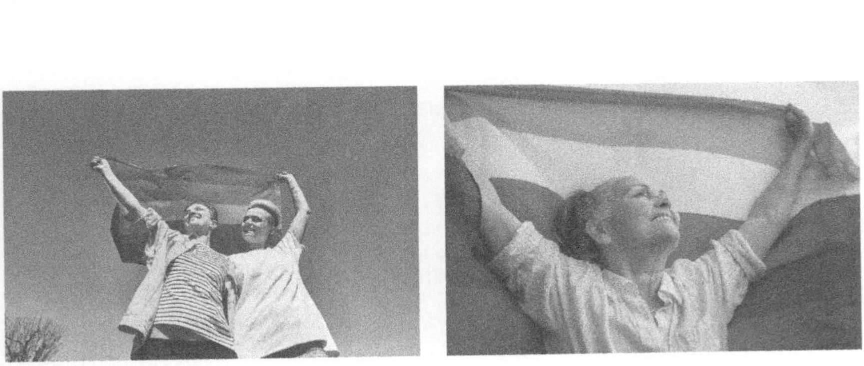

Figure 1.6 Diversity in science is necessary for understanding adulthood.

There Is No "Right" Way to Develop

The world's populations are living longer and becoming more diverse in many ways. This diversity is important because as we have seen from the metatheories of development, culture matters. What creates diversity is not just statistics or groupings, but the ways that culture shapes how we think, what we believe, and the practices that we engage in to live our lives. Therefore, understanding how people differ, especially as they navigate growth and change in adulthood, is important. To move science forward, instead of comparing based on the belief that the "gold standard" or "benchmark" is what we see in W.E.I.R.D. groups, we should look within each group, attempt to understand the factors that lead to change and the factors that promote resilience, and then share those broadly so that we are learning from each other. As Baltes and our other theorists have shown, development is shaped by many intersectional factors and that necessitates a diversity-affirming approach.

Social Determinants of Development

Social factors influence development, both directly and indirectly. A direct example is an individual who does not have the financial resources to go to college and whose professional development may be impacted. An indirect example is a person who is not making a living wage and is living in poverty, and therefore may have poor nutrition that will impact their cognitive, emotional, and physical functioning and create negative mental and physical health outcomes that will hold them back developmentally. Social determinants of

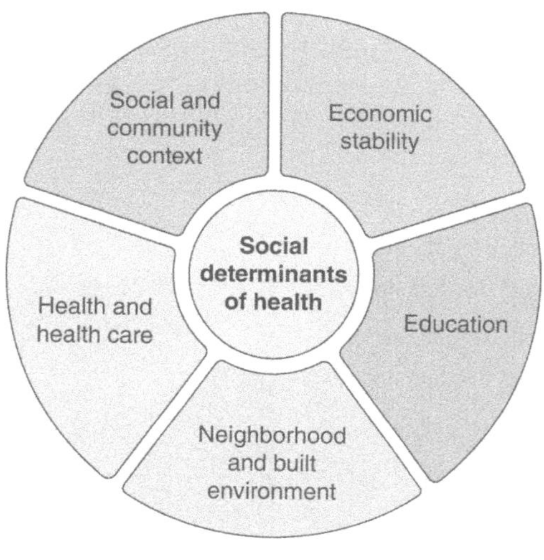

Figure 1.7 Social determinants of development.

development are the conditions or environments in which we live, work, socialize, and grow old, and they influence our mental, cognitive, and physical functioning, our quality of life, and our health risks and outcomes.

Even today, in the United States racial and ethnic segregation influences where people live. There are many regions within large U.S. cities that are still not racially integrated. Black and Hispanic women who live in segregated urban areas have higher incidences of breast cancer (Pruitt et al., 2015). Race and ethnicity are crucial determinants of health because of their enduring links with differences in social and economic resources (Mehta et al., 2013). There is an intersection, then, between race and residential segregation that hinges on socioeconomic status or income. If the socioeconomic status of Blacks were comparable to that of Whites, the White–Black survival gap would disappear (Popescu et al., 2018).

Recent research shows that the gendered developmental outcomes, especially those concerning aging and health, are influenced by the geographic area where people live. Where you live is a context, part of the micro, meso, and exosystems that influence our growth.

Health Disparities in Development

Health disparities refer to the differences in health or aging outcomes that exist among different groups of people as a function of differences in the social and economic resources that they have access to. Health disparities are striking in communities with low income, unstable housing, unsafe neighborhoods, limited access to healthy foods and outdoor recreation, and substandard schools (Jack, 2018). Many organizations, from the American Psychological Association to the Centers for Disease Control and Prevention, are now focused on examining the social determinants of health (SDOH) (see Figure 1.7). These social determinants greatly contribute to health and aging disparities. Socioeconomic status (such as income and level of education), unemployment, racial discrimination, sexual minority stress, social stigma, social networks, and social support are social factors that impact developmental and health outcomes (Coughlin et al., 2019). Other examples of social determinants that influence health and development are immigration status, distrust of medical establishments, inadequate housing, food insecurity, and geographic factors such as where you live (Coughlin et al., 2019).

What may become clear as you think about this is that, oftentimes, several of these factors go together. There is **intersectionality** among social factors. Intersectionality means that a person's life is shaped by their identities, relationships, and social roles and that these things may interact with each other. The concept of intersectionality was developed by Crenshaw (2018) to show how these factors combine to create overlapping forms of privilege or oppression depending on an individual's context and the power structures (e.g., patriarchy, colonialism, imperialism, racism, sexism, ableism, and homophobia) that they exist within.

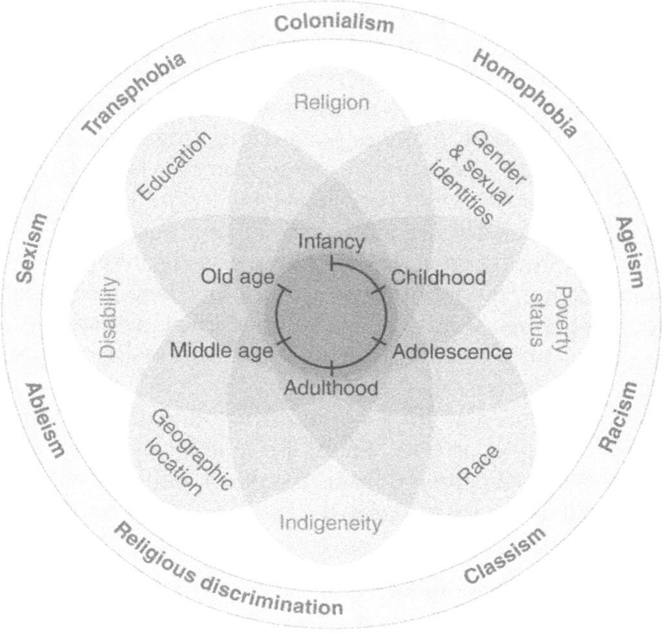

Figure 1.8 The intersectionality wheel.
Source: Adapted from the Equality Institute.

For example, the intersectional nature of race and gender is evident when you consider the health risks for Black women. Black women often have the greatest socioeconomic challenges, and this influences their risk of breast cancer (Mohseny et al., 2016). Intersectionality creates a cascade effect. Gender intersects with racial identity which intersects with level of education (Noonan et al., 2016; Singh et al., 2017) which relates to socioeconomic status which impacts health risks (Coughlin et al., 2019). To understand intersectionality, we must appreciate that while each of these social factors by themselves may elevate risk, when they come together or intersect their influence may be magnified.

Dr. Christy L. Erving

The scholarship of Dr. Christy L. Erving examines how race, ethnicity, gender, and immigrant status intersect to produce differences in health outcomes. She has examined the Black–White mental health paradox; and how status (e.g., gender) shapes the relationship between psychological and physical health. Her research shows that the influence of psychosocial stress associated with discrimination, financial strain, and gendered racial microaggressions impacts both the mental and physical health of Black women. Dr. Erving's research also shows that across the adult life course, the gendered and racialized experiences of Black women can impact their physiological and psychological health both negatively and positively (Erving & Smith, 2022; Robinson et al., 2023). Specifically, her research shows that although U.S. Black and Latinx adults often face more negative health outcomes as they grow older, a paradox exists in which mental health problems are relatively low in Black Americans despite higher levels of psychological distress. Similarly, Latinx adults often show favorable health compared to non-Latinx whites. Dr. Erving and her colleagues argue that in order to understand these complexities we must understand the interaction among social determinants and the value of intersectionality (Thomas Tobin et al., 2023).

From a biopsychosocial perspective it is easy to see how intersectionality can be influential. Adopting an intersectional lens to consider development leads us to ask who is being left behind and why? When we consider the hidden structural barriers that may influence development, we are in a better position to understand how individual experiences differ, especially for those from underrepresented or marginalized groups.

From a developmental perspective, social determinants of health may interact to create inequities in health. These inequities are most often seen in infancy and later life (Mehta et al., 2013). For example, health disparities in midlife and later significantly influence the development of chronic disease. Compared to previous generations, today's older adults are more engaged, more physically fit, and enjoying a higher quality of life due to greater awareness of how to age meaningfully and successfully (Castel, 2018). However, although the death rate from some cancers and heart disease has declined slightly in non-Hispanic whites, it remains constant for Native American/Alaskan Native people. For women in these groups, the rates are increasing. Native American/Alaskan Native people have a 50% higher overall mortality rate annually than non-Hispanic whites and are most likely to die from diabetes and chronic liver disease. A recent large-scale study using Behavioral Risk Factor Surveillance System data from the National Program of Cancer Registries showed that Native Americans/Alaskan Natives were two times more likely to develop liver cancer than age-matched whites, and most of them developed liver cancer nearly 15 years sooner than their white counterparts (Melkonian et al., 2018).

Other factors, such as gender and sexual orientation, relate to health and developmental disparities as well. Although national health initiatives emphasize the importance of eliminating health disparities among historically disadvantaged populations, research has only recently begun to examine health outcomes among LGBTQ+ people (Fredriksen-Goldsen et al., 2014). But it is clear that LGBTQ+ individuals face health disparities that are related to societal stigma, discrimination, and denial of their civil rights (Hatzenbuehler et al., 2010).

There are also health disparities among immigrants to the United States and other countries, who represent a substantial and growing portion of the population (Patterson & Gong, 2009). According to the World Health Organization (WHO), globally there are over one billion people who are immigrants, refugees, or migrants to a new country (WHO, 2022c). That is one out of every seven people around the world. Refugee, immigrant, or migrant (RIM) communities are made up of people with diverse backgrounds and experiences and they often face health and developmental disparities in their new homes (Centers for Disease Control and Prevention [CDC], 2024). Some of the factors that lead to these disparities include language barriers, income/wage gaps, and a lack of social networks and support, health insurance, health care access, education, and employment. One study showed that recent migrants in Europe and North America had higher levels of stress that related to a higher risk of metabolic syndrome and cardiovascular disease (Rosenthal et al., 2022). And the stress effects play forward into the future. First generation adult immigrants and adolescent immigrants developed cardiovascular risk factors later in life (Rosenthal et al., 2022). When you think about the long-term impact of stress on health you can see how later developmental outcomes may be affected. Around the world promoting health equity for RIM groups has become a priority and this will also improve developmental outcomes for these groups.

What is Diversity-affirming, Strengths-based Scholarship?

Above we learned about how the intersection of race and gender can elevate developmental and health risks. But it is also important to recognize the transformative potential of intersectionality as well. Rather than just focusing on the impact of intersecting identities and seeing only risks and comparing outcome to some "ideal" benchmark, when we consider diversity and approach development with an intersectional lens we can strive to achieve equity in our understanding of the varied ways that people grow and change across adulthood. We can be more inclusive and responsive to appreciating the value that diversity brings. Rather than focusing on the differences and deficits and gaps among groups as is common in **deficits-based scholarship**, we can focus on looking within groups at the unique strengths, resources, and resilience that each culture holds that shape development in novel ways. Looking at development from within culture as opposed to outside it represents a **strengths-based approach**. By focusing on diversity, being inclusive, and adopting an intersectional lens, we can better achieve the global pledge to "leave no one behind" in our consideration of adult development.

Chapter Summary

In this chapter we introduced key concepts associated with adult development. First, we considered what developmental scientists who study adult development are interested in. We looked at demographic factors that shape what we know about development in this period. Several new conceptions for understanding the developmental periods within adulthood were presented as well as different ways of thinking about age. We introduced the metatheoretical views that will shape everything we study in this book. We stressed the importance of looking at the social determinants that cause health and developmental disparities, which, in turn, create variability and shape outcomes for different groups of people. Relatedly we introduced the concept of intersectionality and argued for the importance of using an intersectional lens to understand adult development and aging. We followed by stressing the importance of strengths-based, diversity-affirming, and inclusive views of growth and change across the adult years.

Key Takeaways

1 Aging is both a process and a developmental period. We are aging from the moment we are born, so the concept of aging is something that happens throughout the lifespan. Aging is also the period of adulthood later in life.
2 There are different phases of adulthood and different developmental milestones during each one.
3 Individuals are actively involved in shaping their development through the contexts, activities, and people they engage with. We are shaped by our own developmental systems and processes and also actively shape them.
4 The guiding principles of development that shape this book are the biopsychosocial model and the relational developmental systems perspective.
5 It is important to consider the sociocultural context in which a person develops during adulthood because there is no "right" way to develop or age, and contextual influences shape our development in unique ways.

Reflective Questions

1 Which theory of adult development resonates most with you?
2 Can you identify all the different systems that exist in you and your life? Think about how they influence you and how you influence them.
3 How do sociocultural and contextual factors influence developmental outcomes in adulthood?

Suggested Readings

Baltes, P. B. (1987). Theoretical propositions of life-span developmental psychology: On the dynamics between growth and decline. *Developmental Psychology, 23*(5), 611.

Coughlin, S. S. (2019). Social determinants of breast cancer risk, stage, and survival. *Breast Cancer Research and Treatment, 177*(3), 537–548.

Erving, C. L., & Smith, M. V. (2022). Disrupting monolithic thinking about Black women and their mental health: Does stress exposure explain intersectional ethnic, nativity, and socioeconomic differences? *Social Problems, 69*(4), 1046–1067.

Key Terms

Biological age is the age of the physiological systems of your body. It is also sometimes called physiological age.

The **biopsychosocial model** highlights the role of biological, psychological, and social processes in development and considers the interactions between these processes, as well as the entire experience of development.

Chronological age is the number of years that you have been alive since birth.

Deficits-based scholarship refers to a great deal of traditional research that tries to identify and understand the predictors of negative outcomes.

Development is the process through which a human being evolves over time, including progressive changes in one's physical, cognitive, neurological, emotional, and social functioning. It encompasses growth and change from conception to death.

Developmental psychology is the field that studies how people grow, change, and adapt across the lifespan.

Ecological systems theory is a developmental systems theory that depicts how each person's growth and change is nested within various systems.

Emerging adulthood is the developmental period between the ages of 18 and 25, though it has recently been extended to 29.

Established adulthood is the period of adulthood between the ages of 30 and 45.

Functional age is a measure of how well a person is able to perform the basic activities of daily living in order to live independently.

Generational cohort refers to a group of people who were born during the same historical time period and as a result experienced similar sociohistorical events that may have shaped their development in ways that are different from people born before or after their generation.

Health disparities refer to the differences in health or aging outcomes that exist among different groups of people as a function of differences in the social and economic resources that they have access to.

Interindividual differences are differences among people.

Intersectionality means that a person's life is shaped by their identities, relationships, and social roles, and that these things may interact with each other.

Intraindividual change refers to the changes within an individual over time.

The **lifespan developmental perspective** explores the continuity and change in biological, cognitive, and psychosocial processes across the lifespan.

Metatheories are coherent sets of principles that describe and direct what we believe and how we approach understanding it. Metatheories transcend specific theories we might examine and the methods we use to examine them.

Middle adulthood refers to the period of adulthood between the ages of 45 and 64.

Older adults are individuals aged 65 or older.

Relational developmental systems theory (RSD), the leading metatheory in developmental psychology today, posits that it is the interactions among individuals and their environments, reciprocally influencing each other, that cause all aspects of development.

Social age represents the age-normative expectations of society or culture.

Social determinants of development are the conditions or environments in which we live, work, socialize, and grow old. They influence our mental, cognitive, and physical functioning, our quality of life, and our health risks and outcomes.

Sociocultural factors come from the ethnic, gender, religious, socioeconomic, educational, and other contexts that shape the thoughts, feelings, values, beliefs, behaviors, attitudes, and interactions that people have with others around them.

Strengths-based scholarship focuses on identifying and understanding predictors that lead to positive outcomes.

Systems theory conceptualizes something (the human body, the family, or society) as a *system* governed by many different factors. Fundamental to system theory is the belief that a change in any level of the system can ripple outward or inward and influence many other levels of the system.

2 Theoretical Foundations and Models of Adult Development

Learning Outcomes

Give an example to illustrate how the field of adult development and aging is interdisciplinary.

Compare the different fundamental issues in developmental science.

Create a table to summarize the different forms of research covered in this chapter.

Describe the Tuskegee experiment and why we need to have institutional review boards (IRBs).

Around the world, people's lifespans are expanding and they are enjoying living longer and healthier lives. In order to understand how to live rich and meaningful lives we can draw on scientists' studies of older adults as they age.

The field of adult development and aging is an **interdisciplinary** one. It is interdisciplinary because it draws upon theories and research from many fields. Although most of what we know about this phase of the lifespan comes from the work of developmental psychologists, scholars from the social and behavioral sciences, medicine, health care, biology, neurology, social work, economics, and public policy are all interested in understanding how people grow and develop across the adult years.

In Chapter 1 we learned about the guiding theoretical models, such as relational developmental systems **theory** and ecological systems theory, and how they shape the way we think about, study, and understand adult development and aging.

Now we turn our attention to the way we investigate how people grow and change across adulthood. In Chapter 1 we learned about the major world views or metatheories that shape our thinking about human development and adult development and aging. In this chapter we will learn about developmental theories and developmental research methods that can be applied to studying adulthood and aging.

DOI: 10.4324/9781003483809-2

First, what is development anyway? As we learned in Chapter 1, development is the process through which a human being evolves over time, including the progressive changes in their physical, cognitive, neurological, emotional, and social functioning. It encompasses growth and change from conception to death. It used to be that developmental psychologists thought that development stops at the end of childhood.

Do you think that your development stops when you reach adulthood? Do you think that the person you are at 18, is the person you will be for the rest of your life, physically, emotionally, behaviorally, cognitively, socially? You would think that most people would answer "no" to that question. Yet, in my adult development and aging class, when I asked people "do you think you are the same person you have always been or have you changed over time?", 50% said they believe they are the same and the other 50% said they have changed! The issue of stability or change in development across time has been a fundamental focus of developmental psychology.

Similarly, it used to be that some developmental psychologists saw development as either a continuous process, where we keep growing and changing but are fundamentally, essentially the same over time. Others viewed development as a process that is marked by a series of discrete stages, leading to the belief that growth and change over time are discontinuous and that we are fundamentally different once we have mastered a particular developmental challenge. The issue of continuity versus stages of development over time is another fundamental issue in developmental psychology.

What do you think shapes who you are? Your genetic make-up or your environment and the people in it? You have probably already heard about the nature versus nurture controversy in developmental psychology. Across the adult years there are many changes (such as the development of cardiovascular disease, breast cancer, or Alzheimer's disease) that have a genetic component. But there are just as many changes that happen due to contextual and environmental experiences (such as the many people who decided to change their careers after the COVID-19 pandemic, some of these people would argue that the pandemic caused them to think more seriously about whether or not they were happy and to pursue aspirations that improved their lives rather than going back to the status quo).

In the history of developmental science, early theory tended to focus on nature as the force shaping development. Nativists, like Noam Chomsky who believed that humans are born with an innate ability to learn language, believed that maturation would happen in essentially the same way for everyone. Scholars who argued for nature believed that the organism was the center of human development, and they advocated for the **organismic model** – or the theory that genetics and heredity are the primary influences on development and that these influences unfold in a predictable stage-like fashion. Later, behaviorists, like B. F. Skinner, began to argue that the environment and the stimuli within it shape and predict a person's behavior, putting all the emphasis on nurture. Advocates of this position adhered to the **mechanistic model** – or the

Table 2.1 Fundamental issues in developmental psychology

Issue	*Details*	*Examples*
Nature versus nurture	**Nature**: genetics and biological factors that may shape our development. **Nurture**: the experiences and environmental and contextual influences that may shape our development.	**Nature**: genetic predispositions for specific illnesses. Jan has a congenital hearing impairment that her father and paternal grandmother also had. **Nurture**: Diego grew up with two parents who were developmental psychologists and from an early age he has been interested in becoming a developmental scientist.
Continuity versus stages	**Continuity**: development unfolds in a continuous, gradual, and cumulative fashion over time. **Stages**: development occurs through the progression from one discrete stage to the next.	**Continuity**: Leigh was a competitive swimmer through childhood, but when they sustained an injury, they took up playing competitive tournament scrabble. **Stages**: in young adulthood, Kelsey became aware of the intimate bonds she has with certain people. At the age of 42 she realized that what gave her joy was helping her junior colleagues succeed in their academic careers.
Stability versus change	**Stability**: personality traits and personal characteristics are stable and persist through the life span. **Change**: with new experiences and challenges, and at different ages, we acquire new characteristics and may become different people.	**Stability**: Lowell has had a sense of humor his whole life. The things he finds funny may have changed but his playful nature has not. **Change**: in early adulthood Jess was aimless, confused, and did not know what she wanted in life. Then she went to South America and met her partner. She settled down and realized her life's goal was to live in a rural area, become an organic gardener, and have a family.

theory that development occurs when behavior is shaped by environmental forces that continually and gradually act upon an individual over time. What we know now is that these developmental forces work together. Both nature and nurture can influence an individual's development. Most developmental psychologists believe that neither nature nor nurture is more important, and they both contribute to stability and malleability in human growth and development (Shonkoff & Phillips, 2000). For example, a pressing public health

Figure 2.1 Older person feeling lonely.
Source: iStock.

concern, especially for older adults, is loneliness, which has been found to relate to increased likelihood of chronic health conditions. Freilich and colleagues (2024) showed an epigenetic link between DNA and loneliness as a possible mechanism for negative health outcomes in older adults.

These contemporary views are aligned with **interactionist** models of development. The biopsychosocial model, the relational developmental systems theory, and the ecological systems theory that we discussed in Chapter 1 are all interactionist models – they argue that the individual and their environment are reciprocally interacting, shaping and being shaped by each other all the time to direct the course of development.

Today developmental scientists accept that development necessitates both nature and nurture working together over time. Borrowing from evolutionary psychological theory, we know that human beings, regardless of their environments, share 99.9% of the human genome (National Human Genome Research Institute, 2018). We also know the environments that most people develop within share a lot of the same characteristics (e.g., normative developmental environments are characterized by the presence of shelter, caregivers, the use of language, and community support (Narvaez et al., 2022). Despite these commonalities we now know that idiosyncratic experiences unique to specific individuals do shape their development, neurologically, physically, and psychologically. Human brains are characterized by **plasticity** –

the ability to modify, adapt, or flexibly change in response to new experiences. Plasticity, especially in the brain (neuroplasticity) reflects the brain's ability to develop new connections, change, and adapt in the face of developmental challenges. For example, in older adults who suffer a stroke and lose the ability to make connections and recall information, the brain can rewire to create new pathways to recover stored information. Your brain demonstrates neuroplasticity when you navigate around a new city, when you learn a new language, or when you take up a new hobby.

Plasticity is also a characteristic of development writ large. Here the idea is that when the environment or our genetic predisposition or a critical life event that causes trauma poses a challenge for our normative developmental trajectory, we can find a way to blaze a new developmental path, continuing to grow and change and adapt over time. For example, a person with a severe hearing impairment may lose the ability to understand other's speech, their hearing aids may no longer be able to amplify sounds enough for them to be heard. At that point their audiologist may suggest a cochlear implant. A cochlear implant bypasses the damaged parts of the ear. The implant picks up sounds in the environment and converts them to implanted electrodes that automatically stimulate the auditory nerve sending signals to the brain that are then recognized as sound. When someone gets a cochlear implant, they have to learn to hear in a completely new way. That is, nothing sounds the same as it did before. They must learn how to hear for the first time all over again! It takes time and can be very challenging, but eventually "hearing" is restored and functional. Sometimes they can even hear better than they did before. This is a perfect example of both neuroplasticity (the way the brain rewires itself and learns to hear anew) and developmental plasticity (the way that a person can continue to grow, change, and adapt to new challenges). Another example of the concept of plasticity comes from Angie, a 60-year-old woman who was beginning to experience pain, lack of mobility, and a dwindling ability to pursue her livelihood: throwing clay on the wheel to create beautiful pots, dishes, and cups. After consulting her doctor and physical therapist, Angie took up gentle yoga. The practice of yoga gave her stability, flexibility, and greater functionality, especially in her hands and wrists. Now when she sits down at the wheel, she may go a bit slower, but she has accommodated her physical limitations in a way that will support her to age successfully.

Plasticity is an important concept, especially in the context of growth and change over the adult years. In order to optimize our development to live to our fullest potential, we can look for ways to maximize our plasticity for better outcomes.

Now that we have learned more about the history that shaped the developmental theory of adult development and aging, and a few key concepts, let us look at some specific developmental theories that frame our understanding of the adult years.

Developmental Theories of Adult Development and Aging

In most developmental psychology textbooks, whether they concern childhood, adolescence or adulthood, there is usually a refresher on Sigmund Freud's theory of the development of the id, ego, and superego. But there are many more theories of development. Jean Piaget's theory of cognitive development was instrumental in understanding how babies come into the world and, through ongoing, dynamic, interactions with their environment and the people within it, how they develop the basic building blocks of cognitive functioning. Erikson's psychosocial theory of development includes adulthood and aging and is based on eight life stages that a person passes through from birth through death. In Erikson's theory each stage is highlighted by a developmental biopsychosocial challenge and how that crisis is resolved dictates how development unfolds. Bandura's social learning theory emphasizes the role of others in shaping learning and development; and Bowlby's theory of attachment is fundamental to studies of development. All of these theories were developed to understand how children grow and change over time. Few of these theories, including Erikson's, really attempt to understand what happens in adulthood.

In this book we focus on theories that were created to help us understand the developmental period of adulthood. We focus on theories specific to different adult stages because there is a great deal of change between the age of 18 to death! The factors that influence one's sense of self, one's cognitive abilities, and one's health and well-being in emerging adulthood are different in midlife, and even more different at the end of life. People change, relationships change, and the way society, cultures, and institutions interact with adults as they age also change. So, rather than present a set of theories of adult development in this chapter, we will highlight specific theories that apply to cognitive development, emotional and personality development, social and relationship development, and mental and physical development. That said, the core world view of adult development and aging, presented in Chapter 1, is relational developmental systems theory.

How Do We Study Development Across Adulthood?

It has been said that to study development is to study change (Laursen et al., 2012). The process of change is what development is all about. Before we dive into learning about the research methods used to examine age-related differences among people of different ages, or how people grow and change over time, we need to consider some basic and fundamental issues that relate to research methods in any field of psychological science.

Measuring Development

Most of what we know today about adulthood and aging has been generated by scientific research. Scientific research is usually driven by a desire to answer intriguing questions, to solve practical problems, and to test theories. A theory is a set of ideas that explains the world around us. In developmental psychology, theories explain some elements of human growth and behavior. Theories generate testable statements, or **hypotheses**, that we can test to determine whether our theory is supported or not. A hypothesis is a proposed explanation for a phenomenon that a scientist seeks to test in a research study. For example, Bazo Perez and colleagues (2025) hypothesized that middle-aged women are at high risk for eating disorders as a result of the biopsychosocial changes caused by menopause. She set up a study to compare rates of disordered eating behaviors in young and middle-aged women as well as the factors that are shown to elevate risk for eating disorders. The results of her study showed that compared to young women, menopausal women reported more pathological eating behaviors especially when their menopausal symptoms were more bothersome. This study was groundbreaking because it showed that like adolescence, the developmental stage of middle age is a "window of vulnerability" for eating disorders for women. We will revisit this study as we talk about how developmental research is done.

To understand the different research methods used to study age-related changes we must first consider the kinds of evidence that are sought and the variables these methods are designed to test.

Generally, we describe data in one of two ways. **Quantitative data** are gathered through carefully designed examination, with all the possible factors affecting the construct we study determined ahead of time. To remember what quantitative data is, think about the word, quantify – that is what this kind of data does, it quantifies a particular construct. For example, a questionnaire might ask about specific eating behaviors and instruct respondents to answer on a scale from 1 to 10, where 1 is "I rarely engage in this behavior" and 10 is "I always engage in this behavior." When the researcher sums up the respondent's scores to all the questions, they have a number that quantifies how often that person engages in eating behaviors. A high score might indicate greater engagement in pathological behaviors whereas a low score might indicate healthier eating behaviors.

Qualitative data is more open-ended. They are gathered through field observations and open-ended questions, usually with little manipulation of the factors or context. To remember what qualitative data is, think about the word, quality – that is what this kind of data is, it represents the quality of a particular experience, thought, or behavior. An example of qualitative data might come from asking middle-aged women, "Do you think you have an undiagnosed eating disorder? If so, why?" Providing respondents with an opportunity to answer this question in their own words generates data that provides a glimpse into how they view their health, and the quality of their lived experiences as women of a specific age experiencing age-relevant developmental changes.

Compare the following two hypothetical approaches to studying Parkinson's disease, an age-related chronic disorder that makes it difficult for patients to control their movements. In one study, the researchers attended weekly support group meetings for patients with Parkinson's disease. There they asked patients to share their experiences of living with the disease, with only a few prompts from the researcher. Researchers videotaped each conversation. Later, they watched and listened to the videotapes to see what themes emerged, and they recorded what similarities and differences were found across the interviews. From this qualitative data they were able to summarize, from patients' own words, what is it like to live with the disease. These researchers published results from the study and presented their findings in a way that preserves the flavor of subjective experience and qualitative evidence. Meanwhile, a second study of Parkinson's disease produced quantitative data. Again, researchers went to the Parkinson's support group and spoke with patients one-on-one. Except in this case, they asked each participant to answer a series of questions from a standardized questionnaire on stress and coping. These researchers were interested in how older patients cope with the stress of disease. Specifically, in this study, the interviewers asked questions like the following.

- On a scale of 1 to 10, with 1 being *not-at-all stressful* and 10 being *extremely stressful*, how stressful are the symptoms of your illness?
- Please listen to the following common symptoms of Parkinson's disease. For each symptom, please state the level of pain you experience, on a scale where 1 indicates *no pain*, 2 indicates *some pain*, 3 indicates *a great deal of pain*, and 4 indicates *excruciating pain*.

Afterward, based on respondents' answers, researchers categorized the patients into either a low-stress group or a high-stress group. They could then use statistical analyses to determine whether the high-stress group experienced greater levels of pain than the low-stress group. This is an example of a quantitative study. The researchers had a hypothesis that high stress would relate to greater pain in the context of this disease, and they used measures to gather data that would allow them to test that hypothesis.

Once again, in these two types of studies different types of data are gleaned. Qualitative studies aim to explore and describe the quality of experience, while quantitative studies aim to quantify or measure that experience. Qualitative studies seek to record the particulars of experience, while quantitative studies look for generalizations from the data. Quantitative research is almost always *hypothesis driven*: researchers know ahead of time what ideas they are testing.

Variables

In developmental psychology, researchers are interested in the factors that influence age related differences or behavior change over time. In other words, they are interested in how some factors, or *variables* affect others.

Independent variables (IVs) are the factors that researchers manipulate across different groups or conditions within the experiment. Independent variables are used to examine changes in the **dependent variable** (DV). In our study of Parkinson's disease, the stress associated with symptoms is the independent variable. Dependent variables are the observed or expected outcomes that we record or measure. We are looking to see whether the IVs have influenced the DVs. In our example, we want to determine whether those who experience more stress also experience more pain.

Research Designs

There are various ways to understand the influences of IVs on DVs, and we use different research designs to uncover those influences.

Correlational research aims to find associations between variables. For example, a researcher might be interested in the amount of sleep a person gets and their test performance the next day. They might hypothesize that the more hours of sleep (e.g., 7–8 hours) students get the higher their scores on a quiz the next day. Interestingly, the opposite hypothesis is likely as well: the fewer hours of sleep the worse the quiz score is expected to be. This is an example of a **positive correlation** between two variables: as one rises or falls, so does the other. More sleep, higher quiz scores – less sleep, lower quiz scores. In a **negative correlation**, two variables influence each other in the opposite direction: as one rises, the other falls. Researchers might hypothesize that the more hours of sleep the night before a quiz, the lower the test anxiety.

In these examples, quiz score or test anxiety are the DVs, and hours of sleep the night before is the IV, and what we get is a correlation between the IV and the DV. We can quantify a correlation using a **correlation coefficient**. The stronger the correlation, the larger the absolute value of the correlation coefficient. Correlation coefficients range from −1.00 (a perfect negative correlation) to 1.00 (a perfect positive correlation). The closer the

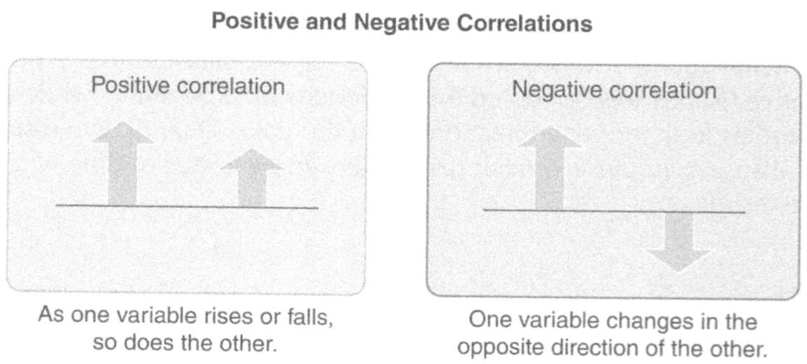

Figure 2.2 Positive and negative correlations.

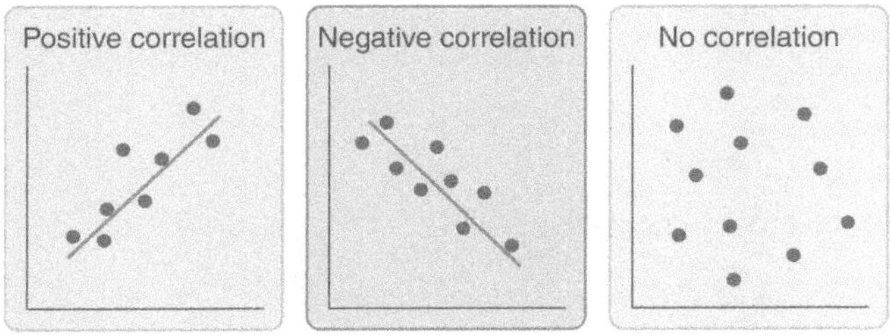

Figure 2.3 Data points to illustrate positive, negative, and no correlation.

coefficient is to 0.00 (no relationship between variables), the weaker the correlation is.

In order to determine the statistical meaningfulness of a correlation, we determine whether or not a correlation is significant or not. We look to see if the correlation meets a predetermined level of significance, reported as a *p value* (or *probability level*). These *p values* represent the likelihood that we would find a correlation at least as large as the one we found, if there were really no relationship between the variables. So, when we say that the correlation had a *p value* below a certain level, we mean that the value reached the threshold at which we are confident that it would be very unlikely if there were truly no relationship. Therefore, the two variables are assumed to influence each other.

As useful as these tools are, keep in mind something important: correlation does not mean causation. In our example, we cannot say that hours of sleep cause quiz scores to be high or that sleep causes test anxiety. Why not? Because maybe it works the other way around. Maybe someone who knows they have studied well can sleep better the night before the quiz. Or perhaps a third factor has caused *both* – perhaps it is hours spent studying or confidence in learning that leads to higher quiz scores and less test anxiety. Only a strictly designed experiment can provide causality, and only when three conditions have been met:

1 there is covariation, or the IV and the DV are related;
2 there is temporal precedence, or the IV (cause) precedes the DV (outcome) in time;
3 and there is a non-spurious relationship, or no plausible alternative explanation (in other words, the influence of the IV on the DV cannot be explained by some other, unstudied third variable).

About our correlational example, all we can say for sure is that in our study sample, the more hours of sleep you get the higher your quiz scores the next day. You would need an experimental study to determine causality. Experimental studies take place in carefully controlled laboratory settings.

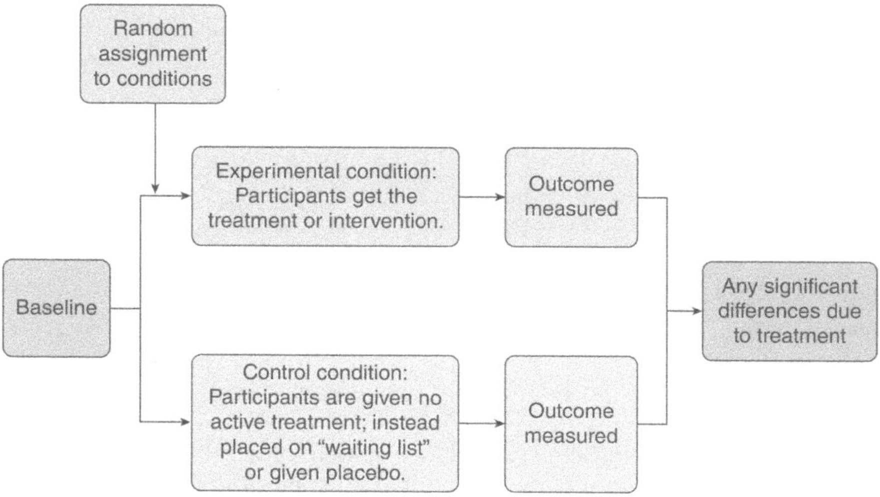

Figure 2.4 Diagram of the experimental process.

Experimental research involves direct manipulation of the variable or variables within a carefully controlled experimental condition (see Figure 2.4). **Quasi-experimental research** resembles experimental studies, but it does not involve random assignment, or IVs that can be controlled by the researcher. Because there is no random assignment of participants in quasi-experimental designs, we cannot rule out the influence of some unexamined third variable and therefore we cannot make claims of causality. Both the examples of Parkinson's disease and of the associations among sleep and quiz scores are quasi-experimental methods. Additionally, these examples both involve self-report questionnaires, another clue that they are collecting quasi-experimental data. In both experimental and quasi-experimental methods, researchers define ahead of time the variables that they want to examine and the hypotheses that they wish to test. Additionally, researchers define the characteristics of the population under study and recruit participants based on whether they meet those criteria. Yet, in quasi-experimental research, there is still room for the complex, subjective nature of experience.

Experimental studies randomly assign participants to different conditions. These studies also make use of a **control group**, or a group that is *not* subjected to the condition we are testing. If we wanted to establish a cause-and-effect relationship among hours of sleep and scores on a quiz the next day, we could bring participants into a lab and carefully control exactly how much sleep they get. Our control group would be people who volunteered but are told they are on a "waitlist" and therefore do not receive any experimental manipulation. Quasi-experimental studies are excellent for establishing differences between groups or associations between variables. They can provide support for hypotheses – or prove them wrong.

Developmental Research Designs: Cross-Sectional and Longitudinal Designs

In developmental research, we usually seek to answer two types of questions: first, how do people compare to one another? For example, how do the fitness levels of 30-year-olds compare to the fitness levels of 70-year-olds? Second, how do people change over time? For example, we follow and test people every two years from age 30 to age 70 to track how their fitness levels ebb and flow over those forty years. There are two common research designs that allow us to address these questions.

Cross-sectional studies generally collect data from a group (or groups) of people at a specific point in time, taking a "snapshot" of behavior. For example, a cross-sectional study might compare how different age groups compare on their fitness levels. In contrast, **longitudinal studies** follow individuals over their lifespan, determining how they change and grow over time. Longitudinal studies help determine how different factors may influence development, growth, stability, and change over time. As Castel (2018) says, "Watching our children grow up or our parents grow old" illustrates how people change over time and is a way to think about longitudinal research. "Comparing ourselves to our children" illustrates how time changes us and how people differ at different ages, a good way to think about cross-sectional research.

Developmental studies are concerned with how age or developmental stage relates to some outcome. Both cross-sectional and longitudinal methods can be used in developmental studies. Say we are interested in whether young adults (between the ages of 18 and 25) or older adults (older than 65) are more likely to practice healthful eating. To find out, we take two "snapshots" or "cross sections" of the population. Developmentally, we are interested in differences between the two age groups. Here age is our IV. We recruit and survey 200 young adults and 200 older adults about their daily eating patterns. We ask "How likely are you to eat each of the following?" We then present choices, such as eating a nutritious breakfast, eating a rainbow of fruits and vegetables daily, and avoiding unhealthy fats. Suppose we find that older adults practice more healthful eating behaviors than younger adults. We might conclude that, as one gets older, one is more likely to adopt healthy eating. After all, older adults might be more concerned with being healthy and living longer than their younger counterparts. Remember, though, that correlation is not causation. Perhaps today's older adults were *always* more health-conscious and have eaten more healthfully all their adult lives. For example, baby boomers, the generation born between 1946 and 1964, enjoyed America's postwar prosperity. They may have been influenced by the health-food craze in America or by nutritional labels that began appearing on food packaging in 1990 or the research evidence that consuming sugar can lead to obesity. We speak of groups with a shared experience or lifestyle as cohorts, and we call factors like these **cohort effects**.

Think about the different generations, from Baby Boomers to Gen Z. Gen Z, or those who were born between 1997 and 2012 are the true digital natives – they were born with tablets in their hands and have never known life without these technologies and the internet. This illustrates how a group of people born at a certain time share historical, cultural, social, and developmental factors that lead to cohort effects.

How then might age influence eating behaviors? To decide, we must look to longitudinal studies.

As we have seen, a cross-sectional study compares groups of participants at a particular point in time. A longitudinal study, however, follows the same participants over time, to determine how their behaviors change as they grow, develop and age. Rather than providing a snapshot, it is more like a movie (see Table 2.1). From a lifespan developmental perspective, this is the ideal way to learn about how personal growth influences health.

Continuing with our example, as we grow older, do we, in fact, become more conscientious about eating more healthy foods? To find out, we would survey a group of young adults and then survey these same participants periodically until they reach old age. We could then see whether and how their eating behaviors change over time.

Table 2.2 Comparisons made in cross-sectional versus longitudinal designs

Cohort Year of Birth	*Age*							
2000	15	16	17	18	19	20	21	22
2001	14	15	16	17	18	19	20	21
2002	13	14	15	16	17	18	19	20
2003	12	13	14	15	16	17	18	19
2004	11	12	13	14	15	16	17	18
2005	10	11	12	13	14	15	16	17
2006	9	10	11	12	13	14	15	16
2007	8	9	10	11	12	13	14	15
2008	7	8	9	10	11	12	13	14
2009	6	7	8	9	10	11	12	13
2010	5	6	7	8	9	10	11	12

Time of Measurement

Indicates a cross-sectional comparison of ages

Indicates a longitudinal comparison of ages

Figure 2.5 Ethics in science.
Source: Shutterstock.

We have now learned about the main research methods used by developmental researchers interested in how people grow and change across adulthood. It is important to understand the factors that shape how research is carried out, including the unfortunate historical problems in scientific research that have led to the strict guidelines we now hold for conducting rigorous scientific research.

Research Ethics

Today, any institution in the United States that conducts research on human or animal subjects requires that research adheres to strict ethical rules. Researchers must gain consent from human participants, and there must be no unnecessary invasive medical procedures. Any scientist planning a study must first gain approval from an **institutional review board** (IRB). The IRB consists of members of the research institution, the institution's legal counsel, and an additional person, usually someone with medical or legal expertise.

This extensive approval is necessary because scientific research has a tainted past. In the name of science, studies have been conducted that seriously harmed and endangered participants. Sometimes participants were forced to take part or unknowingly took part in studies.

One of the most devastating and scandalous medical experiments was also one of the darkest moments in American scientific history. The **Tuskegee**

experiment began in Alabama in 1932 and ran for 40 years. Six hundred poor, rural, African American sharecroppers (all men) were encouraged to participate in a study of "bad blood," a local term for disease. That was all they were told. In exchange for their participation, they were provided free medical care and meals. They were told that for participating they would receive free burial insurance for when they died, but they had to agree to an autopsy. In the course of the experiment, the men were also subjected to painful spinal taps in order to draw fluids for analysis. Only many years later, if they had not already died during the study, did they learn the experiment's real purpose – to examine the effects of untreated syphilis on the human body.

At the start of the study, 399 of the men were diagnosed with the disease but never told, the other 201 men were free of syphilis and served as the control group. When a treatment for syphilis, penicillin, finally became available in 1947, participants in this study were denied it (Perlstadt, 2024a). Dozens of men died, and countless numbers of women, wives, children, and others were infected. In 1972 Peter Buxton who had worked for the U.S. Public Health Service leaked the existence of the study to a U.S. newspaper. There was outcry and, finally, in 1972 the study was halted. At that time, only 74 participants were still alive, 28 had died of the disease, and 100 had died from syphilis-related complications. Forty of their wives were unknowingly infected, and 19 of their children were born with a disabling and often life-threatening form of the disease (Kampmeier, 2000). The U.S. Department of Health, Education and Welfare shut down the study in 1972, but only after it had become a political embarrassment.

On May 16, 1997, President Clinton apologized to the eight survivors of the Tuskegee experiments:

> The eight men who are survivors of the syphilis study at Tuskegee are a living link to a time not so very long ago that many Americans would prefer not to remember, but we dare not forget. It was a time when our nation failed to live up to its ideals, when our nation broke the trust with our people that is the very foundation of our democracy. It is not only in remembering that shameful past that we can make amends and repair our nation, but it is in remembering that past that we can build a better present and a better future.

Another event that led to ethical reform in science came after World War II. German physicians had conducted painful and often deadly medical experiments on concentration camp prisoners without their consent (Annas & Grodin, 1995). These horrific atrocities led to the conviction of camp physicians and administrators for crimes of war and crimes against humanity. It also led to the creation of the Nuremberg Code, a ten-point directive laying out the ethical treatment of human research study participants. However, although this was a step in the right direction, the code lacked the force of the law and served only as a guideline. Later, in 1978, more detailed principles were laid out and codified in the Belmont Report, which came into law three years

Figure 2.6 President Bill Clinton apologizing to the surviving eight men who were coerced into participating in the Tuskegee Experiment.

Source: Alamy.

later. Additional protections were signed into law in 1991. Unfortunately, these measures arrived too late to be applied to many classic psychology experiments. The Stanford prison experiment (1970s), the Milgram obedience experiment (1960s), and Harlow's studies on dependency in monkeys (1950s), for instance, would not be considered ethical today nor would they be allowed to be conducted.

Until 2015, the United States was the only country in the world that continued to use chimpanzees in medical research. Chimps were intentionally infected with diseases, such as hepatitis or HIV, used in live crash test experiments, and subject to painful surgical procedures. In November 2015, the National Institutes of Health announced that it would no longer support any invasive research on chimps, and that the 300 or so chimps remaining in research facilities would move to a federally approved sanctuary. The Endangered Species Act was modified in 2015, listing chimps as an endangered species, thus making it even more difficult for biomedical science to use chimps in experiments (U.S. Fish & Wildlife Service, 2015).

Improving Science

If you read about the results of a study in a blog or hear about something "scientifically proven" on TikTok, how do you know if it is real? Should you believe it? Science has been under fire lately, especially in the United States. But politics aside, science, and particularly psychological science, have been called into question on account of widespread problems in replicating previously published research findings. Advocates of the *replication crisis* suggest that there are many historically significant findings within the field that are taken as fact, but that cannot be reproduced scientifically today; thus, these findings may no longer explain behavior and should not be used to shape theory and practice in the field. The replication crisis involves the culmination of several factors: questionable research practices, flawed research study designs, publication biases toward positive findings, and sometimes even research fraud (when researchers intentionally fabricate or falsify their data).

As we have seen in this chapter, developmental psychology generates knowledge by relying on hypothesis testing and sound empirical methods. However, if a finding from one research study cannot be replicated in another laboratory with a different sample of participants, should the findings be reported and trusted?

For example, suppose you are searching for scientific evidence of the most effective natural sleep aid, and you come across a study that touts the many advantages of listening to opera for 30 minutes before sleeping. Before you stream a new opera performance, you would want to evaluate the study's methods and check if other researchers had tested the hypothesis and come up with the same results. Replication in science is an important issue, and many researchers are now conducting their scientific investigations in ways that allow their empirical methods, hypotheses, data analyses, and findings to be easily tested by others. This is a major and beneficial step to address the replication crisis and to insure more rigorous scientific research. Some researchers now make the dataset that they have collected from their studies available online for free for other scientists to test themselves. This practice, called the **open science** framework, is an important advancement in addressing the replication crisis (Shrout & Rodgers, 2018). Open science involves full disclosure of all the factors that may have influenced researchers' analyses and findings, including those findings that were not statistically significant. Now, many researchers believe that the replication crisis has led to better science – specifically, it has led to new and important insights and practices that can improve psychological science in the twenty-first century and beyond (Shrout & Rodgers, 2018).

Chapter Summary

In this chapter we looked at some adult development theories and how they relate to different kinds of research designs. In addition to research methods for understanding stability, growth, and change across adulthood, we learned about the historical events that led to our currently rigorous research ethics. We also considered the threats to science brought on by the replicability crisis and how contemporary scientists are engaging in open science to conduct better scholarship.

Key Takeaways

1 There are multiple approaches to conceptualizing development across adulthood.
2 Developmental research involves following individuals over time to understand developmental change, as well as comparing individuals at different ages to understand age-related similarities and differences.
3 Developmental scientists use a variety of different methods to study development.
4 Developmental research, like all psychological research, must have IRB approval to protect participants.

Reflective Questions

1 Which model best explains development – the organismic, mechanistic or interactionist model?
2 Can you identify whether a research method is cross-sectional or longitudinal?
3 Why is it important for researchers to gain IRB approval before conducting a study?

Suggested Readings

Narvaez, D., Moore, D. S., Witherington, D. C., Vandiver, T. I., & Lickliter, R. (2022). Evolving evolutionary psychology. *American Psychologist, 77*(3), 424–438. doi: 10.1037/amp0000849.
Perlstadt, H. (2024b). A history of social science ethics and regulations in the United States. In *Assessing Social Science Research Ethics and Integrity: Case Studies and Essays* (pp. 17–39). Springer International Publishing.
Shrout, P. E., & Rodgers, J. L. (2018). Psychology, science, and knowledge construction: Broadening perspectives from the replication crisis. *Annual Review of Psychology, 69*(1), 487–510.

Key Terms/Glossary

A **cohort effect** refers to groups with a shared experience or lifestyle.
A **control group** is a group of participants in an experiment that is *not* subjected to the condition being tested.
The **correlation coefficient** is the statistic that shows the strength among two variables.

Correlational research aims to find associations between variables.

Cross-sectional studies generally collect data from a group (or groups) of people at a specific point in time, taking a "snapshot" of behavior.

Dependent variables (DVs) are the observed or expected outcomes that we record or measure.

Developmental studies are concerned with how age or developmental stage relate to an outcome.

Experimental research involves direct manipulation of the variable or variables within a carefully controlled experimental condition.

A **hypothesis** is a proposed explanation for a phenomenon that a scientist seeks to test in a research study.

Independent variables (IVs) are the factors that researchers manipulate across different groups or conditions within the experiment.

An **institutional review board** (IRB) consists of members of the research institution, the institution's legal counsel, and an additional person, usually someone with medical or legal expertise.

Interactionist models of development are based on the idea that the individual and their environment are reciprocally interacting, shaping, and being shaped by each other, all the time to influence the course of development.

Interdisciplinary is when research draws upon theories and other research from many fields.

Longitudinal studies follow individuals over their lifespan, determining how they change and grow over time.

The **mechanistic model** is the theory that development occurs when behavior is shaped by environmental forces that continually and gradually act upon an individual over time.

A **negative correlation** is when two variables influence each other in the opposite direction: as one rises, the other falls.

Open science is an important advancement in addressing the replication crisis in psychology. It is characterized by researchers sharing their data so others can replicate their methods and results.

The **organismic model** is the theory that genetics and heredity are the primary influences on development and that these influences unfold in a predictable stage-like fashion.

Plasticity, especially in the brain (neuroplasticity), reflects the brain's ability to develop new connections, change, and adapt in the face of developmental challenges.

With a **positive correlation**, when one variable rises or falls, so does the other.

Qualitative data is gathered through field observations and open-ended questions, usually with little manipulation of the factors or context.

Quantitative data are gathered through carefully designed examination, with all the possible factors affecting the construct determined ahead of time.

Quasi-experimental research resembles experimental studies, but it does not involve random assignment or independent variables that can be controlled by the researcher.

A **theory** is a set of ideas that explain the world around us.

The **Tuskegee experiment** began in Alabama in 1932 and ran for 40 years. It tested the effects of untreated syphilis on poor African American men, who were not aware that their health was being manipulated in unethical ways.

3 Biological Aspects of Growth and Change

Learning Outcomes

Describe differences between the programmed aging paradigm and non-programmed aging paradigm theories, and the more recent theories of aging (i.e., mitochondria theory of aging, telomeres, calorie restriction).

Explain the different types of life expectancy (i.e., cohort life expectancy, period life expectancy, maximum life span, active life expectancy, and dependent life expectancy).

Articulate key differences in life expectancy in the United States and across cultures over time.

Describe general changes in vision, hearing, taste, smell, and the vestibular system as we age.

Identify how biological, psychological, and contextual factors are involved in aging.

Theories on Aging

The oldest world record maker in the 100-meter run is Julia "Hurricane" Hawkins. Hawkins completed her 100-meter race in 62 seconds, a record for her age category, which was 105+ in 2021. She was a retired elementary school teacher from Baton Rouge, Louisiana, and an athlete for many years, winning numerous medals in the Senior Olympics in cycling before she began running. Julia was the oldest athlete in the world to compete and win a medal, and she died at age 108 in the fall of 2024.

Why Do We Age?

Everything from plants, to insects, to animals will age over time and die. Why do all living things grow older and die? Is there anything we can do to slow down the aging process? These questions occur for the average person as well as scientists, and there is extensive research on this topic.

DOI: 10.4324/9781003483809-3

Hippocrates (460–377 BC) viewed aging as occurring because of a gradual loss of heat in organisms (Trubitsyn, 2020). By the nineteenth century, Weismann, known as the founder of modern genetics, argued that our longevity comes from natural selection (Trubitsyn, 2020; Weissman, 2010). In the mid-1950s, Medawar argued that genes of aging cannot exist, and instead promoted the idea that aging comes from the "wear and tear" of an organism (Cohen & Holmes, 2014; Trubitsyn, 2020). In the 1950s, the "free radical theory of aging" was discussed as the reason for aging (Son & Lee, 2021). By 1990, there were more than 300 theories proposing explanations on aging, and Medvedev (1990) tried to classify these theories. Today there is still no conclusive evidence to support only one theory of aging in humans and across species (da Costa et al., 2016). Perhaps a combination of parts of different theories may be more beneficial for understanding the aging process, a multidimensional approach (da Costa et al., 2016; Pamplona et al., 2023). This chapter does not provide a conclusive combined theory of why we age; however, we describe a number of theories of aging, some of which have increasing evidence of support.

There has been an ongoing debate over theories addressing the aging process, especially in terms of work on **programmed aging theories**, and **non-programmed theories**, with many studies over time on worms, rodents, and humans (Goldsmith, 2017; Medawar, 1952; Pamplona et al., 2023; Williams, 1957; Winterhalter & Simm, 2022). Researchers today have referred to the theories within each view as a comparison between the programmed aging paradigm and the non-programmed paradigm (e.g., Libertini et al., 2021). Discussion begins with programmed aging theories within the programmed aging paradigm.

Programmed Aging Paradigm

Programmed aging theories refer to aging as something programmed into our bodies (Jin, 2010). Aging is believed to be controlled by genes favoring natural selection at a level beyond the individual, with genes harmful to us as we age. Natural selection affects reproductive success but not overall survival of groups. Programmed aging theories include investigation by researchers looking for a biological clock, involving signaling and biological detection of internal and external conditions responsible for aging (Winterhalter & Simm, 2022). We are genetically programmed to grow older and die, a belief needed for parts of evolution (Goldsmith, 2017).

There are three main programmed aging theories including **endocrine theory**, **programmed senescence**, and **immunological theory**. These theories are based on genetic or biological explanations for why we age. The endocrine theory is based on a biological clock that works through hormones to control the aging process. There are studies showing that aging involves hormone regulation, and the belief that evolutionary conservation is involved in the insulin/insulin-like growth factor 1 (IGF-1) signaling pathway as a key role in hormone regulation associated with aging (American Federation of Aging Research, 2016; van Heemst, 2010). Mice with deficiencies in growth hormone and IGF-1 show association with the regulation of aging (Son & Lee, 2021). Programmed senescence occurs when a sequential switch is triggered to turn on or off certain genes, and senescence is the time period when age-associated reductions in our cells, tissues, organs, and body overall are displayed (Davidovic et al., 2010; Domínguez-Bautista et al., 2021). Immunological theory refers to the immune system being programmed to diminish over time, and allows for an increased likelihood of infectious diseases that result in aging and death. Evidence today comes from our antibodies becoming less effective as we age, resulting in less ability for our bodies to fight a new disease, such as COVID-19 (Li, K., et al., 2020), leading to internal stress (i.e., cellular level) and death (Arvey et al., 2020; Jin, 2010). Modern research shows evidence of immune system issues involved, at least indirectly, in cardiovascular disease, cancer, and Alzheimer's disease (Jyotsna et al., 2023; Martini et al., 2018).

Programmed theories of aging are linked to Charles Darwin's "The Origin of Species" published in 1859. Today, researchers explain that aspects of our biology may limit the lifespan, and this varies by species for specific age limits. It may be an adaptive component because the biological mechanisms that limit the lifespan of different species may provide an evolutionary advantage, what some researchers call a **population benefit** (Pamplona et al., 2023). Some researchers believe that an evolutionary force or drive may be at work to achieve a species-specific best lifespan (Pamplona et al., 2023). Some evidence of an evolutionary drive is lack of variation in lifespan within species. For example, elephants die at approximately 60 to 70 years old, depending on where they live (Lahdenperä et al., 2018), yet the lifespan for over 300 species of octopus is between six months and five years (Mather et al., 2010).

Darwin's work describes evolutionary mechanisms that include mutations, considered random changes in the inheritable design of an organism, and natural selection as an important evolutionary mechanism. If change in an organism causes the organism to live longer and reproduce more, then the change helps production in a population. Long ago researchers showed that traits governed by genes sharing close physical proximity on the same chromosome were generally inherited together as a single unit. In fact, even a gene that is mutated, if it controls a nearby gene, may be able to resist removal by natural selection if it is also linked to a net benefit overall (Williams, 1957). More recently, scientific discoveries show that evolution involves many steps that enable population benefits (Lenski, 2017). For example, **inter-trait linkage** refers to traits linked to increase the difficulty for evolutionary processes to create organisms with only one trait and not other linked traits (Chebib & Guillaume, 2021; Goldsmith, 2014).

Non-programmed Paradigm

Non-programmed theories explain that aging occurs because of the random accumulation of deteriorating experiences that cannot be prevented by natural selection (Libertini et al., 2021). Modern theories within the non-programmed paradigm tend to focus on aging being caused by an accumulation of damage. The damage could be chemical damage from DNA transcription errors, the negative effects of oxidation, mitochondria, or DNA inflammatory issues, and changes in immune functioning (American Federation for Aging Research, 2016; Libertini et al., 2021). This view of aging is negative, harms the organism, and considers natural selection needs to be corrective, not helpful towards aging (Vanhaelen, 2019). Current non-programmed theories are focused on natural deterioration over the lifespan for aging mammals, and the differences between species lifespan based on how well they deal with deteriorative processes. These theories focus on disease-specific damage and mechanisms and ways to correct or repair the damage (Jin, 2010; Libertini et al., 2021).

Current non-programmed theories of aging for mammals, including **mutation accumulation theory**, **antagonistic pleiotropy theory**, and **disposable soma theory**, have no consensus on which theory is the most likely reason for why we age (Cohen et al., 2020; Winterhalter & Simm, 2022). However, damage from an accumulation of DNA mutations, protein aggregates, and/or changes in biological structures appear to have the most support (Cohen et al., 2020; Winterhalter & Simm, 2022).

The mutation accumulation theory is considered the oldest evolutionary theory of aging, and was first discussed by Sir Peter Medawar (1952). This theory is focused on the influence of natural selection decreasing as we age, with individuals having less chances of continuing to produce offspring (Cohen & Holmes, 2014). Medawar (1952) discussed mutation accumulation occurring when natural selection declines enough that it has little effect on repeated harmful mutations that occur in older adults.

The antagonistic pleiotropy theory, considered the most widely cited evolutionary theory of aging, is still receiving support today (Trubitsyn, 2020), and was first discussed by George C. Williams (1957). A gene has antagonistic pleiotropy when it controls more than one trait, at least one of the traits is helpful to the organism early in the lifespan, and another trait is harmful later in life from a decrease in the effect of natural selection (Chebib & Guillaume, 2021; Cohen & Holmes, 2014; Williams, 1957). This theory focuses on the force of natural selection declining as we age. However, Williams (1957) argued that natural selection could actively produce aging, rather than failing to select against aging. Natural selection is expected to work against gene variants that are helpful later in life and harmful early in life (Cohen & Holmes, 2014).

The disposable soma theory, first proposed by Thoms Kirkwood (1977), includes a discussion of balance between maintenance of an organism and the organism's reproductive ability. Not enough self-repair can lead to death of an organism before reaching reproductive age, which is not great for evolution. However, too much focus on self-repair leads to the organism's offspring dying off before they reach their reproductive age, also not beneficial for evolution of organisms (Kirkwood, 2005). Kirkwood explains that finding the balance between repair (cell renewal, intracellular maintenance) and reproductive capability is a challenge for the organism. It could lead to damage in an organism's body repair systems, consequently, leading to cellular damage that worsens as we age (Kirkwood, 2005). For multicellular organisms (e.g., humans), the exact cellular process for reproductive capability to impede the aging process is still unknown.

Theories on Aging Receiving Attention Today

Other Theories on Aging

Some researchers use the term **error theories** of aging to argue that aging is due to a series of accidents. Some error theories include **rate of living theory**, which argues that our bodies only have so many biological moments (e.g., heartbeats) before they will break down, and those with higher metabolic rates have shorter lifespans; **free radical theory** (discussed in detail below) involves reactive atom-oxygen as an explanation for aging and provides some support for the rate of living theory (Harman, 1956); **protein cross-linked theory**, which is based on chemical changes that interact in the body; and **somatic DNA damage theory**, involving our genes controlling our aging until we die. Some theories of aging are receiving more attention in the scientific community today including free radical theory of aging, **mitochondrial theory of aging**, work on **calorie restriction**, and research on **telomeres**. We shall discuss each of these below.

The free radical theory of aging was first brought up by Denham Harman in the 1950s, with most research focused on reactive atom-oxygen, a subtype of reactive oxygen species (ROS) (Son & Lee, 2021; Ziada et al., 2020), though there are reactive atom-nitrogen and reactive atom-sulfur species too (Harman, 1956; Polidori & Mecocci, 2022). The ROS are mostly produced by an organism's mitochondria, and respiratory activity occurs to produce energy that is stored in adenosine triphosphate (ATP). The increased production and buildup of free radicals as organisms age results in damage to organisms nucleic acids, lipids, and proteins; consequently, this damage weakens organisms biological abilities as we age. Some researchers argue against the "universal role of oxidative damage in aging" (Gladyshev, 2014, p. 5), and discuss the idea that there are many forms of damage that could be factors affecting aging.

By the 1970s, Harman had revised his ideas and began focusing on the role of mitochondria with free radicals (Harman, 1972). With his mitochondrial theory of aging, Harman argued that mitochondria show issues with function over time in individuals, leading to an increase of free radicals and oxidation bioproducts with less antioxidants available. Mitochondria are considered multifunctional **organelles** (a specialized part within a cell that has a specific function). Mitochondria produce most of an organism's cellular ATP, and they help regulate and coordinate the cellular processes of an organism (Son & Lee, 2021). Some of the cellular processes include programmed cell death, immune responses, and intracellular and endocrine signaling. Mitochondria transfer electrons from nutrients to oxygen through an electron transfer chain during a process known as oxidative phosphorylation (OXPHOS). It is during this process that organisms' electrons can react with oxygen, creating ROS. Accumulating evidence over time has researchers supporting the idea that mitochondrial dysfunction, involving less oxidative capacity and more oxidative damage, are associated with biological aging (Malek et al., 2018; Polidori & Mecocci, 2022). Mitochondria may affect the aging process by reducing the capacity of energy, cell senescence, and low-grade inflammation (Miwa et al., 2022; Polidori & Mecocci, 2022). Researchers have shown that mitochondrial oxidant signaling is critical for extending the lifespan, and it is involved in the body response to different stressors such as calorie restriction, temperature stress, and physical exertion (Son & Lee, 2021). Work on the Caenorhabditis elegans (known as C. elegans) has shown that early exposure to ROS affects the organisms stress resistance later and is linked to extended lifespan (Ristow & Schmeisser, 2014; Sies, 2020; Son & Lee, 2021). Much work has been done on the C. elegans, and research has shown that a mutation of a gene called the DAF-2 gene is associated with doubling the maximum lifespan of the C. elegans (Son & Lee, 2021; Zhang et al., 2022).

Research over the past few decades has focused more on the role of free radical induced mitochondrial DNA (mtDNA) mutations and the accumulation of mtDNA deletions (Son & Lee, 2021; Ziada et al., 2020). Researchers have shown that mitochondria can repair oxidative mtDNA damage. "Age-dependent mtDNA mutations are considered to be from replication errors by mtDNA polymerase γ (POLG)" (Son & Lee, 2021, p. 161). MtDNA deletion mutations from errors in replication of mitochondrial genome cell loss are considered by scientists to be a feature in aging mammals. Researchers argue the "mtDNA deletion frequency can serve as a marker for electron transport chain (ETC) deficient cells, and the rate of cell loss" (Herbst et al., 2021, p. 1812), and cell loss is associated with negative changes in both tissue structure and function. Numerous unique mtDNA deletion mutations occur at a high level in human cells that are ETC-deficient and associated with aging (Herbst et al., 2021).

Calorie Restriction

There is evidence from research on insects, other animals, and humans that calorie restriction (CR) can extend the lifespan by about one to five years, and even improve brain health in flies (Wilson et al., 2024), though the amount of time by which life is extended depends on the amount of calorie restriction, how it occurs, the species, etc. (Flanagan et al., 2020; Wilson et al., 2024). Calorie restriction is the reduction of dietary consumption below specific energy requirements for weight maintenance while maintaining optimal nutrition. For humans, misuse of CR without proper guidance and supervision by a physician can lead to dangerous situations without adequate intake of nutrients needed for life sustaining functions. Studies that have successfully demonstrated life extension of species with CR have done so under controlled situations maintaining the balance of key nutrients for health (Flanagan et al., 2020). Individuals who are part of the CR Society International are a group of people who have voluntarily restricted their energy consumption for 3 to 15 years with about 30% CR, and maintained recommended nutrients. There is medical evidence for this group that shows improvements in cardiometabolic health, including blood pressure, glucose, cholesterol, and anti-inflammatory markers, comparable to those 15 to 20 years younger than those in the group (Holloszy & Fontana, 2007; Most & Redman, 2017). Other approaches such as alternate-day-fasting (ADF), considered a form of intermittent fasting, have been tried in various ways, altering the number of hours and days. A modified ADF diet seems to provide similar improvements in secondary aging markers to those described above, though no difference in primary aging has been detected yet (Catenacci et al., 2016).

Telomeres

Some researchers have focused their attention on telomeres when trying to explain why we age (Chakravarti et al., 2021). Telomeres are considered the tips of chromosomes (Creighton & McClintock, 1931; Muller, 1938), and they get shorter with each cell replication. Researchers have defined telomeres as repetitive nucleotide sequences (TTAGGG) with a "cap" that keeps the chromosome structure intact (Chakravarti et al., 2021; Trubitsyn, 2020). Telomeres are synthesized in embryonic cells by an enzyme called telomerase, and this enzyme is not present in most somatic cells (Chakravarti et al., 2021; Trubitsyn, 2020). Telomerase can add DNA sequences to chromosome ends and this helps extend telomere length (Greider & Blackburn, 1985). In the 1960s, researchers showed that human fetal cells have a finite ability to replicate, around 50 to 60 times, and this became known as the "Hayflick limit" (Hayflick & Moorhead, 1961; Hayflick, 1965). Researchers have determined that replication of human primary cells in lab cultures show short telomeres that make the Hayflick limit occur (Harley et al., 1990; Trubitsyn, 2020). Extensive research has been conducted on telomeres with insects, mice, and humans, and much research has shown that problems with the telomere are associated with aging (Chakravarti et al., 2021; Lopez-Otin et al., 2013; Trubitsyn, 2020). In fact, extensive research shows a relationship between telomeres, telomerase, inflammation, cellular aging, and various diseases (Chakravarti et al., 2021).

How Long Do We Live?

Do you know how long a person can live? Do you have any relatives who lived to 100 or older?

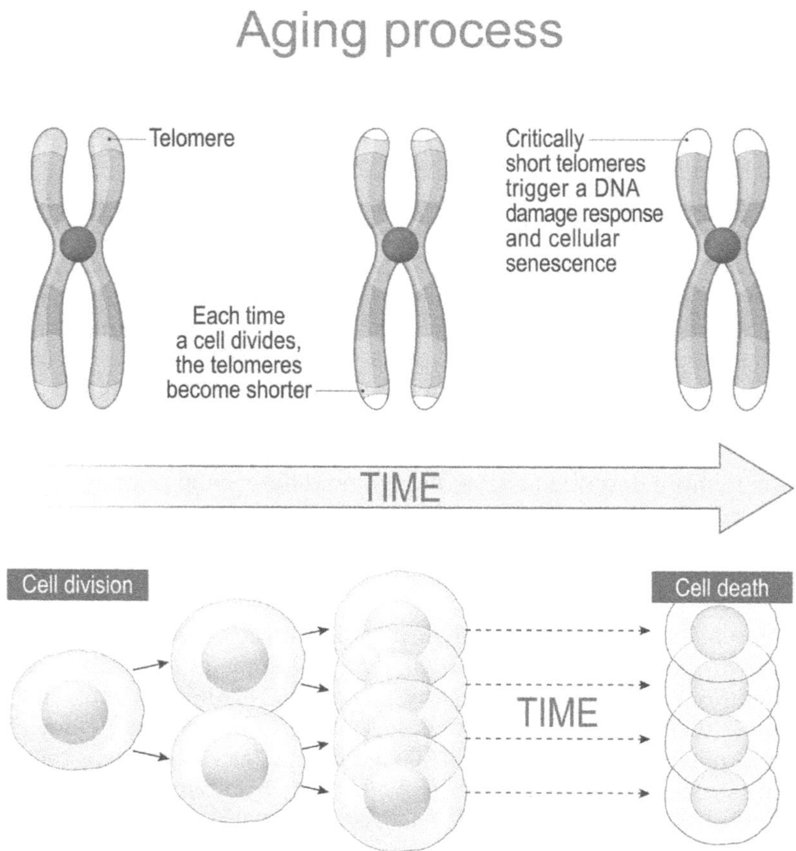

Figure 3.1 This is an illustration of young and old telomeres, showing how the tips are noticeably smaller for the older adult.

Source: Shutterstock.

Studies about how long we live generally refer to concepts such as life expectancy, cohort life expectancy, period life expectancy, maximum lifespan, active life expectancy, and dependent life expectancy. **Life expectancy** is the number of years a person can expect to live, and is based on an estimate. The estimate is the average age that individuals of a specific group will be when they die. **Cohort life expectancy** refers to the average time a group of individuals born in a specific year will live. Many researchers who study life expectancy focus on **period life expectancy**, and period life expectancy is not based on how mortality rates may change over time. Instead, period life expectancy only focuses on the mortality pattern at a specific point in time (Ortiz-Ospina, 2017). **Maximum life span** is the longest an individual can possibly live. Currently, researchers propose that the maximum human life span is close to 150 (Pyrkov et al., 2021). **Active life expectancy** is the number of years an individual can expect to live without disability, with no difficulty in performing activities of daily living (ADLs) such as bathing, dressing, etc. (Jia & Lubetkin, 2020). Active life expectancy is also called **disability-free life expectancy (DFLE)**. **Dependent life expectancy** refers to the number of years an individual is expected to live while they need assistance from others because of disability or illness.

Now that you know some basic definitions for terms related to how long we live, it is time to explore the most recent information on life expectancy in the United States as well as other countries around the world. The most recent life expectancy in the United States (2024) was 79.25 years old, continuing a slow trend upward since the decline during the beginning of the pandemic.[1]

U.S. Studies on Life Expectancy

Research on life expectancy in the United States has consistently shown large differences between racial-ethnic groups, and systemic structural racism has consistently been a core reason for a shorter life expectancy for African Americans, and American Indian or Alaska Natives compared to European Americans (Bailey et al., 2021). Structural racism includes lack of access to healthcare, barriers to employment opportunities, housing, education, and limitations in food resources (just to name a few), and is linked to a much higher mortality rate in African Americans and other minority groups compared to European Americans (Caraballo et al., 2023; Dwyer-Lindgren et al., 2022).

In a study considered the first country-wide assessment of life expectancy with county-level analyses to include non-Latino and non-Hispanic American Indians or Alaska Natives (AIAN), and non-Latino and non-Hispanic Asian or Pacific Islanders (API), researchers shared trends in life expectancy in the United States from 2000 through 2019 (Dwyer-Lindgren et al., 2022). The researchers analyzed death registration data from the U.S. National Vital Statistics System and population data from the U.S. National Center for Health Statistics to assess life expectancy. National data showed an increase in life expectancy for African Americans compared to any other group, including European American, Latinx American, and APIs. African Americans showed an increase in their life expectancy to 75.3 years by 2019. Life expectancy stayed the same for AIANs. Dwyer-Lindgren and colleagues (2022) noted that all racial-ethnic groups showed more increase in their life expectancy across counties from 2000 to 2010 than from 2011 to 2019. The gap in life expectancy between African Americans and European Americans decreased at a national level between 2000 and 2019, because of a larger increase in life expectancy for African Americans and smaller increases or decreases for European Americans. Differences in life expectancy between AIANs and other racial-ethnic groups showed a concerning trend, as AIANs had a significantly lower life expectancy compared to African American, European American and Latinx Americans. The Latinx Americans and APIs had the highest life expectancies, though there was evidence of a decline in life expectancy for Latinx Americans in predominantly minority counties (Dwyer-Lindgren et al., 2022).

In another study on life expectancy in the United States, researchers used data from the Center for Disease Control and Prevention from 1999–2020 that provided comparisons between non-Hispanic European Americans and non-Hispanic African Americans across all age groups (Caraballo et al., 2023). From 1999 to 2011 there was a decline in excess mortality rate for African American males, which appeared to remain at a consistent level from 2011 through 2019, and then increased in 2020. African American females showed a decline in excess mortality rate between 1999 and 2015, no significant change from 2016 through 2019, and an increase in 2020. Rate of excess mortality for African American males and females from 1999 to 2020 resulted in the loss of over 80 million African Americans. Over the lifespan, there was higher mortality for African Americans as a result of heart disease and cancer compared to European Americans, and the researchers argued that structural racism including barriers to health care access and lack of resources likely played a role in this difference (Caraballo et al., 2023). The issue of structural racism quickly became apparent as the pandemic began. African Americans were exposed to more infection from the virus due to their higher likelihood of low socioeconomic status (SES) preventing them from being able to stay home and work (i.e., essential workers at grocery stores, restaurants, etc.), a lack of their own food resources, and lack of access to health care. Over the 22-year period of the study, 1.63 million excess deaths were reported for the U.S. African American population.

Cross-Cultural Studies on Life Expectancy

Studies comparing the United States to other high-income countries have shown a concerning trend in recent research (Barbieri, 2022; Ho, 2022). Barbieri (2022) used death records from the U.S. National Vital Statistics System for 1982 through 2019, examining data for all 3,143 counties in the United States, and data for 20 other high-income countries (Denmark, Finland, Iceland, Norway, Sweden, Austria, Belgium, France, Ireland, Luxembourg, the Netherlands, Switzerland, the United Kingdom, Germany, Italy, Portugal, Spain, Canada, Japan, and Australia), with access to the Human Mortality Database. The United States has shown a noticeable decline in life expectancy compared to other high-income countries. Since the 1980s when this trend was first noticed, even variation in SES does not completely explain the reason for the decline in life expectancy compared to similar high-income countries (Barbieri, 2022). Barbieri reported that by 2019, life expectancy at birth was 73 years for men and 78.7 for women in the lowest SES locations, and 80.2 years for men and 84.5 years for women in the highest SES locations in the United States.

Once COVID-19 arrived, the United States was affected more than other countries with high-income levels, with a big increase in the gap in death rate between SES groups, and people with low SES showing the highest death rate in the United States (COVID-19 Excess Mortality Collaborators, 2022). Barbieri (2022) argued that our previous advantage in the United States for lower mortality rate for those 75 and older has been on a declining trend, and COVID-19 almost eroded that advantage. Overall, gains from improvement in cardiovascular disease in the United States stalling, lack of resources for people with low SES, racial inequality, U.S. public policies for health care, and gun use are all part of the reason for the United States not performing as well as similar high-income countries regarding mortality rate.

Ho (2022) used data from the Human Mortality Database, World Health Organization Mortality Database, and vital statistics agencies to examine life expectancy in the United States and seventeen other high-income countries (Australia, Austria, Belgium, Canada, Denmark, Finland, France, Germany, Italy, Japan, the Netherlands, Norway, Portugal, Spain, Sweden, Switzerland, and the United Kingdom). Ho (2022) found that the U.S. life expectancy is below the other high-income countries, with 2018 life expectancy for men and women in the United States more than five years below world leaders, and over three years lower than the average high-income country. Ho (2022) notes that high mortality in young people due to injury and risky lifestyle choices are part of the reason for a lower life expectancy in the United States compared to other high-income countries. There is a higher mortality rate associated with smoking for those in middle and older adulthood in the United States, as well as cardiovascular disease. Ho (2022) reported that the U.S. life expectancy had a minimal increase from 2010–2013, a decline from 2014 through 2017, and a slight increase from 2017 to 2018. Japan and Switzerland showed gains in life expectancy from 2010 through 2018. The United States has been showing a decline in life expectancy for decades, and continues to decrease over time compared to peer countries, falling to last place in comparison to peer countries for women in 2003 and for men in 2006 (Ho, 2022). Ho (2022) notes that men and women in the United States have death rates that are highest or second highest compared to other high-income countries until ages 70 to 74 for 2008, and 80 to 84 years old for 2018.

In general, some minority groups appear especially at risk of a shorter life expectancy. Indigenous individuals in the United States (Native American, Alaska Natives) have a life expectancy of approximately 74 compared to all ethnicities at approximately 78 years old (Ng et al., 2023). Indigenous groups in Canada have similar concerns regarding lower life expectancy, though it varies across Canadian Indigenous groups (First Nations, Inuit, Métis). Researchers discuss the complex life experiences within the different Indigenous groups in North America, including their experiences with structural racism: loss of land, relocation, trauma, poverty, lack of access to health care, mental health problems, substance abuse, violence, and suicide (Pace & Grenier, 2017). The lack of understanding about cultural differences in the way that Indigenous individuals' view life and death and the many aspects of structural racism continue to place Indigenous people in North America at risk of lower life expectancy (Pace & Grenier, 2017).

Global Life Expectancy

The Global Burden of Diseases, Injuries, and Risk Factors Study (Global Burden of Disease [GBD] 2021 Demographics Collaborators, 2024) included 22,223 data sources for their work on global life expectancy, including vital registration, sample registration, surveys, census, and other sources, to estimate mortality, and provided information on excess mortality from the COVID-19 pandemic (see GBD 2021 Demographics Collaborators, 2024 for details). This global study included 204 countries and territories and 811 subnational areas from 1950 to 2021. Global life expectancy at birth increased from 1950 to 2021 by 22.7 years to a life expectancy of 71.7 years. The exception occurred during COVID-19, with a drop in global life expectancy

Figure 3.2 Global population percentage by age and sex, 2025.

Source: © 2024 by PopulationPyramid.net, made available under a Creative Commons license.

of 1.6 years from 2019 through 2021. The pandemic affected sub-Saharan Africa, the Middle East, South Asia, and Latin America more severely than other parts of the world. There was an increase in life expectancy in 32 of the 204 countries and territories between 2019 and 2021. However, population growth is reported to have slowed across the globe since 2017 (GBD 2021 Demographics Collaborators, 2024). Exceptions to this trend include South Asia, which has a steady population growth, and sub-Saharan Africa, with an increase in population growth. The global evidence of a **"graying world"** shows evidence of an increase in those over 65 years old compared to individuals younger than 15 years old in 188 of 204 nations from the period 2000 to 2021 (GBD 2021 Demographics Collaborators, 2024).

Life Expectancy in Africa

Research on the African continent shows that Tunisia has the highest life expectancy at about 77 years old, with Algeria, Cabo Verde, Morocco, and Mauritius having a life expectancy between 75 and 77 years of age; Nigeria has the lowest life expectancy at about 54 years old (Galal, 2025). Variations in access to nutrition, health care, and safety level/environmental conditions are a few of the factors involved in differences in life expectancy in the African continent.

Who Are Our Longest Living People?

Centenarians

Centenarians, individuals who are 100 or older, are on the increase in the United States and multiple countries around the world. Some research shows that healthy lifestyle may be an important reason for this increase (Li et al., 2024). Research focused on centenarians has been on the rise over the past 20 years, with most studies conducted in Italy, the United States, and China, while Latin American countries and African countries have much less research on centenarians (see Lozada-Martinez et al., 2024 for a review).

There are more than 722,000 centenarians in the world according to the United Nations' work on population projections for 2024. Japan has the most centenarians at 146,000, and the United States has the second largest number at about 108,000. The other three countries in the top five are China with about 60,000, India with 48,000, and Thailand with 38,000 (Schaeffer, 2024).

In the United States most (77%) current centenarians are European American, and significantly fewer minorities are centenarians: 8% are African or Black Americans, 7% are Asian American, 6% are Latinx American, and 1% are multiracial, American Indian, Alaska Native, and Native Hawaiian or other Pacific Islanders (Schaeffer, 2024). In addition, the majority of centenarians are women (78%) rather than men (22%). By 2023, there were more centenarians living in California (8,924), New York (5,666) and Florida (5,530) within the U.S. than other states (Social Security Administration, 2023).

Blue Zones

The places in the world where individuals have a much higher life expectancy are known as **blue zones** because of the use of a blue pen to identify locations with lots of centenarians. Poulain and colleagues (2004) used a blue pen to identify villages of centenarians in the Nuoro Province area of Sardinia, Italy, and showed that the highest number of male centenarians were in this area. This mountainous region in central-eastern Italy, known as the Sardinian blue zone (SBZ), is home to individuals who live well into their 90s and over 100, particularly men (Poulain & Herm, 2024; Poulain et al., 2013). This blue zone was assumed to occur because of a lifestyle that included remaining physically active after 80 years of age, support for the elders from family and community members, and individuals' diet (Poulain et al., 2006). Other researchers suggest that exceptional longevity is the result of diets including high amounts of fruits and vegetables and extremely low consumption of animal proteins (Pes et al., 2022).

Other blue zones are located in the Nicoya Peninsula of Costa Rica; Icaria, Greece; Okinawa Prefecture, Japan (Poulain et al., 2013); and Loma Linda, California in the United States. Loma Linda, California was named a blue zone by Dan Buettner, an American National Geographic Fellow, and founder of a marketing company called Blue Zones LLC. The Seventh-Day Adventist community in this location has extended longevity, believed to be a

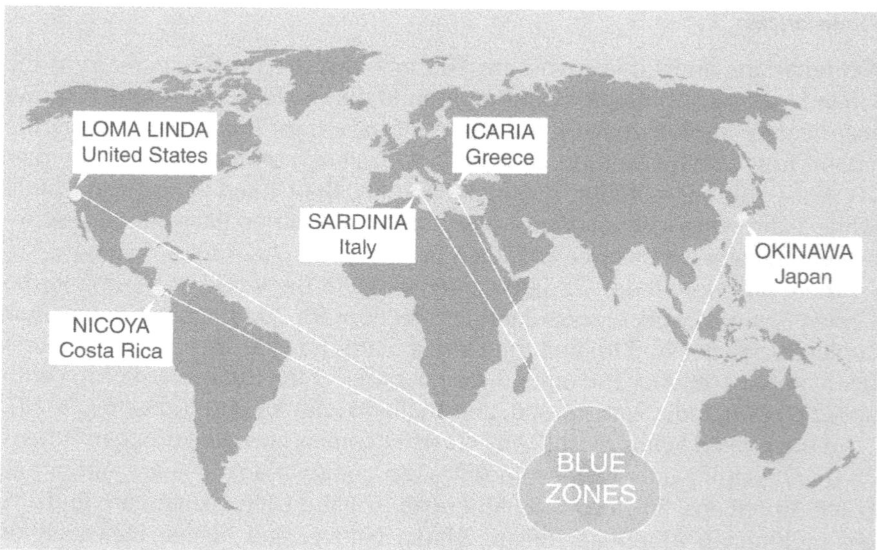

Figure 3.3 Image of the countries with blue zones, which are the five regions of the world with the longest-living populations.

Source: Shutterstock.

result of their lifestyle, including their plant-based diet.[2] Blue zones show that lifestyle, community support, and diet are an important part of an explanation of longevity.

Is Longevity in Our Genes?

It is important to note that there are some biomarkers that may show evidence of a genetic explanation for extreme longevity in individuals, though results on heritability vary across studies (Zatz et al., 2022). For example, researchers assessed individuals from the population-based Apolipoprotein Mortality Risk (AMORIS) cohort with outpatient testing between 1985 and 1996 in Stockholm County, Sweden (Murata et al., 2024). Of the 44,636 participants assessed, 1,224 were centenarians and 43,412 were not centenarians. The findings showed differences in biomarkers between those who became centenarians and those who did not become centenarians, including higher levels of iron and lower levels of glucose, creatinine, and uric acid.

In another study (Bae et al., 2023), researchers conducted a genome-wide association study (GWAS) focused on human participants with extreme longevity past the 99th year of life, and they aggregated data from four centenarian studies including the Long Life Family Study, the New England Centenarian Study, the Southern Italian Centenarian Study, and the Longevity Genes Project. There were 2,304 extreme longevity participants and 5,879 control participants. The findings showed evidence of a unique variant (rs145265196) on chromosome 11 with higher levels of a longevity allele for Ashkenazi Jewish individuals and individuals of Southern Italian ancestry when compared to individuals of other European ancestry.

Biological Changes in Our Sensory System

Sensory Changes

With no single explanation for why we age, we turn now to some of the changes that occur in our bodies as we age. Changes that occur in our bodies include changes in our sensory system (i.e., vision, hearing, smell, taste, balance), which we will discuss below. Other changes such as those that occur in our respiratory system, bone structure and joints, immune system, cardiovascular system, and our reproductive system will be discussed in detail in Chapter 5.

Vision

Unless we live in an environment that can damage our eyes, or we have a familial tendency toward specific eye conditions, most young adults are just starting to notice changes in how well they can see things. However, you may notice your parents holding a menu at a restaurant far away from them and complaining that the print is too small for them to read. If you can see things far away but have trouble seeing things close up, this is known as **presbyopia** or farsightedness. Presbyopia is a visual condition generally occurring at age 40 or older, though it can occur in your mid to late 30s too. Presbyopia involves the lens of your eye hardening as you get older, leading to age-related farsightedness. When the lens of the eyes becomes more rigid, it is more difficult to focus on the retina directly. Blurred vision and issues with seeing things clearly close up, such as menus or newspapers, becomes a problem.

If you can see images well when they are close to you, but the image becomes blurrier as it is moved away from you, that is known as **myopia**, or nearsightedness. This visual condition can develop in childhood and will get worse by middle adulthood. Myopia, much like other visual conditions, may be the result of a combination of genetic and lifestyle factors such as nutrition deficits (Cirone et al., 2023).

There are several common age-related eye conditions that become more frequent as we reach older adulthood including: age-related **macular degeneration**, **cataracts**, **diabetes-related retinopathy**, and glaucoma. Macular degeneration is generally considered an age-related problem with the retina because it affects the **macula**, the central part of your retina. You may lose your central vision, but you will not generally lose all of your vision. Losing your central vision means that you will not be able to see things directly in front of you; however, you will be able to maintain your peripheral vision (ability to see things off to the sides). You will have trouble seeing in low-light environments, and you may have blurred vision, issues with the way you see colors, low vision, difficulty seeing a straight line as wavy, and blank spots or dark spots in your visual field.

When this condition occurs, it is generally in those 50 and older. Macular degeneration can occur in one or both eyes and can have different levels of severity in each eye. The prevalence of macular degeneration in the United States for those aged 40 and older is around 11% for early-stage age-related macular degeneration (AMD) (Rein et al., 2022), though prevalence varies by age group, race and ethnicity, and location. There are less non-Hispanic Black individuals diagnosed with AMD compared to non-Hispanic White individuals, while late-stage AMD was similar for both groups (Rein et al., 2022). About one in eight individuals aged 60 and older have this eye condition in developed countries, with over 200 million individuals around the world diagnosed with AMD (Deng et al., 2022; Vyawahare & Shinde, 2022). While the highest percentage of AMD cases have been found in non-Hispanic Europeans, the rate is about 10% for Hispanic people and 7.5% for African and Asian people (Deng et al., 2022). Almost 20 million U.S. adults have macular degeneration. Globally, the prediction is that 288 million people will have the condition by 2040.

Along with age, the most common risk factors for AMD include a family history, excess weight, smoking, high blood pressure, and a diet high in saturated fats. Changes in lifestyle factors (diet, exercise, and taking

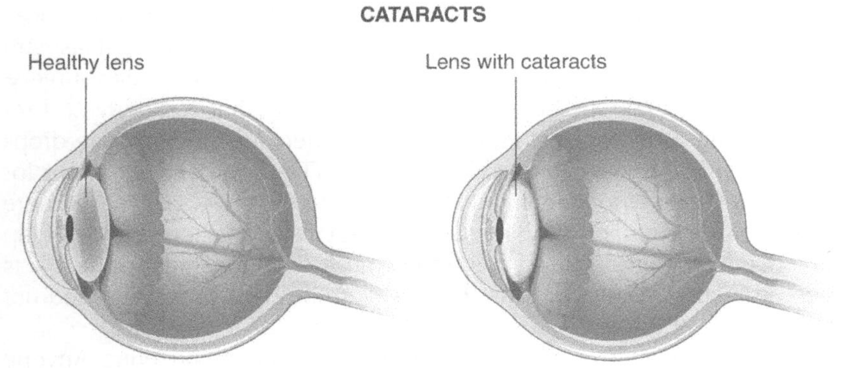

Figure 3.4 Image of healthy lens and lens with cataracts.
Source: Shutterstock.

physician prescribed medications) can improve eye health. Consumption of specific foods or vitamin supplements may slow the progression of AMD – for example, vitamin C, vitamin, E, Lutein, Zinc, Copper Zeaxanthin. There is currently no cure for AMD. Treatments to slow the progression of AMD includes drugs administered by injection in the vitreous area of the eye. Drugs injected can be combined with laser treatment on extra blood vessels in the eye.

Cataracts are cloudy spots that form on the lens portion of your eye. Generally they will not start to appear until we are in our 40s, but are often not noticeable until we reach our 60s. The lens is a clear and flexible structure made up of mostly proteins that are called **crystallins**. As we age, the proteins in the lens will break down, forming cloudy spots that make it harder to see. Individuals report that their vision appears blurry or foggy. There can be changes in perceptions of color, with color appearing faded. Individuals report sensitivity to bright light, including sunlight and the headlights on cars, and glare, including a halo or streaks around lights.

Cataracts are common across the globe, with around 17% of individuals reporting that they interfere with their vision (Hashemi et al., 2020). Prevalence rates vary, with more prevalence in low- to middle-income countries, because of lack of information about cataracts and lack of access to health care and treatment. Global estimates show cases of cataracts increased from 3,492,604 in 1990 to 6,676,281 in 2019, with recent research estimating an increase in cataracts over the next 15 years (Jiang, B. et al., 2023). In the United States about 1 in 5 individuals aged 65 to 74 years old have cataracts, and over 50% of individuals aged 80 and older have cataracts, often requiring surgery to remove them. Health conditions, especially diabetes, are linked to earlier appearance of cataracts, though environmental factors including exposure to certain types of light and other lifestyle factors such as smoking can increase occurrence of visual conditions such as cataracts (Hashemi et al., 2020). Currently, the only way to remove a cataract is through surgery. Cataract surgery is conducted to remove the cataract that is cloudy and replace it with an artificial lens. However, researchers are studying eye drops that may potentially treat cataracts. There are no FDA approved eye drops for cataracts available yet in the United States (De Bruyne et al., 2021), but there are eye drops for cataracts available in Europe. Lifestyle factors that can help you maintain your vision for longer and avoid the development of cataracts include protecting your eyes from the sun with the right sunglasses and not looking directly at the sun.

Diabetes-related retinopathy is an eye disease that affects the retina. Anyone with diabetes can develop this condition. Without treatment, diabetes-related retinopathy can lead to vision loss or blindness. Diabetes-related retinopathy will weaken the blood vessels in your retina. There are two types of diabetes-related retinopathy: **non-proliferative diabetes-related retinopathy (NPDR)** and **proliferative diabetes-related retinopathy (PDR)**. Non-proliferative diabetes-related retinopathy is considered an early disease stage where individuals have blood vessels that leak into their retina, showing fluid hemorrhage in the retina. Over time the blood vessels will close resulting in less blood flow. Proliferative diabetes-related retinopathy is a later stage of eye disease, with abnormal blood vessels that grow, leaking blood into the vitreous fluid that fills your eyes, changing the surface of the retina, and then detaching it, leading to severe vision loss. Your eye symptoms may include blurred vision, colors seeming faded, difficulty with night vision, seeing small dark spots or streaks in your vision, and difficulty seeing things that are far away.

In a systematic review and meta-analysis of 59 population-base studies, researchers found that Hispanic and Middle Eastern individuals with diabetes were more likely to have diabetes-related retinopathy compared to Asians (Teo et al., 2021). They also found that the diabetes-related retinopathy prevalence rate is highest in Africa at about 36% and in North America and the Caribbean at about 33%, and lowest in South and Central America at about 13% (Teo et al., 2021).

A recent review was conducted on the service delivery models to help with eye care for Indigenous individuals from high-income countries and it included 67 studies including individuals from Australia, the United States, Canada, New Zealand, Taiwan, and Greenland (Burn et al., 2021). The researchers found that both the geographic area and the scope of the service delivery models was narrow, with most studies conducted in Australia, and most studies focused on diabetic retinopathy.

To lower your risk of diabetes-related retinopathy consider lifestyle factors such as avoiding smoking, doing your best to control your blood sugar, exercising regularly, maintaining a healthy blood pressure, and taking prescribed medications. The treatments available for diabetes-related retinopathy include injections into your eye to slow the progression of the disease; laser surgery that can help reduce swelling in the retina by shrinking blood vessels or stopping the leakage; or a vitrectomy, which is an outpatient eye surgery involving a small incision in the eye to repair blood vessels and remove scar tissue.

Glaucoma is a term used for a group of eye diseases that involve visual field deficiencies and optic nerve deterioration (Stein et al., 2021). People with glaucoma have optic nerve damage from fluid buildup in their eye. Left untreated, this eye pressure can permanently affect vision. Generally, fluid will build up in the front part of your eye, putting pressure on your eye, and over time will gradually damage your optic nerve. You can have normal eye pressure and end up with glaucoma. If glaucoma is not treated, it will lead to permanent and irreversible loss of vision and blindness. Glaucoma may start off worse in one eye but generally it develops in both eyes. The symptoms of glaucoma include eye pain or pressure, headaches, having a rainbow-colored halo appear around lights, generally low vision, blurred vision, and narrow vision or blind spots, and can be accompanied by nausea and vomiting. Individuals also tend to have red eyes.

Estimates of the age-standardized prevalence of glaucoma are about 3–5% in those 40 years and older worldwide, with an expected increase to 112 million people in 2040 because of a global aging population (Jonas et al., 2017). In the United States, estimates are that about three million people have glaucoma, and it is the second leading cause of blindness after cataracts. Researchers used data from the Global Burden of Diseases, Injuries, and Risk Factors Study 2019 to determine the prevalence and disability-adjusted life years (DALYs) of glaucoma from 1990 to 2019 (Lin et al., 2023). The GBD 2019 study is considered the most comprehensive source on both the levels and trends of health loss for diseases and injuries around the world (GBD, 2020; Santomauro et al., 2021). Lin and colleagues (2023) found that the number of prevalent cases of glaucoma was 3,881,624 in 1990 and prevalence had increased to 7,473,400 by 2019. The highest prevalence of glaucoma is in Mali, and the lowest prevalence is in Taiwan (Chen et al., 2024). As we age, males are more likely to have glaucoma than females.

Understanding ethnic differences in the development and treatment of glaucoma is important for future study of this eye disease. While the risk of glaucoma increases with age, individuals who are of African or Hispanic descent tend to be more likely to end up with glaucoma compared to other ethnic groups, developing the disease earlier in life. Asian and Inuit individuals are susceptible to a specific form of glaucoma known as closed-angle glaucoma. Closed-angle glaucoma is rare. It involves too much pressure building up in your eye because fluid is not flowing out of your eye the way it should. Normally, fluid that is produced in the rear chamber of your eye, behind the iris, flows through your pupil into the front chamber of the eye. If you have a closed angle glaucoma, it is unable to do so. If someone has diabetes, they are over twice as likely to get glaucoma. Other risk factors include a family history of glaucoma, being farsighted or nearsighted, having high blood pressure, and previous eye injuries or surgeries. Currently there are treatments that can slow down vision loss from glaucoma including eye drops, laser treatments, and surgeries. There is an FDA approved implant that will work for several months and is provided by eye care providers. You can also have laser therapy to improve fluid drainage in the eye.

Hearing Loss

According to WHO, by 2050 there will be 2.5 billion individuals who have some amount of hearing loss, and over 700 million individuals that need some form of rehabilitation related to their hearing loss. There are over one billion individuals in young adulthood who practice unsafe listening habits that affect their hearing and may cause permanent avoidable hearing loss (WHO, 2025a; Yang, W. et al., 2023).

About 15% of individuals 18 and over in the United States report issues with their hearing, with about a third of individuals 65 to 74 years old having hearing loss. About 40% of adults aged 75 and older experience hearing loss (National Center for Health Statistics, n.d.). Age-related hearing loss is called

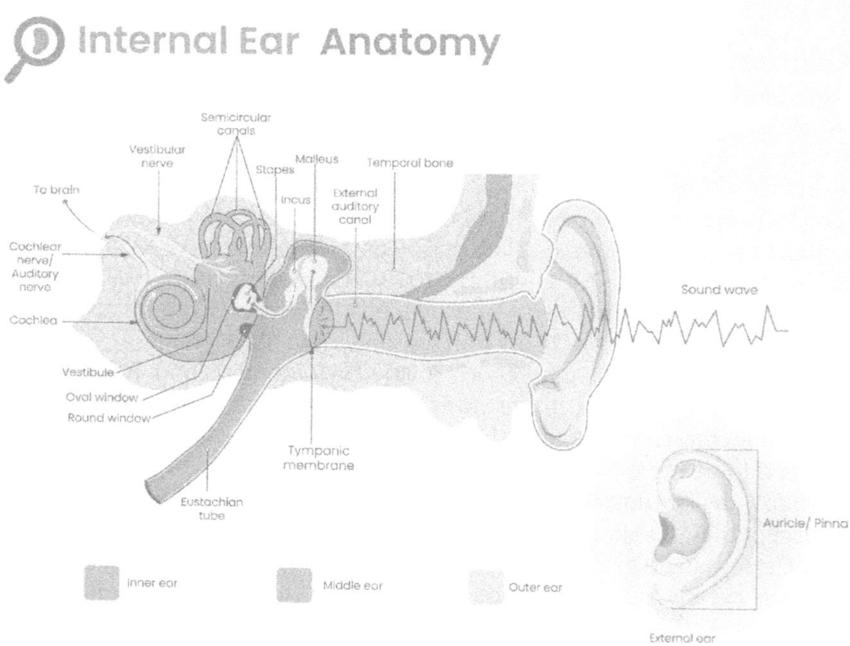

Figure 3.5 Illustration of the ear showing the parts of the ear including the outer ear, middle ear, and inner ear.

Source: Shutterstock.

presbycusis, and it occurs gradually as you age (Yang, W. et al., 2023), generally beginning in our 50s and 60s. With presbycusis you have trouble hearing some high-pitched sounds including alarms. Presbycusis occurs when there is damage to your inner ear, the cochlear organs, and it is frequently linked to central nervous system (CNS) problems that affect your ability to process auditory data. Researchers argue that damage to the cells in the ear that are linked to transmission of auditory information, including changes in the cochlear at a microscopic level, contribute to the development of presbycusis (Noble et al., 2022).

Presbycusis is the most common cause of hearing loss globally, with an estimated 900 million older individuals predicted to have presbycusis by the year 2050 (Lv et al., 2023), and affects around one-third of adults over 65 globally (Sheffield & Smith, 2019). Presbycusis affects about 67% of individuals in the United States. Changes in our hearing, such as changes associated with presbycusis, can happen for many reasons, including genetic influences, health issues, lifestyle factors, medications, and environmental factors (Yang, W. et al., 2023).

One particular factor that could be avoided or reduced is our exposure to loud noises over time. Wearing headphones or earbuds with the volume up high on a regular basis can lead to noise-induced hearing loss, along with exposure to loud work environments such as construction work and lawn mowing. Protection for your ears and reducing the amount of time you are exposed to loud noises can help reduce noise-induced hearing loss. Treatments for hearing loss include hearing aids, cochlear implants (Yang, W. et al., 2023), and assisted listening devices that help with phones and television sets.

Taste

Humans are born with about 10,000 taste buds on our tongues that allow us to experience five primary tastes, including sweet, sour, salty, bitter, and umami (i.e., savory as with meat or fish). As we age the average number of taste buds declines, and the decline is substantial by the time we are 74 to 85 years old (Feng et al., 2014). Global research on our ability to detect bitter taste shows variability across cultures, with Danish individuals showing less detection of bitterness compared to Chinese individuals, and Chinese individuals having more papillae on their tongues to detect bitterness (Cattaneo et al., 2020). There is evidence of a genetic component to tasting bitterness and sweetness in foods and drinks that may be complex, involving multiple alleles, and variations across cultures may affect our taste perceptions too, such as color and shape (Motoki et al., 2023) and texture (Diószegi et al., 2019).

As we age, our sense of taste may be altered, and in the United States about 27% of individuals aged 80 years and older report changes in their sense of taste (Rawal et al., 2016). Older adults often perceive food to lack flavor. Perception of taste may be affected by diseases such as Parkinson's disease or Alzheimer's disease, and infections that make you have a runny nose or congestion, which affect your sense of smell and therefore how you perceive taste – for example, COVID-19 (Sharetts et al., 2024). Other factors include medications (such as blood pressure or depression medicine), lack of nutrients and vitamins such as vitamin B6, zinc, and copper, smoking (which is linked to lower taste sensitivity), and nerve damage from the pathway in the mouth to the brain (Ogawa et al., 2017). **Presbygeusia** is the term for impairment in our taste perception that appears to occur as we age, particularly in older adults. A recent literature review comparing older adults without disease to healthy young adults showed that presbygeusia does occur without disease or side effects from medications and is a natural part of our aging process (Ponzo et al., 2024). However, other factors such as an individual's culture and psychological and social factors may play an important role in eating preferences and habits as we age.

Regardless of the reason for a change in our sense of taste, individuals tend to add more salt and/or sugar to foods that seem to lack flavor. Increases in salt and sugar intake can increase the risk of hypertension and diabetes.

Treating infections can help; however, the more damage to the taste buds, the less likely the injury to a taste bud can be repaired. Researchers are studying promising new ways to repair damaged taste buds (Wang, J. R. et al., 2024), which may be helpful in working with the elderly to improve dietary habits and food consumption.

Smell

The olfactory system is part of the body structures that allow for the sense of smell. The olfactory system includes the nose, the nasal cavities, which have the olfactory mucous membranes that allow for the perception of smell, and the respiratory passage. As you get older, your sense of smell may fade. Researchers in Japan compared younger and older adults results from taste and olfactory assessments and found that older adults had less sensitivity for both taste and olfaction compared to younger adults (Inoue et al., 2022). In the United States about 25% of individuals over the age of 40 perceive a change in their sense of smell, and rates of less sensitivity to smell are highest in older adults – close to one-third for those who are aged 80 years and older (Rawal et al., 2016). Your sense of smell is closely related to your sense of taste (Rawal et al., 2021). When you cannot smell, food may taste bland. You may even lose interest in eating, and as less food is eaten there is a risk of increases in illnesses, including cognitive issues (Olofsson et al., 2021). There are many reasons for the loss of sense of smell, including short-term changes such as with a cold or flu or the COVID-19 infection (Olofsson et al., 2021; Sharetts et al., 2024), allergies, medications, and treatment for cancers including chemotherapy and radiation. Sometimes you experience a loss in your sense of smell that can last a long time, and this might occur with head injuries or diseases such as Parkinson's disease and Alzheimer's disease.

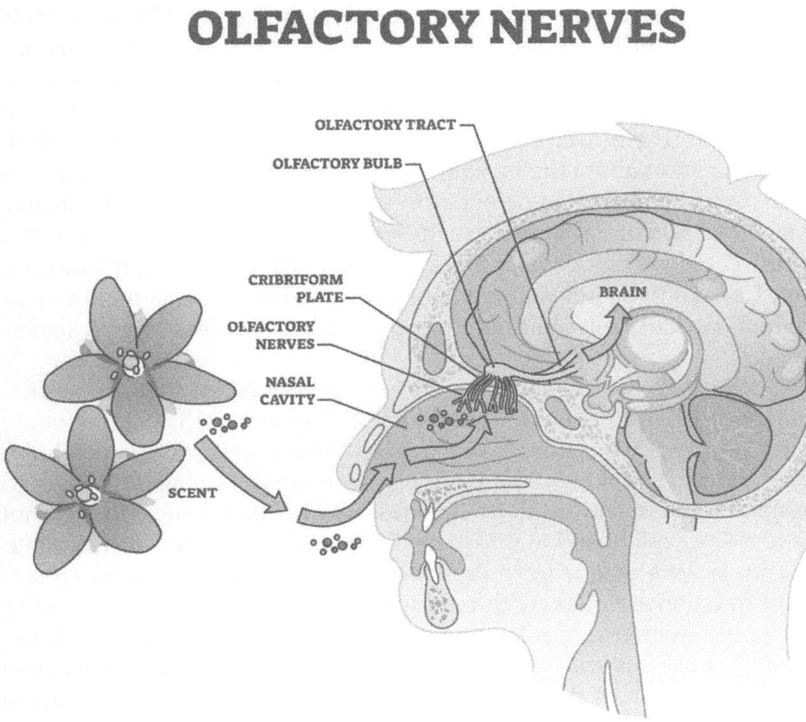

Figure 3.6 Illustration of the **olfactory system**, which involves our nose and naval cavity, that shows a magnified view of the neurons and nerve fibers.

Source: Shutterstock.

In fact, researchers argue that loss of sense of smell may be a precursor to the development of cognitive impairment (Inoue et al., 2022).

Vestibular System

To have normal balance our bodies depend on multiple factors, including multiple systems of the body and external and environmental factors (Wagner et al., 2023). There are three primary sensory systems that help us have postural stability. The vestibular system of the inner ear coordinates with our visual system, and proprioceptors that are able to sense the position and movement of our bodies in space help too. By working together, these systems help us to stand and move in a variety of ways without losing our balance.

The vestibular system within our inner ears includes five vestibular organs: three **semicircular canals**, and two **otolith organs**. The semicircular canals consist of three tubes inside of our inner ears, and they detect rotational head movements. The **superior canal** is able to detect the up-and-down movement of our heads. The **horizontal canal** is able to detect the left-to-right movements of our heads. The **posterior canal** is able to detect side-to-side movements, such as when we tilt our heads toward the left or right shoulder. These three canals end in structures called **ampulla**, which have hair cells that shift when our heads move. The movement triggers the release of nerve signals that allow communication about the position of the heads to the brains. The otolith organs are two chambers that detect movement related to gravity. The **utricle** is able to detect horizontal motion, such as moving forward or backward, and the **saccule** can detect movement that is vertical, such as movement going up or down. The otolith organs house a structure called the macula that has hair cells. When the hair cells shift during movement they release nerve signals to the brain.

As we age, there are changes in our vestibular system that are associated with less ability to maintain our balance (Li et al., 2015; Wagner et al., 2023). By our mid-50s, individuals have less nerve cells in the vestibular system, and the blood flow to the inner ear decreases as we age. Changes to our vestibular system can result in dizziness and balance issues, though not all balance issues are linked to dizziness. Sometimes as we age, if we go into a dark room or walk on an uneven surface, the changes to our vestibular system result in balance issues, with trouble walking, and possibly tripping or falling. There is evidence of bilateral issues with the semicircular canals being linked to problems with our rotational spatial orientation in adults aged 60 years and older from the Baltimore Longitudinal Study of Aging (Anson et al., 2021). There are many reasons for changes in our vestibular system, including impairments in our inner ear functions, health issues (e.g., cardiovascular disease), neurological diseases such as stroke and Alzheimer's disease, nutrition deficits, visual impairments, medications, chemotherapy, lifestyle factors, and environmental factors that can affect brain functioning and the inner ear.

There are multiple ways to support our vestibular system. Maintenance of healthy nutrients can help our senses, including our hearing and sight. Regular eye checkups and proper eyewear prescriptions are an important step to supporting our vestibular system. Training to improve the connection between vision and vestibular function may be helpful too. A study conducted in Canada with a multi-sensory training paradigm that focused on guidance with visual-vestibular training showed improvements in older adults visual heading perception after the training (Gabriel et al., 2022). Other supports include lifestyle changes to help reduce dizziness or vertigo, medications for infections, surgery, and physical therapy for vestibular issues.

Context, Culture, and Biological Changes

One example of how context and culture can play a role in our biological changes is menopause. As we age, menopause is one of the changes that occurs to biological XX or biological female individuals. It is when a biological female stops the monthly menstrual cycle and can no longer provide eggs for the fertilization process. There are wide variations in the perceptions of menopause and the symptoms related to menopause, and culture plays a role in these perceptions (Kabir & Chan, 2023; Kirchengast, 2024). Past research in India showed biological females reporting the transition period in menopause as positive rather than negative (Flint, 1975), though this view was later revised for non-Western biological females. In a recent study by Su and colleagues (2021), researchers compared menopausal symptoms in women from an urban area of Northwest China to women from an urban area of Western Japan. The researchers found that Japanese women reported more severe menopausal symptoms compared to the Chinese women, and they argued that Chinese women's symptoms could be associated with the valued status that is acquired during menopause in China. (A more detailed discussion of menopause is included in Chapter 5.)

Chapter Summary

In this chapter we reviewed theories on why we age. Some newer theories, such as research on mitochondria and telomeres, have the potential to offer a better understanding of the aging process. We discussed life expectancy in humans and factors that can affect our life expectancy, including biological, psychological and contextual factors; cross-cultural research on life expectancy; and blue zones where people live longer. Finally we explored sensory changes as we age (vision, hearing, smell, taste, vestibular), and factors (i.e., biological, psychological, contextual factors) that affect changes in our senses as we age.

Key Takeaways

1. There is a long history of research into and debate around programmed and non-programmed theories on aging, as well as newer theories that have support. There is not one overall theory explaining why we age.
2. There are multiple types of life expectancy. Biological, psychological, and contextual factors influence differences in life expectancy around the globe.
3. Blue zones are places where individuals have longer life expectancies. Explanations for their longevity include personal choice, community support, specific diets, and a healthy environment.
4. There are sensory changes as we age. Multiple factors, including biological, psychological, and contextual, can affect our senses as we age.
5. The sociocultural context in which we develop during adulthood plays an important role in our aging processes and our ability to live a long and healthy life.

Reflective Questions

1 Which theory of why we age do you find most convincing?
2 Identify the biological, psychological, and contextual factors that shape your life. How do they affect your aging processes? What influence do you have on your own aging processes?
3 How do sociocultural and contextual factors affect our aging processes, including our sensory changes in adulthood and aging?

Suggested Readings

Caraballo, C., Massey, D. S., Ndumele, C.D., Haywood, T., Kaleem, S., King, T., Liu, Y., Lu, Y., Nunex-Smith, M., Taylor, H. A., Watson, K. E., Herrin, J., Yancy, C. W., Faust, J. S., & Krumholz, H. M. (2023). Excess mortality and years of potential life lost among the black population in the US, 1999–2020. *JAMA, 329*(19), 1662–1670. doi: 10.1001/jama.2023.7022

da Costa, J. P., Vitorino. R., Silva, G. M., Vogel, C., Duarte, A. C., & Rocha-Santos, T. (2016). A synopsis on aging – Theories, mechanisms and future prospects. *Ageing Research Reviews, 29*, 90–112. doi: 10.1016/j.arr.2016.06.005.

Lozada-Martinez, I. D., Diazgranados-Garcia, M. C., Castelblanco-Toro, S., & Anaya, J.-M. (2024). Global research on centenarians: A historical and comprehensive bibliometric analysis from 1887 to 2023. *Annals of Geriatric Medicine and Research, 28*(2), 144–155. doi: doi: 10.4235/agmr.24.0043.

Key Terms

Active life expectancy is the number of years an individual can expect to live without a disability and while still able to perform activities of daily living without difficulty.

An **ampulla** is a structure with hair cells that shifts when the head moves and triggers a release of nerve signals allowing communication about the position of the head to our brain.

Antagonistic pleiotropy theory argues that one gene controls more than one trait, and at least one of the traits is helpful to an organism early in life, while another trait is harmful later in life, because of a decrease in the effect of natural selection.

Calorie restriction is the reduction of dietary consumption below specific energy requirements for weight maintenance while maintaining optimal nutrition.

Cataracts are cloudy spots that form on the lens portion of the eye, affecting vision.

Cohort life expectancy is the average life expectancy of a group of individuals who are born in the same year.

Crystallins are proteins that make up the structure of the lens portion of the eye.

Dependent life expectancy is the number of years an individual is expected to live while needing assistance from others because of a disability or illness.

Diabetes-related retinopathy is an eye disease that weakens the blood vessels in the retina.

Disability-free life expectancy is another name for active life expectancy.

Disposable soma theory argues that finding a balance between the maintenance of an organism and an organism's reproductive ability could lead to damage in an organism's body repair systems, causing cellular damage to worsen as the body ages.

Endocrine theory is based on the idea of a biological clock working through our hormones to control the aging process.

Free radical theory uses reactive atom-oxygen as an explanation for aging, with increased production and buildup of free radicals as organisms age resulting in damage to organisms' nucleic acids, lipids, and proteins.

Glaucoma is a term used for a group of eye diseases that involve visual field deficiencies and optic nerve deterioration, including optic nerve damage from fluid buildup in the eye.

The **horizontal canal** is able to detect the left-to-right movement of our heads.

Immunological theory is based on the idea that the immune system is programmed to diminish over time.

Inter-trait linkage suggests that traits are linked in a way that would create more difficulty for evolutionary processes to create organisms with only one trait and not the other linked traits.

Life expectancy is the number of years a person can expect to live based on the average age at which individuals within a specific group die.

The **macula** structure is found in otolith organs that have hair cells. When hair cells shift during movement the macula release nerve signals to the brain.

Macular degeneration is considered to be an age-related problem with the retina. It affects the macula, the central part of the retina, and vision.

The **mitochondrial theory of aging** argues that mitochondria show issues with function over time, leading to an increase of free radicals and oxidation bioproducts. Less antioxidants are available over time, which leads to cell death, immune response issues, and intracellular and endocrine signaling issues.

Maximum life span is the longest an individual can possible live.

Mutation accumulation theory is based on natural selection decreasing as individuals age, reducing chances of creating more offspring through the accumulation of mutations.

Myopia is when an individual can see images well when they are close to them, but the image becomes blurrier as it is moved away; also known as nearsightedness.

Non-proliferative diabetes-related retinopathy (NPDR) is an early disease stage where blood vessels leak into the retina. There can be fluid hemorrhage in the retina.

Non-programmed theories argue aging occurs because of the random accumulation of deteriorating experiences that cannot be prevented by natural selection.

The **olfactory system** includes the nose, nasal cavities, and olfactory mucous membranes that allow for the perception of smell, and the lower parts of the respiratory passage.

An **organelle** is a specialized part within a cell that has a specific function.

Otolith organs are two chambers that detect movement related to gravity.

Period life expectancy is based on the mortality pattern at a specific point in time.

A **population benefit** is an adaptive component from the biological mechanisms that limits the lifespan of different species and may provide an evolutionary advantage.

Presbycusis is age-related hearing loss that makes it difficult to hear some high-pitched sounds because of damage to the cochlear organs in the inner ear.

Presbygeusia is impairment in taste perception that appears to occur as individuals age.

Presbyopia is a visual condition involving the lens of the eye hardening as individuals get older, leading to age-related farsightedness.

Programmed aging theories are based on the idea that aging is programmed into bodies.

Programmed senescence is a theory based on the idea of a sequential switch that is triggered to turn on or off certain genes.

Proliferative diabetes-related retinopathy (PDR) is a later stage of eye disease. Abnormal blood vessels that leak blood into the vitreous fluid that fills the eyes can lead to retina detachment and severe vision loss.

Protein cross-linked theory is based on chemical changes that interact in the body.

Rate of living theory argues that bodies only have a set number of biological moments before they break down, and individuals with higher metabolic rates have shorter lifespans.

Saccule can detect movement that is vertical, such as movement going up or down.

The **semicircular canals** are the three tubes inside of the inner ears. They detect rotational head movements.

Somatic DNA damage theory is based on genes controlling aging until individuals die.

The **superior canal** is able to detect the up-and-down movement of the head.

Telomeres are the tips of chromosomes. They get shorter with each cell replication as individuals age.

The **utricle** is able to detect horizontal motion such as moving forward or backward.

Notes

1 This number and current life expectancies for other nations can be found online: https://www.macrotrends.net/global-metrics/countries/USA/united-states/life-expectancy.

2 Buettner's company, Blue Zones LLC, was acquired by the Seventh-Day Adventist health care system in 2020.

4 Brain Structures, Functions, and Cognition as We Age

Learning Outcomes

Describe differences in small and large brain structures as we age, and types of tools used to study the brain.

Explain findings from cross-cultural research on changes to brain structures as we age.

Articulate key differences in cognitive functioning as we age, from healthy adults to those with diseases (such as Alzheimer's disease [AD] and Parkinson's disease [PD]), and cross-cultural research findings.

Describe general models of intelligence used in adulthood and aging research, and how these apply to superagers.

Identify how biological, psychological, and contextual factors are involved in changes in brain structures and cognitive functioning as we age.

Brain Structures

Do you ever wonder about how the brain changes over the lifespan? This question relates to the study of brain structure and function as we age. In the first part of this chapter, we will discuss general findings about brain structure and function, if there are changes, and why changes may occur. We will also discuss cross-cultural research on brain structure and function.

Small Brain Structures

Neurons

Our brains contain billions of cells called **neurons.** Neurons are nerve cells that send and receive signals from your brain and allow for communication between the brain and body. There are different types of neurons, each with specialized functions, located in our brain, spinal cord, and muscles. **Sensory neurons** help us experience sensations such as taste or smell, while **motor**

DOI: 10.4324/9781003483809-4

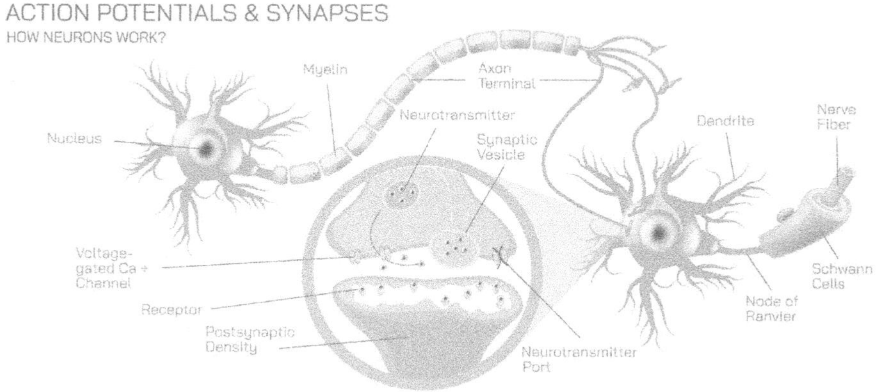

Figure 4.1 Illustration of a neuron and all the parts of the neuron.
Source: Shutterstock.

neurons allow us to coordinate the movement of our muscles. **Interneurons**, the most plentiful neurons in our bodies, are located between other neurons including motor and sensory neurons. They help us control signals by relaying information from different parts of the nervous system (Feltz, 2019; Gosgnach et al., 2017). Neurons interact with other neurons, stimulating or impeding other neuron's activity; communication can occur between two neurons or between a neuron and a muscle or gland.

A process called **neurogenesis**, the creation of new neural stem cells (the precursors of neurons and glial cells), was originally considered to only occur early in life. Now we know that even older adult brains can create new neural stem cells. Adult neurogenesis was first discussed by Josef Altman in 1962. This work was the foundation of the future subfield of **neuroscience** research about the creation of new neurons, but it was the 1990s before most researchers supported the idea of adult neurogenesis with human studies (Eriksson et al., 1998; Owji & Shoja, 2020). Research provides a very different picture of our aging neurons. In fact, researchers have provided much evidence that we make new neurons throughout the lifespan (Shohayeb et al., 2018). There is hope for treatments that could increase neurogenesis, as a way to treat diseases such as **Alzheimer's disease** (AD) and **Parkinson's disease** (PD), through regenerative stem cell therapies and transplants of neural stem cells, though much work still needs to be done (Chen et al., 2023). Research on adult neurogenesis provides room for optimism about aging.

A **synapse** is a junction, a place where one neuron sends a message to another neuron (Foster & Sherrington, 1897). Our brains have ongoing interactions that include billions of neurons and trillions of synapses, with neurons and synapses connecting to networks in the brain, and occurring across multiple brain regions (Mott et al., 2018).

Most of our synapses communicate with chemical messengers called **neurotransmitters**, however, some synapses communicate with electrical signals, and others use both chemical and electrical signals (Feltz, 2019). We have many kinds of neurotransmitters, including glutamatergic (neurotransmitter **glutamate**, frequently excitatory), **GABAergic** (neurotransmitter **gamma-aminobutryic acid** [GAMA], frequently inhibitory), **cholinergic** (neurotransmitter acetylcholine, helps with responses in muscle regions, playing a major role at neuromuscular junctions), and **adrenergic** (neurotransmitter epinephrine or norepinephrine, helps with responses in part of the autonomic nervous system).

An **action potential**, or nerve impulse, triggers the **presynaptic region** or sending region of a neuron to release a neurotransmitter, and it binds to receptors on the **postsynaptic region** or receiving part to allow communication. A neuron can maintain voltage across its membrane (known as the **resting potential**), fire nerve impulses (action potential), and perform metabolic processes that help keep us alive.

Our synapses generally form between nerve terminals known as **axon terminals**, either from the sending portion of a neuron and cell body, or from the receiving neurons, specifically the **dendrites**, which are the part of the neuron responsible for accepting messages (Feltz, 2019). There is some evidence of decreases in the number of dendrites as we age. There may be tangles in fibers of the axons and more deposits of proteins that may interfere with transmission of information from one neuron to the next neuron. This generally occurs much less in those without disease or trauma.

For a chemical messenger or neurotransmitter, electrical activity in the presynaptic region of the neuron is converted to release a neurotransmitter, which binds to receptors on the postsynaptic portion of the cell with activation of a **voltage-gated calcium channel** in the cell membrane known as **Ca^{2+}**. Ca^{2+} occurs at a much higher concentration outside of neurons compared to inside, and it rushes into the cell. Ca^{2+} allows synaptic vesicles to meld with an axon terminal membrane, releasing a neurotransmitter into a region known as the **synaptic cleft** (Feltz, 2019; Levitan & Kaczmarek, 2015).

For an electrical messenger, the presynaptic and postsynaptic portions of the cell membranes are connected by special sections called **gap junctions**, allowing the passage of an electric current, which causes voltage change in the presynaptic cell portion to generate voltage change in the postsynaptic cell regions (Feltz, 2019). Gap junctions allow for communication without neurotransmitters and calcium, facilitating the fast transfer of electrical messenger signals from one neuron to another (Caire et al., 2023; Feltz, 2019).

Research shows that much change occurs with synapses as we age (Cizeron et al., 2020). There is much complexity in synaptic changes (Morrison & Baxter, 2012), and diversity in synapses with the expansion of synapses from birth through early adulthood, which changes to dedifferentiation in synapses in different brain regions in older adulthood (Cizeron et al., 2020). Complexity in synapses includes changes in the number of synapses and level of plasticity in communication in the synaptic region over the lifespan, with some evidence of decline in both, predominantly for those who are more cognitively impaired (Diniz & Crestani, 2023). Though researchers are studying possible treatments for diseases targeting the synapse, much work needs to be done.

Another part of the neuron dictates how fast a neuron communicates. The **myelin sheath**, which covers and protects nerve fibers, speeds up communication between neurons (Feltz, 2019). Some neurons have myelin sheathing and others do not. Over time neurons with myelin sheathing show signs of wearing down, which reduces speed of communication (McNamara et al., 2023; Osso & Hughes, 2024). Research on mice has shown there is a small portion of myelin sheath that continues to be generated throughout the lifespan from **oligodendrocytes**, a type of neural glia that creates myelin sheath, in response to new experiences with the environment, including learning experiences (McNamara et al., 2023; Osso & Hughes, 2024; Pan et al., 2020; Wang et al., 2020). There is promise of techniques to improve memory loss related to **dementia** that help maintain and improve myelin sheathing of neurons (McNamara et al., 2023; Osso & Hughes, 2024).

Tools for Studying the Brain

Much has been learned since the earliest writing about the brain by Edwin Smith in the seventeenth century. Neuroscience involves scientific investigation of the nervous system, which includes the brain, spinal cord, and peripheral nervous system. Neuroscientists who study the brain assess regular changes in the brain as we age, how the brain adapts and compensates for changes, and changes related to disease or trauma to the brain. Study of the structure of the brain and organization of the nervous system is known as **neuroanatomy** (Shaffer, 2019).

Structural neuroimaging includes techniques that take pictures of the brain to understand changes in brain structures as we age. Over 50 years ago, Godfrey Hounsfield (1971) made the first computed tomography (CT) image of the human brain, known as a CT scan. Modern tools such as **x-rays**, CT scans, **positron emission tomography** (PET), and, more recently, **magnetic resonance imaging** (MRI) allow us to look inside a living person's head and examine the structure of their brain. A CT scan is an imaging test that uses a series of X-rays and a computer to create detailed images of the brain. A **PET** scan involves a radioisotope attached to a drug that is injected into the body, allowing scientists and medical practitioners to determine if someone has a tumor or growth (Ter-Pogossian et al., 1975; Vaquero et al., 2015). An **MRI** scan provides clear images of structures inside the body using a large magnet, radio waves, and a computer. Development of MRI stems from early work in the mid 1900s, and multiple researchers are credited with different aspects of the development of MRI, including Raymond Damadian, Paul Lauterbur, and Peter Mansfield (Damadian, 1971; Lauterbur, 1973; Mansfield

& Grannell, 1975; Singh et al., 2023). These modern tools have allowed us to understand healthy brain structures (Bethlehem et al., 2022), and issues with the structure of the brain from damage caused by diseases such as dementia or trauma from an accident or injury (Singh et al., 2023).

Other tools have been developed to help us study brain activity rather than brain structure. Tools developed to study brain activity include techniques for **functional neuroimaging** such as **functional magnetic resonance imaging** (fMRI), and **magnetoencephalography** (MEG).

Functional magnetic resonance imaging was invented in the early 1990s, and is a type of noninvasive brain imaging that allows for detection of brain activity through measurement of changes in blood flow (Whitten, 2012). Researchers are using fMRI for a variety of brain imaging studies, including assessment with cognitive tasks (Finn et al., 2023; Wei et al., 2024).

Magnetoencephalography signals were first measured in 1968 by David Cohen. MEG is a non-invasive technique that provides a measurement of ongoing brain activity quickly, on a millisecond-by-millisecond basis, and shows where brain activity is created. The brain has neuromagnetic signals that are extremely small. MEG scanners use superconducting sensors called **SQUID**, a superconducting quantum interference device developed by James Zimmerman (Zimmerman et al., 1970). The SQUID sensors are kept in a large liquid helium cooling unit at approximately –269°C. The SQUID device detects and then amplifies the magnetic fields generated by neurons a few centimeters away from the sensors. Unlike fMRI, MEG is the only tool that provides both timing and spatial information about brain activity. It is used by researchers and medical practitioners to study cognitive impairment (Scheijbeler et al., 2022).

Larger Brain Structures

As can be seen in Figure 4.2, our brain has multiple structures, including the **frontal lobe**, involved in thinking, problem solving, and personality; the **parietal lobe**, involved with sensation and **perception**, attention, and language; the **temporal lobe**, involved with memory, language, and hearing; the **occipital lobe**, involved with perception and vision; the **cerebellum**, involved with balance and coordination of movement; the **brain stem**, involved in our consciousness and major life sustaining functions such as respiration and heart rate. While there are many other brain structures of importance, these particular brain structures have been studied extensively.

The **prefrontal cortex** and **frontal cortex** portions of the frontal lobe allow us to plan and carry out activities, pay attention to specific items, and switch between different tasks. The prefrontal cortex is involved in personality, emotions, and other aspects of brain functioning called **executive function**; the prefrontal cortex provides much of the higher-order executive function (Deco et al., 2023; Kringelbach & Deco, 2024). The prefrontal cortex has a circular set of regions that researchers have labeled "rings" and that allow for higher levels of brain functioning (Deco et al., 2023). Studies show the important

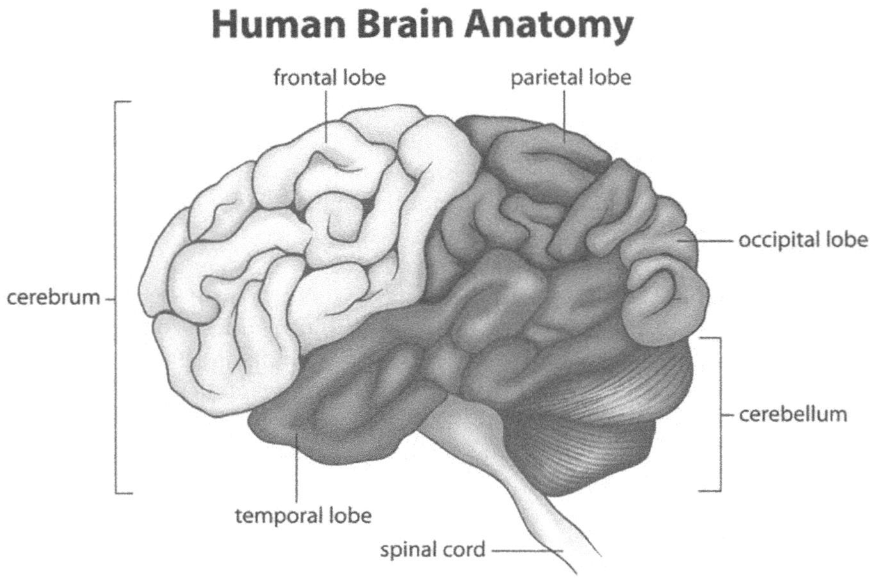

Figure 4.2 Illustration of the human brain.
Source: Shutterstock.

role of the prefrontal cortex in our brain's cognitive flexibility (Kringelbach & Deco, 2024).

Within the medial temporal lobe is the **hippocampus**, a brain structure associated with memory (Daume et al., 2024). Evidence of less hippocampus volume as we age, especially when disease or brain trauma is present, is already well documented. Researchers have shown the role of the hippocampus in various aspects of memory, including executive function and processing speed (O'Shea et al., 2016). Level of hippocampus grey matter (GM) volume decreases as we age, gradually, accompanied by associated age-related changes in our cognitive control, even in those without cognitive impairment (Hu & Li, 2020).

Changes in Brain Structures

Structural decline and functional reorganization of brain structures, generally considered major features of how our brains age, comes with much **inter-individual** (between-subject) variability as we age (Bittner et al., 2019). A brain network has sets of brain regions known as **nodes**; brain regions located in the same network are highly connected to each other compared to networks outside of those specific brain regions. The brain also has areas called **connectome**, which include all connected regions both within and across networks of the brain.

The functional connectome shows evidence of reorganization as we age, moving from a segregated to a more integrated set of brain networks. Both **structural connectivity** (SC) and **functional connectivity** (FC) go through age-related reorganization, and as we age our intra-network FC decreases (Fornito et al., 2013); however, the primary processing networks involved in sensorimotor tasks remain relatively stable. Some researchers have found there are SC decreases as we age that impact the brain, especially the frontal lobe. Researchers have found older adults show problems in their structural connectomes (Li et al., 2020). The connections between our brain structures appear to act as a framework for limiting our brain's functional abilities, with structural connections explaining about 50% of the variance in functional connections (Yang, Y. et al., 2023). Much research has been conducted on changes in our brain structures and functions as we age.

Research on Brain Structures

The National Institutes of Health (NIH), with the help of an Advisory Committee to the Director (ACD), created a report called "Brain 2025: A Scientific Vision." The report includes a framework for funding opportunities for multiyear scientific plans for the Brain Research through Advocacy Initiative Neurotechnologies (BRAIN initiative) that began in 2014, incorporates U.S. and global research research (Maroso, 2023; Mott et al., 2018), and focuses on researchers' understanding of how patterns of neural activity become transformed into cognition, emotion, perception, and actions in health and diseases (Mott et al., 2018).

Bethlehem and colleagues (2022) conducted a study with MRI images from over 100 other studies and found GM volume shows gradual decline from adolescence through late adulthood, while white matter (WM) volume peaks in young adulthood and shows decline after 50 years of age. Research with German samples from two different data sets showed age-related decreases in SC for the whole brain, and especially for the frontal lobe, both within and between brain networks (Stumme et al., 2022). Older adults were more likely to have lower intra-network FC of their primary processing networks, and higher integration between the brain higher-order networks. These findings support other research showing changes in the brain move toward stronger network integration of higher-order networks (Edde et al., 2021). Lower intra-network FC is associated with poorer performance on cognitive tasks (Ewers et al., 2021). Compensation may stop being beneficial, and may be replaced by a dedifferentiated system providing a less distinctive activity pattern in the brain linked to poorer **cognitive functioning** (Edde et al., 2021).

Factors Involved in Brain Changes as We Age

In relation to the biopsychosocial model (Chapter 1), there is evidence of multiple factors involved in changes in our brain structure and function as we age including our genes, education, lifestyle factors (e.g., diet, exercise, smoking and alcohol consumption), and the amount of social support individuals experience over the lifespan (Bittner et al., 2021; Heger et al., 2021; Rolls et al., 2023; Vinodh Kumar et al., 2023; Vints et al., 2024). Our genes are an important factor involved in changes in our brain structure as we age. To determine how much our genes may affect changes in brain structure, researchers calculate **heritability**. Heritability is a statistic used to estimate the ratio of genetic variation between individuals in a population to the total phenotypic variation present in that population (Gazzaniga et al., 2015).

A study conducted in South Korea assessed middle-aged and older adults, and showed intracranial volume, subcortical volume, and cortical thickness are highly heritable (Lee et al., 2023). The researchers found subcortical volume showed heritability at about 42% for the **caudate** volume. The caudate is a C-shaped subcortical structure in the **thalamus** that supports motor skills and executive functions such as inhibitory control (Graff-Radford et al., 2017) and may be involved in diseases such as Parkinson's disease (Niethammer et al., 2013). Lee and colleagues (2023) mentioned high heritability of caudate volume in both middle-aged and older adults, but did not find significant heritability factors for the amygdala, hippocampus, and other portions of the thalamus.

Education may be another factor involved in changes in our brain structures as we age. In a study conducted in Montreal, researchers found that as cognitive task demand increased, older individuals with higher education levels recruited the caudate nucleus portion of the brain for cognitive tasks more than those who reported less education (Ducharme-Laliberté et al., 2022).

Lifestyle factors are involved in changes in our brain structure. For example, Bittner and colleagues (2019) conducted a study with German samples, and found increased alcohol consumption and smoking were linked to decreases in **gyrification** in the left premotor and the right prefrontal cortex. Less physical activity and less social integration were associated with decreases in gyrification. More social integration was associated with more gyrification in the right ventro-lateral prefrontal cortex. Gyrification is the process of forming the folds in the cerebral cortex of our brains (Striedter et al., 2015). Rolls and colleagues (2023) analyses with data from a U.K. Biobank found higher lifestyle risk factors were associated with less cortical thickness in some brain regions, and less subcortical volume in the hippocampus, amygdala, and a subcortical brain structure known as the globus pallidus. Less physical, leisure, and social activity was associated with low connectivity in the somatosensory/motor cortex and hippocampus regions of the brain.

Countries in Africa (e.g., Egypt, Ghana, South Africa, Nigeria Tunisia, and Morocco) are making progress on techniques to assess brain structure and function (Aderinto et al., 2023; Nebli & Rekik, 2021; Spies et al., 2022). Researchers from South Africa conducted a study assessing the relationship of alcohol misuse to brain structure and function in individuals who are HIV positive (Spies et al., 2022). The individuals who were HIV positive and alcohol users showed less brain volume than those who were HIV positive and

Figure 4.3 A "find the hidden objects" picture.
Source: Shutterstock

were not alcohol users for the left and right amygdala, left and right hippocampus, right thalamus, and corpus callosum (Spies et al., 2022).

Activity

Look at Figure 4.3 for 30 seconds and then cover the picture. Without peeking, try to write down each object you remember. This is one of many ways that we can assess individuals' memory.

Cognitive Functioning as We Age

An adult developmental perspective on cognitive functioning extends beyond Piaget's work on cognitive development (Inhelder & Piaget, 1955) with work on postformal thought. **Postformal thought** involves more complex thinking, flexibility in thought, being open to different perspectives outside of our own, and relativistic and dialectical thinking (Riegel, 1973; Sinnott, 1984; Sinnott 1998). Our logical thought processes involve subjectivity as they are self-referential (Sinnott, 1998), pragmatic aspects as they require accepting that there can be multiple causes and solutions to a problem, and the ability to accept contradictions (Sinnott, 1998; Sinnott et al., 2020). There has been controversy over postformal thought, but researchers support relativistic thinking and dialectical thought as necessary parts of postformal thought, differentiating it from earlier work by Piaget (Kramer & Woodruff, 1986).

Cognitive functioning includes the ability to perceive, pay attention to, and react to information or stimuli, process, store, and retrieve information, and make decisions and provide responses to information or stimuli (Kiely, 2014; Morley et al., 2015). There are multiple domains involved in cognitive functioning, including perception, memory, learning, attention, decision making, and language abilities (Kiely, 2014). There are a variety of measures for assessing cognitive functioning, including self-report, in-person interviews, psychometrically tested measures of different aspects of cognition, and the use of neuroimaging techniques to examine the relation between structure and function of the brain with specific cognitive assessments. The main part of the brain involved in memory is located in the medial temporal lobe, the hippocampus, and it interacts with other parts of the brain involved in higher thinking (the prefrontal cortex) and emotions (the amygdala) (Dixon & Dweck, 2022; Murty & Dickerson, 2016; Yavas et al., 2019). However, a traditional one-to-one approach to explain connections between brain structure and function, such as the hippocampus being linked to **episodic memory**, does not truly capture the complexity of our cognitive functioning over the lifespan (Yavas et al., 2019). Our brains handle information for learning and memory with a much more complex interaction between the hippocampus, prefrontal cortex, and the amygdala (Dixon & Dweck, 2022; Yavas et al., 2019).

Much terminology for cognitive functioning comes from the **information-processing model**, which originated in the mid 1950s after the invention of computers (Broadbent, 1958). A U.S. psychologist (George Miller) worked on the information-processing approach to explain how humans process information in our memories (Miller, 1956). Miller also worked on chunking information – being able to hold a specific amount of information in part of our memory system, an amount limited to seven plus or minus two pieces of information (Cowan, 2015).

Later, the **stage theory of information processing** received attention as an explanation for how human memory works. This theory from Atkinson and Shiffrin (1968) includes three stages occurring sequentially – **sensory memory, short-term (or working) memory**, and **long-term memory**. The information processing approach to research on cognitive functioning is based on the following assumptions: (1) individuals actively participate in their memory processes; (2) memory performance includes both quantitative (e.g., how many items can I remember?) and qualitative (e.g., interviews, observations) data but is difficult to define (Aspers & Corte, 2019); and (3) individuals process information through a series of steps.

Our sensory memory requires the use of our senses (sight, sound, touch, taste, smell), and it only lasts for up to three seconds. For information to enter our sensory memory, we must pay attention to that information. We pay attention to information of interest to us or that is important in some way and send this information on to the next stage called short-term memory. Information does not stay in short-term memory for long, approximately 15 to 20 seconds, unless we repeat the information. If we repeat information, known as **maintenance rehearsal**, then information can be stored in short-term memory for a maximum of 20 minutes. How much information or chunks of information can be processed at one time has been the subject of controversy (Cowan, 2015).

Factors affecting our short-term memory include individual cognitive abilities, how much information individuals are trying to process, and individuals' ability to pay attention to information in the first place (Cowan, 2015). The more familiar information is, the easier it is to process the information. If information is considered important, then the person pays more attention to it and is more effective at processing it. One part of memory, **encoding**, involves receiving and processing information in a way that is suitable for storage in memory (Panzeri et al., 2023). **Consolidation**, the stabilization and integration of memory, allows for long-term storage of memory and the ability to resist interference over time, which can occur from stressors in our environment and lack of sleep (Rakowska et al., 2022). Memories can be **reconsolidated**, which involves stored memories becoming reactivated and able to be modified (Asthana et al., 2015). **Retrieval** allows individuals to access information, select information, and reconstruct stored memories, and can be affected by context and how familiar the information is.

The third part of the information processing model is called long-term memory, which unlike sensory and short-term memory does not have a limited capacity (it is considered limitless). Different kinds of information can enter long-term memory and be processed for later use. Researchers provide evidence for three major types of human memory: **declarative memory** (explicit), **non-declarative memory** (implicit), and **working memory**.

Declarative memory is linked to the medial temporal lobe and is involved in conscious recollection of memories. One part of declarative memory is **semantic memory**, which includes facts and concepts (Tulving, 1972; Zemla et al., 2023). There is evidence for semantic memory remaining consistent over time with the use of optimal strategies for retrieval of information (Zemla et al., 2023). Another kind of declarative memory is episodic memory, which includes personal experiences and memories of specific events in our lives. Researchers have shown age-related changes in episodic memory for visual, spatial, auditory, verbal, and tactile memory, with a decrease in performance over time (Blachstein & Vakil, 2016; Kuehn et al., 2018; Lange et al., 2024; Merhav & Wolbers, 2019). However, tactile memory shows only minor changes for precision and bias as we age compared to research conducted on other sensory experiences and memory (Kuehn et al., 2018; Lange et al., 2024).

Non-declarative memory is associated with multiple brain regions, including the premotor cortex, cerebellum, and prefrontal brain regions (Hong et al., 2019). **Non-declarative memory** refers to unconscious learning of information – for example, learning how to perform specific behaviors such as brushing our teeth, riding a bike, or driving a car. This is also known as **procedural** memory, which is maintained as we age (Camina & Güell, 2017; Sridhar et al., 2023).

Other researchers added additional components to the information processing model described above, with the most well-known, the **Baddeley-Hitch**

model (Baddeley & Hitch, 1974), including working memory in the model. Working memory is more detailed – a set of subsystems involved in processing different kinds of information. One subsystem is called the **phonological loop**, this part is able to process information individuals hear. Another subsystem is the **visuospatial sketchpad**, which processes information individuals see. The third subsystem is the **central executive**, and this part coordinates information processing, decision making, and critical thinking, and controls attention. In later work, Baddeley and Hitch added another subsystem to their model, the **episodic buffer**, which is a temporary storage area allowing information from other subsystems of working memory to be integrated and stored for a temporary amount of time (Baddeley, 2000; 2012).

Working memory is associated with the prefrontal cortex and the posterior portion of the parietal cortex; multiple brain structures are involved, with the central executive subsystem coordinating information with the phonological loop, episodic buffer, and visuospatial sketch pad, including the frontoparietal network and the dorsolateral prefrontal cortex (Sridhar et al., 2023; Yu et al., 2023).

Other approaches, including the parallel-distributed processing model, led to Rumelhart and McClelland's **connectionist model** in 1986. The connectionist model is based on the idea that information is stored in a variety of locations in our brains and connected through a network (Rumelhart & McClelland, 1986), and that more neural connections allow individuals to retrieve information with less time and effort (Li et al., 2022). Another working memory model, the **state-based model** (D'Esposito & Postle, 2015), is based on distribution of attention toward internal representations allowing for short-term retention in working memory (Ghaleh et al., 2019; Sridhar et al., 2023).

Aging and Attention

There are many studies on the different parts of memory as we age. For sensory memory, researchers show both younger and older adults take in information in their sensory memory in large amounts, and they lose this information in similar amounts when not paying attention to specific items (Park & Festini, 2017). As we age, changes in our sensory abilities can affect how much auditory, visual, and tactile information we experience, important for sensory memory (Fogerty et al., 2016; Lange et al., 2024).

In order to have a memory of something, one has to go through a process that begins with perception of something in the world. While there are many definitions of perception, for humans, we refer to perception as a process in which sensory experiences such as touch, taste, smell, sight, and hearing are converted into an organized experience (West et al., 2024). In order to perceive something in our world, we use our senses. Distinguishing between perception and sensation has a long and complex history (West et al., 2024), and changes in our sensory experiences influence whether or not we pay attention to or notice something in our environment. Much research has been conducted on age differences in visual attention, especially visuospatial tasks related to memory, with evidence of visuospatial memory skills peaking in individuals in their early 20s and then decreasing linearly as we age (Aul et al., 2023). Researchers have found working memory performance for processing visuospatial information declines in older adulthood (Swanson, 2017).

Factors Involved in Memory

Memory involves many factors, including personal interests and **motivation** (Murty & Dickerson, 2017). For example, if you do not feel particularly interested in doing a specific assignment for a teacher, then you will be less motivated to search your memory for a definition of a concept. Motivation can include external or internal factors that make us initiate actions such as searching our memory for a piece of information (Cofer & Petri, 2024) and can affect our ability to remember and retrieve information from our memory (Murty & Dickerson, 2017). Other factors involved in memory, such as nutrition, exercise, education, geographic location, and age, can affect how well you search your memory (Cadar et al., 2023; Ducharme-Laliberté et al., 2022; Shaw et al., 2022; Zhang et al., 2020). Education has been associated with cognitive reserve capacity, with evidence of older adults with higher education having greater cognitive reserve capacity. Heritability of memory function increases with age, and memory function appears to be influenced by multiple genes (Lee et al., 2023; Mollon et al., 2021), with around half of variance in general cognition a result of genetic factors (Mollon et al., 2021).

Ducharme-Laliberté and colleagues (2022) conducted research on older adults in Canada and assessed working memory. The researchers found older adults who were more educated recruited more neural connections for high demands in working memory tasks, and this did not occur for those with lower education. Education is generally considered a protective factor with regard to our memories and cognitive functioning (Zhang et al., 2020). While education is associated with baseline cognitive performance in older adults in most research, it was not associated with cognitive changes in a systematic review and meta-analysis (Seblova et al., 2020).

Cognitive Impairment and Neurological Disorders

Individuals can have **mild cognitive impairment** (MCI), which can include cognitive impairment in just one domain or in several cognitive domains that does not affect independence (Blanco et al., 2023), though some cognitive issues may eventually lead to diagnosed neurological disorders. However, many of us function well until the end of our lifespan, with minimal changes in our cognitive functioning.

Mild cognitive impairment increases with age, with estimates ranging from about 6% in those over 60 years old (Sachdev et al., 2015) to about 25% in those in their early 80s (Livingston et al., 2017). The prevalence rate of MCI in

Latin America and the Caribbean (LAC) is 14.95% (Ribeiro et al., 2022), similar to estimates of MCI in low- or middle-income countries but higher than high-income countries such as the United States. Not all cases of MCI will become more severe cases of neurological impairment. Approximately 15% of MCI cases become forms of dementia (an umbrella term for many types of advanced neurological impairment, with AD the most common form of dementia; Mitchell et al., 2009), and this increases to 90% after a six-year period (Bruscoli & Lovestone, 2004). Researchers believe it is essential to be able to assess MCI cases that may become AD. They use fluid biomarkers (e.g., blood and saliva), sophisticated assessment techniques involving machine learning (ML) algorithms, neuroimaging techniques (MRI, PET), genetics, and clinical data (cognitive assessments, interviews) to create models that can predict onset and further progression of forms of dementia (Blanco et al., 2023).

What is Alzheimer's Disease?

Research on AD began with work by Dr. Alois Alzheimer, a German physician, who was the first person to describe AD in 1906. Alzheimer's disease is the most common form of dementia worldwide. It is a progressive neurological disorder, with changes in the brain including buildup of proteins, neuronal damage, decay, and neuronal cell death, which is evident in neuroimaging as AD progresses and autopsies that show substantial brain shrinkage in those who died from AD. Damage to the brain appears to begin in areas important to memory (i.e., the hippocampus) before spreading to other areas of the brain. Specifically, **plaques** develop from deposits of protein fragments called **beta-amyloid** that build up in spaces between nerve cells in the brain. **Neurofibrillary tangles** consist of twisted fibers of a protein known as **tau**, which builds up inside cells. Large numbers of plaques and neurofibrillary tangles result in neurons dying and severe brain shrinkage as AD progresses.

Prevalence of Alzheimer's Disease

Though rare, AD can happen in young and middle adulthood, beginning in individuals' 30s. This is considered **early-onset AD**. About 110 of every 100,000 adults between the ages of 30 and 64 have early-onset AD (Mayo Clinic, 2024c). Most cases of AD are **late onset AD** or **sporadic AD** in individuals in their 60s and older. Alzheimer's disease currently affects about 6.7 million Americans aged 65 and older, and it is estimated that this number will grow to about 13.8 million by 2060 unless treatment or cures are developed (Alzheimer's Association, 2023). The prevalence rate of AD in Europe is about 74.5 per million (Gustavsson et al., 2023). More than 55 million individuals around the globe have some form of dementia, with an estimate of between 60 to 70% having AD (Mayo Clinic, 2024a). The African continent prevalence rates of dementia range from 2.3% to 20%, with a need for more investigations on dementia (Akinyemi et al., 2022).

Researchers in the United States have provided prevalence estimates that indicate the eastern and southeastern regions of the United States have the highest prevalence rate of AD. Specific counties in each state with the highest prevalence rate of AD include Miami-Dade county in Florida, Baltimore city in Maryland, and Bronx County in New York. States with more individuals over 85 years old, more women, and more minorities have the highest prevalence rates. African Americans and Hispanic Americans are more likely to experience cognitive impairments and dementia in their middle and older adult years compared to non-Hispanic White people, regardless of gender (Garcia et al., 2019). Alzheimer's disease and related dementia showed an average prevalence rate of 10.9%, ranging from 0.4% to 46% for Asian individuals (Zhu, J. et al., 2024). Prevalence rates for AD are higher in Europe and North America than in Asia, Africa, and South America (Cao et al., 2020). Older individuals and women have a higher prevalence rate.

Symptoms of Alzheimer's Disease

Alzheimer's disease begins with minimal changes in cognition years before individuals are assessed and diagnosed. Moments of confusion and mild memory loss happen infrequently, and will progress to more consistent and problematic issues with both short- and long-term memory, changes in personality, difficulty controlling emotions, and eventually loss of the ability to communicate with others (Alzheimer's Association website, 2026, n.d.). Individuals may begin showing signs of memory loss by forgetting names, or even appointments, and then remembering them later. The frequency of forgetting will increase over time, disrupting daily activities. Individuals will have trouble planning out activities and problem solving, and this will get worse over time. Individuals will forget how to get to the grocery store, forget how to balance a checkbook, lose important memories from their own personal history, and experience language issues and personality changes – for example, someone mild mannered becoming very quick to anger. Once AD reaches parts of the brain involved in respiration and heart-rate, individuals with AD are bedridden and require 24-hour supervision and care (National Institute on Aging, 2022).

Factors Involved in Alzheimer's Disease

Researchers have been investigating possible factors involved in AD for many years. However, we still do not know the cause of or cure for AD. The development of AD may be related to many factors, including multiple genes, biological sex, amount of education, nutrition, exercise, mental engagement, diseases, amount of sleep, weight, drugs and alcohol use, social support, and socioeconomic status (Boukhalfa et al., 2023; Clarens et al., 2020; Dalmasso et al., 2023; Gao et al., 2023; Llera-Oyola et al., 2024; Park, S. Y. et al., 2024; Prajjwal et al., 2024). Evidence of specific genes involved in AD show mutations in the Presenilin gene, of which there are two genes, Presenilin-1

(PSEN1) and Presenilin-2 (PSEN2) (Gao et al., 2023). PSEN1 forms a complex relationship with amyloid precursor protein (APP) in cells and is involved in APP transport. PSEN1 increases with age in the human brain, and it affects our memory as we age. Research shows mutations in PSEN1 lead to greater amounts of amyloid-beta peptides (Gao et al., 2023). Variations in mutations and gene research is complex; however, an association between mutations on PSEN1 and **early-onset AD** is clearer than mutations on PSEN2 (Lanoiselée et al., 2017). Less evidence of AD appears to occur in individuals with higher education who stay mentally engaged (Langa et al., 2017), and those with a healthy diet lower in saturated fat and who maintain regular exercise (Gao et al., 2023).

Interventions/Treatments for Alzheimer's Disease

Researchers focus on treatments that can slow development of AD. A non-invasive treatment for AD is transcranial magnetic stimulation (TMS), which involves a brief discharge of electric current from a coil, inducing a focal magnetic field, and penetrating the scalp and skull. Transcranial magnetic stimulation has not been FDA cleared for commercial use in treatment of AD, because not enough proof of effectiveness for treating AD is available at a clinical trial level. Though a meta-analysis supports TMS effectiveness for improving global cognitive functioning in those with mild-to-moderate AD (Menardi et al., 2022).

Two medications that have been approved to treat early-onset AD are Donanemab (Kisunla™) and Lecanemab (Leqembi®). Both medications have been FDA approved, and both are given as antibody intravenous (IV) infusion therapy that targets and removes beta-amyloid from the brain. These medications are also used to treat MCI or mild dementia due to AD in those with confirmed elevated beta-amyloid in their brain.

Other treatments for AD include cholinesterase inhibitors, which work by treating symptoms related to memory, thinking, language, judgment, and other thought processes. Cholinesterase inhibitors prevent the breakdown of acetylcholine (ACTH), a neurotransmitter important for memory and learning. Two cholinesterase inhibitors of note are drugs that help support communication between nerve cells: Donepezil (Aricept®) is the only drug approved to treat all stages of AD, while Galantamine (Razadyne®) is approved to treat mild-to-moderate stages of AD. Another type of drug used is memantine, which works by binding to N-methyl-D-aspartate receptors (NMDA-receptors), specifically a glutamate receptor and predominantly Ca^{2+} ion channel found in neurons, and blocking effects. Memantine is approved to treat moderate to severe symptoms of dementia related to AD.

Neuroinflammation and abnormalities in astrocytes and microglia may play a role in development and progression of AD, and creating therapeutic approaches focusing on restoring impaired astrocytes could be beneficial for cognitive functioning (Bussian et al., 2018; Valenza et al., 2021). Stem cell therapy may be a promising treatment approach for AD, because it targets neuroinflammation, synaptic loss, oxidative stress, and impairment in neurogenesis (Goncalves et al., 2023).

What is Parkinson's Disease?

The actor Michael J. Fox, known for movies such as *Back to the Future*, was diagnosed with early-onset PD in 1991 at age 29. He created the Michael J. Fox Foundation, which helps fund research to study possible causes of both early- and late-onset PD and treatments. The Michael J. Fox Foundation is considered the world's largest nonprofit funder of Parkinson's research.

Parkinson' s disease is the second most common neurodegenerative disorder in North America and the world, after AD (Safiri et al., 2023b; Willis et al., 2022). The first well-defined evidence of a medical description of PD was written by James Parkinson in 1817. Since then, researchers around the world have learned much about PD. However, we still do not know the specific cause or cure for PD (Parkinson's Foundation website, 2026, n.d.).

Parkinson's disease affects the dopamine-producing neurons in the substantia nigra (Elbaz et al., 2016). Between 60 and 80% of neurons in the substantia nigra are impaired or destroyed before individuals show motor symptoms problems of PD. In those with PD, there is an accumulation of a protein, alpha-synuclein, in neurons of the substantia nigra in Lewy bodies (Mayo Clinic, 2024b).

Motor symptoms of PD include tremors (shaking in hands, arms, and legs), slowness of movement, stiffness, and issues with walking and balance (Elbaz et al., 2016). Tremors generally begin on one side of the body. They can also appear on the other side of the body, but are generally stronger on the side that they first began. Individuals develop significant slowness of movement called **bradykinesia**, and limbs can suddenly become stiff, known as **rigidity**, with individuals often describing feeling locked in place. Individuals with PD have a noticeable problem with walking, including both gait and balance issues. For example, individuals' steps may become shorter as they walk, and they may drag or shuffle their feet rather than lifting them up (Mayo Clinic, 2024b). Non-motor symptoms include depression, anxiety, sleep disturbances, fatigue, cognitive issues, and sensory issues, just to name a few (Kalinderi et al., 2024).

Research provides support for two types of PD, familia and sporadic. The familia form of PD is linked to multiple genetic factors, including mutations on genes affecting alpha-synuclein, and the sporadic form of PD is associated with both genetic and environmental factors, such as pesticides and toxins (Rietdijk et al., 2017). Research with the Braak's hypothesis is associated with the sporadic form of PD. Braak's hypothesis shows evidence of neurons affected in the nasal cavity and the gut, spreading to the central nervous system (CNS) from these places (Del Tredici & Braak, 2016). Research supports Braak's hypothesis for a portion of individuals with an early onset of PD and some individuals with a longer duration of PD (Rietdijk et al., 2017). Much research supports age as a factor in PD, with more cases of PD as we age (Willis et al., 2022).

Prevalence of Parkinson's Disease

The prevalence rate of PD in the United States is about one million, and is expected to increase over time. There is little representation of minority groups in studies on PD in the United States or around the globe. Di Luca and colleagues (2020) conducted a systematic review and meta-analysis focused on minority enrollment in PD clinical trials. Of the 63 clinical trials, only 17.5% provided information on race/ethnicity, with only five African Americans, 16 Latin Americans, and 539 Asian Americans enrolled in studies. The majority of participants in the studies were white (75.8%). Duarte Folle and colleagues (2023) conducted a study in rural Central California, and assessed PD progression in Latino and White Non-Latino (WNL) individuals from three counties. The 18% who identified as Latino had an earlier age for diagnosis of PD and an earlier age for death compared to WNL.

Over 10 million individuals around the world live with PD, and this number may reach 13 million by 2040 (Dorsey & Bloem, 2018). A recent systematic review and meta-analysis of 83 studies from 37 countries showed PD has been increasing over time, especially in countries with higher sociodemographic and/or human development (Zhu, C. et al., 2024). Research on 21 countries in the Middle East and North Africa showed the prevalence of PD was 82.6 per 100,000. The highest prevalence was in Qatar and the lowest prevalence was in Kuwait (Safiri et al., 2023b).

The number of cases of PD increases with age. While most people diagnosed with PD are over 60 years old, about one in ten are under 50 years old (Parkinson's Europe website, 2026, n.d.). There are reports of differences by biological sex, with those who are XY 1.5 times more likely to have PD than those who are XX (Parkinson's Foundation website, 2026, n.d.). Willis and colleagues (2022) showed the incidence of PD increases with age and is higher among males than females. However, results for gender differences are not consistent across countries, in part due to cultural differences in determining prevalence rates, and different criteria for diagnosing PD (Zirra et al., 2023). Zirra and colleagues (2023) found prevalence ratio for biological XY/ biological XX was lowest in Asia.

Treatments for Parkinson's Disease

There are several treatment approaches that target symptoms including tremors, rigidity, slowness of movement, and balance, though not all treat all motor symptoms. Levodopa is well known for treating PD symptoms, as it was the first medication shown to be effective for treating PD over 50 years ago (Cotzias et al., 1967). Once it reaches the brain, Levodopa converts into dopamine. There are many different types of medications available to treat PD including dopamine agonists (DA), which is a chemical that will act like dopamine in the brain, instead of actually converting to dopamine. Recent research indicates a relationship between problems with insulin regulation and the development of PD. Glucagon-like peptide-1 receptor (GLP-1R) agonists that have been used to treat type 2 diabetes mellitus are now considered an important step in treatment for PD, with some success in clinical trials (Kalinderi et al., 2024). Naturally occurring molecules found in curcumin, polyphenols, and nicotine are being studied in treatment for PD (Kalsoom et al., 2023). Deep brain stimulation (DBS) surgery for PD involves the deliverance of pulses of electrical current to deep brain structures by surgically implanted electrodes and a pulse generator. For individuals with PD, parts of the brain most commonly targeted for DBS are the subthalamic nucleus and globus pallidus pars interna (Malvea et al., 2022). However, DBS has been used much less with females and racial and ethnic minorities (Bishay et al., 2024).

Intelligence and Aging

At this point, you have learned about the brain as we age, cognitive functioning, and research on specific neurological disorders such as AD and PD. There are other ways to assess cognitive functioning. The research below is on the concept of intelligence. There is not one definition of intelligence, though many researchers have discussed the term intelligence in relation to performance on standardized tests with the psychometric approach. The term intelligence has quite a turbulent history because of false claims in studies, bias in research, and a history of racism affecting research on intelligence and negatively impacting minority groups, especially African Americans (Serpico, 2021). Researchers who study intelligence in adults tend to focus more on certain types of intelligence, and how these types of intelligence relate to brain structure and function in adults as we age (Kopetzky et al., 2024; Yuan et al., 2018), even as possible early cognitive markers of dementia (Bajpai et al., 2022).

Crystallized and Fluid Intelligence

Charles Spearman hypothesized that there is a general intelligence or **g factor** to explain common aspects of diverse mental abilities (Spearman, 1904). Spearman's student, Raymond Cattell, argued that intelligence is not just one construct, but two different types including **fluid intelligence** (Gf) and **crystallized intelligence** (Gc) (Cattell, 1943). The concepts of Gf and Gc were further developed with Cattell's former student John Horn to study their development across adulthood and aging (Horn & Cattell, 1967). Other types of intelligence have been studied, mostly with children and young adults, using the psychometric approach, which is focused on the relation between intellectual abilities and the way relationships are organized or the structure of intelligence (Sternberg, 2020). Sternberg and his colleagues have done extensive research on different aspects of intelligence (Sternberg, 2022; Sternberg et al., 2023). Sternberg (1988) argued intelligence has several components in his **triarchic mind** theory including: (1) **componential intelligence**, which involves abstract thinking, logical reasoning, and our ability to do verbal and math related skills; (2) **experiential intelligence**, which involves our ability to generate new ideas and handle novel situations; and (3) **contextual intelligence** which involves applying our knowledge to the world around us, and our ability to shape and make choices about our own environment.

While the concept of intelligence continues to evolve over time, much work has been conducted on Gf and Gc in adulthood and aging research.

Fluid Intelligence

Fluid intelligence includes our ability to use abstract thinking, novel problem-solving, working memory, and processing speed (Shakeel et al., 2017). Examples of Gf include classification of figures, number and letter series, and matrices. Raven's Progressive Matrices (RPM) is considered a common measure of Gf. Raven's Progressive Matrices consists of a non-verbal multiple-choice test in which participants examine a series of drawings. Participants complete a drawing or use a computer to select a drawing by first identifying relevant features on the spatial arrangement of prior drawings (see Figure 4.4).

Crystallized intelligence

Crystallized intelligence refers to cognitive abilities that depend on information that has been learned, including culturally relevant rules. An example of Gc could be a crossword puzzle or game shows (i.e., Jeopardy and Wheel of Fortune), because these activities are dependent on accumulated knowledge about topics and culturally relevant rules. Much research indicates Gc can improve until very late in life and remain high, while Gf improves into our 20s, gradually decreasing in adulthood.

Many researchers have examined the relation between brain structure and function and Gf and Gc in adults (Kopetzky et al., 2024). One model receiving support on this relationship is the Parieto-Frontal Integration Theory (P-FIT) (Jung & Haier, 2007). The P-FIT describes a complex network of brain regions that comprise Gf the dorsolateral prefrontal cortex, the inferior and superior parietal lobes, the anterior cingulate gyrus, and areas within the temporal and occipital lobes. Yuan and colleagues (2018) conducted a longitudinal study with a United States sample of healthy adults and found individuals with higher amounts of Gf cortical volume showed slower volume shrinkage over time.

Baltes and colleagues are known for their work on life-span concepts of development (see Chapter 1). They used these concepts to propose a theory of intelligence: the dual-component model of intellectual functioning (Baltes et al., 2006). The first component of their model is known as **mechanics of**

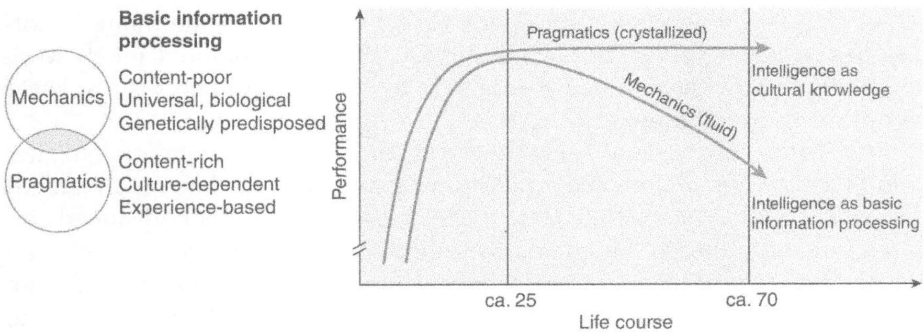

Figure 4.4 Graph showing changes in fluid and crystallized intelligence and the dual component model of intelligence across the lifespan.

intelligence, which includes neurophysiological construction of the mind allowing for thinking, attention, reasoning, etc. The mechanics of intelligence involves the most change earlier in development as the brain grows, and is based on a biological and genetic set of factors that will decrease in adulthood. The second component of their model is known as **pragmatic intelligence** and includes knowledge that is accumulated over the lifespan from culture, such as verbal abilities, wisdom, and the ability to problem solve. Pragmatic intelligence is expected to increase over lifespan. There are some basic similarities between Gf and mechanics of intelligence and Gc and pragmatic intelligence.

Regardless of the labels and definitions of the concept of intelligence, researchers have been studying our intellectual abilities as groups of related skills, and they tend to organize the skills into hypothesized constructs that are called primary mental abilities. The primary mental abilities are then grouped into broader skills known as secondary mental abilities. From many primary mental abilities, around 25, most researchers focus on five including: (1) number, skills for mathematical reasoning; (2) word fluency, how effortlessly we can produce verbal descriptions of things; (3) verbal meaning, our vocabulary; (4) inductive reasoning, how well we can draw conclusions from specific facts to more generalized concepts; and (5) spatial orientation, our skills at understanding the three-dimensional world. The term mental abilities is referenced in the work on Gf and Gc by Horn and Cattell (1967). Early work on mental abilities occurred in the 1940s (Thurstone & Thurstone, 1949).

Perhaps most well-known for his work with primary mental abilities is Dr. Klaus Warner Schaie. Dr. Schaie began work on primary mental abilities with the Seattle Longitudinal Study (SLS) in 1956 for his dissertation research with participants from their early 20s to their late 60s. From 1956 to 2012, participants continued their participation every seven years. In 1983, Dr. Sherry L. Willis became principal co-investigator of the study. There were

26 participants who were in the study for 50 years. Alongside multiple colleagues over the years, Dr. Schaie and Dr. Willis co-authored much work about the SLS (Schaie et al., 2004; Schaie & Willis, 2010) and neuroscience components (Borghesani et al., 2013).

The Seattle Longitudinal Study shows verbal abilities can increase into later adulthood and be maintained, only showing a gradual decline much later in life. Many adults successfully receive their Bachelor's or other advanced certificates later in life. In the United States the number of individuals between 25 and 64 years old who have a college degree or certificate increased from about 38% in 2009 to about 54% in 2021 (Nietzel, 2024). Perceptual speed, also known as processing speed, peaks in young adulthood and shows noticeable decline from middle adulthood and older. This same pattern appears for numeric ability. Individuals highly engaged in work involving numeric skills can maintain those skills.

Training for Cognitive Functioning

Researchers often disagree about brain training programs, and if any changes occur to individuals' cognitive functioning as a result of these programs (Sala & Gobet, 2019). Brain training programs, in general, focus on repair or improvement of specific cognitive abilities, and this is done with repeated practice of specific tasks (Nguyen et al., 2022). Devices used to repeatedly engage individuals with specific cognitive tasks include smartphones, tablets such as iPads, and computers. If brain training works, then it should be applicable to tasks individuals were not trained on repeatedly yet reflect similar cognitive ability, and this is known as **near-transfer**. Training applicable to tasks that are not similar for cognitive ability is known as **far-transfer** (Jaeggi & Buschkuehl, 2014).

Research on Interventions to Improve Cognitive Functioning

Researchers conducted a meta-analysis with 43 studies including North America, Europe, Australia, and Asia to determine if brain training programs are helpful for healthy older adults and for those with MCI (Nguyen et al., 2022). Almost all significant effects for brain training were for healthy adults, not those with MCI. One exception was near-transfer, which occurred for both healthy adults and those with MCI. Healthy adults showed improvement in executive functioning (specifically working memory) and processing speed with brain training.

Researchers have assessed musical instrument training, meditation practices, and mindfulness-based programs for their effects on cognitive functioning (Bhattacharyya et al., 2024; Rogers & Metzler-Baddeley, 2024; Whitfield et al., 2022). A review and meta-analysis included 13 studies from around the world and showed musical instrument training affected executive functioning (attention switching, distractor inhibition, and category switching of verbal fluency) and processing speed (Rogers & Metzler-Baddeley, 2024).

Research on mind–body practices (e.g., deep breathing techniques, yoga, tai chi, music therapy, aroma therapy, and meditation) document their connections to health and well-being (e.g., Bhattacharyya et al., 2024; Crego et al., 2021), with meditation associated with improvements in episodic memory, but not executive function (Bhattacharyya et al., 2024), and mindfulness-based programs improving executive function and working memory (Whitfield et al., 2022).

Superagers

Do All Brains Age the Same?

Researchers have shown that individuals have brain structure and function that is similar to individuals much younger than them. These individuals are known as **superagers**!

Superagers

Superagers have been broadly defined by researchers as individuals over 80 years old with episodic memory performance that is the same as or superior to individuals in middle adulthood (de Godoy et al., 2021; Fili et al., 2024; Harrison et al., 2012; Zhou et al., 2023), and brain structures similar to those in middle adulthood, with some studies showing similar brain structures to individuals in young adulthood too (Sun et al., 2016; Zhang et al., 2020). Support for

Figure 4.5 Photograph of four participants in the SuperAgers Study from the SuperAging Research Initiative.

Source: SuperAging Research Initiative.

superagers comes from research from around the world, including the United States, Canada (Harrison et al., 2012; Rogalski et al., 2022), Australia (Maccora et al., 2021), Germany (Zhou et al., 2023), Spain (Garo-Pascual et al., 2024), Switzerland and Korea (Park et al., 2022), Argentina (Calandri et al., 2020), Prague (Heissler et al., 2023), India (Batra et al., 2024), and China (Lin et al., 2024). Not all research provides support for superagers (Keenan et al., 2024).

One group of researchers is collecting data from participants at sites in the United States and Canada as part of the SuperAging Research Initiative (Rogalski et al., 2022). This initiative is a multicenter study designed to help identify factors associated with superaging, including behavioral, genetic, environmental, socioeconomic, psychosocial, and neurological factors (Rogalski et al., 2023). The U.S. sites include Illinois (University of Chicago), Wisconsin (University of Wisconsin-Madison), Michigan (University of Michigan), and Georgia (Emory University), and there is a Canadian Site in Southwest Ontario (Western University). An important focus of the Super Aging Research Initiative is enrollment of Black superagers and a comparison to a control group formed of typical elderly people with similar demographics.

Brain Structure of Superagers

In 2016, a study conducted in the United States showed superagers had preserved volume in the anterior temporal cortex, medial prefrontal cortex, anterior midcingulate cortex, and the hippocampus compared to typical older adults, and these preserved regions were correlated positively with memory performance (Sun et al., 2016).

Researchers conducted a study in Spain and found superagers have greater GM volume in the motor thalamus area and the medial temporal lobe compared to average older adults (Garo-Pascual et al., 2023). In another recent study in Spain, researchers provided both cross-sectional and longitudinal assessments of superagers compared to average older adults (Garo-Pascual et al., 2024). The results showed superagers did not differ from the average older adult on total WM volume. However, superagers had better WM microstructures compared to the average older adult group, and superagers showed much slower decreases over time in WM microstructures, with greater differences between groups on the anterior portion of the brain.

Factors Involved in Superagers

Researchers are investigating factors associated with being a superager, including genetics, diet, education, sleep, mental health, drug and alcohol use, physical activity level, and environmental factors (Garo-Pascual et al., 2024; Lin et al., 2024; Trammell et al., 2024). Being physically active and maintaining mental functioning are important factors positively associated with superagers (Garo-Pascual et al., 2024), and specific dietary preferences such as alkaline diets are also positively associated with superagers (Lin et al.,

2024). Researchers conducted a study on African Americans aged 80 years and older (Trammell et al., 2024). About 5% were identified as superagers if their cognitive performance was similar to individuals aged 50 to 60 years old with no cognitive impairment. Superagers were primarily female, with higher education, less sleep issues, less depression, and less alcohol use.

Chapter Summary

In this chapter we discussed small and large brain structures, cross-cultural research on the brain, and factors that influence brain changes as we age. We discussed cognitive functioning, factors involved in changes in cognitive functioning, and cross-cultural research on cognitive functioning, as well as changes in our memory as we age. We explored prevalence and cross-cultural research for MCI, AD, PD, and possible treatments. Finally, we compared intelligence models for adulthood and aging research, and discussed training for cognitive functioning, cross-cultural research on cognitive training, and superagers.

Key Takeaways

1. There is evidence of both growth and decline in the brain as we age, and changes at the cellular level.
2. There are multiple factors involved in changes in the brain, and cross-cultural research on these factors.
3. Cognitive functioning shows changes over the lifespan. However, some parts of cognitive functioning are stable or improve as we age.
4. There are biological, psychological, and contextual factors that affect our cognitive functioning as we age, as shown with cross-cultural research.
5. The sociocultural context in which we develop during adulthood plays an important role in the structure and function of our brains, our cognitive functioning as we age, and the resources available for us.

Reflective Questions

1. Which factors influencing cognitive functioning as we age do you find most convincing?
2. Identify biological, psychological, and contextual factors that are relevant to your life. How will they impact your brain structures and functions as you age?
3. How do sociocultural and contextual factors affect the cross-cultural research on cognition as we age?

Suggested Readings

Garo-Pascual, M., Zhang, L., Valentí-Soler, M., & Strange, B. A. (2024). Superagers resist typical age-related white matter structural changes. *Journal of Neuroscience, 44*(25), e2059232024. doi: 10.1523/JNEUROSCI.2059-23.2024.

Owji, S., & Shoja, M. M. (2020). The history of discovery of adult neurogenesis. *Clinical Anatomy, 33*(1), 41–55. doi: 10.1002/ca.23447.

Yuan, P., Voelkle, M. C., & Raz, N. (2018). Fluid intelligence and gross structural properties of the cerebral cortex in middle-aged and older adults: A multi-occasion longitudinal study. *Neuroimage, 172*, 21–30. doi: 10.1016/j.neuroimage.2018.01.032.

Key Terms

An **action potential** is a nerve impulse that triggers specific regions of a neuron to release a neurotransmitter, which binds to receptors on specific regions to allow for communication.

An **adrenergic** neurotransmitter (epinephrine or norepinephrine) can help with responses in part of the autonomic nervous system.

Alzheimer's disease (AD) is a progressive neurological disorder that is the result of changes in the brain, including the buildup of proteins, and changes that lead to neuronal damage, decay, and cell death.

Axon terminals are nerve terminals from the sending portion of a neuron and cell body.

Bradykinesia is when individuals develop significant slowness of movement.

The **brain stem** is the brain structure involved in consciousness and major life sustaining functions such as respiration and heart rate.

Ca^{2+} is a voltage-gated calcium channel in the cell membrane of a neuron.

Caudate is a C-shaped subcortical structure in the brain region known as the thalamus that helps with motor skills and executive functions such as inhibitory control.

The **central executive** is a subsystem of working memory that coordinates information processing, decision making, and critical thinking, and controls attention.

The **cerebellum** is the brain structure involved with balance and coordination of movement.

Cholinergic refers to the neurotransmitter acetylcholine that can help with responses in muscle regions. It plays a major role at neuromuscular junctions.

Cognitive functioning includes the ability to perceive, pay attention to, and react to information or stimuli, process, store, and retrieve information, and decisions and provide responses to information or stimuli.

Componential intelligence involves abstract thinking, logical reasoning, and the ability to practice verbal and math-related skills.

Computerized tomography (CT) refers to imaging tests that use a series of X-rays and a computer to create detailed images of the brain.

The **connectionist model** is based on the idea that information is stored in a variety of locations in the brain, and connected through a network. More neural connections allow individuals to retrieve information with less time and effort.

Connectomes are brain areas that include all connected regions within and across networks of the brain.

Consolidation refers to the stabilization and integration of memory that allows for storage of long-term memory that is able to resist interference over time.

Contextual intelligence involves applying knowledge to the world around us, and the ability to shape and make choices about our own environment.

Crystallized intelligence (Gc) refers to cognitive abilities that depend on information that has been learned, including culturally relevant rules.

Declarative memory is linked to the medial temporal lobe and is involved in the conscious recollection of memories.

Dementia is an umbrella term for many types of advanced neurological impairment.

A **dendrite** is the part of the receiving neurons responsible for accepting messages.

Early-onset Alzheimer's disease, though rare, can occur in young and middle adulthood, beginning in the 30s.

Encoding involves receiving and processing information in a way that is suitable for storage in memory.

The **episodic buffer** is a temporary storage area that allows information from other subsystems of working memory to be integrated and stored for a temporary amount of time.

Episodic memory includes memories of specific events.

Experiential intelligence involves the ability to generate new ideas and handle novel situations.

Fluid intelligence (Gf) is the ability to use abstract thinking and novel problem-solving. It generally refers to cognitive abilities that do not depend on general information that has been learned.

The **frontal lobe** is the brain structure involved in thinking, problem solving, and personality.

Functional connectivity involves the relation of spatially remote neurophysiological events.

Functional Magnetic Resonance Imaging (fMRI) is a type of noninvasive brain imaging that allows for the detection of brain activity through a measurement of changes in blood flow.

Functional neuroimaging techniques allow brain activity to be studied.

Gamma-aminobutryic acid (GABA) is the most common inhibitory neurotransmitter.

Gap junctions are special sections of a neuron that facilitate communication without neurotransmitters and calcium, allowing for fast transfer of electrical messenger signals from one neuron to another.

Glutamate is the most common excitatory neurotransmitter.

Gyrification is the process of forming folds in the cerebral cortex of the brain.

Heritability is a statistic used by researchers to estimate the ratio of genetic variation between individuals in a population to the total phenotypic variation present in that population.

The **hippocampus** is the brain structure in the medial temporal lobe associated with memory.

The **information-processing model** helps to explain how humans process information in our memories.

Inter-individual means between subjects.

Interneurons are located between other neurons and help to control signals in the body and relay information from different parts of the nervous system.

Late onset Alzheimer's disease or **sporadic Alzheimer's disease** generally begins in individuals in their 60s and older.

Long-term memory does not have a limited capacity; it is considered limitless.

Magnetic Resonance Imaging (MRI) is a test that creates a clear image of the structures inside the body using a large magnet, radio waves, and a computer.

Magnetoencephalography (MEG) is a non-invasive technique that records millisecond-by-millisecond measurements of brain activity, providing both timing and spatial information on brain activity.

Maintenance rehearsal is when information is repeated, allowing it to be stored in short-term memory for a maximum of 20 minutes.

The **mechanics of intelligence** includes the neurophysiological construction of the mind that allows for thinking, attention, reasoning, etc.

Motivation can include external or internal factors that initiate actions, such as searching memory for a concept, and can impact the ability to remember and retrieve information from the memory.

Motor neurons help to coordinate movement of muscles.

The **myelin sheath** covers and protects nerve fibers to allow fast communication between neurons.

Neuroanatomy refers to the structure of the brain and the organization of the nervous system.

Neurofibrillary tangles consist of twisted fibers of a protein known as tau that build up inside the cells.

Neurogenesis is the creation of new neural stem cells, considered the precursors to neurons and glial cells.

Neurons are nerve cells that send and receive signals from the brain and allow for communication.

Neuroscience refers to the scientific investigation of the nervous system, including the brain, spinal cord, and the peripheral nervous system.

Neurotransmitters are chemical messengers that help synapses to communicate.

Nodes are brain regions located in the same network that are highly connected to each other.

Non-declarative memory refers to unconscious learning of information – for example, such as learning how to perform specific behaviors such as brushing our teeth.

The **occipital lobe** is the brain structure involved in perception and vision.

Oligodendrocytes are a type of neural glia that forms the myelin sheath. They are created throughout the lifespan in response to new experiences with the environment, including learning experiences.

The **parietal lobe** is the brain structure involved in sensation, perception, attention, and language.

Parkinson's disease (PD) is the second most common neurodegenerative disorder in North America and the world, affecting the dopamine-producing neurons in the substantia nigra.

Perception in humans is the process by which our sensory experiences, such as touch, taste, smell, sight, and hearing, are converted into an organized experience.

A **phonological loop** is a subsystem of working memory that is able to process information individuals hear.

Plaques develop from the deposit of protein fragments called beta-amyloid that build up in the spaces between the nerve cells in the brains.

Positron Emission Tomography (PET) refers to a radioisotope attached to a drug, injected into the body, allowing scientists and medical practitioners to determine if someone has a tumor or growth.

Postformal thought refers to more complex thinking, flexibility in thought, being open to different perspectives outside of our own, and relativistic and dialectical thinking.

Postsynaptic region is the receiving part of a neuron where a neurotransmitter binds to receptors, allowing for communication.

Pragmatic intelligence includes knowledge that is accumulated over a lifespan from culture, such as verbal abilities, wisdom, and the ability to problem solve.

The **prefrontal and frontal cortex** are the parts of brain involved in planning and carrying out activities, paying attention to specific items, and switching between different tasks. The prefrontal cortex is also involved in personality, emotions, and higher-order executive functions.

Presynaptic region is the sending region of the neuron that is triggered by an action potential to release a neurotransmitter into the synapse.

Procedural memory such as riding a bike or driving a car is maintained as we age.

Reconsolidated refers to stored memories becoming reactivated, allowing the memories to be modified.

Resting potential refers to a neuron maintaining voltage across its membrane.

Retrieval allows individuals to access information, select information, and reconstruct stored memories, and can be affected by the context and how familiar the information is.

Rigidity is when limbs suddenly become stiff and feel locked in place.

Semantic memory is one part of declarative memory that includes facts and concepts.

Sensory memory requires the use of the senses and it only lasts for a very brief amount of time – up to 3 seconds.

Sensory neurons help individuals experience sensations such as taste, smell, and pain.

Short-term memory is where information that is of interest to us ends up, for about 15 to 20 seconds, unless we repeat it to store it for later.

The **stage theory of information processing** is based on three stages that occur sequentially: sensory memory, short-term (or working memory), and long-term memory.

The **state-based model** refers to the distribution of attention toward internal representations that allow for short-term retention in working memory.

Structural connectivity refers to connections between brain structures.

Structural neuroimaging is a technique that takes pictures of the brain.

Superagers are individuals who are more that 80 years old but have episodic memory performance that is the same as or superior to individuals in middle adulthood, and brain structures similar to those in middle adulthood. Some studies show similar brain structures to individuals in young adulthood too.

A **superconducting quantum interference device** (SQUID) is a collection of superconducting sensors that detect and amplify magnetic fields generated by neurons that are only a few centimeters away from the sensors.

A **synapse** is a junction, a place where one neuron sends a message to another neuron using chemical messengers or electrical signals.

A **synaptic cleft** is an area where axon terminal membrane allows the release of a neurotransmitter.

The **temporal lobe** is the brain structure involved in memory, language, and hearing.

The **visuospatial sketchpad** is a subsystem of working memory that processes information individuals can see.

Working memory has a set of subsystems that are involved in processing different kinds of information.

5 Bodily Changes and Acute and Chronic Illnesses

Learning Objectives

Describe changes in skin, hair, bones/joints, muscles, hormones, and other body systems across adulthood.
Explain differences in acute and chronic illnesses in adults across cultures.
Articulate general findings on communication and treatment for acute and chronic illnesses and differences across cultures.
Describe functional health and functional abilities.
Identify how biological, psychological, and contextual factors are involved in bodily changes, acute and chronic illnesses, and functional abilities as we age.

Activity

Can you see differences in your skin compared to when you were 10 years old? Describe the changes you have noticed.

Bodily Changes

Skin

Skin changes over the lifespan, both in appearance and function. There are two types of aging that occur with skin: **intrinsic aging** and **extrinsic aging** (Lawton, 2023; Sales et al., 2022). Intrinsic aging includes changes in the structure and function of skin, viewed as a normal part of development for all individuals. Intrinsic aging occurs, in part, because of our genetic makeup, and proceeds at different rates in different species. There is a buildup of reactive oxygen species (ROS), leading to damage to DNA, enzymes, and membranes (Farage et al., 2013). Changes result in skin that is drier, thinner, and

DOI: 10.4324/9781003483809-5

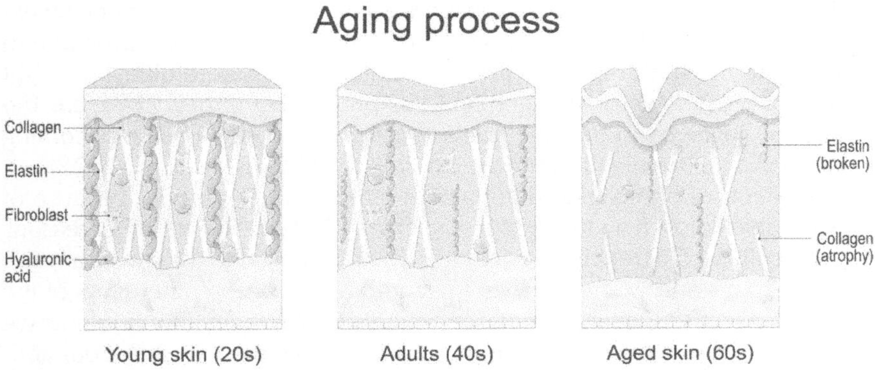

Figure 5.1 Illustration of the different layers of skin as they change over the adult lifespan.

Source: Shutterstock

has less elasticity, increased wrinkles over time, **telangiectasias** (small, dilated blood vessels near the surface of the skin, otherwise known as spider veins), and changes in pigment (Sales et al., 2022). Extrinsic aging includes lifestyle factors (e.g., smoking) and the environment (e.g., pollution) (Lawton, 2023; Sales et al., 2022).

There are also changes to our **epidermis**, which is the top layer of skin. The epidermis becomes thinner, which leads to skin becoming dryer and needing more moisturizer over time. The epidermis becoming thinner is generally viewed as the first step in the formation of wrinkles. Some cells in the epidermis, including **melanocytes** (one of many types of cells involved in melanin production), decrease, and this affects our immune system response, making us more susceptible to infections and skin cancer, and increasing the time it takes wounds to heal (Cichorek et al., 2013; Lawton, 2023).

The **dermis** is the middle layer of skin. Changes within the dermis in **collagen fibers** is considered the second step in the formation of wrinkles. These fibers make up connective tissue and lose flexibility over time, resulting in skin with reduced ability to regain shape after it is squeezed. Changes within the dermis in **elastin fibers** occur, with the dermis showing less mass. Changes in elastin fibers is the third step in wrinkle formation, as elastin fibers lose their ability to maintain skin in a stretched form, which results in sagging. Cells within the dermis decrease over time, reducing the dermis' protective capacity and limiting the wound healing process when we have wounds (Lawton, 2023; Sales et al., 2022). There is a decrease in the protective padding provided to our bodies, which is the fourth step in wrinkle formation, alongside less skin elasticity. The padding from the underlying layer of fat diminishes over time, reducing the ability to smooth out contours in the skin.

Premature aging of skin is associated with the environment, especially exposure to the sun. This is known as "**photoaging**" because skin ages due to exposure to the sun's rays over time. Continued exposure to ultraviolet light leads to a breakdown of collagen and less production of new collagen. The sun is also involved in damage to elastin, and this results in skin becoming looser and more wrinkled over time (Asyi et al., 2023; Sales et al., 2022).

The effects of photoaging differ across ethnic groups, in part, because of different skin colors (Lawton, 2023; Asyi et al., 2023). However, other reasons include cultural differences in how long we are exposed to the sun as a result of occupations and where we live. In addition, diseases in other parts of the body can affect skin aging, socioeconomic status can affect the nutrients we consume or absorb over time, and physiological changes may affect our ability to properly care for our own skin (Asyi et al., 2023; Lawton, 2023).

Treatments for changes in the skin due to photoaging vary from Chinese herbal formulas (He et al., 2021; Zhang et al., 2023) to intense pulsed light (IPL) (Sales et al., 2022). A systematic review included 16 studies showing IPL is effective as a treatment for skin rejuvenation (Sales et al., 2022). The specific parameters for the best effects of IPL on skin rejuvenation are not known, in part, because of much variability across studies.

Another factor that influences skin aging is hormones. Skin cells including melanocytes are affected by hormones and decreases in estrogen levels (e.g., as a result of **menopause**) affect skin (Owen et al., 2016). In a five-year study with randomized placebo-controlled trial design, researchers investigated the relationship between hormone therapy (HT) and the amount of wrinkles and the rigidity of skin in early postmenopausal women with participants from the Kronos Early Estrogen Prevention Study (KEEPS) (Owen et al., 2016). The early menopausal women did not show results from HT in protection against wrinkle formation over the four-year period assessed. However, total wrinkle score and skin rigidity were significantly different across ethnic groups, with African American women having the lowest wrinkle scores over time compared to White American women.

Skin sensitivity also changes over time. **Tactile sensitivity** refers to our ability to perceive physical characteristics with the fingertips, and shows changes over the lifespan. There is evidence of a decline in touch sensitivity. However, positive touch experiences such as a light touch like a caress appear to be maintained. Researchers from Canada conducted a study on individuals aged 18 to 71 years old, with a vibration-emitting smartphone application called the Vibratus App (Lindsay et al., 2024). Smartphones with the Vibratus App showed a significant age difference, with less tactile sensitivity in older participants.

Hair

Hair goes through both intrinsic and extrinsic changes over time. One visible sign of intrinsic aging is hair becomes grayer over time. Up to 25% of individuals generally have about 50% of their hair turn gray by the time they are

50 years old (Villani et al., 2023). Loss of melanin-producing melanocytes in the base of the hair follicle is associated with a decrease in the pigment of hair, resulting in hair that becomes grayer over time (Maymone et al., 2021).

Hair becoming grayer generally occurs in the mid to late forties; however, variability in onset is associated with ethnicity. Both intrinsic factors such as genetics and extrinsic factors including geographic location affect age of onset for gray hair. White individuals tend to have onset in their mid-thirties, Asian individuals begin showing gray hair in their late thirties, and Africans do not generally show graying until their mid-forties (Maymone et al., 2021; Villani et al., 2023).

Besides graying, there are ethnic differences in hair structure and changes in hair over the lifespan. There are gradual changes including changes in diameter, density, shape, and growth patterns of hair, with ethnic differences as we age (Csuka et al., 2023; Maymone et al., 2021; Villani et al., 2023). In a review of 59 studies, researchers assessed lipid and other hair structures across ethnic groups (Csuka et al., 2023). Lipids are considered fatty, waxy, or oily compounds, and there are ethnic differences in lipid content with most lipid percentage in African hair (6%), followed by White hair (3%), and then Asian hair (2%). African hair is considered the most fragile, in part, because of disorder in lipid composition, and Asian hair is considered the strongest and most resistant to ultraviolet damage (Csuka et al., 2023). Cultural differences in the treatment of hair (i.e., an extrinsic factor) show White and Asian individuals have more hair damage at the hair shaft and African individuals have more hair damage closer to the hair root (Maymone et al., 2021).

Some individuals will develop different types of baldness as they age. One common type of balding is known as **androgenetic alopecia**, or male pattern baldness, though it can affect biological males and females at any age (Villani et al., 2023). It involves progressive reduction in the hair follicle. The specific pattern of distribution appears to be genetic, occurring in about 80% of males and about 50% of women, with greater prevalence as they age (Lolli et al., 2017; Villani et al., 2023).

Bones, Joints, and Muscles

Bones, joints, muscles, and nerves degenerate over time, leading to problems with movement such as going up and down stairs and standing and sitting (Cordeiro et al., 2023; Fink et al., 2020). Decrease in muscle mass as we age is called **sarcopenia** (Cho et al., 2022; Cordeiro et al., 2023). Prevalence of sarcopenia is about 29% in older adults, and can range up to 50% in adults over 80 years old (Cruz-Jentoft et al., 2014). **Locomotive syndrome,** first coined in Japan, is a term for decline in bones, joints, muscles, and nerves that can increase risk of disease and death, because such changes weaken bones and increase the risk of falls and accidents (Nakamura, 2008; Nakamura & Ogata, 2016). Research on individuals aged 60 years and older from the Baltimore Longitudinal Study of Aging (BLSA) showed that African American adults' physical performance (assessed by gait speed) was significantly poorer than non-Hispanic White adults, after controlling for socioeconomic status (Chiles Shaffer et al., 2020).

There are ethnic differences in the amount of muscle compared to adipose tissue in the body, with a greater amount of intermuscular adipose tissue (IMAT) in African American adults compared to Asian and White American adults (Gallagher et al., 2005). A study on the U.S. national prevalence of sarcopenia in individuals aged 50 to 80 years old was conducted (Bigman & Ryan, 2021), and showed non-Hispanic African American adults were less likely to have sarcopenia if assessed by body mass index, more likely to have it if assessed by gait speed, and showed no difference in prevalence by grip strength. Hispanic adults and Asian/other adults were more likely to have sarcopenia if assessed by grip strength, gait speed, and body mass compared to non-Hispanic White adults.

There is evidence of behaviors that can increase muscle strength capacity, in particular, resistance training (RT). Resistance training involves a planned exercise program to achieve an increase in one's muscle strength and thickness (Coratella, 2022). A systematic review and meta-analysis conducted on individuals aged 50 and older, with 27 studies, showed an effect for voluntary activation of specific muscles from RT interventions (James et al., 2021). Another systematic review and meta-analysis (Cordeiro et al., 2023) showed that RT had a significant effect on muscle development and strength for participants aged 60 and older.

Hormones

Declines in the hormone estrogen when women reach menopause can have an effect on their overall mental and physical health. Menopause is generally defined as the 12 months after a woman's last menstrual cycle. The end of the menstrual cycle begins with fluctuations in monthly menstrual cycle during the menopause transition period, known as **perimenopause**. During perimenopause a biological female has fluctuations in production of estrogen and progesterone. While the transition period can begin somewhere between 45 and 55 years old, some women experience it much earlier or later. The transition period lasts about seven years, but can last as many as 14 years (Strelow et al., 2024). Multiple factors may be involved in the duration of the transition including age at onset, ethnicity, and lifestyle factors (e.g., smoking).

Symptoms that occur during perimenopause can vary, with some women having little to no symptoms, and other women experiencing severe effects of symptoms, including hot flashes (e.g., sudden heat in the neck and face, all over the body, heavy sweating followed by feeling very cold and shivering), trouble sleeping, painful sexual experiences, mood changes and irritability, and depression, with ethnicity and different cultural experiences affecting perceptions and experiences with symptoms (Kabir & Chan, 2023; Shea, 2020). Early menopause can also be triggered by removal of ovaries and/or a hysterectomy (removal of uterus), as hormones involved in the menstrual cycle will drop rapidly without hormone replacement therapy (HRT).

Lifestyle factors such as diet and physical activity level are important for maintaining good health and better quality of life when dealing with symptoms of menopause, though cultural differences in perception of symptoms and views about perimenopausal symptoms vary (Kabir & Chan, 2023; Kirchengast, 2024). Nonpharmacological techniques can be helpful as HRT has known risk factors, such as cancer, stroke, heart disease, blood clots, and dementia (from early research on HRT) (Anderson et al., 2004; Rossouw et al., 2002), and malignant melanoma (from a systematic review and meta-analysis of sixteen studies) (Chiavarini et al., 2022). Not all studies support evidence of a risk from HRT for different forms of cancer (Bae, 2021). Hormone replacement therapy can be estrogen by itself or estrogen can be combined with progestin, which is a synthetic form of progesterone.

After menopause, women reach a new phase called **postmenopause**, making them more susceptible to health conditions like **osteoporosis** (Mayo Clinic, 2025b). Osteoporosis, where bones become brittle, is associated with the postmenopausal period and the reduction in hormones such as estrogen in women, but osteoporosis can also occur in men. While osteoporosis does affect men and women of all ethnicities, it is considered most common in White and Asian women past menopause (Kabir & Chan, 2023). Non-Hispanic African Americans have a lower amount of bone loss compared to non-Hispanic White and Hispanic and Asian adults in the United States, though results vary across studies and within ethnic groups, and fewer studies are available on non-Hispanic African Americans and Hispanic and Asian adults compared to non-Hispanic White adults in the United States (Noel et al., 2021). The prevalence rate of osteoporosis globally (based on a systematic review and meta-analysis) is 18.3%, with the highest prevalence rate of osteoporosis in Africa at 39.5% (Salari et al., 2021).

If an individual's bones become brittle, they are more susceptible to a break from a fall. Bone loss leading to osteoporosis starts before menopause. There is a period of fast bone loss that begins one year before the last menstrual period. Bone loss is rapid for a few years and then continues at a slower rate, though other variables can play a role in symptoms of perimenopause (Kirchengast, 2024) and amount of bone loss, such as health conditions (e.g., obesity and hypertension) (Greendale et al., 2021; Kirchengast, 2024).

Secondary reasons for osteoporosis are associated with endocrine problems (e.g., pituitary disorders, **diabetes mellitus** (DM), and rheumatic disorders), and cancers (e.g., lymphoma), as well as lifestyle factors (e.g., smoking, excessive consumption of alcohol) (Hudec & Camacho, 2013). Secondary causes of osteoporosis affect more than 60% of older men, more than 50% of women who have not reached menopause yet, and about 30% of women who have finished menopause (Ganesan et al., 2023; Hudec & Camacho, 2013). In a systematic review, research showed that nonpharmacological techniques to prevent osteoporosis, including physical activity and educational sessions, are helpful to prevent osteoporosis in individuals during menopause (Mohammadi et al., 2022).

Chemicals in our environment can lead to decreases in bone mass and increases in the number of individuals with osteoporosis. One such chemical is cadmium (Cd), which occurs naturally in the environment, but can also be released by human activities (Center for Disease Control [CDC], 2021; Leconte et al., 2021). People can be exposed to Cd in many ways (e.g., eating plants and food sources that absorb Cd) (CDC, 2021). Individuals who smoke are exposed to higher quantities of Cd, and some jobs such as industrial work can lead to more exposure to Cd inhalation. Researchers have found that exposure to Cd is associated with an increase in osteoporosis, and about 16% of U.S. osteoporosis cases in those aged 50 to 79 years old may be from exposure to Cd (Pouillot et al., 2022).

Other Hormone Changes

While men do not have such a dramatic drop in hormones, they do have a gradual decline in testosterone over time (Zouhal et al., 2022), known as **andropause**. Andropause is considered a partial deficit of androgen and is associated with testicular problems as men age (Fink et al., 2020). The link between bones, joints, and hormones is complex, and individuals with arthritis do show lower levels of testosterone compared to healthy adults (Lashkari et al., 2018).

Another hormone issue that affects older adults is **hyperthyroidism**, which is excessive amounts of thyroid hormone that speed up the body's metabolism too much, affecting body mass. **Hypothyroidism**, a condition where there is not enough thyroid hormone in the body, slows down the metabolism, which can cause mental and physical health issues. Researchers assessed data from the BLSA, and individuals with a median age of 68 had higher FT4 (i.e., unbound thyroxine hormone) associated with less leg lean mass and greater risk of sarcopenia (Ibad et al., 2023). Abasilim and colleagues (2024) found that thyroid-related hormones were associated with changes in blood pressure and more hypertension in the Hispanic/Latino adult sample.

Treatments for hormone issues as a result of aging can include medications, and also exercise training programs. Zouhal and colleagues (2022) conducted a systematic review of the impact of exercise training on hormones in individuals over 40 years old with 33 studies. Findings showed testosterone, insulin-like growth factor-1 (IGF-1), human growth hormone, and dehydroepiandrosterone increased in both males and females over the age of 40 with exercise training programs.

Respiratory System

Our respiratory system includes an **upper respiratory tract** and a **lower respiratory tract**. The **upper respiratory tract** includes the nose and mouth, nasal cavity, sinuses, and larynx. It transports air into the body, helps move air to the lungs, and adds moisture to air that is breathed in; and it includes our nose and mouth, nasal cavity, sinuses, and larynx. The **lower respiratory tract** includes the trachea, bronchi, and lungs. The trachea, bronchi and bronchioles (small airways) are part of the tracheobronchial area, which includes increasingly smaller tubes responsible for transport of air from our upper respiratory tract to the small air sacs in our lungs called **alveoli** (Smith, 2024; Sobhan, 2024).

Over time it becomes more difficult to maintain a high level of physical activity. One of the major causes of decrease in activity is the decrease in the ability of respiratory organs to acquire and deliver oxygen to arterial blood. There are a number of structural changes that occur in the respiratory system. The cartilage in the walls of the trachea and bronchi undergoes increased hardening making the walls more rigid. These changes cause a gradual decrease in maximum breathing capacity. Next, the walls of the alveoli deteriorate over time, resulting in a reduction of the surface area of the alveoli, which is where gas exchange takes place. Finally, the lungs lose some of their elastic ability to contract, and this leads to less resistance to expansion. The lungs have two main functions. One of their functions is to get oxygen from air into the body, and the other function is to remove carbon dioxide. Once airways are filled, stretchy tissue and bands of muscle will lose elasticity over time, and this affects our ability to take in oxygen and remove carbon dioxide (Smith, 2024; Sobhan, 2024).

In humans, lungs are the organ in the body with the largest surface area. There are ongoing stressors to lungs, including chemical, mechanical, biological, and immunological effects (Schneider et al., 2021). Individuals who live with allergies or asthma have an increased risk of infections as they age. Individuals in older adulthood who show deterioration in their lung capacity are at greater risk of respiratory infections (Bruce et al., 2021), obstructive lung disease (Budinger et al., 2017), and lung cancer (Budisan et al., 2021).

Lower respiratory tract infections (LRTI) are associated with increased disease and death amongst older adults in American Indian (AI) and Alaska Native (AN) populations in the United States (Holman et al., 2011). Bruce and colleagues (2021) conducted a study with AI/AN adults aged 18 years or older and found that the rate of increase of infection over time was significantly higher for Alaska compared to non-Alaska Indian Health Service regions, and the rate substantially increased for older adults. For those aged 85 and older from Alaska the rate was 70.1, compared to older adults from non-Alaska with a rate of 56.9 for hospitalizations for LRTI. Some factors involved in increase in LRTI in AI and AN older adults include use of tobacco, crowded homes, more air pollution in homes, and poverty (Thomas et al., 2016). Equatorial Guinea, Chile, and Albania had the greatest decreases in LRTIs from 1990 through 2019. However, Guinea, Chad, and India had the most increase in incidence rates for LRTIs. Safiri and colleagues (2023a) mentioned air pollution in homes and lack of hand-washing facilities as two factors involved in LRTIs.

Many conditions such as allergies, asthma, and chronic obstructive pulmonary disease (COPD) can affect organs and tissues that make up the respiratory system. Any pollutants or germs that are breathed in from air can be linked to these health conditions, and other factors such as genetic diseases (e.g., cystic fibrosis) can play a role too. Individuals can have an allergic reaction to tree pollen, pet hair, and dust affecting their airways and nasal passages.

There are ethnic disparities in Asthma and COPD, with African American, AI/AN, and multi-ethnic American adults having a higher prevalence of Asthma compared to non-Hispanic White Americans (i.e., Forno et al., 2023). Chronic obstructive pulmonary disease is less likely in African Americans and Hispanic Americans compared to White non-Hispanic Americans (American Lung Association, 2025). However, individuals from a minority background are less likely to be diagnosed and treated for COPD compared to White Americans, leaving them more likely to experience severe symptoms and death related to COPD at an earlier age (Odhiambo et al., 2023). The use of a church community may help with early detection and treatment of these diseases (Odhiambo et al., 2023). Hospitals and doctor's offices are not always readily available or used by individuals of many minority backgrounds and cultures.

There are treatments for asthma, COPD, and other related conditions, including corticosteroids, antibiotic medications, antihistamines, and more advanced techniques such as surgery for blockages or tumors and lung transplants. In addition, behavior therapy and pulmonary rehabilitation are non-pharmacological approaches to treating conditions such as COPD that also help those individuals with a history of smoking (Yawn et al., 2021).

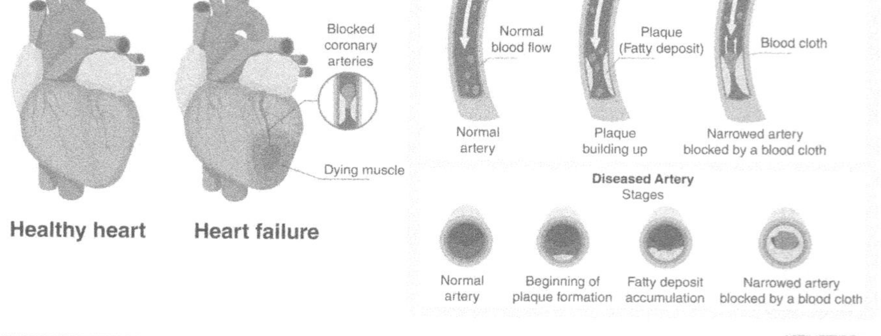

Figure 5.2 Changes in the heart when disease is present in the arteries.
Source: Shutterstock.

Cardiovascular System

Over time, there are changes in our heart and our blood vessels. **Resting heart rate**, the number of heart beats per minute at rest, does not change much. However, gradually, over time, our hearts are not able to beat as fast during physical activities or stressors. There may be times when we feel our heart skip a beat or feel like it is beating too hard. If this kind of experience happens often, then this could mean that you have an abnormal rhythm in your heart known as **arrhythmia**, which will require treatment (Adhikary et al., 2022; National Institute on Aging, 2024).

The chambers of the heart can increase in size, because the heart wall thickens leading to a decrease in the amount of blood the chamber can hold. This increases the risk of **atrial fibrillation**, a type of heart rhythm condition common in older adults, and it can increase risk of a stroke. In addition, valves responsible for controlling flow of blood between chambers of the heart can become thicker and less flexible. Valves that are more rigid can limit blood flow out of the heart. More rigid valves can also lead to leaks that cause fluid buildup in other parts of the body, including the legs and abdomen (Adhikary et al., 2022; National Institute on Aging, 2024).

As is evident from this description, changes in blood vessels put us at increased risk of cardiovascular conditions. **Arteriosclerosis** is when the arteries have become more rigid. This can result in hypertension (known as high blood pressure), the risk of which increases with age. When our coronary arteries show a gradual increase in fatty deposits on the walls of arteries, often labeled plaques, this is known as **atherosclerosis**. We can also have this plaque buildup in the arteries in our brain and legs, and this can increase our risk of a stroke (National Institute on Aging, 2024).

When there is decreased blood flow to the heart because of plaque buildup in coronary arteries, we may feel pain in our chests, neck, or left arm. The pain we feel is known as **angina**. If blood flow to the heart is blocked, then we do not get sufficient oxygen and nutrients. This situation is labeled a heart attack by physicians and cardiologists (National Institute on Aging, 2024; Wurm et al., 2019).

Cardiovascular disease (CVD) is the leading cause of death in the United States and globally (Martin et al., 2024; Roth et al., 2020; Zhang et al., 2021). About one-third of deaths in the United States are believed to be from CVD (Benjamin et al., 2018). There are ethnic differences in prevalence of CVD in the United States, with non-Hispanic African American adults having more risk factors for CVD compared to non-Hispanic White adults (Benjamin et al., 2018). However, African immigrants showed a lower prevalence rate of CVD risk factors compared to African Americans, including less hypertension, less diabetes mellitus, less high cholesterol, and less smoking (Turkson-Ocran et al., 2020).

Researchers used data from the Global Burden of Disease (GBD) 2019 to assess prevalence of CVD in 21 Middle East and North Africa (MENA) countries (Alhuneafat et al., 2024). The prevalence rate for CVD showed a decrease from 1990 to 2019, with males having higher rates of CVD than females in 1990 and 2019. Ischemic heart disease, stroke, and peripheral artery disease were the most prevalent types of CVD, which is consistent with the latest global findings (Martin et al., 2024).

Factors involved in CVD include genetic risk factors (The China Kadoorie Biobank Collaborative Group, 2024); a sedentary lifestyle; diets high in meat consumption, saturated fats, and junk food; excessive consumption of alcohol; smoking (Zhang et al., 2021); environmental factors (e.g., pollutants and lead); and metabolic risk factors (e.g., hypertension, high levels of fasting glucose, and high LDL cholesterol; Martin et al., 2024).

Treatments for different kinds of cardiovascular conditions can include medications such as alpha-beta blockers, anticoagulants, and calcium channel blockers, with some designed to control blood pressure, reduce blood clotting, or regulate heartbeat (American Heart Association, 2024). Sometimes individuals undergo a **catheterization**, which involves a tube being guided through a blood vessel to the heart's arteries and dye being injected through the tube to the arteries, making them and any blockages show up on X-ray images. This allows doctors to determine the amount of blockage in a blood vessel (Mayo Clinic, 2023a).

If there is significant blockage from blood clots or plaques from atherosclerosis, then doctors may place a stint (a tiny tube) into the blood vessel to keep the blood vessel open and improve blood flow. Catheterizations are done for a variety of heart problems, including symptoms like chest pain. Sometimes individuals have blood vessels that are mostly or completely blocked and they need cardiac bypass surgery, which involves a healthy blood vessel from another part of the body, such as the chest or leg area, being connected below the blocked heart artery to improve blood flow to the heart (Mayo Clinic, 2023a).

Individuals with irregular heartbeats can take medications for this condition, and many also have an implantable cardioverter-defibrillator (ICD). The ICD is a small device that is battery-powered; it can detect irregular heartbeats or arrhythmias, stop irregular heartbeats, and, when necessary, deliver electric shocks to restore an individual's regular heart rhythm (Mayo Clinic, 2025a).

Of course, the best way to help an individual is to get them to a maintain healthy lifestyle to prevent CVD or reduce further risk of additional cardiovascular events. Longitudinal research with the German Ageing Survey included individuals aged 40 to 95 years old and showed that changing perceptions of oneself because of cardiovascular issues may lead to a decrease in health-related behaviors (Wurm et al., 2019). Increased smoking is linked to increased risk of CVD as well as cancer (Sun et al., 2013; Zhang et al., 2021). In contrast, a study conducted in Accra, Ghana (Asiamah et al., 2023), showed individuals who had moderate to high levels of physical activity had more likelihood of CVD, perhaps because of increased risk of injury or excess demand on the heart. A review of literature on Chinese immigrants to Western countries (e.g., U.S., Canada) showed that they take an active role in managing their diet and activity level to manage their likelihood of CVD (Zeng et al., 2023a). Communication about health can be difficult because of language barriers in Western countries (Zeng et al., 2023a).

With few exceptions, regardless of country or culture, it appears that there is a need to support and encourage those with cardiovascular conditions to maintain health promoting behaviors as they age. In fact, supporting health promoting behaviors in early adulthood may reduce risk of both cardiovascular issues and cognitive decline late in life (Yaffe et al., 2021). There is evidence of benefits from physical training that can improve health markers in both young and older adults. High-intensity interval training (HIIT) helps with gains in physical fitness and overall health. In a systematic review and meta-analysis, researchers assessed if HIIT was beneficial for older adults (Oliveira et al., 2024). Twenty-nine trials with participants 65 years old and older showed improvement in multiple health outcomes from HIIT, including less fat, better control of glycemia, improved blood pressure, and overall cardiorespiratory gains (Oliveira et al., 2024).

Temperature Regulation

Normal body temperature decreases over time, with a lower body temperature evident in older adults when compared to younger adults (Geneva et al., 2019). **Thermoregulation** is a biological mechanism that helps us maintain our internal body temperature (98.6°F (37°C). Thermoregulation includes multiple systems in our bodies, including our cardiovascular system, respiratory system, and musculoskeletal system. The hypothalamus is part of the brain involved in temperature regulation, and the circulatory system, sweat glands, and skin also help us maintain body temperature. When we sweat it helps to lower body temperature, and when we shiver it helps to raise body temperature, because sweating and shivering can narrow or relax blood vessels, which affects the flow of blood in our bodies. When we are not able to regulate our body temperature we may overheat or become too cold. When we overheat, this can lead to hyperthermia, and when we become too cold, this can lead to hypothermia (Kurz, 2008).

There are multiple ways we can thermoregulate body temperature. One way is through **efferent responses**, which are behaviors that can help us regulate temperature in our bodies, such as wearing a warm sweater or coat on a cold day, and using a fan or going into an air-conditioned building to cool off on a hot day. Another way we can regulate our body temperature is with **afferent** sensing, which involves temperature receptors in our body that help to determine if core body temperature is getting too hot or too cold. The receptors send this information to the hypothalamus. The hypothalamus is known as the central control, and it helps to regulate temperature. The hypothalamus uses information sent from afferent sensing to produce hormones our body uses to alter temperature. These hormones send signals to different parts of our bodies, so we can respond to heat or cold (Kurz, 2008).

Older adults are more sensitive to cold and less sensitive to heat, and this is especially true for extremities (e.g., legs, arms, hands, feet). In a study conducted in Campina Grande in Paraíba/Brazil, research on older adults showed they were more sensitive to cold than heat (de Farias Panet et al., 2022). In Canada, older adults showed core temperature and strain on their cardiovascular system occurred once temperature indoors was above 26°C (Meade et al., 2024). Changes in weather and room conditions affect thermoregulation, and infection and genetic factors may play a role.

Digestive System

Our digestive system goes through changes that can affect absorption of liquids and solid food, and can cause body concerns such as constipation, heartburn, gas, and bloating; as a result we need to better understand our diet and protein absorption (Gallego et al., 2022; Gorissen et al., 2020; Lutz et al., 2019). How we chew and swallow can change, leading to safety concerns for older adults. We can experience **dysmasesis**, which is difficulty in chewing our food and may be caused by loss of teeth. We can experience **dysphagia**, which is difficulty swallowing in a safe manner, and this issue increases in older adults. Factors that contribute to dysphagia include a decrease in saliva production and less strength in the area called the esophageal sphincter. While it is more likely with some diseases such as Parkinson's disease (PD), degeneration of our nerves and muscles can impair swallowing. All of these factors can affect our ability to coordinate the swallowing process as we age. Losses in taste and/or smell of food and drinks, loss in appetite, loss of bone, and changes in our gastrointestinal system affect our ability to properly digest liquids and solids and absorb nutrients. Regular dental visits and maintaining teeth and gum health is important in reducing digestive issues. A healthy lifestyle including a diet rich in vitamins such as vitamin D and calcium and nutrients such as proteins, lots of fluids (especially water), regular exercise, and sleep can all help maintain a better digestive system (Gallego et al., 2022; Gorissen et al., 2020).

Sleep

A good night's sleep is beneficial to our mental and physical health. Over time our bodies go through changes that can affect how much sleep we get, as well as the quality of our sleep. There are many sleep problems experienced including insomnia (difficulty falling or staying asleep), obstructive sleep apnea (a decrease or complete stop in our airflow), feeling very tired during the day, sleep-related movement disorders (repetitive movement that interferes with sleep), and sleep-wake disorders associated with our circadian rhythm (sleep cycle can be too short, too long, etc.) (Bubu et al., 2020;

Canever et al., 2024; Jalali et al., 2022). A recent systematic review and meta-analysis was conducted on worldwide prevalence of sleep problems in older adults living in the community. There were 252 studies (1988 to 2023) with individuals over 60 years old from 36 countries (Canever et al., 2024), and researchers found that obstructive sleep apnea was the most frequent sleep concern worldwide at 46%.

There are many recommendations regarding what to do when you have trouble sleeping, including the type and timing of food and drink consumption, regular exercise, and relaxation techniques such as listening to soothing music (Alruwaili et al., 2023; Chen et al., 2021; Yajima et al., 2014). Sedative music is music with a slow tempo and a soft sound and melody (Wang et al., 2016). Rhythmic music includes a fast tempo, loud volume, and rhythmic patterns (Jiang et al., 2013). A systematic review and meta-analysis on the effect of music therapy on improving the quality of sleep in older adults showed that when older adults listened to music they had better sleep quality than those who did not listen to music, and sedative music provided better quality sleep than rhythmic music (Chen et al., 2021).

Urinary Tract Concerns

Over time our immune system has an increased risk of infections, and one of the most common is infections in the urinary tract (Kalhori et al., 2024; Khatony et al., 2021; Medina et al., 2019). A urinary tract infection (UTI) is a bacterial infection, and it can affect the lower urinary tract, upper urinary tract, and the bladder. Urinary tract infections can show an increase in females from ages 14 to 24 years old (Schmiemann et al., 2010), however, prevalence is much higher in older women over age 65 at about 20% (Chu & Lowder, 2018). Urinary tract infections occur in millions of individuals every year, and UTIs that are not treated can have severe health consequences (Salari et al., 2022). Researchers conducted a systematic review and meta-analysis to determine the global prevalence of UTIs in older adults for 1982–2022 (Kalhori et al., 2024). The global prevalence rate of UTIs in older adults was 23.6%, and the highest prevalence rate was for Africans, older women, and people in nursing homes (Kalhori et al., 2024).

To treat a UTI, antibiotics are generally the first approach, with intravenous antibiotics used for more severe UTIs. Individuals should drink plenty of water to flush out bacteria, but avoid liquids that irritate the bladder, including coffee, alcohol, and drinks with citrus juice or caffeine. Cranberry juice may be helpful in moderation, but be careful of home remedies without proof of safety.

Immune System

Over time one of the changes in our bodies involves the immune system. Our immune system is the first area of defense against possible injuries and infections. Changes in our bodies occur at the cellular level, including changes in the telomere and mitochondria (see Chapter 3). Changes that occur at the intercellular level affect communication between cells and tissue, lead to less response from the immune system, increased inflammation, and less **T** and **B cell** production; these changes are known as **immunosenescence** (Ford & Savitz, 2022; Mathot et al., 2021; Soma & Nagata, 2022; Tran Van Hoi et al., 2023). Immunosenescence leads to greater risk of auto-immune issues and infections and reduced benefits for older adults from vaccinations, such as the one for COVID-19 (Ward et al., 2022). There is evidence of a link between immunosenescence and frailty (Tran Van Hoi et al., 2023), and chronic diseases such as CVD, asthma, and cancer in older adults (Sadighi Akha, 2018; Soma & Nagata, 2022). A systematic review of immune system functioning and frailty in individuals aged 60 years old and older with 44 studies (Tran Van Hoi et al., 2023) showed that elevated levels of **Interleukin 6 protein** (IL-6) and **C-reactive protein** (CRP) were associated with frailty. IL-6 helps to support the growth rate of B cells, and it is known to react negatively towards regulatory T cells (Tanaka et al., 2014). CRP is a protein that is made by the liver, and it increases when there is inflammation in the body. The B cells are white blood cells called **lymphocytes**, and they make proteins called antibodies to fight off bacteria or viruses that enter the body. The T cells are white blood cells known as lymphocytes. There is a T cell known as **Cytotoxic T cell**, which can destroy an infected cell, and **Helper T cells** that send signals telling other immune cells to fight an infection.

There is some evidence for a connection between exercise and improvements in cellular immunosenescence markers such as T cells. A systematic review was conducted on the relationship between physical exercise and cellular markers that are part of our immunosenescence (Mathot et al., 2021). Of 55 studies included in their review, 15 articles showed the effects of long-term physical exercise on young and middle adults, with some results showing an increase in T cells, but others showing no effect. Only four articles provided the relationship between long-term exercise on older adults over 65 years old, showing an effect of long-term exercise on T cells and the effect was associated with intensity level of exercise.

Acute Illnesses

An **acute illness** may occur for only a brief amount of time, sometimes a few days or weeks. Acute illness or conditions may be caused by viruses or infections, and typical examples of acute conditions include the common cold or flu. Adults typically experience the common cold two or three times a year, with symptoms such as a runny nose, headache, sore throat, and a cough. However, sometimes an acute illness can cause more serious life-threatening symptoms that can require hospitalization or lead to death. **Respiratory syncytial virus** (RSV) is an acute illness that can have severe complications. Respiratory syncytial virus causes infections of both the lungs and respiratory tract.

Respiratory syncytial virus is common in children and can infect adults (Ali et al., 2020). While it can generally be mild, RSV is associated with complications in health for those with weakened immune systems and older adults. Within about a week, RSV symptoms appear, including a runny nose, sneezing, headache, dry cough, and low grade fever. If RSV infects the lower respiratory tract then it can cause pneumonia or bronchiolitis, which is inflammation of small airway passages entering the lungs. Symptoms of more severe RSV include a fever, a severe cough, rapid or difficult breathing, and skin tone becoming bluish because of lack of oxygen (Mayo Clinic, 2023b). In a systematic review of RSV in adults aged 18 and older in Latin America, Ali and colleagues (2020) included 18 studies, and found that there was much variability across studies for RSV detection from 0 to about 78%. Respiratory syncytial virus may be an important cause of hospitalization for adults in Latin America.

As noted with RSV, sometimes acute illnesses require a hospital stay, and some acute illnesses such as COVID-19 can be life-threatening. The **severe acute respiratory syndrome** (SARS-CoV-2), COVID-19, appeared in December of 2019 in Wuhan, China, and quickly became a pandemic with a high mortality rate (Lavrentieva et al., 2023; Taylor et al., 2020). There were over 776 million cases with seven million deaths globally by 2024 (World Health Organization [WHO], 2024a). The country with the highest number of new cases was the Russian Federation, followed by Poland, Czechia, Greece, and the United Kingdom. The country with the highest number of new 28-day reported deaths was the United States, followed by Sweden, the Russian Federation, Greece, Czechia, and Denmark (WHO, 2024a).

Varying vaccination rates are a global concern for acute respiratory illnesses. Researchers assessed the vaccination rate for acute respiratory illness in the United States with a systematic review and meta-analysis (Shehadeh et al., 2020). The researchers found that overall pooled vaccination rate for influenza was about 49%, but there were variations by ethnicity. European Americans had a rate of about 51%, African Americans of about 36%, and Latinx Americans of about 42%. Vaccination rates were higher among adults over 65 years old at about 78% compared to children aged 0 to 17 years old, about 37%.

Though there are still deaths from COVID-19, the mortality rate has been drastically reduced because of vaccinations. In a meta-analysis of seven studies from the United States with COVID-19 patients, researchers found that unvaccinated individuals who were infected with COVID-19 were 2.46 times more likely to have severe symptoms leading to death from COVID-19 compared to individuals who were vaccinated for the virus (Ikeokwu et al., 2023). Both variability in amount of access to health care and vaccinations and mistrust about vaccinations lead to less vaccinations. Researchers in the United Kingdom conducted a systematic review on enrollment of ethnic minority adults in trials of the COVID-19 vaccination in the United Kingdom, with a primary focus on Black adults (Herieka et al., 2024). The researchers assessed seven studies and found that Black adults were underrepresented in trials, and other adult ethnic minorities were underrepresented too.

Chronic Illnesses

Sometimes an acute illness can become a chronic condition. A **chronic health condition** is a long-term condition that can require regular doctor or hospital visits, medications, and may limit mobility and **activities of daily living** (ADL) (Goodman et al., 2013). One condition that progressed from an acute fatal

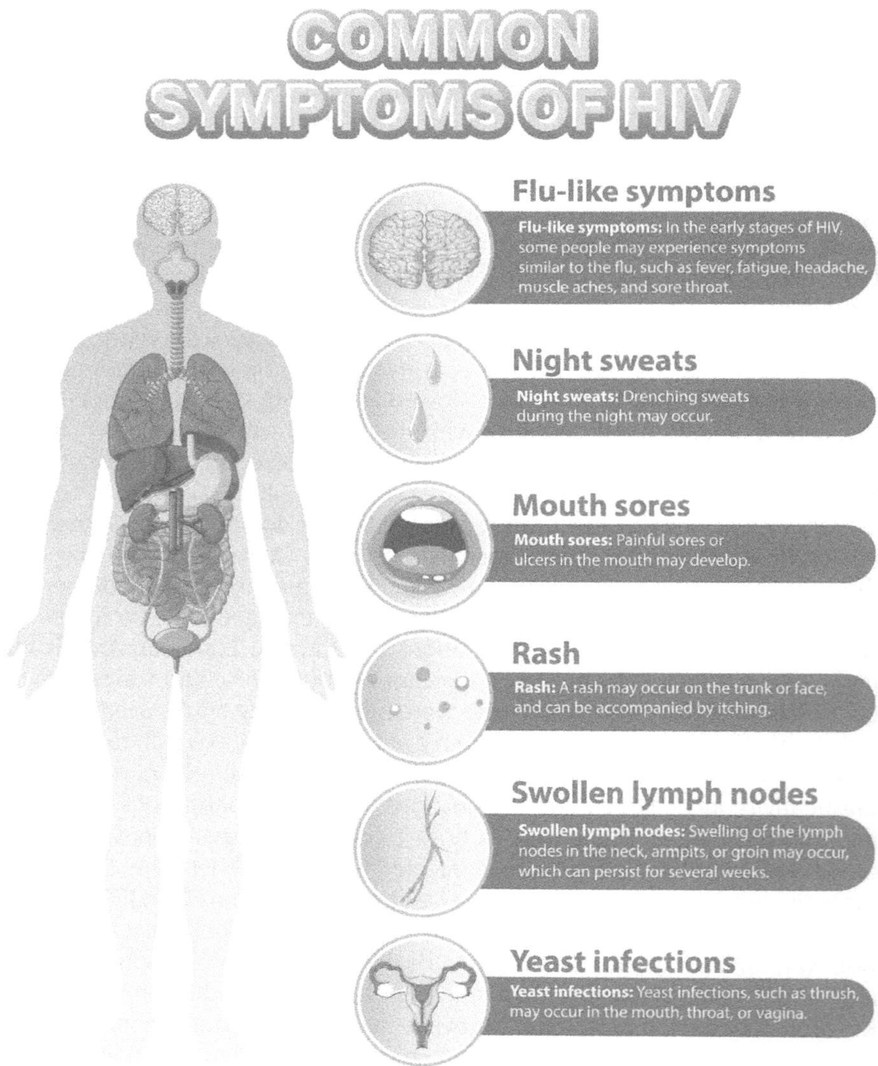

Figure 5.3 The common symptoms of HIV.

Source: Shutterstock.

illness to a chronic health condition was **human immunodeficiency virus** (HIV). The first known case of HIV was found in the blood work of a man from Kinshasa, Democratic Republic of the Congo back in 1959 (Faria et al., 2014). As a result of travel around the globe, HIV showed up in the United States from 1979–1981 as rare cases of pneumonia, cancer and other illnesses. HIV became a pandemic in 1981. Before we had medications to treat HIV, it could develop into **acquired immunodeficiency syndrome** (AIDS), which is still deadly today. A combination of medications in the mid-1990s helped those with HIV. Currently, options include medications for long-term health. Individuals can live for decades with HIV, making this once acute fatal illness a chronic disease. Since many people live a long time with HIV before it becomes AIDS, researchers study self-management for living with HIV. Researchers conducted a review of individuals who were self-managing HIV, in which there were 27 studies (Sematlane et al., 2024). There were challenges to individuals' identity once they received a diagnosis of HIV. Issues such as HIV stigma, individuals' culture, and social context appear to play a role in identity, self-management of HIV, and actions individuals take to protect their health (Sematlane et al., 2024).

Not everyone has easy access to medications here in the United States or around the world. Globally, over 40 million individuals live with HIV, and 39 million adults (adults were defined as 15 years old and over) were infected with HIV in 2024. In 2024, approximately 31 million people living with HIV were receiving antiretroviral therapy (UNAIDS Fact Sheet, 2025). In 2024, sub-Saharan Africa had the most new cases of HIV, about 63% were women and girls (UNAIDS Fact Sheet, 2025).

Some chronic conditions can last for one's entire lifespan (Lee et al., 2020), because some individuals can be born with a chronic disease. The risk of developing a chronic condition increases over time, with about 93% of individuals in older adulthood having at least one chronic condition, and about 78% of them with two or more chronic health conditions (Watson et al., 2025). Some chronic conditions tend to develop gradually over time, and can take months or years to become a condition that affects our ability to move around freely or prevents us from maintaining our daily functioning. Chronic conditions can worsen over time, and can lead to death. Chronic conditions may be the result of genetic predispositions, lifestyle factors (e.g., diet, exercise, smoking and alcohol consumption) or environmental factors (e.g., pollutants); however, often chronic conditions occur from a combination of these different factors (Al Wachami et al., 2024; Folkmann et al., 2024). Chronic conditions that are common in the United States and around the globe include hypertension, CVD, cancers, chronic respiratory conditions such as COPD, arthritis, and diabetes (Al Wachami et al., 2024; Folkmann et al., 2024; Lee et al., 2020; Yang, Y. et al., 2024).

A recent review article on chronic diseases was conducted with satellite imagery and included 43 studies. Researchers showed where most satellite imagery was focused around the globe when monitoring the presence of chronic diseases (Folkmann et al., 2024). Most satellite imagery was from high income countries. Folkman and colleagues (2024) emphasize that locations with the greatest amount of burden from death resulting from chronic diseases, low income countries, appear to have the least amount of satellite data. There are other issues with assessment of chronic diseases around the globe. A systematic review and meta-analysis with 42 studies showed prevalence of COPD varied across countries because of many differences in diagnostic standards (Al Wachami et al., 2024).

Chronic kidney disease (CKD) involves a gradual loss of kidney function, and affects more than 10% of the global population (Kovesdy, 2022). Our kidneys help us to filter out waste and excess fluid from our blood; the filtered fluid is then removed from our bodies in urine output. At first, individuals may have few, if any, signs or symptoms of CKD. Over time, with progressive damage to kidneys, signs and symptoms of CKD appear, including urinating more or less, sleep issues, fatigue, swollen ankles and feet, very dry and itchy skin, hypertension that is difficult to treat, lack of appetite, vomiting, shortness of breath, and chest pain. When individuals have an advanced case of CKD, they may have dangerous levels of fluids and wastes in their bodies. Health care providers treat CKD by trying to slow the progression of kidney damage. However, kidney damage may still progress to end-stage kidney failure, and this is fatal unless individuals have dialysis treatment (artificial filtering) or a kidney transplant. Nisar and colleagues (2024) conducted a systematic literature review of CKD in 13 countries, and found that expenditure on dialysis, hospitalizations, medications, physician office visits, and laboratory work is high in Asian countries.

Diabetes mellitus is considered a major chronic disease, with global estimates for those who are aged 20 to 79 years old at over 536 million (Sun et al., 2022). Diabetes mellitis is a disorder involving carbohydrate metabolism that

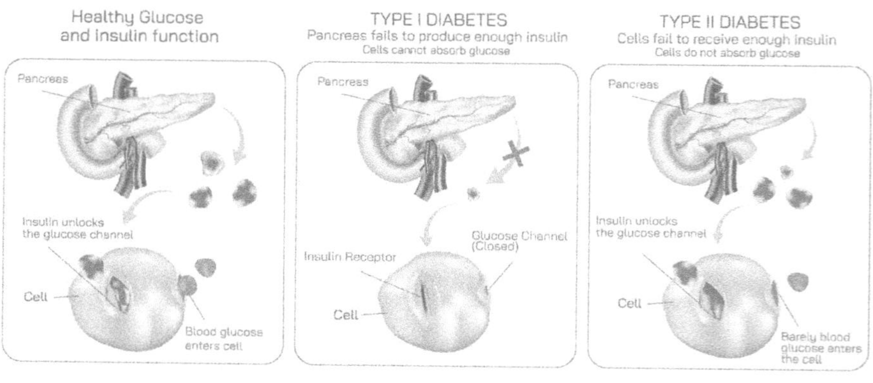

Figure 5.4 A comparison between healthy glucose and insulin function and type I and type II diabetes.

is characterized by impaired ability of the body to produce or respond to insulin and to maintain proper levels of sugar (glucose) in the blood. Recent U.S. information shows prevalence for **type 2 diabetes mellitus** (T2DM) is 90% of cases of diabetes. Individuals with T2DM have a higher amount of glycemia because of increasing deterioration of their B-cell function and insulin resistance (Yang et al., 2024; Yong et al., 2021). Close to a third of individuals with T2DM develop kidney disease. There are often complications from kidney disease and increased risk of death. Risk factors include being overweight, high blood pressure, and old age. Older age is associated with both diabetes and increased risk of kidney disease as a result of T2DM (Nanayakkara et al., 2021; Yang et al., 2024). Minority elderly people are at increased risk of T2DM that becomes more complicated with the development of kidney disease (Yang et al., 2024), and this may be due to reduced access to health care, nutrition, and medicines for those on low income (Golden et al., 2019).

A systematic review and meta-analysis on race and ethnicity, socioeconomic status, and quality of life was conducted on adults with T2DM (Lee et al., 2020). The researchers found that individuals of African ancestry had less sugar control when measured for HbA1c and less blood pressure control compared to those of European or European American background. For individuals of African and Latin ancestry, poorer health control was associated with lack of access to health care and lack of insurance in multiple studies.

Racial/ethnic health disparities are evident around the globe and within the United States (Esdaille et al., 2024; Moore & Hayes, 2023; Spencer et al., 2023). Individuals of African ancestry who have lived in the United States for multiple generations have the highest death rate from most cancers of all racial/ethnic groups and this is much higher than for African and Caribbean individuals who are recent immigrants to the United States (American Cancer Society, 2022; Pinheiro et al., 2020). Exposure to environmental stressors (e.g., racism, low socioeconomic status [SES]) may lead to **allostatic load** (AL), which is when the body is exposed to chronic stress that wears out the body (McEwen & Stellar, 1993). This activates the hypothalamic-pituitary-adrenal (HPA) axis and sympathetic nervous system, releasing cortisol and epinephrine, which is linked to inflammation, disruption to immune system functions, and changes in major organs over time, with increased risk of cardiovascular issues and cancers (Stabellini et al., 2024).

Approaches to Communication

It is important when trying to treat patients to communicate with health care providers in a safe and equitable way, with interpreters when necessary. In a review of individuals' perception of care that included 16 studies (Yu et al., 2021), researchers showed that cross-cultural communication was considered an important factor in how patients viewed their care in hospital settings. Communication issues excluded individuals from discussion of their own health concerns. In addition, the culture of the patient affected their view of the types of treatments offered. In a systematic review of communication between health care providers and patients with acute illnesses (aged 18 years or older), researchers included 52 articles from multiple countries (Gross & Koffman, 2024). The findings showed the need for a shared understanding between health care providers and their patients regarding treatment plans. Sometimes the issue may be a communication barrier due to language differences and difficulty communicating. However, there is no consistency in health care providers' views about the importance of communicating all aspects of care to patients, and not all health care providers have a patient-centered approach to communication. Some health care providers lack confidence in their ability to communicate treatment plans because of fear of conflict with patients who hold a different point of view.

Factors involved in Treatment

Treatments for Chronic Illness

There are many treatment approaches used for chronic illnesses, and these approaches can vary based on the type of chronic illness and by cultures involved in treatment. Researchers conducted a systematic review of strategies to improve adherence to treatment for multiple chronic health conditions including HIV, hypertension, and DM for individuals in sub-Saharan Africa (Gumede et al., 2024). The researchers included 82 studies with adults aged between 30 and 40 years old. The findings indicate the importance of a connection between health care facilities and communities in which patients reside, with community- and home-based adherence interventions helpful in meeting chronic care management needs. The researchers found that mobile health is an initiative gaining attention because it is helpful for promoting adherence to treatment regimens. Adherence to counseling interventions depended on cultural barriers, attitudes about health conditions, perceived stigma, and cognitive abilities.

There are various cultural practices for treatment of illnesses, including herbal medicines, yoga, acupuncture, and massage. In a systematic review of traditional and complimentary treatments, researchers provided results from ten articles primarily from Malaysia (Yusoff et al., 2019). The Malay massage, acupuncture, Tai Chi (a Chinese exercise with slow rhythmic movements), yoga, Ai Chi, and ayurveda are often used to help with management of chronic illnesses. The Malay massage is perceived as helpful for muscle tone and blood circulation; Tai Chi, is helpful for reducing pain and fatigue; acupuncture is very popular with individuals from a Chinese background, for pain associated with headaches, stroke, and other psychological conditions. In a systematic review of traditional, complimentary, and alternative medicines (TCAM), researchers assessed 17 studies from multiple countries with a focus on ethnic minority samples (Agu et al., 2019). The researchers found that a great number of ethnic minority individuals were using TCAM for their health.

Functional Health

Functional health includes both our body and our mind. It is viewed as an interconnected system involving our genetics, the environment, and our lifestyles all interacting together. Functional health is our ability to perform self-care and other tasks necessary for independent living (Barman et al., 2024; Vaish et al., 2020). Some individuals can be born with health issues that may require assistance over time, while others may develop conditions that can affect their ability to perform tasks as they age (Boer & deBeer, 2019; Verbrugge & Yang, 2002). We may develop conditions that require some assistance to help us perform daily functions including dressing, feeding, moving around, and more complex cognitive tasks such as remembering to take medications, preparing meals, and taking care of our finances. Functional health is an important aspect of chronic conditions, because chronic conditions can affect our ability to function over time. There is global research on individuals based on their **functional abilities** and disabilities including South Africa (Boer & DeBeer, 2019), Latin America, and China (Gao et al., 2024).

Functional Ability

According to WHO, functional ability is an individual's ability to perform activities of value to them within the constraints of their environment (WHO, 2015). For example, if an individual has the functional ability to buy groceries at a food

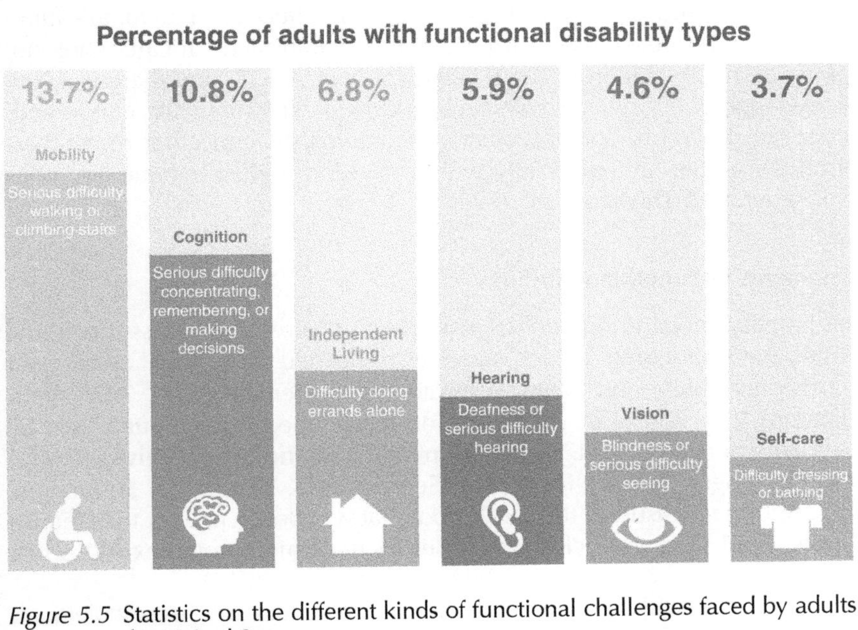

Figure 5.5 Statistics on the different kinds of functional challenges faced by adults in the United States.

Source: abilitymagazine.com.

market, the lack of a food market within walking distance or lack of transportation to that market can impede success at this activity. Researchers in Ghana provided evidence of transportation difficulties from the WHO Study on Global AGEing and Adult Health Ghana Wave 1 (Awuviry-Newton et al., 2022), and found that over half of the women in the study had difficulty accessing and using transportation. A few of the factors involved in transportation difficulties were advanced age, low SES, lack of trust in individuals, and chronic disease.

Individuals' functional abilities require **intrinsic capacity**, environmental characteristics, and ongoing interaction between intrinsic capacity and environmental characteristics. Intrinsic capacity is the amount of mental and physical capacity an individual has available to use, including their senses, mobility, and cognition. WHO describes the environment as including individuals' homes, their community, and society, and the values, relationships, and policies within these environments that can help or hurt the ability to use them.

The International Classification of Functioning, Disability and Health (ICF) is a specific classification system developed by WHO (2001). The ICF is based on a standardized reference system and provides specific basic terms for the classification of an individual's functioning related to their health conditions (Habenicht et al., 2023; WHO, 2001). The ICF was meant to be a standard that is used by health care practitioners and by researchers. There are classifications for impairments based on structures and functions and limitations in individual's ability to perform specific activities. As part of the ICF, health care practitioners are involved with rehabilitating individuals, and researchers explore personal and contextual factors that may affect an individual's functional health. However, use of ICF standards within medical care when not working on rehabilitation is rare (Habenicht et al., 2023) and there is a lack of knowledge of classification systems worldwide among health care practitioners, psychologists, social workers, gerontologists, and other researchers around the globe, and especially within low and middle-income countries (Venkatapuram & Thiyagarajan, 2023).

Assessments of Functional Abilities

Most practitioners and researchers use questionnaires that assess functional abilities and disabilities, lacking consistency needed for a global assessment of functional ability and treatment protocols (Habenicht et al., 2023; Venkatapuram & Thiyagarajan, 2023). For example, one measure often used by researchers to address ADL and **instrumental activities of daily living** (IADL) is the Groningen Activity Restriction Scale (GARS, Kempen & Suurmeijer, 1990). Another measure is the a-ADL tool that was developed for the Flemish Belgian population and helps with assessment of more complex ADLs that may indicate cognitive impairment (De Vriendt et al., 2013).

Health care practitioners, gerontologists, and psychologists assess individuals based on ADL and IADL. Activities of daily living include an individual's ability to perform basic activities, such as dressing, moving around, bathing, eating, being able to get out of bed, being able to use a bathroom, getting up, and sitting down. Activities of daily living require cognitive skills from procedural memory, which is generally protected unless trauma or diseases such as dementia are present. Activities of daily living require the ability to physically do these tasks. Instrumental activities of daily living include an individual's ability to perform more complex activities, such as preparing meals that require cooking, being able to go grocery shopping, taking medications, and managing finances. Instrumental activities of daily living require more advanced cognitive skills, some of which may not be as protected, including prospective memory that requires remembering what you will need to do at a future time period. Instrumental activities of daily living require the ability to physically do these more complex tasks.

Researchers in China developed and provided validation of a measure of functional ability based on the definition from WHO (Chang et al., 2024). The researchers developed and tested the measure on a large sample of individuals aged 60 years and older from the China Health and Retirement Longitudinal Study. Chang and colleagues (2024) provided evidence of internal reliability and external validity for their measure, which was called the functional ability index (FAI) and intended for use by health care practitioners in determining functional health.

WHO collaborated with the United Nations (UN) on the Decade of Healthy Ageing (2020–2030). Rudnicka and colleagues (2020) provided details on the initiative, including both positive and negative aspects. While there is still much work needed to improve consistency in assessment of functional ability standards around the world, these kinds of initiatives may lead to a global standard of functional assessment.

Chapter Summary

In this chapter we discussed changes in skin, hair, bones/joints/muscles, hormones, and other bodily systems across adulthood, and cross-cultural research on these changes in adulthood and the factors involved in the changes. We investigated differences in acute and chronic illnesses in adulthood and across cultures, and research on communication and treatment for acute and chronic illnesses and differences across cultures. We explored functional health and functional abilities. Throughout we discussed how biological, psychological, and contextual factors are involved in changes in our bodies over time.

Key Takeaways

1. There is evidence of changes in our skin, hair, bones/joints/muscles, hormones, and other bodily systems across adulthood.
2. There are multiple factors involved in bodily changes, and cross-cultural research about these factors.

3 There are differences in acute and chronic illnesses, and a need for better communication and access to treatments across cultures.
4 Biological, psychological, and contextual factors affect bodily changes and acute and chronic illnesses as we age, as shown with cross-cultural research.
5 The sociocultural context in which we develop during adulthood plays an important role in our functional abilities throughout adulthood.

Reflective Questions

1 Which factors that impact bodily changes as we age do you think are the most influential?
2 Identify biological, psychological, and contextual factors that are relevant to your life. How will they affect your body over time?
3 How do sociocultural and contextual factors impact cross-cultural research on acute and chronic illnesses as we age?

Suggested Readings

Adhikary, D., Barman, S., Ranjan, R., & Stone, H. (2022). A systematic review of major cardiovascular risk factors: A growing global health concern. *Cureus, 14*(10), e30119. doi: 10.7759/cureus.30119.

Esdaille, A. R., Kuete, N. K., Anyaeche, V. I., Kalemoglu, E., & Kucuk, O. (2024). The interplay between structural inequality, allostatic load, inflammation, and cancer in Black Americans: A narrative review. *Cancers (Basel), 16*(17), 3023. doi: 10.3390/cancers16173023.

Martin, S. S., Aday, A. W., Almarzooq, Z. I., Anderson, C. A. M., Arora, P., Avery, C. L., Baker-Smith, C. M., Gibbs, B. B., Beaton, A. Z., Boehme, A. K., Commodore-Mensah, Y., Currie, M. E., Elkind, M. S. V., Evenson, K. R., Generoso, G., Heard, D. G., Hiremath, S., Johansen, M. C., Kalani, R., Kazi, D. S., Ko, D., Liu, J., Magnani, J. W., Michos, E. D., Mussolino, M. E., Navaneethan, S. D., Parikh, N. I., Perman, S. M., Poudel, R., Rezk-Hanna, M., Roth, G. A., Shah, N. S., St-Onge, M.-P., Thacker, E. L., Tsao, C. W., Urbut, S. M., Van Spall, H. G. C., Voeks, J. H., Wang, N.-Y., Wong, N. D., Wong, S. S., Yaffe, K., Palaniappan, L. P., & American Heart Association Council on Epidemiology and Prevention Statistics Committee and Stroke Statistics Subcommittee (2024). 2024 Heart disease and stroke statistics: A report of US and global data from the American Heart Association. *Circulation, 149*(8), e347–e913. doi: 10.1161/CIR.0000000000001209.

Key Terms

Acquired Immunodeficiency Syndrome (AIDS) is the most advanced, and fatal, stage of HIV.

Activities of daily living (ADL) include the ability to perform basic activities such as dressing, moving around, bathing, eating, getting out of bed, using the bathroom, getting up and sitting down.

Acute illness happens suddenly and may occur for only a brief amount of time.

Allostatic load is when the body is exposed to chronic stress and is worn down.

Alveoli are small air sacs in the lungs.

Androgenetic alopecia is also known as male pattern baldness, though it can affect biological males and females at any age. It is progressive reduction in the hair follicle.

Andropause is a partial deficit of androgen and is associated with testicular problems as men age.

Angina is pain in the chest, neck, or left arm that is caused by decreased blood flow to the heart because of plaque buildup in the coronary arteries.

Arrhythmia is an abnormal rhythm in the heart, which may skip a beat.

Arteriosclerosis describes arteries that have become more rigid.

Atherosclerosis describes coronary arteries that show a gradual increase in fatty deposits on their walls, often referred to as plaques. It can increase risk of heart issues and stroke.

Atrial fibrillation is a heart rhythm condition that is common in older adults and can increase risk of stroke.

B cells are white blood cells called lymphocytes. They make proteins called antibodies to fight off bacteria or viruses that enter your body.

C-reactive protein (CRP) is made by the liver. It increases when there is inflammation in the body.

Catheterization involves a tube being guided through a blood vessel to the heart's arteries and dye being injected through the tube to the arteries, making them and any blockages show up on X-ray images. This allows doctors to determine the amount of blockage in a blood vessel.

A **chronic health condition** is a long-term condition that can require regular doctor or hospital visits and medications, and may limit mobility and activities of daily living.

Chronic kidney disease (CKD) is gradual progressive loss of kidney function.

Collagen fibers make up the connective tissue of the dermis and lose flexibility over time.

A **cytotoxic T cell** can destroy an infected cell.

The **dermis** is the middle layer of skin.

Diabetes mellitus (DM) is a disorder involving carbohydrate metabolism that is characterized by impaired ability of the body to produce or respond to insulin and to maintain proper levels of sugar (glucose) in the blood.

Dysmasesis is difficulty chewing food, which may be caused by loss of teeth.

Dysphagia is difficulty swallowing in a safe manner.

Efferent responses are behaviors that can help to regulate the temperature in the body, such as wearing a warm sweater or coat on a cold day, and using a fan to cool down.

Elastin fibers within the dermis are responsible for the skin's ability to maintain a stretched form.

The **epidermis** is the top layer of skin.

Extrinsic aging is the result of lifestyle factors and the environment (e.g., smoking, drinking alcohol, toxins in the environment such as pollution).

Functional ability includes the ability to perform activities of value within the constraints of an environment (e.g., grocery shopping).

Functional health includes both the body and mind. It is viewed as an interconnected system comprised of genetics, the environment, and lifestyle. It describes the ability to perform self-care tasks necessary for independent living.

Helper T cells send signals telling other immune cells to fight an infection.

Human immunodeficiency virus (HIV) was once an acute fatal illness but now it can be treated and is considered a chronic health condition. The virus can be passed on through sexual contact, drug use, or blood transfusions.

Hyperthyroidism is excessive amounts of thyroid hormone, which speeds up the body's metabolism too much affecting body mass.

Hypothyroidism is an insufficient amount of thyroid hormone in the body, slowing down metabolism.

Immunosenescence describes changes that occur at the intercellular level that affect communication between cells and tissue. This leads a less responsive immune system, increased inflammation, and less T and B cell production.

Instrumental activities of daily living (IADL) include the ability to perform more complex activities such as preparing meals that require cooking, grocery shopping, taking medications, and managing finances.

Interleukin 6 protein (IL-6) helps to support the growth rate of B cells, and it is also known to react negatively toward regulatory T cells.

Intrinsic aging describes changes in the structure and function of skin, partly from genetic makeup, and proceeds at different rates in different species.

Intrinsic capacity is the amount of mental and physical capacity an individual has available, including their senses, mobility, and cognition.

Locomotive syndrome describes a decline in bones, joints, muscles, and nerves that can increase the risk of disease and death.

The **lower respiratory tract** includes the trachea, bronchi, and lungs, which are part of the tracheobronchial area. Increasingly smaller tubes are responsible for the transport of air from the upper respiratory tract to the lungs.

Menopause is the twelve months after a female's last menstrual cycle.

Osteoporosis is a skeletal disease associated with a low bone mass and increased risk of fractures.

Perimenopause is the period before menopause, which is characterized by fluctuations in monthly menstrual cycle and in the production of estrogen and progesterone.

Photoaging is the premature aging of skin from exposure to the sun's rays over time.

Postmenopause is the period after menopause where women are more susceptible to health conditions such as cardiovascular disease and bone fractures.

Respiratory syncytial virus (RSV) is an acute illness that can have severe complications, causing infections in both the lungs and the respiratory tract.

Resting heart rate is the number of heart beats per minute at rest.

Sarcopenia describes the decrease in muscle mass.

Severe acute respiratory syndrome (SARS-CoV-2) is more commonly known as COVID-19. It causes respiratory and gastrointestinal sickness and is transmitted via the air through direct or indirect contact.

T cells are white blood cells known as lymphocytes.

Tactile sensitivity is the ability to perceive physical characteristics with the fingertips.

Thermoregulation is a biological mechanism that helps maintain internal body temperature.

Type 2 diabetes mellitus (T2DM) makes up about 90% of diabetes cases. It is characterized by a higher amount of glycemia because of the increasing deterioration of B-cell function and insulin resistance.

The **upper respiratory tract** transports air into the body, helps move air to the lungs, and adds moisture to air that is breathed in. It includes the nose, mouth, nasal cavity, sinuses, and larynx.

6 Personality and Emotional Regulation

Learning Objectives

Define personality and the different historical approaches to personality.
Compare the different contemporary theories of personality.
Explain what emotional regulation is and the process model of emotion regulation.

As a graduate student I was a teaching assistant for Dr. Karen Hooker in her Adult Development and Aging course. One day she asked the class, "raise your hand if you think you are the same person you've always been." In a class of nearly 100 students, about half raised their hands. Then she said, "Now if you think that you've experienced something and that has led you to change and become a different person than you were before the experience, raise your hand." Again, half the class raised their hands. Dr. Hooker then talked about the important developmental issue of stability versus change over time, especially in the context of how we view our self-concepts, our personalities, and the essence of who we are. If you remember from Chapter 1, this issue – whether we are stable or changing over time – is one of the critical foci of the field of developmental psychology and it is especially important across adulthood.

At the heart of Dr. Hooker's question is the idea that we each have a unique personality that has developed over time. As adults we have a sense of who we are and what our personality traits are. Whether we think we are the same person we have always been or that certain life events have shaped who we are represents an important way in which we have come to know ourselves.

Our **personality** is a unique collection of interrelated cognitive, emotional, and behavioral ways of being. Personality develops over time through a blend of innate dispositions and environmental or experiential factors that shape our distinctive ways of thinking, feeling, and behaving in the world. Cutting to the chase, personality can be both stable and enduring over time and responsive and changing as a result of our experiences. Our core personality traits may be quite consistent over time in adulthood, but a lifetime of experiences can certainly lead to change.

DOI: 10.4324/9781003483809-6

First, it is important to know that the history of personality theory goes back a very long time in the field of psychology. Over 2,000 years ago Hippocrates and the ancient Greeks were interested in personality and developed a theory that there were four basic personality types. First, the Sanguine personality referred to people who were pleasure-seeking and sociable, present-oriented, emotional, enthusiastic, and optimistic. Next, the Choleric personality type referred to people who were ambitious, leaders, focused, assertive, fearless, and intense. The Melancholic person was someone who was analytical and literal, introverted, sensitive, abstract thinking, and sensitive. Finally, Phlegmatic referred to people who were relaxed and thoughtful, reserved, self-sufficient, consistent, and conservative.

Some of the major historical theoretical approaches to personality are listed in Table 6.1.

Table 6.1 Historical theories of personality development

Personality Theory	*Theorists*	*Assumptions*	*View of Personality*	*How Personality is Assessed*
Psychoanalytic	Freud	Human behavior results from interactions among the three components of the mind: id (instinctual drives/pleasure principle), ego (mediator of id based on reality principle), and superego (mind's morality and conscience).	Personality develops out of pleasure-seeking (id), a reality principle (ego), and an internal set of ideals (superego).	Free association, projective tests, dream analysis.
Humanistic	Maslow, Rogers	People strive for self-realization.	When basic human needs are met, people strive toward self-actualization. When people exist in a climate of unconditional positive regard, they can develop self-awareness and a realistic and positive self-concept.	Questionnaires, psychotherapy.

(*Continued*)

Table 6.1 (Continued)

Personality Theory	*Theorists*	*Assumptions*	*View of Personality*	*How Personality is Assessed*
Trait theory	Allport, Eysenck, McCrae & Costa	People develop certain stable and enduring characteristics or traits that are partly influenced by genetic predispositions.	Different theorists identify different traits, such as the Big Five traits (neuroticism, extraversion, openness to experience, agreeableness, and conscientiousness).	Personality inventories designed to assess traits.
Social cognitive	Bandura	Characteristics develop from our interactions with our social environments that reinforce certain traits.	Conditioning and observational learning interact with cognitive processes to develop into behavioral patterns.	Behavior is predicted by past reinforcements.

Historically, the psychodynamic perspective, developed by Freud, was highly focused on how our unconscious processes and hidden emotions, impulses, and motivations may shape how we experience the world and interact with it. Psychodynamic theory places a great deal of emphasis on the impact of early development on how personality manifests later in adulthood (Calarusso & Nemiroff, 1981). In fact, Freud believed that an individual's personality is essentially set in stone by the tender age of five. From a psychodynamic perspective your personality might change a little, but you are expected to be the same person at 20, 40, 60 and 80 as you were at 4 (Calarusso & Nemiroff, 1981). You have probably learned about Freud's concepts of the id, ego, and superego in other psychology courses, and in our present discussion we mention them only as historical artifacts. What is important to know is that currently developmental scholars do not place much weight on Freud's theory or the early psychodynamic theory of development.

The Humanistic approach to development emphasizes the importance of self-actualization, free will, and the intrinsic human capacity for positive growth and development. The humanistic approach became prominent in the middle of the twentieth century, in part, in reaction to the psychodynamic perspective and behaviorism. Focusing primarily on how healthy people grow as a result of their drive toward creativity and self-actualization, Rogers and the humanists emphasized the importance of human potential and the ability for change. They strongly rejected the concept of biological determinism and focused on how the self develops over time. Rogers' personality theory proposed an ongoing interactive process in which an individual takes in and responds to things in their subjective reality (also called the phenomenal field). This reality is constantly changing and therefore people can grow and change. The main tenant of this developmental approach is the development of the self-concept.

Humanists equate personality and self-concept. Self-concept represents our thoughts, feelings, and beliefs about ourselves. In essence, when you answer the question "Who am I?", you answer with your self-concept: "I am an artist," "I am a mother," "I am a good person." These are examples of the self-concept expressed. They reflect fundamental aspects of your identity. How you see yourself can be mainly positive and you may feel good about who you are and that will lead to feeling that the world is a safe and positive place. However, if you feel primarily negative about who you are you are likely to feel unhappy and pessimistic about the world and your place within it. Rogers distinguished between two aspects of the self-system – the **real self** (who you actually are) and the **ideal self** (who you would like to be). He believed that we are motivated to minimize the discrepancy among the real and the ideal. These ideas are still relevant and can be seen in current theories such as self-discrepancy theory (Higgins, 1987) and possible selves theory (Frazier & Hooker, 2006; Hooker, 1999: Markus & Nurius, 1986). For Rogers, development does not unfold in stages but rather is characterized by dynamic processes. He believed that individuals are motivated to strive to reach their full potential through these processes in order to achieve what he called "the good life" (Rogers, 1961, pp. 186–187). He believed that through these processes several traits or tendencies emerge: 1) an openness to experience; 2) an existential lifestyle characterized by living fully in the moment; 3) trust in one's own judgement and behavior; 4) self-determination and freedom of choice; 5) desire to strive toward creativity and lower need for conformity; 6) fundamental reliability and constructiveness; and 7) a rich life encompassing a wide range of positive and negative emotions (Rogers, 1961).

Trait theories of personality focus on the idea that personality is comprised of stable characteristics or dispositions that are relatively consistent over time. From a trait perspective, the question "Who am I?" is answered with adjectives such as "I am outgoing," "I am nerdy," "I am playful," "I am ambitious," or "I am conscientious." As you can see, these responses differ from those we give when we are talking about our self-concept. From a trait perspective, it would be likely that your best friend, your father, your boss, or your professor might describe you with these same traits; our characteristics are who we are to ourselves and to the world. The trait theory argues that our personalities are a constellation of traits that are consistent and enduring over time and come to represent our psychological makeup. Our traits shape our behaviors. Like James, who believed that personality developed and was "set in stone" by the time we are 30, trait theorists argue for continuity in personality over time. By far the most influential trait theory was developed by Costa and McCrae in 1984. Their theory is called **The Five Factor Model** and it argues that any individual can be characterized as having some level of five basic personality traits (Costa & McCrae, 1999). Their theory is also often referred to as the "Big Five."

Originally, Costa & McCrae (1999) developed a measure of personality called the NEO Personality Inventory (NEO-PI). It measures that five facets of neuroticism (a tendency to experience negative emotions), extraversion (a tendency to be outgoing and social), openness (a tendency to seek novelty and aesthetic experiences), agreeableness (a tendency to get along and go along with others), and conscientiousness (a tendency to feel comfort with rules, details, and organization). Everyone is either higher or lower on each of the five basic personality traits. The NEO-PI and a recently revised version, NEO-PI-R, have been used to derive an individual's traits for use in clinical and counselling, business and industrial, and research settings. Overall, research shows that there is a high degree of consistency in an individual's traits over time and across adulthood.

Contemporary Theories of Personality

At the beginning of the chapter we introduced the developmental scientist, Dr. Karen Hooker. Dr. Hooker, together with Dr. Dan McAdams, developed the **six foci of personality** model of personality (Hooker & McAdams, 2003). Grounded in developmental systems theory (Ford & Lerner, 1992), which by now you are familiar with, the six foci model articulates the complexity of personality in adulthood and allows for the investigation of stability and change over time. This model highlights the importance of considering both the structure as well as the process of personality. The six foci are embedded in an integrative model of personality. Three of the foci represent structural levels of personality (traits, states, life story) and three of the foci represent the processes (personal action constructs, self-regulatory processes, self-narration). Traits are the dispositional part of personality that is stable over time and states vary by situation or context. Examples of traits are outgoing, confident, shy, or caring. Examples of states are mood, fatigue, hunger, or anxious (Hooker & McAdams, 2003). Personal action constructs are the goals, motivations, and tasks that we are working toward. They are embedded in time, place, and our social roles, and they are the "doing" part of our personalities. Self-regulatory processes are the actions that are a product of our personalities and personal action constructs. The life story part of personality refers to our own unique personal narrative of ourselves. It is the story we create to bridge our pasts with our present and the goals we have for the future. Our life stories often provide our lives with meaning, unity, and purpose (Hooker & McAdams, 2003). These stories help us understand who we were, are, and will be in the future, and they are constantly evolving with time. Finally, our life stories develop as we change our personal narratives of our experiences.

Self-narration is the process through which we create our life stories. Our traits and states, and our personal action constructs and self-regulatory behaviors, help us to self-narrate our experiences and create our life stories. The six foci model is a useful framework for studying personality.

Social cognitive theories of personality development originally suggested that personality develops early in life as a function of observational learning, modelling, **self-efficacy**, and the interaction between situational influences and cognitive processes. Theorists like Bandura emphasized the importance of social learning and learning through observing others to the process of internalizing ways of being. For Bandura, our conscious thoughts and especially our sense of self-efficacy – or how capable we feel of achieving or avoiding certain outcomes – are crucial for how we behave and interact with those around us (Bandura, 1977). In early social cognitive theory our beliefs and abilities were crucial to who we are. In this theory our personality is evidenced by our behaviors and our behaviors are shaped by an interaction between the social environment and our cognitive processes or what we attend to and believe about the social world. An example of early social cognitive theory was evidenced by the Bobo doll experiment. We preface this example by saying that this experiment could not be done today because it likely inflicted distress upon the children who participated, and it would never be approved by a modern internal review board. That said, in the experiment, children were required to watch an adult violently interact with a Bobo doll (Bandura et al., 1961). After watching this interaction, children were left with the Bobo doll. Many of the children who had observed the aggressive and violent interaction between the adult and the doll imitated this behavior, demonstrating that the children had learned how to behave by observing the adults (Bandura et al., 1961). The idea behind early social cognitive theories of personality was that personality is manifested as behavior and is learned through social observation.

More recent evolution of the social cognitive theory is found in **socioemotional selectivity theory**. This theory, developed by Carstensen (1993; 2006) is a theory of life span development that is focused on the perception of time. Noticing the high levels of social and emotional well-being in aging adults in spite of many and varied losses related to aging, Carstensen argued that as people age, their perspectives of time change, the future time horizon changes, and this leads older adults to selectively choose how to allocate their cognitive resources, to selectively choose how to engage in prosocial behaviors and what subjective experiences they would like to have. This theory was a positive spin on how people age and focused on personality as socioemotional development. It was tested and study after study showed that when compared to younger adults, older adults reported having more positive emotional experiences (Mroczek & Kolarz, 1998) and more control over their emotions (Gross et al., 1997). This demonstrated that there were emotional advantages that accrued with age and experience. Older adults were more empathic, expressed more gratitude, and were more inclined to forgive others compared to their younger counterparts (Chopik et al., 2019; Sze et al.,

2012). Large scale studies show that older adults experience less worry, anger, disgust, and sadness than young adults (Stone et al., 2010). Carstensen and colleagues (2020) also showed that in the midst of the COVID-19 pandemic, older adults reported more positive and less negative emotions compared to younger age groups. The socioemotional selectivity theory demonstrated that despite many losses associated with growing older, older adults' emotional well-being and their ability to regulate their emotions actually improves with age. Put a different way, despite the fact that "virtually all the presumed factors that make people happy – social status, physical health, broad and diverse social networks, and high levels of social engagement – decline with chronological age [...] psychological well-being improves" (Carstensen, 2021, p. 1189). This is the paradox of aging and Dr. Carstensen's socioemotional selectivity theory helps to explain why it exists.

The time perspective is a fundamental underpinning in socioemotional selectivity: specifically, a shift from time since birth to time left to live. This subtle shift in time perspective instigates a selective pruning of activities, social networks, and other changes that allow an older adult to focus on that which is truly most meaningful to them. It is a conservation of social and emotional resources and an allocation of those resources to the aspects of life that bring the most meaning and joy, which leads to the well-being paradox in later life. This theory is supported by decades of research including longitudinal studies that demonstrate these changes (Carstensen, 2021). As time perspectives change with age, goals change too, in ways that lead to the selective deployment of resources toward things that really matter and make life meaningful.

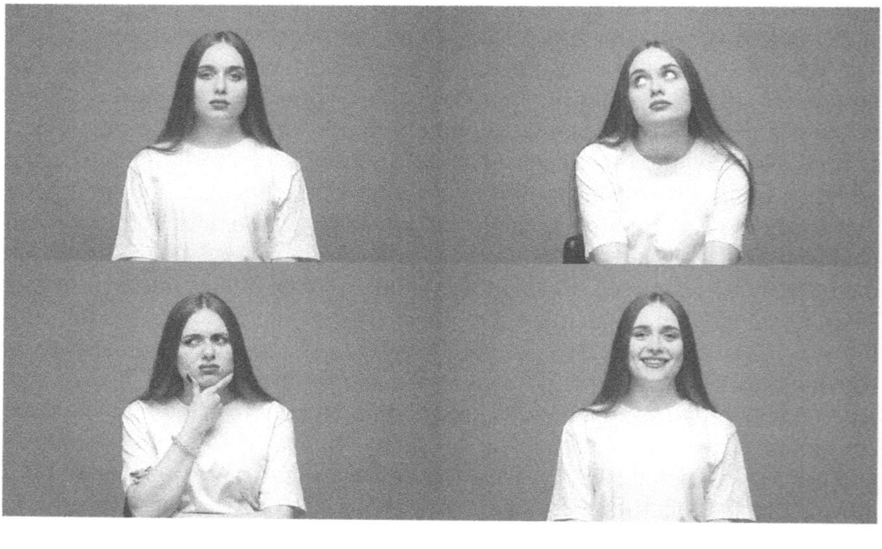

Figure 6.1 Each of us experience a wide range of emotions.

Source: Shutterstock.

Emotions Across Adulthood

"The longer I live the more beautiful life becomes." (Frank Lloyd Wright)

Research shows that contrary to what we might expect, especially given the socioemotional selectivity theory, older people are not more happy than younger people. Rather, they are less unhappy than younger people (Burr et al., 2021; Carstensen, 2021). The "**positivity effect**," which refers to a developmental pattern of attentional bias that favors negative information, actually shows that attentional biases become more positive as people age (Baumeister et al., 2001). Surprisingly, the positivity effect that operates subconsciously at the level of memory and attention, leading to the well demonstrated research finding that older adults recall more positive memories than negative ones, simply shows that as we grow older we may focus more on the "bright side of things" and we might be more inclined to look for "silver linings" in events and experiences that are negative.

Emotion Regulation

Emotions are complex at any age and one of the keys to successful coping and adaptation is to be able to manage one's emotions well. We do not just passively experience emotions, rather we often notice them and attempt to manage them, especially when experiencing them is a source of distress for us. **Emotion regulation** is the process through which we attempt to influence or manage our experience of emotions. Better emotional regulation leads to improved health, relationships, work success and overall well-being across the adult years (Doerwald et al., 2016; Kotsou et al., 2011).

The process model of emotion regulation (McRae & Gross, 2020) identifies five types of strategies involved in the regulation of emotions. These strategies are focused on when emotion regulation is needed, what strategy to use to regulate it, and how to monitor the success of the emotion regulation strategy. Typically, the need to regulate our emotions begins when there is a discrepancy between a desired emotional state and the actual emotional state. For example, Julie is about to give a professional presentation, and she desires to project a calm, knowledgeable, professional emotional state, but inside she is anxious, her stomach is in knots, she is sweating, and she is afraid that her voice will quiver when she speaks revealing her inner turmoil. Once she identifies this discrepancy, she will likely initiate emotional regulation strategies to manage her negative and anxious emotions to better achieve her goals. According to the process model of emotion regulation, strategies can be antecedent-focused and occur before an emotional response has been expressed or they can be response-focused and occur after an emotional response has been expressed (Gross, 1998). Examples of antecedent-focused strategies are distraction, cognitive reappraisal (e.g., changing the meaning of the situation) or modification of the situation. An example of a response-focused strategy is suppressing emotional expression (e.g., inhibiting one's emotional expression).

Here is how these emotion regulation strategies might be used in a social situation. Alfie has a party to go to. They might go to the party because they anticipate that they will have a good time (situation selection). While they are there, two friends begin to argue. Alfie could tell a joke to break the tension (situation modification), or they could focus on how great the food tastes instead of thinking about the conflict (distraction). Alfie could choose to interpret the friends' argument as the result of one of them having a bad day rather than acting like a rude person (reappraisal). In the end, Alfie could choose not to express their negative emotions about the argument to either of them (suppression). Typically, antecedent-focused strategies lead to better emotional well-being whereas response-focused strategies lead to lower well-being (Eldesouky & English, 2018).

Table 6.2 shows the six emotion regulation strategies proposed by Gross and colleagues (McRae & Gross, 2020), with examples applied to a job interview situation.

As individuals grow older, they get better at regulating their emotions more proactively (Hay & Diehl, 2011; Scheibe & Carstensen, 2010). Specifically, older adults select environments, social interactions, and people they interact

Table 6.2 Emotion regulation strategies and examples

The Five Families of ER Strategies, Strategy, and Tactic Examples From the Job Interview Context, Organized by the Stage in the Emotion Generation Cycle in Which They First Intervene

Strategy family	*Selected strategies*	*Example tactics (in job interview context)*
Situation selection	Avoidance	Declining initial engagement with emotional situations (e.g., declining interview request)
Situation modification	Direct request	Taking action to influence a situation once engaged (e.g., asking to move interview to a private location)
Attentional deployment	Distraction	Directing attention (internal or external) away from the emotional situation toward nonemotional aspects of the situation or nonemotional situations (e.g., glancing at notes rather than the interviewer's face)
	Rumination	Recurrently directing attention toward causes and consequences of emotion (e.g., mentally replaying a moment in which the interviewer appeared to frown at your response)
Cognitive change	Cognitive reappraisal	Reinterpreting or reevaluating the emotional situation and/or your goals (e.g., telling yourself the interviewer was likely coached to not give overt positive feedback to applicants)

(*Continued*)

Table 6.2 (Continued)

	Acceptance	Welcoming emotions with nonevaluative judgment (e.g., noticing and cultivating curiosity about manifestations of anxiety in the interview)
Response modulation	Expressive suppression	Preventing outward expression of internal emotional state (e.g., keeping face neutral to avoid expressing disappointment)
	Physiological intervention	Directly altering emotion-relevant physiology using actions or substances (e.g., slowing one's breathing rate)

Source: McRae & Gross [2020]
Note. ER = emotion regulation.

with that will support their emotional well-being (Aspinwall & Taylor, 1997; Diamond & Aspinwall, 2003). Older adults report that they have more control over their emotions, and that they are more flexible, selected and targeted in their ways of coping with emotions (Blanchard-Fields et al., 2007). They also report relying less on confrontation when they are upset than their younger counterparts (Birditt & Fingerman, 2005). Emotional regulation may improve as we age, in part due to the increased emotional complexity that older adults have. Emotional complexity has been conceptualized as the co-occurrence of both positive and negative emotions at the same time (Carstensen et al., 2000) – for example, feeling happiness and sadness simultaneously. Emotional complexity also increases with age. For example, developmental research shows that with age and life experiences, emotions become more mixed and nuanced (Hay & Diehl, 2011; Labouvie-Vief & Medler, 2002; Magai et al., 2006). Starting in midlife and into later life, adults are better able to integrate and tolerate contradictions in their emotions (Labouvie-Vief & Medler, 2002).

Emotion regulation patterns change across adulthood for a variety of reasons. First, there are parallel shifts in patterns of physiological reactivity. As we age, we become less physiologically reactive, which that can lead to less intensity in the experience of emotions (Cacioppo et al., 2011). Second, life experience may lead to better emotional regulation. For example, as we age we gain experience with emotion regulation strategies and know which ones are better at regulating emotions and making us feel better (English & Carstensen, 2013). Finally, cognitive resources change with age and as a result older adults may focus on changing the situation or on distraction because they are less cognitively demanding (Sheppes & Gross, 2011).

Figure 6.2 Feeling positive emotions is good for well-being.
Source: Shutterstock.

However, it is important to mention that some studies (Allen & Windsor, 2019; Isaacowitz 2022) have failed to find emotional regulation stability in the later years.

Nevertheless, emotion regulation is an important developmental phenomenon across the adult years. Moreover, the preponderance of evidence suggests that with life experience and self-introspection, emotion regulation is one of the positive psychological constructs that leads to better quality of life and well-being. In terms of strengths-based outcomes, focusing on being better in tune with and more effective at managing our emotional life is a good thing at any age.

Chapter Summary

In this chapter we explored the various ways we can understand and conceptualize personality across adulthood. We looked at historical theories of personality development and considered contemporary views of personality that best fit with the dynamic processes of both stability and change over time. Our emotions and how they change in adulthood are also related to personality. We looked at several theories of emotion and how we manage emotions through emotion regulation.

Key Takeaways

1. Personality can remain stable and change over the course of the lifespan.
2. With age, people tend to focus on and remember more of the positive aspects of life.
3. Emotion regulation is important for responding to life events.

Reflective Questions

1. Do you think that you are the same person you have always been or have you changed over time?
2. What is your real self, and what is your ideal self?
3. Have you noticed that your perception of time has changed?

Suggested Readings

Carstensen, L. L. (2021). Socioemotional selectivity theory: The role of perceived endings in human motivation. *The Gerontologist, 61*(8), 1188–1196.

Blanchard-Fields, F. (2007). Everyday problem solving and emotion: An adult developmental perspective. *Current Directions in Psychological Science, 16*(1), 26–31.

Frazier, L. D., & Hooker, K. (2006). Possible selves in adult development: Linking theory and research. In C. Dunkel & J. Kerpelman (Eds.), *Possible Selves: Theory, Research and Applications* (pp. 41–59). Nova Science Publishers.

Key terms

Emotion regulation is the process by which we attempt to influence or manage our experience of emotions.

The five factor model or "the big five" model argues that any individual can be characterized as having some level of each of the five basic personality traits.

Ideal self refers to who we would like to be.

Personality is a person's unique collection of interrelated cognitive, emotional, and behavioral ways of being.

Positivity effect refers to a developmental pattern of attentional bias that favors negative information and shows that attentional biases become more positive as people age.

Real self refers to who we actually are.

Self-efficacy is how capable we feel we are of achieving or avoiding certain outcomes.

The **six foci of personality** model of personality articulates the complexity of personality in adulthood. It allows for the investigation of stability and change over time and highlights the importance of considering both the structure and the process of personality.

The **socioemotional selectivity theory** is a theory of life span development that is focused on the perception of time.

Trait theories of personality focus on the idea that personality is comprised of stable characteristics or dispositions that are relatively consistent over time.

7 Interpersonal Relationships

Learning Objectives

Explain the focus of developmental science in relation to adult interpersonal relationships.

Define attachment theory and the way it may manifest in adult relationships.

Generate an example of social penetration theory for your own relationships.

Describe the characteristics of the following life events: finding a partner, marriage, and the end of a marriage.

Create a table to summarize the different types of relationships and what we know about them.

Think about the Convoy Model and how it explains your social network.

One of the hallmarks of a life well lived is meaningful relationships. Our relationships develop and change across adulthood in interesting and important ways. Understanding the characteristics of adult relationships and how they change as we age is important so that we can make the most of these relationships. This is key because a vast amount of research shows that positive relationships are associated with better outcomes for mental and physical health and life satisfaction (Braithwaite & Holt-Lunstad, 2017; Gustavson et al., 2016; Ogolsky et al., 2025), and lower levels of loneliness (Flora & Segrin, 2000).

One of the salient, socially normative developmental tasks of adulthood is finding a partner and settling into a relationship. Most people hope that this relationship will be long term. Many people also anticipate that once they have settled into this relationship, they will consider beginning a family. Having children, parenting them through childhood, launching them into adulthood, and then living with them as adult children is a developmental process that involves a lot of changes as it unfolds over time. Later in life, one may become a grandparent. At any stage, one may experience the death of a spouse – a major relationship status change. Alongside familial relationships,

DOI: 10.4324/9781003483809-7

there are often relationships with friends, which grow and change over time just as we do.

In this chapter we will examine all these relationships, and the developmental expectations associated with them. Developmental theory associated with relationships is really about the intersection of the developing adult and the social forces that shape their relationships. To understand these important developmental milestones, we will look at each developmental task and consider some specific theories associated with it. But keep in mind that the developmental theories can and do apply to relationships at any stage of the adult lifespan.

Figure 7.1 Examples of families. (*continued*)

Source: Shutterstock.

Figure 7.1 (Continued)

The Changing Nature of the Adult Child–Parent Relationship

One of the most significant relationships that figures prominently in emerging adulthood is the relationship young adults have with their parents. With demographic changes meaning that people are living longer, parents and children are also alive at the same time for longer (Lauterbach, 1995). Because of the unique type of intimacy, the parent–child relationship is very specific and differs from all other relationships that adults have, such as those with partners, friends, and other family members (Troll & Fingerman, 1996). The relationship between a child and their parents begins at birth and progresses through all of the child, teenager, and adult's developmental changes. A positive, solid, nurturing relationship between a parent and child in early development can shape future cognitive, emotional, and social development (Antonucci et al., 2004).

Attachment theory offers one way to think about the adult child–parent relationship. **Attachment theory** focuses on the early emotional bonds between infants and their caregivers and how these early forms of attachment shape social and emotional development and later relationships (Bowlby, 1988). Bowlby (1988) and his colleague Ainsworth based the theory on the idea that human beings are born with an innate need to develop close emotional relationships with their primary caregivers. These relationships are fundamental to ensuring the survival of the child as well as its healthy emotional development. The primary caregiver who is consistently present and responsive becomes a safe, comforting, and secure base for the child, from which the child begins to explore its world. The theory posits that it is the quality of these early attachments that forms the internal working model of relationships that shapes the child's expectations of relationships, which they carry forward throughout their lives. From their research, Ainsworth and Bowlby suggested that there are four basic attachment styles.

The four attachment styles as they manifest in adult relationships are summarized below.

1 **Secure attachment**: Individuals with this attachment style are self-assured, direct, and responsive. They are comfortable with intimacy and can balance dependence and independence in relationships.
2 **Preoccupied attachment**: Individuals with this attachment style can be anxious, self-doubting, and sensitive. These individuals crave intimacy and may become overly dependent and demanding in relationships.
3 **Dismissive attachment**: Individuals with this attachment style tend to be avoidant, self-reliant, and dismissive. This translates into a strong sense of self-sufficiency, which may appear as detachment. They highly value their independence and may seem uninterested in close relationships.
4 **Fearful attachment**: Individuals with this attachment style tend to be self-sabotaging, unpredictable, and isolated. They desire close relationships but fear being vulnerable. Therefore, they may act unpredictably in their relationships because of their internal conflict between a desire for intimacy and fear of it.

There are many sociocultural factors that shape young people's relationships, including, more recently, the COVID-19 pandemic. Many young adults who were attending college or living away from home, had to move back home to shelter-in-place with their parents when their campuses closed, or they lost their jobs and income and could no longer afford to live on their own. For many of these emerging adults the move home was experienced as a regression leading some to feel a sense of failure due to their loss of autonomy and a sense of control over their lives and futures (Jiang, Y. et al., 2023; Regnoli et al., 2022; Vehkalahti et al., 2021). Sometimes moving home exacerbated conflict between adult children and their parents. There were lots of stressors for the whole family at that time, including employment disruptions and the shift to remote work and learning, for example (Hensley & Harris, 2022). Many young adults have had to or chosen to remain living at home with their parents. Evidence shows that these relationships vary, in part depending on the economic situations of the adult children and their parents (Fingerman et al., 2011). These living arrangements and continued financial associations have contributed to the later age at which adults are beginning their independent lives and long-term romantic relationships. Since the acceptance of adult responsibilities, such as becoming financially independent, making decisions for oneself, and being responsible for one's self are the hallmark of becoming an adult, the changing timeline of reaching adulthood, especially during an historically impactful period such as the COVID-19 pandemic, has had consequences for the individuation of emerging adults.

A look at parent–adult child relationships shows that parents are very involved in the lives of their emerging adult children, and this involvement is reciprocal (Fingerman et al., 2011). Even when parents and their adult children do not live in the same home, they see or speak to (or text) each other regularly. Parents also frequently provide emotional, practical, and financial support. This amount of communication and contact represents an increase from 40 years ago (Fingerman et al., 2011). Fingerman and her colleagues (2011) showed that this support and involvement is related to higher life satisfaction in adult children.

However, there are both positive and negative emotional experiences that are the hallmark of ties between parents and their adult children (Hay et al., 2007). Adult children and their parents often worry about one another (Hay et al., 2007) and that can influence how positively or negatively they perceive their relationship.

From a developmental systems framework, a primary task during emerging adulthood is recentering (Tanner, 2006). Recentering refers to the rearrangement of relations between young adults and their parents and families. Specifically, it concerns the changing dynamics such as shifts in power, agency, responsibility, and dependency, and the transition from parental regulation to self-regulation. The recentering process has three stages: 1) the individual is still embedded in the family and parents are making decisions and controlling the child's behavior; 2) the individual gains more independence through entering new relationships, a college environment, and/or work context, which causes parental influence to wane; 3) the individual accepts and takes on full responsibility for themselves as an adult independent of their family of origin (Serido et al., 2020). Recentering happens within the context of one's relationship with their parents and involves a reciprocal, dynamic interplay between the adult child and their parents. The processes of recentering and individuation from one's parents are keys to establishing a relationship with one's life partner.

Finding a Life Partner

Traditionally and historically reaching adulthood was inferred, in part, from the socio-demographic milestones of marriage and parenthood (Wright et al., 2025). These milestones were based upon research observations from the 1950s and 60s on white, middle-class men. These observations about normative development were gleaned at a time in history when the normative pathways to adulthood were relatively uniform and socially expected (Wright et al., 2025). Typically a young adult would land a job, find a spouse, and start a family in their early twenties (Blatterer, 2007).

That model of development and those milestones of adulthood are no longer the norm. Specifically, that model of early adult relationships is no longer representative of the wider population of young adults and that image of their transition to adulthood is outdated. In fact, today, the transition to adulthood happens in a world that is "increasingly characterized by volatility, uncertainty, complexity, and ambiguity (Johansen & Euchner, 2013). Today there is great variation in the timing and nature of major life transitions (Wright et al., 2025). Evidence shows that in developed countries, on average, emerging adults are not fully assuming adult responsibilities until the third decade of life (Arnett, 2004; Côté 2000; Settersen & Ray, 2010). For example, the average age of first marriage is now in the thirties. But before we look at marriage and other long-term intimate relationships, we should first consider what contemporary relationships look like in young adulthood.

What do Relationships Look Like in Young Adulthood?

Theories of the development of relationships, especially in young adulthood, show some interesting patterns. Specifically, **social penetration theory** states that relationships develop and progress linearly over time as intimacy builds from communication processes (Altman & Taylor, 1973). First, individuals get acquainted with each other, then they progress to mutually exchanging affections, and these processes increase the depth and disclosure in the relationship. Dyadic crystallization happens as partners move through the following stages: the evaluation of perceived similarities, rapport building and self-disclosure, and the mutual perception of good "role-fit." This process was articulated in Lewis's (1972) premarital dyadic formation model. The problem with these models is that they are over 50 years old. How well do they fit with today's dating and relationship development?

In the early 2000s, young adult relationships were focused on hookups. Hookup culture was the norm on college campuses (Garcia et al., 2012). Defining hookups was problematic because it could range from kissing to penetrative sex (Olmstead et al., 2018). Demographically speaking though, college students tend to have less sex and fewer sexual partners than their generational peers. Interestingly, college students who are sexually active are more likely to have sex with a close friend than a one-night stand with a stranger or casual acquaintance (Monto & Carey, 2014). What is important to note here is that college students may be leaning toward having sex with someone they already have a rapport or established relationship with. The intimacy of these hookups could represent one stage of a deeper developing relationship. This fits with a study that showed that 65% of women and 45% of men reported that they would like their casual sexual relationships to develop into a committed relationship (Owen & Fincham, 2011).

A 2023 study showed that sex was actually decreasing in young adults (Taylor, 2023). In 2019 the percentage of sexually active U.S. adults fell to the lowest rate in 30 years, with 30% of young men and 20% of young women reporting that they were not having sex (Taylor, 2023). One study proposes that the reduction in young adult sexual intimacy is due to a decline in romantic relationships, a reduction in alcohol consumption, declining earnings, and an increased use of computer games (Lei & South, 2021). The demographic and sociocultural changes that are happening in the United States may be shifting the landscape of relationships. Comparative studies show that young adults in the United States today are beginning romantic and sexual relationships later than in previous decades and a growing number of people are postponing or avoiding getting legally married altogether (Twenge & Campbell, 2018). Despite these societal changes, findings from historical comparative research also shows that the stages of romantic relationships have not changed in the last ten years (Ogolsky et al., 2025).

Other changes in young adult relationships include online dating, social networking, and social media, which are ubiquitous for social life, dating, and access to potential partners. Today many people are using online platforms to research potential partners prior to actually meeting them (Chan, 2021) and this can impact both the timeline and development of early stages of relationship building.

One longitudinal study conducted by *eHarmony* from 2005 to 2012 showed that more than 30% of marriages began online, and this was an increase from even a few years earlier (Cacioppo et al., 2013). By 2022, 20% of partnered adults under the age of 30 and 25% of partnered LGBTQ+ adults met their partners online (Vogels & McClain 2023). Today the number of people meeting romantic partners online has surpassed the number meeting romantic partners through friends or family, and it is anticipated that these rates will continue to grow over time (Rosenfeld et al., 2019).

What has caused these shifts? Well, data from the American Time Use Survey shows that adults are spending most of their waking hours online (Perrin & Atske, 2021). That said, it has been argued that the reason for the increase in online dating could be due to the pool of available partners being considerably larger online compared to one's own personal networks. Meeting potential partners online allows individuals to feel more in control when choosing a partner as well as more confident in their decisions (Sharabi, 2024). Yet, in an early study of online dating, Finkel and colleagues (2012) showed a downside – in the face of too many choices, people are more inefficient and become disinterested more quickly.

There has also been a shift in the social understanding of what constitutes a romantic relationship (see Figures 7.2 and 7.3). Between 2020 and 2025 the number of U.S. adults identifying as LGBTQ+ doubled to 9.3% of the total population (Jones, 2025). The same Gallup Poll also showed that one in five Gen Z adults identify as LGBTQ+. More than half (56%) of those reporting identified as bisexual and this sexual identity is more common in younger adults (Jones, 2025). We will discuss marriage in more detail below but in terms of the types of relationships that exist today, the number of same sex couples is approximately 1.3 million in the United States in 2022.

Figure 7.2 Americans' self-identification as Lesbian, Gay, Bisexual, Transgender or something other than Heterosexual 2012–2024.

Source: Gallup.

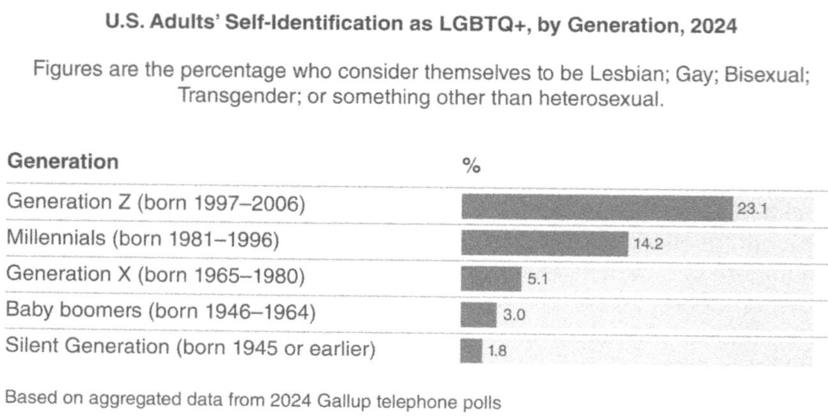

Figure 7.3 U.S. adults' self-identification as LGBTQ+, by generation, 2024.

Figure 7.4 Gay pride flag.
Source: Shutterstock.

Many of the factors that shape intimate relationships in hetero- and cis-normative individuals are similar for LGBTQ+ partnerships, though this group does face some unique challenges (Van Acker et al., 2025). These challenges relate to the stigma, prejudice, and discrimination that affect the lives, relationships, and mental health of sexual minority individuals (Van Acker et al., 2025). Specifically, on top of typical day-to-day stressors that all adults face, the pervasive impact of sexual minority stress has a detrimental impact on relationship satisfaction (Song et al., 2024). Similarly to their hetero- and cis-normative counterparts, LGBTQ+ partnered people have higher self-esteem, greater thriving, higher life satisfaction, and lower levels of loneliness and depression than single people (Elizabeth et al., 2025).

Young adults are choosing to marry later. Another change that has happened over time represents an alternative to marriage. Over the last 50 years there has been a marked increase in non-marital cohabitation (i.e., committed couples living together) and the biggest ever decrease in the percentage of people reporting being married (Courtney, 2025). Another interesting change is that traditionally romantic partnerships moved to cohabitation through marriage, whereas now that it is more acceptable to do so (Courtney, 2025), many couples live together on the road to marriage or never do get legally married. Developmentally, eventually individuals home in on one person and that relationship becomes committed and long term.

Love and Passion

What is love, anyway? Despite the fact that people have been trying to describe, define, measure, and experience love almost since the beginning of time, we may not be any closer to answering that question than we ever were. That said, in the field of psychology there have been some attempts to measure and theorize about love. Understanding what love is in the context of adult relationships is important to understanding those relationships. Before we discuss the psychology of love, you can assess the strength of one of your relationships below.

Sternberg's Triangular Love Scale

Think about one person you love or care for deeply. Read each of the following statements, filling in the blank spaces with their name.

Rate your agreement with each statement according to the scale and enter the appropriate number on the right-hand side.

1 = Not at all 2 3 4 5 = Moderately 6 7 8 9 = Extremely

	Score:
1. I am actively supportive of ________'s well-being.	______
2. I have a warm relationship with ________.	______
3. I am able to count on ________ in times of need.	______
4. ________ is able to count on me in times of need.	______
5. I am willing to share myself and my possessions with ________.	______
6. I receive considerable emotional support from ________.	______
7. I give considerable emotional support to ________.	______
8. I communicate well with ________.	______
9. I value ________ greatly in my life.	______
10. I feel close to ________.	______
11. I have a comfortable relationship with ________.	______
12. I feel that I really understand ________.	______
13. I feel that ________ really understands me.	______
14. I feel that I can really trust ________.	______
15. I share deeply personal information about myself with ________.	______
16. Just seeing ________ excites me.	______

17. I find myself thinking about ________ frequently during the day. ________
18. My relationship with ________ is very romantic. ________
19. I find ________ to be very personally attractive. ________
20. I idealize ________. ________
21. I cannot imagine another person making me as happy as ________ does. ________
22. I would rather be with ________ than with anyone else. ________
23. There is nothing more important to me than my relationship with ________. ________
24. I especially like physical contact with ________. ________
25. There is something almost "magical" about my relationship with ________. ________
26. I adore ________. ________
27. I cannot imagine life without ________. ________
28. My relationship with ________ is passionate. ________
29. When I see romantic movies and read romantic books, I think of ________. ________
30. I fantasize about ________. ________
31. I know that I care about ________. ________
32. I am committed to maintaining my relationship with ________. ________
33. Because of my commitment to ________, I would not let other people come between us. ________
34. I have confidence in the stability of my relationship with ________. ________
35. I could not let anything get in the way of my commitment to ________. ________
36. I expect my love for ________ to last for the rest of my life. ________
37. I will always feel a strong responsibility for ________. ________
38. I view my commitment to ________ as a solid one. ________
39. I cannot imagine ending my relationship with ________. ________
40. I am certain of my love for ________. ________
41. I view my relationship with ________ as permanent. ________
42. I view my relationship with ________ as a good decision. ________
43. I feel a sense of responsibility toward ________. ________
44. I plan to continue my relationship with ________. ________
45. Even when ________ is hard to deal with, I remain committed to our relationship. ________

Scoring: Sternberg, who developed the triangular theory of love, conceptualized love as being composed of three components: *intimacy*, *passion*, and *commitment*. The first 15 items in the scale measure intimacy, the second 15 reflect passion, and the final 15 assess commitment. Add up your scores for each group of 15 items. Find the scores closest to your three totals in the appropriate column below to determine the degree to which you experience each of these three components of love.

Intimacy (Items 1–15)	**Passion** (Items 16–30)	**Commitment** (Items 31–45)	
93	73	85	Significantly below average
102	85	96	Somewhat below average
111	98	108	Average
120	110	120	Somewhat above average
129	123	131	Significantly above average

High scores in all three components, according to Dr. Sternberg, indicate *consummate* love. Keep in mind, all relationships have ups and downs, and the nature of any relationship may change over time. Uneven or low scores do not necessarily mean that a relationship is not strong.

According to Sternberg (1997), love is comprised of three components that make up a triangle.

- Intimacy: The emotional closeness and deep connection that partners in a loving relationship share.
- Passion: The romance, physical attraction, and desire that partners in a loving relationship feel.
- Commitment: The decision that one loves one's partner and wants to maintain and nurture a loving relationship long term.

The interplay among these components gives rise to different forms of love. **Romantic love** is made up of passion and intimacy. **Companionate love** is made up of intimacy and commitment. **Fatuous love** is made up of passion and commitment. The triangular theory of love provides valuable insights into how relationships evolve and provides guidance on how individuals and couples can strengthen their bonds as passion ebbs and flows over time.

Passion is an important component of love in Sternberg's theory. Romantic passion (or passionate love) has been defined by Hatfield and Walster (1978) as an intense longing for being with another person. It is a psychological state featuring intense and powerful emotions that can be focused on being with another person as well as being sexually involved with that person. Sexual desire is strongly correlated with romantic passion in contemporary Western cultures (see Hatfield et al., 2012). However, people can feel sexual desire without feeling passionate romantically. Passion tends to peak early in a relationship and then steadily declines in a long-term relationship, though it can be rekindled from time to time.

According to Baumeister and Bratslavsky (1999) passion is derived as intimacy builds over time. Specifically, according to the Rate of Change in Intimacy Model (Baumeister & Bratslavsky, 1999) as romantic partners learn more about each other, begin to share affectionate communications, and enjoy new experiences together intimacy increases, and as intimacy increases feelings of romantic passion do too. This model suggests that the rate at which intimacy rises influences how much passion is felt. In long-term relationships there is a point beyond which learning new things about a partner begins to level off. At this point passion levels off too. This is when intense passion plateaus in a romantic relationship. The way to bring more passion into a relationship then is to cultivate greater intimacy. This can be done by sharing novel experiences or new things about yourself or finding new ways to be affectionately communicative.

Intimate Relationships, Marriage, and Cohabitation

Although in 2025 young adults are reaching the developmental milestones of finding a life partner, marriage, and parenthood later than their parent's generation did, most Americans who are between the ages of 18 and 34 would like to marry someday (Aragãgo, 2024). A study from the Pew Research Center showed that in 2022 30% of adults in the United States were not married, living with a partner, engaged, or in a committed relationship and half of young adults were single (34% of women and 63% of men).

Another factor that has shifted is the social understanding of what constitutes a romantic relationship and the acceptance of a broader definition of what marriage is. **Marriage equality** is the legal recognition of marriage between two people regardless of their sex. Same-sex couples can marry legally and enjoy the same legal and financial protections as heterosexual couples. In the United States and many other countries same-sex relationships and marriage between two people of the same sex are accepted. In fact, as of 2025 marriage equality exists in 38 countries, all of which have legalized same-sex unions.

Marriage is perhaps one of the most significant life events that a person experiences. It plays a key role in shaping psychosocial development. But why do people choose to marry? Well, the most obvious reason is that they feel love for their partner and would like to share their lives. The factors that influence the choice to marry are multifaceted, and include emotional needs, personal values, social expectations, and cultural norms. The motivations that drive the choice to marry influence the stability of family life. Factors that predict marital success are good communication, flexibility, emotional closeness, mechanisms for conflict resolution, shared leisure activities, cohesive spiritual beliefs, and a satisfying sexual relationship (Olson et al., 2013).

In a qualitative study of marriage, Wallerstein (2019) identifies four different types of marriages. The first is called the romantic marriage. At its core it is an enduring passionate sexual relationship. Another feature is the core belief that two people were destined to be together. The spouses interviewed shared that their marriage was exciting and they still had vivid memories of their first meeting and courtship, which retained their glow over the years and strengthened the bond between them.

The second type of marriage that Wallerstein identified was the companionate form of marriage. It was most common among younger couples and is characterized by friendship, a shared value of feminism, and a goal of balancing the partners' emotional investments in the relationship with each other and their children with their investments in their professions. This form of marriage is counter to the next: the traditional marriage. The traditional marriage, at its core, features a division of labor and responsibilities along traditional gender lines. That is, the woman is responsible for the home and family and the man is the primary wage earner. Wallerstein found that in contemporary times, women in this kind of marriage define their lives as the time before marriage and children, then the time with young children, then the time when they returned to employment. A final form of marriage that Wallerstein identifies is the retirement marriage. These couples spend a lot of time together, more than they had before retirement, and they report that their togetherness both enriches and challenges their relationship.

Long-term Intimate Relationships Across Adulthood

There are many inherent benefits associated with being in a long-term committed relationship, whether one is married or not. However, research on marriage shows that the benefits of marriage are contingent upon the quality of the marriage. Specifically, the greatest benefits are associated with the happiest marriages (Brown & Wright, 2017). Research shows that the personalities of the partners in the relationship are the driver of marital quality (Malouff et al., 2010). Being part of a couple becomes part of one's identity over time and when older couples share a couple-related sense of self they experience greater well-being (Schindler et al., 2010). As you will recall from previous chapters, socioemotional selectivity theory suggests that older adults with a shifting perspective of time based on their end of life drawing nearer invest more emotionally in their relationships, which become more important to them. Marital communication is key to long-term marital satisfaction as well (Lavner et al., 2016). In later life, older adults have more emotional empathy and more positivity, and practice more prosocial behavior, which may contribute to better marital functioning (Bell & Harsin, 2018). In general, older couples have less conflict and a greater potential for pleasure than younger couples (Levenson et al., 1993), and older couples tend to be more affectionate with one another (Carstensen et al., 1995). In a longitudinal study of marriage, a greater sense of connection and greater interpersonal boundaries at midlife was associated with less depression and greater levels of warmth and support in later life (Bell & Harsin, 2018).

Another important ingredient for a happy long-term relationship across adulthood is a satisfying sex life. Even in later life, older adults, especially those who enjoy good health, continue to desire and engage in sexual relations, though many report that the emotional intimacy is just as important (Lindau & Gavrilova, 2010).

Marriage is still considered an important developmental milestone for young adults and is an important part of the developmental scaffolding that helps adults as they grow and change across adulthood. But it is important to consider that alternative forms of long-term committed relationships are just as valid. The important part developmentally is committing to one person with whom you share your life and with whom you may want to start a family – another important developmental milestone. Before we look at the developmental changes associated with becoming parents, let us first consider that not all first marriages last, and many people divorce and remarry.

Figure 7.5 An older couple.
Source: Shutterstock.

When Marriages End

The dissolution or end of a marriage, or a divorce, is a significant life change with profound implications for individuals, their families, and their larger social networks. The longtime trend has been that 50% of marriages in the United States end in divorce (Lebow, 2019). This statistic reflects the dissolution of first marriages. The rates of second or third marriages are higher, 60% and 70% respectively. Estimating divorce rates is actually complex, a more refined way of thinking is provided by the Centers for Disease Control and Prevention (CDC) who estimate that the probability is 36% that a woman aged 15–44 will experience divorce in the first 10 years of her first marriage (National Center for Health Statistics, 2010). Some data show that the typical length of a first marriage that ended in divorce was approximately eight years. Typically, divorce is most likely to happen when partners are in their late 20s to early 30s. Many people do remarry after divorce. Over half of men (52%) and just under half of women (44%) remarry within five years of their divorce (National Center for Health Statistics, 2010).

There is evidence that divorce rates have been dropping. One reason relates to the fact that people are waiting longer to get married. Another reason is that the actual number of marriages is dropping as well. In the 2020s there were fewer marriages than in previous decades, and this is partly due to the impact of the COVID-19 pandemic, as well as other societal changes that have been discussed above. However, despite evidence that overall divorce rates are dropping, divorce rates are rising rapidly in people aged 65 and older (Brouk, 2025). This trend is called "gray divorce" and relates to the increased longevity of older people. As people live longer, they feel less inclined to stay in an unhappy marriage and more optimistic that they will find a more suitable partner in their later years. This leads to older adults being more willing to dissolve unhappy marriages than they have been in the past. Living longer has led to greater opportunities to develop new romantic partnerships across adulthood, including after divorce or widowhood.

There are many relationship challenges that lead to divorce. Every relationship is different, and all have their own unique challenges. However, some common themes include lack of commitment or not being ready for the commitment of marriage; infidelity – both sexual and emotional; domestic violence; substance abuse issues; and incompatibility. The common reasons for "gray divorces" are similar to those at earlier ages. The most common reason is emotional and physical abuse (Brown & Lin, 2022). Gray divorce is most often initiated by the woman, but older men are more likely to remarry more quickly in later life.

Some evidence suggests that a partner or couple who want to end a marriage may wait until the children leave home. But research shows that leaving a bad or unhappy relationship is better for one's health than staying in it. This is true not only for the married couple but also for the children. Although divorce necessitates a transition and invokes change, living without conflict is

Figure 7.6 Starting a family.
Source: Shutterstock.

often a better situation. Within a family most adults and children experience divorce as a high-stress state, especially during the marital dissolution transition (Lebow, 2019). Divorce significantly impacts family dynamics.

Parenting and Family

The transition to parenthood is a developmental milestone in adults' lives. This transition includes a lot of psychosocial changes to both partners and invokes changes in many domains of life. Becoming a parent is a powerful impetus for change (Hooker et al., 1996). Developmentally speaking, incorporating the new role of parent into one's sense of self is a process (Hooker et al., 1996). The emotional experiences of parents may vary from euphoria, excitement, and joy, to anxiety, fear, and dread. Especially for women after giving birth, emotional distress can be common, and it may impair the quality of life of the mother and the baby in a variety of ways (Alexander & Higgins, 1993). Many of the immediate emotions, and their fluctuation, can be tied to fatigue and hormonal changes. The period after the birth of a baby can be an intense emotional experience for both parents (Alexander & Higgins, 1993) and one that impacts parents' marital satisfaction. Research shows that between 10% and 20% of new mothers and 10% of new fathers suffer from postpartum depression (Holopainen & Hakulinen, 2019). However, not all new parents experience negative emotions and some even have a decrease in their emotional distress (Hackel & Ruble, 1992).

Becoming a father is also an emotional, life-changing experience. Research shows that fathers often feel unsupported and overlooked during the transition to parenthood (Leanderz et al., 2025). In a qualitative study carried out by Leanderz and colleagues (2025) on what it means to become a father, participants reported that being a father means a new feeling of connection with their child, their partner, and their social network. A heightened sensitivity, feeling of stress (Solberg et al., 2023; Vidaurreta et al., 2022), and diminished mental health are common for new fathers (Barrett & Charlton, 2025). Fathers who look back on the transition to becoming a father report feelings of guilt and a sense of being ill-equipped for parenthood (Barrett & Charlton, 2025). Barrett and Charlton (2025) developed the concept of "passive parenting" to capture what some fathers report experiencing with regard to the quest to become an authentic father, to overcome a sense of lack of agency and voice, and to engage more in caring for a baby. It is clear that fathers are deeply affected by the experience of becoming a parent.

It is hard to describe how individuals are affected by the experience of becoming a parent or how being a parent changes their lives because there are so many individual differences in the experience. The transition to being a parent may be particularly challenging for individuals who had difficult relationships with their own parents. Becoming a parent provokes considerable changes in personal identity, partner relationships, and family dynamics, and can create new relational experiences that relate to the attachment system. Attachment theory suggests that insecure attachment combined with interpersonal stress may elevate the risk for individuals more prone to developing depressive symptoms (Bowlby, 2008). Research on attachment theory also shows that parents with more avoidant attachment styles experienced greater stress after the birth of their first child and perceived parenting as less personally meaningful and satisfying (Rholes et al., 2006). Another study showed that parents who had insecure attachments with their primary caregivers may have difficulty forming an emotional connection to their own child (Simpson & Rholes, 2019). But the arrival of children does not just impact each individual, but the dynamic of the relationship too.

One of the most fundamental and life-changing experiences for a couple is that of becoming parents. The impact on one's sense of self and on one's relationships is similar for same-sex couples when they become parents. Just as the experience of the birth or adoption of a child is a cause for joy and celebration in the lives of a heterosexual couple and their family, the same is true for same-sex couples. All parents, regardless of the nature of their parental relationship, must work out the transition to parenting and caregiving. There are certainly unique factors that gay and lesbian couples face that heterosexual couples do not. But the transition to becoming a parent will challenge each individual's identity in similar ways. The impact of how an individual was parented and one's attachment style may influence their relationship with their children in similar ways. However, LGBTQ+ couples who become parents have to live with minority stress (Meyer, 2003) – institutionalized, interpersonal, and sometimes internalized discrimination and stigma that heterosexual couples do not (Everett et al., 2021). Moreover, an individual's experience of developing sexuality and subsequent coming out may also affect the way they parent (Sandor, 2025). However, there are also some protective factors for same-sex couples with children, including strong practical and emotional support (Möllborn et al., 2025).

Historically, marital satisfaction has displayed an inverted U pattern during the trajectory of parenthood. It is high before the arrival of children, dips during the years of parenting, and rises again when the last child moves out of the family home. From a developmental systems perspective, there are many reasons that may explain this pattern. One factor that may impact marital satisfaction is the perception of equity in household and parenting tasks. Parenting can impact the division of labor within the family and this is an important factor that impacts the relationship of the parents.

The allocations of tasks within a family has been consistently gendered (Schmitz & Trübner, 2025). In the United States in the 1960s married women did seven times more household labor and four times more childcare than their male partners (Bianchi et al., 2012; Milkie et al., 2025). However, recent research shows that the traditional gender breakdown of household labor has changed. By the mid-1990s women were still doing twice the amount of childcare and housework as men, and despite the fact that many mothers are now working outside the home, they are still doing most of the childcare (Milkie et al., 2025). Analyzing data from the 2003–2023 American Time Use Survey, Milkie and colleagues (2025) showed that the historically significant gender gap in time spent on household chores had diminished a bit, especially in core household work areas such as cooking and laundry. Time spent on childcare also showed greater parity among mothers and fathers. These social dynamics represent factors that may influence and shape individuals' identities and their satisfaction within their relationships and the family.

The Modern American Family

According to the Pew Research Center, the last several decades have led to many changes in the makeup of the American family. There is no longer one typical form of family but rather a great deal of variations and a lot of diversity in what constitutes family in the United States today. Figure 7.7 illustrates how families have changed over time.

What is evident from Figure 7.7 is that whereas in 1970 67% of adults aged 25 to 49 were living with their partner and one or more children under the age of 18, over the past five decades that percentage has dropped to 37% (Aragão et al., 2023). Simultaneously, there has been an increase in the percentage of other types of families, such as unmarried adults raising children

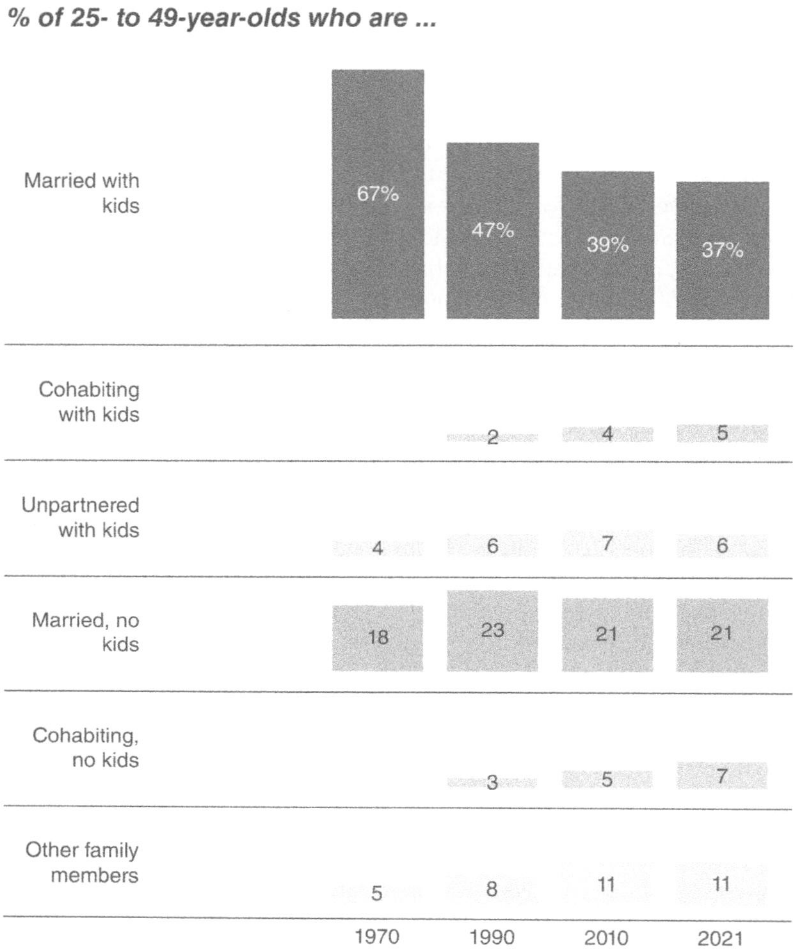

Figure 7.7 Trends in the American family.

Source: Pew Research Center.

together and multifamily or multigenerational families. These changes in the structure of the American family are in part due to some of the factors we have discussed above, such as the decline of heterosexual marriages and the increase of same-sex marriages. Changes in decisions to have children have had a significant impact on the structure of the family too. Couples in general are having fewer children now than in the 1970s. Figure 7.8 shows that being married and having children are seen as less important to leading a fulfilling life today than they were in the past (Parker & Minkin, 2023).

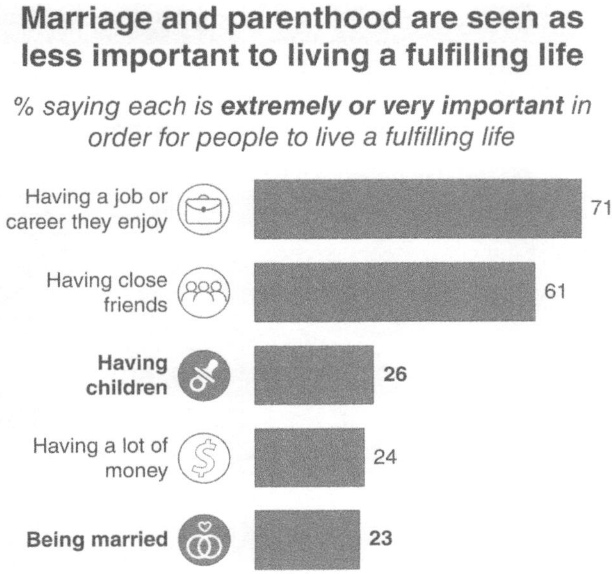

Figure 7.8 Marriage and parenthood are seen as less important to living a fulfilling life.

Note: Response options also included "Somewhat important," "Not too important" and "Not at all important."

Source: Survey of U.S. adults conducted April 10–16, 2023.

"Public Has Mixed Views on the Modern American Family"

Pew Research Center

Figure 7.9 shows diversity in the family unit as a function of family composition, such as opposite-sex couple, same-sex couple, mother and children only, father and children only, and also as a function of ethnicity. From this graph you can see that families are very diverse in terms of multiethnic composition and they are no longer mainly made up of an opposite-sex couple with children.

Another type of family that is common worldwide is the stepfamily – a family created when a two individuals who have children from previous unions come together and blend their families. Blended families also have several different forms, including when a new couple is formed and in addition to their children from a previous relationship, they have a new child together. Merging into a blended family takes time and effort from all members of the stepfamily, but cohesion and a new sense of family are possible (Ganong et al., 2019). Many people from blended families are close with their stepparent and their stepsiblings. When a child's parents divorce and one remarries and has a child with a new partner, the half siblings can also form meaningful sibling relationships. Half siblings who share a residence, are the same

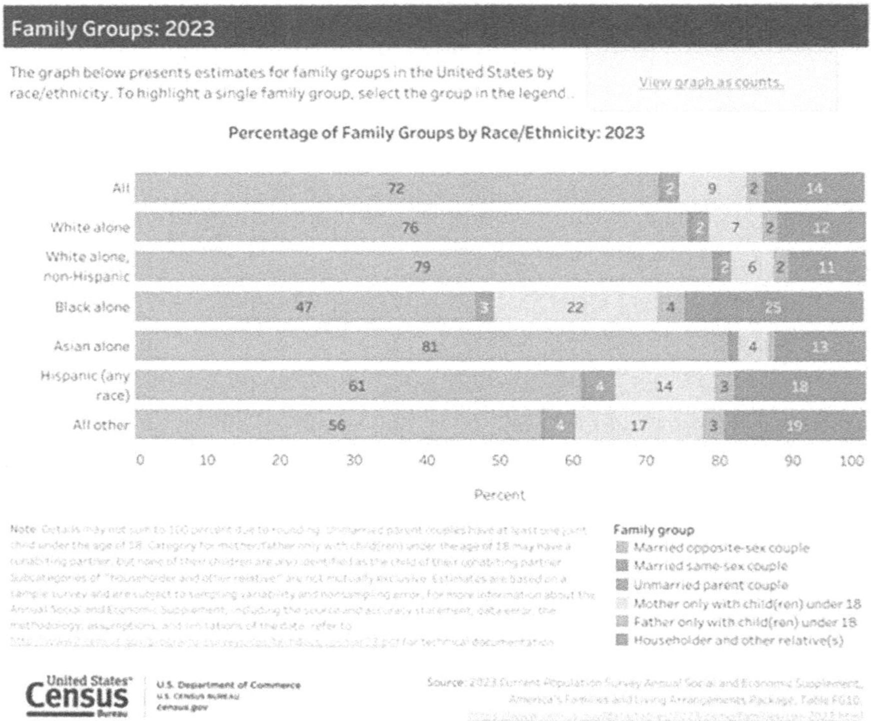

Figure 7.9 Family groups in 2023.

Source: U.S. Department of Commerce, U.S. Census Bureau

gender, and are closer in age tend to be closer emotionally and report positive relations within the family (Oliver-Blackburn, 2024).

Launching Children – The Empty Nest

One of the biggest moments in family life is when children move out of the home. The **empty nest** refers to the moment when the last child leaves home and the parents, who have spent the last 18 or more years caring for them, are once again living as a couple by themselves.

Early research on the empty nest called it a syndrome and characterized the emotional changes brought about by children leaving home. This developmental transition was thought to be harder on mothers than fathers because at that time motherhood was considered a primary role for many women (Raup & Myers, 1989). The empty nest happens when parents launch their children into the real world – they leave home to go to college or to take a job somewhere else, to move into their own place, to get married. In many ways, this moment signifies that parents have "done their job," they have raised their children to become individuals who are beginning their own adult lives. This developmental transition most often occurs when children reach the age of 18 or older and when parents are middle aged. The transition naturally involves a reorganization, readjustment, and redefinition of parental roles and familial relationships.

Is the empty nest a syndrome? Most research on this developmental period has focused on several factors: 1) the emotional impact on parents and their reactions to their children moving out; 2) the impact of the empty nest on the couple's relationship; 3) the impact of the empty nest on intergenerational and familial relationships; and 4) the socioeconomic impact of the change in living arrangements when children leave home. Although as children are leaving home later than in previous generations or returning home after living away, the complete transition to a fully empty nest has been delayed and become less linear, less permanent (Mitchell et al., 2019). Nevertheless, as mentioned above, research has found that marital satisfaction takes a U-shape over time, being highest before children, being relatively low during the active parenting period, and rising again when children leave home (Mitchell, 2022). There is research evidence that shows that when children leave home there are positive changes in the parents' relationships. The changes in roles and the reallocation of time can improve the relationship (Bouchard & McNair, 2016). There are fewer daily physical and emotional burdens associated with running a household and providing for children, which leads to greater freedom and more time to spend together as a couple, and this can increase life and relationship satisfaction. Family dynamics shift and there can be a reduction in familial conflict when children leave home. The empty nest creates a greater parity and equity in the parent's relationship, which is also related to greater satisfaction, especially for mothers (Kulik et al., 2010). However, research has also shown that the empty nest transition can increase marital conflict and increase the risk of marital dissolution (Mitchell, 2022). Some parents stay in unhappy marriages for the sake of the children, so when children leave home the parents are free to end their relationship (Bouchard, 2014).

Although the cultural myth of the empty nest as a syndrome marked by depression was popular in the 1970s, and it is true that many parents experience sadness and a sense of loss when their children leave home, the stereotype of the empty nest as a syndrome has been debunked (Mitchell et al., 2019). Rather, even stay-at-home moms can feel a sense of relief and of freedom after launching their children, and research shows that the majority of parents' emotional experiences are neither severe nor long-lasting (Mitchell, 2022). The empty nest syndrome is also not universal, as parents in other cultures, especially those that are collectivistic in nature, feel a sense of pride from launching their children, and many also know that the nest is never really empty because of intergenerational family connections that continue through the developmental changes of emerging adulthood.

Familial Relationships

Adult–child and parent relationships change during emerging adulthood and especially as a function of the empty nest. **Interdependence theory** (Rusbult & van Lange, 2003) suggests that the linked lives and the mutual influence that continues despite the changes in the parent–child dyad relate to relationship satisfaction. Specifically, according to this theory, in a dyadic relationship an individual's satisfaction with the relationship they have with others influences not only their own well-being but the well-being of the person with whom they are in a relationship. In terms of familial relationships, when a family member is unsatisfied or unhappy with their relationship with another member of the family, those negative emotions impact their own psychological distress and create distress for others as well. Research shows that when parents are satisfied with their relationships with their adult children, they experience less distress (Lowenstein et al., 2007). However, as adult children individuate and form new social roles and relationships outside the family – with partners and peers, for example – the salience of their relationships with their parents diminishes and the new and evolving relationships become more impactful on their emotional lives (Galambos et al., 2018). There are, however, some ethnic variations to be noted. Specifically, ethnicity is an important factor for understanding the psychosocial implications of intergenerational relationships (Hong et al., 2021). Familism, a sense of strong kinship and the importance of family that is a hallmark of Hispanic-American families, emphasizes that the family is at the center of one's life and familial goals are central to and come before one's individual goals (Baca Zin, 1982). Consequently, the relationships among parents and adult children may continue to have a profound impact on the lives of adult children even as they launch their own adult lives.

Sibling Relationships

Our relationships with our siblings may well be the longest lasting relationships that we will have in our lives. How good those relationships are and how close we feel to our siblings may change over time. Yet, sibling relationships are largely understudied, especially during adulthood (Gilligan et al., 2020). There are several theories that help us understand the dynamics of sibling relationships across adulthood. The first, social exchange theory, states that relationships can be understood in terms of the perceptions individuals have of the costs and benefits that come from the relationship. We typically engage and invest in relationships where the rewards outweigh the costs or where there is equity in what we give and what we receive. In family relationships the notions of "justice" and "fairness" are also relevant (Gilligan et al., 2020). In adulthood, siblings report exchanging both emotional and instrumental support (Gilligan et al., 2020). Across the lifespan, from childhood to later life, sibling relationships are marked by several dimensions:

affection–warmth, hostility–conflict, and rivalry–parental favoritism (McHale et al., 2012). In mid- to late-adulthood individuals report having more positive relationships with their siblings and levels of conflict and parental favoritism are diminished compared to earlier periods of the lifespan (Stocker et al., 2020). In general, adult siblings are also less likely than their younger selves to experience their relationships as ambivalent (Fingerman et al., 2004). Over time, in familial relationships and especially in sibling relationships, adults are less likely to engage in negative interactions and more likely to focus on maintaining positive relationships with those they are close to (Carstensen et al., 1999).

Across adulthood people feel more favorably toward their sibling relationships than they did at any other point in the lifespan. This is why adult siblings report having regular contact, either in person, on the phone, via email or text, or through social media – at an average of once per week to several times per week (Stocker et al., 2020). Older adults who are more comfortable with technology have more communications with siblings and the frequency and regularity of contact can lead to closer relationships.

Grandparent Relationships

The type of relationships that adult children have with their grandparents depends on different personal and situational factors. Age, for example, is a factor that influences those relationships. Specifically, as grandmothers grow older, they tend to have less significant contact with their grandchildren than younger grandmothers do (Roberto & Stroes, 2019). Younger grandmothers tend to be more fun-loving and more engaged, often seeing themselves as too young to fit the image of the traditional grandmother (Roberto & Stroes, 2019). Young adults value their relationships with their grandparents greatly and report that these relationships are very important to them. Young adults maintain these relationships because they get enjoyment, emotional support, and value from their grandparents, despite also feeling a sense of obligation to them (Roberto & Stroes, 2019). During the transition to adulthood, when young adults are establishing their lives, contact with grandparents may decrease but the emotional bond endures (Wetzel & Hank, 2020). In general, grandparent–adult grandchild relationships are characterized by warmth, intimacy, emotional connection, communication, and companionship (Scharf, 2016).

The majority of older adults are grandparents. This role is central to the lives of people over the age of 50 who have experienced becoming a grandparent (Di Gessa et al., 2020). Many grandparents become caregivers for their young grandchildren – for example, to help alleviate the economic strains facing parents. Evolutionary theory suggests that becoming a grandparent should be associated with emotional benefits for older adults since grandparenting has a direct effect on genetic fitness (Hilbrand et al., 2017). The transition to becoming a grandparent brings with it the positive benefits of nurturing, protecting, and passing on their knowledge to their younger offspring (Di Gessa et al., 2020). Grandparents may also welcome the opportunity to improve upon their parenting, and the opportunity to provide emotional or financial support to their children and grandchildren (Wells & Kendig, 1997). However, becoming a grandparent has also been found to be associated with negative psychosocial outcomes. Specifically, dealing with the negative stereotypes of aging and ageism that come with being a grandparent may negatively impact well-being. Grandparents report feeling older than non-grandparents, especially if they became grandparents at a younger age when it is less common to be a grandparent (Bordone & Arpino, 2016). Another potential negative impact is when becoming a grandparent is associated with the resurfacing of long-standing conflicts within the family (Clarke & Roberts, 2004).

Surprisingly, little research has explored the impact of becoming a grandparent on the grandparents' life satisfaction or well-being. However, longitudinal research by Di Gessa and colleagues (2020) shows that becoming a grandparent has positive effects on well-being but only for grandmothers whose daughters had a child for the first time. These results did not apply to grandfathers. More recent research showed that, for some, grandparenthood actually reduces well-being but does not affect physical or cognitive functioning or mental health (Leimer & Van Ewijk, 2022). Specifically, the results of a study by Leimer and van Ewijk (2022) showed that a reduction in well-being occurred for those grandparents with relatively little regular contact with family and no childcare experiences, and for grandmothers who provide daily caregiving for their grandchildren. Grandparenting in the context of close regular family contact, and the opportunity to provide occasional childcare, led to improved health but not improved well-being. Interestingly, grandparenting was associated with increases in family contact and increased decisions to retire. In sum, becoming a grandparent did not confer benefits or disadvantages to well-being. A recent study showed an increased sense of meaning and purpose in an individual's life during the transition to becoming a grandparent, but that after becoming a grandparent these values diminished and there was no difference compared to older adults who were not grandparents (Chereches et al., 2025). These findings may seem surprising, but let us not forget that an experience is what you make it! The research findings may not be capturing those ephemeral aspects of grandparenting that make it meaningful for each unique individual person.

Friendships Across Adulthood

The 2025 World Happiness Report (see Pei & Zaki, 2025) shows that social connections are vital to happiness in young adulthood. They buffer the toxic effects of stress and they significantly enhance psychological well-being. Happiness is inherently social and it comes from our ties with others and the friendships we form.

The friendships that characterize young adulthood usually form early in the college experience, and these friendships are linked to increased flourishing and reduced rates of depression. These findings are important because mental health issues are rising among young adults. During the transition to adulthood, as young adults strive for independence they become less reliant on family and focus on developing new friendships and expanding their social lives. The benefits of positive friendships are conferred throughout adulthood, including health benefits. In fact, studies continuously show that for older adults friendships are more important to offset loneliness than relations with family and close relatives (Thompson et al., 2024).

Friends are different from family and provide a unique and vital source of social relation across all stages of adult development (Ajrouch et al., 2024). Research has shown how friendships made in childhood have long-term positive impacts on health in adulthood (Narr et al., 2019). There is a great deal of evidence that shows the positive effects of friendship on well-being (Blieszner et al., 2019). Friends provide so much – from emotional support and validation, to comradery and fun activities, to new ways of thinking and information that shapes who we are (Ajrouch et al., 2025). We know from the socioemotional selectivity theory that beginning in early adulthood and through later life there is a pruning of social networks. When we begin to feel the pressure of the amount of time we have left to live, we prioritize spending that time with the people with whom we feel closest and who make our lives most meaningful. Older adults reduce their social networks to focus on the people with whom they are closest emotionally (English & Carstensen, 2013). This highlights the importance of close friendships throughout adulthood.

One way to conceptualize the importance of friends in our social networks through adulthood is the **convoy model of social relations** (Antonucci et al., 2014). In this model, a convoy is the assembly of social connections, including with family and friends, that surrounds us throughout our lives. This theoretical framework allows us to consider the hierarchical importance of social relationships, with an emphasis on emotional closeness. Essentially, we are all surrounded by supportive people who travel with us through life. Emotional closeness becomes more important as we age because the older we get the more we prioritize emotional goals as opposed to instrumental goals (Carstensen, 1995). Figure 7.10 shows the social convoy diagram that was developed by Antonucci. You can use it to map your social convoy. Just think about those people who are meaningful in your life and position their names in relation to you. People who are more meaningful should be closer to you in the diagram.

Our social convoy is responsive to what we are dealing with at any point in our lives and provides stability or change depending on the personal or situational aspects of our lives. Our social convoy influences our health across our lifespan, working against stress and negative health outcomes (Ajrouch et al., 2024). As we grow and change our convoy does too. The specific people in the convoy may change and the qualities of our social relations with

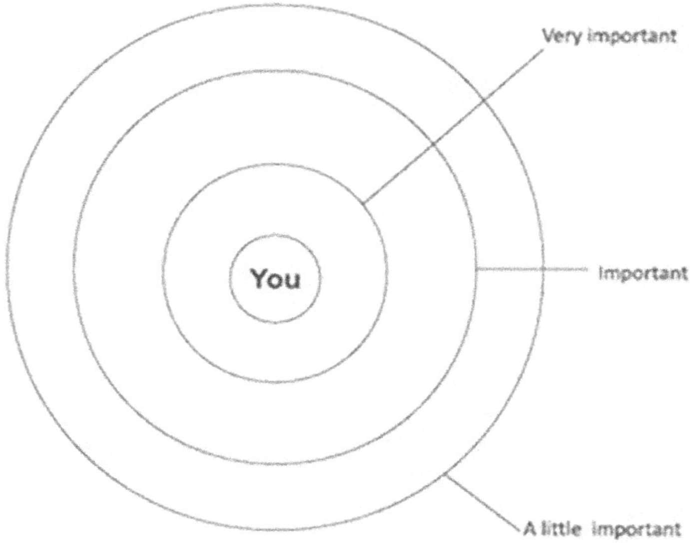

Figure 7.10 Social convoy diagram.
Source: Based on Kahn and Antonucci (1980).

those people may vary as well. Unlike family ties, though, friendship ties are more likely to require active maintenance over time (Huxhold et al., 2022).

Friendships are incredibly beneficial and relate to personal growth and well-being. Our friends can influence us in many ways and act as our "chosen family" (Anderson & Chen, 2002). These people have the power to impact how we perceive ourselves and the shape of our lives (Baumeister & Leary, 1995). Friends help us to progress toward our ideal selves and provide us with opportunities for self-growth (Aron et al., 2022).

Interestingly, little research has focused on how stressful some relationships can be. Many relationships with family or friends can be a mix of positive and negative experiences and emotions. Some relationships that lack emotional support can be stressful in and of themselves (Rouxel et al., 2022). Moreover, some people with whom we have relationships can be downers: they can be critical, undermining, competitive, hostile, and create drama and conflict. These tend to be the relationships that are not supportive and can lead to distress and anxiety. In part because we choose our friends voluntarily, our relationships with them are typically assumed to be characterized by positive interactions, not negative ones (Blieszner, 2014). Typically, younger adults who are forging new friendships prioritize new connections that require them to tolerate more negative elements, compared to older adults who spend time with friends who know them well and treat them well (Rouxel et al., 2022).

Chapter Summary

Across the adult lifespan people individuate from their families of origin, to embark on college, new jobs, new friendships, and new partners, and to pursue their own paths. This is the first developmental relational milestone of adulthood. The second major milestone is finding a life partner, settling in, and eventually starting a family. Parenthood is a major task of adulthood that spans an average of two decades. At that point, parents experience the empty nest as their adult children leave home to forge their own lives. We have looked at factors that influence the selection of partners, the quality of intimate relationships, and how those relationships may change over time. Finally, in midlife or beyond adults become grandparents. This may not always be the life-changing event that it is made out to be, but these relationships can provide a source of love, comfort, fun, and support. Finally, we explored the role of friends across the lifespan.

Key Takeaways

1 There are several important developmental tasks in adulthood that pertain to relationships, such as finding a life partner, starting a family, the empty nest, and widowhood.
2 There are different types of love that may correspond to the duration of a relationship, and some that positively influence the longevity of relationships.
3 Adult friendships change over time for a variety of reasons.

Reflective Questions

1 Which of the development relationship benchmarks of adulthood are most important to you?
2 Does the convoy model make sense to you?
3 What evidence is most compelling for the socioemotional selectivity theory?

Suggested Readings

Antonucci, T. C., Ajrouch, K. J., & Birditt, K. S. (2014). The convoy model: Explaining social relations from a multidisciplinary perspective. *The Gerontologist, 54*(1), 82–92. doi: 10.1093/geront/gnt118.

Baumeister, R. F., & Leary, M. R. (2017). The need to belong: Desire for interpersonal attachments as a fundamental human motivation. *Psychological Bulletin, 117*(3), 497–529. doi: 10.1037/0033-2909.117.3.497.

Wallerstein, J. (2019). *The Good Marriage: How and Why Love Lasts.* Plunkett Lake Press.

Key Terms

Attachment theory focuses on the early emotional bonds between infants and their caregivers and how these early forms of attachment shape social and emotional development and later relationships.

A **commitment** is a decision to maintain and nurture a loving relationship long-term with a partner that you love.

The **convoy model of social relations** is a theoretical framework that considers the hierarchical importance of social relationships with an emphasis on emotional closeness.

Empty nest refers to the moment when the last child leaves home and the parents are left in the home alone.

Interdependence theory suggests that the linked lives and the mutual influence that continues despite the changes in the parent–child dyad relate to relationship satisfaction.

Intimacy is the emotional closeness and deep connection that partners in a loving relationship share.

Marriage equality is the legal recognition of marriage between two people regardless of their sex.

Passion is the romance attraction and physical desire that partners in a loving relationship feel.

Social penetration theory states that relationships develop and progress linearly over time as intimacy builds as a result of communication processes.

8 Life Tasks, Work, Retirement, and Leisure

Learning Objectives

Explain what the developmental tasks of adulthood are.
Describe Super's theory of career development.
Identify the features of Holland's theory of vocational development.
Describe how age bias and age discrimination affect individual's lives.
Define leisure and give some examples of what you do for leisure.

Figure 8.1 Falling in love.
Source: Shutterstock

DOI: 10.4324/9781003483809-8

Figure 8.2 Stress at work.
Source: Shutterstock.

Figure 8.3 Leisure activities in later life.
Source: Shutterstock.

In this chapter, we turn our attention to the notion that there are developmental life tasks that we seek to achieve as we move through the stages of adulthood.

Developmental Life Tasks

Havighurst believed that learning is a fundamental aspect of human development and that it continues across the life span (1948). He proposed a set of **developmental tasks** for each period or stage of the life span, and he believed that individuals are motivated independently and through sociocultural forces to achieve each of the tasks assigned to that period before moving on to the next. Developmental tasks are age-graded normative experiences based upon societal expectations of the developmental milestones that are supposed to be reached in that specific life phase (Havighurst & Glasser, 1972). Havighurst believed that when these tasks are achieved, they lead to happiness and to success in later tasks. The age-specific tasks of adulthood are broken down into early, middle, and late adulthood. Although the time frame for adolescence has expanded and we now have the developmental period of emerging adulthood, Havighurst's tasks are still relevant for conceptualizing the activities that mark each period of adulthood. Let us take a look at them.

Although Havighurst laid out tasks from birth through death, here we will focus on those relevant to adult development. As can be seen in Table 8.1, the first relevant stage is Early Adulthood (18–30 years) and the developmental tasks during this period are mainly focused on establishing romantic and social relationships and securing employment. Specifically, the relationship-related developmental tasks are finding a partner, learning to live with a marriage partner, becoming a parent, having and raising children, and managing the family and one's home. In young adulthood, a developmental task that takes an enormous amount of time relates to the achievement of an occupational career. During this time, young adults may be continuing their education to earn advanced degrees or beginning to establish themselves in their work roles. There may be conflict between the desire to achieve the life tasks in the relationship sector and trying to pursue the life tasks in the work sector. Many young adults may postpone one task in order to secure the achievement of another. For example, establishing a career before focusing on finding a partner, getting married, and beginning a family. Social life at this time is focused on forming new friendships and assuming responsibility in the larger community. Some of the challenges of this period are the pressure to find a partner and "settle down." This can be the most exciting and also the most stressful task of this stage, especially if parents or well-meaning aunts are pressuring the emerging adult. That said, learning to live with a partner is also often an unexpected challenge, in both positive and negative ways. People who have been living independently for most of their early adulthood may find it challenging to have their lives hitched to another. This is a period focused on learning how to fit two lives together. The decision to begin a family

Table 8.1 Havighurst's developmental life tasks

Type of Developmental Task					
Life Phase	*Romantic Relationships*	*Family Life*	*Work Life*	*Social Life*	*Physical Changes*
Early Adulthood (18–30 years)	Selecting a partner Learning to live with a partner	Starting a family Becoming a parent Raising children Managing a home	Continuing higher education Starting an occupation Taking on civic responsibilities	Finding a congenial social group	Peak fertility
Middle Adulthood (30–60 years)	Relating to one's partner Maintaining a satisfactory romantic relationship	Promoting the growth of teenage children into responsible happy adults Adjusting to parents' aging	Reaching and maintaining satisfactory performance in one's occupation/career Achieving adult social and civic responsibility	Developing adult leisure activities Establishing a satisfactory work–life balance	Adapting to the physiological changes of midlife (i.e., menopause, visible signs of aging)
Late Adulthood (60+ years)	Adjusting to the failing health or death of one's partner	Adapting to changing social roles (i.e., becoming a grandparent) Caring for grandchildren	Adjusting to retirement and the reduction of income	Establishing an explicit affiliation with one's age group	Establishing satisfactory living arrangements Adapting to decreasing physical strength and health changes
Non-normative tasks	Adjusting to divorce Finding a new partner/remarrying	Caring for chronically ill family member Family separation due to migration or job opportunities	Coping with changes in employment status/loss of work	Establishing new social contacts after relocation	Dealing with severe illness

Note: Some of these tasks have been modified to better reflect current life circumstances (Huttemann et al., 2014). These tasks may differ across cultures and time.

is a big one and it causes many changes to the individual's sense of self, their relationship with their partner, and their career goals and future plans. Becoming parents may cause both the individual person and the young couple to take on a responsibility far greater than any they have ever experienced before. They are now responsible for a human life that is not their own, and to be able to fulfil this responsibility they must master the physical and emotional tasks of the period.

The developmental tasks of middle age grow out of the previous stage and are marked by a new maturity. This period is also defined by a deepening of existing roles and the development of some new ones as relationships change. There is likely to be continuity in the transition from parenting an infant in young adulthood to raising and then launching one's children in midlife. There are changes in the relationship with one's own parents that happen at this time as well. Specifically, as parents age and their health status changes, middle-aged children often become caregivers for them. In many cultures aging parents come to live with or near the middle-aged couple and their family. In the work sector, many middle-aged adults are ascending to the peak of their professional careers, with more responsibilities and changing roles within the workplace. Middle-aged adults may become more active members of their communities as well as taking actions to invest in the future of coming generations. Following the launching of their children and the new experience of the "empty nest," oftentimes in midlife people begin to develop new friendships and activities outside of family life and work. They may begin to travel or to take up new hobbies or become involved in new activities, and so their leisure lives become more salient. One of the marked changes in midlife are the physical changes associated with aging. Especially for those at the upper end of this period, they may begin to look and feel differently as they notice the physical signs of growing older. It is especially hard to avoid this realization for women who enter menopause.

In later adulthood, traditionally, people become grandparents. While this is a normative change for most people, not everyone is psychologically prepared for it. While it is exciting to see one's family growing and to begin to develop relationships with a new generation, for some people, the idea that they are "old enough" to be grandparents is a bit shocking. For them, it may take time to adjust to the new role and acclimatize their identities to their new role. A similar identity-related challenge in the later years is tied to this, historically, being the time when many individuals begin to consider and then move toward **retirement** from their careers. Retirement can have many different impacts on aging individuals, including the loss of a steady income. Older adults during this period also may develop some concerns about their physical and psychological health.

Later in the older years, many people experience losses. Friends, family, and spouses may die, and this can change relationships, affect living situations, and impact emotional and financial stability. The individual's own health may be changing as well. With losses in physical capabilities, many older adults may begin to consider changing their living arrangements, downsizing their homes, and moving into retirement communities. One thing to keep in mind is that although old age has often been characterized as a period of loss and decline, there is a great deal of variation in how people age and how their lives are affected by growing older. In fact, development in any period of life consists of both gains and losses, although the gain–loss ratio becomes increasingly negative with advancing age (Baltes, 1987; Heckhausen et al., 1989).

Havighurst's developmental task theory provides a useful framework for thinking about how biopsychosocial factors interact to influence development during the adult years. It is important to keep in mind that in the 50 years since Havighurst developed his theory sociocultural and historical factors have influenced how and when tasks become salient. For example, the period of young adulthood is changing and many individuals are postponing tasks such as leaving home, marriage, and starting a family (Arnett, 2000; Seiffge-Krenke & Gelhaar, 2008; Shanahan, 2000). When the timing of the tasks in young adulthood is pushed back, it has a ripple effect on the "normative" time period for future tasks. Our society now has different perspectives associated with gender, gender roles, and sexual identity that have impacted the timing of relationship and parenting tasks. Similarly, with people living longer and healthier lives, the tasks of middle and late adulthood have shifted to later in life. There are also many ways in which culture and historical cohort can influence the timing of life tasks. However, taken together there is evidence that Havighurst's theory has shaped what we anticipate as normative developmental benchmarks across adulthood.

With Havighurst's theory in mind we now turn to the factors that shape career choice and development in young adulthood.

Super's Theory of Career Development

Our careers are often in the making throughout our childhood and into adulthood. A career is a combination and trajectory or sequence of the roles that a person plays over the course of their lifetime (Super, 1980). In Chapter 1 we covered Erikson's stage theory of development and we discussed the important role that one's sense of self and one's future self-representations hold for adult identity development. Think about ice breakers at events with adults. Many adults introduce themselves like this: "Hi, I'm Juan, and I'm a forensic accountant." Our professional identity is often one of the core aspects of our self-concept and our identity. Through most of adulthood our goals for the future pertain to achievements in our careers as well. So, how does this come to be? How does our sense of self, our self-concept, and our identity come to be influenced by our chosen professional path?

Super is a developmental psychologist who focuses on career development. His theory is a lifespan view of career development that has been used in vocational counselling for 75 years. The assumption guiding this theory is

Table 8.2 Super's five stages of career development

Stage	*Age*	*Characteristics*
Growth	birth–14	Development of self-concept, attitudes, needs and general world of work
Exploration	15–24	"Trying out" through classes, work hobbies; tentative choice and skill development
Establishment	25–44	Entry-level skill building and stabilization through work experience
Maintenance	45–64	Continual adjustment process to improve position
Decline	65+	Reduced output, prepare for retirement

that our different abilities and interests are key to our choice of occupation and our success within that occupation. The core tenet of Super's theory is that self-concept changes over time as a result of our experiences.

Occupational choices and competencies are a function of an individual's life experiences. As people grow and change over time, their work experiences evolve and they develop vocational maturity. Table 8.2 shows Super's five stages of career development.

The idea behind Super's developmental theory of career development is that through our interactions with and our experiences within our environment we engage in self-assessments, explore potential professional pathways, and set goals and plans of action that eventually lead us to our chosen career. The development of our self-concept is the central focus and the aspect that influences our choices. Self-concept is shaped by our perception of our abilities, our interests, and our values. The key here is that career development is a life-long, ongoing process that shifts and changes based upon life experiences and our evolving self-concept. It is important then for individuals to have a sense of their own strengths, weaknesses, and interests in order to make the choices that suit them best. Career maturity is conceptualized as the ability to make appropriate professional and career decisions grounded upon one's self-concept and developmental stage. We can and do revisit these actions when we strive for career advancement, pursue new directions, or prepare to leave the workforce in later years. In summary, Super's theory (2012) posits that career self-concept is shaped by personal experience, education experiences, and early career experiences (Vondracek & Porfeli, 2011). Since career experiences may be highly impactful, changes may occur in career choice and pathways, especially within the first five years of beginning an occupation. This is an important period of discovery when mismatches between what students learned in school or were trained to do and their workplace experiences will occur. Take, for example, the very common experience of a person who graduated with a bachelor's degree in psychology and went to work in their first professional job as a human resources specialist. While this position might draw on their learned knowledge of human behavior, they might quickly feel that they are not able to help people as much as they had hoped and that advanced graduate training would increase their career opportunities. One study of students who earned bachelor's level degrees in marketing showed that there was a significant gap between the college training and what they perceived would be needed to feel useful and exercise influence in their careers (Montano & Mercado, 2025). As a consequence many graduates returned to school for advanced degrees. The authors of this study also showed that bachelor's level graduates were highly adaptable, especially with technology, and that they took initiative regarding decision-making and working with teams, demonstrating Super's exploration stage of career development.

Across adulthood many people may struggle to land on a career that suits them, and it can be difficult to imagine or anticipate what kind of career will fit better than another. Although historically one's profession was shaped by the family trade (Bui & Miller, 2017) and/or one's sex assigned at birth (Marlowe, 2007), with advances in social movements and technology, those simplistic influences are no longer as influential (Gulliford et al., 2025). Recently efforts have prioritized the needs of the self in occupational goals and career counselling (Gulliford et al., 2025). Gulliford and colleagues (2025) propose that the focus should be on better understanding individual differences in sense of self, beyond that of self-concept. Specifically, they suggest that self-construals or the ways that people define themselves, are the foundational process shaping decision-making and behaviors. They conceptualize self-construals in the same way that Markus & Kitayama (1991) did and argue that people's self-construals are derived from their social experiences and culture and can fall into two major domains. If a person is grounded in a collectivistic or interdependent culture they are likely to form an interdependent self-construal in which they see themselves as an important part of a social fabric. If someone is from an individualistic culture, they are more likely to form an independent self-construal in which they see themselves as separate or less bound to the social structures around them. People with strongly independent self-construals are less sensitive to social contexts and are more likely to prioritize self-consistency and emphasize personal control compared to those who have strongly interdependent self-construals (Gulliford et al., 2025). Gulliford and colleagues (2025) sought to determine if these different self-construals would differentially map on to career areas while controlling for sex assigned at birth. They found that people who were high in independent self-construals were more drawn to science, law, and art; and people with interdependent self-construals were more drawn to business and human relations. Their findings are important for career counsellors who rely on Super's theory of career development because they have shown the very important influence of culture on self-concept or self-construals. They argue that taking into account the background and culture a person comes from can help to find them a career that better matches with their self-concept.

Holland's Theory of Vocational Personalities and Work Environments

Another theory that addresses how people match their identities and goals to the pursuit of fitting careers is Holland's (1997) theory of vocational personalities and work environments. The basic idea in Holland's theory is that most people are a combination of six personality types. Each personality type is characterized by specific interests, preferred activities, unique abilities, beliefs and values, and other individual characteristics. Using Holland's assessment a person is assigned a code that represents their three most prevalent or dominant personality characteristics. This code can be checked against the codes attributed to "personalities" that best suit different careers or work environments. When there is a close match a person should thrive in that work environment because it should be a good fit for their vocational personality. You can find the test online.

Holland Code Quiz

Each question is an opportunity for you to describe the kinds of things you as a person can do, might like to do, or the action that most suits you.

Are you...	
Helpful?	Sociable?
Assertive?	Outgoing?
A nature lover?	Mechanically inclined?
Well groomed?	Friendly?
Inventive, original?	Idealistic?
Efficient?	Practical?
Understanding?	Analytical (like to figure things out)?
Persuasive?	Observant?
Self-confident?	Free spirit or a rebel?
Curious?	Straightforward?
Able to do your own thing?	Imaginative?
Energetic?	Creative?
Enthusiastic?	Intuitive?
Able to operate tools and machinery?	Precise?
Responsible?	Methodical?

Scientific-use information to solve new problems?	Athletic?
Insightful?	Mechanical?
Can you...	
Sing, act or dance?	Lead a group discussion?
Sell things or promote ideas?	Do complex calculations?
Start projects?	Write useful business letters?
Pitch a tent?	Work well within a system?
Think abstractly?	Keep accurate records?
Sketch, draw, paint?	Teach/train others?
Operate mechanical equipment or power tools?	Convince people to do things your way?
Mediate disputes?	Fix electrical things?
Cooperate well with others?	Understand science-use information to figure things out?
Suggest a better way to accomplish a task?	Lead a group?
Use a computer?	Play a sport?
Use machines and power tools?	Write stories, poetry, music?
Plan and supervise an activity?	Organize activities and events?
Solve math problems?	Solve mechanical problems?
Design fashions, interiors, or quilts?	Give talks or speeches?
Use a microscope?	Make original crafts, dinners, school, or work projects?
Express yourself clearly?	Play a musical instrument?
Do a lot of paperwork in a short time?	Tolerate weather conditions?
Do you like to...	
Cook?	Push through to task completion?
Win a leadership or sales award?	Be in the center of activity?
Express your own style?	Read fiction, plays, poetry?

Read scientific or technical magazines?	Make sure things get done?
Tinker or work with your hands?	Work with young people?
Cook without a recipe to guide you?	Work with numbers?
Be physically active?	Do volunteer service?
Work on cars, lawnmowers, or sewing machines; repair kids' toys?	Perform experiments?
Be responsible for details?	Work outdoors?
Explore ideas?	Attend concerts, theaters, art exhibits?
Start your own political campaign?	Be outdoors?
Work in groups?	Help people with problems?
Take photographs?	Meet important people?
Keep detailed records?	Follow clearly defined procedures?
Type, file, use a ten-key pad?	Participate in meetings?
Work independently (by yourself with little direction)?	Make decisions affecting others?
Play team sports?	Work on crafts, make gifts for friends and relatives?
Be elected to office or make your opinions heard?	Use computers?

Source: John Holland (1997).

The Holland codes make up a system that can be used to classify people's work personalities, interests, or attributes. In the Holland model, these categories represent work personalities.

The six work personalities are described here.

- **Realistic** people are often competitive, assertive, and interested in activities that require motor coordination, skills, and strength. People with a realistic orientation usually prefer to work a problem through by actively doing something, rather than talking about it or thinking about it. They prefer concrete approaches to problem solving, rather than abstract theory. They may be drawn to scientific or mechanical fields rather than cultural and aesthetic fields. They like to work with THINGS.

- **Investigative** people like to think and observe rather than act. They prefer to digest, organize, and understand information rather than to persuade. They are drawn to individual activities rather than people-oriented activities. They like to work with DATA.
- **Artistic** people are usually creative, independent, open, inventive, original, perceptive, sensitive, and emotional. They prefer less structure and fewer rules, and like tasks that involve people. They like to use their physical skills, and are also more likely to express their emotions than others. They are motivated to engage in thinking, organizing, and understanding artistic and cultural things. They are drawn to work with IDEAS and THINGS.
- **Social** people are drawn to teaching or helping fields. They differ from realistic and investigative people in the way they seek close relationships with other people and are less likely to want to be focused on intellectual or physical tasks They like to work with PEOPLE.
- **Enterprising** people are good at communication and use this skill to lead or persuade others. They also value reputation, prestige, power, money, and status, and tend to pursue it. They like to work with PEOPLE and DATA.
- **Conventional** people feel most comfortable with rules, clear expectations, and regulations, and focus on self-control. They are drawn to structure and order, and do not like unstructured or unclear work and interpersonal situations. They place high value on reputation, power, or status. They like to work with DATA.

Using the codes from the Holland personality styles and vocational interests assessment you can work out your own two or three-letter RIASEC or Holland code. Research the Holland codes online to find out more about the relationship between job personalities and key characteristics, college majors, hobbies, abilities, and related careers.

Holland's theory is one of the most extensively examined theories in career development. Holland (1997) argued that individuals search for and enter work environments that allow them to "exercise their skills and abilities, express their attitudes and values, and take on agreeable problems and roles" (p. 4). The goal is to achieve "congruence" – which is the degree of fit between an individual's personality type and the work environment type. Holland argued that congruence is related to several important outcomes, including job satisfaction, stability, and performance (see also Nauta, 2010).

Surprisingly, there have not been any new developmental theories that speak to how adults choose their professions. However, there have been many influences that shape how satisfied people are with their work and their work–life balance, and their decisions to retire or change careers.

COVID-19 and Work

The COVID-19 pandemic prompted colossal changes in the way people think about and live their lives. These changes are especially apparent in how

Figure 8.4 Working during the COVID-19 pandemic.
Source: Shutterstock

people think about and engage with work. Findings show that over half (56%) or nearly 125 million workers who are employed full-time now conduct their jobs from home (Clifton & Harter, 2023). Over 90% of U.S. workers who had office jobs do not want to return to the office and of those 40% said they would change jobs to keep the option of working (full or part time) from a non-office location (Clifton & Harter, 2023). Researchers at Gallup Survey Group have assessed people's satisfaction with work post-pandemic and found that the following factors are critical: feeling that one is treated with respect at work, that one's organization cares about and works to improve employee's well-being with an emphasis on improving mental health, receiving some meaningful feedback on a regular basis, and feeling that one's employer also cares about the company's clients, customers, or users (Clifton & Harter, 2023).

Many of the changes brought on by the COVID-19 pandemic are still unfolding five years later. Location of work, remote and hybrid working situations, a tight labor market, and a focus on creating a positive office culture and promoting employee wellness are trends that have been prominent.

Alongside the pandemic, the impact of artificial intelligence (AI) on work life is still unknown. It appears that the future of work will be characterized by increased automation, greater reliance on and integration of AI, and flexibility in working arrangements. These changes to the world of work brought on by AI will require employees to learn new skills and retrain to keep pace with technological advances. This could be especially problematic for older workers.

Several scholars monitored the effect of the pandemic on technology use in older adults (Zapletal et al., 2023). They noted that digital technology had become prevalent in our work and personal lives, with computers, the internet, smart phones, video streaming, and social media being a common component of modern life. Back in 2019, 62% of older adults described themselves as daily internet users (Davidson & Schimmele, 2019). The digital divide exists because compared to younger age groups, older adults have fewer technology skills, less comfort with various forms of technology, and lower technology usage (Zapletal et al., 2023). Prior to the COVID-19 pandemic, some older adults may have lacked digital literacy but during the pandemic many people of all ages relied more on technology for social connection (Vargo et al., 2021). For those older adults who were not avid users of technology, there was a sense of exclusion and isolation (Seifert et al., 2021).

Consequences of the COVID-19 Pandemic on the Work Lives of Adults

As we have seen, the transition in young adulthood from being in school to being in the work force full time is a sort of "right of passage" or "coming of age" milestone in most developed economies (Garret & Eccles, 2009, Li et al., 2023). In addition to the developmental implications, it often means a change in one's income and financial and work responsibilities that are characteristic of becoming an adult (Arnett, 2014). The COVID-19 pandemic created tremendous economic uncertainty and impacted the employment of many adults of all ages. By late 2020, there was a 4.7 point increase in unemployment for young adults (age 15–24) but no change for older adults (Grzegorczyk & Wolff, 2020). COVID-19 may have shaped emerging adults' work expectations, experiences, and financial stability.

Once people began to return to work after the pandemic, there were many and varied changes in how and where work was carried out. Many people returned to work arrangements with greater flexibility that have challenged traditional relationships between employers and employees, working hours, and work–life balance (Vyas, 2022). More recently, workers have been asked to return to in-person work and this has been seen as positive by some and a negative by others. One survey (that was not conducted by trained researchers) showed that 91% of all workers were dissatisfied with the return-to-the-office mandate, and many (73%) were looking for new jobs (Castrillon, 2024). Research shows that during the pandemic, remote work led to workers feeling that they had more authority over their work, could personalize their working environment and routines, and feel a greater sense of independence (Lara-Pulido & Martinez-Cruz, 2023). When employers pushed for a return to the workplace, many employees experienced stress and anxiety (Fan & Moen, 2023), and felt apprehensive about how their positions, tasks, and approaches to work would have to change to adapt to the in-person environment again (Bennett & McWhorter, 2021). In fact, one of the factors increasing the stress of returning to work was having to return to toxic and stressful working climates in person (Parker et al., 2022). These are some of the factors that have led to "The Great Resignation," which refers to the record numbers of people who resigned from or quit jobs that they did not wish to return to after the COVID-19 pandemic. Data shows that the wave of people quitting their jobs in 2021–2022 was experienced across all industries and demographic groups, however there were more younger people, women, people from non-White ethnicities, and people without college degrees who chose to stop working during that time (Michaels, 2024).

Job Satisfaction

If people are happy in their work they usually stick with it. Factors associated with long-term work satisfaction can be internal or external. Examples of intrinsic work values are seeing your work as interesting, with opportunities to learn (Chow et al., 2017). Extrinsic work values include salary, job security, or job title. Longitudinal research shows that both intrinsic and extrinsic work values at age 21 predict rewards derived from work 10 years later (Johnson & Mortimer, 2011). However, it is only intrinsic work values consistent over adulthood that predict work rewards in midlife (Chow et al., 2017). Work rewards are seen as proximal predictors of job satisfaction and may be more important than intrinsic or extrinsic work values (Kalleberg, 2011). Career satisfaction, which is thought of as a subjective indicator of career success, is a function of early intrinsic work values, work rewards, and career satisfaction.

Thinking back to the person-job fit we discussed above, you might be wondering how one's personal characteristics influence job satisfaction. Heintz and Ruch (2020) found that in a large sample of adults from the ages of 18 to over 60 (N = 12,499), with jobs in many different occupations (e.g., nurses, physicians, clinical psychologists, social workers, supervisors, office workers, economists, educators, secondary school teachers), a sense of zest, hope, curiosity, gratitude, and life satisfaction generally related to higher levels of job satisfaction. Of course, work satisfaction is shaped by working conditions but the individual influences their own satisfaction with their work both directly (through personality characteristics) and indirectly (through how well they "fit" in their job) (Heintz & Ruch, 2020).

Burnout

You have likely heard the term **burnout**, which refers to a psychological syndrome related to chronic exposure to interpersonal or other kinds of work-related stressors. Burnout is recognized as an occupational hazard in some high-stress professions, such as health care, education, and human service industries (Maslach & Leiter, 2016). Research on burnout in the healthcare field shows that it is typically associated with feelings of depersonalization, emotional exhaustion, and lack of personal accomplishments (Maslach &

Leiter, 2016). Maslach and Leiter (2016) showed that in work domains that have high demands and limited resources workers can feel that there is an imbalance between their work values and their work environments. That is, what they hope to achieve and accomplish in their work is not supported by the work environment and this can lead to burnout and especially emotional exhaustion (Kjos et al., 2025). Typically, when an individual feels that their workload is more than they can handle, they are likely to get burned out. Also when people feel that they have little control over their work, or that the work they do is not ethical, that they are not connected with co-workers, or are being treated unfairly – burnout is a risk. People can experience burnout at high-stress times or it can build over time, leading to a desire to not go to work, exhaustion just thinking about work, and a cynical attitude toward work. Research shows that during the COVID-19 pandemic burnout was as high as 52% for health care workers, and over 66% for physicians and nurses in particular (Ghahramani et al., 2021). Post pandemic, burnout is still high. In a 2024 poll by the National Alliance on Mental Health (NAMI), over 2,000 U.S. adults who work full-time responded and over half reported feeling burned out over the past year (NAMI, 2025). Burnout is a significant problem because it can lead to mental health issues such as depression, anxiety, substance abuse, memory problems, and sleep disturbances (Kjos et al., 2025). Burnout is also a factor that influences how people feel about work, their work satisfaction, and their overall quality of life.

So what can you do if you are experiencing burnout? Ideally, workplaces and organizations should support positive mental health. However, there are things that you can do to help yourself. It is important to remember that burnout can vary from person to person, but a useful first step is to recognize which parts of your work are within your control and which are not. Speaking up when your workload is causing you to feel overwhelmed is helpful to prevent burnout. When you have a good rapport with your supervisors and colleagues it can promote engagement and make it easier to speak up when things are challenging. Sometimes the best way to prevent burnout is to have activities, relationships, and things that are important to you outside of work. Finding a "work–life balance" that works for you can be critical for offsetting burnout.

Age Bias and Discrimination

Although it is illegal in many countries, age bias and discrimination are still present in the workplace globally. With the age wave, older workers are the fastest growing segment in the global workforce. Some have called this group "the new unemployables" (Wanberg et al., 2016). Ageism refers to stereotypes, prejudice, or discrimination against individuals based upon their age (Burnes et al., 2019). Experiencing ageism is related to higher rates of depression, reduced life satisfaction, and poorer mental and physical health (Marchiondo et al., 2019; Shippee et al., 2019). Ageism, age discrimination, and age-related bias in the workplace can be direct or indirect. An example of

Figure 8.5 Age discrimination is illegal but still prevalent.

Source: Shutterstock.

direct age discrimination is when an older applicant is treated unfairly due to their age. One experimental study showed that applicants to an advertised position had up to a 46% greater likelihood of being selected for an interview if their otherwise identical resumes showed that they were under the age of 50, compared to those who were over 50 (Lahey, 2008). Indirect age discrimination is when the systems in place within work organizations have unequal impacts on older and younger workers – for example, eliminating a position held by an older worker and opening a job search for a new position with a similar title and hiring a younger employee, or not promoting older employees who do not having currently relevant job skills that a younger employee may have.

Research shows that older workers are allocated poorer quality of work than their younger counterparts (Chou & Choi, 2011), they are given less access to training (Grima, 2011), they have a lower likelihood of promotion and pay raises, and they experience pressure to take early retirement (Yang, 2012). Older workers are often stereotyped as being less competent, less productive, and less willing to undertake training to develop new skills (Harris et al., 2018; Sinclair et al., 2024). Exposure to ageism and discrimination at work is associated with poorer performance, reduced knowledge sharing among younger and older workers, greater job dissatisfaction, more frequent absenteeism, and a greater intention to retire (Sinclair et al., 2024).

Retirement

Work has a very integral and central role in people's lives. Many people come to see themselves, in large part, according to the work that they do. In fact, our occupation is the single most important element of our social identity (Hooker, 1991). Our job or job title is often part of our self-concept, and we often introduce ourselves with our occupation. Therefore, the decision to retire or the transition to retirement can be one of the role changes that creates the biggest impact in one's life.

Retirement, when people leave their jobs due to age, choice, or other reasons, is a major milestone in the life course that can pose many opportunities and challenges for older adults (Wang & Shultz, 2010). Worldwide people are retiring later than they did in the past due to economic demands (Desjardins et al., 2013). However, despite the great variability in the reasons why people choose or are forced to retire, how this transition affects them is of critical importance, especially to their mental and physical well-being (Nazar et al., 2025). A systematic review of longitudinal studies showed that retirement is consistently linked to declining physical functioning, the prevalence of disease, and elevated risks for mortality (Nazar et al., 2025). This means that retirement negatively impacts a person's health. However, there are also often pre-retirement health issues that may worsen after leaving work. Research shows that the effect of retirement on health is worse for men (who show a 25% increase in mean physical dysfunction post-retirement) than women (who show a 17% mean increase in physical dysfunction post-retirement) (Nazar et al., 2025). Type of job is also a factor. Jobs that are less physically demanding and of higher quality or status have less of an impact on health compared to physically demanding jobs and afford people the economic resources they need to retire early. For these individuals, health is less likely to be poor and therefore may not worsen as much after retirement (Böckerman & Ilmakunnas, 2020). Some have also argued that the transition to retirement leads to changes in lifestyle that may elevate risk for poor health outcomes (Eibich, 2015; Vigezzi et al., 2021). Changes in levels of physical activity and increases in passive **leisure activities**, such as reading, watching TV, or playing cards, may affect health (Sharifi et al., 2023). Research also shows that involuntary retirement is related to increased alcohol consumption, poorer sleep quality and poorer self-reported health (Storeng et al., 2020).

For many people, economic concerns increase post-retirement. Research shows that financial concerns and feelings of financial insecurity are higher after retirement and are predictive of post-retirement health and mortality (Chetty et al., 2016; Cruwys et al., 2019). Financial concerns will be more likely if involuntary retirement is a result of being dismissed from a job or ill health (Rhee et al., 2016).

Having a retirement plan and planning for retirement promotes a smoother transition and mitigates many of the negative impacts on health post-retirement. Deciding when to retire and planning ahead for that event are critical. A retirement plan may involve goals that focus on adjustment to retired life and ensuring you have the means to fund a satisfying retired lifestyle (Wang & Shultz, 2010). Developing an effective retirement plan can provide realistic and practical expectations for what retired life will be like and also allows adults to anticipate and plan for the next stage of life (Moen, 1996). Part of the retirement plan might be to establish a financial plan, to think about how to spend one's time, and to integrate activities to keep the mind and body and personal relationships healthy. At its very basic level a retirement plan focuses on when and how a person will retire (e.g., full or partial withdrawal from work, timing of withdrawal).

Figure 8.6 Planning for retirement is key to satisfaction in retirement.

Source: iStock.

Retirement marks a developmental milestone in older people's lives, it marks the end of a person's professional career, and can trigger shifts in goals, identity, and perceptions of aging. While this developmental transition can have negative influences on health and well-being, it can also be a positive transition that provides a healthier, less stressful, more leisurely and socially engaging lifestyle (Han, 2025).

Leisure Across Adulthood

Engaging in and enjoying leisure activities is a hallmark of successful aging. It also promotes physical health and well-being (Paggi et al., 2016). But participating in leisure activities is something we do throughout our lives. Leisure activities are activities we engage in during our free time. So they can be anything from walking the dog to playing frisbee to going to the ballet. Regardless of our age, participation in leisure activities relates to better mental and physical well-being (Taylor-Piliae et al., 2010). Engaging in leisure activities enriches our lives and provides quality of life (Takiguchi et al., 2023). From a developmental perspective, the cumulative effects of leisure activities throughout the lifespan influence both the present and the future (Elder et al., 2015). Understanding how our leisure activities influence our lives in positive ways is important and can promote development across adulthood. From the field of leisure studies we know that leisure is a "good enhancer" of subjective well-being and it increases our positive emotions, quality of life, and sense of happiness (Takiguchi et al., 2023). Leisure engagement also builds psychological resilience and buffers against negative mental and physical health outcomes (Iwasaki et al., 2005). For example, leisure engagement reduces stress, anxiety, and depressive symptoms (Takiguchi et al., 2023).

You might be wondering if some kinds of leisure activities are better for positive outcomes. You could be thinking, for example, that getting a massage or playing golf would be especially good for reducing stress, but what about sky-diving, bungee jumping or extreme snowboarding? A wide range of activities are associated with the positive impact of leisure on well-being. Social activities such as going out with friends or family, activities involving others, and spending time with others, relate to higher well-being. Physical leisure activities such as sports, fishing, hiking, gardening, biking, or kayaking are also good for elevating well-being. Cognitive leisure activities such as engaging in creative work, art, reading, playing games, making puzzles, knitting, crafting, and other activities that involve thought also increase well-being. The bottom line is that the type of leisure activity does not really matter – if it is leisure, it has a positive influence on well-being (Menec & Chipperfield, 1997; Yarnal et al., 2008). Newman and colleagues (2014) argued that what matters is how much satisfaction a person obtains from leisure activities – the more satisfying it is, the more it will positively influence well-being. These authors also suggested that the degree of satisfaction we take from our leisure activities is highly correlated with the value we place on that activity. These authors went so far as to say that when we perform highly valued leisure activities it gives our lives meaning. The higher the subjective value we place on the leisure activity, the more satisfaction it provides – giving us a sense of self-worth and meaning in our life, and promoting mental and physical health over time (Watters et al., 2013).

Below is the Leisure Satisfaction Scale (Beard & Ragheb, 1980), which is a way to measure how much satisfaction leisure activities provide you. For each question select the answer that best represents how strongly you agree or disagree. When you are done you can add up your score. A higher score indicates greater satisfaction from leisure activities. You can also look at your mean (add the scores and divide by the number of questions) for each domain (i.e., psychological, educational, social, relaxation, physiological, and aesthetic). By looking at your mean scores on the different dimensions of leisure you can understand which types of activities bring you the most satisfaction.

Psychological	1. My leisure activities are very interesting to me 1 = strongly disagree, 2 = disagree, 3 = neutral, 4 = agree, 5 = strongly agree
	2. My leisure activities give me self-confidence 1 = strongly disagree, 2 = disagree, 3 = neutral, 4 = agree, 5 = strongly agree
	3. My leisure activities give me a sense of accomplishment 1 = strongly disagree, 2 = disagree, 3 = neutral, 4 = agree, 5 = strongly agree
	4. I use many different skills and abilities in my leisure activities 1 = strongly disagree, 2 = disagree, 3 = neutral, 4 = agree, 5 = strongly agree
Educational	5. My leisure activities increase my knowledge about things around me 1 = strongly disagree, 2 = disagree, 3 = neutral, 4 = agree, 5 = strongly agree
	6. My leisure activities provide opportunities to try new things 1 = strongly disagree, 2 = disagree, 3 = neutral, 4 = agree, 5 = strongly agree
	7. My leisure activities help me to learn about myself 1 = strongly disagree, 2 = disagree, 3 = neutral, 4 = agree, 5 = strongly agree

	8. My leisure activities help me to learn about other people 1 = strongly disagree, 2 = disagree, 3 = neutral, 4 = agree, 5 = strongly agree
Social	9. I have social interaction with others through leisure activities 1 = strongly disagree, 2 = disagree, 3 = neutral, 4 = agree, 5 = strongly agree
	10. My leisure activities have helped me to develop close relationship with others 1 = strongly disagree, 2 = disagree, 3 = neutral, 4 = agree, 5 = strongly agree
	11. The people I meet in my leisure activities are friendly 1 = strongly disagree, 2 = disagree, 3 = neutral, 4 = agree, 5 = strongly agree
	12. I associate with people in my free time who enjoy doing leisure activities a great deal 1 = strongly disagree, 2 = disagree, 3 = neutral, 4 = agree, 5 = strongly agree
Relaxation	13. My leisure activities help me to relax 1 = strongly disagree, 2 = disagree, 3 = neutral, 4 = agree, 5 = strongly agree
	14. My leisure activities help relieve stress 1 = strongly disagree, 2 = disagree, 3 = neutral, 4 = agree, 5 = strongly agree
	15. My leisure activities contribute to my emotional well being 1 = strongly disagree, 2 = disagree, 3 = neutral, 4 = agree, 5 = strongly agree
	16. I engage in leisure activities simply because I like doing them 1 = strongly disagree, 2 = disagree, 3 = neutral, 4 = agree, 5 = strongly agree
Physiological	17. My leisure activities are physically challenging 1 = strongly disagree, 2 = disagree, 3 = neutral, 4 = agree, 5 = strongly agree

	18. I do leisure activities which develop my physical fitness 1 = strongly disagree, 2 = disagree, 3 = neutral, 4 = agree, 5 = strongly agree
	19. I do leisure activities which restore me physically 1 = strongly disagree, 2 = disagree, 3 = neutral, 4 = agree, 5 = strongly agree
	20. My leisure activities help me to stay healthy 1 = strongly disagree, 2 = disagree, 3 = neutral, 4 = agree, 5 = strongly agree
Aesthetic	21. The areas or places where I engage in my leisure activities are fresh and clean 1 = strongly disagree, 2 = disagree, 3 = neutral, 4 = agree, 5 = strongly agree
	22. The areas or places where I engage in my leisure activities are interesting 1 = strongly disagree, 2 = disagree, 3 = neutral, 4 = agree, 5 = strongly agree
	23. The areas or places where I engage in my leisure activities are beautiful 1 = strongly disagree, 2 = disagree, 3 = neutral, 4 = agree, 5 = strongly agree
	24. The areas or places where I engage in my leisure activities are well designed 1 = strongly disagree, 2 = disagree, 3 = neutral, 4 = agree, 5 = strongly agree

Chapter Summary

In this chapter we examined the factors that influence our choice of work and what leads to work satisfaction. We explored stress at work, how our work lives were impacted by the COVID-19 pandemic, and other factors that may contribute to burnout at work. We also considered how ageism and age discrimination can impact older people's work lives, and the factors that lead to retirement and how retirement impacts our health and well-being. We concluded that retirement planning is crucial for an easy transition to post work life. We then explored what we do in our non-working hours – and the factors that link leisure activities to life satisfaction.

Key Takeaways

1. There are many potential reasons to explain why people choose their career paths – several theories explain how we select our occupation.
2. Retirement can have negative or positive impacts on people's lives. This may depend on why someone retires and what they do after they retire, as well as to what extent the work they did was part of their identity.
3. Leisure is critically important across adulthood.

Reflective Questions

1. Did the theories of career choice help you identify the work you may be drawn to?
2. Do you know people who have retired? How did they respond to the process of retiring and to be retired?
3. What are your leisure activities?

Suggested Readings

Montano, V., & Mercado, J. L. (2025). Career exploration stage and employment outcome of marketing management graduates: An exploratory factor analysis. *American Journal of Multidisciplinary Research & Development (AJMRD)*, *7*(01), 19–33.

Shultz, K. S., & Wang, M. (2011). Psychological perspectives on the changing nature of retirement. *American Psychologist, 66*(3), 170.

Wanberg, C. R., Ali, A. A., & Csillag, B. (2020). Job seeking: The process and experience of looking for a job. *Annual Review of Organizational Psychology and Organizational Behavior*, *7*(1), 315–337.

Key Terms

Burnout is as an occupational hazard in some high-stress professions, such as health care, education, and human service industries.

Developmental tasks are age-graded normative experiences and based upon societal expectations of the developmental milestones that are supposed to be reached in that specific life phase.

Leisure activities are pastimes people engage in during their free time.

Retirement is when people stop working due to age, choice, or other reasons.

9 Mental Health, Psychological Well-Being, and Resilience

Learning Outcomes

Define mental health, well-being, and mental disorders, and the role of lifespan developmental perspective within these definitions.

Explain the key findings of cross-cultural research on mental health, well-being, and mental disorders.

Articulate the key symptoms and diagnoses for major depressive disorder, generalized anxiety disorder, post-traumatic stress disorder (PTSD), substance use disorder (SUD), and psychotic disorders, and they key findings from cross-cultural research on these mental health disorders.

Describe Alzheimer's disease, define stress, coping, and resilience, and summarize the key findings from cross-cultural research on these topics.

Identify key treatments for different mental disorders, and cross-cultural research on these treatment approaches.

Activity

Maria is 67 years old, has a full-time job working for a publishing company, has always maintained a good diet, exercises regularly, and visits her children, other family members, and friends regularly. Lately, she has been having trouble sleeping, difficulty concentrating on her work, and has lost her appetite. She was generally a very happy person until her husband passed away after a sudden heart attack. Write down what you think Maria might experiencing based only on the information provided.

We do not know anything about Maria's personal history of **mental health**. Perhaps Maria is showing signs of depression? How do we figure this out? In general, to determine what Maria might be experiencing, you would first seek

DOI: 10.4324/9781003483809-9

a medical evaluation to rule out a medical condition. If there are no signs of a medical condition, then the next step would be to refer Maria to a licensed clinician.

It is important to be aware of the qualifications that someone needs in order to be able to diagnose a mental health disorder. There are different kinds of licensed clinicians including psychologists with a master's degree or doctoral degree in clinical or counseling psychology, psychiatrists with a doctoral degree in medicine, and licensed clinical social workers with a master's degree or doctoral degree. Those who provide professional help with mental health disorders should have a license, training with supervised hours, and at least a master's degree.

Defining Mental Health

According to the World Health Organization (WHO), mental health exists on a continuum and encompasses individuals' **well-being** and ability to manage **stressors**, meet goals, learn, work, and participate in community (WHO, 2022a).[1] The American Psychological Association defines mental health as "a state of mind characterized by emotional well-being, good behavioral adjustment, relative freedom from anxiety and disabling symptoms, and a capacity to establish constructive relationships and cope with the ordinary demands and stresses of life" (2025). Both WHO and the American Psychological Association describe mental health as more than the absence of **mental disorders**. Mental health can be influenced by genetics, personal characteristics, social networks, social class, education level, and geographic location.

According to the lifespan approach to mental health, an individual's age, culture, and context play a role in their perceptions about their mental health, views on mental disorders, views about treatment for mental disorders, and accessibility to mental health treatments (American Psychological Association, 2018d; Gautam et al., 2024; WHO, 2022a). A lifespan developmental perspective on mental health recognizes the importance of genetic factors, life experiences from different time periods, social support, economic status, and individual resources, including personality and coping skills, when making assessments of mental health and treatment approaches (Pachana, 2024).

Well-being

Researchers and practitioners often refer to "good" mental health as well-being, and WHO provides a global framework for well-being in relation to public health (WHO, 2023a). WHO describes well-being as a positive state including an individual's quality of life and ability to contribute to society, providing meaning and purpose in their life (WHO, 2023a). Well-being is generally viewed as having two dimensions – objective and subjective; however, there are various models of well-being including a neurobiological model (Gautam et al., 2024). Well-being is measured using a variety of instruments, with most of them being self-report questions on factors that encompass well-being (Gautam et al., 2024). For example, the Psychological Well-Being Scale by Carol Ryff (1989) assesses six factors (self-acceptance, positive relationships with others, autonomy, environmental mastery, purpose in life, and personal growth), and the WHO-Five Well-Being Index (2024e) assesses five items (cheerful, calm, active, rested, and things of interest). According to a study on primarily White adults, well-being improves in our twenties and thirties, is mostly stable in our forties and fifties, and shows stability in older adults with a slight decline in the later part of older adulthood (Charles et al., 2023). Findings from research on more diverse samples are discussed below.

Cross-Cultural Research on Well-being

Researchers analyzed data from two different studies to assess well-being in low- and middle-income countries and compared them to high-income countries (Moreno-Agostino et al., 2020). The first wave of the Study on Global Ageing and Adult Health (SAGE) included data from low- and middle-income countries. The Collaborative Research on Ageing in Europe (COURAGE) study included data from high-income countries. Individuals in the samples were aged 50 years older. Moreno-Agostino and colleagues (2020) found retired individuals reported higher positive affect and lower negative affect than individuals who were still working, and this was consistent for both studies. Less time working was associated with higher positive affect, and watching higher amounts of television was associated with higher negative affect. For low- and middle-income countries, individuals who listened to the radio more reported higher positive affect than those who listened less. For high-income countries listening to the radio more was associated with lower positive affect.

In a study conducted in Nigeria, which is considered the largest populated country in Africa and where poverty is a major issue, researchers assessed subjective well-being in community dwelling older adults (Togonu-Bickersteth et al., 2023). The study included data from a national survey of factors affecting older adults in Nigeria, including three states (Imo, Lagos, and Kano) representing the three major ethnic groups in Nigeria. Data was analyzed on individuals aged between 60 and 101 years old. Togonu-Bickersteth and colleagues (2023) found that despite most of the individuals being from low-income households, the majority of the sample had a medium level of subjective well-being.

Many factors influence well-being besides socioeconomic status, such as social support and maintaining activities of daily living (Briggs et al., 2023; Crealey et al., 2023; Moreno-Agostino et al., 2020; Viola et al., 2023). For example, researchers conducted a systematic review and meta-analysis of the effects of group gardening interventions on well-being in individuals aged 18 and older (Briggs et al., 2023). Researchers included 20 studies from multiple countries, and individuals with an average age of about 51 years old. Briggs and colleagues (2023) found gardening interventions may be beneficial for increasing well-being.

Mental Disorders

WHO defines a mental disorder as "a clinically significant disturbance in an individual's cognition, emotional regulation, or behaviour" (WHO, 2022b). The American Psychological Association defines a mental disorder as "any condition characterized by cognitive and emotional disturbances, abnormal behaviors, impaired functioning, or any combination of these. Such disorders cannot be accounted for solely by environmental circumstances and may involve physiological, genetic, chemical, social, and other factors" (American Psychological Association, 2018c). This definition closely supports the view expressed in the American Psychiatric Association's latest manual on the diagnosis of mental disorders – the *Diagnostic and Statistical Manual of Mental Disorders*, Fifth Edition, Text Revision (DSM-5-TR) (American Psychiatric Association, 2022).

WHO states that one in eight individuals around the world is living with a mental disorder, including about 5% of adults with a depressive disorder, and about 4% of adults with an anxiety disorder (WHO, 2022b). About 3.9% of adults experience **post-traumatic stress disorder** (PTSD) at some time in their lives (WHO, 2024c). According to the United Nations Office on Drugs and Crime (UNODC) (2024), the number of drug users increased to 292 million people worldwide in 2022, which was a 20% increase over a ten-year period. UNODC (2024) also states that, globally, 65 million individuals have drug use disorders.

The line between mental health and mental disorders is not a clear one, and many factors can affect our mental health in adulthood (see the biopsychosocial model framework in Chapter 1). The terms mental health and mental disorders can mean different things to people from different developmental cohorts and cultures around the world. For example, ethnic minority individuals face specific problems, such as discrimination and racism, that do not impact ethnic majority individuals. These life experiences are extremely stressful and are associated with mental health issues and less trust in the health care systems (Ricci et al., 2023; Schouler-Ocak & Moran, 2022). Ethnic minority individuals and individuals from low-income environments are at greater risk of mental health disorders. Within the United States there is a history of racial trauma involving emotional reactions to stressors such as humiliation, threats of harm, and unfair treatment that is associated with mental health conditions in minority groups (Comas-Díaz et al., 2019). Sometimes mental health issues occur because of increased risk of **cultural race-related stress**, the impact of living in a majority culture that views itself as better than other cultures and is promoted and normalized in societies (Williams et al., 2019), and **institutional race-related stress**, systematic limits to rights, privileges, and access to opportunities (including food, safety, health care, education, jobs, and housing) that

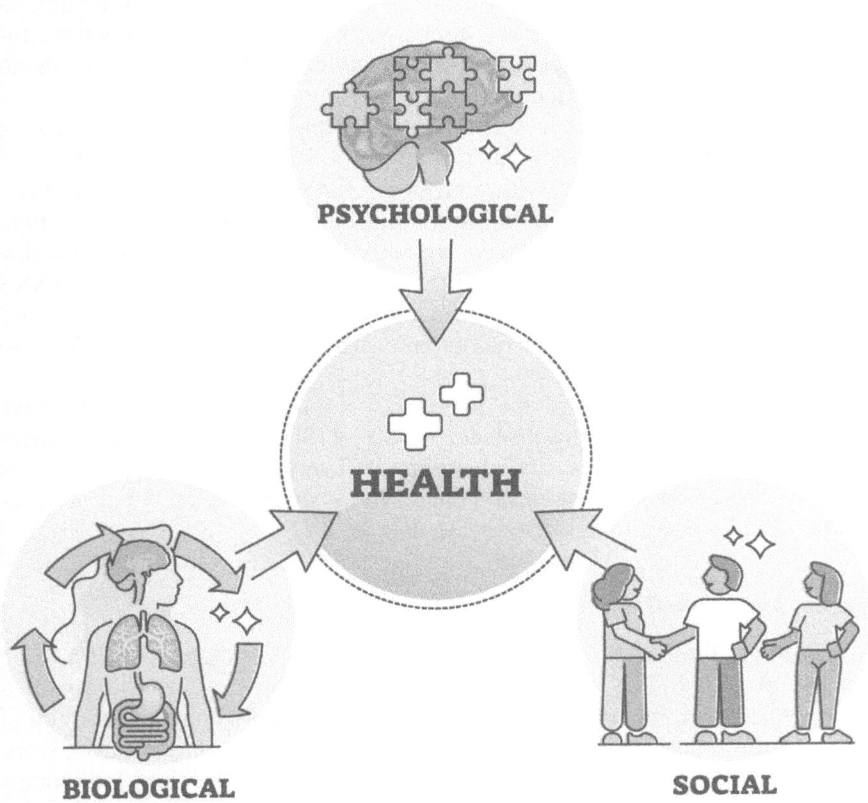

Figure 9.1 Biopsychosocial and contextual factors contribute to healthy aging.
Source: Shutterstock.

restrict individuals' ability to achieve upward mobility (Needham et al., 2023; Williams & Mohammed, 2013). In an online study conducted from 2018 to 2020, researchers assessed the effect of cultural and institutional race-related stressors on the mental health of young adults in the United States aged 18 to 35 years old (Brown et al., 2024). The sample of young adults were primarily African American, Asian American, or multi-racial, with a smaller proportion of Latinx, Native American/Alaskan Native (AN). Both cultural and institutional race-related stress predicted more depressive symptoms.

Cross-Cultural Research on Mental Health Disorders

Culture plays a role in how we perceive mental health. A study on Latinx college students from a Southeastern university was conducted with focus groups on mental health and help-seeking behavior (Geegan et al., 2023).

The findings showed Latinx Gen Z college students did not view the campus mental health resources as useful to themselves. Latinx students view the family as the only source of support they need for their mental health, and outside help is not sought out (Zhou et al., 2022).

A risk factor for mental health disorders is the use of social networking sites (SNS). Researchers investigated the role of SNS in the mental health of young adults in Bangladesh with a cross-sectional study conducted in 2021 (Islam et al., 2021). The sample of individuals ranged from 15 (adolescence) to 40 years old. Individuals who reported more than three hours of SNS a day had more depressive symptoms than those with less than three hours of SNS a day. Those in young adulthood who were female, unmarried, students, and lived in an urban area reported higher amounts of mental health problems in association with SNS usage.

Below is a discussion of the symptoms for **major depressive disorder** (MDD), **generalized anxiety disorder** (GAD), PTSD, **substance use disorder** (SUD), **psychotic disorder**, and **dementia**. All information on symptoms is from the DSM-5-TR (American Psychiatric Association, 2022), which we recommend individuals review for further details.

Major Depressive Disorder

According to the DSM-5-TR (American Psychiatric Association, 2022), to be diagnosed with MDD, individuals must have five or more symptoms for a two-week period, including a change in prior functioning, and a minimum of one symptom must be depressed mood or loss of interest or pleasure. Symptoms must also not be the result of a different medical condition. Individuals must have symptoms most of the day, almost every day.

The MDD symptom list includes depressed mood (e.g., feeling sad); less interest in most or all activities; significant weight loss (not from dieting), or weight gain; insomnia or hypersomnia; psychomotor agitation or lack of movement; fatigue or loss of energy; feelings of worthlessness or excessive guilt; difficulty concentrating or indecisiveness; and recurrent thoughts of death, suicidal ideation without a plan, or suicide attempt or plan. Yan and colleagues (2024) found the highest rates of MDD were from low-income countries, with Uganda and Palestine reporting the highest rates. The United States had the highest increase in rates from 1990 through 2019. Globally, females had a higher rate of MDD than males in over 21 regions.

Other forms of depression include **dysthymia** and **minor depression**. Dysthymia is also known as persistent depressive disorder (PDD). Although the symptoms are less severe than those of major depression, they last a long time – at least two years. Minor depression symptoms are less severe than both major depression and dysthymia, and symptoms do not last long. Depression declines as we age, with the lowest percentage of occurrence found in adults aged 60 and older (8.7% for 2021–2023 in the U.S.)

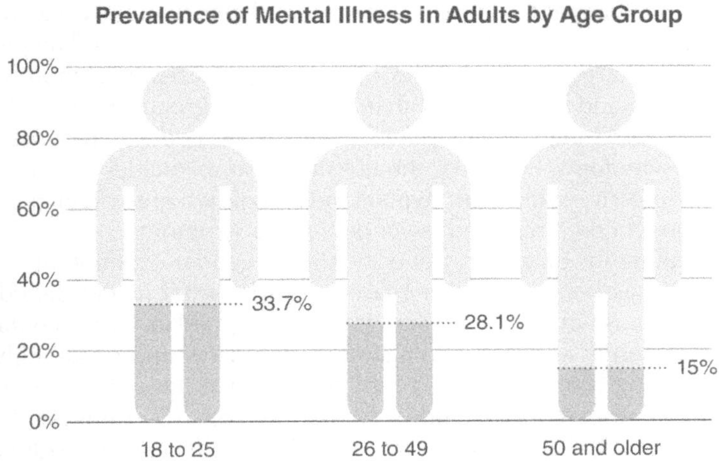

Figure 9.2 Percentage of U.S. adults with a mental health disorder by age group.
Source: National Institutes of Health.

(Brody & Hughes, 2025). Depression is not a normal part of aging, and should be recognized as a mental health concern in older adults.

Cross-Cultural Research on Depression

Nan Wang and colleagues (2024) used data from the National Health and Nutrition Examination Survey (2017–2020) to analyze U.S. individuals aged 20 years and older and found that the pre-pandemic rate of MDD was 16.5%. Factors that influenced likelihood of MDD included being female and/or non-Hispanic Black, a low income, a lack of physical activity, and health concerns. Nan Wang and colleagues (2024) also found that younger individuals without a partner, who took part in less physical activity, consumed more alcohol, and have diabetes were more likely to have MDD than others.

Researchers used data from the Study on Global Ageing and Adult Health to assess prevalence rate of depression in Ghana and South Africa (Adjaye-Gbewonyo et al., 2019). Adjaye-Gbewonyo and colleagues (2019) found that individuals aged 50 and older had a prevalence rate of depression of 7.5% in Ghana and 4% in South Africa. Individuals in urban areas were more likely to be unemployed, despite education and a wealthier family background, and also more likely to be part of the Akan or Gur ethnic groups.

Culture can also interact with socio-structural factors (Quashie & Andrade, 2018). For example, Indigenous Chilean individuals with a low socioeconomic status (SES) and less education are marginalized. However, cultural values of respect for older members and the value that is attributed to the knowledge of the elder members can be beneficial. Research on Indigenous

Mapuche and Aymara older adults from the North and South of Chile included interviews and assessment for depressive symptoms, health, and medications (Gallardo-Peralta et al., 2019). The Mapuche group reported more depressive symptoms and health issues than the Aymara group. For the Mapuche group, visits with Indigenous physicians were associated with reports of more depressive symptoms. However, the use of herbal medicines was associated with less depressive symptoms. Aymara individuals who provided knowledge to their grandchildren reported fewer depressive symptoms.

Intersectionality of ethnic minority status, gender identity, and sexual orientation is associated with increased risk of mental health disorders, in large part because of discrimination, persecution, and lack of acceptance in societies (Egbert et al., 2024). In a systematic review and meta-analysis on MDD including individuals from mid-adolescence through early 40s (Cai et al., 2024), researchers included 48 studies from 15 countries. Cai and colleagues (2024) found the prevalence of MDD in the LGBTQIA+ samples was 32.2%, much higher than the global estimates provided by WHO (2022b).

Generalized Anxiety Disorder

According to the DSM-5-TR (American Psychiatric Association, 2022), individuals with GAD experience excessive and uncontrollable worry about a variety of things in their lives, such as going to school, taking tests, learning to drive, ability to do a job, and interacting with other people. To be diagnosed with GAD individuals must experience excessive worry and anxiety, and it must occur for most of the time for at least six months. Individuals must show symptoms of GAD, and at least three of the symptoms must be present. The GAD symptom list includes trouble controlling one's worry, restlessness, fatigue, muscle tension, trouble concentrating, feeling irritable, and sleep disturbances. Symptoms of anxiety can change over the lifespan. A study with a U.S. sample showed that GAD symptoms of anxiety decline in a gradual pattern over the lifespan (Miloyan et al., 2014).

Other types of anxiety disorders include **panic disorder** and different types of **phobias**. Panic disorder includes recurring and unexpected panic attacks that can have sudden periods of very intense fear, and individuals may sweat, shake, have shortness of breath, and even experience numbness (National Institute of Mental Health [NIH], 2022). There are many kinds of phobias. In general, a phobia is an anxiety disorder characterized by irrational, unrealistic, excessive fear of a specific object or situation, and it is persistent over time (American Psychiatric Association, 2022). Phobias generally occur for more than six months, and individuals with phobias try to avoid the object or situation. If individuals cannot avoid the object or situation, then this causes the individual to have a significant amount of stress. We recommend consulting the DSM-5-TR to learn about additional anxiety disorders.

Cross-Cultural Research on Anxiety

Researchers evaluated several mental health disorders including GAD in individuals aged 15 to 69 years old in Bhutan with secondary data analyses (Pengpid & Peltzer, 2021), using data from the Bhutan STEPS Noncommunicable Disease Risk Factor Survey (WHO, 2019). Pengpid and Peltzer (2021) found a low prevalence of GAD (1.7%) compared to the prevalence in Afghanistan, Pakistan, Malaysia, and overall global prevalence in that time period. Researchers found no significant difference in GAD by rural or urban location; however, women had a higher prevalence of GAD than men. Researchers also found that both psychosocial and environmental stressors were associated with increased occurrences of GAD, including family alcohol problems and health concerns such as heart attack or stroke. Individuals aged 45 to 69 years old reported less GAD than those in younger age groups.

Much research has been carried out on the effects of the pandemic on anxiety levels around the world. The prevalence of GAD in the United States was assessed using pre-pandemic data from the 2019 National Health Interview Survey on adults, and after the pandemic began using the Understanding America Study on adults (Daly & Robinson, 2021). For individuals aged 60 and older the pre-pandemic sample had a prevalence rate of 6.4% for GAD, and by the beginning of April 2020, during the pandemic, the rate was 14.3%, more than double the pre-pandemic rate.

In a study conducted in East Azerbaijan Province, Tabriz, Iran, researchers assessed adults aged 60 years older for the prevalence of psychiatric disorders, using a cross-sectional sample of individuals from before the pandemic in 2019 (Fakhari et al., 2023), and 5.3% of the sample had GAD. In a study conducted during the pandemic, researchers assessed GAD in Rafsanjani located in Southeastern Iran, primarily in nurses in young to middle adulthood (Zakeri et al., 2021). Data was collected during March 2020 using a cross-sectional web-based study, and the rate of GAD was 27.8%. The prevalence rates of GAD within countries before and after the pandemic show the significant effect of the pandemic on anxiety levels. However, it appears that the pandemic's impact on mental health is declining.

Post-Traumatic Stress Disorder

Post-traumatic stress disorder is a mental health disorder that is caused by witnessing or experiencing something traumatic. Multiple criteria are involved in diagnosing PTSD, including stressors, **intrusion symptoms**, **avoidance**, **negative alterations in mood**, and **alterations in arousal/reactivity**. An example of a stressor is direct or indirect exposure to a real or threatening experience, such as an injury or assault. An example of intrusion symptoms is reoccurring thoughts that are involuntary and relate to a traumatic event. An example of avoidance is avoiding or trying to avoid memories or thoughts that are related to a traumatic experience. An example of a negative alteration in mood is persistent and distorted beliefs that are negative toward the individual or the world. An example of alterations in arousal/reactivity is having reckless or self-destructive behavior. Individuals must have symptoms that reflect these criteria for more than one month, and the symptoms cannot be the result of another medical illness, medication, or substance use. We recommend reviewing the DSM-5-TR for more information on the symptoms, diagnosis, and treatment of PTSD, including greater detail about the criterion and the specific number of criterion required for a diagnosis (American Psychiatric Association, 2022).

Cross-Cultural Research on Post-traumatic Stress Disorder

Within the United States, there is evidence of more trauma and more PTSD among minority ethnic groups than the majority culture (Alegría et al., 2013; Walsh et al., 2022). Some ethnic minority groups are exposed to greater risk of victimization from violence from someone within their own ethnic or cultural group, known as **cultural betrayal**, and/or from someone close to them, known as **high betrayal** (Gómez, 2019). A researcher assessed both types of betrayal in relation to PTSD in a sample of ethnic minority college students from a primarily White public university in the Pacific Northwest of the United States, including Asian American, Latinx American, Black/African American, Native Hawaiian or other Pacific Islander, American Indian/Alaska Native (AN), and Middle Eastern individuals (Gómez, 2021). More than half of the students reported being exposed to violence at some point in their lifespans. About 44% reported experiencing high betrayal, and about 43% reported experiencing cultural betrayal with trauma at a medium level of betrayal. Over one-third of the individuals reported experiencing cultural betrayal with trauma at a high level of betrayal (Gómez, 2021).

There are a variety of experiences that can trigger PTSD, including violence and natural disasters. Military veterans tend to have a higher prevalence of PTSD. Merians and colleagues (2023) assessed data from the 2019–2020 National Health and Resilience in Veterans Study (NHRVS) to determine ethnic differences in prevalence of mental health conditions. The sample of individuals had an average age of 63 years old, ranged from 22 to 99 years old, and included non-Hispanic White, non-Hispanic Black, and Hispanic military veterans. Merians and colleagues (2023) found that both Hispanic and non-Hispanic Black military veterans were more likely to screen positive for PTSD compared to White veterans, and ethnic minority status, low income, younger age, and biological XX or female sex predicted more mental health conditions.

Researchers assessed internally displaced people from Africa who had lost their homes as a result of war or disaster (Tesfaye et al., 2024). There were 14 studies included in the analysis. Tesfaye and colleagues (2024) found the highest prevalence was in Nigeria at 62%, and the lowest prevalence was in Sudan at 15%. Females were at twice as much risk of PTSD compared to males, and some other risk factors included unemployment, injury, exposure to more traumatic events, poor health, presence of other mental health conditions (e.g., depression), and repeated incidences of displacement.

As a result of individuals' changes in stress sensitivity over the life course (Cougle et al., 2009), exposure to adverse conditions in childhood may elevate risk for mental health problems in adulthood – this is known as **stress sensitization** (Hammen, 2005). In a longitudinal birth cohort study in Soweto, South Africa, researchers investigated the link between trauma in childhood and adult exposure to COVID-19 (Kim et al., 2023). Information on childhood trauma was provided by caregivers, individuals aged 11 to 18 years old provided self-reports, and the original time frame was 1990–2008. The adult assessments occurred during COVID-19, with an average age of 30. Kim and colleagues (2023) found that individuals exposed to more trauma in childhood and more stress from COVID-19 had more severe PTSD in adulthood than those with less exposure to trauma.

Substance Use Disorders

There are different types of substances that can lead to SUDs, including alcohol, cannabis, hallucinogens, inhalants, opioids, sedatives, hypnotics, stimulants, tobacco, and caffeine. There are 11 criteria for SUDs, including drug cravings, inability to reduce drug use, increased use of drug beyond intended amount, and continual drug use regardless of negative outcomes (McLellan, 2017). To have a SUD, individuals must experience cognitive, behavioral, and physiological effects from the substance, and show evidence of changes within their brain, even after they have gone through a detoxification process, which is a type of cleansing for drugs (American Psychiatric Association, 2022). The worldwide prevalence of SUDs was about 2% in 2019, with alcohol-use disorder at a higher prevalence rate than other drug-use disorders, and higher-income countries reported more SUDs than low-income countries (Castaldelli-Maia & Bhugra, 2022).

Substance Abuse

Criteria for determining **substance abuse** includes a pattern of substance use that leads to a clinically relevant amount of impairment as a result of one or more symptoms within a 12-month time period. The symptoms include: (1) reoccurring substance use results in inability to fulfill roles at work, school, or home, (2) reoccurring substance use when in situations considered physically dangerous, (3) reoccurring legal problems from substance use, and (4) reoccurring substance use regardless of social or interpersonal issues arising from the use of the substance

Substance Dependence

Substance dependence is defined by a pattern of substance use that harms or can harm the individual, results in significant amounts of damage or distress, and causes the individual to exhibit three or more symptoms that occur at any time during a 12-month period (American Psychiatric Association, 2022).

Some of the symptoms include: (1) **tolerance**, which involves the need for greater amounts of a substance to have a desired effect, (2) **withdrawal symptoms** for a specific substance and the need to take the same or a similar drug to reduce or avoid such withdrawal symptoms, which can include anxiety, tremors (known as "the shakes"), nausea, **hallucinations**, and seizures, and (3) the substance being taken in larger amounts or over a longer period than was originally intended.

Cross-Cultural Research on Substance Use Disorders

In a study on Jamaican individuals, researchers assessed prevalence of polysubstance use (i.e. use of more than one drug) and sociodemographic factors related to polysubstance use (Lalwani et al., 2022). Lalwani and colleagues (2022) conducted a secondary data analysis of the Jamaica National Drug Prevalence Survey 2016 (Younger-Coleman et al., 2017). The sample included individuals aged 12 to 65 years old. Lalwani and colleagues (2022) found that about 20% of individuals reported the use of two or more drugs during their lifetime. Polysubstance use was higher in males than females and higher in rural areas. The most frequently used drug was marijuana when assessing polysubstance use, indicating a need to focus interventions earlier in the lifespan because marijuana is often the initial drug used by youth in Jamaica. Individuals aged 18 to 34 years old were more likely to report polysubstance use than individuals aged 35 to 65 years old.

Daejun Park and colleagues (2024) assessed data from the National Epidemiologic Survey of Alcohol and Related Conditions-III (NESARC-III) (Grant et al., 2015) to assess patterns of both family trauma and racial trauma in relation to SUDs in racial/ethnic minority adults. The sample included individuals of minority background including Hispanic, Black, Asian American and Pacific Islander, and American Indian or Alaska Native (AN) individuals aged 18 years or older, with about one-third of the sample aged 50 years or older. Daejun Park and colleagues (2024) found that Black and American Indian/AN adults reported higher amounts of discrimination, higher amounts of adverse childhood experiences, higher amounts of trauma, and more drug disorders including alcohol, opioid, and other drug disorders than the other groups, and recommend interventions tailored to their specific trauma experiences.

Chiang and colleagues (2024) assessed Latin American immigrants in the United States to better understand the relation between discrimination and SUDs. With data from the NESARC-III (Park, D. et al., 2024), Chiang and colleagues (2024) assessed a sample of Latin American immigrants, ranging from 18 to 60 years old. Discrimination during the past year was linked to more reports of an SUD in young and middle adult Latin American immigrants, providing support for **cultural stress theory**. Cultural stress theory refers to cultural stressors, including discrimination, having a negative effect on immigrants and increasing the likelihood of an SUD (Salas-Wright & Schwartz, 2019).

Psychotic Disorders

According to the DSM 5-TR, when individuals have a psychotic disorder, they have psychopathology in one or more of five domains, including **delusions**, hallucinations, disorganized thought or language, disorganized or unusual motor behavior such as catatonia, and expressing no emotion (American Psychiatric Association, 2022). Delusions include beliefs that cannot be changed despite evidence against the belief being presented. For example, delusions can include beliefs about being persecuted or feeling very important. Hallucinations are intense perceptions of something that no one else can perceive.

Schizophrenia is one type of psychotic disorder; an individual must experience delusions, hallucinations, and disorganized speech to be diagnosed, according to DSM-5-TR criteria. There are different types of schizophrenia, but individuals can have unusual motor behavior, express no emotions, and show no interest in performing any goal-directed behaviors. To be diagnosed with schizophrenia, the main symptoms must be present for at least a month, with other symptoms present for six months. Schizophrenia appears between the ages of 16 and 35 years old, and generally before the age of 30 (Immonen et al., 2017). Physicians will need to rule out other medical conditions first. As schizophrenia generally occurs in adolescence and young adulthood, older adults showing signs of schizophrenia should be assessed for medical and neurological conditions including dementia. Sometimes individuals with Parkinson's disease who are receiving too much Levo-dopa medication can have hallucinations, because the presence of too much of the neurotransmitter dopamine is associated with schizophrenia.

Cross-Cultural Research on Psychotic Disorders

Different types of trauma may be associated with different symptoms of psychosis. In a cross-cultural study on types of trauma and psychotic symptoms, Stevenson and colleagues (2024) analyzed data from NeuroGAP-Psychosis, a study on both genetic and environmental factors for psychotic disorders in Sub-Saharan Africa (2019). Individuals in the study were from Ethiopia, Kenya, and Uganda, and aged 18 and older, with data collection taking place between 2018 and 2023. Stevenson and colleagues' (2024) sample included individuals with an average age of 36. The findings showed exposure to a war zone was directly associated with individuals having visual hallucinations, unusual beliefs, and disorganized speech.

Researchers assessed the relationship between adverse childhood experiences and psychosis in adults (Ranu et al., 2023). There were 15 studies, 11 of which were part of the quantitative analyses. Ranu and colleagues (2023) found that individuals who had been physically abused when they were children or had a violent or criminal parent were twice as likely to develop psychosis and become violent themselves. The combination of violence and psychosis in adulthood was also seen in individuals who were sexually abused as children, and/or exposed to family members who used drugs or alcohol.

Dementia

Adults can experience mild cognitive impairment (MCI) to severe cognitive impairment; however, cognitive impairment that impedes daily functioning is not a normal part of aging. The typical healthy adult does not automatically develop MCI and then become severely cognitively impaired. Instead, disease or trauma that affects the brain leads to MCI or more severe cognitive impairments. Current research includes evidence of neurogenesis throughout adulthood, and research on older adults known as superagers (see Chapter 4). It is important to have an understanding of dementia and **Alzheimer's disease** (AD) but, we reiterate, dementia is not a normal part of aging for a healthy adult.

Dementia is a term often used interchangeably with AD. Dementia is a general descriptive term, and it includes multiple different subtypes caused by a variety of different disorders, or injuries, with AD being the most common disorder. Other types of dementia include, to name a few, vascular dementia, Lewy body dementia, frontotemporal dementia, Huntington's disease, Parkinson's disease (PD), and Creutzfeldt-Jakob disease. Many factors may be involved in dementia, including genetic factors, hypertension, and/or diabetes, health risk behaviors such as smoking, alcohol or being physically inactive, social isolation, and mental health conditions such as depression (Ghondaghsaz et al., 2024; WHO, 2023c).

According to WHO, over 55 million individuals around the globe have dementia, and at least 60% of these individuals with dementia are living in low- and-middle income countries (WHO, 2023c). A systematic review and meta-analysis of dementia prevalence rate was conducted by Farina and colleagues (2020) based on the STRiDE program (STrengthening Responses to Dementia in DEveloping Countries), which took place in middle-income countries, including Brazil, India, Indonesia, Jamaica, Kenya, Mexico, and South Africa. Farina and colleagues' (2020) findings include a pooled prevalence rating that ranged from 2% in India to 9% in Jamaica.

Dementia involves the loss of cognitive functioning, which can include how we think, what we can remember, and how we reason about our world. It also interferes with activities of daily living (e.g., remembering how to put on clothes, or remembering how to make dinner). Sometimes people with different forms of dementia have trouble controlling their emotions, and some forms of dementia show changes in personality.

Though memory loss is an important common symptom of dementia, physicians do not diagnose dementia if that is the only symptom. Individuals must have two or more problems with their brain function, including a decline in memory, coherent speech, ability to recognize or identify objects, motor function, sensory function, ability to make judgments, and ability to carry out complex tasks. If memory loss occurs along with one of these symptoms and the individual does not lose consciousness, then a physician is likely to diagnose the individual with dementia. Physicians must rule out other medical conditions and the possibility of medication causing the symptoms too.

There has been extensive research on factors involved in the development of cognitive decline. Diabetes has been considered as a risk factor for dementia, with insulin resistance a possible link between diabetes and cognitive decline (Livingston et al., 2020). A recent study was conducted on a possible connection between the triglyceride-glucose index and cognitive decline (Ghondaghsaz et al., 2024). Research on cognitive decline and triglyceride-glucose (TyG) index, with TyG index as a substitute for insulin resistance, included seventeen studies in analyses (Ghondaghsaz et al., 2024). Higher levels of the TyG index were associated with more cognitive decline and dementia, even in groups of nondiabetic individuals.

Alzheimer's Disease

The most common type of dementia is AD, with an estimated 6.9 million individuals aged 65 years or older living with AD in the United States in 2024 (Alzheimer's Association, 2024; Rajan et al., 2021). As mentioned earlier (see Chapter 4), we do not know the exact cause of AD, and there is no cure for AD. The brain changes involved in the symptoms that eventually occur may begin more than 20 years before the symptoms first appear. There is evidence of neuron damage in the parts of the brain involved in memory, language, and thinking, in particular the hippocampus. Beta-amyloid changes may damage neurons by interfering in the communication between neurons at the synapse. These changes include **amyloid plaques** and **tau tangles**. Amyloid plaques are fragments of beta-amyloid that form outside of neurons, blocking the spaces between nerve cells. Tau tangles are when the protein tau appears in an unusual form in accumulating amounts inside the neuron. The tau tangles appear to block the movement of nutrients needed for normal function of neurons and this harms communication with other neurons too (Alzheimer's Association, 2024; Beyene & Berha, 2023; Ghondaghsaz et al., 2024). The amyloid plaques and tau tangles lead to damage and death of neurons known as **neurodegeneration** (see Chapter 4 for more details on beta-amyloid and tau). The presence of these abnormalities in the brain leads to an immune system response in the brain that cannot keep up with the damage and destruction of the neurons. Individuals with AD will show a noticeable shrinkage of their brains, well beyond the typical gradual changes in brain volume of healthy adults over the lifespan.

Current discussion of AD includes research on both early onset AD, occurring before the age of 65, and late onset AD, occurring at age 65 or older. Early onset AD has a larger genetic predisposition than late onset AD, with an autosomal dominant AD that runs within the family on PSEN1, PSEN2, and APP (Mendez, 2019). Early onset AD tends to occur more rapidly than late

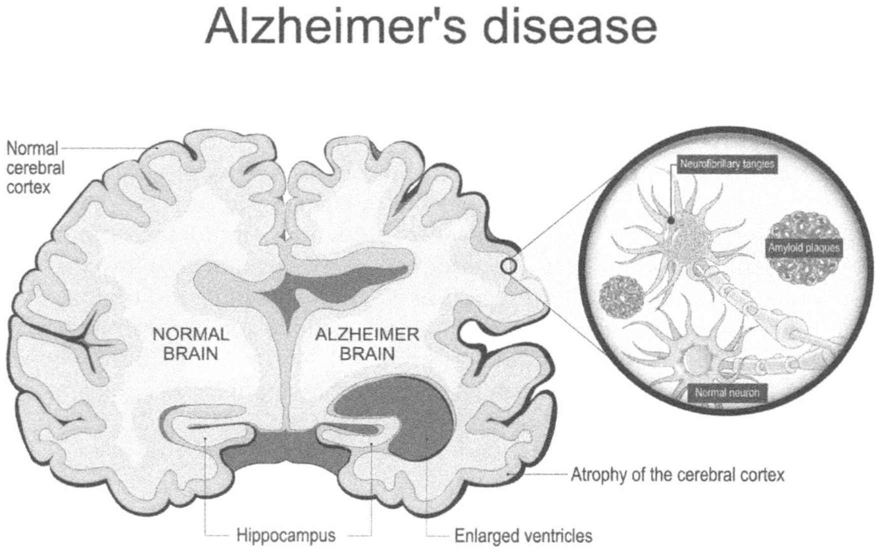

Figure 9.3 Image of normal brain and Alzheimer's brain.
Source: Shutterstock.

onset AD. Early onset AD appears to affect posterior portions of the neocortex, including the parietal and temporoparietal areas, much more than the hippocampus, which is generally the first area of shrinkage in late onset AD (Mendez, 2019). The differences in areas of the brain affected and the rapid progression of early onset AD tend to delay diagnosis and affect how symptoms are displayed. Early onset AD has a prevalence rate of 5 to 6% (Mendez, 2019); late onset AD is more common, with the prevalence rate increasing into the eighth and ninth decade of life. In a study conducted in China, researchers presented a prevalence rate of over 48% in older adults aged 95 to 99 years old (Chan et al., 2013).

Cross-Cultural Research on Dementia and Alzheimer's Disease

In a systematic review of dementia in Arab countries, researchers included 18 studies from seven countries: Egypt, Lebanon, Qatar, Tunisia, United Arab Emirates, Saudi Arabia, and Jordan (El-Metwally et al., 2019). Older individuals were more likely to have cognitive decline, dementia, or AD. Prevalence ranged from 1% to about 2% for individuals aged 50 years or older, and increased to 13% to 18% for individuals aged 80 years or older. The prevalence rate of dementia for Egyptian studies ranged from 2% to about 2.3%, with studies in Lebanon at 3.3% to 7.4%, about 1% in Qatar, and over 58% in Tunisia.

There is evidence of increased risk of dementia in minority ethnic groups in the United States and in the United Kingdom (Adelman et al, 2009; Mehta & Yeo, 2017). Researchers assessed racial/ethnic differences in the survival and mortality of minority groups with dementia (Co et al., 2021). There were 22 articles included in the qualitative analyses, with average age ranging from 72 to 87 years old. The meta-analysis included six studies from the United States. Co and colleagues (2021) found the Indigenous group and Asian American group had higher mortality rates from dementia. The Black/African American group and the Latinx American group showed evidence of a lower mortality risk from dementia than other groups. In a review of underrepresented older adults in research on cognitive disorders and AD in National Institutes of Health sponsored research in the United States, researchers included 436 articles in their analyses (Godbole et al., 2023). There was little evidence of recruitment of individuals from ethnic minorities and rural areas, with low SES or disabilities, or from the LGBTQ community, providing evidence of additional important gaps in research on underrepresented groups.

In research on the prevalence of MCI in Latin America researchers included 11 studies in their analyses (Ribeiro et al., 2022). Individuals aged 50 years or older were included from nine countries (Brazil, Mexico, Argentina, Colombia, Peru, Cuba, Dominican Republic, Venezuela, and Costa Rica). Ribeiro and colleagues (2022) found prevalence rates for MCI between about 7% and about 26%, with older individuals and lower-educated individuals having higher prevalence rates.

Stress and Coping

Dr. Richard Lazarus (1966) discussed the relation between psychological stress and coping processes. In the 1980s, Dr. Lazarus and his colleague, Dr. Susan Folkman, developed their **transactional model of stress and coping**. In this model, stress is considered the result of an interaction between an individual and their environment, with the model including individual's appraisal of stressors and the coping techniques used to respond to the stressors (Folkman & Lazarus, 1988; Lazarus & Folkman, 1984). Later research on the model included the importance of positive emotions even when dealing with stress, and positive emotion role in the coping process (Folkman & Moskowitz, 2004). More recently, stress and coping research has included the important role of technology in the assessment of stress and in how to manage stressors, ethnic minority older adult samples, effects on well-being during COVID-19, and the mediating role of rumination on relation of stress and coping (Lee & Williams, 2022; Saidi et al., 2024; Wu et al., 2023).

Stressors are external events that create demands on an individual that could activate stress responses. Stressors can be from physical, emotional, and even environmental events, range from hassles in daily life to major life experiences, and may show variability in strength and how long they last. **Daily hassles** are of especial importance in this model – daily events that individuals find annoying and distressing on a regular basis (Lazarus & DeLongis, 1983; Lazarus, 1993).

Stress and coping research addresses **acute stressors** and **chronic stressors**. Acute stressors are defined as abrupt, brief events that trigger stress, such as having a fight with your partner. Chronic stressors are defined as ongoing events that trigger stress for a longer duration. Examples of chronic stressors include stress related to an individual's occupation, stress from financial worries, and stress related to chronic mental or physical health issues, such as depression or living with a heart condition.

Within the transactional model, individuals use **cognitive appraisal** when they encounter a possible stressor. Cognitive appraisal means assessing a situation and determining if it is a threat, a harm or loss, a possible challenge, considered gain or growth, or not relevant at all. For individuals to perceive something as a stressor, they must view it as something of importance that may exceed their resources for coping with a stressor. How a situation is viewed can influence the coping mechanisms used to deal with stressors. Lazarus and Folkman (1984) discussed a **primary appraisal**, which involves an individual determining if a stressor may affect their well-being – is the stressor a threat to me or a challenge towards improving myself? **Secondary appraisal** involves an individual determining if available resources will help them deal with the stressor. Resources available may include physical health, support from family and friends, and an individual's confidence level or and finances.

Coping is viewed as cognitive and behavioral attempts to manage stressors viewed as exceeding an individual's resources. Lazarus and Folkman (1984) discussed coping with stressors as something flexible, showing change over time, with individuals making updated assessments of the stressor and their coping resources. Two types of coping strategies are **problem-focused** and **emotion-focused**. Problem-focused coping strategies help to change a stressful situation and reduce or eliminate the stressor. For example, if you find yourself very unhappy at your current job, using problem-focused coping strategies might involve checking the job market to determine what is available and if you should get additional training or education to pursue a different career path. You are taking action to deal with a stressful situation. Emotion-focused coping strategies help to manage emotions that may be related to the stressor, rather than actually reducing or eliminating the event causing the stress. An example of an emotion-focused coping strategy would be reaching out to your best friend to talk about a negative situation at work. The negative situation at work will still be there, but reaching out to someone for emotional support may help you feel less anxious for a while.

Coping Measures

Folkman and Lazarus developed a measure to assess coping called the Ways of Coping Questionnaire, which measures eight different dimensions – confrontive coping, distancing, self-controlling, seeking social support, accepting responsibility, escape-avoidance, planful problem-solving, and positive reappraisal (Folkman & Lazarus, 1988). Other coping strategies have been proposed over time, and other measures on coping. For example, the Coping Style Questionnaire features five types of coping – active-cognitive, active-behavioral, avoidance, problem-focused, and emotion-focused (Billings and Moos, 1981); the Miller Behavioral Style Scale includes monitoring and blunting strategies (Miller, 1987); and the Coping Orientations to Problems Experienced (COPE) measure includes 15 different coping approaches in the categories for problem-focused and emotion-focused coping, including a coping strategy considered maladaptive coping (Carver et al., 1989). Even when using the theoretical ideas from the transactional model, other researchers may use different measures of coping to assess parts of this model in their research.

Cross-Cultural Research on Stress and Coping

Lee and Williams (2022) assessed data from the Well Elderly2 study from Los Angeles, California, spanning 2004 to 2008 (Jackson et al., 2009). Coping was measured using COPE (Carver et al. 1989). The sample ranged from age 60 to 90 years old and included White Americans, African Americans, Latinx Americans, Asian Americans, and multi-ethnic Americans. Lee and Williams (2022) found that older minority individuals reported more stressors than White individuals, and stressors were related to health, finances, and social relationships. The top coping technique of minority older adults was religious coping, and the top coping technique of White older adults was active coping.

Researchers conducted a review of African immigrants in the United States regarding mental health and coping strategies (Nyanamba et al., 2024). The 22 studies were on African immigrants from Sub-Saharan Africa. There were a wide variety of coping strategies. For example, to deal with discrimination-related stress, African immigrants learn to adapt their ethnic/racial identity, use strategies to avoid discrimination, or turn to maladaptive coping techniques such as substance use. Some individuals concentrate on their academic coursework and achievements, which is a positive focus for them. Other coping strategies included religion/faith and social support from other African immigrants and African Americans.

In a study conducted during COVID-19, researchers assessed the transactional model of stress and coping in Chinese college students (Wu et al., 2023). The sample included Chinese college students, with an average age of 20 years old, from a Southwestern University in Chengdu, Sichuan, China. Coping was assessed using the Coping Flexibility Scale (CFS) (Kato, 2012). Wu and colleagues (2023) found that positive stress appraisal, hope, core self-evaluations, and **resilience** were important to students' wellbeing.

In a systematic review of coping strategies for those from conflict-affected areas in low- and middle-income countries (Seguin & Roberts, 2017), researchers included 50 studies. Seguin and Roberts (2017) found that both gender and trauma exposure were key factors that affected individual's coping strategies. Social support seeking behavior was the most common coping strategy reported, other coping techniques included positive cognitive restructuring of events, using problem-solving techniques, and escape-avoidance and distraction.

Resilience

Resilience involves successfully adapting to life experiences that may be difficult or to adverse events; it requires the ability to adapt and be flexible to deal with demands (American Psychological Association, 2018f; Clark et al., 2018). Resilience is not viewed as simply the absence of pathology, individuals need to be able to develop strength when exposed to adverse situations (Phillips et al., 2016). Resilience involves personal characteristics and contextual factors, which may affect an individual's ability to adapt to changing demands in adulthood and aging (Górska et al., 2022). For example, researchers investigated resilience in response to adversity in a community sample of adult Pacific Islanders aged 50 years or older from Southern California (Rainer et al., 2024). Individuals reported multiple adverse events in their lives, including substance abuse, bereavement, loss of homes, abuse, and migration. Individuals used strategies such as making a plan of action, considered an internal strategy. However, most individuals used external strategies such as support from family and friends and religion when dealing with adverse situations.

Cross-Cultural Research on Resilience

In a study on older adult individuals from the north and south of Chile, researchers assessed variables related to successful aging including resilience (Gallardo-Peralta et al., 2022). The average age of the sample participants was 72 years old, and the sample was made up primarily of two indigenous communities, the Mapuche and Aymara. The findings showed that resilience had a strong positive association with both physical and psychosocial domains of successful aging and was the leading predictor variable in the study.

In a study on older adults in four countries (Canada, Colombia, Brazil, and Albania), researchers assessed life events, environments, and resilience (Phillips et al., 2016). The adults in this study were part of the longitudinal International Mobility in Aging Study (IMIAS) Zunzunegui et al., 2015). Phillips and colleagues (2016) found that economic disadvantage in childhood was associated with lower resilience in adulthood, and current social engagement was associated with resilience in women.

Researchers assessed resilience in adults aged 55 years and older (Górska et al., 2022). There were 49 studies from ten countries included in the meta-analysis. Personal factors were associated with resilience. Higher scores on a health-promoting lifestyle, optimism, purpose in life, self-efficacy, self-transcendence, and sense of coherence were all positively associated with resilience despite variation in the measures of resilience. Contextual factors were also associated with resilience, including higher education, income, family and friend network size, and social support.

Treatment Approaches

It is important to understand that treatment of any sort can only occur if the individual is willing to seek help when needed and receive help when offered, and if help is available and accessible. Help-seeking behavior can differ across cohorts and across cultures. Generation Z college students are displaying different views on seeking help for mental health compared to Millennials and Generation X (Geegan et al., 2023; Rue, 2018; Twenge, 2017). In a study comparing Generation X to Millennials (DePew & Gonzeles, 2020), researchers analyzed data from the 2000 and 2016 National Health Interview Survey. Millennials were more likely to report moderate to severe levels of distress than individuals from Generation X. Millennials perceived less stigma around health and mental health.

Individuals providing treatment need to understand the cultural variables that may help or hinder effective treatment. Clinicians have assessed the American Psychiatric Association PTSD Guideline and found a need for better inclusion of cultural needs as part of training methods (Henning & Brand, 2019). Ethnic minority groups are at increased risk of mental health disorders, and understanding the reasons they do or do not seek help for a mental health disorder or SUD is important for effective treatment (Smith et al., 2025).

Researchers in the United Kingdom assessed personal experiences, meaning, and context of help-seeking in relation to depressive symptoms in Black Caribbean adults aged 65 to 79 years old using semi-structured interviews (Bailey & Tribe, 2021). Individuals reported that they need to try to help themselves feel better before recognizing that they may need external help. Individuals mentioned that religion plays a role in their feelings about depressive symptoms and if they should seek help. In the Black Caribbean community religious beliefs can deter people from seeking help, because of beliefs about depressive symptoms being linked to bad spirits. Individuals in the study also reported that they do not trust health care professionals to do their best to help the individual.

In a cross-sectional study on 154 individuals with psychosis in the United States, researchers assessed early contacts for help with the early stages of psychosis, including formal (e.g., doctors/nurses or school counselors) and informal (e.g., spiritual leaders, friends) (Oluwoye & Weeks, 2024). The multiethnic sample included non-Hispanic White America, Black/African American, Asian American, American Indian/Alaska Native (AN), multi-racial and other racial minority individuals including Hispanic Americans. The average age for non-Hispanic White Americans was 53 years old, and across ethnoracial minority individuals was 47 years old. Oluwoye and Weeks (2024)

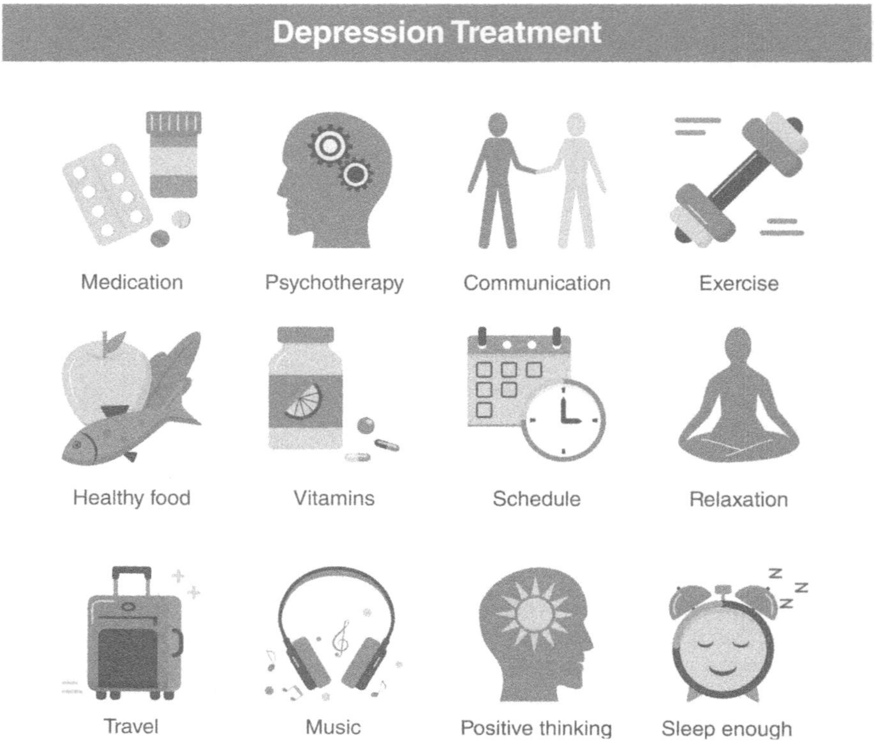

Figure 9.4 Ways to treat depression.

Source: Shutterstock.

found that Black/African American and Hispanic American family members were more likely to make early contact with their religious or spiritual leaders, friends, and online groups for support with the early stages of psychosis compared to non-Hispanic White Americans whose family members made early contact with doctors and nurses.

Types of Treatment Approaches

There are a variety of different treatment approaches used to treat mental health disorders and SUDs. For example, **cognitive behavioral therapy** (CBT) is often used to treat depression, and psychoeducational groups can be used to treat depression and anxiety. Different types of group psychotherapy are effective for treating SUDs in adults (Lo Coco et al., 2024). Substance use disorders can be treated with relapse prevention groups, group drug counseling, and interpersonal process groups.

Cognitive behavioral therapy is a treatment approach that combines different theories about cognition and learning to help reduce maladaptive thoughts and behaviors. It employs cognitive restructuring techniques and behavioral techniques (American Psychological Association, 2018a). Cognitive behavioral therapy has also been shown to improve language memory domains in individuals with dementia in Sub-Saharan Africa, including those with HIV-associated dementia (Beyene & Berha, 2023). Some other approaches include **mindfulness**, **interpersonal psychotherapy (IPT)**, and **eye movement desensitization and reprocessing (EMDR)**. Mindfulness is a technique that helps individuals to be more aware of their thoughts, feelings, and the external environment, and learn how to control automatic responses to internal and external experiences without automatic negative responses such as stress (American Psychological Association, 2018e). Interpersonal psychotherapy helps individuals to explore the details of their interactions with significant others in their lives, including the therapist, and possible environmental experiences that may affect their thinking and behavior (American Psychological Association, 2018b). Eye movement desensitization and reprocessing involves incorporating eye movements and other rhythmic stimulation such as tapping while focusing on a traumatic memory to reduce the intensity of the memory and emotional connection with the memory. Eye movement desensitization and reprocessing is used to change the way a memory is stored in the brain (American Psychological Association, 2017).

Researchers conducted a systematic review of culturally adapted treatment approaches on adult refugees and/or asylum seekers (McDermott et al., 2024). The review included 18 articles with refugees and/or asylum seekers in young and middle adulthood who were assessed in eleven countries. There were eight studies with **transdiagnostic intervention**, which are interventions that target common aspects of multiple co-occurring illnesses that require a combination of treatment approaches. An example is the combined use of psychological education, relaxation techniques, and behavioral techniques. There were six studies with CBT and four studies with other approaches, including mindfulness, IPT, or EMDR. McDermott and colleagues (2024) found that transdiagnostic interventions and CBT were the approaches most often adapted to suit different cultures, and other types of treatment approaches were culturally adapted to some extent. Cognitive behavioral therapy and other forms of psychotherapy were most effective, with less evidence for transdiagnostic interventions.

In research on psychotherapy treatments for adult depression, researchers compared Western to non-Western psychotherapy trials (Tong et al., 2023). Tong and colleagues (2023) included 405 randomized control trials, with 105 studies from non-Western countries and 300 studies from Western countries. Tong and colleagues (2023) found that non-Western countries psychotherapy trial studies showed a larger treatment effect than Western trials. There was much variability in study design, including high risk of bias and low validity, and other factors that may explain the larger treatment effect in non-Western trials compared to Western trials.

Other Treatment Approaches

In addition to different forms of therapy, other treatment approaches for mental health conditions include interactions with children, **tai chi**, yoga, other forms of exercise, herbal medicines, mindfulness, relaxation techniques such as meditation, and self-regulation techniques that can reduce stress (Lisowska, 2024). Some of these treatment approaches are discussed below.

In a study conducted in South Africa, researchers assessed ten individuals aged 60 years or older with a semi-structured interview and quantitative measurements of anxiety and depression (Earl & Marais, 2023). Individuals were living at a retirement facility in the Cape Peninsula Organization for the Aged complex. Twice a week individuals at the facility could interact with children aged three to five years old who attended a playschool on the property. Older adults could also volunteer to work with the children. Forty percent of the sample showed symptoms of depression, and 30% of the sample showed symptoms of anxiety. Individuals in the study reported a positive view of the children and their interactions with them. Individuals felt a sense of belonging and felt they had purpose in their lives because of their interactions with the children. Spending some consistent amount of time with the children helped to create a more positive mood in the older adults.

There are different forms of tai chi. In general, tai chi involves learning to connect your mind and body, and to slow down your mind and your body through the repetition of rhythmic specific workouts, including breathing techniques, aspects of martial arts, and meditation. Tai chi comes from Chinese cultural practices and medicines. Researchers conducted a systematic review and meta-analysis of tai chi in relation to depression in middle-aged and older adults (Zeng et al., 2023b). The meta-analysis included 12 trials with individuals aged 45 years or older, and the trials were from two countries: 11 from China and one from a Central American state. Zeng and colleagues (2023b) found that tai chi reduced depressive symptoms in middle-aged and older adults.

Regular exercise is associated with many health benefits including improvements in mental health. For example, research that included 218 studies in adulthood found that depression was reduced for those who exercised with walking, jogging, yoga, or strength training when compared to other types of exercise (Noetel et al., 2024).

Medications

When different forms of therapy and alternative treatment approaches do not work by themselves, medications may be necessary to treat various disorders. Caution is warranted before using medications to self-treat some disorders such as cognitive decline from AD. A meta-analysis was conducted on the role of nonsteroidal anti-inflammatory drugs in helping to slow down cognitive decline in those with AD (Asthana et al., 2024). Asthana and colleagues (2024) found no significant relationship between the use of nonsteroidal anti-inflammatory drugs and slowing down cognitive decline in AD.

Medications for different disorders should be prescribed by a licensed medical doctor. Selective serotonin reuptake inhibitors (SSRI) are the most common medication for depression, and are sometimes prescribed for anxiety disorders too. All medicines have side effects – of particular concern for older adults is the association between SSRIs and bone loss (Mercurio et al., 2022). Medications for schizophrenia generally help with hallucinations and delusions; haloperidol and chlorpromazine are two of the most common.

Chapter Summary

In this chapter we reviewed descriptions of mental health, well-being, and mental health disorders, and cross-cultural research on well-being and mental health disorders. We explored factors (biological, psychological, and contextual) that affect individuals' mental health, stress, and coping techniques, and resilience across adulthood. Finally, we discussed factors involved in help-seeking behavior, and treatment approaches for different mental health disorders in adulthood.

Key Takeaways

1. Definitions on mental health and well-being from the World Health Organization and American Psychological Association are consistent with key parts of the lifespan developmental perspective.
2. There is cross-cultural research on many factors (biological, psychological, and contextual) involved in mental health and mental disorders in adulthood.
3. Minority individuals across cultures are at greater risk of mental health disorders in adulthood compared to those of a majority culture.
4. Coping techniques used to deal with stressors show variability within and across cultures. However, the use of religion as a coping technique is more common as we age.
5. The sociocultural context in which we develop during adulthood plays an important role in our mental health, help-seeking behavior, and treatment options.

Reflective Questions

1 Which definition of mental health do you think is most relevant to the developmental perspective?
2 Can you identify the biological, psychological, and contextual factors in your life that affect your mental health? How will they influence your mental health as you age?
3 How do sociocultural and contextual factors affect our coping techniques in response to stressors, resilience, and help-seeking behaviors?

Suggested Readings

Bailey, N. V., & Tribe, R. (2021). A qualitative study to explore the help-seeking views relating to depression among older Black Caribbean adults living in the UK. *International Review of Psychiatry, 33*, 113–118. doi: 10.1080/09540261.2020.1761138.

Charles, S. T., Rush, J., Piazza, J. R., Cerino, E. S., Mogle, J., & Almeida, D. M. (2023). Growing old and being old: Emotional well-being across adulthood. *Journal of Personality and Social Psychology, 125*(2), 455–469. doi: 10.1037/pspp0000453.

Schouler-Ocak, M., & Moran, J. K. (2022). Racial discrimination and its impact on mental health. *International Review of Psychiatry, 35*(3–4), 268–276.

Key Terms

Acute stressors are abrupt, brief events that trigger stress, such as having a fight with a partner.

Alterations in arousal/reactivity leads to reckless or self-destructive behavior.

Alzheimer's disease (AD) is the most common form of dementia. It is caused by two specific changes in the brain – amyloid plaques and tau tangles.

Amyloid plaques are fragments of the protein beta-amyloid that form outside of neurons, blocking the spaces between nerve cells.

Avoidance means avoiding or trying to avoid memories or thoughts that are related to a traumatic experience.

Chronic stressors are ongoing events that trigger stress for a longer duration.

Cognitive appraisal means assessing a situation to determine if it is a threat, a harm, a loss, or a possible challenge, a gain or a growth, or not relevant at all.

Cognitive behavioral therapy (CBT) combines different theories about cognition and learning to help reduce maladaptive thoughts and behaviors with cognitive restructuring techniques and behavioral techniques. It is often used to treat depression.

Cultural betrayal refers to victimization from violence enacted by someone within an individual's own ethnic or cultural group.

Cultural race-related stress refers to the impact of living in a majority culture that views itself as better than other cultures and is promoted and normalized in society.

Cultural stress theory refers to the negative effect that cultural stressors, such as discrimination, have on immigrants.

Daily hassles are daily events that individuals find annoying and distressing on a regular basis.

Delusions include beliefs that cannot be changed despite evidence against the belief being presented.

Dementia is a general descriptive term, and it includes multiple different subtypes caused by a variety of different disorders, or injuries, with AD as the most common disorder. It involves the loss of cognitive functioning which can include how we think, what we can remember, and how we reason about our world.

Dysthymia, also known as persistent depressive disorder, is a form of depression. Symptoms are less severe than those of major depression but they last a long time, at least two years.

Emotion-focused coping strategies help to manage emotions that may be related to the stressor, rather than actually reducing or eliminating the event causing the stress.

Eye movement desensitization and reprocessing (EMDR) incorporates eye movements and other rhythmic stimulation such as tapping while focusing on a traumatic memory to reduce the intensity of the memory and emotional connection of the memory.

Generalized anxiety disorder (GAD) is excessive and uncontrollable worry about a variety of things in life, such as going to school, taking tests, learning to drive, doing a job, and interacting with other people.

Hallucinations are intense perceptions of something that no one else can perceive.

High betrayal refers to victimization from violence enacted by someone close to you.

Institutional race-related stress refers to systematic limits to rights, privileges, and access to opportunities, including food, safety, health care, education, jobs, and housing, that limit individuals' ability to achieve upward mobility.

Interpersonal psychotherapy helps individuals to explore the details of their interactions with significant others in their lives, including the therapist, and possible environmental experiences that may affect their thinking and behavior.

Intrusion symptoms include reoccurring thoughts that are involuntary and relate to a traumatic event.

Major depressive disorder (MDD) is diagnosed when a person experiences five or more symptoms for a two-week period. The person must exhibit a change in prior functioning, and a minimum of one symptom must be depressed mood or loss of interest or pleasure.

Mental disorders are clinically significant disturbances in an individual's cognition, emotional regulation, or behavior.

Mental health refers to an individuals' well-being. It allows them to be able to manage stressors, meet their goals, learn, work, and participate in their community.

Mindfulness is a technique that helps individuals become more aware of their thoughts, feelings, and the external environment, and learn how to control automatic responses to internal and external experiences without automatic negative responses such as stress.

Minor depression is less severe than major depression and dysthymia, and symptoms do not last long.

Negative alteration in mood refers to persistent and distorted beliefs that are negative about the individual or the world.

Neurodegeneration refers to the damage and death of a neuron.

Panic disorder is an anxiety disorder that includes recurring and unexpected panic attacks that can cause sudden periods of very intense fear. Individuals may sweat or shake, and experience shortness of breath or even numbness.

A **phobia** is an anxiety disorder characterized by irrational, unrealistic, and excessive fear of a specific object or situation.

Post-traumatic stress disorder (PTSD) is a mental health disorder that is caused by witnessing or experiencing something traumatic. It is diagnosed when an individual experiences stressors, intrusion symptoms, avoidance, negative alterations in mood, and arousal/reactivity for more than one month.

Primary appraisal involves an individual determining if a stressor may affect their well-being – for example, by asking, "Is the stressor a threat to me or a challenge towards improving myself?"

Problem-focused coping strategies help to change a stressful situation and reduce or eliminate the stressor.

Psychotic disorder refers to psychopathology in one or more of five domains, including delusions, hallucinations, disorganized thoughts or language, disorganized or unusual motor behaviors, and expressing no emotion.

Resilience involves successfully adapting to life experiences that may be difficult or to adverse events, and requires the ability to adapt and be flexible in order to deal with demands.

Schizophrenia is a psychotic disorder that is characterized by delusions, hallucinations, and disorganized speech.

Secondary appraisal involves individuals determining if available resources will help them to deal with the stressor.

Stress sensitization refers to exposure to adverse conditions in childhood that may elevate an individual's risk for mental health problems in adulthood.

A **stressor** is a real or threatening experience, such as an injury or assault, that an individual is exposed to. It is considered an external event that creates demands on an individual that could activate stress responses.

Substance abuse is a pattern of substance use that leads to a clinically relevant amount of impairment by within a 12-month time period.

Substance dependence is a pattern of substance use that harms or can harm the individual, results in significant amounts of damage or distress, and causes the individual to exhibit three or more specific symptoms during a 12-month period.

Substance use disorders (SUDs) are diagnosed when individuals experience cognitive, behavioral, and physiological effects as a result of taking a substance. They are defined by specific criteria, including drug cravings, inability to reduce drug use, increased use of drug beyond intended amount, and continually using the drug regardless of negative outcomes.

Tai chi is a practice that involves learning to connect your mind and body and to slow down your mind and your body through the repetition of rhythmic specific workouts that include breathing techniques, aspects of martial arts, and meditation.

Tau tangles are created when the protein tau appears in an unusual form, accumulating inside the neuron. They block the movement of nutrients needed for normal function of neurons and this harms communication with other neurons.

Tolerance is when an individual is no longer as sensitive to a substance and must consume greater amounts of the substance in order for it to have the desired effect.

The **transactional model of stress and coping** includes a person's appraisal of stressors and the techniques of coping they use to respond to the stressors.

A **transdiagnostic intervention** targets common aspects of multiple co-occurring illnesses, requiring a combination of treatment approaches.

Well-being is a positive state that encompasses a person's quality of life and ability to contribute to society, allowing for both meaning and purpose.

Withdrawal symptoms occur when a person suddenly stops taking a drug. They can include anxiety, tremors (known as "the shakes"), nausea, hallucinations, and seizures.

Note

1 You can access the most recent data portal from WHO online (https://www.who.int/Data/Gho/Data/Major-Themes/Health-and-Well-Being), which also provides access to public health information on mental health.

10 The Impact of Changing Health Conditions in Later Life

Learning Outcomes

Define chronic illness and describe the physical and emotional symptoms that chronically ill patients often experience.

Identify the factors that influence coping with chronic illness.

Explain the factors that influence development and management of disease over time.

Describe treatment seeking and how patient–practitioner relations influence medical management.

Identify the different options for managing medical conditions through changes in living arrangements in later life.

Figure 10.1 An older person with chronic illness.
Source: Shutterstock.

DOI: 10.4324/9781003483809-10

Activity

Marnee Lee is a middle-aged single mother of three emerging adult children. They live in the same neighborhood as Marnee's aging mother, Fumiko. Fumiko is now in her 80s and is in frail health with mobility issues due to severe arthritis, lingering respiratory issues after a bout of COVID-19, moderate age-related hearing loss that she refuses to wear hearing aids for, and signs of worsening dementia. Marnee and her children are active caregivers for Fumiko. The children joke about how gross it is that their grandma has condiments in the refrigerator that have a "best by" date of 2005! Marnee is concerned because when the home health aide arrived yesterday morning she found Fumiko still asleep, her pillow was covered with dried blood, and there was a large gash on Fumiko's head. Although she was otherwise fine, Fumiko had no recollection of what might have happened in the night to cause the injury. Today Marnee has spoken to her children and her siblings, and everyone agrees that it is no longer safe for Fumiko to live independently in her home. So, what are their choices? Given Fumiko's various progressive chronic conditions Marnee and her family have several options. But whatever they choose Marnee knows that the changes will be hard on her mother, and the stress of the transition will affect them all.

What impact do you think these changes will have on Fumiko? What impact do you think these changes will have on Marnee and her children? How would you feel if you had to make a decision about moving a family member into a residential care setting?

In this chapter we will consider what it is like to live with **chronic illness** in adulthood. We will explore the impact of chronic illness on the patient and their family and how illness trajectories unfold over time and into later life. We will think about how we relate to health care professionals and models of care for illness management in the later years.

Chronic Illness

When you have a cold, an upset stomach, or a headache, you may feel dreadful in the moment, but you know from experience that you will likely feel better soon. As we learned in Chapter 5, acute illnesses may be intense and serious, and they may cause pain and disability, but they are often curable and of limited duration – in other words, they go away. On the other hand, chronic illnesses are conditions that, once you have them, are not curable and may last the rest of your life, requiring medical management and creating significant life changes, stress, and discomfort.

The Impact of Chronic Illness

The impact of chronic conditions can be vast and affect many domains of a person's life, from physical health to work and social life to emotional health, well-being, and **quality of life**. They can cause pain, fatigue, mobility and functional limitations, distress, anxiety and depression, social isolation, reduced capacity to work leading to financial strain; and they can take a toll on the patient, their family and caregivers.

Many people live with chronic conditions such as hearing and visual impairments, mobility and perceptual impairments, and emotional and intellectual impairments. Often these conditions lead to disability. There are also many types of chronic illnesses, including cardiovascular disease (CVD), diabetes, arthritis, Alzheimer's (AD) and Parkinson's diseases (PD), amyotrophic lateral sclerosis (called ALS or Lou Gehrig's disease), multiple sclerosis, asthma, cystic fibrosis, some types of cancers, eating disorders, and osteoporosis (to mention just a few). Although there is great variability in what is considered a chronic condition (specifically, in the amount of time that someone must live with a condition for it to be considered "chronic"), here we will adopt the Centers for Disease Control and Prevention definition that chronic conditions are conditions that last one year or longer and often require ongoing medical attention (Centers for Disease Control [CDC], 2025).

People can be born with conditions (such as genetic hearing impairment, autism, blindness) or they can develop a condition at some point in their lifespan. For example, polycystic ovary syndrome (PCOS), a condition that stems from hormonal imbalance, menstrual irregularities, and the development of cysts on the ovaries, is usually diagnosed during puberty. But PCOS can cause infertility later in life, and increased risk of diabetes or metabolic syndrome in midlife. Many chronic illnesses emerge in mid and later life, such as CVD, AD, and PD. Regardless of when they emerge, whether they are stable or characterized by periods of remission or a progressive trajectory, living with a chronic condition places a tremendous amount of stress on a person and their loved ones. Living with disability associated with chronic conditions is one of the understudied areas of adult development and aging.

The Global Burden of Chronic Illness

Chronic illnesses are also a global health challenge – perhaps the greatest health challenge we face today. Diseases like diabetes, cancer, heart disease, and stroke are the major causes of morbidity and mortality worldwide (Hacker, 2024; Murphy et al., 2024). By 2030, the estimated cost of chronic illness will reach $47 trillion globally. It is important to note that in the recent past, COVID-19 and diseases of despair (Ahmad et al., 2023; Cohen, 2018) such as drug overdose, suicide, excessive alcohol use) have significantly negatively impacted the lives of Americans (Hacker, 2024). Nevertheless, chronic illnesses are the leading causes of death in the United States and around the world (Ahmad et al., 2023; World Health Organization [WHO], 2024d). Even within the context of the COVID-19 pandemic, 40% of all deaths in the United States in 2022 were attributed to heart disease and cancer, and COVID-19 was a risk factor that elevated deaths from those chronic conditions (Hacker, 2024).

The most recent global data from 2021 shows the top 10 leading causes of death (see Figure 10.2). In terms of lives lost, the top three disease categories are CVD (including ischaemic heart disease and stroke), which accounts for

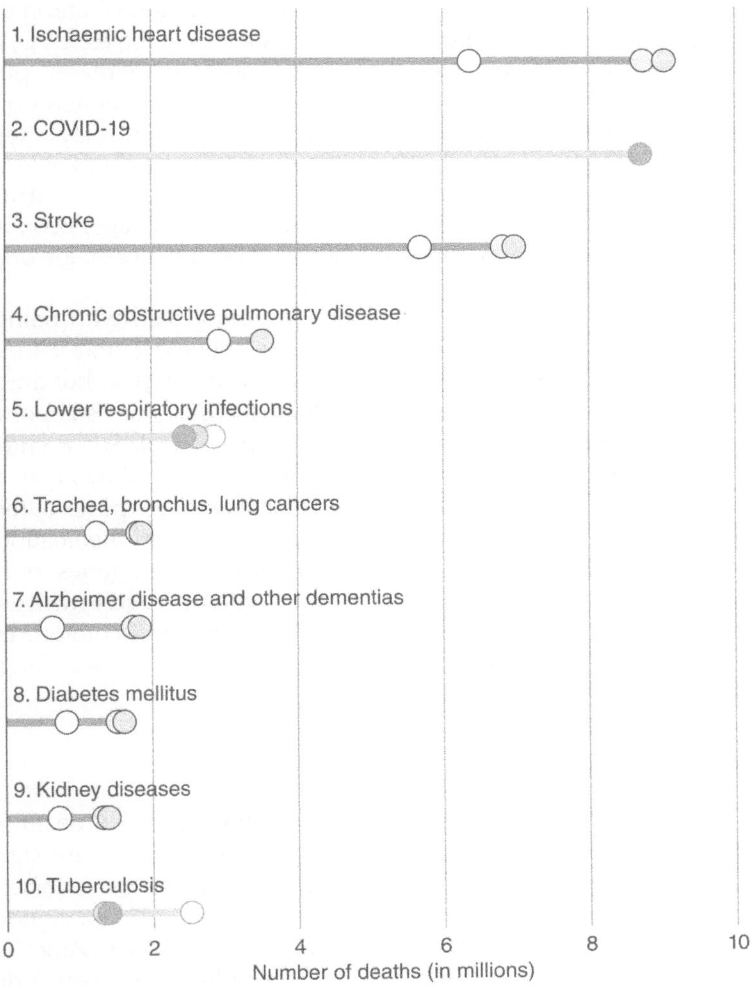

Figure 10.2 Leading causes of death in 2021 globally.
Source: World Health Organization.

13% of deaths worldwide, respiratory diseases (including COVID-19, chronic obstructive pulmonary disease and other respiratory infections), and AD and dementias, which account for 68% of deaths globally. The burden of chronic illness is apparent in the statistic showing that 60% of all Americans have at least one chronic condition, and 40% have multiple chronic conditions – and this proportion increases with age (CDC, 2025). The National Council on Aging shows that 94.9% of adults over age 60 have at least one condition, while 78.7% have two or more. (National Council on Aging, 2022). This is due, as we saw in Chapter 1, to an increasing population of older adults, who are living longer than ever before.

What is striking when you think about the global burden of chronic illness is that many preventable chronic conditions such as diabetes, CVD, and cancer are modifiable through lifestyle changes, such as increased physical activity, improved nutrition, reduced alcohol use, and elimination of tobacco. Adverse childhood experiences, poverty, and stress all play roles as well (Bauer et al., 2014; Borja et al., 2019). Physiological, psychological, and sociocultural factors can influence the risks and trajectory of illness and affect how people cope with conditions. These factors include sex, age, economic stability, ethnicity, and religion. A biopsychosocial perspective helps understand the impact of chronic illness on a person's life.

On a personal level, the pain and discomfort associated with being ill can vary by disease. Some chronic conditions are noticeable and felt every day, such as chronic back pain. Others may not cause any pain but are still dangerous, such as high cholesterol, high blood pressure, or osteoporosis. The trajectory over time of chronic illness can vary as well. Some chronic conditions are marked by long periods of stability, interrupted by acute episodes or flare-ups. Others are progressive, and each new stage poses different challenges. Some diseases require self-management through medication or lifestyle changes, while others require repeated treatments, surgeries, or hospitalizations. There may also be differences in the intensity and invasiveness of treatments, and these treatments may themselves create discomfort. Even the same disease may not be experienced in the same way by two different patients (Frazier, 2025).

Health Disparities in Chronic Illness

Both the prevalence of chronic illness and the leading causes of death vary as a function of sociodemographic factors. For example, there are significantly higher rates of chronic kidney disease among African Americans compared to other groups in the United States (Lissanu et al., 2019). Although the prevalence of early-stage kidney disease is similar for African Americans and Whites, African Americans reach the threshold of life-threatening kidney failure more quickly than Whites do (Lissanu et al., 2019). Why? While it is the case that many African American kidney patients are more likely to have comorbid chronic conditions, such as obesity, diabetes, and hypertension, which put them at greater risk for severe kidney disease, they are also more likely to encounter socioeconomic obstacles to receiving medical care and social support, making self-care and disease management more problematic (Lissanu et al., 2019). These biopsychosocial factors all come together to create a significant health disparity.

Health disparities also adversely affect other racioethnic groups in the United States. For example, in the Latinx population there are higher rates of childhood obesity, adult diabetes, advanced and terminal cancers, and suicide attempts compared to non-Latinx groups (Ramírez Garcia, 2019). These disparities can be attributed to social determinants of health, such as economic and social resources, living conditions, social context, and cultural beliefs (Ramírez Garcia, 2019). Among all minority populations, health inequities increase vulnerability to both acute and chronic illnesses.

From a biopsychosocial perspective health disparities can be, in part, attributed to economic disadvantage. Despite the Affordable Care Act (ACA), Americans with low income or who live with poverty are likely not to have health insurance. Although people without the financial resources for medical care can use free clinics that provide medical services for little or no expense, not everyone in need of this care can access it (Frazier, 2025). For residents of rural communities, where lower incomes are combined with distance from resources, visiting a clinic may be extremely challenging (Theeke et al., 2019). Additionally, low socioeconomic status (SES) and financial insecurity are associated with higher levels of stressful experiences, such as instability in work, divorce, death of a child, and threat or experience of violence (Cohen et al., 2019). Like dominos, the experience of one stressor can lead to another (Cohen et al., 2019), and the more stressors a person experiences, the more vulnerable that person becomes to chronic illness.

In order to understand the challenges faced by people across the adult lifespan we must understand how social determinants and health disparities impact the experience of chronic illness. Biopsychosocial factors also influence the development, progression, and mortality of chronic and terminal conditions. The first step in addressing these disparities is to understand them.

Emotional Responses to Chronic Illness

No matter how old you are, having a chronic illness can set off a cascade of physical and emotional changes. Finding a way to manage the emotions associated with living with a chronic condition is key to managing the illness. While many conditions cannot be cured, the stress, depression, and anxiety related to illness can be addressed. For most people, a diagnosis of a chronic condition comes after the experience of symptoms, various doctors' visits, medical tests, and often a prolonged period of not knowing what is wrong. And once a patient has been given a diagnosis, new and different kinds of stressors emerge. Receiving a diagnosis is likely to lead to a flood of emotions: grief, shame, guilt, emptiness, loneliness, and sadness (Stanton

& Revenson, 2013). According to Frazier (2025) a common first reaction is shock and there may be a sense of disbelief and disconnection from the situation. However, if feelings of shock do not give way to reality, the patient cannot begin to cope with the diagnosis. Although chronic conditions unfold differently for each person and their impact varies from person to person, for many people, in addition to the physical pain and symptoms of illness, they may face relationship strains, possible loss of employment, and serious financial burden. People who have already experienced a lot of stressful life events or who have a history of depression can be at risk for greater distress upon diagnosis (Cohen et al., 2019).

Stress may have both direct and indirect impacts on aging, health, and chronic illness. Stress directly increases the risk of developing a chronic condition, the progression and severity of symptoms, and, ultimately, mortality associated with the condition. Poor emotional regulation, anxiety, fear, and depression may contribute to both stress and chronic illness. Stress may not cause disease – but it may weaken the immune system, create inflammation, and disrupt the balance of gut microbiota, all of which make the development of a chronic condition more likely. But living with a chronic illness is also stressful. Stressful experiences that are a threat to a person's sense of self, competence, and social status – such as being diagnosed with or living with chronic illness – are especially "costly" in terms of negative health outcomes (Cohen et al., 2016; Frazier, 2025). Over 70 years of research shows the association between stressful life events, perceived stress, and subsequent chronic illness (Cohen et al., 2019).

Figure 10.3 In the context of chronic illness, anxiety and depression may be a reaction to the illness or a co-morbid symptom of it.

Source: Shutterstock.

Depression and Anxiety

Depression and anxiety are common emotional responses to chronic illness. In patients with rare chronic conditions, 42% reported moderate to severe depression and 23% reported regularly experiencing anxiety (Uhlenbusch et al., 2019). Chronic illness can be associated with depression in two ways: illness can involve neurochemical and structural changes in the brain and/or deficiencies in the immune system, all of which can trigger depression (Liew, 2012); and the pain, physical limitations, loss of independence and sense of self, feelings of helplessness, and interpersonal difficulties in living with illness can also lead to depression (Friedman, Lyness, Delavan, Li, & Barker, 2008; Liew, 2012). Diagnosing depression in patients with chronic illness is hard because depression may be mistaken for a normal reaction to living with chronic illness, and symptoms such as fatigue, lack of appetite, or malaise can be seen as part of the illness itself. Patients themselves may not realize they are depressed because they are more focused on their physical health.

Sometimes negative emotions are a reaction to the illness, but sometimes they are **comorbid symptoms**: they exist alongside the illness and interact with it. In other words, chronic illness may cause depression, and depression may exacerbate chronic illness (Clarke & Currie, 2009). Each one can exacerbate the other. For example, depression is a common symptom of PD and it may result from the neurological changes caused by the disease as much as from the impact of the disease on the patient's life. Depression may lessen as the patient learns to cope with and adapt to the illness. Or it may appear intermittently in response to changes in symptoms, prognosis, or treatments. For instance, someone with PD may experience bouts of depression with each new loss of motor function (Frazier, 2002; 2025).

Feelings of Loss

Chronic illness is often associated with feelings of loss – loss of identity, self-esteem and self-confidence, goals, activities, social connections, sleep, independence, and more (Carel, 2017; Frazier, 2000; 2002; Frazier et al., 2003; Frazier & Hooker, 2006; Frazier et al., 2000; Frazier et al., 2002; Turvey & Klein, 2008). These feelings may fluctuate from day to day, depending on levels of pain and discomfort, visits to the doctor, changes in symptoms or changes to medications and treatments, as well as perceived competence at managing the illness. People living with HIV, for example, often report a loss of their very sense of self (Golub et al., 2013), which has a significant impact on perceptions of illness and health. This loss can worsen depression and lower quality of life. Although these emotions are a normal reaction to living with chronic illness, managing them is challenging all the same. People respond to these challenges in many different ways, depending on their personal, social, and economic resources.

Figure 10.4 Adjusting to changes brought on by chronic illness can be akin to riding an emotional roller coaster of stress, depression, and anxiety. Fortunately, adaptation to any condition is possible.

Source: Shutterstock.

Chronic illness has the potential to create dramatic changes in the lives of patients and their families (de Ridder et al., 2008), affecting sense of self, work, productivity, economic stability, and social networks. The sense of loss stemming from chronic illness can take two forms. **Clear loss** is the sense of loss associated with tangible changes, such as the loss of mobility, eyesight, or motor abilities. **Ambiguous loss** is the sense of uncertainty that chronic illness causes, such as a lack of clarity about the course of the illness or fluctuating pain levels and capabilities (Boss & Couden, 2002).

Coping Along the Trajectory of Chronic Illness

As we keep learning, there is a lot of variability in how people adjust to living with chronic illness. Some patients will shift from the initial shock of diagnosis to denial. Some may become paralyzed at the prospect of a lifelong illness and refuse to accept the diagnosis: "This can't be true." Others may simply withdraw. These emotional reactions may provide a protective buffer while the person is still not ready to accept their situation. However, these responses can also stand in the way of coping with inevitable stress, depression, anxiety, and feelings of loss, or of getting needed medical treatment (Frazier, 2002; Golub et al., 2014; Stanton & Revenson, 2013).

Ambiguity, or not knowing what to expect, causes the greatest distress (Dunkel-Schetter et al., 1992; Frazier, 2002). After that comes fear of future physical limitations and loss of functioning (Dunkel-Schetter et al., 1992; Frazier, 2002), fear of pain, fear of lifestyle changes, and fear of other forms of clear loss. Fortunately, active, problem-focused strategies can help patients cope more effectively, develop a sense of self-efficacy, and live a fuller life.

How do people cope with living with chronic illness? Generally speaking, chronically ill patients are less likely than others to adopt active, problem-focused coping strategies. That is because there may be little that they can control. The best approach is, then, to focus on managing emotions (Frazier, 2002; 2025). When people cope through avoidance, distractions, or withdrawal they tend to experience greater distress, more problematic symptoms, poorer adjustment, and a poorer prognosis. In contrast, when patients perceive a strong sense of control over their lives despite their illness, they are more likely to cope better.

When the stress of chronic illness relates to physical problems, a problem-focused strategy is especially beneficial. For an 80-year-old woman with balance issues after a stroke, using a walker might help. When the stress of living with chronic illness is emotional, managing those emotions is key; a weekly support group can help by inviting patients to share their experiences of their disease. Some patients can avoid feeling like victims by making their illness part of their sense of self (Frazier, 2002). They may not be able to change the prognosis, but they can still find a way to accept and even master it. Sometimes just remembering that each day brings a new morning can provide a sense of optimism.

Adjusting to life with chronic illness requires flexibility (Cheng et al., 2014). When patients tailor their coping to the situation, they can face it better. This is true for patients with PD (Frazier, 2002). The symptoms of PD include physical impairments (shaking, tremors, and difficulty writing, walking, brushing teeth, or chewing food), emotional impairments (loneliness, anxiety, depression, or fear of the future), and social impairments (less social engagement, smaller social networks, or fewer opportunities to socialize). When patients with PD match their coping strategies to the type of stressor, they have a greater sense of well-being.

A Parkinson's patient who had been a dancer and dance instructor, for example, felt distress in simply rising from a chair and walking across the room. She was able to rise to a standing position, but that first step was torture: she felt paralyzed. One day, as she rose from the chair, her husband took her arms, placed one on his shoulder and the other on his waist, and asked her to dance. Much to their amazement, they waltzed easily across the room. Obviously, she could not waltz everywhere. Still, whenever she wanted to walk, she focused on making her first few steps fluid and dance-like, and she was able to get where she needed to go without freezing or tremors. She had found a creative way of coping.

For some, adjusting to life with a chronic illness can be similar to living with post-traumatic stress (Hefferon et al., 2009). For others, the stress, depression, and anxiety will abate. Patients may even come to see the experience of illness as a positive influence on their lives – an effect sometimes called post-traumatic growth (Carver, 1998; Golub et al., 2013; Nolen-Hoeksema & Davis, 2004). In one study of arthritis patients, those who had social support and a sense of spirituality were more likely to transition from feelings of trauma to post-traumatic growth (Sörensen et al., 2021). It may seem surprising that resilience and other positive outcomes can result from negative health situations, as we will explore in Chapter 12.

Human beings are resourceful, and most find a way to adapt to their illness. **Adaptation** is the process of coming to terms with and adjusting to illness. Clearly, adaptation depends on effective coping strategies, good medical care and self-care, and a supportive and understanding family and social network. Adaptation can help the patient maintain their lifestyle and functional abilities in the face of progressing disease and changing symptoms. It also helps to preserve a positive mind-set and to avoid distress (Stanton et al., 2007). We will explore adaptation further in Chapter 12.

Quality of Life

At any point in the human lifespan a person can sense that they are living life to the fullest, or not. If one feels that in most domains of their lives, things are good, we can say that they have quality of life. Quality of life is one of the measures of the impact of living with chronic conditions and one of the barometers of aging well. Quality of life has been traditionally linked to health and, in the past, was primarily assessed by physicians. A person was assumed to have high quality of life if they were free of disease and low quality of life if they had a disease, with no grey area in between. However, a biopsychosocial approach can be used to understand which aspects of a person's life are most at risk in the face of aging, disease, disability, and death.

Quality of life refers to the degree of satisfaction that people feel for their lives. Domains of quality of life include intimacy and relationships, work, school, leisure activities, hobbies, intellectual growth, how bodies feel, what people are capable of doing, and goals for the future. Finding the right balance among all of these domains of life gives rise to an overall quality of life. WHO defines quality of life as individuals' perception of their lives within the context of the culture and value systems in which they live, and in relation to societal expectations, standards, concerns, and goals (Saxena et al., 1997). The different components of quality of life are presented in Table 10.1.

Of course, people can feel differently about different aspects of their lives. You might think, "My relationship with my adult children makes my life rich and satisfying" – and, at the same time, be thinking, "I hate my dead-end job." You may be thinking "I am so happy with where I am in life now" but "the global problems of the world today distress me so greatly." These factors also affect one another. For example, illness influences not just our physical self, but our emotional, social, and spiritual selves as well.

Table 10.1 Facets of quality of life

Physical	Energy and fatigue
	Pain and discomfort
	Sleep and rest
Psychological	Body image and appearance
	Negative feelings
	Positive feelings
	Self-esteem
	Thinking, learning, memory, and concentration
Level of independence	Mobility
	Activities of daily living (ADL)
	Dependence on medical substances and medical aids
	Work capacity
Social relationships	Personal relationships
	Social support
	Sexual activity
Environment	Financial resources
	Freedom, physical safety, and security
	Health and social care (accessibility and quality)
	Home environment
	Opportunities for acquiring new information and skills
	Participation in and opportunities for recreation and leisure
	Physical environment (pollution, noise, traffic, climate)
	Transport
Spirituality	Religion
	Spirituality
	Personal beliefs

Source: WHO (1997).

In the context of acute illness, medical professionals focus on minimizing impairment and finding a cure. In the context of chronic conditions that cannot be cured, the goal is to preserve **health-related quality of life**. Health-related quality of life focuses on physical functioning, emotional well-being, fatigue, social functioning, pain, any limitations due to health-related problems, and overall health (Ahlström & Sjöden, 1996; Koplas et al., 1999; Lawton, 1991; Stewart et al., 1988). Like quality of life in general, it relies on the patient's self-assessment of how they feel about their lived experiences.

One of the most widely used health-related quality of life assessment tools is the Rand Health Survey. This questionnaire was developed to measure self-reported health-related quality of life in eight health domains: physical functioning, bodily pain, role limitations due to physical health, role limitations due to emotional problems, social functioning, mental health, vitality, and general health perceptions. In essence, it is a measure of the burden of disease (Ware, 2000). Below are some examples of the questions on the 20-item Rand Short Form.

Examples of Questions in the Rand Health Survey

Patients are asked to choose one option for each questionnaire option.

1. In general, would you say your health is:

1 Excellent
2 Very good
3 Good
4 Fair
5 Poor

2. For how long (if at all) has your **health limited you** in **each** of the following activities?

	Limited for more than 3 months	Limited for 3 months or less	Not limited at all
a. The kinds or amounts of **vigorous** activities you can do, like lifting heavy objects, running or participating in strenuous sports	1	2	3
b. The kinds or amounts of **moderate** activities you can do, like moving a table, carrying groceries, or bowling	1	2	3
c. Walking uphill or climbing a few flights of stairs	1	2	3
d. Bending, lifting, or stooping	1	2	3
e. Walking one block	1	2	3
f. Eating, dressing, bathing, or using the toilet	1	2	3

3. How much **bodily** pain have you had **during the past 4 weeks**?

1 None
2 Very mild
3 Mild
4 Moderate
5 Severe
6 Very severe

4. Does your health **keep** you from working at a job, doing work around the house, or going to school?

1 YES, for more than 3 months
2 YES, for 3 months or less
3 NO

5. Have you been unable to do **certain kinds or amounts** of work, housework, or schoolwork because of your health?

1 YES, for more than 3 months
2 YES, for 3 months or less
3 NO

For **each** of the following questions, please mark the circle for the **one** answer that comes **closest** to the way you have been feeling **during the past month**.

	All of the time	Most of the time	A good bit of the time	Some of the time	A little of the time	None of the time
6. How much of the time, during the past month, has your **health limited your social activities** (like visiting with friends or close relatives)?	1	2	3	4	5	6
7. How much of the time, during the past month, have you been a **very nervous person**?	1	2	3	4	5	6
8. How much of the time, during the past month, have you felt **calm and peaceful**?	1	2	3	4	5	6
9. How much of the time, during the past month, have you felt **downhearted and blue**?	1	2	3	4	5	6

10. How much of the time, during the past month, have you been a **happy person**?	1	2	3	4	5	6
11. How often, during the past month, have you felt so **down in the dumps that nothing could cheer you up**?	1	2	3	4	5	6

12. Please mark the circle that **best** describes whether **each** of the following statements is **true** or **false** for you.

	Definitely true	Mostly true	Not sure	Mostly false	Definitely false
a. I am somewhat ill	1	2	3	4	5
b. I am as healthy as anybody I know	1	2	3	4	5
c. My health is excellent	1	2	3	4	5
d. I have been feeling bad lately	1	2	3	4	5

As we age our perceptions of our quality of life change and the emphasis on preserving health becomes more important. If you ask older people who have lost family and friends to illness – and who may have a chronic illness themselves – they will tell you, "If you don't have your health, you don't have anything." They may mention how a diagnosis of cancer or heart disease or diabetes was a "wake-up call" – a call to eat healthier and get more exercise. They know the importance of how they feel each and every day.

Because anxiety and depression are three times more common in patients with chronic illness, cultivating good mental health is especially important for maintaining quality of life (National Collaborating Centre for Mental Health [U.K.], 2010). As the stages of illness progress, preserving patients' independence becomes paramount. Many patients' greatest fears for the future are that they will become dependent on others (Frazier, 2002). From driving to feeding to dressing, most patients want to be able to perform daily tasks on their own. However, for many older adults and their families there may come a time when they can no longer manage their illnesses by themselves, at home, and the time comes to consider available options.

Care Options and Living Arrangements in Later Life

If there came a time when you could no longer manage your illness by yourself, and you needed more help than your spouse or family could provide, where would you like to live and what kind of care would you like to receive? Many adults never think about these things until the day comes when they are face-to-face with making these difficult decisions for their aging parents, their loved ones, or themselves. Interestingly, some people who have experience of watching a family member or friend navigate these age-related challenges, may start to think about how they would like to live in their later years well before a health crisis happens.

Consider these two scenarios. Beth and Ben are in their late 70s and both have some significant chronic conditions that are likely to worsen with time. They have been overseeing the care for Ben's sister who is now living in a skilled nursing facility due to her mobility issues. Experiencing her health, living, and financial transitions and anticipating their future health needs, they have decided to be proactive and have sold their home to move into an independent living unit at a continuing care retirement community. Buying into this community means that when they can no longer live independently, they can easily move to an apartment in another wing that provides more daily caregiving and medical care. But for now, they can enjoy the vast array of activities that the community offers for seniors. They are happy having made this decision and relieved that their future is planned for. Joan and Jack are also in their late 70s. Jack has mobility issues and vascular dementia, and Joan is developing signs of AD. They have a lovely home and do not want to have to ever leave it. As their illnesses progress, there are lots of conflicts, but their children persevere and hire home health aides to come to their home and help cook and clean and keep an eye on them, and they install cameras to monitor them at night when there is no caregiver coverage. Of course there are health scares, falls, and trips to the emergency room, but they are able to maintain this lifestyle for many years until both Joan and Jack get COVID-19. Once they get COVID-19, the home health agencies can no longer provide caregivers. Jack is hospitalized, develops pneumonia, and dies within a few weeks. Joan, who is very ill and whose dementia progresses rapidly as a result of COVID-19, remains at home and is cared for by her daughter. Joan's children decide to move her to an assisted living facility as soon as she is well enough. It is very traumatic for everyone. However, round the clock supervision, prepared meals and activities, and on-site medical care are provided, and Joan eventually adjusts to this new living arrangement.

Obviously, there are many ways that aging, health, and living arrangements can play out in the later years. Of the many factors that people consider when thinking about these things, maintaining a person's quality of life is often at the top of the list. Considering what steps to take is often fraught for the older individual themselves and their loved ones. Planning for the future and having the resources to support the desired lifestyle are critical.

The Psychological Impact of Changes in Living Arrangements in Later Life

One of the most critical considerations when contemplating changes in living arrangements in later life is the concept of the "goodness of fit" between the older person's situation and needs and the home environment (Hays, 2002). The older person's physical and social environment within the household can either inhibit or promote the prevention of health crises and maintenance of health and quality of life (Hays, 2002). Moreover, although most people choose their living situation based upon their physical and social needs while considering the resources they have at their disposal, for many older adults these decisions are often made during challenging health difficulties when their physical and medical needs escalate as their socioeconomic resources diminish (Hays, 2002). This was the case for Joan and Jack, in the example above, who wanted desperately to "age in place," that is, to grow old and die in their own home.

Aging in place is the primary goal of most aging adults and most older adults want to remain living in their homes as they age (Farber et al. 2011). In 2022, 88% of older adults reported that it was important to them to continue living safely in their homes for as long as possible (National Poll on Healthy Aging, 2022). An older study (McAuley & Blieszner, 1985) asked people what they would prefer if they "became sick or disabled for a long time" (p. 189) and receiving care in their own home from a family member (66%) or a paid caregiver (70%) were the most frequently chosen answers. Less than 30% of the sample selected nursing home care as a desirable option. Across ranges of in-home care options, and variability in level of physical limitations and disability, people want to age at home (Kasper et al., 2019). Kasper and colleagues (2019) found that the majority of older adults still prefer aging in place but close to one-third chose assisted living or continuing care retirement communities, which suggests that people are beginning to appreciate other options for their later years.

To some extent, aging in place often means living alone. Keep in mind that in 2022, those who were aged 65 had an average life expectancy of approximately 19 more years (20.2 for women and 17.5 for men). In 2023 68% of older men were married whereas only 47% of older women were married; and 29% of all older women were widows. There are still three times as many women who are widows (9 million) than men who are widowers (2.9 million). Similarly, approximately 16% of older people were divorced/separated or had never married in 2023. Although aging in place is the preference of most people, there are some concerns about the mental and physical well-being of older adults who live alone. According to a recent U.S. Census Bureau Report, approximately 1 in 10 young adults (between the ages of 18–34) and 3 in 10 older adults (over the age of 65) lived alone in 2022 (Hemez et al., 2024).

Age and sex interact with living arrangements in later life. Specifically, approximately 27% of women aged 65–74, and 43% of women over the age of 75 live alone, compared to 21% of men aged 65–74 and 24% of men over the age of 75. More men across the later years have the benefit of living with a spouse compared to age-matched women. Taken together that is nearly one third of all seniors living by themselves. This is a concern not only for long-term health problems and quality of life, but for risk of isolation and loneliness. Research shows that isolation and feelings of loneliness can negatively impact health for older adults. One study showed that older adults who experienced loneliness or isolation had significantly higher risks of disability, and those who reported feeling both isolated and lonely were at the greatest risk (Shimada et al., 2025). A study carried out in 2020 during the COVID-19 pandemic found that 56% of seniors said that they felt isolated (Piette et al., 2023). Social isolation can lead to poor health habits such as smoking, drinking in excess, poor diet, and little physical activity (American Psychological Association [APA], 2020). Balanced diets are often a challenge for seniors living alone, in part because of loss of appetite, sometimes due to the side effects of medications or age- or illness-related physical changes, but financial challenges also pose a threat. Stress results from loneliness and researchers have found that levels of stress and blood pressure are significantly higher in older people who report loneliness (Cacioppo et al., 2015). Loneliness has also been found to increase the rate of cognitive decline and elevate the risks of AD (Bennett et al., 2012).

Some other concerns for those living at home are unexpected medical events, accidents, and declines in health, which can sometimes make living independently at home a challenge. Falls are the leading cause of injury among older adults. Data from 2018 showed that 28% of adults aged 65 years and older reported at least one fall in the past year (35.6 million falls), and 10% reported a fall-related injury (8.4 million fall-related injuries) (Moreland et al., 2020). While falls are not often fatal, the older one is the higher the risk of a fatality, and there has been an increase in deaths due to falls in people over the age of 85 (James et al., 2020). Many older adults have difficulty with at least one area of functioning that may affect their ability to live independently, yet, only 10% of U.S. homes are set up to accommodate an older person's physical needs. Specifically, 21% of seniors have difficulty with mobility (walking or climbing stairs), 6% are blind or have serious difficulty seeing (even if wearing glasses), and 7% have difficulty with self-care (bathing or dressing). Given that many older adults plan to remain in their homes as they age, it is important for older adults and their family members to better understand the preventive measures they can take and the modifications they can make to help improve the safety of their homes.

What factors influence older adults' decisions to relocate in their later years? On the surface, age, gender, household income level, driving status, characteristics of the home, and ability to carry out upkeep in home are all significant factors predicting consideration of relocation (Weeks et al., 2012). Historically, spouses and adult children have provided the most immediate support and caregiving for late life adults (National Academies of Science, Engineering, and Medicine, 2016; Skoblow & Gilligan, 2025). With the growth of options related to traditional nursing home care, trends are changing.

Some of the options within planned elder housing include different types of elder communities and residential care – for example, independent or assisted living in a continuous care community, a nursing home, or other residential care setting.

For those living at home, assistance can be provided by others who live in the home (i.e., family caregivers) or by non-family caregivers who are brought in to provide help with cooking, cleaning, laundry, transportation, supervision of medicines or medical treatments, or companionship. Hiring a home health aide can be expensive but Medicare and long-term care insurance may partially cover these expenses.

Costs of these different options vary by geographic region, levels of required care, whether one has a private or shared room, and training and services provided (including how many additional services are provided – e.g.,

Table 10.2 Types of living arrangements and characteristics associated with them

Type of Living	*Who Might Benefit?*	*What Services are Associated*
Aging in place with home care	People who live at home but need supervision and help with household chores, meal preparation, activities of daily living, transportation	Housekeeping, meal preparation, assistance with medications and ADLs, companionship and supervision
Senior or 55+ apartments	Active, independent, and healthy older adults enjoying their retirement years but who want to be with others their age	Community, grounds maintenance
Independent living within a retirement community	Active, independent, and healthy older adults enjoying their retirement years but who want to live in a community setting	Facilities for activities, games, theatre, social activities, dining; often housekeeping and grounds maintenance are provided
Assisted living	Older adults who can live independently but need assistance with ADLs	Social and fitness programming, healthy dining, transportation assistance, housekeeping, grounds maintenance
Memory care/ Alzheimer's care	Older adults who have some type of dementia or AD	Specialized memory/dementia care and support, special meal preparation, secured environment
Skilled nursing/ Nursing home facilities	Older adults who need 24-hour medical care/ supervision	Provides the highest level of care for patients who need 24/7 medical care
Adult day care	Older adults who desire socialization and require help with meals during work hours	Meals, assistance with ADLs, social activities

beauty salon home treatments, foot care nursing visits). In general, in-home care is the least expensive and skilled nursing facilities are the most expensive.

Aging in place in one's own home may take the form of living independently with minimal need for assistance or supervision from others. Or it may take the form of any level of functional impairment, disability, or poor health that requires caregiving provided by family or home health aides. Independent living communities are an option for active older adults who require little assistance, but who would like to join a senior community. These retirement communities are for people aged 55 or older who want to live in a senior-friendly environment with an easy-to-manage lifestyle and access to amenities and social activities such as a pool, golf course, club house, dining, theatre, gaming, libraries, and social events. Living in this type of community frees one up from home maintenance and often housekeeping and transportation can be arranged. These living accommodations may range from a detached single-family home within a community to a luxury condo or apartment within a building on a campus.

Assisted living refers to a lifestyle and amenities that fall between independent living and supportive nursing care. When an older person no longer feels safe living at home or has significant mobility issues, health concerns or early signs of dementia, assisted living is a good choice. Seniors in assisted living may need a little help with some ADLs (e.g., bathing, supervision of medicines, having meals provided) but do not need constant medical care or supervision. These facilities offer lots of opportunities for social engagement and are a great way to offset loneliness. They also offer daily activities, entertainment, wellness and enrichment classes, local excursions, on-site spas and beauty salons, and transportation. Seniors who live in assisted living will not have to worry about housekeeping, laundry, or home maintenance and they will have access to 24/7 emergency assistance if required.

Memory care units may be stand-alone residential spaces or specific buildings on the campus of a retirement community. They provide dedicated specialized care for seniors with AD and other forms of dementia. Memory care units are designed to provide safe residential settings with 24/7 support from health care providers trained to care for patients with conditions characterized by memory loss. They provide personal care for ADLs, medication management, programs to enhance cognitive functioning, activities that promote sensory experiences, and movement, music, and art classes at a level that is appropriate for dementia patients. Memory units are usually secure units so that dementia patients prone to wandering are safe and cannot hurt themselves.

Skilled nursing facilities are often called nursing homes. Like hospitals, skilled nursing units provide the highest level of medical care and supervision 24/7. When seniors need ongoing daily medical care that cannot be provided through assisted living or home care, skilled nursing is often the best option. They provide meals, health management, and activities. Sometimes skilled nursing units are suited for people recovering from surgery or stroke who are there for short-term rehabilitation, as well as those who need medically complicated long-term care. Skilled nursing facilities have a registered nurse (RN) on staff 24/7, and they often have an in-house medical practitioner, occupational and physical therapy specialists, social workers, and aides. This facility is an option for seniors with chronic or terminal conditions.

Popping up all over the United States are continuing care retirement communities (CCRC). These communities offer access to all levels of care, from independent living to assisted living, to memory care and skilled nursing care, all on the same campus or within the same building. The purpose of these communities is to allow residents to seamlessly transition from one living arrangement to the next, shifting between levels of care as their health needs change with age. Most often people opt in when they want independent living and as their care needs change, their support and services change too.

Adult day care is often an option for older adults living at home with family who do not want to be home alone during the day while their loved ones are at work. Adult day care centers provide activities, supervision, and meals and keep the older person engaged and active.

Although it is not mentioned in Table 10.2, another important type of care is respite care. Respite care is short-term care provided to allow the full-time or primary caregiver to take a break. This is critically important because research shows that caregivers often become ill themselves while providing care for their spouses or loved ones (Frazier & Hooker, 2006). Respite care can offer a temporary relief from the responsibilities of caregiving and allow the caregiver to focus on self-care or stress management, take a vacation, or tend to their own medical and health care needs. Respite care can be provided in the home or in independent, assisted, or skilled nursing settings. Respite caregivers will step in and provide the day-to-day care that the chronically ill care recipient needs so that the primary caregiver can take a break.

Chapter Summary

In this chapter we extended our understanding of chronic health conditions and when health conditions become chronic. We examined the biopsychosocial factors that influence the development and management of disease over time. We also considered psychological conceptions of illness and disease, and how these are affected by aging. We explored how changes in health impact quality of life in all domains, including when functional status necessitates a change in living arrangements. Finally, we discussed factors associated with caregiving for someone with a chronic condition.

Key Takeaways

1 Chronic illness at any point in adulthood is a major life event that causes stress and requires good coping mechanisms.

2 Both well-being and quality of life are important for managing chronic illness over time.
3 When chronic conditions lead to functional impairments that make living independently a challenge, there are living arrangements that can support chronically ill patients in the long term.

Reflective Questions

1 Have you ever had a chronic condition? If yes, how did it impact your life?
2 What contributes to your psychological well-being?
3 How do you think biopsychosocial factors interact to influence your quality of life?

Suggested Readings

Schetter, C. D., Feinstein, L. G., Taylor, S. E., & Falke, R. L. (1992). Patterns of coping with cancer. *Health Psychology*, *11*(2), 79–87.

Skoblow, H. F., & Gilligan, M. (2025). Stressors and resources among adult child caregivers in the presence or absence of siblings. *The Gerontologist*, *65*(3), gnaf006.

Key Terms

Adaptation is the process of coming to terms with and adjusting to illness.

Ambiguous loss is the sense of uncertainty that chronic illness causes – for example, a lack of clarity regarding the course of the illness or fluctuating pain levels and capabilities.

Chronic illnesses are conditions that are not curable and may last an entire life, requiring medical management and creating significant life changes, stress, and discomfort.

Clear loss is the sense of loss associated with tangible changes, such as the loss of mobility, eyesight, or motor abilities.

Comorbid symptoms exist alongside an illness and interact with it.

Health-related quality of life focuses on physical functioning, emotional well-being, fatigue, social functioning, pain, limitations due to health-related problems, and overall health.

Quality of life refers to how satisfied people are with their lives. Domains of quality of life include intimacy and relationships, work, school, leisure activities, hobbies, intellectual growth, how bodies feel, capabilities, and our goals for the future.

11 Terminal Illness, Death, and Bereavement

Learning Outcomes

Describe cardiocirculatory death, brain death, and a persistent vegetative state.

Explain what is meant by "do not resuscitate," cultural differences in the use of do not resuscitate orders, and how other important documents can provide instructions about dying.

Articulate key differences in the death rate in the United States compared to other countries around the globe, and factors involved in death across the lifespan.

Describe developmental differences in views about death across the lifespan, and how culture plays a role in views about death and how we grieve and mourn.

Identify how biological, psychological, and contextual factors are involved in decisions about end-of-life care.

An Introduction to Death and Dying

Activity

Read the true story below and reflect on your own response to the story.

Charlie and Francie Emerick were married for 66 years, and they were in a happy and loving relationship throughout their marriage. By the end of their lives, Francie had a severely weakened heart, and Charlie was living with two life threatening diseases, prostate cancer and Parkinson's disease (PD). They had both been struggling with their diseases for a long time. Francie and Charlie made a choice to exercise some control over their deaths by planning to die together with the use of the **death with dignity** law in their state, Portland,

DOI: 10.4324/9781003483809-11

Oregon. Because of this law, they were able to obtain a medication that could cause their deaths. They died together in their bed on April 20, 2017, after they each took a lethal dose of the medication they obtained. Francie who was 88 years old died within 15 minutes of taking her lethal dose. Charlie who was 87 years old died an hour later after he took his lethal dose. It was reported that they were holding hands at the end of their lives. One of their three grown daughters, Sher Safran, who was 62 years old at the time, stated that her parents had no regrets, and no unfinished business. Being able to end their suffering together in their own way, under their own control, was reported as a comfort to both of them and their daughters.

Write down your reaction to reading this story. How did it make you feel? Were there any concerns you had upon reading the story? If so, what were these concerns?

Views about death and dying vary across cultures and within families. The customs and traditions of an individual's culture and their religious views may affect their perception of the above story (Karumathil & Tripathi, 2022). Some individuals may be happy that the couple made a choice that was right for them and were able to die together. Other individuals may think that the death with dignity law and the choice made by this couple was wrong, something they fundamentally disagree with and would not do. Later in the chapter we will discuss the death with dignity law, and the states within the United States and countries around the world where this law is in place. First, we begin the chapter with a discussion of how death is defined.

Definitions of Death

There are many philosophical debates about what really defines death, including loss of heart and circulatory function and of brain activity. However, there are cases in which someone would be declared dead based on a specific definition but would still be kept in some state of life with the use of machines. There are legal and medical definitions of death (World Health Organization [WHO], 2017), and some differences in terminology reflect the cultures in which those definitions occur and/or the period of the lifespan involved (Adjei et al., 2023; Garcini et al., 2021; Karumathil & Tripathi, 2022; Kochen et al., 2020; Moore et al., 2022). One example is from the Akan people, the largest population in Ghana, Africa. The Akan believe death occurs once in an individual's life, but they do not believe that everything ceases with the individual's death. The Akan believe that an ancestral world exists, the afterworld, and souls of departed loved individuals go to live in the ancestral world known as asamando (Adinkrah, 2022).

During 2014, the members of the Department of Service Delivery and Safety at the WHO worked together to agree on the clinical criteria for determining death (WHO, 2017). Members of this group came up with criteria for **cardiocirculatory death** and **brain death**. For cardiocirculatory death there are a number of criteria that must be met. First, all individuals, regardless of where individuals are located (e.g., home, hospital, nursing home), must show an absence of circulation with a clinical diagnosis. This includes: 1) absence of central pulse; 2) absence of heart sound with instrument such as a stethoscope; 3) absence of breathing; and 4) absence of pupil response to light. In addition, specific additional tests for declaring individuals dead are required for individuals who had been on life support machines, including: 1) no electrical activity on a continuous electrocardiogram (ECG) display; 2) no pulse flow when using an intra-arterial pressure monitoring device; and/or 3) absence of contractile activity when using echocardiography. Once all of this has been confirmed, there is a minimal waiting period of five minutes to ensure no spontaneous return of cardiac or respiratory functions. The waiting period might be longer, depending on the culture, and if the waiting period involves a child rather than an adult.

In situations where it cannot be determined that there has been cardiocirculatory death, brain death needs to be confirmed. The criteria for brain death include: 1) examination of coma; 2) confirmation that there is an absence of brain stem reflexes; and 3) an apnea test (WHO, 2017). Professionals on the scene of a possible brain death, regardless of location, will look for no spontaneous response to any stimuli, no spontaneous respiration, no eye movements including blinking and pupil responsiveness, no postural activity, no swallowing, no yawning, no vocalization, no motor reflexes, and a flat electroencephalogram (EEG). The length of time these responses are required to be absent in order to confirm brain death varies based on the amount of brain trauma, the age of the individual, and cultural differences in how assessments are made and in definitions of brain death (Starr et al., 2024). Professionals carry out these tests to make sure that there is a clear absence of cerebral and brainstem functions and that death is not reversible. If medical intervention restores life functions, then the individual is not brain dead.

Persistent Vegetative State

When an individual is in a **persistent vegetative state** (PVS) after a coma (post-coma) they are unresponsive; they may appear to be awake but will show no evidence of awareness of their surroundings (Jennett & Plum, 1972; Kondziella et al., 2020). Another name for PVS is unresponsive wakefulness syndrome (UWS) Bender et al., 2015; Laureys et al., 2010). Regardless of the term used, it is considered a clinical condition that involves the individual being completely unaware of themselves and their environment (Multi-Society Task Force on PVS, 1994). Persistent vegetative state is considered a chronic disorder involving severe brain damage. Even though cranial-nerve and spinal reflexes may be intact, there is no evidence of cognitive functions and no responses to any visual, auditory, tactile or painful stimuli (Multi-Society Task Force on PVS, 1994). Individuals with PVS have normal functions such as heartbeat and breathing, sleep and wake patterns, and they may chew and swallow food. They may even have a startle reflex, reacting to sudden stimuli in their environment, however, they do not have the usual signs of consciousness. They do not speak in any clear language, and they do not respond to commands. Individuals with PVS do not move with any specific purpose, and do not avoid painful stimuli. To be diagnosed with PVS, someone must show these symptoms for four weeks (Multi-Society Task Force on PVS, 1994). It should be noted that recent research and much controversy exists regarding different states of consciousness and diagnosis and treatment of these different states of consciousness (Mudrik et al., 2025; Sattin et al., 2021).

Decisions about Death

Now that we have defined death, we will turn to a discussion of some of the important decisions involved in the dying process. Death is defined in different ways according to laws and religious and cultural views. Therefore, decisions about whether or not someone would like to be resuscitated if they do die can be complicated (Ding et al., 2020). A **do not resuscitate** (DNR) medical order is either written or oral depending on where someone lives and indicates that the individual should not receive cardiopulmonary resuscitation if the individual's heart stops beating.

Individuals can have a DNR in place and file a copy with their physicians and lawyers, and still have issues enforcing it. For example, if someone with a DNR is an organ donor, how long should they be kept alive in order to harvest their organs? What if the individual dies in a location where there is no access to the individual's DNR document and/or organ donor information? Sometimes patients can be transferred from one facility to another, and the paperwork can be misplaced during the transfer. Individuals' religious beliefs, family values, and the laws of a society can sometimes interfere with an individual's DNR status (Ding et al., 2020; Wang et al., 2023). If DNR orders cannot be found, then physicians will try to resuscitate a patient. In general, most people with a DNR order want compassionate care involving pain-free and emotionally supportive end-of-life care.

Cross-cultural Research on DNR

A study conducted in the United States on 23,402,637 patient records between 2016 and 2019, showed an increase in DNR over that time period (Rachoin et al., 2024). However, patients whose ethnicity was Black/African American and who were male were less likely to have a DNR status, and they had higher inpatient death, a longer length of stay in a hospital, and more hospital charges.

A study conducted in China assessed individuals with or without do not attempt resuscitation (DNAR) orders at the emergency department of a large comprehensive teaching hospital (Wang et al., 2023). When compared to patients without a DNAR order, those with DNAR orders (53% of sample) were older, more likely to be female, had a higher comorbidity score on a health measure, and a higher number had a primary diagnosis of cancer or a history of neurological issues.

Even within a culture, personal preferences of health care professionals can affect the decision to support or ignore a DNR order (Amacher et al., 2024). Researchers in Switzerland conducted a nationwide multicenter survey with healthcare professionals (Amacher et al., 2024). They provided case vignettes about DNR status, and found that a main factor in a healthcare professional's decision to support the DNR status of a patient is the healthcare professional's personal preferences.

Other Documents Helpful for Dying

It can be helpful to those we leave behind to have documents that clearly state our specific requests related to our own dying process. Individuals can create a **living will**, which states how, when, and under what circumstances they want to receive life-sustaining treatments and when they want them to be withheld. It is a type of **advance directive**, a document that explains to their health care providers what medical treatments they do or do not want if they become permanently unconscious or find themself at the end of a terminal illness.

Individuals can also have a **medical directive**, which is a document that summarizes decision about any special treatment for specific healthcare scenarios before they occur. Individuals can have a **durable power of attorney**, which is a document that allows them to select a surrogate person to make decisions on their behalf when they can no longer make such decisions, or it can be part of family-shared decision making (health care proxy).

Statistics on Death

U.S. Death Rates

The death rate in the United States decreased in 2023 compared to 2022 by 6% to approximately 750 deaths per 100,000 individuals (Murphy et al., 2024). Life expectancy in the United States was 78.4 years in 2023, which was a small increase of 0.9 from the previous year (Murphy et al., 2024). There were 3,046,569 deaths in the United States in 2024, and this was an increase of about 2.4% compared to 2023 (database.earth, 2025).

Murphy and colleagues (2024) presented the death rate for the total U.S. population, providing information on race and ethnicity too. There was a decrease in death rate for multiple minority groups for both males and females from 2022 to 2023. While the ten leading causes of death in the United States were consistent with those from 2022, there were some changes. COVID-19 dropped from the fourth leading cause of death in the previous year to the tenth in 2023 (Murphy et al., 2024). In 2023, stroke became the fourth leading cause of death, followed by chronic lower respiratory diseases, Alzheimer's disease (AD), diabetes, and kidney disease; chronic liver disease and cirrhosis came in at ninth place (Murphy et al., 2024). It is important to note that African Americans and other ethnic minorities in the United have been at an increased risk of contracting COVID-19 and dying from it because of inequity in health care access, discrimination, and lack of trust in the health care system due to a history of mistreatment (Kennedy, 2021).

Global Death Rates

Globally, for the ten leading causes of death, the distribution remained the same for 2019, 2020, and 2021. There was an important exception. COVID-19 became the third and then the second leading cause of death globally as it spread around the world. COVID-19 was responsible for approximately 4.1 million deaths in 2020 and 8.8 million deaths in 2021 (WHO, 2024a; 2025c).

COVID-19 was responsible for the most deaths in 2020 and 2021 in the Americas, and in 2021 in the South-East Asia region (WHO, 2024a). COVID-19 was the second leading cause of death in 2020 and 2021 in both the European and Eastern Mediterranean regions. In the African region, COVID-19 was the sixth leading cause of death in 2021. COVID-19 was not in the top ten leading causes of death in the Western Pacific region in 2020 or 2021 (WHO, 2024a). COVID-19 dropped to the tenth leading cause of death in 2023 in the United States (Murphy et al., 2024).

Prior to COVID-19, the Global Burden of Disease (GBD) Study 2017 assessed global, regional, and national mortality and life expectancy from 1950 to 2017 (GBD 2017 Mortality Collaborators, 2018). The research included multiple age groups and 195 countries and territories. The researchers found that life expectancy increased from 48.1 years to 70.5 years for men and from 52.9 years to 75.6 years for women. However, there was much variation across different parts of the world. For example, males born in 2017 showed a life expectancy of 49.1 years in the Central African Republic, while females born in 2017 showed a life expectancy of 87.6 years in Singapore (GBD 2017 Mortality Collaborators, 2018).

A systematic review of attitudes towards death and dying in relation to COVID-9 included nine studies, and showed moderate to high amounts of death anxiety surrounding COVID-19 for individuals aged 50 years and older (Officer et al., 2024a). Studies included in the review were from Turkey, Jordan, Iran, Israel, Germany, and China, and results showed increased death anxiety resulted from fears of the risk and consequences of COVID-19, but not the preventative measures that were used to try and stop the spread of the virus.

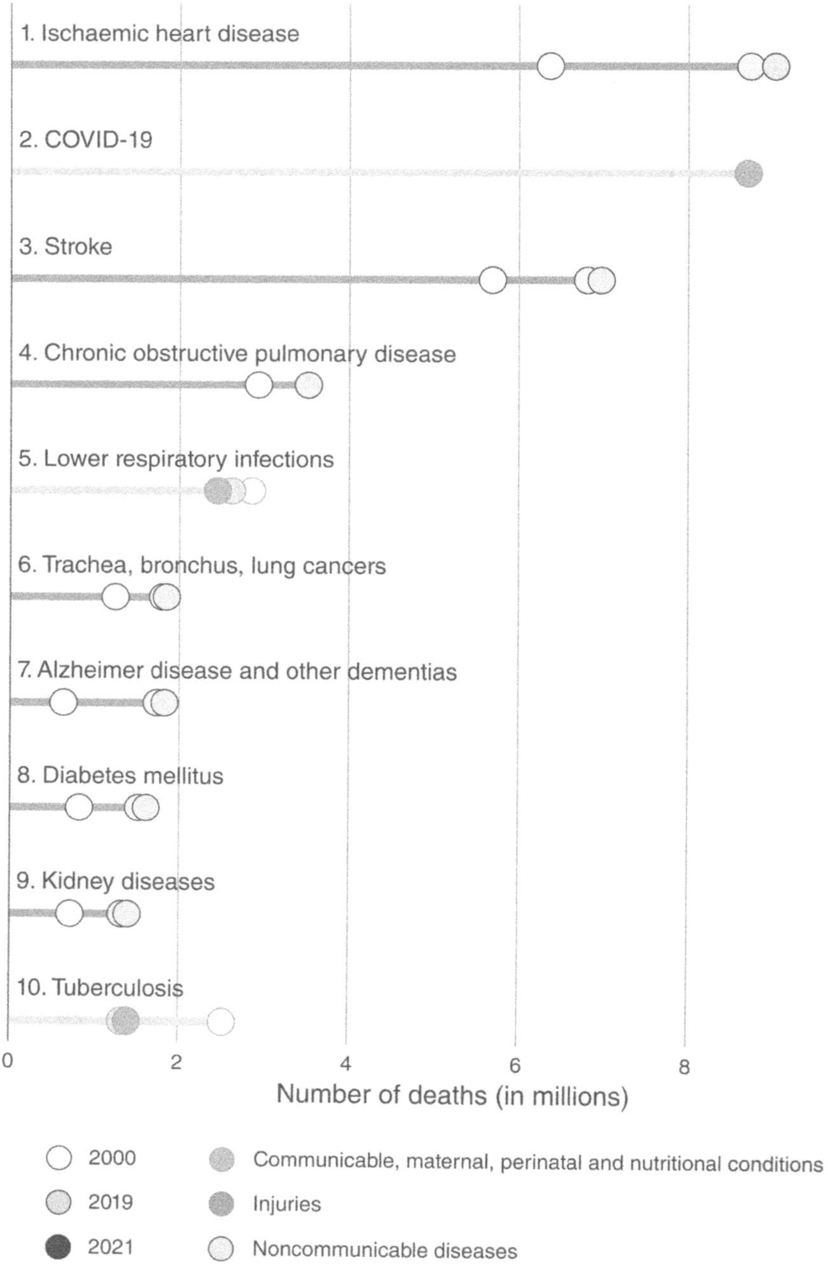

Figure 11.1 The top ten leading causes of death in 2021 globally.
Source: World Health Organization.

Statistics on Death Across the Lifespan

Death can occur at any time in the lifespan, and researchers study death rates from the neonatal period to the end of the lifespan. The infant mortality rate did not significantly differ from 2022 to 2023 – approximately 560 infant deaths per 100,000 lives births in 2023 (Murphy et al., 2024). Overall, there is good news regarding the mortality rate for children under 5 years old. The number of deaths for children under 5 around the globe declined to approximately 4.9 million in 2022, which was a 51% decline in mortality for this age group (WHO, 2024a). However, in the African region, children under five still have the highest risk of dying, and this region made up more than half of the total number of deaths for children under 5 in 2022, according to the estimates developed by the United Nations Inter-agency Group for Child Mortality Estimation in 2023 (WHO, 2024a).

Unfortunately, since the reduction in maternal mortality rates of 2015, progress in reducing maternal mortality has slowed. An estimated 287,000 women died globally from maternal causes in 2020, with the African region still having the highest maternal mortality rate over the past two decades. South-East Asia has achieved the largest decline, and reduced maternal mortality rate to 117 deaths per 100,000 live births in 2020. There were increases in maternal mortality rates in the Americas, Europe, and Western Pacific regions between 2016 and 2020; however, levels of maternal mortality are still below 80 deaths per 100,000 lives births in these regions and have been since the year 2000 (WHO, 2024a).

Within the United States, maternal mortality rates are notably high, and some researchers argue that this is based on the current National Vital Statistics System and National Center for Health Statistics (NVSS/NCHS) method. This method includes identification of maternal deaths based on information from the pregnancy, with a checkbox on the death certificate. The NCHS reports a high increasing rate of maternal mortality in the United States, which may be due to less specific and related causes of death (Joseph et al., 2024). Joseph and colleagues (2024) recommend an approach to identifying maternal deaths based on a definition that requires at least one mention of pregnancy among multiple causes of death. This definition-based approach for identification of maternal deaths showed lower and more stable maternal mortality rates in the United States. However, Joseph and colleagues (2024) point out that rates of maternal mortality are still much higher for non-Hispanic Black women compared to other groups.

The death rate for the United States over the lifespan for 2022 and 2023 shows a decrease for all age groups from age one to 85 years and older (Murphy et al., 2024). As a result of improvements in prevention and how quickly and accurately individuals are diagnosed and treated for chronic diseases, there has been a decline in mortality from chronic diseases before the age of 70. The risk of dying before the age of 70 from one of the four major chronic diseases (i.e., cardiovascular disease (CD), cancer, chronic respiratory disease, diabetes) dropped from 22.7% in 2000 to 18.2% in 2019 (WHO, 2024d; 2025c).

Despite evidence of positive progress in reducing mortality before the age of 70, there are differences around the globe. The Eastern Mediterranean region still had the highest risk of death before the age of 70 for these chronic diseases in 2019, compared to other regions. The Americas consistently maintained the lowest risk of mortality before the age of 70 for these chronic diseases between 2000 and 2019, showing about a 24% reduction over that time period. Europe and the Western Pacific regions showed the quickest declines in these chronic diseases from 2000 through 2019 (WHO, 2024d; 2025c).

There are many causes of death besides acute or chronic diseases, including vehicle fatalities, environmental hazards such as air pollution, unsafe washing, suicide, and homicide. For example, the global estimate of mortality due to unsafe washing in 2019 was about 395,000 deaths in children under 5 years old (WHO, 2023a; 2024d).

Factors Involved in Death Across the Lifespan

The relationship between our age and our death is generally shown with a J-shaped diagram. First, death rates are high in infancy, decline rapidly in childhood, start to increase again in adolescence, increase more as we become adults, and accelerate in older adulthood (Dattani, 2023). Factors that are involved in this J-shaped diagram vary across the lifespan.

For infants the death rate is high for a variety of reasons, including birth defects, complications at birth, premature births, and infections. Death rates are lower during childhood and tend to rise in adolescence, with accidents, drug overdoses, and violence contributing to death rates during these years of development (Dattani, 2023). From young adulthood through middle adulthood (20s through early 60s), there is a gradual increase in the death rate for a variety of reasons, including the most recent opioid epidemic, accidents, and chronic diseases. For individuals aged 65 to 84 years old the death rate rises due to the effects of aging on the body, chronic diseases, and less ability to recover from illness and injury. Heart disease, cancer, and AD are major contributing factors to death in this age range (Lleras-Muney & Moreau, 2022). For individuals aged 85 years and older the death rate is the highest because of frailty, greater susceptibility to illness because of more weakened immune systems, and living with multiple chronic conditions simultaneously.

Some deaths are preventable, including those related to drug use and accidents. Health-promoting behaviors can reduce and eliminate some risk factors linked to death in those in young and middle adulthood. Falls are the leading cause of accidental injury and death in older adults (Guirguis-Blake et al., 2024). There are many reasons for the increase in falls in older adults, including poorer eyesight, diseases, foot problems, medications, gait and balance issues, and environmental hazards that can lead to falls (Colón-Emeric et al., 2024). Health care providers and researchers agree that there are many things we can do to reduce the risk of falls as we get older, including exercise and diet. Staying physically active is very important, because regular exercise helps us maintain our muscle strength longer, maintain our flexibility, slows bone loss, and reduces risk of diseases linked to balance issues and falls (Colón-Emeric et al., 2024; Guirguis-Blake et al., 2024; National Institute on Aging, 2025). There are exercise programs that can improve balance and muscle strength, such as yoga, pilates, and tai chi. Also, it is important to make your home safe to prevent falls as you age, including removing flooring that is slippery, not using rugs without secure backing, providing a clear visual contrast for differences in flooring heights (including better lighting), and installing lights that come on automatically as older adults move around rooms. Annual eye and ear exams will also reduce the risk of falls related to poor eyesight or hearing.

Now that we have discussed statistics and patterns to death, we turn to how we each view dying from a life course perspective. There are many factors that can affect how we each view dying, including personal characteristics such as age, temperament and personality, level of cognitive functioning, gender, education level, socioeconomic status (SES), geographic location, religious and spiritual beliefs, and other cultural influences (Moore et al., 2022; Officer et al., 2024b).

Life Course Approach to Dying

Once a child can communicate and form an attachment to others, researchers can study their understanding of death. While young children may not have a clear understanding of death regarding the loss of a loved one, recent research shows that they have a continual bond with the deceased person, even though, the loved one has died (Harris, 2023). Children will discuss the absent loved one, showing signs of attachment to them (Harris, 2023; Zhang & Harris, 2022).

When adolescents or emerging and young adults are dealing with the death of someone close to them, such as a sibling, friend, or parent, the experience can be very disruptive in their lives, with both short and long-term effects that require professional help and more family support (Feigelman et al., 2017). How close the adolescent or emerging and young adult was to the person, and the type of death (suicide, drug-related, an illness), can affect their mental health, with increased reports of anxiety and/or depression (Pham et al., 2018).

Learning to deal with the death of other individuals over time, including siblings, parents, and grandparents, can help individuals learn to think about their own death. The death of a parent is considered one of the most common losses during adulthood, and a normative life event by middle adulthood (Kim et al., 2019). Middle-aged adults begin to confront their own mortality, and they undergo a change in their sense of time lived and time until death. When middle-aged adults deal with the death of their parents, they realize that they are the oldest generation in the family.

As we age, losing a spouse or life partner can be one of the most difficult experiences to deal with, besides losing a child. While it is often assumed that older adults are more accepting of death, facing our own death in a positive way depends on a variety of factors, including acceptance of our impending death and a positive view of the life we have lived. Culture plays an important role in an individual's perception of dying and death. For example, within the Black community death is viewed as a natural part of life, and individuals who are dying may be more accepting of death and give less effort to slowing down the dying process (Barrett & Heller, 2002). Support from family, friends, and their community are provided when a member of the Black community is dying, providing help with activities of daily living and singing and praying with them and for them (Moore et al., 2022). Within the Black community, faith is an important part of the dying process. For those who are dying and for individuals who are dealing with the loss of a loved one, spirituality and the church play an important role in dying and death (Moore et al., 2022).

Cross-Cultural Research on Dealing with Death

In a qualitative study on adolescents and emerging adults, a researcher assessed their perspectives of death and dying with semi-structured interviews (Naik, 2024). Naik (2024) conducted this study in India and included nine participants with an age range of 16 to 22 in the interviews. The participants were from Hindu and Islamic religious backgrounds, had all experienced the loss of at least one family member, mostly grandparents but also some siblings, friends, or neighbors. Overall themes emerged, including an understanding of death, especially with regard to spirit stories, learning to manage grief and anxiety, and discussion of social and cultural views about death education. The adolescents and emerging adults were aware of how individuals in their cultures proceed with burial or cremation, and felt they could talk about it with family members, friends, and neighbors.

Our perspective of death can be affected by the type of death, and sudden traumatic death such as homicide can have significant and long-lasting effects on surviving family members and friends. In a review of literature on coping strategies of Black survivors of homicide, researchers included 35 articles (Sharpe et al., 2025). While most of the studies were conducted in the United States, there were studies from other countries (Canada; Trinidad and Tobago, Port of Spain; Trinidad and Tobago, Dar es Salaam and Tanzania; and Johannesburg, South Africa). Most of the participants were Black mothers, Black men, and youth within the Black community. Sharpe and colleagues (2025) pointed out the long history of racism and discrimination that created barriers to dealing with the loss of a family member or friend to homicide, especially in the United States. Black survivors lack trust in doctors, lawyers, and the mental health care system. The pain of losing a loved one to homicide can cause anger, helplessness, and fear, with some individuals trying to suppress these feelings. Sharpe and colleagues (2025) also noted that Black mothers experienced much internal and external blame, and that this can result in a very difficult, long, and complicated grief experience for them. While spirituality is an important part of the Black community, it is not consistently helpful with regard to homicide. Some individuals feel less connected to their faith and spirituality after experiencing the homicide of a loved one.

In a systematic review of attitudes toward death and dying in individuals in middle adulthood and older, researchers included 74 studies from 1961 to 2022 from 30 countries (Officer et al., 2024b). The researchers found that having close relationships helped individuals deal with anxiety.

A systematic review was conducted on the transition from a caregiver role for a dying spouse to a widow or widower (Baumbach et al., 2024). The researchers included 22 studies from multiple countries, including the United States, Australia, Canada, England, Germany, and one in Europe that did not specify a country. Baumbach and colleagues (2024) found that new widows or widowers can experience depressive symptoms, guilt, health issues, financial issues, and difficulty trying to transition away from a caregiver role. Individual coping strategies ranged from seeking support from family and friends, seeking community service help, and engaging in spirituality, to more negative approaches such as substance abuse and rumination about the spouse's illness, the dying process, and the caregiver role.

Researchers conducted a systematic literature review of older adults confronting their own end of life and individuals facing a life-threatening disease (Kukla et al., 2021). The researchers included 49 studies from 2010 to 2020, with studies from the United States, China, Japan, Australia, Poland, Canada, the United Kingdom., Denmark, Italy, Portugal, Spain, Switzerland, Singapore, and Germany. Kukla and colleagues (2021) found a wide variety of approaches to confronting one's own impending death, including the use of psychotherapy, being involved in educational programs, and the use of psychosocial narratives as a form of intervention. Kukla and colleagues (2021) found that coping strategies that can help promote a more positive view of one's impending death include active confrontation with death topics and recognition of personal accomplishments during one's life.

Ethical Issues

We have discussed definitions of death, statistics on death, and how death varies across the lifespan. We turn next to ethical issues involved in dying and death. **Bioethics** involves examining the interaction between human values and technological advances. The most important bioethical issue is **euthanasia**, which is the practice of ending life for reasons of mercy. Euthanasia has often been known as "the good death" (Lewy, 2011). **Active euthanasia** is the deliberate, intentional action to end life. For example, a physician giving an individual a lethal dose of a sedative. As of 2025, active euthanasia is legal in several countries, including Belgium, Canada, Colombia, Luxembourg, the Netherlands, New Zealand, and Spain (World Population Review, 2025a).

Passive euthanasia involves withholding or withdrawing a life-sustaining medicine or machine. Many countries allow passive euthanasia, including Belgium, Canada, Colombia, Luxembourg, the Netherlands, New Zealand, Spain, India, Nigeria, the United States, Brazil, Ethiopia, Mexico, Turkey, Germany, Thailand, the United Kingdom, France, South Africa, Italy, South Korea, Argentina, Ukraine, Poland, Venezuela, Taiwan, Zambia, Kazakhstan, Chile, Romania, Bolivia, the Dominican Republic, the United Arab Emirates, Sweden, the Czech Republic, Azerbaijan, Greece, Hungary, Israel, Austria, Switzerland, Hong Kong, Nicaragua, Bulgaria, Serbia, El Salvador, Denmark, Singapore, Finland, Norway, Slovakia, Ireland, Costa Rica, Panama, Croatia, Georgia, Uruguay, Puerto Rico, Bosnia and Herzegovina, Namibia, Moldova, Armenia, Lithuania, Albania, Slovenia, Latvia, North Macedonia, Trinidad and Tobago, Cyprus, Estonia, Guyana, Montenegro, Malta, Iceland, Andorra, the Faroe Islands, Greenland, Gibraltar, and Monico (World Population Review, 2025a).

Within the United States euthanasia is illegal under federal law. However, there are some states that allow individuals to die with dignity. **Physician-assisted suicide** generally falls under the term "death with dignity," which is also known as medical aid in dying. This end-of-life option, which is controlled by state legislation, allows eligible individuals to legally request and obtain medications from a physician that will enable them to end their own life in a manner that is dignified and peaceful. The wording of the legislation varies from state-to-state, and individuals need to clearly understand the wording of the document in their state (Koepp, 2024). States that allow individuals to "die with dignity" include Oregon, Hawaii, Washington State, Maine, Colorado, Vermont, New Jersey, New Mexico, Montana, and California. Death with dignity is also legal in the District of Columbia (World Population Review, 2025b).

Physician-assisted suicide involves a physician providing the patient with medical supplies and specific prescription medications to end their life by suicide. In many states throughout the United States this is viewed as homicide simply because the physician provides the drugs that the individual is going to use to end their own life. This is an ongoing debate because there are many different moral views relating to the issue. In general, the medical community does not support physician-assisted suicide. Because the medications provided to individuals to commit suicide are under tight control, the prescriptions for these medications are flagged and would be stopped in most states. In order to have a physician-assisted suicide, the patient must be experiencing suffering that is "irremediable and unbearable", a second physician must agree after a thorough evaluation of the individual, the individual must be aware of all other available options for help, and the patient must be of sound mind (Twycross, 2024).

Cross-Cultural Research on Euthanasia

Karumathil and Tripathi (2022) conducted an integrative review on euthanasia, the first one to examine how aspects of culture help shape our public opinion about euthanasia across many world views. The researchers included 40 studies in their qualitative summaries from countries in Asia (Turkey, China, Hong Kong, Japan, Iran), Europe (the United Kingdom, Germany, the Netherlands, Italy, Greece, Belgium, France, Spain, Sweden, Norway, Portugal), North America (the United States and Canada), and multi-cultural studies. The findings on views about euthanasia varied across cultures and within cultures. For example, in some Asian cultures the Taoists belief that maintaining balance in life includes staying alive through any effort and do not support euthanasia (Qin & Xia, 2015). Students studying healthcare and law in Turkey support euthanasia, while those in other disciplines do not (Karaahmetoglu & Kutahyalioglu, 2019).

Another study incorporating a review of views on assisted dying was conducted across diverse racial, ethnic and cultural perspectives and included 17 studies (the United States, Belgium, Australia, Austria, Canada, and Finland; Bloomer et al., 2024). The researchers found that support of assisted dying varied both within and across cultures. For example, in the United States and Austria, individuals with stronger religious viewpoints, from multiple religious backgrounds including Christianity and Judaism, do not support assisted dying, and this is true for Muslim women living in Belgium too. Bloomer and colleagues (2024) also found that views about intolerable suffering could be used as an argument in support of assisted dying for others, even if not for oneself, depending on how influential other aspects of religious and cultural views were.

Palliative Care and Hospice Care

Palliative care focuses on improving the quality of an individual's life when they have a serious illness, and can include their care partners too. Palliative care can occur for any part of the lifespan, involves effective symptom management and coordination of care, and is generally interdisciplinary, including a team of doctors, nurses, and other care providers who coordinate care for the ill individual and their family based on the individual's specific values (Fields et al., 2023; National Institute on Aging, 2021; Radbruch et al., 2020). Palliative care can occur at any point in an individual's illness, and can include end-of-life care and **bereavement** support for the whole family. Palliative care can occur in many places, including hospitals, assisted living facilities, nursing homes, outpatient clinics, and home.

Hospice care is a specific type of palliative care that is provided in the final weeks or months of someone's life. Hospice care involves an approach to assisting dying that prioritizes pain management and death with dignity (i.e., palliative care). Hospice care emphasizes quality of life rather than quantity of life, and the goal is to de-emphasize the prolongation of death for terminally ill patients. Hospice care supports a dignified death for patients and emotional support for the family (National Institute on Aging, 2021). Both inpatient and outpatient hospice care is available. The role of staff is to be with the patient but not to treat the patient. Hospice patients often refuse to eat or drink to starve themselves to death. Hospice programs can be set in nursing homes, where the greatest number of individuals are there due to dementia; in one's home, though this is more common in urban areas; or in hospitals, where the greatest number of chronically ill individuals may be (National Institute on Aging, 2021). Benefits of hospice programs include professional support to family and caregivers, financial savings for the family, and the patient being able to die at home in familiar surroundings.

Cross-Cultural Research on Palliative Care and Hospice Care

Research on palliative care for adolescents and young adults was conducted with a review that included 51 studies (Abdelaal et al., 2023). The researchers noted that 34 studies were conducted in the United States, and there were also studies from Lebanon, France, Canada, Australia, South Africa, the United Kingdom, Thailand, India, the Netherlands, and Italy. The researchers' findings indicated that adolescents and young adults experiences more severe symptoms and extensive medical treatment in end-of-life care, particularly cancer patients, and that there was a need for better palliative care for this age range.

It is important to acknowledge, understand, and respect the role culture plays in palliative care in order for it to be a positive and successful experience for the individual and their family (Narayanan et al., 2025; Qureshi et al., 2022). Palliative care is most successful when an individual's cultural beliefs and values are understood, respected, and integrated into the approach. Researchers conducted a review of palliative care for Indigenous individuals in the United States (Isaacson & Lynch, 2018). The researchers found 17 studies that met criteria for their review, and findings indicated a need for better communication about practices and policies between health care professionals/organizations and Indigenous individuals. Indigenous individuals often felt that they had little opportunity to ask questions about the diagnosis of their illnesses. Health care professionals did not appear sensitive to or aware of body language and nonverbal cues, and a need was identified for better understanding of the beliefs, customs, and values of the variety of Indigenous individuals they encounter during palliative care. The need for better understanding about different cultural beliefs, customs, and values should also be extended to those from other minority groups and those from low and middle-income countries (Narayanan et al., 2025), with a special need for focus on palliative care for individuals with neurodiverse challenges (Bruun et al., 2025).

In countries around the world, individuals view a good death as one that includes dignity through end-of-life care (Järviö et al., 2023), and hospice care can contribute to a positive experience. In a systematic review, researchers included 25 studies (the majority from India, but also Pakistan, Bangladesh, Sri Lanka, and Bhutan) to better understand what it means to have a "good death" in the South Asian region (Wijeyaratne et al., 2025). Four themes emerged from the review: (1) mutual care and connection support a continued sense of self; dignity and support are required from others to still feel like a valued person. Giving helps patients maintain a sense of self, which includes making sure the family will be cared for when they are gone (e.g., finances, who will care for children) and not wanting to be a burden to the family; (2) Freedom to choose is both a privilege and a burden, and includes being able to decide if you receive care for excessive pain. However, individuals are not always able to obtain care because of financial reasons and sometimes family members want to be the ones to provide this care; (3) Important opportunities in the last days include being pain-free, feeling safe, and gathering one's family; (4) After death matters, including an individual's need to leave a legacy behind – for example, through acknowledgements of their contributions to specific organizations, communities, countries, and their families, and by leaving a will or documents with specific guidelines for family members after they have died, including ceremonies they would like to be performed.

In another review, researchers included 18 studies from countries around the world, including New Zealand, the Netherlands, Western Australia, the United States, Lebanon, India, Canada, South Africa, and a study with both South Africa and Uganda (Herbstsomer & Stahl, 2020). The researchers identified important themes in the review: (1) communication is very important when working with minority individuals in hospice settings; (2) lack of knowledge about hospice care and/or palliative care can cause some individuals to experience stigma from family and friends; and (3) non-Western and minority individuals from Western countries have specific needs that need to be met with hospice care that can often only be met at home.

As can be seen from the above research, understanding the importance of different cultural beliefs, customs, and values is essential to providing the best possible palliative care, both for those who will get better and those in need of end-of-life care in a hospice setting. This is true across the globe, and especially for minority individuals. In fact, this is very important as some countries are starting to offer palliative care within Sub-Saharan Africa, and they require a better understanding of the specific cultures they will encounter, how to respect these cultures, and how to provide effective palliative care (Heller, 2024).

End-of-Life Issues

One aspect of accepting one's own impending death is dealing with end-of-life issues. Individuals may wish to create a **final scenario**, which involve deciding how they want their body disposed of after death, (e.g., buried in the ground at a specific location). Some individuals will create a detailed description of how they want to be memorialized and will make decisions about the distribution of their assets. One important aspect of a final scenario is saying goodbye to family and friends – helping themself and their family through the separation and bringing closure to a relationship. However, religious and cultural values will also play a role in whether or not individuals believe that relationships end with death (Watson-Jones et al., 2017).

Funeral Arrangements

One end-of-life issue that must be considered is funeral arrangements. Decisions must be made regarding viewing and burial or **cremation** (burning of the body until only small amounts of bone fragments remain), depending on culture, family preferences and traditions, and the cost of the funeral experience. The National Funeral Directors Association (NFDA) was founded in 1882, and it is the largest association in the world that provides funeral services, with over 20,000 members that represent about 11,000 funeral homes in 49 countries (NFDA, 2024). The NFDA reported a projected cremation rate of about 62%, and burial rate of about 33% (NFDA, 2024). The median cost for a funeral with viewing and burial in 2023 was $8,300, and the median cost of a funeral with cremation was $6,280 (NFDA, 2024).

Research on those in mourning in Japan showed that when families perceive a funeral to be good, it helps them to cope with their grief. Grief-related issues with low productivity are reduced, as is the need for costly public services such as counselling and medical interventions (Becker et al., 2022). Barriers to a good funeral experience can include low income and less equitable funeral care, particularly for individuals in the LGBTQIA+ community (Wright-Berryman & Huber, 2024). Researchers interviewed 23 funeral providers and consumers in the United States. They found that both fear of and actual religious discrimination were frequently reported by providers and consumers involved in the funeral arrangements for individuals in the LGBTQIA+ community, leading to feeling less safe and the need for safe spaces (Wright-Berryman & Huber, 2024).

In some cultures, people who work in the funeral industry will gloss over death and make dead individuals appear beautiful and alive (Slominski, 2023). Even the terms we use to discuss death such as "passing on" or "no longer with us," rather than the use of the term "dead," can be linked to personal, religious, and cultural views about death (Beard & Burger, 2017).

Grief, Mourning, Bereavement, Near Death Experiences

Grief

What is grief? Grief encompasses all of the feelings associated with loss. Individuals may feel sad and cry after the loss of a loved one. Individuals can have feelings of anger or they can idealize the loved one who has died.

They can have guilt pangs, which are often experienced as physical feelings that include shortness of breath, feeling like there is a knot in the stomach, or emptiness. Grief is a universal reaction to the loss of a loved one. Some behavioral aspects of grief can include active distress, and searching for the lost loved one. Some theoretical ideas about grief were shaped by Freud, who discussed the need to withdraw emotional attachments or energy from the lost loved one and form new attachments (Hamilton, 2016). The loss of an attachment is also described by Bowlby, who identified four phases: shock and disbelief; protest and obsessive yearning; despair, intense sadness, and social withdrawal; and learning to reorganize one's life and adjust (Bowlby, 1982).

Many of us gradually begin to adapt to the loss of our loved ones and get back into the daily routines of our lives. However, sometimes when individuals grieve, they may have difficulty adjusting. Individuals who are so overwhelmed with feelings of sadness sometimes develop a more complex and chronic form of grief known as **prolonged grief disorder** (PGD) (Prigerson et al., 2009). Prolonged grief disorder includes feelings of intense yearning and emotional pain, preoccupation with the deceased person, a disruption in their identity, feelings of disbelief, avoidance, numbness, and loneliness, and trouble getting back to their daily routine after the death of their loved one (Prigerson et al., 2021). Sometimes grief can be extensive and more complicated because of the loss of an infant or young child (Kochen et al., 2020), or a sudden death due to homicide (Moore et al., 2022).

Much like other aspects of death and dying, the experience of grief can differ across cultures. Within Western cultures such as the United States, grief is often focused on the individual. When someone has trouble dealing with the loss of a loved one, they are referred to grief counseling or support groups alone. However, even within the United States, there are many subcultures that view grieving in different ways. Native American culture encompasses many tribes (Brave Heart et al., 2011). The Lakota tribe elders consider the death of one member to be felt by all members of the tribe (Stone, 1998). Grief is not viewed as an individual experience but from a collectivistic view, and the whole tribe grieves. Another example is the African American community. In the African American community grieving is complicated by the history of slavery and racism, which causes an ongoing state of grief for African Americans that impacts their grief after the loss of a loved one (Moore et al., 2022).

Acknowledging historical aspects of trauma is something already recognized within Indigenous communities too (Brave Heart et al., 2011). Ongoing intergenerational trauma, which includes discrimination, racism, and oppression of Indigenous individuals in both the United States and Canada, was assessed with a systematic review (Gone et al., 2019). The researchers included 32 articles on historical trauma in their review, however, they could not integrate findings into a coherent theme across studies. Gone and colleagues (2019) recommended the development of a clearer definition of historical trauma for Indigenous individuals, and more consistency regarding how variables are measured to better integrate findings in a coherent way across studies for future reviews.

During the 1960s, Dr. Kübler-Ross conducted more than 200 interviews over the course of about three years at a Chicago hospital with individuals who had been diagnosed with a terminal illness, and the interviews resulted in the publication of her book *On Death and Dying* (1969). Dr. Kübler-Ross is known for the **five stages of grief** that were derived from these interviews: denial (this is not true, it must be a mistake), anger (this is so unfair!), bargaining (trying to negotiate with a higher power, I will do better), depression, and acceptance (I feel okay about what is going to happen). There has been much discussion about whether all of the interviewees actually experienced all five stages, if they did so in that sequence, if there is a specific, correct way to move through the stages, and if there really are any stages at all (Corr, 2015; Stroebe et al., 2017)? To celebrate the fiftieth anniversary of the publication of *On Death and Dying*, a new edition was published with an update from her children (Barbara Ross Rothweiler and Ken Ross) who reflected on the five stages individuals encounter when dealing with their own mortality (Ross Rothweiler & Ross, 2019). Commentary from Dr. Kübler-Ross's adult children included the importance of communicating with an individual about their emotional experiences throughout the dying process, and doing so across cultures.

In a recent article, Corr (2021) assessed 47 textbooks from 10 different countries outside the United States to address some of the criticisms of the five stages of grief. Corr points out that Dr. Kübler-Ross never meant to imply that the experiences of the interviewees from which the five stages were derived were happening in some kind of specific linear order, and that the five stages were not considered to be occurring across all cultures (Corr, 2021; Kübler-Ross & Kessler, 2005).

More recent research on how people experience and cope with their own dying is viewed through process-based models (Fiore, 2019). In the **dual-process model** of grief, Stroebe and Schut (1999; 2010) discuss the view that individuals fluctuate between "loss oriented" and "restoration oriented" phases while they are processing their grief experiences. In the **loss-oriented phases**, individuals feel grief and yearn for the person they have lost, and they may dwell on thoughts about the person they have lost and feel much distress. In the **restoration phases**, grief moves to the background, and individuals try to do new things and meet new people. Individuals try to use strategies to help them perform tasks and to distract them from dwelling on more negative aspects of the grieving process. This movement back and forth between "loss focused" and "restoration focused" phases can also be viewed as going back and forth between emotion-focused coping strategies and problem-focused coping strategies, as discussed previously in Chapter 9.

Mourning

What is mourning? Mourning is an expression of grief through acts and gestures that are accepted and defined by specific cultures following the death of another individual (Gire, 2014). Some eastern cultures with a collectivistic view, such as China, Japan, and Korea, focus on collective mourning; entire communities are involved in mourning rituals and support each other through grief.

Mourning Rituals

There are many kinds of mourning rituals around the world. For example, there is the **Qingming Festival** in China, where individuals visit the grave of their ancestors to offer food, burn incense, and keep the site clean to show respect for the ancestor and stay connected to them. In Latin America death is viewed as part of a cycle that continues after life. In places such as Mexico individuals participate in **Día de los Muertos** (Day of the Dead), by celebrating life and taking time to honor the dead. Individuals prepare altars of food, photographs, and special souvenirs to encourage the spirits of their dead family members to return for a brief visit with them (Gutiérrez et al., 2015).

Sometimes mourning rituals are different based on whether someone is male or female. One example involves the Akan people of Ghana. Their mourning rituals are of important cultural significance to them, and much of the rituals are determined by gender (Adjei et al., 2023). Bereaved men, widowers, are strongly encouraged to avoid excessive displays of feelings in public. Males organize and supervise death and mourning rites and given specific roles, with one male acting as the key person to be informed of deaths. The chief mourner is generally a male, and he must choose a successor to the deceased family member and oversee all aspects of rites involved in the death, including a funeral that best reflects the social status of the family and the deceased family member (Adjei et al., 2023). The Akan females must openly display feelings of grief. Akan women who do not cry repeatedly in public are viewed in a negative manner, often considered possibly responsible in some way for the death (Adinkrah, 2015).

Bereavement

What is bereavement? Bereavement is when an individual has lost a loved one due to death. "Bereaved" refers to the status of a person who survives the death of a loved one. Social status can change because of the loss of a loved one – for example, taking on a new role as the only child when your sibling dies, or becoming the matriarch in a family when you are the only surviving female. Bereavement is linked to increased risk of disease and death in the bereaved, especially for those who already have health problems (Buckley et al., 2010). Individual differences in bereavement can include varying periods of grief and a variety of mourning experiences depending on individuals' personal characteristics, coping techniques, and cultural differences.

In a systematic review of bereavement in widowed Latinos in the United States, researchers found 19 studies on the experience of bereavement (Garcini et al., 2021). There were ten quantitative studies, three qualitative studies, and six narrative reviews. Only four studies had samples that included only Latino participants, and most participants in those four studies were of Mexican-American origin. The rest of the samples had a mixture of different ethnic groups. A common theme in the qualitative studies and narrative reviews was discussion of a continued connection with the deceased person and/or viewing death as an extension of life. Garcini and colleagues (2021) found that there were a number of risk factors related to decreased well-being in their systematic review, including a greater risk if the individual was male because of not expressing grief. In the Latin community males may instead suppress emotional responses to loss of a loved one because of the cultural value of **machismo**, which is the need to show strength rather than noticeable outward signs of sorrow. Other risk factors for less well-being in the bereaved included financial strain due to the loss of income from the loved one, changes in social status, an undocumented legal status, experiencing widowhood at a younger age, poor health behaviors, and issues with physical health.

In a systematic review of parent-focused bereavement interventions after the loss of a child, researchers included 21 articles with 15 interventions (Kochen et al., 2020). Countries included in the systematic review included Finland, the United States, Denmark, Australia, and the United Kingdom. The researchers found that there were five key components of bereavement intervention after the loss of a child. One component was the acknowledgement of being a parent and their child's life. Kochen and colleagues (2020) included examples of washing the child, holding and dressing the child, and a blessing ceremony that celebrates the child's life. A second component was needing to establish keepsakes such as keeping a lock of the child's hair or items that belonged to the child. A third component included follow-up contact from those involved in the intervention. For example, phone calls, visits with the parents, and sending condolence letters. A fourth component was education and information related to coping and grief and providing folders with information such as financial advice, support meetings available for relatives, and workshops on coping. The fifth component was remembrance activities such as special ceremonies and attending the funeral.

Near Death Experiences

What is a **near death experience** (NDE)? Near death experiences are unique experiences that sometimes occur when individuals face life threatening events. An NDE, as described by people who have experienced one, varies across individuals and cultures. An NDE can include feeling as if one is moving toward a destination, experiencing what feels like a recording of one's life, or recalling specific events in a room or space outside the area in which the life-threatening event was occurring (Parnia et al., 2022).

While NDEs may be considered with skepticism by many and turned into dramatic movies or stories by others, researchers have been studying NDEs for quite a while, and much scientific work continues on this topic. For example, in a review of the literature on NDEs following a cardiac arrest, researchers used 11 studies from multiple countries, including the United States, Slovenia, the United Kingdom, Austria, the Netherlands, Sweden (Kovoor et al., 2024). The researchers found that the most common descriptions of an NDE included feeling peace, sensing light, and external visual and/or auditory experiences. In another article, Martial and colleagues (2025) reviewed literature on NDEs and proposed a model for NDEs that includes psychological and neurophysiological processes and explains them using an evolutionary frame of reference. It is evident from the research already conducted that researchers and health practitioners consider brain chemistry to be an important part of the NDE experience.

Chapter Summary

In this chapter we reviewed definitions of different types of death and the role of culture and other factors in determining death and making decisions about DNRs. We discussed death rate statistics in the United States and around the globe, and how culture and context play a role in the death rate across the lifespan. We explored developmental differences in views on death and dying, and how culture influences our views. We discussed active and passive euthanasia, grieving, mourning, and bereavement, and factors (i.e., biological, psychological, contextual factors) that affect our views, decisions, and experiences regarding these topics. There were consistent themes of disadvantage for minority individuals related to accessing help in health care settings and receiving support during death and dying.

Key Takeaways

1. Decisions about death involve specific procedures based on how death is defined and the role of culture and other factors (e.g., age).
2. Documents involved in life sustaining functions, medical care, the dying process, and death arrangements are important; however, culture and context can affect the use of such documents.
3. Biological, psychological, and contextual factors can affect our views about dying and death.
4. Grieving, mourning, and bereavement are affected by multiple factors, including culture and context.
5. The sociocultural context in which we develop during adulthood plays an important role in death rates across the lifespan and across the globe.

Reflective Questions

1 Which definition of death do you think is the most influential?
2 Can you identify the biological, psychological, and contextual factors that influence your life and think about how they affect your views about dying and death?
3 How do sociocultural and contextual factors affect our decisions about do not resuscitate status, euthanasia, and palliative care?

Suggested Readings

Adinkrah, M. (2022). If you die a bad death, we give you a bad burial: Mortuary practices and "bad death" among the Akan of Ghana. *Death Studies, 46*(3), 695–707. doi: 10.1080/07481187.2020.1762264.

Bloomer, M. J., Saffer, L., Hewitt, J., Johns, L., McAuliffe, D., & Bonner, A. (2024). Maybe for unbearable suffering: Diverse racial, ethnic and cultural perspectives of assisted dying. A scoping review. *Palliative Medicine, 38*(9), 968–980. doi: 10.1177/02692163241268449.

Moore, S. E., Jones-Eversley, S. D., Tolliver, W. F., Wilson, B., & Harmon, D. K. (2022). Cultural responses to loss and grief among Black Americans: Theory and practice implications for clinicians. *Death Studies, 46*(1), 189–199. doi: 10.1080/07481187.2020.1725930.

Key Terms

Active euthanasia is the deliberate, intentional action to end life.

An **advance directive** is a document that explains to a health care provider what medical treatments an individual does or does not want if they become permanently unconscious or find yourself at the end of a terminal illness.

Bereavement is the status of a person who survives the death of a loved one.

Bioethics involves examining the interaction between human values and technological advances.

Brain death is confirmed when there is an absence of brain stem reflexes.

Cardiocirculatory death is the absence of a central pulse, heart sounds observable with an instrument such as a stethoscope, breathing, and pupil response to light.

Cremation is the burning of a dead body until only small amounts of bone fragments remain.

Death with dignity, also known as medical aid in dying, is an end-of-life option that is controlled by legislation in each state. Physicians supply medications that individuals use to end their life.

Día de los Muertos (Day of the Dead) is viewed as part of cycle that continues after life in Latin America. Individuals celebrate life and take time to honor the dead, and prepare altars of food, photographs, and special souvenirs to encourage spirits of their beloved dead family members to return for a brief visit with them.

Do not resuscitate is a medical order, either written or oral depending on where someone lives, indicating that the individual should not receive cardiopulmonary resuscitation if the individual's heart stops beating.

The **dual-process model** suggests that individuals oscillate or fluctuate between "loss oriented" and "restoration oriented" phases while they are processing their grief experiences.

Durable power of attorney is a document that specifies a surrogate person who should make decisions on an individual's behalf when they can no longer make such decisions themselves, or it can be part of family-shared decision making.

Euthanasia is the practice of ending life for reasons of mercy.

The **final scenario** refers to how individuals want their body to be disposed after death, such as buried in the ground at a specific location, or cremated.

The **five stages of grief** are denial, anger, bargaining, depression, and acceptance.

Grief is the feeling associated with loss, and can include sadness, anger, and guilt.

Hospice care is a specific type of palliative care that is provided in the final weeks or months of someone's life that emphasizes pain management and death with dignity.

A **living will** is a document that states how, when, and under what circumstances an individual wants to have life-sustaining treatments and when they want such treatments to be withheld.

Loss-oriented phases are when individuals feel grief and yearn for the person they have lost. They may dwell on thoughts about the person they have lost and feel much distress.

Machismo, in Latin communities, causes males to suppress emotional responses to loss of a loved one because of the need to present strength and not show noticeable outward signs of sorrow.

A **medical directive** is a document that outlines any special treatment an individual wants to receive in specific healthcare scenarios before they occur.

Mourning is an expression of grief through acts and gestures that are accepted and defined by specific cultures following a death.

Near death experiences are unique experiences that sometimes occur when individuals are experiencing life threatening events. For example, it can include feeling as if one is moving toward a destination or experiencing what feels like a recording of one's life.

Palliative care aims to improve the quality of an individual's life when they have a serious illness, and can include their care partners too.

Passive euthanasia involves withholding or withdrawing a life-sustaining medicine or machine.

A **persistent vegetative state** (PV) is unresponsiveness after a coma (post-coma). They may appear to be awake but show no evidence of awareness of their surroundings.

Physician-assisted suicide involves a physician providing a patient with medical supplies and specific prescription medications needed to allow the individual to end their life by suicide.

Prolonged grief disorder is when an individual is so overwhelmed with feelings of sadness as a result of the loss of a loved one that they develop a more complex and chronic form of grief. Symptoms include feelings of intense yearning, emotional pain, preoccupation with the deceased person, and a disruption in identity.

Qingming festival in China is when individuals visit the grave of their ancestors. They offer food, burn incense, and keep the site clean to show respect for the ancestor and to stay connected to them.

Restoration phases are when grief moves to the background of a person's life, and they try to do new activities and meet new people.

12 A Life Well Lived: Enriching the Experiences of Growing Older

Learning Outcomes

Define positive psychology and explain why we study it.

Outline the biopsychosocial, developmental, and sociocultural influences on well-being and resilience across the adult years.

Identify potential interventions for increasing well-being during adulthood.

Describe the future of adult development and aging.

Identify the global and sociocultural challenges the field of adulthood and aging will face in the future.

Name some of the field's emerging areas.

Explain how a person would become a developmental psychologist/gerontologist studying adult development and aging, and identify other careers in the field.

There is a Cherokee parable called Two Wolves that describes a conversation between a grandfather and his grandson:

> An old Cherokee man is teaching his grandson about life. "A fight is going on inside me," he says to the boy.
>
> "It is a terrible fight and it is between two wolves. One is evil," he continues. "He is anger, envy, sorrow, regret, greed, arrogance, self-pity, guilt, resentment, inferiority, lies, false pride, superiority, and ego. The other one is good. He is joy, peace, love, hope, serenity, humility, kindness, benevolence, empathy, generosity, truth, compassion, and faith. The same fight is going on inside you – and inside every other person, too."
>
> The grandson thinks about this for a minute and then asks his grandfather, "Which wolf will win?"
>
> His grandfather simply replies, "The one you feed."

DOI: 10.4324/9781003483809-12

As graduate students interviewing individuals who were living with Alzheimer's disease (AD) or Parkinson's disease (PD) and their caregivers, our aims were to learn about what made them resilient and helped them to adjust to these devastating, chronic, progressive, and life-altering conditions.

Growing older is marked by many biopsychosocial and developmental changes and **successful aging** means adapting well and maintaining quality of life. From our personal experiences interacting with these older people and our research on these topics, we learned that an individual's mood and approach to managing emotions are critical to adjustment to living with a chronic condition and maintaining high quality of life. Our research was relevant not only to people with chronic conditions but also those facing age-related challenges as well.

But what does it mean to age well? Why, we kept asking ourselves, do some people become the masters of their age-related conditions and others the victims? Why do some people see their aging or health as a conquerable challenge, while others feel overwhelmed by it? Is personality the key? Is it values? Is it faith? Is it social support and valuable resources? Who chooses which wolf to feed, and why? We wondered if, perhaps, the biopsychosocial model could help tease apart these questions.

What is it about our personalities, our experiences, and the cultural milieu that we develop within that influences who we become and how we grow and change over time? We sought to understand how people facing developmental changes make meaning out of their lived experiences.

It is common to human nature that most of us want to be happy and live satisfying lives. Good health and aging well contribute to a fulfilling life, and age-related challenges such as poor health impairs our quality of life. In turn, genetic predisposition, environmental factors, and risky behaviors may all have negative health outcomes and make the older years more challenging. Throughout this book, we have explored the process of growth and change across the adult years from a biopsychosocial approach. Although it is important to understand the role of biological, psychological, and social factors in development, it is equally important to explore these links in the context of positive developmental outcomes. How we adapt to life's challenges depends in large part on which wolf we feed, as the Cherokee parable says. Knowing which cognitive styles and personal resources lead to better developmental outcomes can help us all make choices that contribute to emotional health and well-being and aging successfully.

In this chapter, we explore the **positive psychology** of aging and health. And then we turn to the future of the field of adult development and aging. We look at how biopsychosocial factors influence our approach to and management of our development across the adult years, and how we can achieve positive outcomes – high quality of life and well-being, a life well lived. We also examine the characteristics, types, and qualities of **happiness**, well-being, and **resilience** in the United States and around the world. As we have seen so often in previous chapters, personality, culture, spirituality, and humor intersect with genetics, health, and illness.

Positive Psychology, Well-Being, and Adult Development

"If psychologists wish to improve the human condition, it is not enough to help those who suffer. The majority… also need examples and advice to reach a richer and more fulfilling existence," wrote Martin Seligman, the father of the positive psychology movement (Seligman & Csikszentmihalyi, 2000).

The field of psychology is changing. We are moving toward a strengths-based approach and away from a deficits-based approach. We no longer seek to understand psychological dysfunction but also how psychologically healthy people can live happier and more fulfilled lives (Frazier, 2025). This approach is embodied in the field of positive psychology, which focuses on understanding optimal human functioning (Seligman & Csikszentmihalyi, 2000) and what makes life most worth living (Peterson et al., 2008). Positive psychology seeks to uncover the factors that relate to what is best in life and what remedies the worst in life, and it challenges scientists, practitioners, and students alike to think about strengths as well as weaknesses. Here we consider what makes life good and explore how we adapt to developmental challenges across the adult years.

The Development of Positive Psychology

Positive psychology was born in 1998 when Martin Seligman, then president of the American Psychological Association (APA), made it the centerpiece of his presidency. In the three decades since, positive psychology has become a crucial pillar in the field and its popularity is still growing among the general public, the academic community, and mental health providers. Because of its focus on the intraindividual, interpersonal, and sociocultural factors, it has helped identify and promote positive approaches to living within the context of economic, sociocultural, developmental, mental, and physical health challenges.

Positive psychology goes hand in hand with the biopsychosocial model. Both are based on the idea that happiness, or a good life, is not just the absence of what is bad, problematic, or emotionally challenging (Frazier, 2025). Instead, learning how to be happy is just as important as learning how to avoid feeling bad. Keep in mind, though, that we are discussing evidence-based, empirically sound psychological science – not untested self-help.

Since its inception the area of positive psychology has experienced several waves of theory and research. The first wave was focused simplistically on understanding well-being and flourishing (Lomas & Ivtzan, 2016; van Zyl et al., 2024). The second wave pursued the complexity of flourishing, integrating the dynamic nature of both positive and negative experiences as influences on positive outcomes, such as post-traumatic growth. The third wave focused on broadening the concept of positive psychology to think about the interactional and intersectional nature of individuals within their social systems, cultures, and contexts (van Zyl et al., 2024).

This approach is timely. Our society is aging rapidly. Estimates are that 50% of the U.S. population will be age 65 or older by 2036 (Kim et al., 2021). Most research efforts in the biomedical and social science fields have focused on prevention and treatment of chronic diseases. Still the number of years lost to disability continues to increase, and the gains that we have made in life expectancy are reversing in some racioethnic groups (Kim et al., 2021). It has never been more important to examine psychological assets like resilience, adaptation, and well-being that may promote longevity and quality of life.

Adaptation

How people adapt to the complex nature of aging, health, and illness has been likened to a desert mirage. From a distance, aging well, good health, and adaptation to living with illness appear clear, and yet, just as researchers and clinicians try to define them, they can seem to disappear (Dubos, 1961; Walker et al., 2004).

Adaptation is a dynamic process; we are always changing. As we change, we adapt and adjust our thoughts and behaviors to make our situations as favorable as we can for ourselves. We use conscious awareness and personal choices to create greater consistency in our lives (Roy & Andrews, 1999; Weinert et al., 2008). Like the mirage, adaptation is sometimes hard to grasp

Figure 12.1 A desert mirage.
Source: Shutterstock.

and harder still to measure scientifically. Although an optimal state of health, aging well, and high quality of life may appear to be easily understood, researchers and clinicians find it difficult to define how we adapt to achieve each.

Successful Aging is Adaptation

In the context of development, adaptation has been a topic of interest to gerontologists for a long time. Think back to Chapters 1 and 2 where we talked about Baltes and his concept of successful aging as a process of selective optimization with compensation. That is exactly what adaptation is. We adapt by selectively choosing aspects of ourselves, our personalities, cognitions, emotions and behaviors to optimize in order to compensate for aspects of ourselves that are changing. For example, a woman in her 60s who is losing her hearing due to age-related hearing loss may be sad that she has difficulties hearing her grandchildren's giggles and stories. She may choose to spend time with them in situations where they can be together without extraneous noise and where she can sit close and have them repeat things. This change in her behavior will allow her to preserve her meaningful social interactions with her grandchildren, just as getting hearing aids would. We can find many ways to compensate for developmental changes, and doing so allows us to adapt better to those changes, and to age more successfully.

People make lifestyle choices and behavioral changes to be healthier, to have more energy, and to improve their mood and self-esteem. As we know, in midlife many people develop health conditions that require medical management, such as changes in vision and hearing, high blood pressure and high cholesterol, and diabetes. Adaptation is also necessary when one is diagnosed with a chronic condition, must undergo surgery, develops physical disabilities, or becomes a caregiver for a loved one with a chronic illness. All of these are highly stressful situations, demanding significant adjustment to a new distressing reality (Kleftaras & Psarra, 2012; Psarra & Kleftaras, 2013). In each, depression is a common symptom. Although some people manage to adapt successfully, others fail to adjust to and accept their circumstances (Psarra & Kleftaras, 2013).

Many factors may assist in adaptation – from positive personality traits, such as optimism and resilience, to a sense of control or meaning in life. In one study, researchers examined factors that promoted positive adaptation during a major life transition that confronts millions of college freshmen every year – adapting to college. Students who had an optimistic thinking style were more likely to have a positive adjustment to college (Leary & DeRosier, 2012; Umucu et al., 2024).

In this chapter we are thinking about what it means to age well, no matter where you are in adulthood. Like the opening parable, how we achieve that depends a lot on what we choose for ourselves.

Aging, Wellness, and Well-Being

Many people do not feel their age until they experience age-related changes that bring it into focus for them. For example, noticing that you are not able to lift as much weight at the gym when you are 40 as you did when you were 20; looking in the mirror and noticing the smile lines that give your face a new character; reflecting that you are more committed to mentoring and helping your junior colleagues than competing with them; realizing that you see yourself in the last third of your life rather than the first two thirds.

Many people sense that they are growing older when they notice physical changes. As we have seen throughout this book, aging and health go hand-in-hand. Our health affects and is affected by many facets of our lives, from age, employment, and income to social activities, moods, and overall well-being (Binder & Coad, 2013).

Linkages between health and living a long life relate to our health-promoting behaviors and good coping strategies, and the positive impact they have on our health. We know about the importance of getting enough sleep, eating well, exercising, fostering a sense of control, being connected to others, having financial stability, and not smoking. These factors and others come together to create **wellness**. We have also considered health-compromising behaviors and poor lifestyle choices, and their negative impact on aging, health, and wellness. We have examined how developmental stressors such as changes in relationships, employment status, living arrangement, becoming a caregiver, and living with chronic illness in its terminal phase can challenge one's sense of self and quality of life. Yet people facing developmental changes and health crises can adapt and grow in the face of these challenges, attaining well-being. To better understand how and why, it helps to know the differences between wellness and well-being.

Wellness

Wellness is good physical and mental health. Aging well means having good physical and mental health, so to a degree aging well is synonymous with wellness. Wellness is a continuum. There are varying degrees of wellness, even for those who are ill. For a high level of wellness, good health is important; stress, chronic disorders, poor health, and pain significantly reduce wellness. Wellness is a dynamic concept, as our mental and physical health change over time according to our experiences; so too does wellness. However, wellness hinges on integrating and balancing one's physical and mental states (Dunn, 1977), including body, mind, and spirit (Bezner et al., 1997).

The **wheel of wellness** (Kauppi et al., 2023; Sweeney & Witmer, 1991; Witmer & Sweeney, 1992; Witmer et al., 1998) is comprised of seven factors that contribute to an optimal state of health. They cover every domain of our lives: spiritual, emotional, intellectual, physical, social, environmental, and financial. Regardless of your age, there are simple things that you can do to live better and achieve greater wellness. The ability to self-regulate, identify with one's work, and maintain valuable friendships are the strongest predictors of wellness (Hermon & Hazler, 1999).

Other research on wellness has identified as many as 12 different factors. A sense of self-worth and a sense of control over one's life are crucial, and poor health and illness can take a toll on both. Emotional awareness, coping effectively, and realistic beliefs are important, so too are stress management and creative problem solving. Having a strong sense of identity, including cultural identity, helps to strengthen one's sense of self in the face of aging and health challenges. Aspects of wellness can vary by gender, culture, and point in the lifespan.

As you might imagine, maintaining a sense of humor is essential in the face of crises of any kind (Tandler & Proyer, 2022; Proyer et al., 2018). When we recognize and appreciate something funny (Solomon, 1996), it leads to beneficial physical changes: a hearty laugh causes the skeletal muscles to relax and stimulates heart rate and circulation bringing an influx of energy and nutrients to vital organs, and also boosts the immune system. A sense of humor assists in digestion and, through the release of endorphins in the brain, enhances wellness and a sense of well-being (Erdman, 1991). Even better, it lessens symptoms of depression, provides pain relief (Carroll, 1990), boosts self-esteem, and lowers perceived stress (Kuiper et al., 1993). People who

Figure 12.2 Laughter is the best medicine.

Source: Shutterstock.

have a good sense of humor are often more positive and respond better to both positive and negative life events (Martin et al., 1993; Solomon, 1996). Finally, looking on the bright side of things helps promote self-awareness and social cohesion and diffuses conflicts and feelings of hostility (Burns, 1989; Burns et al., 1996; Morreall, 1991; Richman, 1995).

Related to having a good sense of humor, playfulness across the life span and especially in adulthood is linked to many positive outcomes, from better coping and increased life satisfaction and well-being, to better relationships with others, higher work–life balance, and greater satisfaction at work (Clifford et al., 2024; Lubbers et al., 2023; Shen, 2020; Tandler et al., 2024).

No matter where you are in the adult lifespan, greater wellness may be one of the factors that differentiates a person who sees opportunities for growth even in the face of life's challenges from someone who feels helpless and overwhelmed. As the old Cherokee story goes, where you fall on the illness–wellness continuum may be, in large part, due to which wolf you choose to feed.

Well-Being

Wellness and well-being are intertwined. Whereas wellness refers to our state of mental and physical health, well-being is how we feel about ourselves and our lives, including our health. Well-being, too, has many components.

Well-being is characterized by a sense of fulfillment and purpose in life (Whitbourne & Ebmeyer, 2013). People who are high in well-being are curious about the world around them and enjoy their lives and relationships. They tend to have positive relationships with others and a sense of control in their lives.

Well-being is a biopsychosocial concept – the physical, psychological, and social aspects interact and influence one another. Well-being is influenced by the environment and our socioeconomic status (SES) too. Like wellness, well-being is related to aging and health. Physical well-being is the knowledge that we can function typically in such activities as bathing, dressing, eating, and moving around (U.S. Department of Health and Human Services, 2000). Emotional well-being is a result of having intact cognitive capacities and minimal fear, anxiety, stress, depression, or other negative emotions. Finally, social well-being is the ability to derive fulfillment from social, familial, and intimate engagement with others.

Psychology began to focus on well-being in 1989, when Carol Ryff saw a gap in research on aging and health: no one focused on the positive outcomes. Like the wheel of wellness, Ryff's concept of well-being encompasses many different factors.

- Autonomy: living in accord with one's personal convictions.
- Environmental mastery: the ability to manage one's own life.
- Personal growth: reaching full potential.

- Positive relationships: fulfilling relations with others.
- Purpose in life: a sense that life has meaning and direction.
- Self-acceptance: self-awareness and acceptance of oneself.

Ryff's model is outlined in Table 12.1. As you can see, many factors can influence well-being – from gender, age, and education, to income, employment status, social and intimate relationships, and personality (Binder & Coad, 2013). Health is a strong correlate of well-being, which is relevant as we age. The healthier you feel, the higher your well-being is likely to be (Dolan & Peasgood, 2008; Easterlin, 2003). Aging and disabilities lower overall well-being (Brickman et al., 1978; Oswald & Powdthavee, 2008; Uppal, 2006), as does living with chronic conditions such as rheumatoid arthritis, gastric distress, migraines, epilepsy, pain, and drug and alcohol abuse (Binder & Coad, 2013). The treatments for chronic and life-threatening illnesses may also affect well-being. Although there are no treatments or cures for aging, one can certainly strive to age well to maintain a high psychological well-being.

Table 12.1 Dimensions of the psychological well-being scale

Autonomy	
High scorer	Is self-determining and independent; resists social pressures to think and act in certain ways; regulates behavior from within; evaluates self by personal standards
Low scorer	Is concerned about the expectations and evaluations of others; relies on judgment of others to make important decisions; conforms to social pressures to think and act in certain ways
Environmental Mastery	
High scorer	Has a sense of mastery and competence in managing the environment; controls a complex array of external activities; makes effective use of surrounding opportunities; is able to choose or create contexts suitable to personal needs and values
Low scorer	Has difficulty managing everyday affairs; feels unable to change or improve surrounding context; is unaware of surrounding opportunities; lacks sense of control over external world
Personal Growth	
High scorer	Has a feeling of continued development; sees self as growing and expanding; is open to new experiences; has sense of realizing potential; sees improvement in self and behavior over time; is changing in ways that reflect more self-knowledge and effectiveness
Low scorer	Has a sense of personal stagnation; lacks sense of improvement or expansion over time; feels bored and uninterested with life; feels unable to develop new attitudes or behaviors

(*Continued*)

Table 12.1 (Continued)

Positive Relationships	
High scorer	Has warm, satisfying, trusting relationships with others; is concerned about the welfare of others; is capable of strong empathy, affection, and intimacy; understands give and take of human relationships
Low scorer	Has few close, trusting relationships with others; finds it difficult to be warm, open, concerned about others; is isolated and frustrated in interpersonal relationships; is not willing to make compromises to sustain important ties with others
Purpose in Life	
High scorer	Has goals in life and a sense of direction; feels there is meaning to present and past life; holds beliefs that give life purpose; has aims and objectives for living
Low scorer	Lacks a sense of meaning in life; has few goals or aims; lacks sense of direction; does not see purpose in past life; has no outlooks or beliefs that give meaning
Self-Acceptance	
High scorer	Possesses a positive attitude toward the self; acknowledges and accepts multiple aspects of self, including good and bad qualities; feels positive about past life
Low scorer	Feels dissatisfied with self; is disappointed with what has occurred in past life; is troubled by certain personal qualities; wishes to be different

Source: Ryff (2014).

Well-Being Across the Lifespan

How does well-being change across the adult lifespan? Younger and middle-aged adults see themselves as improving over time in well-being, whereas older adults often anticipate declines (Frazier et al., 2012; Ryff, 2014) and personal growth and purpose in life do appear to decline with age. Whenever we face a challenge, whether it be a move or change in our living, work, or marital and familial situations, age-related problems, or chronic illness, our well-being is at stake. Adverse outcomes, whether a hearing or visual impairment, mobility issues, or unemployment can cause a decline in the overall quality of life, independent of age, sex, education, or frailty (Andrew et al., 2012). People who have higher environmental mastery, autonomy, and personal growth tend to navigate changes better (Frazier et al., 2012). People with greater well-being have fewer chronic conditions, are more productive in life and work, and are less likely to need or use health care services (Keyes & Grzywacz, 2005). Lower levels of well-being are associated with greater mortality five years after a life challenge (Andrew et al., 2012).

Older adults' perceptions of their own aging and being older influences well-being and quality of life (Hausknecht et al., 2020). We have seen throughout this book that what it means to be "old," or to feel whatever age you happen to be, is the product of an ongoing, dynamic interaction between oneself and sociocultural and historical influences. When societies or the structures and people within them view aging negatively, it perpetuates ageist, ableist perceptions that are internalized by those who are aging, causing physical and psychological consequences (Levy, 2009; Wurm et al., 2013). Ageism is a prejudice against older people and the aging process and it is one of the most pervasive and widely accepted forms of prejudice throughout the world (Palmore, 2001; World Health Organization [WHO], 2015). Ageism has three components (Hausknecht et al., 2020) – the cognitive (focused on stereotypes of aging and older people); the affective (focused on the prejudicial attitudes and the emotions associated with them), and the behavioral (such as any words or actions that are discriminatory to older people). In addition, ageism along these three dimensions can be implicit (unconscious and not openly articulated) or explicit (conscious and articulated) (Iversen et al., 2009). Ageism and the stereotyping and discrimination that result from it create stigma against older people that they then can internalize, creating negative self-perceptions of one's age, being older, and the aging process. Needless to say, age-stereotype internalization and negative perceptions of aging can undermine successful aging and well-being in later life.

The way that societies frame aging can impact how individuals perceive their own age and the positive and negative aspects of the aging process. In adults older than 65, feeling younger leads to higher well-being, perhaps because feeling younger late in life is tied directly to health. Older adults who feel better also tend to feel younger (Ward, 2010). At any age, however, higher well-being depends on having a realistic perspective of ourselves, our aging, and our health (Frazier et al., 2012; Lachman et al., 2008). Theoretical frameworks of growing older that emphasize successful, positive, and active ways of aging can help individuals age better and enjoy a higher quality of life (Hausknecht et al., 2020).

Successful Aging

The renowned architect Frank Lloyd Wright once said, "The longer I live, the more beautiful life becomes." Gerontologists, who focus on studying the aging process, argue that now that people are living longer, maintaining well-being and quality of life for as long as possible, rather than just avoiding disease or disability, is the key goal. The idea is to "add life to years," not merely to add years to your life. We have seen throughout this book how important successful aging is in terms of reducing our probability of disease and disability and aiming for high cognitive and physical functioning and active engagement throughout the later years (Rowe & Kahn, 1997; Friedman et al., 2019).

Interestingly, gerontologists have also uncovered the well-being paradox, in which older adults who have significant health challenges (including disease and disability) still report high levels of subjective well-being. Those of us who are younger might wonder: how can you be happy with all those aches and pains? Research shows that younger and older adults do not hold the same expectations about what later life and the aging process will be like (Castel, 2019). For instance, in one large-scale study of people aged 75 or older, 80% said they were "happy" or "very happy" (Castel, 2019; Taylor, 2009). The emotional effect for older adults may skew more positively.

Many theories and models of successful aging that we have covered in this book capture and articulate what people can do to offset disease, prolong functioning, and remain actively engaged in life. From the perspective of developmental science, we can make lifestyle choices at any age that will increase our chances of successful aging. In the words of jazz musician Eubie Blake, "If I knew I was going to live this long, I would have taken better care of myself" (Castel, 2019). This quotation captures what we have tried to emphasize in this book – that we can all live a life that leads to good health, growth, and successful aging. Our attitudes and beliefs, happiness and life satisfaction, engagement in mental enrichment and physical exercise, and positive social relationships are the keys to successful aging and adding life to our years.

Figure 12.3 Resilience.

Source: Shutterstock.

Resilience

Another important positive psychological trait is resilience. Resilience is the ability to successfully adapt and recover in the face of acute stress, trauma, or chronic adversity (Charney, 2004). Given the many changes that a person faces as they navigate adulthood and aging, including chronic health conditions, retirement, relocation, and loss of loved ones, resilience is a key characteristic for successful aging. Resilience is how we recover or rebound from stressors, and how long it takes to regain equilibrium (Zautra et al., 2010b). It is our "ordinary magic" (Frazier, 2025; Masten, 2001). Resilience has also been referred to as a "constellation of risk factors and resources that predict developmental outcomes" (Staudinger & Greve, 2015, p. 1). Its aim is to achieve and hold on to well-being in the face of developmental challenges and stressors.

An emphasis on resilience is part of a major shift in thinking about aging, health, and wellness – and it could be a novel way to conceptualize growth and change over the adult life course. The concept of resilience originated from the study of children who survived difficult or abusive home environments (adverse childhood experiences). Resilience is not simply the absence of stressful life events, but the process of cultivating healthy mental, emotional, and physical habits to help us cope with them when they arise.

Resilience has three overlapping steps (Zautra et al., 2010a). The first step is recovery, or a return to baseline functioning. The second step is moving forward with minimal disruption. Finally, when we can move beyond previous levels of adaptation, we can experience growth. Each step is important to facing the unexpected challenges associated with growing older.

Sources of Resilience

Where does resilience come from? Resilience stems from the interaction between internal capacities, such as optimism or a sense of control, and external resources, such as family, friends, and community. While some initial distress in the face of a stressful situation is normal and even beneficial for adaptation, to cope with stress over time we need additional resources.

Resilience is a personal resource but is not a personality trait. Unlike personality traits, which are internal and unchanging, resilience is dynamic, and resilient people can change how they cope with stress. Here are just some of the resources on which they can draw (Dunkel Schetter & Dolbier, 2011).

- Dispositional resources, such as emotional stability and empathy.
- Ego-related resources, such as a sense of autonomy and a positive self-image.
- Interpersonal resources, such as family support and quality relationships.
- Culturally based beliefs, such as spirituality and concerns for benevolence and justice.
- Behavioral and cognitive skills, such as mindfulness, social skills, and creativity.
- Other resources, such as SES, a healthy diet, and exercise.

Resilience is better thought of as a process that encapsulates recovery, forward movement, and positive growth after stressful or traumatic experiences (Frazier, 2025).

Though it does not get a lot of recognition, a propensity for resilience is the norm and may even be universal (Gallo et al., 2007; Zautra et al., 2010a), and feats of resilience are common across the lifespan (Bonanno, 2004; Garmezy, 1991; Greve & Staudinger, 2006). People who have faced poverty, childhood emotional abuse, war, or natural disaster, or who live with disability or a chronic condition do not always develop mental or physical health problems. Rather, they may develop a strong sense of growth in adversity, and that sense provides a buffer against future stressors and health challenges.

Although the concept of resilience arose from studies of children who were invincible in the face of traumatic, high-risk, or adverse situations, people of all ages can think about "finding a silver lining," "discovering what really matters in life," "learning how much others cared," or "uncovering hidden strengths" (Zautra, 2003).

Sociocultural influences are also important to resilience. Communities matter. Think about the resilience of Los Angeles residents after the fires in California in January 2025, or of Kyoto Animation staff after the arson attack in July 2019, where neighbors or even strangers helped one another in the face of trauma. In addition, how ethnic minorities adapt to illness and infirmity may relate to how they sustain themselves in the face of the trauma from racism (Becker & Newsom, 2005). For example, Hispanic people with a strong attachment to their heritage have significantly better health outcomes (Fuentes-Afflick et al., 1999; Gould et al., 2003).

It might seem that the burdens of aging are greater for racial and ethnic minorities (Dowd & Bengtson, 1978), but all groups can overcome adversity through self-determination and community (Becker & Newsom, 2005; James, 1994). Adesogan examined data from a large longitudinal study of African American families (the Protecting Strong African American Families program or ProSAAF) (Barton et al., 2018) and found that three systems were critical for resilience in Black Americans: 1) the individual, which includes one's religious and/or spiritual beliefs; 2) the relational, which includes one's romantic partner, family, and social circle; and 3) the community, which includes one's neighborhood and larger sociocultural context. Each of these systems was important independently for predicting resilience but the additive effect was even more profound (Adesogan et al., 2024).

Resilience, Aging, and Health

Although life is filled with stress, chronic long-term stress is bad for health (Baum et al., 1999; Dunkel Schetter & Dolbier, 2011; Thoits, 2010). It can be devastating to live with a life-threatening medical condition, such as cancer, human immunodeficiency virus (HIV), or AD. In these cases, resilience can literally be a matter of life and death (Bower & Hayes, 1998; Dunkel Schetter

& Dolbier, 2011; Pakenham & Cox, 2009; Park et al., 2010; Xu & Roberts, 2010). Positive emotions, like those that give rise to resilience, are linked in many ways to longevity and survival (Xu & Roberts, 2010). Positive adaptation to breast cancer, which is common in many middle-aged and older women, gives women a greater sense of control over the disease, bolsters their self-esteem, and increases their optimism for the future (Taylor, 1993). They are attempting to find balance between the good and the bad in their lives – much like the Cherokee belief in "the one you feed." That balance in mind, body, and spirit is what leads to the overall experience of a high quality of life (Albrecht & Devlieger, 1999; Ubel et al., 2005). It is the ability to adapt, to find meaning, and to maintain emotional health in the face of disability, and it is crucial to resilience.

Across adulthood, and especially in the later years, resilience can be seen in how people adapt to many age-related changes, whether they are cognitive, physical, emotional, functional, relational, social, or other kinds of changes. Some of the resources critical to resilience are a sense of control, **agency**, adaptability of goals, and the ability to reframe stressors and cope with them in adaptive ways (Staudinger & Greve, 2015).

Happiness and Hope

Although we all think we know what happiness is, psychologists define happiness as the appreciation of life as a whole – or how much you like the life you lead (Veenhoven, 2008). It is essentially having lots of positive affect and little negative affect (Diener, 2000; Diener & Lucas, 1999). And that turns out to be important to good health and successful development during the adult years.

Happiness stems from having good relationships, fulfilling work, spirituality, and a passion for life. What does not matter, surprisingly, is money (Vohs & Baumeister, 2011), although spending money on others can make us happy (Dunn et al., 2008). You might feel happy if you are having "a good day." What does it mean to have a good day? Well, it touches on three common features: autonomy, competence, and connection to others. That means that happiness is the freedom to make our own decisions, to feel competent at whatever we are doing, and to share our lives with others. College students who took an online course in positive psychology that taught them how to maximize their happiness and wellbeing had less anxiety and depression and higher levels of happiness (Smith et al., 2023). This shows that we can improve our lives by focusing on being happy. Yale University's Dr. Laurie Santos has taught what is, without a doubt, the most popular college course ever. Yale University does not even have a room big enough for all the students who want to take her "The Science of Well-being" course each semester. Based on the data that Dr. Santos has collected on over four million students who have taken her course, the results are astounding: students are, on average, 17% happier after taking her course than they were on the first day (Yaden et al.,

2021). Luckily, Dr. Santos's class at Yale is available online for free for anyone who would like to learn to be happier. You can also learn how to be happier through "Pursuit-of-Happiness" programs, which are also available online.

Even in the face of late life, centenarians report high levels of happiness, especially the positive feeling of having a good laugh (Jopp & Smith, 2006). These older adults have not just beaten the odds, and they do not necessarily benefit from higher levels of education, income, or social status. Rather, both prospective and longitudinal studies show that happiness serves as a protective factor in relation to health and mortality (Steptoe, 2019). Some researchers theorize that we each have a set point of happiness, much like a thermometer. They argue that we return to that set point as we adapt to changing circumstances. It may be a genetic predisposition, and it may account for as much as 50% of our happiness, as opposed to the 10% that can be attributed to life circumstances. But that still leaves 40% that we can hope to control through the power of change (Lyubomirsky et al., 2005). In one novel study that used ecological momentary assessment, participants reported their levels of happiness at scheduled or random times during the day, week, and month to demonstrate day-to-day fluctuations in happiness. Results from these assessments show that happiness, even over the course of a single day, has an impact on survival (Steptoe & Wardle, 2011). One thing to remember is that happiness requires both daily, and lasting, commitments (Lyubomirsky, 2008).

Hope goes hand-in-hand with happiness. Hope is the feeling that occurs you expect or desire something to happen in the future. When you are faced with an obstacle, what do you do? Do you actively look for ways around it? Do you persist, or give up? If you are often able to find another path to your goals, chances are you have a hopeful outlook on life. How hopeful are you? Complete the State Hope Scale to find out (Snyder et al., 1996).

The State Hope Scale

Read each item carefully. Using the scale shown below, please select the number that best describes how you think about yourself right now.

Please take a few moments to focus on yourself and what is going on in your life at this moment. Once you have this "here and now" mindset, go ahead and answer each item using the following scale.

1 = Definitely false
2 = Mostly false
3 = Somewhat false
4 = Slightly false
5 = Slightly true

6 = Somewhat true
7 = Mostly true
8 = Definitely true

1 If I should find myself in a jam, I could think of many ways to get out of it.
2 At the present time, I am energetically pursuing my goals.
3 There are lots of ways around any problem that I am facing now.
4 Right now I see myself as being pretty successful.
5 I can think of many ways to reach my current goals.
6 At this time, I am meeting the goals I have set for myself.

Scoring: Combine your scores on each item. Higher scores indicate a greater sense of hope. If you have a score of 36 or higher, you are a hopeful individual.

What is hope? There is actually no agreed-upon definition of hope. Hope can be seen as a trait, sometimes a state, a personal attribute, an experience, an emotion, or even a life force (Southerland et al., 2016). What we do know is that hope has affective, cognitive, and behavioral components. Whereas fear is an automatic emotional response, hope is an emotional and cognitive process. Hope involves having goals for each day and for the future. It derives from a sense of success, along with the energy and the ability to find pathways to get there (Snyder, 2002; Snyder et al., 2002).

It is probably not surprising that hope is found to consistently relate to better outcomes, whether in academics, athletics, psychological adjustment, or physical health. It is associated with greater adherence to medical regimens and higher levels of satisfaction with medical treatment (Makarem et al., 2010; Nekolaichuk, 2015). When a doctor tells a middle-aged patient that he needs to lose weight to avoid a heart attack, hope assists with the challenge of sticking to a new diet and exercise regimen.

Related to hope is agency – the sense that our behavior is under our control. In the hope scale above, agency is also assessed (add up your scores on the even items only to find out how high you rate in agency). Agency includes a belief that we can change our environment, as well as be changed by it. We do so not only through what we think and feel but also through what we choose to do or not do.

Positive Emotions and Positive Outcomes

There are many benefits of positive emotional states (Steptoe, 2019; Zautra, 2003) when navigating life's challenges at any point in the adult lifespan. Happiness opens doors to other desirable outcomes, such as good performance at school, satisfaction at work, close and fulfilling intimate and social relationships, good health, and a long life. It is also an important buffer against the damaging effects of disappointments and setbacks experienced throughout life, including health crises (Peterson, 2006).

There is plenty of evidence that the happier you are, the better your health (Steptoe, 2019; Veenhoven, 2008; Veenhoven & Hagerty, 2006) and the longer your life (Lyyra et al., 2006; Veenhoven, 2008). This association exists at the personal and global levels. For example, a longitudinal study of Catholic nuns found that happiness, love, and hope at an early age were predictive of longer life (Siahpush et al., 2008). Similarly, a 20-year longitudinal study of Finnish twins found that happiness was associated with lower mortality (Koivumaa-Honkanen et al., 2000). The correlation holds regardless of age, gender, SES, and personality – and across nations (Helliwell, 2001; Helliwell et al., 2015; Helliwell et al., 2019; Pierewan & Tampubolon, 2015). The correlation is also higher in people with illness than those without, making the importance of happiness to health outcomes clearer still; not that happiness cures disease and makes people well again – it does not (Veenhoven, 2008). But being a happy person can help us adjust to aging, maintain health, and adapt to chronic illness.

How do positive emotions such as happiness protect us? First, chronic unhappiness triggers the fight-or-flight response, which can elevate blood pressure and lower immune functioning. Conversely, a positive mood may lead to better immune functioning (Pressman & Cohen, 2005). Second, happy people appear to take better care of themselves and be more health conscious, at least in part because they are more self-confident and open to new experiences (Zautra, 2003). They are more likely to have a well-balanced diet, watch their weight, engage in sports, and attend to symptoms of illness (Ormel, 1980; Schulz & Decker, 1985; Veenhoven, 2008). Happy people engage in fewer health-compromising behaviors, as well, with lower rates of drinking and smoking (Veenhoven, 2008). Finally, happy people have more friends and more satisfying close relationships. A 2010 paper, "What's love got to do with it?", reported on the daily happiness, social functioning, and perceived health of married octogenarians. Although happiness may decline with age for both men and women, marital satisfaction buffers the day-to-day impact of poor health (Waldinger & Schulz, 2010). In our experiences as graduate student researchers (see the chapter's opening story), we certainly saw this firsthand in the spouse caregivers of patients with devastating illnesses. Our conversations with hundreds of patients about their experiences taught us that, as the Cherokee saying goes, coping with stress and adapting to aging depends on whichever wolf – positive or negative – you feed.

The Future of the Field of Adult Development and Aging

Like any science, the field of adult development and aging is always changing and always teaching us something new.

Many people who work in the field of adult development and aging are focused on research and clinical practice in order to understand how people

Figure 12.4 Success is a journey not a destination.
Source: Shutterstock.

grow and change across the adult years, and how to optimize development and promote good mental and physical health. Today, promoting healthy and successful aging, promoting education, and providing evidence-based guidance for helping people make the most of their later years is crucially important. With the changing demographics of the world, and the global age wave, people who work with adults and especially older adults need to be culturally sensitive and aware of the intersectional nature of social determinants of health and aging.

The lifespan developmental perspective is required to truly understand development holistically across the lifespan. Developmental psychologists who focus on adulthood and aging are interested in understanding the varied ways in which people grow and change over time and how to cultivate good developmental outcomes no matter where you are in the lifespan. Developmental research that begins early in childhood and follows people into later life is critical to the success of aging and aging well. Throughout this book, we have recognized the value of longitudinal studies to understanding health.

What Does It Take to Be a Developmental Psychologist Who Studies Adult Development and Aging?

Most developmental psychologists have earned a Doctorate in Philosophy (PhD) in Developmental Psychology, and through this training are prepared to carry out scientific research and teach at universities and colleges. As you

Figure 12.5 Gerontologists focus on improving the lives of older people.
Source: Shutterstock.

know, developmental psychologists, regardless of what part of the lifespan they are interested in, are focused on understanding changes in physical, cognitive, intellectual, emotional, perceptual, personality, and social growth over time. Developmental scientists who conduct research are focused on providing evidence-based information to help people reach their full potential.

Developmental psychologists and gerontologists work in a variety of different settings, from academia (colleges and universities) to government or other agencies concerned with aging, to the health care sector and residential facilities. People who work in academia focus on research and teaching, and people who work in applied settings such as clinics, assisted living facilities, hospitals, and mental health clinics, focus on providing care.

What Is Gerontology and What Do Gerontologists Do?

While geriatrics is the medical field concerned with aging, the aging body, and age-related medical conditions, gerontology is the study of the biopsychosocial aspects of later life. Gerontologists have a multidisciplinary focus on the physical, emotional, cognitive, social, and societal implications of aging. Whether you think of it as the "gray wave" or the "silver tsunami," people are aging around the world at an astounding rate. Students interested in gerontology might tackle some of the most pressing issues facing older adults today with a proactive focus on strengths-based applications to help people age well despite disease and disability. Gerontologists focus on improving quality of life for older people through health care and public policy. A gerontologist might assess the needs of the elderly by considering their physical and mental health, their well-being and social engagement, and the sociocultural context in which they live. As the population ages the important role of gerontologists is becoming increasingly apparent. The great news about this field is that you can become a gerontologist without having to complete a doctorate. There are many masters level programs that offer certificates for training in gerontology.

Population Aging and Careers in Gerontology

Population aging is taking place in nearly all countries (United Nations, 2017). In 2017, 962 million people around the world were older than 60 years, more than twice as many as in 1980. By 2050, the number of older adults will double again to reach over 2 billion people. That means that there will be more older adults than children. The fastest-growing segment of the older population worldwide is people over the age of 80 years old, who will represent 425 million people by 2050.

The aging of the population presents important challenges to medicine, health care, and health psychology. In developed countries, older adults are the main consumers of healthcare, and they have an increasing number of chronic conditions that need long-term medical and behavioral management. With the growing population of older adults, the focus on identifying and changing health behaviors becomes more important as well (Siegler et al., 2012). Health psychology must address risk factors for chronic illness and identify and promote successful aging.

While many of the health problems faced by older adults are the same as those for other age groups, aging presents several unique challenges. First among these is AD, the sixth leading cause of death in the United States today. Currently, one out of nine older people has AD, and as the population grows, this number will reach an alarming 13.8 million by 2050. Providing appropriate care to AD patients and their caregivers is crucial to maintaining health, well-being, and quality of life for as long as possible.

Dementia is another age-related illness that gerontologists address. Because it impacts a person's memory, attention, and communication skills, dementia makes carrying out ADLs difficult. Dementia is very common in later life and likelihood increases with age. According to the Health and Retirement Survey, 5% of people in their seventies have dementia, while nearly 38% of people in their nineties suffer from it (Kuchibhatla et al., 2020). Dementia can be comorbid with a number of different diseases, such as type 2 diabetes. Older adults with diabetes are at greater risk for dementia and heart disease and can suffer from many other disease-related complications that negatively impact their quality of life.

Gerontologists include psychologists, physicians, social workers, nursing home administrators, and any other career that specializes in aging and later life. There are many training programs in gerontology that can lead to fulfilling and impactful careers in the health sector, and, as the world population ages, employment opportunities will continue to increase.

If you would like to learn more about a future career in adult development and aging or gerontology you should consult the American Psychological Association's Division 20 for Adult Development and Aging. You may also be interested in looking at the resources available on the website for the Gerontological Society of America. The National Council on Aging is another great source of information.

Chapter Summary

Positive psychology has helped us recognize how individuals can live a healthy life, reduce the risk of negative physical and mental health outcomes, and cope more effectively when dealing with age-related challenges. Many interpersonal factors influence well-being and wellness. They include personality factors, such as positive affect, extraversion, optimism, and an internal locus of control. They also include tailoring one's coping efforts to the specific situation and finding social support. Resilience is not just the avoidance of stress or the absence of poor health but also the "everyday magic" of recovery. It differentiates people who, when faced with life-altering challenges, see them as opportunities for growth. Together, these ideas can help us maintain happiness, hope, and good mental and physical health. The field of adult development and aging is changing because the world is changing. Our aging and diversifying population points to the need for a biopsychosocial and lifespan developmental approach to health care and public policy, while global and national health disparities point to the necessity of focusing on the social and economic determinants of health and aging. Developmental psychologists who focus on adult development address these issues. For those who want to work in the field, innovative careers are available, especially in the field of gerontology.

Key Takeaways

1. There are many positive psychological outcomes that we can strive for across adulthood.
2. A strengths-based approach to development in aging should focus on the positive things one can do to age well.
3. The fields of developmental psychology and gerontology will be important in the future as global populations age.

Reflective Questions

1 What are some of your own positive psychological resources?
2 Do you think having hope and agency are important to your well-being?
3 What do you find appealing about the field of adult development and aging? Would you consider a career that involves working with older people?

Suggested Readings

Seligman, M., & Csikszentmihalyi, M. (2000). Positive psychology. *American Psychologist, 55*(1), 5–14.

van Zyl, L. E., Gaffaney, J., van der Vaart, L., Dik, B. J., & Donaldson, S. I. (2024). The critiques and criticisms of positive psychology: A systematic review. *The Journal of Positive Psychology, 19*(2), 206–235.

Hausknecht, S., Low, L. F., O'loughlin, K., McNab, J., & Clemson, L. (2020). Older adults' self-perceptions of aging and being older: A scoping review. *The Gerontologist, 60*(7), e524–e534.

Key Terms

Agency is the sense that an individual's behavior is under their control.

Happiness is appreciation of life as a whole – or how much an individual enjoys the life they lead.

Hope is expecting or desiring something to happen in the future.

Positive psychology focuses on understanding optimal human functioning.

Resilience is the ability to successfully adapt and recover in the face of acute stress, trauma, or chronic adversity.

Successful aging involves reducing the probability of disease and disability and aiming for high cognitive and physical functioning and active engagement throughout the later years.

Wellness is good physical and mental health.

The **wheel of wellness** is comprised of seven factors that contribute to an optimal state of health: spiritual, emotional, intellectual, physical, social, environmental, and financial.

References

Abasilim, C., Persky, V., Sargis, R. M., Argos, M., Daviglus, M., Freels, S., Cai, J., Tsintsifas, K., Isasi, C. R., Peters, B. A., Talavera, G. A., Thyagarajan, B., & Turyk, M. E. (2024). Thyroid-related hormones and hypertension incidence in middle-aged and older Hispanic/Latino adults: The HCHS/SOL study. *Journal of the Endocrine Society*, *8*(6), bvae088. doi: 10.1210/jendso/bvae088.

Abdelaal, M., Avery, J., Chow, R., Saleem, N., Fazelzad, R., Mosher, P., Hannon, B., Zimmermann, C., & Al-Awamer, A. (2023). Palliative care for adolescents and young adults with advanced illness: A scoping review. *Palliative Medicine*, *37*(1), 88–107. doi: 10.1177/02692163221136160.

Adelman, S., Blanchard, M., & Livingston. G. (2009). A systematic review of the prevalence and covariates of dementia or relative cognitive impairment in the older African-Caribbean population in Britain. *International Journal of Geriatric Psychiatry*, *24*(7), 657–665.

Aderinto, N., Abdulbasit, M., Olatunji, G., & Edun, M. (2023). The landscape of neuroscience research in Africa: Current state, progress, and challenges; A perspective. *Annals of Medicine and Surgery*, *85*(10), 5267–5274. doi: 10.1097/MS9.0000000000000001219.

Adesogan, O., Lavner, J. A., Carter, S. E., & Beach, S. R. (2024). Additive benefits of individual, relational, and community factors on physical- and mental-health trajectories among Black Americans. *Clinical Psychological Science*.

Adhikary, D., Barman, S., Ranjan, R., & Stone, H. (2022). A systematic review of major cardiovascular risk factors: A growing global health concern. *Cureus*, *14*(10), e30119. doi: 10.7759/cureus.30119.

Adinkrah, M. (2015). Suicide and mortuary beliefs and practices of the Akan of Ghana. *OMEGA – Journal of Death and Dying*, *74*(2), 138–163. doi: 10.1177/0030222815598427.

Adinkrah, M. (2022). If you die a bad death, we give you a bad burial: Mortuary practices and "bad death" among the Akan of Ghana. *Death Studies*, *46*(3), 695–707. doi: 10.1080/07481187.2020.1762264.

Adjaye-Gbewonyo, D., Rebok, G. W., Gallo, J. J., Gross, A. L., & Underwood, C. R. (2019). Urbanicity of residence and depression among adults 50 years and older in Ghana and South Africa: An analysis of the WHO Study on Global AGEing and Adult Health (SAGE). *Aging Mental Health*, *23*(6), 660–669. doi: 10.1080/13607863.2018.1450839.

Adjei, S. B., Adinkrah, M., & Mpiani, A. (2023). Gendered mourning: A perspective of Akan death culture in Ghana. *Death Studies*, *48*(5), 478–488. doi: 10.1080/07481187.2023.2236983.

Agu, J. C., Hee-Jeon, Y., Steel, A., & Adams, J. (2019). A systematic review of traditional, complementary and alternative medicine use amongst ethnic minority populations: A focus upon prevalence, drivers, integrative use, health outcomes, referrals and use of information sources. *Journal of Immigrant and Minority Health, 21*(5), 1137–1156. doi: 10.1007/s10903-018-0832-4.

Ahlström, G., & Sjöden, P. O. (1996). Coping with illness-related problems and quality of life in adult individuals with muscular dystrophy. *Journal of Psychosomatic Research, 41*(4), 365–376.

Ahmad, F. B., Cisewski, J. A., Xu, J., & Anderson, R. N. (2023). Provisional mortality data—United States, 2022. *Morbidity and Mortality Weekly Report, 72*(18), 488–492. doi: 10.15585/mmwr.mm7218a3.

Ajrouch, K. J., Hu, R. X., Webster, N. J., & Antonucci, T. C. (2024). Friendship trajectories and health across the lifespan. *Developmental Psychology, 60*(1), 94.

Akinyemi, R. O., Yaria, J., Ojagbemi, A., Guerchet, M., Okubadejo, N., Njamnshi, A. K., Sarfo, F. S., Akpalu, A., Ogbole, G., Ayantayo, T., Adokonou, T., Paddick, S. M., Ndetei, D., Bosche, J., Ayele, B., Damas, A., Coker, M., Mbakile-Mahlanza, L., Ranchod, K., Bobrow, K., Anazodo, U., Damasceno, A., Seshadri, S., Pericak-Vance, M., Lawlor, B., Miller, B. L., Owolabi, M., Baiyewu, O., Walker, R., Gureje, O., Kalaria, R. N., Ogunniyi, A., & African Dementia Consortium (AfDC) (2022). Dementia in Africa: Current evidence, knowledge gaps, and future directions. *Alzheimer's & Dementia, 18*(4), 790–809. doi: 10.1002/alz.12432.

Al Wachami, N., Guennouni, M., Iderdar, Y., Boumendil, K., Arraji, M., Mourajid, Y., Bouchachi, F. Z., Barkaoui, M., Louerdi, M. L., Hilali, A., & Chahboune, M. (2024). Estimating the global prevalence of chronic obstructive pulmonary disease (COPD): A systematic review and meta-analysis. *BMC Public Health, 24*(1), 297. doi: 10.1186/s12889-024-17686-9.

Albrecht, G. L., & Devlieger, P. J. (1999). The disability paradox: High quality of life against all odds. *Social Science & Medicine, 48*(8), 977–988.

Alegría, M., Fortuna, L. R., Lin, J. Y., Norris, F. H., Gao, S., Takeuchi, D. T., Jackson, J. S., Shrout, P. E., & Valentine, A. (2013). Prevalence, risk, and correlates of posttraumatic stress disorder across ethnic and racial minority groups in the United States. *Medical Care, 51*(12), 1114–1123. doi: 10.1097/MLR.0000000000000007.

Alexander, M. J., & Higgins, E. T. (1993). Emotional trade-offs of becoming a parent: How social roles influence self-discrepancy effects. *Journal of Personality and Social Psychology, 65*(6), 1259.

Alhuneafat, L., Ta'ani, O. A., Jabri, A., Tarawneh, T., ElHamdan, A., Naser, A., Al-Bitar, F., Alrifai, N., Ghanem, F., Alaswad, K., Alqarqaz, M., Van't Hof, J. R., Adabag, S., & Virani, S. S. (2024). Cardiovascular disease burden in the Middle East and North Africa region. *Current Problems in Cardiology, 49*(3). doi: 10.1016/j.cpcardiol.2023.102341.

Ali, A., Lopardo, G., Scarpellini, B., Stein, R. T., & Ribeiro, D. (2020). Systematic review on respiratory syncytial virus epidemiology in adults and the elderly in Latin America. *International Journal of Infectious Diseases, 90*, 170–180. doi: 10.1016/j.ijid.2019.10.025.

Allen, V. C., & Windsor, T. D. (2019). Age differences in the use of emotion regulation strategies derived from the process model of emotion regulation: A systematic review. *Aging Mental Health, 23*(1), 1–14.

Altman, I., & Taylor, D. A. (1973). *Social Penetration: The Development of Interpersonal Relationships*. Holt, Rinehart & Winston.

Alruwaili, N. W., Alqahtani, N., Alanazi, M. H., Alanzi, B. S., Aljrbua, M. S., & Gatar, O. M. (2023). The effect of nutrition and physical activity on sleep quality among adults: A scoping review. *Sleep Science Practice, 7*, 1–13. doi: 10.1186/s41606-023-00090-4.

Alzheimer's Association (n.d.) 10 early signs and symptoms of Alzheimer's and dementia. www.alz.org/alzheimers-dementia/10_signs. Accessed November 13, 2025.

Alzheimer's Association (2023). 2023 Alzheimer's disease facts and figures. *Alzheimer's & Dementia, 19*(4), 1598–1695. doi: 10.1002/alz.13016.

Alzheimer's Association (2024). 2024 Alzheimer's disease facts and figures. *Alzheimer's & Dementia,* 1–114. doi: 10.1002/alz.13809.

Alzheimer's Association (2025). Alzheimer's disease facts and figures. www.alz.org/alzheimers-dementia/facts-figures#:~:text=Seventy%2Dthree%20percent%20are%20age,other%20dementias%20as%20older%20Whites.

Amacher, S. A., Gross, S., Becker, C., Arpagaus, A., Urben, T., Gaab, J., Emsden, C., Tisljar, K., Sutter, R., Pargger, H., Marsch, S., & Hunziker, S. (2024). Misconceptions and do-not-resuscitate preferences of healthcare professionals commonly involved in cardiopulmonary resuscitations: A national survey. *Resuscitation Plus, 17,* 100575. doi: 10.1016/j.resplu.2024.100575.

American Cancer Society (2022*)*. Cancer facts & figures for African American/Black people 2022–2024. www.cancer.org/content/dam/cancer-org/research/cancer-facts-and-statistics/cancer-facts-and-figures-for-african-americans/2022-2024-cff-aa.pdf.

American Federation of Aging Research (2016). Theories of aging. www.afar.org/imported/AFAR_INFOAGING_GUIDE_THEORIES_OF_AGING_2016.pdf.

American Heart Association (2025). Types of heart medications. www.heart.org/en/health-topics/heart-attack/treatment-of-a-heart-attack/cardiac-medications. Accessed November 18, 2025.

American Lung Association (2025). Trends in COPD by race/ethnicity, sex and age. www.lung.org/research/trends-in-lung-disease/copd-trends-brief/data-tables/trends-copd-race-ethnicity-sex-age. Retrieved July 26, 2025.

American Psychiatric Association (2022). *Diagnostic and Statistical Manual of Mental Disorders* (5th ed., Text Revision).

American Psychological Association (2017). Eye movement desensitization and reprocessing. *Clinical Practice Guideline for the Treatment of Posttraumatic Stress Disorder.* Adapted from: www.apa.org/ptsd-guideline/treatments/eye-movement-reprocessing. Accessed January 21, 2025.

American Psychological Association (2018a). Cognitive behavior therapy. *APA Dictionary of Psychology.* Adapted from: https://dictionary.apa.org/cognitive-behavior-therapy. Accessed January 21, 2025.

American Psychological Association (2018b). Interpersonal psychotherapy. *APA Dictionary of Psychology.* Adapted from: https://dictionary.apa.org/interpersonal-psychotherapy. Accessed January 21, 2025.

American Psychological Association (2018c). Mental disorders. *APA Dictionary of Psychology*. Available from: https://dictionary.apa.org/mental-disorder. Accessed January 5, 2025.

American Psychological Association (2018d). Mental health. *APA Dictionary of Psychology.* Available from: https://dictionary.apa.org/mental-health. Accessed January 3, 2025.

American Psychological Association (2018e). Mindfulness. *APA Dictionary of Psychology*. Adapted from: https://dictionary.apa.org/mindfulness. Accessed January 21, 2025.

American Psychological Association (2018f). Resilience. *APA Dictionary of Psychology*. Available from: https://dictionary.apa.org/resilience. Accessed February 20, 2025.

American Psychological Association (2020, October). Stress in America 2020: A national mental health crisis [Press release]. www.apa.org/news/press/releases/stress/2020/report-october.

American Psychological Association (2025). Mental health. *APA Dictionary of Psychology*. Adapted from: https://dictionary.apa.org/mental-health. Accessed January 5, 2025.

Anderson, G. L., Limacher, M., Assaf, A. R., Bassford, T., Beresford, S. A. A., Black, H., Bonds, D., Brunner, R., Brzyski, R., Cann, B., Chlebowski, R., Curb, D., Gass, M., Hays, J., Heiss, G., Hendrix, S., Howard, B. V., Hsia, J., Hubbell, A., Jackson, R., Johnson, K. C., Judd, H., Kotchen, J. M., Kuller, L., LaCroix, A. Z., Lane, D., Langer, R. D., Lasser, N., Lewis, C. E., Manson, J., Margolis, K., Ockene, J., O'Sullivan, M. J., Phillips, L., Prentice, R. L., Ritenbaugh, C., Robbins, J., Rossouw, J. E., Sarto, G., Stefanick, M. L., Horn, L. V., Wactawski-Wende, J., Wallace, R., Wassertheil-Smoller, S., & Women's Health Initiative Steering Committee (2004). Effects of conjugated equine estrogen in postmenopausal women with hysterectomy: The Women's Health Initiative randomized controlled trial. *JAMA, 291*(14), 1701–1712.

Anderson, S. M., & Chen, S. (2002). The relational self: An interpersonal social-cognitive theory. *Psychological Review, 109*(4), 619–645. doi: 10.1037/0033-295X.109.4.619.

Andrew, M. K., Fisk, J. D., & Rockwood, K. (2012). Psychological well-being in relation to frailty: A frailty identity crisis? *International Psychogeriatrics, 24*(8), 1347–1353.

Annas, G. J., & Grodin, M. A. (Eds.) (1995). *The Nazi Doctors and the Nuremberg Code: Human Rights in Human Experimentation*. Oxford University Press.

Anson, E., Ehrenburg, M. R., Simonsick, E. M., & Agrawal, Y. (2021). Association between vestibular function and rotational spatial orientation perception in older adults. *J Vestib Res, 31*(6), 469–478. doi: 10.3233/VES-201582.

Antonucci, T., Akiyama, H., & Takahashi, K. (2004). Attachment and close relationships across the life span. *Attachment & Human Development, 6*(4), 353–370.

Antonucci, T. C., Ajrouch, K. J., & Birditt, K. S. (2014). The Convoy Model: Explaining social relations from a multidisciplinary perspective. *The Gerontologist, 54*(1), 82–92. doi: 10.1093/geront/gnt118.

Aragão, C. (2024, February 15). Among young adults without children, men are more likely than women to say they want to be parents someday. *Pew Research Center*. www.pewresearch.org/short-reads/2024/02/15/among-young-adults-without-children-men-are-more-likely-than-women-to-say-they-want-to-be-parents-someday/#:~:text=Here%20are%20the%20questions%20used,their%20parents%20to%20do%20so.

Aragão, C., Parker, K., Greenwood, S., Baronavski, C., & Mandapat, J. C. (2023, September 14). The modern American family. *Pew Research Center*. www.pewresearch.org/social-trends/2023/09/14/the-modern-american-family/.

Arnett, J. J. (1997). Young people's conceptions of the transition to adulthood. *Youth & Society, 29*(1), 3–23.

Arnett, J. J. (1998). Learning to stand alone: The contemporary American transition to adulthood in cultural and historical context. *Human Development, 41*(5–6), 295–315.

Arnett, J. J. (2000). Emerging adulthood: A theory of development from the late teens through the twenties. *American Psychologist, 55*(5), 469.

Arnett, J. J. (2004). *Emerging Adulthood: The Winding Road from the Late Teens to the Early Twenties*. Oxford University Press.

Arnett, J. J. (2014). Presidential address: The emergence of emerging adulthood: A personal history. *Emerging Adulthood, 2*(3), 155–162.

Arnett, J. J. (Ed.). (2015). *The Oxford Handbook of Emerging Adulthood*. Oxford University Press.

Aron, A., Lewandowski Jr., G. W., Branand, B., Mashek, D., & Aron, E. (2022). Self-expansion motivation and inclusion of others in self: An updated review. *Journal of Social and Personal Relationships, 39*(12), 3821–3852. doi: 10.1177/02654075221110630.

Arvey, A., Rowe, M., Legutki, J. B., An, G., Gollapudi, A., Lei, A., Colston, B., Putterman, C., Smith, D., Stiles, J., Tarasow, T., & Ramamoorthy, P. (2020). Age-associated changes in the circulating human antibody repertoire are upregulated in autoimmunity. *Immunity & Ageing*, 17, 28. doi: 10.1186/s12979-020-00193-x.

Asiamah, N., Kouveliotis, K., Petersen, C., Eduafo, R., & Borkey, R. (2023). Physical activity time and lifestyle correlates of cardiovascular disease status in older adults in Accra. *Journal of Public Health, 31*, 1453–1462. doi: 10.1007/s10389-022-01712-4.

Aspers, P., & Corte, U. (2019). What is qualitative in qualitative research. *Qualitative Sociology, 42*(2), 139–160. doi: 10.1007/s11133-019-9413-7.

Aspinwall, L. G., & Taylor, S. E. (1997). A stitch in time: Self-regulation and proactive coping. *Psychological Bulletin, 121*(3), 417.

Asthana, A., Tripathi, S., & Agarwal, R. (2024). Role of nonsteroidal anti-inflammatory drugs as a protective factor in Alzheimer's disease: A systematic review and meta-analysis. *Neurology India, 72*(6), 1144–1151. doi: 10.4103/ni.ni_1073_22.

Asthana, M. K., Brunhuber, B., Mühlberger, A., Reif, A., Schneider, S., & Herrmann, M. J. (2015). Preventing the return of fear using reconsolidation update mechanisms depends on the met-allele of the brain derived neurotrophic factor val66met polymorphism. *International Journal of Neuropsychopharmacoly, 19*(6), pyv137. doi: 10.1093/ijnp/pyv137.

Asyi, M. S., Syahrizal, D., Sary, N. L., & Husna, F. (2023). The impact of photoaging on skin: A systematic review analysis. *Journal of Social Research, 3*, 209–215. http://ijsr.internationaljournallabs.com/index.php/ijsr.

Atkinson, R. C., & Shiffrin, R. M. (1968). Human memory: A proposed system and its control processes. In K. W Spence & J. T. Spence (Eds.), *The Psychology of Learning and Motivation: Advances in Research and Theory. Vol. 2*. (pp. 89–195). Academic Press.

Aul, C., Brau, J. M., Sugarman, A., DeGutis, J. M., Germine, L. T., Esterman, M., McGlinchey, R. E., & Fortenbaugh, F. C. (2023). The functional relevance of visuospatial processing speed across the lifespan. *Cognitive Research: Principles and Implications, 8*(1).

Awuviry-Newton, K., Kwadwo Ofori-Dua, K., & Newton, A. (2022). Understanding transportation difficulty among older adults in Ghana from the perspective of World Health Organisation's Healthy Ageing framework: Lessons for improving social work practice with older adults. *The British Journal of Social Work, 52*, 416–436. doi: 10.1093/bjsw/bcaa247.

Baca Zinn, M. (1982). Familism among Chicanos: A theoretical review. *Humboldt Journal of Social Relations, 10*(1), 224–238.

Baddeley, A. (2012). Working memory: Theories, models, and controversies. *Annual Review of Psychology, 63*, 1–29.

Baddeley, A. D. (2000). The episodic buffer: A new component of working memory? *Trends in Cognitive Sciences, 4*, 417–423.

Baddeley, A. D., & Hitch, G. (1974). Working memory. In G. H. Bower (Ed.), *The Psychology of Learning and Motivation: Advances in Research and Theory*. Vol. 8. (pp. 47–89). Academic Press.

Bae, H., Gurinovich, A., Malovini, A., Atzmon, G., Andersen, S. L., Villa, F., Barzilai, N., Puca, A., Perls, T. T., & Sebastiani, P. (2018). Effects of FOXO3 Polymorphisms on survival to extreme longevity in four centenarian studies. *The Journals of Gerontology Series A: Biomedical Sciences and Medical Sciences, 73*(11),1439–1447. doi: 10.1093/gerona/glx124.

Bae, J.-M. (2021). Hormonal replacement therapy and risk of thyroid cancer in women: A meta-epidemiological analysis of prospective cohort studies. *Journal of Menopausal Medicine, 27*, 141–145. doi: 10.6118/jmm.21023.

Bailey, N. V., & Tribe, R. (2021). A qualitative study to explore the help-seeking views relating to depression among older Black Caribbean adults living in the UK.

International Review of Psychiatry, 33, 113–118. doi: 10.1080/09540261.2020.1761138.

Bajpai, S., Upadhayay, A. D., Banerjee, J., Chakrawarthy, A., Chatterjee, P., Lee, J., & Dey, A. B. (2022). Discrepancy in fluid and crystallized intelligence: An early cognitive marker of dementia from the LASI-DAD Cohort. *Dementia and Geriatric Cognitive Disorders Extra, 12*(1), 51–59. doi: 10.1159/000520879.

Baltes, P. B. (1987). Theoretical propositions of life-span developmental psychology: On the dynamics between growth and decline. *Developmental Psychology, 23*(5), 611.

Baltes, P. B., Lindenberger, U., & Staudinger, U. M. (2006). Life span theory in developmental psychology. In R. M. Lerner & W. Damon (Eds.), *Handbook of Child Psychology: Theoretical Models of Human Development* (6th ed.). (pp. 569–664). John Wiley & Sons, Inc.

Baltes, P. B., Reese, H. W., & Nesselroade, J. R. (1997). *Life-span Developmental Psychology: Introduction to Research Methods*. Brooks/Cole.

Bandura, A. (1977). Self-efficacy: Toward a unifying theory of behavioral change. *Psychological Review, 84*(2), 191–215.

Bandura, A., Ross, D., & Ross, S. A. (1961). Transmission of aggression through imitation of aggressive models. *The Journal of Abnormal and Social Psychology, 63*(3), 575–582.

Barbieri, M. (2022). Socioeconomic disparities do not explain the U.S. international disadvantage in mortality. *The Journals of Gerontology Series B: Psychological Sciences and Social Sciences, 77*, S158–S166. doi: 10.1093/geronb/gbac030.

Barman, P., Rahut, D. B., & Mishra, R. (2024). Mediating role of social disengagement and loneliness in the nexus between functional health and mental well-being in older individuals. *Scientific Reports, 14*,16232. doi: 10.1038/s41598-024-66919-9.

Barnes, D. E., Yaffe, K., Byers, A. L., McCormick, M., Schaefer, C., & Whitmer, R. A. (2012). Midlife vs late-life depressive symptoms and risk of dementia: Differential effects for Alzheimer disease and vascular dementia. *Archives of General Psychiatry, 69*, 493–498. doi: 10.1001/archgenpsychiatry.2011.1481.

Barrett, N., & Charlton, E. (2025). Passenger parenting, role conflict and guilt: The transition to parenthood from new and experienced fathers. *Journal of Family Studies*, 1–24.

Barrett, R. K., & Heller, K. S. (2002). Death and dying in the Black experience. *Journal of Palliative Medicine, 5*(5), 793–799. doi: 10.1089/109662102320880714.

Barton, A. W., Beach, S. R., Wells, A. C., Ingels, J. B., Corso, P. S., Sperr, M. C., Anderson, T. N., & Brody, G. H. (2018). The Protecting Strong African American Families Program: A randomized controlled trial with rural African American couples. *Prevention Science, 19*(7), 904–913. doi: 10.1007/s11121-018-0895-4.

Batra, R., Kumar, D. A., Rao, A., Kaloiya, G. S., Khan, M. A., Satapathy, S., Chakrawarty, A., Soni, N., Kumar, P. & Chatterjee, P. (2024). Clinical and neuropsychological characterization of SuperAgers residing in Delhi and National Capital Region of India – A cross-sectional study. *Aging Medicine*, 7(1), 67–73. doi: 10.1002/agm2.12285.

Bauer, U. E., Briss, P. A., Goodman, R. A., & Bowman, B. A. (2014). Prevention of chronic disease in the 21st century: Elimination of the leading preventable causes of premature death and disability in the USA. *The Lancet, 384*(9937), 45–52.

Baum, A., Garofalo, J. P., & Yali, A. (1999). Socioeconomic status and chronic stress: Does stress account for SES effects on health? *Annals of the New York Academy of Sciences, 896*(1), 131–144.

Baumbach, A., Hughes, M. C., & Liu, Y. (2024). Challenges and coping strategies in transitioning from caregiving to widowhood: A systematic review. *Research on Aging, 46*(9–10), 535–547. doi: 10.1177/01640275241254396.

Baumeister, R. F., & Bratslavsky, E. (1999). Passion, intimacy, and time: Passionate love as a function of change in intimacy. *Personality and Social Psychology Review*, 3, 49–67.

Baumeister, R. F., Bratslavsky, E., Finkenauer, C., & Vohs, K. D. (2001). Bad is stronger than good. *Review of General Psychology*, *5*(4), 323–370.

Baumeister, R. F., & Leary, M. R. (1995). The need to belong: Desire for interpersonal attachments as a fundamental human motivation. *Psychological Bulletin*, *117*(3), 497–529. doi: 10.1037/0033-2909.117.3.497.

Bazo Perez, M., de Carvalho, P., & Frazier, L. D. (2025) Examining the factor structure and measurement invariance of the eating disorder examination-questionnaire and the Eating Attitudes Test-26 in young and middle-aged women [Unpublished manuscript]. Under review at *Eating and Weight Disorders – Studies on Anorexia, Bulimia and Obesity.*

Beard, J. G., & Ragheb, M. G. (1980). Measuring leisure satisfaction. *Journal of Leisure Research*, *12*(1), 20–33.

Beard, V., & Burger, W. (2017). Change and innovation in the funeral industry: A typology of motivations. *OMEGA – Journal of Death and Dying*, *75*(1), 47–68. doi: 10.1177/0030222815612605.

Becker, C. B., Taniyama, Y., Kondo-Arita, M., Yamada, S., & Yamamoto, K. (2022). How grief, funerals, and poverty affect bereaved health, productivity, and medical dependence in Japan. *OMEGA – Journal of Death and Dying*, *85*(3), 669–689. doi: 10.1177/0030222820947573.

Becker, G., & Newsom, E. (2005). Resilience in the face of serious illness among chronically ill African Americans in later life. *The Journals of Gerontology Series B: Psychological Sciences and Social Sciences*, *60*(4), S214–S223.

Bell, L. G., & Harsin, A. (2018). A prospective longitudinal study of marriage from midlife to later life. *Couple and Family Psychology: Research and Practice*, *7*(1), 12–21. doi: 10.1037/cfp0000096.

Bender, A., Jox, R. J., Grill, E., Straube, A., & Lulé, D. (2015). Persistent vegetative state and minimally conscious state: A systematic review and meta-analysis of diagnostic procedures. *Deutsches Ärzteblatt International*, *112*(14), 235–42. doi: 10.3238/arztebl.2015.0235.

Benjamin, E. J., Virani, S. S., Callaway, C. W., Chamberlain, A. M., Chang, A. R., Cheng, S., Chiuve, S. E., Cushman, M., Delling, F. N., Deo, R., de Ferranti, S. D., Ferguson, J. F., Fornage, M., Gillespie, C,., Isasi, C. R., Jiménez, M. C., Jordan, L. C., Judd, S. E., Lackland, L., Lichtman, J. H., Lisabeth, L., Liu, S., Longenecker, C. T., Lutsey, P. L., Mackey, J. S., Matchar, D. B., Matsushita, K., Mussolino, M. E., Nasir, K., O'Flaherty, M., Palaniappan, L. P., Pandey, A., Pandey, D. K., Reeves, M. J., Ritchey, M. D., Rodriguez, C. J., Roth, G. A., Rosamond, W. D, Sampson, U. K. A., Gary M. Satou, Shah, S. V., Spartano, N. L., Tirschwell, D. L., Tsao, C. W., Voeks, J. H., Willey, J. Z., Wilkins, J. T., Wu, J. H., Alger, H. M., Wong, S. S., & Muntner, P. (2018). Heart disease and stroke statistics – 2018 update: A report from the American Heart Association. *Circulation*, *137*, e67–e492.

Bennett, D. A., Schneider, J. A., Buchman, A. S., Barnes, L. L., Boyle, P. A., & Wilson, R. S. (2012). Overview and findings from the rush Memory and Aging Project. *Current Alzheimer Research*, *9*(6), 646–663.

Bennett, E. E., & McWhorter, R. R. (2021). Virtual HRD's role in crisis and the post Covid-19 professional lifeworld: Accelerating skills for digital transformation. *Advances in Developing Human Resources*, *23*(1), 5–25.

Bertalanffy, L. V. (1968). General systems theory as integrating factor in contemporary science. Akten des XIV. *Internationalen Kongresses für Philosophie*, 2, 335–340.

Bethlehem, R. A. I., Seidlitz, J., White, S. R., Vogel, J. W., Anderson, K. M., Adamson, C., Adler, S., Alexopoulos, G. S., Anagnostou, E., Areces-Gonzalez, A., Astle, D. E., Auyeung, B., Ayub, M., Bae, J., Ball, G., Baron-Cohen, S., Beare, R., Bedford, S.

A., Benegal, V., Beyer, F., Blangero, J., Blesa Cábez, M., Boardman, J. P., Borzage, M., 3R-BRAIN, AIBL, Alzheimer's Disease Neuroimaging Initiative, Alzheimer's Disease Repository Without Borders Investigators, CALM Team, Cam-CAN, CCNP, COBRE, cVEDA, ENIGMA Developmental Brain Age Working Group, Developing Human Connectome Project, FinnBrain, Harvard Aging Brain Study, IMAGEN, KNE96, Mayo Clinic Study of Aging, NSPN, POND, PREVENT-AD Research Group, & VETSA (2022). Brain charts for the human lifespan. *Nature, 604*(7906), 525–533. doi: 10.1038/s41586-022-04554-y.

Beyene, D. A., & Berha, A. B. (2023). Management practice and clinical outcomes of dementia in Sub-Saharan Africa: A systematic review. *Behavioural Neurology*, 2307443. doi: 10.1155/2023/2307443.

Bezner, J., Adams, T. B., & Steinhardt, M. A. (1997). Relationship of body dissatisfaction to physical health and wellness. *American Journal of Health Behavior, 21*(2), 147–155.

Bhattacharyya, K. K., Gupta, D. D., Schwartz, S., Molinari, V. & Fauth, E. B. (2024). Protective roles of meditation practice and self-esteem on cognitive functions over time: Findings from the Midlife in the United States study. *Psychogeriatrics, 24*(1), 94–107. doi: 10.1111/psyg.13046.

Bianchi, S. M., Sayer, L. C., Milkie, M. A., & Robinson, J. P. (2012). Housework: Who did, does or will do it, and how much does it matter? *Social Forces, 91*(1), 55–63.

Bigman, G., & Ryan, A. S. (2021). Implications of race and ethnicity in Sarcopenia US national prevalence of Sarcopenia by muscle mass, strength, and function indices. *Gerontology and Geriatric Research, 4*(1), 126.

Billings, A. G., & Moos, R. H. (1981). The role of coping response and social resources in attenuating the stress of life events. *Journal of Behavioral Medicine, 4*, 139–157. doi: 10.1007/BF00844267.

Binder, M., & Coad, A. (2013). "I'm afraid I have bad news for you…": Estimating the impact of different health impairments on subjective well-being. *Social Science & Medicine, 87*, 155–167.

Birditt, K. S., & Fingerman, K. L. (2005). Do we get better at picking our battles? Age group differences in descriptions of behavioral reactions to interpersonal tensions. *The Journals of Gerontology Series B: Psychological Sciences and Social Sciences, 60*(3), P121–P128.

Bishay, A. E., Hughes, N. C., Zargari, M., Paulo, D. L., Bishay, S., Lyons, A. T., Morkos, M. N., Ball, T. J., Englot, D. J., & Bick, S. K. (2024). Disparities in access to deep brain stimulation for Parkinson's disease and proposed interventions: A literature review. *Stereotactic and Functional Neurosurgery, 102*(3), 179–194. doi: 10.1159/000538748.

Bittner, N., Jockwitz, C., Franke, K., Gaser, C., Moebus, S., Bayen, U. J., Amunts, K., & Caspers, S. (2021). When your brain looks older than expected: Combined lifestyle risk and BrainAGE. *Brain Structure and Function, 226*, 621–645. doi: 10.1007/s00429-020-02184-6.

Bittner, N., Jockwitz, C., Muhleisen, T. W., Hoffstaedter, F., Eickhoff, S. B., Moebus, S., Bayen, U. J., Cichon, S., Zilles, K., Amunts, K., & Caspers, S. (2019). Combining lifestyle risks to disentangle brain structure and functional connectivity differences in older adults. *Nature Communications, 10*, 62.

Blachstein, H., & Vakil, E. (2016). Verbal learning across the lifespan: An analysis of the components of the learning curve. *Neuropsychology, Development, and Cognition. Section B, Aging, Neuropsychology and Cognition, 23*, 133–153.

Blanchard-Fields, F. (2007). Everyday problem solving and emotion: An adult developmental perspective. *Current Directions in Psychological Science, 16*(1), 26–31.

Blanchard-Fields, F., Mienaltowski, A., & Seay, R. B. (2007). Age differences in everyday problem-solving effectiveness: Older adults select more effective strategies for interpersonal problems. *The Journals of Gerontology Series B: Psychological Sciences and Social Sciences, 62*(1), P61–P64.

Blanco, K., Salcidua, S., Orellana, P., Sauma-Pérez, T., León, T., Steinmetz, L.C.L., Ibañez, A., Duran-Aniotz, C. & de la Cruz, R. (2023). Systematic review: Fluid biomarkers and machine learning methods to improve the diagnosis from mild cognitive impairment to Alzheimer's disease. *Alzheimer's Research & Therapy, 15*(1), 176. doi: 10.1186/s13195-023-01304-8.

Blatterer, H. (2007). Adulthood: The contemporary redefinition of a social category. *Sociological Research Online, 12*(4), 1–11. doi: 10.5153/sro.1563.

Blieszner, R. (2014). The worth of friendship: Can friends keep us happy and healthy? *Generations, 38*(1), 24–30.

Blieszner, R., Ogletree, A. M., & Adams, R. G. (2019). Friendship in later life: A research agenda. *Innovation in Aging, 3*(1), Article igz005. doi: 10.1093/geroni/igz005.

Bloomer, M. J., Saffer, L., Hewitt, J., Johns, L., McAuliffe, D., & Bonner, A. (2024). Maybe for unbearable suffering: Diverse racial, ethnic and cultural perspectives of assisted dying. A scoping review. *Palliative Medicine, 38*(9), 968–980. doi: 10.1177/02692163241268449.

Böckerman, P., & Ilmakunnas, P. (2020). Do good working conditions make you work longer? Analyzing retirement decisions using linked survey and register data. *The Journal of the Economics of Ageing, 17*, 100192.

Boer, P.-H., & DeBeer, Z. (2019). The effect of aquatic exercises on the physical and functional fitness of adults with Down syndrome: A non-randomised controlled trial. *Journal of Intellectual Disability Research, 63*, 1453–1463. doi: 10.1038/s41430-021-00957-8.

Bonanno, G. A. (2004). Loss, trauma, and human resilience: Have we underestimated the human capacity to thrive after extremely aversive events? *American Psychologist, 59*(1), 20–28.

Bordone, V., & Arpino, B. (2016). Do grandchildren influence how old you feel? *Journal of Aging and Health, 28*(6), 1055–1072.

Borghesani, P. R., Madhyastha, T. M., Aylward, E. H., Reiter, M. A., Swarny, B. R., Schaie, K. W., & Willis, S. L. (2013). The association between higher order abilities, processing speed, and age are variably mediated by white matter integrity during typical aging. *Neuropsychologia, 51*(8), 1435–1444. doi: 10.1016/j.neuropsychologia.2013.03.005.

Borja, S., Nurius, P. S., Song, C., & Lengua, L. J. (2019). Adverse childhood experiences to adult adversity trends among parents: Socioeconomic, health, and developmental implications. *Children and Youth Services Review, 100*, 258–266.

Boss, P., & Couden, B. A. (2002). Ambiguous loss from chronic physical illness: Clinical interventions with individuals, couples, and families. *Journal of Clinical Psychology, 58*(11), 1351–1360.

Bouchard, G. (2014). How do parents react when their children leave home? An integrative review. *Journal of Adult Development, 21*, 69–79.

Bouchard. G., & McNair J. L. (2016) Dyadic examination of the influence of family relationships on life satisfaction at the empty-nest stage. *Journal of Adult Development, 23*, 174–182.

Boukhalfa, W., Jmel, H., Kheriji, N., Gouiza, I., Dallali, H., Hechmi, M. & Kefi, R. (2023). Decoding the genetic relationship between Alzheimer's disease and type 2 diabetes: Potential risk variants and future direction for North Africa. *Frontiers in Aging Neuroscience, 15*, 1114810. doi: 10.3389/fnagi.2023.1114810.

Bower, A. M., & Hayes, A. (1998). Mothering in families with and without a child with disability. *International Journal of Disability, Development and Education*, 45(3), 313–322.

Bowlby, E. J. M. (2008). *Loss-Sadness and Depression: Attachment and Loss* (Vol. 3). Random House.

Bowlby, J. (1982). *Attachment and Loss: Vol. 1. Attachment*. Basic Books. (Original work published 1969.)

Bowlby, J. (1988). *A Secure Base: Parent-child Attachment and Healthy Human Development*. Basic Books.

Braithwaite, S., & Holt-Lunstad, J. (2017). Romantic relationships and mental health. *Current Opinion in Psychology, 13,* 120–125. doi: 10.1016/j.copsyc.2016.04.001.

Brave Heart, M. Y., Chase, J., Elkins, J., & Altschul, D. B. (2011). Historical trauma among Indigenous Peoples of the Americas: Concepts, research, and clinical considerations. *Journal of Psychoactive Drugs, 43*(4), 282–290. doi: 10.1080/02791072.2011.628913.

Brickman, P., Coates, D., & Janoff-Bulman, R. (1978). Lottery winners and accident victims: Is happiness relative? *Journal of Personality and Social Psychology, 36*(8), 917–927.

Briggs, R., Morris, P. G., & Rees, K. (2023). The effectiveness of group-based gardening interventions for improving wellbeing and reducing symptoms of mental ill-health in adults: A systematic review and meta-analysis. *Journal of Mental Health, 32*(4), 787–804. doi: 10.1080/09638237.2022.2118687.

Broadbent, D. E. (1958). *Perception and Communication*. Pergamon Press.

Brody, D. J., & Hughes, J. P. (2025). Depression prevalence in adolescents and adults: United States, August 2021–August 2023. (NCHS Data Brief. No. 527, 1–11). *Center for Disease Control*. doi: 10.15620/cdc/174579.

Brody, H. (2014). Stories and the biopsychosocial model. *Philosophy, Psychiatry, & Psychology, 21*(3), 191–193.

Bronfenbrenner, U. (1979) *The Ecology of Human Development: Experiments by Nature and Design*. Harvard University Press.

Bronfenbrenner, U., & Morris, P. (2006). The bioecological model of human development. In W. Damon (Series Ed.) & R. M. Lerner (Series/Volume Ed.), *Handbook of Child Psychology: Vol. 1. Theoretical Models of Human Development* (6th ed.) (pp. 793–828). John Wiley.

Brouk, T. (2025, March 11). Purdue expert: Overall divorce rates lowest in decades but "gray divorce" soars. *College of Health and Human Sciences*. www.purdue.edu/hhs/news/2025/03/purdue-expert-overall-divorce-rates-lowest-in-decades-but-gray-divorce-soars/.

Brown, K. L., Banks, D. E., & Zapolski, T. C. B. (2024). The impact of cultural and institutional race-related stress on mental health outcomes among ethnic/racially minoritized young adults: Ethnic identity as a protective factor. *The Americal Journal of Orthopsychiatry*. doi: 10.1037/ort0000767.

Brown, S. L., & Lin, I. F. (2022). The graying of divorce: A half century of change. *The Journals of Gerontology Series B: Psychological Sciences and Social Sciences, 77*(9), 1710–1720. doi: 10.1093/geronb/gbac057.

Brown, S. L., & Wright, M. R. (2017). Marriage, cohabitation, and divorce in later life. *Innovation in Aging, 1*(2), igx015.

Bruce, M. G., Bressler, S. S., Apostolou, A., & Singleton, R. J. (2021). Lower respiratory tract infection hospitalizations among American Indian/Alaska Native adults, Indian Health Service and Alaska region, 1998–2014. *International Journal of Infectious Diseases, 111,* 130–137. doi: 10.1016/j.ijid.2021.08.033.

Bruscoli, M., & Lovestone, S. (2004). Is MCI really just early dementia? A systematic review of conversion studies. *International Journal of Psychogeriatry, 16*(2), 129–140. doi: 10.1017/s1041610204000092.

Bruun, A., Jordan, L., Giles, J., Hughes, R., Anderson-Kittow, R., & Tuffrey-Wijne, I. (2025). Don't assume, ask! A focus group study on end-of-life care planning with people with intellectual disabilities from minoritised ethnic groups. *BMC Palliative Care, 24,* 13. doi: 10.1186/s12904-025-01646-0.

Bubu, O. M., Andrade, A. G., Umasabor-Bubu, O. Q., Hogan, M. M., Turner, A. D., de Leon, M. J., Ogedegbe, G., Ayappa, I., Giradin, J.-L. G., Jackson, M. L., Varga, A. W., & Osorio, R. S. (2020). Obstructive sleep apnea, cognition and Alzheimer's disease: A systematic review integrating three decades of multidisciplinary research. *Sleep Medicine Reviews, 50*, 101250. doi: 10.1016/j.smrv.2019.101250.

Buckley, T., McKinley, S., Tofler, G., & Bartrop, R. (2010). Cardiovascular risk in early bereavement: A literature review and proposed mechanisms. *International Journal of Nursing Studies, 47*(2), 229–238. doi: 10.1016/j.ijnurstu.2009.06.010.

Budinger, G. R. S., Kohanski, R. A., Gan, W., Kobor, M. S., Amaral, L. A., Armanios, M., Kelsey, K. T., Pardo, A., Tuder, R., Macian, F., Chandel, N., Vaughan, D., Rojas, M., Mora, A. L., Kovacs, E., Duncan, S. R., Finkel, T., Choi, A., Eickelberg, O., Chen, D., Agusti, A., Selman, M., Balch, W. E., Busse, P., Lin, A., Morimoto, R., Sznajder, J. I., & Thannickal, V. J. (2017). The intersection of aging biology and the pathobiology of lung diseases: A joint NHLBI/NIA workshop. *The Journals of Gerontology Series A: Biomedical Sciences and Medical Sciences, 72*, 1492–1500.

Budisan, L., Zanoaga, O., Braicu, C., Pirlog, R., Covaliu, B., Esanu, V., Korban, S. S., & Berindan-Neagoe, I. (2021). Links between infections, lung cancer, and the immune system. *International Journal of Molecular Sciences, 22*(17), 9394. doi: 10.3390/ijms22179394.

Bui, Q., & Miller, C. C. (2017). The jobs you're most likely to inherit from your mother than father. *The New York Times*. www.nytimes.com/interactive/2017/11/22/upshot/the-jobs-youre-mostlikely-to-inherit-from-your-mother-and-father.html.

Burn, H., Hamm, L., Black, J., Burnett, A., Harwood, M., Burton, M. J., Evans, J. R., & Ramke, J. (2021). Eye care delivery models to improve access to eye care for Indigenous peoples in high-income countries: A scoping review. *BMJ Global Health, 6*(3), e004484. doi: 10.1136/bmjgh-2020-004484.

Burnes, D., Sheppard, C., Henderson Jr., C. R., Wassel, M., Cope, R., Barber, C., & Pillemer, K. (2019). Interventions to reduce ageism against older adults: A systematic review and meta-analysis. *American Journal of Public Health*, 109(8), e1–e9.

Burns, D. D. (1989). *The Feeling Good Handbook*. Penguin Group.

Burns, J. W., Johnson, B. J., Mahoney, N., Devine, J., & Pawl, R. (1996). Anger management style, hostility and spouse responses: Gender differences in predictors of adjustment among chronic pain patients. *Pain, 64*(3), 445–453.

Burr, D. A., Castrellon, J. J., Zald, D. H., & Samanez-Larkin, G. R. (2021). Emotion dynamics across adulthood in everyday life: Older adults are more emotionally stable and better at regulating desires. *Emotion, 21*(3), 453.

Bussian, T. J., Aziz, A., Meyer, C. F., Swenson, B. L., van Deursen, J. M., & Baker, D. J. (2018). Clearance of senescent glial cells prevents tau-dependent pathology and cognitive decline. *Nature, 562*, 578–582. doi: 10.1038/s41586-018-0543-y.

Cacioppo, J. T., Berntson, G. G., Bechara, A., Tranel, D., & Hawkley, L. C. (2011). Could an aging brain contribute to subjective well-being? The value added by a social neuroscience perspective. *Social Neuroscience: Toward Understanding the Underpinnings of the Social Mind, 249*, 262.

Cacioppo, J. T., Cacioppo, S., Gonzaga, G. C., Ogburn, E. L., & VanderWeele, T. J. (2013). Marital satisfaction and break-ups differ across on-line and off-line meeting venues. *Proceedings of the National Academy of Sciences, 110*(25), 10135–10140.

Cacioppo, S., Grippo, A. J., London, S., Goossens, L., & Cacioppo, J. T. (2015). Loneliness: Clinical import and interventions. *Perspectives on Psychological Science, 10*(2), 238–249.

Cadar, D., Brocklebank, L., Yan, L., Zhao, Y., & Steptoe, A. (2023). Socioeconomic and contextual differentials in memory decline: A cross-country investigation between England and China. *The Journals of Gerontology Series B: Psychological Sciences and Social Sciences, 78*(3), 544–555. doi: 10.1093/geronb/gbac163.

Cai, H., Chen, P., Zhang, Q., Lam, M. I., Si, T. L., Liu, Y. F., Zheng, W. Y., Su, Z., Cheung, T., Jackson, T., Ungvari, G. S., Ren, Z., Li, X., Li, X. H., & Xiang, Y. T. (2024). Global prevalence of major depressive disorder in LGBTQ+ samples: A systematic review and meta-analysis of epidemiological studies. *Journal of Affective Disorders, 360*, 249–258. doi: 10.1016/j.jad.2024.05.115.

Caire, M. J., Reddy, V., & Varacallo, M. (2023). Physiology, Synapse. *StatPearls*. StatPearls Publishing. https://pubmed.ncbi.nlm.nih.gov/30252303/. Retrieved January 1, 2024.

Calandri, I. L., Crivelli, L., Martin, M. E., Egido, N., Guimet, N. M., & Allegri, R. F. (2020). Environmental factors between normal and superagers in an Argentine cohort. *Dementia & Neuropsychologia, 14*(4), 345–349.

Camina, E., & Güell, F. (2017). The neuroanatomical, neurophysiological and psychological basis of memory: Current models and their origins. *Frontiers in Pharmacology, 8*, 438. doi: 10.3389/fphar.2017.00438.

Canever, J. B., Zurman, G., Vogel, F., Sutil, D. V., Diz, J. B. M., Danielewicz, A. L., Moreira, B. S., Cimarosti, H. I., & de Avelar, N. C. P. (2024). Worldwide prevalence of sleep problems in community-dwelling older adults: A systematic review and meta-analysis. *Sleep Medicine, 119*, 118–134. doi: 10.1016/j.sleep.2024.03.040.

Cao, Q., Tan, C. C., Xu, W., Hu, H., Cao, X. P., Dong, Q., Tan, L., & Yu, J. T. (2020). The prevalence of dementia: A systematic review and meta-analysis. *Journal of Alzheimer's Disease, 73*(3), 1157–1166. doi: 10.3233/JAD-191092.

Caraballo, C., Massey, D. S., Ndumele, C. D., Haywood, T., Kaleem, S., King, T., Liu, Y., Lu, Y., Nunex-Smith, M., Taylor, H. A., Watson, K. E., Herrin, J., Yancy, C. W., Faust, J. S., & Krumholz, H. M. (2023). Excess mortality and years of potential life lost among the black population in the US, 1999–2020. *JAMA, 329*(19), 1662–1670. doi: 10.1001/jama.2023.7022.

Carel, H. (2017). Illness and its experience: The patient perspective. In *Handbook of the Philosophy of Medicine* (pp. 93–108).

Carroll, J. L. (1990). The relationship between humor appreciation and perceived physical health. *Psychology: A Journal of Human Behavior, 27*(2), 34–37.

Carstensen, L. L. (1993). Motivation for social contact across the life span: A theory of socioemotional selectivity. In *Nebraska Symposium on Motivation. Vol. 40*. (pp. 209–254).

Carstensen, L. L. (1995). Evidence for a life-span theory of socioemotional selectivity. *Current Directions in Psychological Science, 4*(5), 151–156.

Carstensen, L. L. (2006). The influence of a sense of time on human development. *Science, 312*(5782), 1913–1915.

Carstensen, L. L. (2021). Socioemotional selectivity theory: The role of perceived endings in human motivation. *The Gerontologist, 61*(8), 1188–1196.

Carstensen, L. L., Gottman, J. M., & Levenson, R. W. (1995). Emotional behavior in long-term marriage. *Psychology and Aging, 10*, 140–149.

Carstensen, L. L., Isaacowitz, D. M., & Charles, S. T. (1999). Taking time seriously: A theory of socioemotional selectivity. *American Psychologist, 54*(3), 165–181.

Carstensen, L. L., Pasupathi, M., Mayr, U., & Nesselroade, J. R. (2000). Emotional experience in everyday life across the adult life span. *Journal of Personality and Social Psychology, 79*(4), 644.

Carstensen, L. L., Shavit, Y. Z., & Barnes, J. T. (2020). Age advantages in emotional experience persist even under threat from the COVID-19 pandemic. *Psychological Science, 31*(11), 1374–1385.

Carver, C. S. (1998). Resilience and thriving: Issues, models, and linkages. *Journal of Social Issues, 54*(2), 245–266.

Carver, C. S., Scheier, M. F., & Weintraub, J. K. (1989). Assessing coping strategies: A theoretically based approach. *Journal of Personality and Social Psychology, 56*(2), 267–283. doi: 10.1037//0022-3514.56.2.267.

Castaldelli-Maia, J. M., & Bhugra, D. (2022). Analysis of global prevalence of mental and substance use disorders within countries: Focus on sociodemographic characteristics and income levels. *International Review of Psychiatry, 34*(1), 6–15. doi: 10.1080/09540261.2022.2040450.

Castel, A. D. (2018). *Better with Age: The Psychology of Successful Aging*. Oxford University Press.

Castrillon, C. (2024, October 6). The real impact of return-to-office mandates on productivity at work. *Forbes*. www.forbes.com/sites/carolinecastrillon/2024/10/06/impact-of-return-to-office-mandates-on-productivity/.

Catenacci, V. A., Pan, Z., Ostendorf, D., Brannon, S., Gozansky, W. S., Mattson, M. P., Martin, B., MacLean, P. S., Melanson, E. L., & Donahoo, W. T. (2016). A randomized pilot study comparing zero-calorie alternate-day fasting to daily caloric restriction in adults with obesity. *Obesity, 24,* 1874–1883.

Cattaneo, C., Liu, J., Bech, A. C., Pagliarini, E., & Bredie, W. L. P. (2020). Cross-cultural differences in lingual tactile acuity, taste sensitivity phenotypical markers, and preferred oral processing behaviors. *Food Quality and Preference, 80,*103803. doi: 10.1016/j.foodqual.2019.103803.

Cattell, R. B. (1943). The measurement of adult intelligence. *Psychological Bulletin, 40*(3), 153–193.

Centers for Disease Control (2021). Cadmium factsheet. In *U.S. Department of Health and Human Services, Vol. 2021.* wwwn.cdc.gov/tsp/substances/ToxSubstance.aspx?toxid=15.

Centers for Disease Control and Prevention (2024, October 4). About chronic diseases: Chronic disease in America. www.cdc.gov/chronic-disease/about/index.html#:~:text=Chronic%20diseases%20are%20defined%20broadly,of%20daily%20living%20or%20both.&text=Six%20in%2010%20Americans%20have,two%20or%20more%20chronic%20diseases.

Centers for Disease Control and Prevention (2024). About immigrant and refugee health. www.cdc.gov/immigrant-refugee-health/about/index.html.

Centers for Disease Control and Prevention (2025, June 11). People with certain medical conditions and COVID-19 risk factors. www.cdc.gov/coronavirus/2019-ncov/need-extra-precautions/people-with-medical-conditions.html.

Chakravarti, D., LaBella, K. A., & DePinho, R. A. (2021). Telomeres: History, health and hallmarks of aging. *Cell, 184*, 306–322. doi: 10.1016/j.cell.2020.12.028.

Chan, K. Y., Wang, W., Wu, J. J., Liu, L., Theodoratou, E., Car, J., Middleton, L., Russ, T. C., Deary, I. J., Campbell, H., Wang, W., Rudan, I., & Global Health Epidemiology Reference Group (2013). Epidemiology of Alzheimer's disease and other forms of dementia in China, 1990–2010: A systematic review and analysis. *The Lancet, 381*(9882), 2016–2023. doi: 10.1016/S0140-6736(13)60221-4.

Chan, L. S. (2021). Looking for politically like-minded partners: Self-presentation and partner-vetting strategies on dating apps. *Personal Relationships*, 28(3), 703–720. doi: 10.1111/pere.12375.

Chang, Y., Sapkota, S., Thapa, B., Ma, L., Sheng, L., Wang, C., Chhetri, J. K., & Chan, P. (2024). Development and validation of a functional ability index for older adults: A multicohort study. *Age & Ageing, 53*(10), 1–11. doi: 10.1093/ageing/afae231.

Charles, S. T., Rush, J., Piazza, J. R., Cerino, E. S., Mogle, J., & Almeida, D. M. (2023). Growing old and being old: Emotional well-being across adulthood. *Journal of Personality and Social Psychology, 125*(2), 455–469. doi: 10.1037/pspp0000453.

Charney, D. S. (2004). Psychobiological mechanisms of resilience and vulnerability: Implications for successful adaptation to extreme stress. *American Journal of Psychiatry, 161*(2), 195–216.

Chebib, J., & Guillaume, F. (2021). Pleiotropy or linkage? Their relative contributions to the genetic correlation of quantitative traits and detection by multitrait GWA studies. *Genetics, 219*(4), 159. doi: 10.1093/genetics/iyab159.

Chen, C. T., Tung, H. H., Fang, C. J., Wang, J. L., Ko, N. Y., Chang, Y. J., & Chen, Y. C. (2021). Effect of music therapy on improving sleep quality in older adults: A systematic review and meta-analysis. *Journal of the American Geriatrics Society, 69*(7), 1925–1932. doi: 10.1111/jgs.17149.

Chen, W., Xu, Y., Liu, Z., & Zhao, J. (2024). Global, regional and national burden of Glaucoma: An update analysis from the Global Burden of Disease Study 2019. *International Journal of Ophthalmoly, 44*, 234. doi: 10.1007/s10792-024-03222-6.

Chen, X., Jiang, S., Wang, R., Bao, X., & Li, Y. (2023). Neural stem cells in the treatment of Alzheimer's Disease: Current status, challenges, and future prospects. *J Alzheimers Dis, 94*(s1), S173–S186. doi: 10.3233/JAD-220721.

Cheng, C., Lau, H. P. B., & Chan, M. P. S. (2014). Coping flexibility and psychological adjustment to stressful life changes: A meta-analytic review. *Psychological Bulletin, 140*(6), 1582.

Chereches, F. S., Ballhausen, N., Brehmer, Y., & Olaru, G. (2025). Sense of purpose and meaning in life during the transition to grandparenthood. *European Journal of Personality, 39*(3), 357–376.

Chetty, R., Stepner, M., Abraham, S., Lin, S., Scuderi, B., Turner, N., Bergeron, A., & Cutler, D. (2016). The association between income and life expectancy in the United States, 2001–2014. *JAMA, 315*(16), 1750–1750. doi: 10.1001/jama.2016.4226.

Chiavarini, M., Naldini, G., Giacchetta, I., & Fabiani, R. (2022). Exogenous hormone factors in relation to the risk of malignant Melanoma in women: A systematic review and meta-analysis. *Cancers, 14*, 3192. doi: 10.3390/cancers14133192.

Chiles Shaffer, N., Simonsick, E. M., Thorpe, R. J., & Studenski, S. A. (2020). The roles of body composition and specific strength in the relationship between race and physical performance in older adults. *The Journals of Gerontology Series A: Biomedical Sciences and Medical Sciences, 75*(4), 784–791. doi: 10.1093/gerona/glz103.

The China Kadoorie Biobank Collaborative Group (2024). Joint impact of polygenic risk score and lifestyles on early- and late-onset cardiovascular diseases. *Nature Human Behaviour, 8*, 1810–1818. doi: 10.1038/s41562-024-01923-7.

Cho, M. R., Lee, S., & Song, S. K. (2022). A review of Sarcopenia pathophysiology: Diagnosis, treatment and future direction. *J Korean Med Sci, 37*(18), e146. doi: 10.3346/jkms.2022.37.e146.

Chopik, W. J., Newton, N. J., Ryan, L. H., Kashdan, T. B., & Jarden, A. J. (2019). Gratitude across the life span: Age differences and links to subjective well-being. *The Journal of Positive Psychology, 14*(3), 292–302.

Chou, R. J. A., & Choi, N. G. (2011). Prevalence and correlates of perceived workplace discrimination among older workers in the United States of America. *Ageing & Society, 31*(6), 1051–1070.

Chow, A., Galambos, N. L., & Krahn, H. J. (2017). Work values during the transition to adulthood and mid-life satisfaction: Cascading effects across 25 years. *International Journal of Behavioral Development, 41*(1), 105–114.

Chu, C. M., & Lowder, J. L. (2018). Diagnosis and treatment of urinary tract infections across age groups. *The American Journal of Obstetrics and Gynecology, 219*, 40–51. doi: 10.1016/j.ajog.2017.12.231.

Cichorek, M., Wachulska, M., Stasiewicz, A., & Tymińska, A. (2013). Skin melanocytes: Biology and development. *Advances in Dermatology and Allergology, 30*(1), 30–41. doi: 10.5114/pdia.2013.33376.

Cirone, C., Cirone, K. D., & Malvankar-Mehta, M. S. (2023). Linkage between a plant-based diet and age-related eye diseases: A systematic review and meta-analysis. *Nutrition Review, 81*(4), 428–440. doi: 10.1093/nutrit/nuac067.

Cizeron, M., Qiu, Z., Koniaris, B., Gokhale, R., Komiyama, N. H., Fransén, E., & Grant, S. G. N. (2020). A brainwide atlas of synapses across the mouse life span. *Science, 369*(6501), 270–275. doi: 10.1126/science.aba3163.

Clarens, M. F., Crivelli, L., Calandri, I., Chrem Méndez, P., Martin, M. E., Russo, M. J., Campos, J., Surace, E., Vázquez, S., Sevlever, G., & Allegri, R. F. (2020). Neuropsychological profile of Alzheimer's disease based on amyloid biomarker findings results from a South American cohort. *Applied Neuropsychology: Adult, 29*(3), 345–350. doi: 10.1080/23279095.2020.1756816.

Clarke, D. M., & Currie, K. C. (2009). Depression, anxiety and their relationship with chronic diseases: A review of the epidemiology, risk and treatment evidence. *Medical Journal of Australia, 190*, S54–S60.

Clarke, L., & Roberts, C. (2004). The meaning of grandparenthood and its contribution to the quality of life of older people. In A. Walker & C. H. Hennessy (Eds.), *Growing Older: Quality of Life in Old Age* (pp. 188–208). McGraw Hill.

Clark, P. G., Burbank, P. M., Greene, G., Owens, N., & Riebe, D. (2018). What do we know about resilience in older adults? An exploration of some facts, factors, and facets. In B. Resnick, L. P. Gwyther, & K. A. Roberto (Eds.), *Resilience in Aging Concepts, Research and Outcomes* (pp. 51–66). Springer.

Clifford, C., Paulk, E., Lin, Q., Cadwallader, J., Lubbers, K., & Frazier, L. D. (2024). Relationships among adult playfulness, stress, and coping during the COVID-19 pandemic. *Current Psychology, 43*(9), 8403–8412.

Clifton, J., & Harter, J. (2023). *Culture Shock: An Unstoppable Force is Changing How We Work and Live. Gallup's Solution to the Biggest Leadership Issue of our Time*. Simon & Schuster.

Co, M., Couch, E., Gao, Q., Martinez, A., Das-Munshi, J., & Prina M. (2021). Differences in survival and mortality in minority ethnic groups with dementia: A systematic review and meta-analysis. *International Journal of Geriatric Psychiatry, 36*(11), 1640–1663. doi: 10.1002/gps.5590.

Cofer, C. N., & Petri, H. L. (2024). Motivation. *Encyclopedia Britannica*. www.britannica.com/topic/motivation. Accessed June 25, 2024.

Cohen A. A., & Holmes D. J. (2014) *Evolution and the Biology of Aging. Reference Module in Biomedical Sciences*. Elsevier.

Cohen, A. A., Kennedy, B. K., Anglas, U., Bronikowski, A. M., Deelen, J., Dufour, F., Ferbeyre, G., Ferrucci, L., Franceschi, C., Frasca, D., Friguet, B., Gaudreau, P., Gladyshev, V. N., Gonos, E. S., Gorbunova, V., Gut, P., Ivanchenko, M., Legault, V., Lemaître, J.-F., Liontis, T., Liu, G.-H., Liu, M., Maier, A. B., Nóbrega, O. T., Rikkert, M. G. M., Pawelec, G., Rheault, S., Senior, A. M., Simm, A., Soo, S., Traa, A., Ukraintseva, S., Vanhaelen, Q., Raamsdonk, J. M. V., Witkowski, J. M., Yashin, A. I., Ziman, R., & Fülöp, T. (2020). Lack of consensus on an aging biology paradigm? A global survey reveals an agreement to disagree, and the need for an interdisciplinary framework. *Mechanisms of Ageing and Development, 191*, 111316. doi: 10.1016/j.mad.2020.111316.

Cohen, D. (1968). Magnetoencephalography: Evidence of magnetic fields produced by alpha-rhythm currents. *Science, 161*, 784–786. doi: 10.1126/science.161.3843.784.

Cohen, J. P. (2018, July 19). Diseases of despair contribute to declining U.S. life expectancy. *Forbes Healthcare*. www.forbes.com/sites/joshuacohen/2018/07/19/diseases-of-despair-contribute-to-declining-u-s-life-expectancy/?sh=58fef150656b.

Cohen, S., Gianaros, P. J., & Manuck, S. B. (2016). A stage model of stress and disease. *Perspectives on Psychological Science, 11*(4), 456–463.

Cohen, S., Murphy, M. L., & Prather, A. A. (2019). Ten surprising facts about stressful life events and disease risk. *Annual Review of Psychology*, 70(1), 577–597.

Colarusso, C. A., & Nemiroff, R. A. (1981). *Adult Development: A New Dimension in Psychodynamic Theory and Practice*. Plenum.

Colón-Emeric, C. S., McDermott, C. L., Lee, D. S., & Berry, S. D. (2024). Risk assessment and prevention of falls in older community-dwelling adults: A review. *JAMA, 331*(16), 1397–1406. doi: 10.1001/jama.2024.1416.

Comas-Díaz, L., Hall, G. N., & Neville, H. A. (2019). Racial trauma: Theory, research, and healing: Introduction to the special issue. *Americal Psychologist, 74,* 1–5.

Convertino, A. D., Brady, J. P., Albright, C. A., Gonzales IV, M., & Blashill, A. J. (2021). The role of sexual minority stress and community involvement on disordered eating, dysmorphic concerns and appearance-and performance-enhancing drug misuse. *Body Image*, 36, 53–63.

Coratella, G. (2022). Appropriate reporting of exercise variables in resistance training protocols: Much more than load and number of repetitions. *Sports Medicine Open, 8*(1), 99. doi: 10.1186/s40798-022-00492-1.

Cordeiro, L. S., Linhares, D. G., Barros Dos Santos, A. O., Lima Dos Santos, L., de Castro, J. B. P., & Vale, R. G. S. (2023). Influence of resistance training on muscle architecture in older adults: A systematic review and meta-analysis of randomized controlled trials. *Archives of Gerontology and Geriatrics, 112,* 105020. doi: 10.1016/j.archger.2023.105020.

Corr. C. A. (2015). Let's stop "staging" persons who are coping with loss. *Illness, Crisis and Loss*, 23(3), 226–241. doi: 10.1177/1054137315585423.

Corr, C. A. (2021). Elisabeth Kübler-Ross and the "Five Stages" Model in a sampling of recent textbooks published in 10 countries outside the United States. *Omega (Westport), 83*(1), 33–63. doi: 10.1177/0030222819840476.

Costa, P. T., & McCrae, R. R. (1999). A five-factor theory of personality. *Handbook of Personality: Theory and Research, 2*(01), 1999.

Costa, P. T., McCrae, R. R., & Holland, J. L. (1984). Personality and vocational interests in an adult sample. *Journal of Applied Psychology, 69*(3), 390.

Côté, J. E. (2000). *Arrested Adulthood: The Changing Nature of Maturity and Identity*. NYU Press.

Cotzias, G. C., Van Woert, M. H., & Schiffer, L. M. (1967). Aromatic amino acids and modification of parkinsonism. *The New England Journal of Medicine, 276*(7), 374–379. doi: 10.1056/NEJM196702162760703.

Coughlin, S. S., Caplan, L., Stewart, J. L., & Young, L. (2019). Do breast cancer survivorship care plans improve health outcomes? *Journal of Cancer Treatment & Diagnosis*, 3(1), 28.

Cougle, J. R., Resnick, H., & Kilpatrick, D. G. (2009). Does prior exposure to interpersonal violence increase risk of PTSD following subsequent exposure? *Behaviour Research and Therapy, 47*(12), 1012–1017.

Courtney, M. G. (2025). "Trends in cohabitation and marriage by experience of economic vulnerability in the United States. In Blair, S. L. and Z. Mu (Eds.), *The Retreat from Marriage and Parenthood: Examining the Causes and Consequences of Declining Rates. Vol. 30*. (pp. 259–288). Emerald Publishing Limited. doi: 10.1108/S1530-353520250000030015.

COVID-19 Excess Mortality Collaborators (2022). Estimating excess mortality due to the COVID-19 pandemic: A systematic analysis of COVID-19-related mortality, 2020–21. *The Lancet, 399,* 1513–1536. doi: 10.1016/S0140-6736(21)02796-3.

Cowan, N. (2015). George Miller's magical number of immediate memory in retrospect: Observations on the faltering progression of science. *Psychological Review, 122*(3), 536–541. doi: 10.1037/a0039035.

Crealey, G., McQuade, L., O'Sullivan, R., & O'Neill, C. (2023). Arts and creativity interventions for improving health and wellbeing in older adults: A systematic literature review of economic evaluation studies. *BMC Public Health, 23*(1), 2496. doi: 10.1186/s12889-023-17369-x.

Crego, A., Yela, J. R., Gómez-Martínez, M. Á., Riesco-Matías, P., & Petisco-Rodríguez, C. (2021). Relationships between mindfulness, purpose in life, happiness, anxiety, and depression: Testing a mediation model in a sample of women. *International Journal of Environmental Research and Public Health, 18*(3), 925. doi: 10.3390/ijerph18030925.

Creighton, H. B., & McClintock, B. A. (1931). Correlation of cytological and genetical crossing-over in Zea Mays. *Proceedings of the National Academy of Sciences of the United States of America, 17*(8), 49249–7. doi: 10.1073/pnas.17.8.492.

Crenshaw, K. (2018). Demarginalizing the intersection of race and sex: A Black feminist critique of antidiscrimination doctrine, feminist theory, and antiracist politics. In K. T. Bartlett & R. Kennedy (Eds.), *Feminist Legal Theory* (pp. 57–80). doi: 10.4324/9780429500480-5. (Original work published 1989.)

Cruwys, T., Haslam, C., Steffens, N. K., Haslam, S. A., Fong, P., & Lam, B. C. (2019). Friendships that money can buy: Financial security protects health in retirement by enabling social connectedness. *BMC Geriatrics, 19*, 1–9.

Cruz-Jentoft, A. J., Landi, F., Schneider, S. M., Zúñiga, C., Arai, H., Boirie, Y., Chen, L.-K., Fielding, R. A., Martin, F. C., Michel, J.-P., Sieber, C., Stout, J. R., Studenski, S. A., Vellas, B., Woo, J., Zamboni, M., & Cederhold, T. (2014). Prevalence of and interventions for sarcopenia in ageing adults: a systematic review. Report of the International Sarcopenia Initiative (EWGSOP and IWGS). *Age Ageing, 43*(6): 748–759. doi: 10.1093/ageing/afu115.

Csuka, D. A., Csuka, E. A., Juhász, M. L. W., Sharma, A. N., & Mesinkovska, N. A. (2023). A systematic review on the lipid composition of human hair. *International Journal of Dermatoly, 62*(3), 404–415. doi: 10.1111/ijd.16109.

da Costa, J. P., Vitorino. R., Silva, G. M., Vogel, C., Duarte, A. C. & Rocha-Santos, T. (2016). A synopsis on aging-theories, mechanisms and future prospects. *Ageing Research Reviews*, 29, 90–112. doi: 10.1016/j.arr.2016.06.005.

Dalmasso, M. C., de Rojas, I., Olivar, N., Muchnik, C., Angel, B., Gloger, S., Sanchez Abalos, M., Chacón, M. V., Aránguiz, R., Orellana, P., Cuesta, C., Galeano, P., Campanelli, L., Novack, G. V., Martinez, L. E., Medel, N., Lisso, J., Sevillano, Z., Irureta, N., Castaño, E. M., Montrreal, L., Thoenes, M., Hanses, C., Heilmann-Heimbach, S., Kairiyama, C., Mintz, I., Villella, I., Rueda, F., Romero, A., Wukitsevits, N., Quiroga, I., Gona, C., Lambert, J., Solis, P., Politis, D. G., Mangone, C. A., Gonzalez-Billault, C., Boada, M.,Tárraga, L., Slachevsky, A., Albala, C., Fuentes, P., Kochen, S., Brusco, L. I., Ruiz, A., Morelli, L., & Ramírez, A. (2023). The first genome-wide association study in the Argentinian and Chilean populations identifies shared genetics with Europeans in Alzheimer's disease. *Alzheimer's & Dementia, 20*, 1298 –1308. doi: 10.1002/alz.13522.

Daly, M., & Robinson, E. (2021). Anxiety reported by US adults in 2019 and during the 2020 COVID-19 pandemic: Population-based evidence from two nationally representative samples. *J Affect Disord, 286*, 296–300. doi: 10.1016/j.jad.2021.02.054.

Damadian, R. (1971). Tumor detection by nuclear magnetic resonance. *Science, 171 (3976)*, 1151–1153. doi:10.1126/science.171.3976.1151.

Database.earth (2025). https://database.earth/population/united-states-of-america/deaths. Retrieved March 16, 2025.

Dattani, S. (2023). How does the risk of death change as we age – and how has this changed over time? *Our World in Data*. https://ourworldindata.org/how-do-the-risks-of-death-change-as-people-age. Retrieved March 18, 2025.

Daume, J., Kamiński, J., Schjetnan, A. G. P., Salimpour, Y., Khan, U., Kyzar, M., Reed, C. M., Anderson, W. S., Valiante, T. A., Mamelak, A. N., & Rutishauser, U. (2024). Control of working memory by phase–amplitude coupling of human hippocampal neurons. *Nature, 629*, 393–401. doi: 10.1038/s41586-024-07309-z.

Davidovic, M., Sevo, G., Svorcan, P., Milosevic, D. P., Despotovic, N., & Erceg, P. (2010). Old age as a privilege of the "selfish ones". *Aging and Disease, 1*, 139–146.

Davidson, J., & Schimmele, C. (2019). Evolving internet use among Canadian seniors. *Statistics Canada*. https://epe.bac-lac.gc.ca/100/201/301/weekly_acquisitions_list-ef/2019/19-28/publications.gc.ca/collections/collection_2019/statcan/11f0019m/11f0019m2019015-eng.pdf?nodisclaimer=1.

de Bruyne, S., van Schie, L., Himpe, J., De Somer, F., Everaert, I., Derave, W., Van den Broecke, C., Huizing, M., Bostan, N., Speeckaert, M., Callewaert, N., Van Aken, E., & Delanghe, J. R. (2021). A potential role for fructosamine-3-kinase in Cataract treatment. *International Journal of Molecular Science, 22*(8), 3841. doi: 10.3390/ijms22083841.

de Godoy, L. L., Alves, C. A. P. F., Saavedra, J. S. M., Studart-Neto, A., Nitrini, R., da Costa Leite, C., & Bisdas, S. (2021). Understanding brain resilience in superagers: A systematic review. *Neuroradiology, 63*(5), 663–683. doi: 10.1007/s00234-020-02562-1.

de Farias Panet, M., de Araújo, V. M. D., & de Araújo, E. H. S. (2022). Thermal sensation index for elderly people living in Brazil. *International Journal of Biometeorology, 66*(3), 469–480. doi: 10.1007/s00484-021-02194-x.

de Oliveira, F., Bertolucci, P. F., Chen, E., & Smith, M. (2015). Assessment of risk factors for earlier onset of sporadic Alzheimer's disease dementia. *Neurology India, 62*, 625–630. doi: 10.4103/0028-3886.149384.

De Ridder, D., Geenen, R., Kuijer, R., & Van Middendorp, H. (2008). Psychological adjustment to chronic disease. *The Lancet, 372*(9634), 246–255.

De Vriendt, P., Gorus, E., Cornelis, E., Bautmans, I., Petrovic, M., & Mets, T. (2013). The advanced activities of daily living: A tool allowing the evaluation of subtle functional decline in mild cognitive impairment. *The Journal of Nutrition, Health & Aging, 17*, 64–71.

Deco, G., Perl, Y. S., Ponce-Alvarez, A., Tagliazucchi, E., Whybrow, P. C., Fuster, J., Kringelbach, M. L. (2023). One ring to rule them all: The unifying role of prefrontal cortex in steering task-related brain dynamics. *Progress in Neurobiology, 227*, 102468. doi: 10.1016/j.pneurobio.2023.102468.

Del Tredici, K., & Braak, H. (2016). Review: Sporadic Parkinson's disease: Development and distribution of α-synuclein pathology. *Neuropathology and Applied Neurobioly, 42*, 33–50. doi: 10.1111/nan.12298.

Deng, Y., Qiao, L., Du, M., Qu, C., Wan, L., Li, J., & Huang, L. (2022). Age-related macular degeneration: Epidemiology, genetics, pathophysiology, diagnosis, and targeted therapy. *Genes & Diseases, 9*, 62–79.

DePew, R., & Gonzales, G. (2020). Differences in health outcomes between millennials and generation X in the USA: Evidence from the National Health Interview Survey. *Population Research and Policy Review, 39*, 605–616. doi: 10.1007/s11113-019-09563-w.

Desjardins, R., Thorn, W., Schleicher, A., Quintini, G., Pellizzari, M., Kis, V., & Chung, J. E. (2013). OECD skills outlook 2013: First results from the survey of adult skills. *OECD*. www.oecd.org/en/publications/2013/10/oecd-skills-outlook-2013_g1g3451c.html. Accessed November 8, 2025.

D'Esposito, M., & Postle, B. R. (2015). The cognitive neuroscience of working memory. *Annual Review of Psychology, 66*, 115–142. doi: 10.1146/annurev-psych-010814-015031.

Di Gessa, G., Bordone, V., & Arpino, B. (2020). Becoming a grandparent and its effect on well-being: The role of order of transitions, time, and gender. *The Journals of Gerontology Series B: Psychological Sciences and Social Sciences, 75*(10), 2250–2262.

Di Luca, D. G., Sambursky, J. A., Margolesky, J., Cordeiro, J. G., Dlaz, A., Shpiner, D. S., Moore, H. P., Singer, C., & Luca, C. (2020). Minority enrollment in Parkinson's disease clinical trials: Meta-analysis and systematic review of studies evaluating treatment of neuropsychiatric symptoms. *Journal of Parkinson's Disease, 10*(4), 1709–1716. doi: 10.3233/JPD-202045.

Diamond, L. M., & Aspinwall, L. G. (2003). Emotion regulation across the life span: An integrative perspective emphasizing self-regulation, positive affect, and dyadic processes. *Motivation and Emotion*, 27, 125–156.

Diener, E. (2000). Subjective well-being: The science of happiness and a proposal for a national index. *American Psychologist, 55*(1), 34–43.
Diener, E., & Lucas, R. E. (1999). Personality and subjective well-being. In D. Kahneman, E. Diener, & N. Schwarz (Eds.), *Well-being: Foundations of Hedonic Psychology* (pp. 213–229). Russell Sage Foundation.
Diniz, C. R. A. F. & Crestani, A. P. (2023). The times they are a-changin': A proposal on how brain flexibility goes beyond the obvious to include the concepts of "upward" and "downward" to neuroplasticity. *Molecular Psychiatry, 28*, 977–992 (2023). doi: 10.1038/s41380-022-01931-x.
Ding, C.-Q., Zhang, Y.-P., Wang, Y.-W., Yang, M.-F., Wang, S., Cui, N.-Q., & Jin, J.-F. (2020). Death and do-not-resuscitate order in the emergency department: A single-center three-year retrospective study in the Chinese mainland. *World Journal of Emergency Medicine, 11*, 231–237. doi: 10.5847/wjem.j.1920-8642.2020.04.005.
Diószegi, J., Llanaj, E., & Ádány, R. (2019). Genetic background of taste perception, taste preferences, and its nutritional implications: A systematic review. *Frontiers in Genetics, 10*, 1272. doi: 10.3389/fgene.2019.01272.
Dixon, M. L., & Dweck, C. S. (2022). The amygdala and the prefrontal cortex: The co-construction of intelligent decision-making. *Psychological Review, 129*(6), 1414–1441. doi: 10.1037/rev0000339.
Doerwald, F., Scheibe, S., Zacher, H., & Van Yperen, N. W. (2016). Emotional competencies across adulthood: State of knowledge and implications for the work context. *Work, Aging and Retirement*, 2(2), 159–216.
Dolan, P., & Peasgood, T. (2008). Measuring well-being for public policy: Preferences or experiences? *Journal of Legal Studies, 37*(S2), S5–S31.
Domínguez-Bautista, J. A., Acevo-Rodríguez, P. S., & Castro-Obregón, S. (2021). Programmed cell senescence in the mouse developing spinal cord and notochord. *Fronters in Cell and Developmental Biology*, 9, 587096.
Dorsey, E., & Bloem, B. R. (2018). The Parkinson pandemic—a call to action. *JAMA Neurology, 75*, 9–10.
Dowd, J. J., & Bengtson, V. L. (1978). Aging in minority populations. An examination of the double jeopardy hypothesis. *Journal of Gerontology, 33*(3), 427–436.
Duarte Folle, A., Flores, M. E. S., Kusters, C., Paul, K. C., Del Rosario, I., Zhang, K., Ruiz, C., Castro, E., Bronstein, J., Ritz, B., & Keener, A. M. (2023). Ethnicity and Parkinson's disease: Motor and nonmotor features and disease progression in Latino patients living in rural California. *The Journals of Gerontology Series A: Biomedical Sciences and Medical Sciences, 78*, 1258–1268. doi: 10.1093/gerona/glad016.
Dubos, R. (1961). *Mirage of Health: Utopias, Progress and Biological Change*. Doubleday.
Ducharme-Laliberté, G., Mellah, S., Boller, B., & Belleville, S. (2022). More flexible brain activation underlies cognitive reserve in older adults. *Neurobiology of Aging, 113*, 63–72. doi: 10.1016/j.neurobiolaging.2022.02.001.
Dunkel Schetter, C., & Dolbier, C. (2011). Resilience in the context of chronic stress and health in adults. *Social and Personality Psychology Compass, 5*(9), 634–652.
Dunkel Schetter, C. D., Feinstein, L. G., Taylor, S. E., & Falke, R. L. (1992). Patterns of coping with cancer. *Health Psychology, 11*(2), 79–87.
Dunn, E. W., Aknin, L. B., & Norton, M. I. (2008). Spending money on others promotes happiness. *Science, 319*(5870), 1687–1688.
Dunn, H. L. (1977). High Level Wellness: A Collection of Twenty-nine Short Talks on Different Aspects of the Theme "High-level Wellness for Man and Society." Charles B. Slack.
Dwyer-Lindgren, L., Kendrick, P., O Kelly, Y., O Sylte, D., Schmidt, C., Blacker, B. F., Daoud, F., Abdi, A. A., Baumann, M., Mouhanna, F., Kahn, E., Hay, S. I., Mensah, G. A., Nápoles, A. M., Pérez-Stable, E. J., Shiels, M., Freedman, N., Arias, E., George, S. A., Murray, D. M., Phillips, J. W., Spittel, M. L., Murray, C, J., Mokdad,

A. H. (2022). Life expectancy by county, race, and ethnicity in the USA, 2000–19: A systematic analysis of health disparities. *The Lancet, 400,* 25–38. doi: 10.1016/S0140-6736(22)00876-5.
Earl, E. J., & Marais, D. (2023). The experience of intergenerational interactions and their influence on the mental health of older people living in residential care. *PLoS One, 18,* 1–20. doi: 10.1371/journal.pone.0287369.
Easterlin, R. A. (2003). Building a better theory of well-being. *IZA Discussion Paper, 742.* https://ssrn.com/abstract=392043.
Edde, M., Leroux, G., Altena, E., & Chanraud, S. (2021). Functional brain connectivity changes across the human life span: From fetal development to old age. *Journal of Neuroscience Research, 99*(1), 236–262. doi: 10.1002/jnr.24669.
Egbert, J., Luke, A., & Qeadan, F. (2024). Intersectionality of demographic characteristics in self-reported anorexia nervosa, bulimia nervosa, and probable eating disorders among college students. *International Journal of Eating Disorders, 57,* 132–145. doi: 10.1002/eat.24090.
Eibich, P. (2015). Understanding the effect of retirement on health: Mechanisms and heterogeneity. *Journal of Health Economics, 43,* 1–12.
Elbaz, A., Carcaillon, L., Kab, S., Moisan, F. (2016). Epidemiology of Parkinson's disease. *Revue Neurologique, 172*(1), 14–26.
Elder, G. H., Shanahan, M. J., & Jennings, J. A. (2015). Human development in time and place. *Handbook of Child Psychology and Developmental Science, 4,* 6–54.
Eldesouky, L., & English, T. (2018). Another year older, another year wiser? Emotion regulation strategy selection and flexibility across adulthood. *Psychology and Aging, 33*(4), 572.
Elizabeth, H. S., Wongsomboon, V., & Clark, M. S. (2025). Links between partnering, relationship quality and mental well-being among sexual minority and straight individuals. *Psychology & Sexuality,* 1–23. doi: 10.1080/19419899.2025.2490913.
Elliz, P., Scheijbeler, D. N., Schoonhoven, M., Engels, M. A., Scheltens, P., Stam, C. J., Gouw, A. A., & Hillebrand, A. (2022). Generating diagnostic profiles of cognitive decline and dementia using magnetoencephalography. *Neurobiology of Aging, 111,* 82–94. doi: 10.1016/j.neurobiolaging.2021.11.002.
El-Metwally, A., Toivola, P., Al-Rashidi, M., Nooruddin, S., Jawed, M., AlKanhal, R., Razzak, H. A., & Albawardi, N. (2019). Epidemiology of Alzheimer's disease and dementia in Arab countries: A systematic review. *Behavioural Neurology,* 3935943. doi: 10.1155/2019/3935943.
Engel, G. L. (1977). The need for a new medical model: A challenge for biomedicine. *Science,* 196, 129–136.
Engel, G. L. (1980). The clinical application of the biopsychosocial model. *American Journal of Psychiatry, 137,* 535–544.
English, T., & Carstensen, L. L. (2013). Shifts in emotional experience and regulation across adulthood. *Changing Emotions,* 31–36.
Erdman, L. (1991). Laughter therapy for patients with cancer. *Oncology Nursing Forum, 18*(8), 1359–1363.
Erickson, K. I., Voss, M. W., Prakash, R. S., Basak, C., Szabo, A., Chaddock, L., Kim, J. S., Heo, S., Alves, H., White, S. M., Wojcicki, T. R., Mailey, E., Vieira, V. J., Martin, S. A., Pence, B. D., Woods, J. A., McAuley, E., & Kramer, A. F. (2011). Exercise training increases size of hippocampus and improves memory. *Proceedings of the National Academy of Sciences, 108*(7), 3017–3022. doi: 10.1073/pnas.1015950108.
Eriksson, P. S., Perfilieva, E., Björk-Eriksson, T., Alborn, A. M., Nordborg, C., Peterson, D. A. & Gage, F. H. (1998). Neurogenesis in the adult human hippocampus. *Nature Medicine, 4,* 1313–1317.
Erving, C. L., & Smith, M. V. (2022). Disrupting monolithic thinking about Black women and their mental health: Does stress exposure explain intersectional ethnic, nativity, and socioeconomic differences? *Social Problems, 69*(4), 1046–1067.

Esdaille, A. R., Kuete, N. K., Anyaeche, V. I., Kalemoglu, E., & Kucuk, O. (2024). The interplay between structural inequality, allostatic load, inflammation, and cancer in Black Americans: A narrative review. *Cancers (Basel), 16*(17), 3023. doi: 10.3390/cancers16173023.

Everett, B. G., Wall, M., Shea, E., & Hughes, T. L. (2021). Mortality risk among a sample of sexual minority women: A focus on the role of sexual identity disclosure. *Social Science & Medicine, 272*, 113731.

Ewers, M., Luan, Y., Frontzkowski, L., Neitzel, J., Rubinski, A., Dichgans, M., Hassenstab, J., Gordon, B. A., Chhatwal, J. P., Levin, J., Schofield, P., Benzinger, T. L. S., Morris, J. C., Goate, A., Karch, C. M., Fagan, A. M., McDade, E., Allegri, R., Berman, S., Chui, H., Cruchaga, C., Farlow, M., Graff-Radfrod, N., Jucker, M., Lee, J.-H., Martins, R. S., Mori, H., Perrin, R., Xiong, C., Rossor, M., Fox, N. C., O'Connor, A., Salloway, S., Danek, A., Buerger, K., Bateman, R. J., Habeck, C., Stern, Y., Franzmeier, N., Alzheimer's Disease Neuroimaging Initiative, & the Dominantly Inherited Alzheimer Network (2021). Segregation of functional networks is associated with cognitive resilience in Alzheimer's disease. *Brain, 144*(7), 2176–2185. doi: 10.1093/brain/awab112.

Fakhari, A., Herizchi, S., Sadeghi-Bazargani, H., Shahrokh, A., Noorazar, S. G., Mirzajanzade, M., Barzegar, H., Farahbakhsh, M., & Azizi, H. (2023). Prevalence of psychiatric disorders in the aging population in the northeastern of Iran. *Middle East Current Psychiatry, 30*, 1–7. doi: 10.1186/s43045-023-00287-4.

Fan, W., & Moen, P. (2023). Ongoing remote work, returning to working at work, or in between during COVID-19: What promotes subjective well-being? *Journal of Health and Social Behavior, 64*(1), 152–171.

Farage, M. A., Miller, K. W., Elsner, P., & Maibach, H. I. (2013). Characteristics of the aging skin. *Advances in Wound Care* (New Rochelle), *2*(1), 5–10. doi: 10.1089/wound.2011.0356.

Farber, N., Shinkle, D., Lynott, J., Fox-Grage, W., & Harrell, R. (2011, December). Aging in place: A state survey of livability policies and practices. National Conference of State Legislatures & AARP Public Policy Institute.

Faria, N. R., Rambaut, A., Suchard, M. A., Baele, G., Bedford, T., Ward, M. J., Tatem, A. J., Sousa, J. D., Arinaminpathy, N., Pépin, J., Posada, D., Peeters, M., Pybus, O. G., & Lemey, P. (2014). HIV epidemiology: The early spread and epidemic ignition of HIV-1 in human populations. *Science, 346* (6205), 56–61. doi: 10.1126/science.1256739.

Farina, N., Ibnidris, A., Alladi, S., Comas-Herrera, A., Albanese, E., Docrat, S., Ferri, C. P., Freeman, E., Govia, I., Jacobs, R., Astudillo-Garcia, C. I., Musyimi, C., Sani, T. P., Schneider, M., Theresia, I., Turana, Y., Knapp, M., Banerjee, S. & STRiDE Team (2020). A systematic review and meta-analysis of dementia prevalence in seven developing countries: A STRiDE project. *Global Public Health, 15*(12), 1878–1893. doi: 10.1080/17441692.2020.1792527.

Feigelman, W., Rosen, Z., Joiner, T., Silva, C., & Mueller, A. S. (2017). Examining longer-term effects of parental death in adolescents and young adults: Evidence from the national longitudinal survey of adolescent to adult health. *Death Studies, 41*(3), 133–143. doi: 10.1080/07481187.2016.1226990.

Feltz, A. (2019). *Physiology of Neurons* (1st ed.) Garland Science. doi: 10.1201/9780429292972.

Feng, P., Huang, L., & Wang, H. (2014). Taste bud homeostasis in health, disease, and aging. *Chemical Senses, 39*, 3–16.

Fields, D., Fraser, L. K., Taylor, J., & Hackett, J. (2023). What does 'good' palliative care look like for children and young people? A qualitative study of parents' experiences and perspectives. *Palliative Medicine, 37*(3), 355–371. doi: 10.1177/02692163231154300.

Fili, M., Mohammadiarvejeh, P., Klinedinst, B. S., Wang, Q., Moody, S., Barnett, N., Pollpeter, A., Larsen, B., Li, T., Willette, S. A., Mochel, J. P., Allenspach, K., Hugh, G., & Willette, A. A. (2024). A machine learning approach for potential Super-Agers identification using neuronal functional connectivity networks. *Alzheimer's Dementia, 16*, e12595. doi: 10.1002/dad2.12595.

Fingerman, K. L., Cheng, Y. P., Tighe, L., Birditt, K. S., & Zarit, S. (2011). *Relationships between young adults and their parents*. In A. Booth, S. L. Brown, N. S. Landale, W. D., Manning, & S. M. McHale (Eds.), *Early Adulthood in a Family Context* (pp. 59–85). Springer New York.

Fingerman, K. L., Hay, E. L., & Birditt, K. S. (2004). The best of ties, the worst of ties: Close, problematic, and ambivalent social relationships. *Journal of Marriage and Family, 66*(3), 792–808. doi: 10.1111/j.0022-2445.2004.00053.x

Fingerman, K. L., Kim, K., Birditt, K. S., & Zarit, S. H. (2016). The ties that bind: Midlife parents' daily experiences with grown children. *Journal of Marriage and Family, 78*(2), 431–450.

Fink, J. E., Hackney, A. C., Matsumoto, M., Maekawa, T., & Horie, S. (2020). Mobility and biomechanical functions in the aging male: Testosterone and the Locomotive Syndrome. *Aging Male, 23*(5), 403–410. doi: 10.1080/13685538.2018.1504914.

Finkel, E. J., Eastwick, P. W., Karney, B. R., Reis, H. T., & Sprecher, S. (2012). Online dating: A critical analysis from the perspective of psychological science. *Psychological Science in the Public Interest, 13*(1), 3–66. doi: 10.1177/1529100612436522.

Finn, E. S., Poldrack, R. A. & Shine, J. M. (2023). Functional neuroimaging as a catalyst for integrated neuroscience. *Nature, 623*, 263–273. doi: 10.1038/s41586-023-06670-9.

Fiore, J. (2019). A systematic review of the Dual Process Model of coping with bereavement (1999–2016). *OMEGA – Journal of Death and Dying, 84* (2), 414–458. doi: 10.1177/0030222819893139.

Flanagan, E. W., Most, J., Mey, J. T., & Redman, L. M. (2020). Calorie restriction and aging in humans. *Annual Review of Nutrition*, 40, 105–133. doi: 10.1146/annurev-nutr-122319-034601.

Flint, M. (1975). The menopause: Reward or punishment? *Psychosomatic J. Consult. and Liaison Psychiatry, 16*(4), 161–163.

Flora, J., & Segrin, C. (2000). Relationship development in dating couples: Implications for relational satisfaction and loneliness. *Journal of Social and Personal Relationships, 17*(6), 811–825. doi: 10.1177/0265407500176006.

Fogerty, D., Humes, L. E. & Busey, T. A. (2016). Age-related declines in early sensory memory: Identification of rapid auditory and visual stimulus sequences. *Frontiers in Aging Neuroscience, 8*, 90. doi: 10.3389/fnagi.2016.00090.

Folkman, S., & Lazarus, R. S. (1988). *Manual for the Ways of Coping Questionnaire*. Consulting Psychologist Press.

Folkman, S., & Moskowitz, J. T. (2004). Coping: Pitfalls and promise. *The Annual Review of Psychology, 55*, 745–774. doi: 10.1146/annurev.psych.55.090902.141456.

Folkmann, E. J., Hughes, M. C., Khan, U. A. & Vaezi, M. (2024). Examining noncommunicable diseases using satellite imagery: A systematic literature review. *BMC Public Health, 24*, 2774. doi: 10.1186/s12889-024-20316-z.

Ford, B. N., & Savitz, J. (2022). Depression, aging, and immunity: Implications for COVID-19 vaccine immunogenicity. *Immunity & Ageing, 19*(1), 32. doi: 10.1186/s12979-022-00288-7.

Ford, D. H., & Lerner, R. M. (1992). *Developmental systems theory: An integrative approach*. Sage Publications, Inc.

Fornito, A., Zalesky, A., & Breakspear, M. (2013). Graph analysis of the human connectome: Promise, progress, and pitfalls. *NeuroImage, 80*, 426–444.

Forno, E., Ortega, V. E., & Celedón, J. C. (2023). Asthma and chronic obstructive pulmonary disease. *Clinics in Chest Medicine, 44*(3), 519–530. doi: 10.1016/j.ccm.2023.03.008.

Foster, M., & Sherrington, C. S. (1897). *Textbook of Physiology. Vol. 3*. (7th ed.). Macmillan.

Frazier, L. D. (2000). Coping with disease-related stressors in Parkinson's disease. *The Gerontologist*, 40(1).

Frazier, L. D. (2002). Stability and change in patterns of coping with Parkinson's disease. *The International Journal of Aging and Human Development, 55*(3), 207–231.

Frazier, L. D. (2025). *The Psychology of Health and Illness: A Multicultural Perspective*. Routledge; Taylor & Francis.

Frazier, L. D., Barreto, M. L., & Newman, F. L. (2012). Self-regulation and eudaimonic well-being across adulthood. *Experimental Aging Research, 38*(4), 394–410.

Frazier, L., Cotrell, V., & Hooker, K. (2003). Possible selves and illness: A comparison of individuals with Parkinson's disease, early-stage Alzheimer's disease, and healthy older adults. *International Journal of Behavioral Development, 27*(1), 1–11.

Frazier, L. D., Gonzalez, G. K., Kafka, C. L., & Johnson, P. M. (2002). Psychosocial influences on possible selves: A comparison of three cohorts of older adults. *International Journal of Behavioral Development, 26*(4), 308–317.

Frazier, L. D., & Hooker, K. (2006). Possible selves in adult development: Linking theory and research. In C. Dunkel & J. Kerpelman (Eds.), *Possible Selves: Theory, Research and Applications* (pp. 41–59). Nova Science Publishers.

Frazier, L. D., Hooker, K., Johnson, P. M., & Kaus, C. R. (2000). Continuity and change in possible selves in later life: A 5-year longitudinal study. *Basic and Applied Social Psychology, 22*(3), 237–243.

Frazier, L. D., & Bazo Perez, M. (2024). Unpacking eating disorder risk and resilience during menopause: A biopsychosocial perspective. *Menopause, 32*(5), 443–452. doi: 10.1097/GME.0000000000002511.

Frazier, L. D., & Saunders, J. F. (2025) *Women of a Certain Age: Stories from the Other Side of Youth.* [Manuscript in preparation.]

Fredriksen-Goldsen, K. I., Simoni, J. M., Kim, H.-J., Lehavot, K., Walters, K. L., Yang, J., Hoy-Ellis, C. P., & Muraco, A. (2014). The health equity promotion model: Reconceptualization of lesbian, gay, bisexual, and transgender (LGBT) health disparities. *American Journal of Orthopsychiatry, 84*(6), 653–663. doi: 10.1037/ort0000030.

Friedman, B., Lyness, J. M., Delavan, R. L., Li, C., & Barker, W. H. (2008). Major depression and disability in older primary care patients with heart failure. *Journal of Geriatric Psychiatry and Neurology, 21*(2), 111–122.

Friedman, S. M. (2019). The interface between healthy aging, longevity, disease, and disability. In P. Coll (Ed.), *Healthy Aging: A Complete Guide to Clinical Management* (pp. 23–29). Springer.

Freilich, C. D., Markon, K. E., Mann, F. D., Cole, S. W., & Krueger, R. F. (2024). Associations between loneliness, epigenetic aging, and multimorbidity through older adulthood. *The Journals of Gerontology Series B: Psychological Sciences and Social Sciences, 79*(12), gbae169. doi: 10.1093/geronb/gbae169.

Fuentes-Afflick, E., Hessol, N. A., & Pérez-Stable, E. J. (1999). Testing the epidemiologic paradox of low birth weight in Latinos. *Archives of Pediatrics and Adolescent Medicine, 153*(2), 147–153.

Gabriel, G. A., Harris, L. R., Henriques, D. Y. P., Pandi, M. & Campos, J. L. (2022). Multisensory visual-vestibular training improves visual heading estimation in younger and older adults. *Frontiers in Aging Neuroscience, 14,* 816512. doi: 10.3389/fnagi.2022.816512.

Galal, S. (2025). Life expectancy in African countries 2025. *Statista*. www.statista.com/statistics/1218173/life-expectancy-in-african-countries/?srsltid=AfmBOoqL44ul0lPWLuX7cZ0qvAqVk7TTsUErOGtN6AxeCXvCVFwqK94p. Accessed November 22, 2025.

Galambos, N. L., Fang, S., Horne, R. M., Johnson, M. D., & Krahn, H. J. (2018). Trajectories of perceived support from family, friends, and lovers in the transition to adulthood. *Journal of Social and Personal Relationships*, 35(10), 1418–1438. doi: 10.1177/0265407517717360.

Gallagher, D., Kuznia, P., Heshka, S., Aibu, H., Heymsfield, S. B., Goodpaster, B., Visser, M., & Harris, T. B. (2005). Adipose tissue in muscle: A novel depot similar in size to visceral adipose tissue. *The American Journal of Clinical Nutrition, 81*, 903–910. doi: 10.1093/ajcn/81.4.903.

Gallardo-Peralta, L. P., Mayorga Muñoz, C., & Soto Higuera, A. (2022). Health, social support, resilience and successful ageing among older Chilean adults. *International Social Work, 65*(2), 283–299. doi: 10.1177/0020872819901147.

Gallardo-Peralta, L. P., Sánchez-Moreno, E., & Rodríguez-Rodríguez, V. (2019). Strangers in their own world: Exploring the relation between cultural practices and the health of older adults in native communities in Chile. *The British Journal of Social Work, 49*, 920–942. doi: 10.1093/bjsw/bcz045.

Gallego, M., Barat, J. M., Grau, R., & Talens, P. (2022). Compositional, structural design and nutritional aspects of texture-modified foods for the elderly. *Trends in Food Science & Technology, 119*, 152–163. doi: 10.1016/j.tifs.2021.12.008.

Ganesan, K., Jandu, J. S., Anastasopoulou, C., Ahsun, S., & Roane, D. (2023). Secondary osteoporosis. *StatPearls*. StatPearls Publishing.

Ganong, L., Jensen, T., Sanner, C., Russell, L., & Coleman, M. (2019). Stepfathers' affinity-seeking with stepchildren, stepfather-stepchild relationship quality, marital quality, and stepfamily cohesion among stepfathers and mothers. *Journal of Family Psychology, 33*(5), 521–531. doi: 10.1037/fam0000518.

Gao, Q., Chua, K.-C., Mayston, R., & Prina, M. (2024). Longitudinal associations of loneliness and social isolation with care dependence among older adults in Latin America and China: A 10/66 dementia research group population-based cohort study. *International of Journal of Geriatric Psychiatry*, e6115. doi: 10.1002/gps.6115.

Gao, Y., Wen, D., Wang, S., & Wang, J. (2023). Presenilin and Alzheimer's disease interactions with aging, exercise and high-fat diet: A systematic review. *BIOCELL, 47*(1), 41–49. doi: 10.32604/biocell.2022.022689.

Garcia, J. R., Reiber, C., Massey, S. G., & Merriwether, A. M. (2012). Sexual hookup culture: A review. *Review of General Psychology, 16*(2), 161–176.

Garcia, M. A., Downer, B., Chiu, C. T., Saenz, J. L., Rote, S., & Wong, R. (2019). Racial/ethnic and nativity differences in cognitive life expectancies among older adults in the United States. *The Gerontologist, 59*(2), 281–289. doi: 10.1093/geront/gnx142.

Garcini, L. M., Brown, R. L., Chen, M. A., Saucedo, L., Fite, A. M., Ye, P., Ziauddin, K., & Fagundes, C. P. (2021). Bereavement among widowed Latinos in the United States: A systematic review of methodology and findings. *Death Studies, 45*(5), 342–353. doi: 10.1080/07481187.2019.1648328.

Garmezy, N. (1991). Resiliency and vulnerability to adverse developmental outcomes associated with poverty. *American Behavioral Scientist, 34*(4), 416–430.

Garo-Pascual, M., Gaser, C., Zhang, L., Tohka, J., Medina, M., & Strange, B. A. (2023). Brain structure and phenotypic profile of superagers compared with age-matched older adults: A longitudinal analysis from the Vallecas Project. *The Lancet Healthy Longevity, 4*, 374–385.

Garo-Pascual, M., Zhang, L., Valentí-Soler, M., & Strange, B. A. (2024). Superagers resist typical age-related white matter structural changes. *Journal of Neuroscience, 44*(25), e2059232024. doi: 10.1523/JNEUROSCI.2059-23.2024.

Garrett, J. L., & Eccles, J. S. (2009). Transition to adulthood: Linking late-adolescent lifestyles to family and work status in the mid-twenties. In I. Schoon & R. K. Silbereisen (Eds.), *Transitions from School to Work: Globalization, Individualization, and Patterns of Diversity* (pp. 243–264). Cambridge University Press. doi: 10.1017/CBO9780511605369.011.

Gautam, S., Jain, A., Chaudhary, J., Gautam, M., Gaur, M., & Grover, S. (2024). Concept of mental health and mental well-being, its determinants and coping strategies. *Indian Journal of Psychiatry*, *66*(Suppl 2), S231–S244. doi: 10.4103/indianjpsychiatry.indianjpsychiatry_707_23.

Gazzaniga, M. S., Heatherton, T. F., & Halpern, D. F. (2015). *Psychological Science* (5th ed.). New York.

Geegan, S. A., Parker, K. A., Pfeiffer S. N., Rodriguez, D., & Tristan, A. (2023). The complexities of mental health help seeking among Latinx college students: Qualitative inquiry using the Theory of Planned Behavior. *Hispanic Journal of Behavioral Sciences*, *45*(2), 91–120. doi: 10.1177/07399863231214104.

Geneva, I. I., Cuzzo, B., Fazili, T., & Javaid, W. (2019). Normal body temperature: A systematic review. *Open Forum Infect Dis*, *6*(4), ofz032. doi: 10.1093/ofid/ofz032.

Ghahramani, S., Lankarani, K. B., Yousefi, M., Heydari, K., Shahabi, S., & Azmand, S. (2021). A systematic review and meta-analysis of burnout among healthcare workers during COVID-19. *Frontiers in Psychiatry*, *12*, 758–849.

Ghaleh, M., Lacey, E. H., Fama, M. E., Anbari, Z., DeMarco, A. T., & Turkeltaub, P. E. (2019). Dissociable mechanisms of verbal working memory revealed through multivariate lesion mapping. *Cerebral Cortex*, *30*, 2542–2554. doi: 10.1093/cercor/bhz259.

Ghondaghsaz, E., Khalaji, A., Mahalleh, M., Masrour, M., Mohammadi, P., Cannavo, A., & Behnoush, A H. (2024). Exploring the association between cognitive decline and Triglyceride-Glucose Index: A systematic review and meta-analysis. *Brain and Behavior*, *14*(11), e70131. doi: 10.1002/brb3.70131.

Gilligan, M., Stocker, C. M., & Jewsbury Conger, K. (2020). Sibling relationships in adulthood: Research findings and new frontiers. *Journal of Family Theory & Review*, *12*(3), 305–320.

Gire, J. (2014). How death imitates life: Cultural influences on conceptions of death and dying. *Online Readings in Psychology and Culture*, *6*(2), 1–22. doi: 10.9707/2307-0919.1120.

Gladyshev, V. N. (2014). The free radical theory of aging is dead. Long live the damage theory! *Antioxidants & Redox Signaling*, *20*, 727–731. doi: 10.1089/ars.2013.5228.

Global Burden of Disease 2017 Mortality Collaborators (2018). Global, regional, and national age-sex-specific mortality and life expectancy, 1950–2017: A systematic analysis for the Global Burden of Disease Study 2017. *The Lancet*, *392*, 1684–1735.

Global Burden of Disease 2019 Diseases and Injuries Collaborators (2020). Global burden of 369 diseases and injuries in 204 countries and territories, 1990–2019: A systematic analysis for the Global Burden of Disease Study 2019. *The Lancet*, *396*(10258), 1204–1222. doi: 10.1016/S0140-6736(20)30925-9.

Global Burden of Disease 2021 Demographics Collaborators (2024). Global age-sex-specific mortality, life expectancy, and population estimates in 204 countries and territories and 811 subnational locations, 1950–2021, and the impact of the COVID-19 pandemic: A comprehensive demographic analysis for the Global Burden of Disease Study 2021. *The Lancet*, *403*(10440), 1989–2056. doi: 10.1016/S0140-6736(24)00476-8.

Godbole, N., Kwon, S. C., Beasley, J. M., Roberts, T., Kranick, J., Smilowitz, J., Park, A., Sherman, S. E., Trinh-Shevrin, C., & Chodosh, J. (2023). Assessing equitable inclusion of underrepresented older adults in Alzheimer's disease, related cognitive disorders, and aging-related research: A scoping review. *The Gerontologist*, *63*(6), 1067–1077. doi: 10.1093/geront/gnac060.

Golden, S. H., Yajnik, C., Phatak, S., Hanson, R. L., & Knowler, W. C. (2019). Racial/ethnic differences in the burden of type 2 diabetes over the life course: A focus on the USA and India. *Diabetologia*, *62*(10), 1751–1760. doi: 10.1007/s00125-019-4968-0.

Goldsmith, T. (2014). *The Evolution of Aging* (3rd ed.). Azinet Press.

Goldsmith, T. C. (2017). Externally regulated programmed aging and effects of population stress on mammal lifespan. *Biochemistry (Moscow), 82*(12), 1430–1434. doi: 10.1134/S0006297917120033.

Golub, S. A., Gamarel, K. E., & Rendina, H. J. (2014). Loss and growth: Identity processes with distinct and complementary impacts on well-being among those living with chronic illness. *Psychology, Health & Medicine, 19*(5), 572–579.

Golub, S. A., Rendina, H. J., & Gamarel, K. E. (2013). Identity-related growth and loss in a sample of HIV-positive gay and bisexual men: Initial scale development and psychometric evaluation. *AIDS and Behavior, 17*, 748–759.

Gómez, J. M. (2019). What's the harm? Internalized prejudice and intra-racial trauma as cultural betrayal among ethnic minority college students. *American Journal of Orthopsychiatry, 89*, 237–247. doi: 10.1037/ort0000367.

Gómez, J. M. (2021). Cultural betrayal as a dimension of traumatic harm: Violence and PTSS among ethnic minority emerging adults. *Journal of Child & Adolescent Trauma, 14*(3), 347–356. doi: 10.1007/s40653-020-00314-0.

Gonçalves, R. G. J., Vasques, J. F., da Silva-Junior, A. J., Gubert, F., & Mendez-Otero, R. (2023). Mesenchymal stem cell- and extracellular vesicle-based therapies for Alzheimer's disease: Progress, advantages, and challenges. *Neural Regeneration Research, 18*(8), 1645–1651. doi: 10.4103/1673-5374.361546.

Gone, J. P., Hartmann, W. E., Pomerville, A., Wendt, D. C., Klem, S. H., & Burrage, R. L. (2019). The impact of historical trauma on health outcomes for indigenous populations in the USA and Canada: A systematic review. *Americal Psychologist, 74*(1), 20–35. doi: 10.1037/amp0000338.

Goodman, R. A., Posner, S. F., Huang, E. S., Parekh, A. K., & Koh, H. K. (2013). Defining and measuring chronic conditions: Imperatives for research, policy, program, and practice. *Preventing Chronic Disease, 10*, E66. doi: 10.5888/pcd10.120239.

Gorissen, S. H. M., Trommelen, J., Kouw, I. W. K., Holwerda, A. M., Pennings, B., Groen, B. B. L., Wall, B. T., Churchward-Venne, T. A., Horstman, A. M. H., Koopman, R., Burd, N. A., Fuchs, C. J., Dirks, M. L., Res, P. T., Senden, J. M. G., Steijns, J., de Groot, L. C. P. G. M., Verdijk, L. B., & van Loon, L. J. C. (2020). Protein type, protein dose, and age modulate dietary protein digestion and phenylalanine absorption kinetics and plasma phenylalanine availability in humans. *Journal of Nutrition, 150*(8), 2041–2050. doi: 10.1093/jn/nxaa024.

Górska, S., Singh Roy, A., Whitehall, L., Irvine Fitzpatrick, L., Duffy, N., & Forsyth, K. (2022). A systematic review and correlational meta-analysis of factors associated with resilience of normally aging, community-living older adults. *The Gerontologist, 62*(9), e520–e533. doi: 10.1093/geront/gnab110.

Gosgnach, S., Bikof, J. B., Dougherty, K. J., El Manira, A., Lanuza, G. M., & Zhang, Y. (2017). Delineating the diversity of spinal interneurons in locomotor circuits. *Journal of Neuroscience, 37*(45), 10835–10841. doi: 10.1523/JNEUROSCI.1829-17.2017.

Gould, J. B., Madan, A., Qin, C., & Chavez, G. (2003). Perinatal outcomes in two dissimilar immigrant populations in the United States: A dual epidemiologic paradox. *Pediatrics, 111*(6 Pt 1), e676–e682.

Graff-Radford, J., Williams, L., Jones, D. T., & Benarroch, E. E. (2017). Caudate nucleus as a component of networks controlling behavior. *Neurology, 89*(21), 2192–2197. doi: 10.1212/WNL.0000000000004680.

Grant, B. F., Goldstein, R. B., Saha, T. D., Chou, S. P., Jung, J., Zhang, H., Pickering, R. P., Ruan, W. J., Smith, S. M., Huang, B., & Hasin, D. S. (2015). Epidemiology of DSM-5 alcohol use disorder: Results from the National Epidemiologic Survey on Alcohol and Related Conditions III. *JAMA Psychiatry, 72*(8), 757–766. doi: 10.1001/jamapsychiatry.2015.0584.

Greenberg, G., & Tobach, E. (2014). *Behavioral Evolution and Integrative Levels: The T.C. Schneirla Conference Series, Vol. 1*. Psychology Press.

Greendale, G. A., Jackson, N. J., Han, W., Huang, M., Cauley, J. A., Karvonen-Gutierrez, C., & Karlamangla, A. S. (2021). Increase in c-reactive protein predicts increase in rate of bone mineral density loss: The study of women's health across the nation. *JBMR Plus, 5*(4), e10480.

Greider, C. W., & Blackburn, E. H. (1985). Identification of a specific telomere terminal transferase activity in Tetrahymena extracts. *Cell, 43*(2 Pt. 1), 405–413. doi: 10.1016/0092-8674(85)90170-9.

Greve, W., & Staudinger, U. M. (2006). Resilience in later adulthood and old age: Resources and potentials for successful aging. In D. Cicchetti & D. J. Cohen (Eds.), *Developmental Psychopathology, Vol. 3. Risk, Disorder, and Adaptation* (2nd ed.) (pp. 796–840). Wiley.

Grima, F. (2011). The influence of age management policies on older employee work relationships with their company. *The International Journal of Human Resource Management, 22*(06), 1312–1332.

Gross, J., & Koffman, J. (2024). Examining how goals of care communication are conducted between doctors and patients with severe acute illness in hospital settings: A realist systematic review. *PLoS One, 19*(3), e0299933. doi: 10.1371/journal.pone.0299933.

Gross, J. J. (1998). Antecedent-and response-focused emotion regulation: Divergent consequences for experience, expression, and physiology. *Journal of Personality and Social Psychology, 74*(1), 224.

Gross, J. J., Carstensen, L. L., Pasupathi, M., Tsai, J., Götestam Skorpen, C., & Hsu, A. Y. (1997). Emotion and aging: Experience, expression, and control. *Psychology and Aging, 12*(4), 590.

Grzegorczyk, M., & Wolff, G. (2020). The scarring effect of COVID-19: Youth unemployment in Europe. *Bruegel Blog*, 28.

Guirguis-Blake, J. M., Perdue, L. A., Coppola, E. L., & Bean, S. I. (2024). Interventions to prevent falls in older adults: Updated evidence report and systematic review for the US Preventive Services Task Force. *JAMA, 332*(1), 58–69. doi: 10.1001/jama.2024.4166.

Gulliford, M., Gore, J. S., & Incera, S. (2025). Who I am and what I want to do: Linking self-construals and career interests. *Journal of Career Development*, doi: 10.1177/08948453251319021.

Gumede, S. B., de Wit, J. B. F., Venter, W. D. F., Wensing, A. M. J., Lalla-Edward, S. T. (2024). Intervention strategies to improve adherence to treatment for selected chronic conditions in sub-Saharan Africa: A systematic review. *Journal of the International AIDS Society, 27*(6), e26266. doi: 10.1002/jia2.26266.

Gustavson, K., Røysamb, E., Borren, I., Torvik, F. A., & Karevold, E. (2016). Life satisfaction in close relationships: Findings from a longitudinal study. *Journal of Happiness Studies, 17*, 1293–1311. doi: 10.1007/s10902-015-9643-7.

Gutiérrez, I. T., Rosengren, K. S., & Miller, P. J. (2015). Día de los Muertos: Learning about death through observing and pitching in. *Advances in Child Development and Behaviour, 49*, 229–249. doi: 10.1016/bs.acdb.2015.08.004.

Habenicht, R., Fehrmann, E., Blohm, P., Ebenbichler, G., Fischer-Grote, L., Kollmitzer, J., Mair, P., & Kienbacher, T. (2023). Machine learning based linking of patient reported outcome measures to WHO international classification of functioning, disability, and health activity/participation categories. *Journal of Clinical Medicine, 12*, 5609. doi: 10.3390/jcm12175609.

Hackel, L. S., & Ruble, D. N. (1992). *Changes in the Marital Relationship after the First Baby is Born: Predicting the Impact of Expectancy Disconfirmation*. [Unpublished manuscript]. New York University.

Hacker, K. (2024). The burden of chronic disease. *Mayo Clinic Proceedings: Innovations, Quality & Outcomes, 8*(1), 112–119.

Hamilton, I. J. (2016). Understanding grief and bereavement. *Br J Gen Pract, 66*(651), 523. doi: 10.3399/bjgp16X687325.

Hammen, C. (2005). Stress and depression. *Annual Review of Clinical Psychology, 1,* 293–319.

Han, M. (2025). Prediction model for post-retirement depression in the older population: A cross-sectional study. *Journal of Korean Gerontological Nursing, 27*(1), 21–34.

Harley, C. B., Futcher, A. B., & Greider, C. W. (1990). Telomeres shorten during ageing of human fibroblasts. *Nature, 345,* 458–460.

Harman, D. (1956). Aging: A theory based on free radical and radiation chemistry. *Journal of Gerontology, 11,* 298–300.

Harman, D. (1972). The biological clock: The mitochondria? *Journal of the American Geriatrics Society, 20,* 145–147.

Harris, K., Krygsman, S., Waschenko, J., & Laliberte Rudman, D. (2018). Ageism and the older worker: A scoping review. *The Gerontologist, 58*(2), e1–e14.

Harris, P. L. (2023). Young children's representation of people who are elsewhere—Or dead. *International Journal of Behavioral Development, 47*(3), 265–274. doi: 10.1177/01650254221144268.

Harrison, T. M., Weintraub, S., Mesulam, M. M., & Rogalski, E. (2012). Superior memory and higher cortical volumes in unusually successful cognitive aging. *Journal of the International Neuropsycholy Society, 18,* 1081–1085. doi: 10.1017/S1355617712000847.

Hashemi, H., Pakzad, R., Yekta, A., Aghamirsalim, M., Pakbin, M., Ramin, S., & Khabazkhoob, M. (2020). Global and regional prevalence of age-related cataract: A comprehensive systematic review and meta-analysis. *Eye (London), 34*(8), 1357–1370. doi: 10.1038/s41433-020-0806-3.

Hatfield, E., Bensman, L., & Rapson, R. L. (2012). A brief history of social scientists' attempts to measure passionate love. *Journal of Social and Personal Relationships, 29,* 143–164.

Hatfield, E., & Walster, G. W. (1978). *A New Look at Love*. University Press of America.

Hatzenbuehler, M. L., McLaughlin, K. A., Keyes, K. M., & Hasin, D. S. (2010). The impact of institutional discrimination on psychiatric disorders in lesbian, gay, and bisexual populations: A prospective study. *American Journal of Public Health, 100*(3), 452–459.

Hausknecht, S., Low, L. F., O'loughlin, K., McNab, J., & Clemson, L. (2020). Older adults' self-perceptions of aging and being older: A scoping review. *The Gerontologist, 60*(7), e524–e534.

Havighurst, R. J. (1948). *Developmental Tasks and Education*. The University of Chicago Press.

Havighurst, R. J., & Glasser, R. (1972). An exploratory study of reminiscence. *Journal of Gerontology, 27*(2), 245–253. doi: 10.1093/geronj/27.2.245.

Hay, E. L., & Diehl, M. (2011). Emotion complexity and emotion regulation across adulthood. *European Journal of Ageing, 8,* 157–168.

Hay, E. L., Fingerman, K. L., & Lefkowitz, E. S. (2007). The experience of worry in parent–adult child relationships. *Personal Relationships, 14*(4), 605–622.

Hayflick, L. (1965). The limited in vitro lifetime of human diploid cell strains. *Experimental Cell Research, 37,* 614–636. doi: 10.1016/0014-4827(65)90211-9.

Hayflick, L., & Moorhead, P. S. (1961). The serial cultivation of human diploid cell strains. *Experimental Cell Research, 25,* 585–621.

Hays, J. C. (2002). Living arrangements and health status in later life: A review of recent literature. *Public Health Nursing, 19*(2), 136–151.

He, J.-Y., Yv, X.-Y., Wu, J.-D., Lv, L., Zhang, X.-Q., Ma, T.-M., & Zhang, Y. (2021). The effectiveness and safety of Chinese herbal formulas on skin photoaging: A protocol for systematic review and meta-analysis. *Medicine, 100,* e24197. doi: 10.1097/MD.0000000000024197.

Heckhausen, J., Dixon, R. A., & Baltes, P. B. (1989). Gains and losses in development throughout adulthood as perceived by different adult age groups. *Developmental Psychology, 25*(1), 109.

Hefferon, K., Grealy, M., & Mutrie, N. (2009). Post-traumatic growth and life threatening physical illness: A systematic review of the qualitative literature. *The British Journal of Health Psychology, 14*(2), 343–378.

Heger, I. S., Deckers, K., Schram, M. T., Stehouwer, C. D. A., Dagnelie, P. C., van der Kallen, C. J. H., Koster, A., Eussen, S. J. P. M., Jansen, J. F. A., Verhey, F. R. J., van Boxtel, M. P. J., & Köhler, S. (2021). Associations of the lifestyle for brain health index with structural brain changes and cognition: Results from the Maastricht Study. *Neurology, 97*(13), e1300–e1312. doi: 10.1212/WNL.0000000000012572.

Heintz, S., & Ruch, W. (2020). Character strengths and job satisfaction: Differential relationships across occupational groups and adulthood. *Applied Research in Quality of Life, 15*(2), 503–527.

Heissler, R., Georgi, H., Kožený, J., & Kopeček, M. (2023). Competing factor models of cognition of healthy older adults: Support for superagers identification. *Československá Psychologie, 67*(1), 30–49. doi: 10.51561/cspsych.67.1.30.

Heller, L. D. (2024). Palliative care in Sub-Saharan Africa: A narrative review. *J Palliat Med, 27*(8), 1083–1089. doi: 10.1089/jpm.2023.0501.

Helliwell, J. F. (2001). Social capital, the economy and well-being. In K. Banting, A. Sharpe, F. St-Hilaire (Eds.), *The Review of Economic Performance and Social Progress: The Longest Decade: Canada in the 1990s* (pp. 43–60). Centre for the Study of Living Standards, The Institute for Research on Public Policy; McGill-Queen's University Press.

Helliwell, J. F., Layard, R., & Sachs, J. (Eds.). (2015). World happiness report 2015. *World Happiness Report*. www.worldhappiness.report/ed/2015/.

Helliwell, J., Layard, R., & Sachs, J. (2019). World happiness report 2019. *World Happiness Report*. www.worldhappiness.report/ed/2019/

Hemez, P. F., Washington, C. N., & Kreider, R. M. (2024). America's families and living arrangements: 2022. US Census Bureau. www.census.gov/library/stories/2024/05/living-arrangements.html.

Henning, J. A., & Brand, B. L. (2019). Implications of the American Psychological Association's posttraumatic stress disorder treatment guideline for trauma education and training. *Psychotherapy (Chicago), 56*(3), 422–430. doi: 10.1037/pst0000237.

Hensley, S., & Harris, V. W. (2022). Impacts of the Coronavirus pandemic on families: A family systems perspective. *Advances in Social Sciences Research Journal, 9,* 230–238.

Herbst, A., Lee, C.C., Vandiver, A.R., Aiken, J.M., McKenzie, D., Hoang, A., Allison, D., Liu, N., & Wanagat, J. (2021). Mitochondrial DNA deletion mutations increase exponentially with age in human skeletal muscle. *Aging Clinical and Experimental Research, 33*(7), 1811–1820. doi: 10.1007/s40520-020-01698-7.

Herbstsomer, R., & Stahl, S. (2020). Cross-cultural experiences of hospice and palliative care services: A thematic analysis. *OMEGA – Journal of Death and Dying, 84,* 551–566. doi: 10.1177/0030222820904205.

Herieka, H., Babalis, D., Tzala, E., Budhathoki, S., & Johnson, N. A. (2024). How inclusive were UK-based randomized controlled trials of COVID-19 vaccines? A systematic review investigating enrolment of Black adults and adult ethnic minorities. *Trials, 25,* 255. doi: 10.1186/s13063-024-08054-4.

Hermon, D. A., & Hazler, R. J. (1999). Adherence to a wellness model and perceptions of psychological well-being. *Journal of Counseling and Development, 77*(3), 339–343.

Higgins, E. T. (1987). Self-discrepancy: A theory relating self and affect. *Psychological Review, 94*(3), 319.
Hilbrand, S., Coall, D. A., Gerstorf, D., & Hertwig, R. (2017). Caregiving within and beyond the family is associated with lower mortality for the caregiver: A prospective study. *Evolution and Human Behavior, 38*(3), 397–403.
Ho, J. Y. (2022). Causes of America's lagging life expectancy: An international comparative perspective. *The Journals of Gerontology: Series B: Psychological Sciences and Social Sciences, 77*, S117–S126. doi: 10.1093/geronb/gbab129.
Holland, J. L. (1997). *Making of Vocational Choices: A Theory of Vocational Personalities and Work Environments* (3rd ed.). Psychological Assessment Resources.
Holloszy, J. O., & Fontana, L. (2007). Caloric restriction in humans. *Experimental Gerontology, 42*, 709–712.
Holman, R. C., Folkema, A. M., Singleton, R. J., Redd, J. T., Christensen, K. Y., Steiner, C. A., Schonberger, L. B., Hennessy, T. W., & Cheek, J. E. (2011). Disparities in infectious disease hospitalizations for American Indian/Alaska Native people. *Public Health Reports®, 126*(4), 508–521. doi: 10.1177/003335491112600407.
Holopainen, A., & Hakulinen, T. (2019). New parents' experiences of postpartum depression: A systematic review of qualitative evidence. *JBI Evidence Synthesis, 17*(9), 1731–1769.
Hong, J. Y., Gallanter, E., Müller-Oehring, E. M., & Schulte, T. (2019). Phases of procedural learning and memory: Characterization with perceptual-motor sequence tasks. *Journal of Cognitive Psychology, 31*(5–6), 543–558. doi: 10.1080/20445911.2019.1642897.
Hong, P., Cui, M., Ledermann, T., & Love, H. (2021). Parent-child relationship satisfaction and psychological distress of parents and emerging adult children. *Journal of Child and Family Studies, 30*, 921–931.
Hooker, K. (1991). Change and stability in self during the transition to retirement: An intraindividual study using P-technique factor analysis. *International Journal of Behavioral Development, 14*(2), 209–233.
Hooker, K. (1999). Possible selves in adulthood: Incorporating teleonomic relevance into studies of the self. In T. M. Hess & F. Blanchard-Fields (Eds.), *Social Cognition and Aging* (pp. 97–122). Academic Press.
Hooker, K., Fiese, B. H., Jenkins, L., Morfei, M. Z., & Schwagler, J. (1996). Possible selves among parents of infants and preschoolers. *Developmental Psychology, 32*(3), 542.
Hooker, K., & McAdams, D. P. (2003). Personality reconsidered: A new agenda for aging research. *The Journals of Gerontology Series B: Psychological Sciences and Social Sciences, 58*(6), P296–P304.
Horn, J. L., & Cattell, R. B. (1967). Age differences in fluid and crystallized intelligence. *Acta Psychologica, 26(2)*, 107–129. doi: 10.1016/0001-6918(67)90011-X.
Hu, S., & Li, C.R. (2020). Age-related structural and functional changes of the hippocampus and the relationship with inhibitory control. *Brain Science, 10*(12), 1013. doi: 10.3390/brainsci10121013.
Hudec, S. M., & Camacho, P. M. (2013). Secondary causes of osteoporosis. *Endocrine Practice, 19*(1), 120–128. doi: 10.4158/EP12059.RA.
Hutteman, R., Hennecke, M., Orth, U., Reitz, A. K., & Specht, J. (2014). Developmental tasks as a framework to study personality development in adulthood and old age. *European Journal of Personality, 28*(3), 267–278.
Huxhold, O., Fiori, K. L., & Windsor, T. (2022). Rethinking social relationships in adulthood: The differential investment of resources model. *Personality and Social Psychology Review*, 26(1), 57–82. doi: 10.1177/10888683211067035.
Ibad, H. A., Mammen, J. S., Simonsick, E. M., Kwoh, C. K., Guermazi, A., & Demehri, S. (2023). Higher thyroid hormone has a negative association with lower limb lean

body mass in euthyroid older adults: Analysis from the Baltimore Longitudinal Study of Aging. *Frontiers in Aging, 4,* 1150645. doi: 10.3389/fragi.2023.1150645.

Ikeokwu, A. E., Lawrence, R., Osieme, E. D., Gidado, K. M., Guy, C., & Dolapo, O. (2023). Unveiling the impact of COVID-19 vaccines: A meta-analysis of survival rates among patients in the United States based on vaccination status. *Cureus, 15*(8), e43282. doi: 10.7759/cureus.43282.

Immonen, J., Jääskeläinen, E., Korpela, H., & Miettunen, J. (2017). Age at onset and the outcomes of schizophrenia: A systematic review and meta-analysis. *Early Intervention in Psychiatry, 11*(6), 453–460. doi: 10.1111/eip.12412.

Inhelder, B., & Piaget, J. (1955). *De La Logique de l'enfant à La Logique de l'adolescent: From the Logic of the Child to the Logic of the Adolescent*. Presses Universitaires de France. https://search.ebscohost.com/login.aspx?direct=true&db=psyh&AN=1955-07000-000&lang=es&site=ehost-live.

Inoue, S., Watanabe, J., & Wada, Y. (2022). Subjective health awareness and sensory ability of taste and olfaction: A case study of a health promotion class for older people. *PLoS One, 17*(10), e0275093. doi: 10.1371/journal.pone.0275093.

Isaacowitz, D. M. (2022). What do we know about aging and emotion regulation? *Perspectives on Psychological Science, 17*(6), 1541–1555.

Isaacson, M. J., & Lynch, A. R. (2018). Culturally relevant palliative and end-of-life care for U.S. Indigenous populations: An integrative review. *Journal of Transcultural Nursing, 29*(2), 180–191. doi: 10.1177/1043659617720980.

Islam, M. R., Jannath, S., Moona, A. A., Akter, S., Hossain, M. J., & Islam, S. M. A. (2021). Association between the use of social networking sites and mental health of young generation in Bangladesh: A cross-sectional study. *Journal of Community Psychology, 49*(7), 2276–2297. doi: 10.1002/jcop.22675.

Iversen, T. N., Larsen, L., & Solem, P. E. (2009). A conceptual analysis of ageism. *Nordic Psychology, 61*(3), 4–22.

Iwasaki, Y., Mannell, R. C., Smale, B. J., & Butcher, J. (2005). Contributions of leisure participation in predicting stress coping and health among police and emergency response services workers. *Journal of Health Psychology, 10*(1), 79–99.

Jack, L. (2018). Advancing Health Disparities Research in Population Health. *Preventing Chronic Disease*, 15. doi: 10.5888/pcd15.180588.

Jackson, J., Mandel, D., Blanchard, J., Carlson, M., Cherry, B., Azen, S., Chou, C.-P., Jordan-Marsh, M., Forman, T., White, B., Granger, D., Knight, B., & Clark F. (2009). Confronting challenges in intervention research with ethnically diverse older adults: The USC Well Elderly II trial. *Clinical Trials,* 6(1), 90–101. doi: 10.1177/1740774508101191.

Jaeggi, S. M., & Buschkuehl, M. (2014). Working memory training and transfer: Theoretical and practical considerations. In B. Toni (Ed.), *New Frontiers of Multidisciplinary Research in STEAM-H (Science, Technology, Engineering, Agriculture, Mathematics, and Health)* (pp. 19–43). Springer International Publishing.

Jalali, R., Mohammadi, M., Vaisi-Raygani, A., & Salari, N. (2022). The prevalence of sleep disorders among Iranian older adults: A systematic review and meta-analysis. *Current Psychology, 41,* 8002–8009. doi: 10.1007/s12144-020-01252-8.

James, E., Nichols, S., Goodall, S., Hicks, K. M., & O'Doherty, A.F. (2021). The influence of resistance training on neuromuscular function in middle-aged and older adults: A systematic review and meta-analysis of randomized controlled trials. *Experimental Gerontology, 149,* 111320. doi: 10.1016/j.exger.2021.111320.

James, S. A. (1994). John Henryism and the health of African-Americans. *Culture, Medicine, and Psychiatry, 18*(2), 163–182.

James, S. L., Lucchesi, L. R., Bisignano, C., Castle, C. D., Dingels, Z. V., Fox, J. T., Hamilton, E. B., Henry, N. J., Krohn, K. J., Liu, Z., McCracken, D., Nixon, M. R., Roberts, N. L. S., Sylte, D. O., Adsuar, J. C., Arora, A., Briggs, A. M., Collado-Mateo, D., Cooper, C., Dandona, L., Dandona, R., Ellingsen, C. L., Fereshtehnejad, S.-M.,

Gill, T. K., Haagsma, J. A., Hendrie, D., Jürisson, M., Kumar, G. A., Lopez, A. D., Miazgowski, T., Miller, T. R., Mini, G., Mirrakhimov, E. M., Mohamadi, E., Olivares, P. R., Rahim, F., Riera, L. S., Villafaina, S., Yano, Y., Hay, S. I., Lim, S. S., Mokdad, A. H., Naghavi, A., & Murray, C. J. (2020). The global burden of falls: Global, regional and national estimates of morbidity and mortality from the Global Burden of Disease Study 2017. *Injury Prevention, 26*(Suppl 2), i3–i11. doi: 10.1136/injuryprev-2019-043286.

Järviö, T., Nosraty, L., & Aho, A. L. (2023). Older individuals' perceptions of a good death: A systematic literature review. *Death Studies, 47*(4), 476–489. doi: 10.1080/07481187.2022.2092787.

Jennett, B., & Plum, F. (1972). Persistent vegetative state after brain damage. A syndrome in search of a name. *The Lancet, 1*, 734–737.

Jia, H., & Lubetkin, E. I. (2020). Life expectancy and active life expectancy by marital status among older U.S. adults: Results from the U.S. Medicare Health Outcome Survey (HOS). *SSM Popul Health*, 12, 100642. doi: 10.1016/j.ssmph.2020.100642.

Jiang, B., Wu, T., Liu, W., Liu, G., & Lu, P. (2023). Changing trends in the global burden of cataract over the past 30 years: Retrospective data analysis of the global burden of disease study 2019. *JMIR Public Health and Surveillance*, 9, e47349. doi: 10.2196/47349.

Jiang, J., Zhou, L., Rickson, D., & Jiang, C. (2013). The effects of sedative and stimulative music on stress reduction depend on music preference. *The Arts in Psychotherapy, 40*(2), 201–205. doi: 10.1016/j.aip.2013.02.002.

Jiang, Y., Tan, Y., Wu, D., Yin, J., & Lin, X. (2023). The double-edged impact of the COVID-19 pandemic on Chinese family relationships. *Journal of Family Issues, 44*, 91–111.

Jin, K. (2010). Modern biological theories of aging. *Aging and Disease, 1*(2), 72–74.

Johansen, B., & Euchner, J. (2013). Navigating the VUCA world. *Research-Technology Management, 56*(1), 10–15.

Johnson, M. K., & Mortimer, J. T. (2011). Origins and outcomes of judgments about work. *Social Forces, 89*(4), 1239–1260.

Jonas, J. B., Aung, T., Bourne, R. R., Bron, A. M., Ritch, R., & Panda-Jonas, S. (2017). Glaucoma. *The Lancet, 390*(10108), 2183–2193. doi: 10.1016/S0140-6736(17)31469-1.

Jones, J. H. (2012). *Tuskegee's Truths: Rethinking the Tuskegee Syphilis Study*. UNC Press Books.

Jones, J. M. (2025, February 20). LGBTQ+ identification in U.S. rises to 9.3%. *Gallup*. https://news.gallup.com/poll/656708/lgbtq-identification-rises.aspx.

Jopp, D., & Smith, J. (2006). Resources and life-management strategies as determinants of successful aging: On the protective effect of selection, optimization, and compensation. *Psychology and Aging, 21*(2), 253–265.

Joseph, K. S., Lisonkova, S., Boutin, A., Muraca, G. M., Razaz, N., John, S., Sabr, Y., Chan, W.-S., Mehrabadi, A., Brandt, J. S., Schisterman, E. F., & Ananth, C. V. (2024). Maternal mortality in the United States: Are the high and rising rates due to changes in obstetrical factors, maternal medical conditions, or maternal mortality surveillance? *The American Journal of Obstetrics and Gynecology, 230*, 440.e1–440.e13.

Jung, R. E., & Haier, R. J. (2007). The Parieto-Frontal Integration Theory (P-FIT) of intelligence: Converging neuroimaging evidence. *Behavioral and Brain Sciences, 30*(2), 135–154. doi: 10.1017/S0140525X07001185.

Jyotsna, F., Ikram, J., Nageeta, F., Komal, F., Anjlee, F., Patel, H., Nassri, T., Kumari, M., Kumar, R., Shah, S. U., Kashif, M., Varrassi, G., Kumar, S., & Patel T. (2023). Unlocking the potential of immunotherapy in cardiovascular disease: A comprehensive review of applications and future directions. *Cureus, 15*(8), e42790. doi: 10.7759/cureus.42790.

Kabir, M. R., & Chan, K. (2023). Menopausal experiences of women of Chinese ethnicity: A meta-ethnography. *PLoS One, 18*(9), e0289322. doi: 10.1371/journal.pone.0289322.

Kahn, R. L., & Antonucci, T. C. (1980). Convoys over the life course: Attachment, roles, and social support. In P. B. Baltes & O. Brim (Eds.), *Life-span Development and Behavior*. Vol. 3. (pp. 254–283). Academic Press.

Kalhori, R. P., Faraji, A., Yari, M., Ganjabi, M., & Kazeminia, M. (2024). Global prevalence of urinary tract infections in the older persons: A systematic review and meta-analysis. *Ageing International, 49,* 813–835. doi: 10.1007/s12126-024-09569-6.

Kalinderi, K., Papaliagkas, V., & Fidani, L. (2024). GLP-1 receptor agonists: A new treatment in Parkinson's disease. *International Journal of Molecular Science, 25,* 3812. doi: 10.3390/ijms25073812.

Kalleberg, A. L. (2011). *Good Jobs, Bad Jobs: The Rise of Polarized and Precarious Employment Systems in the United States, 1970s–2000s*. Russell Sage Foundation.

Kalsoom, I., Wang, Y., Li, B., & Wen, H. (2023). Research progress of α-Synuclein aggregation inhibitors for potential Parkinson's disease treatment. *Mini-Reviews in Medicinal Chemistry, 23*(20), 1959–1974. doi: 10.2174/138955752366623051716 3501.

Karaahmetoglu, U., & Kutahyalioglu, N. S. (2019). Attitudes toward euthanasia among Turkish university students. *OMEGA – Journal of Death and Dying, 79*(2), 174–190.

Karumathil, A. A., & Tripathi, R. (2022). Culture and attitudes towards euthanasia: An integrative review. *Omega (Westport), 86*(2), 688–720. doi: 10.1177/0030222820984655.

Kasper, J. D., Wolff, J. L., & Skehan, M. (2019). Care arrangements of older adults: What they prefer, what they have, and implications for quality of life. *The Gerontologist, 59*(5), 845–855.

Kato, T. (2012). Development of the coping flexibility scale: Evidence for the coping flexibility hypothesis. *Journal of Counseling Psychology, 59,* 262–273. doi: 10.1037/a0027770.

Kauppi, K., Vanhala, A., Roos, E., & Torkki, P. (2023). Assessing the structures and domains of wellness models: A systematic review. *International Journal of Wellbeing, 13*(2).

Keenan, H. E., Czippel, A., Heydari, S., Gawryluk, J. R., Mazerolle, E. L., & Alzheimer's Disease Neuroimaging Initiative (2024). Intrinsic functional connectivity strength of superagers in the default mode and salience networks: Insights from ADNI. *Aging Brain, 5,* 100114.

Kempen, G. I. J. M., & Suurmeijer, T. P. B. M. (1990). The development of a hierarchical polychotomous adl-iadl scale for noninstitutionalized elders. *The Gerontologist, 30,* 497–502. doi: 10.1093/geront/30.4.497.

Kennedy, B. R. (2021). African Americans and Covid-19: A multifaceted model of biopsychosocial-spiritual/cultural factors addressing disparities in increased COVID-19 infection. *Journal of Cultural Diversity, 28*(4), 88–97.

Keyes, C. L., & Grzywacz, J. G. (2005). Health as a complete state: The added value in work performance and healthcare costs. *Journal of Occupational and Environmental Medicine, 47*(5), 523–532.

Khatony, A., Mohammadi, M., Jafari, F., Vaisi-Raygani, A., Jalali, R., & Salari, N. (2021). Urinary tract infection among Iranian older adults: A systematic review and meta-analysis. *Ageing International, 46,* 170–181. doi: 10.1007/s12126-020-09384-9.

Kiely, K. M. (2014). Cognitive function. In Michalos, A. C. (Ed.), *Encyclopedia of Quality of Life and Well-Being Research* (pp. 974–978). Springer, Dordrecht. doi: 10.1007/978-94-007-0753-5_426.

Kim, A. W., Said Mohamed, R., Norris, S. A., Naicker, S., Richter, L. M., & Kuzawa, C. W. (2023). Childhood adversity during the post-apartheid transition and COVID-19 stress independently predict adult PTSD risk in urban South Africa: A biocultural analysis of the stress sensitization hypothesis. *The American Journal of Bioogical Anthropology, 182*(4), 620–631. doi: 10.1002/ajpa.24791.

Kim, E. S., Tkatch, R., Martin, D., MacLeod, S., Sandy, L., & Yeh, C. (2021). Resilient aging: Psychological well-being and social well-being as targets for the promotion of healthy aging. *Gerontology and Geriatric Medicine, 7,* doi: 10.1177/23337214211002951.

Kim, Y., Kim, K., Boerner, K., Birditt, K. S., Zarit, S. H., Fingerman, K. L. (2019). Recent parental death and relationship qualities between midlife adults and their grown children. *Journal of Marriage and Family, 81*(3), 616–630. doi: 10.1111/jomf.12549.

Kirchengast, S. (2024). Menopause in a globalized world – A systematic literature review focussing on the challenge of health problems associated with menopausal transition among women with a migration background. *Maturitas, 187,* 108045. doi: 10.1016/j.maturitas.2024.108045.

Kirkwood, T. B. (2005). Understanding the odd science of aging. *Cell, 120*(4), 437–47. doi: 10.1016/j.cell.2005.01.027.

Kirkwood, T. B. L. (1977). Evolution of ageing. *Nature, 270,* 301–304.

Kjos, A. L., Gnacinski, S. L., & Wahl, C. A. (2025). An exploratory model of how ethical indicators predict health professional burnout. *Research in Nursing & Health, 48*(3), 310–323. doi: 10.1002/nur.22453.

Kleftaras, G., & Psarra, E. (2012). Meaning in life, psychological well-being and depressive symptomatology: A comparative study. *Psychology, 3*(4), 337–345.

Knecht, M., & Freund, A. M. (2016). Boundary management: A time-sampling study on managing work and private life in middle adulthood. *Research in Human Development, 13*(4), 297–311.

Kochen, E. M., Jenken, F., Boelen, P. A., Deben, L. M. A., Fahner, J. C., van den Hoogen, A., Teunissen, S. C. C. M., Geleijns, K., & Kars, M. C. (2020). When a child dies: A systematic review of well-defined parent-focused bereavement interventions and their alignment with grief- and loss theories. *BMC Palliative Care, 19*(1), 28. doi: 10.1186/s12904-020-0529-z.

Koepp, R. (2024). Death with dignity: States in US. *Center for Mental Health and Aging*. www.mentalhealthandaging.com/death-with-dignity-states-in-us/. Retrieved April 3, 2025.

Koivumaa-Honkanen, H., Honkanen, R., Viinamäki, H., Heikkilä, K., Kaprio, J., & Koskenvuo, M. (2000). Self-reported life satisfaction and 20-year mortality in healthy Finnish adults. *American Journal of Epidemiology, 152*(10), 983–991.

Kondziella, D., Bender, A., Diserens, K., van Erp, W., Estraneo, A., Formisano, R., Laureys, S., Naccache, L., Ozturk, S., Rohaut, B., Sitt, J. D., Stender, J., Tiainen, M., Rossetti, A. O., Gosseries, O., Chatelle, C. & EAN Panel on Coma, Disorders of Consciousness (2020). European Academy of Neurology guideline on the diagnosis of coma and other disorders of consciousness. *European Journal of Neurology, 27,* 1–16. doi: 10.1111/ene.14151.

Koplas, P. A., Gans, H. B., Wisely, M. P., Kuchibhatla, M., Cutson, T. M., Gold, D. T., Taylor, C. T., & Schenkman, M. (1999). Quality of life and Parkinson's disease. *The Journals of Gerontology Series A: Biomedical Sciences and Medical Sciences, 54*(4), M197–M202.

Kopetzky, S. J., Li, Y., Kaiser, M., Butz-Ostendorf, M., & Alzheimer's Disease Neuroimaging Initiative (2024). Predictability of intelligence and age from structural connectomes. *PLoS One, 19*(4), e0301599. doi: 10.1371/journal.pone.0301599.

Kotsou, I., Nelis, D., Grégoire, J., & Mikolajczak, M. (2011). Emotional plasticity: Conditions and effects of improving emotional competence in adulthood. *Journal of Applied Psychology, 96*(4), 827.

Kovesdy, C. P. (2022). Epidemiology of chronic kidney disease: An update 2022. *Kidney International Supplements* (2011), *12*(1), 7–11. doi: 10.1016/j.kisu.2021.11.003.

Kovoor, J. G., Santhosh, S., Stretton, B., Tan, S., Gouldooz, H., Moorthy, S., Pietris, J., Hannemann, C., Yu, L. K., Johnson, R., Reddi, B. A., Gupta, A. K., Wagner, M., Page, G. J., Kovoor, P., Bastiampillai, T., Maddocks, I., Perry, S. W., Wong, M. L., Licinio, J., & Bacchi, S. (2024). Near-death experiences after cardiac arrest: A scoping review. *Discover Mental Health*, *4*(1),19. doi: 10.1007/s44192-024-00072-7.

Kramer, D. A., & Woodruff, D. S. (1986). Relativistic and dialectical thought in three adult age-groups. *Human Development, 29*(5), 280–290. doi: 10.1159/000273064.

Kringelbach, M. L., & Deco, G. (2024). Prefrontal cortex drives the flexibility of whole-brain orchestration of cognition. *Current Opinion in Behavioral Sciences, 57*, 101394. doi: 10.1016/j.cobeha.2024.101394.

Kübler-Ross, E. (1969). *On Death and Dying*. Macmillan.

Kübler-Ross, E., & Kessler, D. (2005). *On Grief and Grieving: Finding the Meaning of Grief Through the Five Stages of Loss*. Scribner.

Kuchibhatla, M., Hunter, J. C., Plassman, B. L., Lutz, M. W., Casanova, R., Saldana, S., & Hayden, K. M. (2020). The association between neighborhood socioeconomic status, cardiovascular and cerebrovascular risk factors, and cognitive decline in the Health and Retirement Study (HRS). *Aging Mental Health*, *24*(9), 1479–1486.

Kuehn, E., Perez-Lopez, M. B., Diersch, N., Döhler, J., Wolbers, T., & Riemer, M. (2018). Embodiment in the aging mind. *Neuroscience and Biobehavioral Reviews, 86*, 207–225. doi: 10.1016/j.neubiorev.2017.11.016.

Kuiper, N. A., Martin, R. A., & Olinger, L. J. (1993). Coping humour, stress, and cognitive appraisals. *Canadian Journal of Behavioural Science*, *25*(1), 81–96.

Kukla, H., Herrler, A., Strupp, J., & Voltz, R. (2021). The effects of confronting one's own end of life on older individuals and those with a life-threatening disease: A systematic literature review. *Palliative Medicine*, *35*(10), 1793–1814. doi: 10.1177/02692163211042528.

Kulik, L., Shilo-Levin, S., & Liberman, G. (2010). Work family role conflict and well-being among women and men. *Journal of Career Assessment, 24*(4), 651–668.

Kurz, A. (2008). Physiology of thermoregulation. *Best Practices and Research Clinical Anaesthesiology*, *22*, 627–644. doi: 10.1016/j.bpa.2008.06.004.

Labouvie-Vief, G., & Medler, M. (2002). Affect optimization and affect complexity: Modes and styles of regulation in adulthood. *Psychology and Aging, 17*(4), 571.

Lachman, M. E., Röcke, C., Rosnick, C., & Ryff, C. D. (2008). Realism and illusion in Americans' temporal views of their life satisfaction: Age differences in reconstructing the past and anticipating the future. *Psychological Science, 19*(9), 889–897.

Lahdenperä, M., Mar, K. U., Courtoil, A., & Lummaa, V. (2018). Differences in age-specific mortality between wild-caught and captive-born Asian elephants. *Nature Communications*, *9*, 3023.

Lahey, J. N. (2008). Age discrimination and hiring. In R. W. Eberts & R. A. Hobbie (Eds.), *Older and Out of Work: Jobs and Social Insurance for a Changing Economy* (pp. 45–58). WE Upjohn Institute for Employment Research.

Lalwani, K., Whitehorne-Smith, P., Walcott, G., McLeary, J.-G., Mitchell, G., & Abel, W. (2022). Prevalence and sociodemographic factors associated with polysubstance use: Analysis of a population-based survey in Jamaica. *BMC Psychiatry, 22*, 513. doi: 10.1186/s12888-022-04160-2.

Langa, K. M., Larson, E. B., Crimmins, E. M., Faul, J. D., Levine, D. A., Kabeto, M. U., Weir, D. R. (2017). A comparison of the prevalence of dementia in the United States in 2000 and 2012. *JAMA Internal Medicine, 177*(1), 51–58. doi: 10.1001/jamainternmed.2016.6807.

Lange, L. S., Chrysidou, A., Liu, P., & Kuehn, E. (2024). Tactile memory impairments in younger and older adults. *Scientific Reports, 14*, 11766. doi: 10.1038/s41598-024-62683-y.

Lanoiselée, H. M., Nicolas, G., Wallon, D., Rovelet-Lecrux, A., Lacour, M., Rousseau, S., Richard, A. C., Pasquier, F., Rollin-Sillaire, A., Martinaud, O., Quillard-Muraine,

M., de la Sayette, V., Boutoleau-Bretonniere, C., Etcharry-Bouyx, F., Chauviré, V., Sarazin, M., le Ber, I., Epelbaum, S., Jonveaux, T., Rouaud, O., Ceccaldi, M., Félician, O., Godefroy, O., Formaglio, M., Croisile, B., Auriacombe, S., Chamard, L., Vincent, J. L., Sauvée, M., Marelli-Tosi, C., Gabelle, A., Ozsancak, C., Pariente, J., Paquet, C., Hannequin, D., Campion, D., & Collaborators of the CNR-MAJ Project (2017). APP, PSEN1, and PSEN2 mutations in early-onset Alzheimer disease: A genetic screening study of familial and sporadic cases. *PLoS Medicine, 14*(3), e1002270. doi: 10.1371/journal.pmed.1002270.

Lara-Pulido, J. A., & Martinez-Cruz, A. L. (2023). Stated benefits of teleworking in Mexico City: A discrete choice experiment on office workers. *Transportation, 50*(5), 1743–1807.

Lashkari, M., Noori, A., Oveisi, S., & Kheirkhah, M. (2018). Association of serum testosterone and dehydroepiandrosterone sulfate with rheumatoid arthritis: A case control study. *Electronic Physician, 10,* 6500.

Laureys, S., Celesia, G. G., Cohadon, F., Lavrijsen, J., León-Carrión, J., Sannita, W. G., Sazbon, L., Schmutzhard, E., von Wild, K. R., Zeman, A., Dolce, G., & the European Task Force on Disorders of Communication (2010). Unresponsive wakefulness syndrome: A new name for the vegetative state or apallic syndrome. *BMC Medicine,* 8, 68.

Laursen, B., Little, T. D., & Card, N. A. (Eds.) (2012). *Handbook of Developmental Research Methods*. Guilford Press.

Lauterbach, W. (1995). Die gemeinsame Lebenszeit von Familiengenerationen [The period of life that family generations spend together]. *Zeitschrift für Soziologie, 24,* 22–43.

Lauterbur, P.C. (1973). Image formation by induced local interactions: Examples of employing nuclear magnetic resonance. *Nature, 242 (5394):* 190–191. doi: 10.1038/242190a0.

Lavner, J. A., Karney, B. R., & Bradbury, T. N. (2016). Does couples' communication predict marital satisfaction, or does marital satisfaction predict communication? *Journal of Marriage and Family, 78*(3), 680–694.

Lavrentieva, A., Kaimakamis, E., Voutsas, V., & Bitzani, M. (2023). An observational study on factors associated with ICU mortality in Covid-19 patients and critical review of the literature. *Scientific Reports, 13,* 7804. doi: 10.1038/s41598-023-34613-x.

Lawton, M. P. (1991). A multidimensional view of quality of life in frail elders. In J. E. Birren, J. C. Rowe, J. E. Lubben, & D. E. Deutchman (Eds.), *The Concept and Measurement of Quality of Life in the Frail Elderly* (pp. 3–27). Academic Press.

Lawton, S. (2023). Skin changes associated with ageing. *British Journal of Community Nursing, 28*(10), 504–508. doi: 10.12968/bjcn.2023.28.10.504.

Lazarus, R. S. (1966). *Psychological Stress and the Coping Process*. McGraw Hill.

Lazarus, R. S. (1993). From psychological stress to the emotions: A history of changing outlooks. *Annual Review of Psychology, 44,* 1–21. doi: 10.1146/annurev.ps.44.020193.000245.

Lazarus, R. S., & DeLongis, A. (1983). Psychological stress and coping in aging. *American Psychologist, 38*(3), 245–254. doi: 10.1037//0003-066x.38.3.245.

Lazarus, R. S., & Folkman, S. (1984). *Stress, Appraisal, and Coping*. Springer.

Leanderz, Å., Henricson, M., Lygnegård, F., Bäckström, C., & Larsson, M. (2025). What it means to become a father. *American Journal of Men's Health, 19*(2), doi: 10.1177/15579883251323251.

Leary, K. A., & DeRosier, M. E. (2012). Factors promoting positive adaptation and resilience during the transition to college. *Psychology, 3*(12A), 1215–1222.

Lebow, J. L. (2019). Divorce today. In *Treating the Difficult Divorce: A Practical Guide for Psychotherapists* (pp. 35–55). American Psychological Association. doi: 10.1037/0000116-003.

Leconte, S., Rousselle, C., Bodin, L., Clinard, F., & Carne, G. (2021). Refinement of health-based guidance values for cadmium in the French population based on modelling. *Toxicology Letters, 340*, 43–51. doi: 10.1016/j.toxlet.2020.12.021.

Lee, E., & Williams, J. M. (2022). Examining coping skills as a mediating factor in perceived stress and life satisfaction: A comparison between minority and nonminority older adults. *International Journal of Aging and Human Development, 95*(1), 72–90. doi: 10.1177/00914150211024178.

Lee, W., Lloyd, J. T., Giuriceo, K., Day, T., Shrank, W., Rajkumar, R. (2020). Systematic review and meta-analysis of patient race/ethnicity, socioeconomics, and quality for adult type 2 diabetes. *Health Services Research, 55*(5), 741–772. doi: 10.1111/1475-6773.13326.

Lee, Y., Park, J. Y., Lee, J. J., Gim, J., Do, A. R., Jo, J., Park, J., Kim, K., Park, K., Jin, H., Choi, K. Y., Kang, S., Kim, H., Kim, S., Moon, S. H., Farrer, L. A., Lee, K. H., & Won, S. (2023). Heritability of cognitive abilities and regional brain structures in middle-aged to elderly East Asians. *Cereberal Cortex, 33*(10), 6051–6062. doi: 10.1093/cercor/bhac483.

Lei, L., & South, S. J. (2021). Explaining the decline in young adult sexual activity in the United States. *Journal of Marriage and Family, 83*(1), 280–295.

Leimer, B., & Van Ewijk, R. (2022). Are grandchildren good for you? Well-being and health effects of becoming a grandparent. *Social Science & Medicine, 313*, 115392.

Lehman, B. J., David, D. M., & Gruber, J. A. (2017). Rethinking the biopsychosocial model of health: Understanding health as a dynamic system. *Social and Personality Psychology Compass, 11*(8), e12328.

Lenski, R. E. (2017). What is adaptation by natural selection? Perspectives of an experimental microbiologist. *PLoS Genetics, 13*(4), e1006668.

Lerner, R. M. (2012). Developmental science: Past, present, and future. *International Journal of Developmental Science*, 6(1–2), 29–36.

Lerner, R. M. (2021). *Individuals as Producers of Their Own Development: The Dynamics of Person-context Coactions*. Taylor & Francis.

Lerner, R. M., & Lerner, J. V. (2019). The development of a person: A relational–developmental systems perspective. In D. P. McAdams, R. L. Shiner, & J. L. Tackett (Eds.), *Handbook of Personality Development* (pp. 59–75). The Guilford Press.

Levenson, R. W., Carstensen, L. L., & Gottman, J. M. (1993). Long-term marriage: Age, gender, and satisfaction. *Psychology and Aging, 8*, 301–313.

Levitan, I. B., & Kaczmarek, L. K. (2015). T*he Neuron: Cell and Molecular Biology* (4th ed.). Oxford University Press.

Levy, B. (2009). Stereotype embodiment: A psychosocial approach to aging. *Current Directions in Psychological Science, 18*(6), 332–336.

Lewis, R. A. (1972). A developmental framework for the analysis of premarital dyadic formation. *Family Process, 11*(1), 17–48. doi: 10.1111/j.1545-5300.1972.00017.x.

Lewy, G. (2011). *Assisted Suicide in US and Europe*. Oxford University Press.

Li, C., Layman, A. J., Geary, R., Anson, E., Carey, J. P., Ferrucci, L., & Agrawal, Y. (2015). Epidemiology of vestibulo-ocular reflex function: Data from the Baltimore Longitudinal Study of Aging. *Otology & Neurotology, 36*, 267–272.

Li, K., Huang, B., Wu, M., Zhong, A., Li, L., Cai, Y., Wang, Z., Wu, L., Zhu, M., Li, J., Wang, Z., Wu, W., Li, W., Bosco, B., Gan, Z., Qiao, Q., Wu, Wang, Q., Wang, S., & Xia, X (2020). Dynamic changes in anti-SARS-CoV-2 antibodies during SARS-CoV-2 infection and recovery from COVID-19. *Nature Communications*, 11, 6044.

Li, L., Serido, J., Vosylis, R., Sorgente, A., Lep, Ž., Zhang, Y., Fonseca, G., Crespo, C., Relvas, A. P., Zupančič, M., & Lanz, M. (2023). Employment disruption and wellbeing among young adults: A cross-national study of perceived impact of the COVID-19 lockdown. *Journal of Happiness Studies, 24*(3), 991–1012. doi: 10.1007/s10902-023-00629-3.

Li, N., Baldermann, J. C., Kibleur, A., Treu, S., Akram, H., Elias, G. J. B., Boutet, A., Lozano, A. M,. Al-Fatly, B., Strange, B., Barcia, J. A., Zrinzo, L., Joyce, E., Chabardes, S., Visser-Vandewalle, V., Polosan, M., Kuhn, J., Kühn, A., & Horn, A. (2020). A unified connectomic target for deep brain stimulation in obsessive-compulsive disorder. *Nature Communications, 11*, 3364. doi: 10.1038/s41467-020-16734-3.

Li, T., Zheng, Y., Wang, Z., Zhu, D. C., Ren, J., Liu, T., & Friston, K. (2022). Brain information processing capacity modeling. *Scientific Reports, 12*, 2174. doi: 10.1038/s41598-022-05870-z.

Li, Y., Wang, K., Jigeer, G., Jensen, G., Tucker, K. L., Lv, Y., Shi, X., & Gao, X. (2024). Healthy lifestyle and the likelihood of becoming a Centenarian. *JAMA Network Open, 7*(6), e2417931. doi: 10.1001/jamanetworkopen.2024.17931.

Libertini, G., Shubernetskaya, O., Corbi, G., & Ferrara, N. (2021). Is evidence supporting the Subtelomere–Telomere Theory of Aging? *Biochemistry Moscow, 86*, 1526–1539. doi: 10.1134/S0006297921120026.

Liew, H. P. (2012). Depression and chronic illness: A test of competing hypotheses. *Journal of Health Psychology, 17*(1), 100–109.

Lin, C. Y., Li, F., An, H. H., Zhai, Y. J., Li, J. B., Qiu, H. N., Wu, F., Chen, T., & Lin, J. N. (2024). The impact of dietary acid load on super-agers with exceptional cognitive abilities: A propensity score analysis of national health and nutrition examination survey (NHANES) 2011–2014. *The Journal of Nutrition, Health & Aging, 28*(6), 100238.

Lin, Y., Jiang, B., Cai, Y., Luo, W., Zhu, X., Lin, Q., Tang, M., Li, X., & Xie, L. (2023). The global burden of Glaucoma: Findings from the Global Burden of Disease 2019 Study and predictions by Bayesian Age-Period-Cohort Analysis. *Journal of Clinical Medicine, 12*(5), 1828. doi: 10.3390/jcm12051828.

Lindau, S. T., & Gavrilova, N. (2010). Sex, health, and years of sexually active life gained due to good health: Evidence from two US population based cross sectional surveys of ageing. *BMJ*, 340.

Lindsay, O. R., Hammad, H., Baysic, J., Young, A., Osman, N., Ferber, R., Culos-Reed, N., & Peters, R. M. (2024). Age related changes in skin sensitivity assessed with smartphone vibration testing. *Scientific Reports, 14*(1), 17836. doi: 10.1038/s41598-024-68579-1.

Lisowska, K. (2024). Ways of coping with stress in (no)increased risk situations – Examples of effective ways of proceeding. *Medical Science Pulse, 18*(2), 53–59. doi: 10.5604/01.3001.0054.6845.

Lissanu, L., Lopez, F., King, A., Robinson, E., Almazan, E., Metoyer, G., Quinn, M., Peek, M. E., & Saunders, M. R. (2019). "I try not to even think about my health going bad": A qualitative study of chronic kidney disease knowledge and coping among a group of urban African-American patients with CKD. *Journal of Racial and Ethnic Health Disparities, 6*(3), 625–634. doi: 10.1007/s40615-019-00561-4.

Livingston, G., Huntley, J., Sommerlad, A., Ames, D., Ballard, C., Banerjee, S. (2020). Dementia prevention, intervention, and care: 2020 report of the Lancet Commission. *The Lancet, 396*(10248), 413–446. doi: 10.1016/S0140-6736(20)30367-6.

Livingston, G., Sommerlad, A., Orgeta, V., Costafreda, S. G., Huntley, J., Ames, D., Ballard, C., Banerjee, S., Burns, A., Cohen-Mansfield, J., Cooper, C., Fox, N., Gitlin, L. N., Howard, R., Kales, H. C., Larson, E. B., Ritchie, K., Rockwood, K., Sampson, E. L., Samus, Q., Schneider, L. S., Selbæk, G., Teri, L., & Mukadam, N. (2017). Dementia prevention, intervention, and care. *The Lancet, 390*, 2673–2734.

Llera-Oyola, J., Carceller, H., Andreu, Z., Hidalgo, M. R., Soler-Sáez, I., Gordillo, F., Gómez-Cabañes, B., Roson, B., de la Iglesia-Vayá, M., Mancuso, R., Guerini, F. R., Mizokami, A., & García-García, F. (2024). The role of microRNAs in understanding sex-based differences in Alzheimer's disease. *Biology of Sex Differences, 15*(1), 13. doi: 10.1186/s13293-024-00588-1.

Lleras-Muney, A., & Moreau, F. (2022). A unified model of cohort mortality. *Demography, 59*(6), 2109–2134. doi: 10.1215/00703370-10286336.

Lo Coco, G., Graffeo, M. T., & Albano, G. (2024). Implementing group therapy for adults with substance use disorders: What research-based evidence? *Group Dynamics: Theory, Research, and Practice, 28*(3), 199–215. doi: 10.1037/gdn0000222.

Lohman, T., Bains, G., Berk, L., & Lohman, E. (2021). Predictors of biological age: The implications for wellness and aging research. *Gerontology and Geriatric Medicine*, 7. doi: 10.1177/23337214211046419.

Lolli, F., Pallotti, F., Rossi, A., Fortuna, M. C., Caro, G., Lenzi, A., Sansone, A., & Lombardo, F. (2017). Androgenetic alopecia: A review. *Endocrine, 57*, 9–17. doi: 10.1007/s12020-017-1280-y.

Lomas, T., & Ivtzan, I. (2016). Second wave positive psychology: Exploring the positive–negative dialectics of wellbeing. *Journal of Happiness Studies*, 17, 1753–1768.

Lowe, K., & Arnett, J. J. (2020). Failure to grow up, failure to pay? Parents' views of conflict over money with their emerging adults. *Journal of Family Issues, 41*(3), 359–382.

López-Otín, C., Blasco, M, A., Partridge, L., Serrano, M., & Kroemer, G. (2013). The hallmarks of aging. *Cell, 153*, 1194–1217.

Lowenstein, A., Katz, R., & Gur-Yaish, N. (2007). Reciprocity in parent-child exchange and life satisfaction among the elderly: A cross-national perspective. *Journal of Social Issues, 63*(4), 865–883. doi: 10.1111/j.1540-4560.2007.00541.x.

Lozada-Martinez, I. D., Diazgranados-Garcia, M. C., Castelblanco-Toro, S:, & Anaya, J.-M. (2024). Global research on centenarians: A historical and comprehensive bibliometric analysis from 1887 to 2023. *Annals of Geriatric Medicine and Research*, 28(2), 144–155. doi: 10.4235/agmr.24.0043.

Lubbers, K., Cadwallader, J., Lin, Q., Clifford, C., & Frazier, L. D. (2023). Adult play and playfulness: A qualitative exploration of its meanings and importance. *The Journal of Play in Adulthood, 5*(2).

Lutz, M., Petzold, G., & Albala, C. (2019). Considerations for the development of innovative foods to improve nutrition in older adults. *Nutrients, 11*, 1275. doi: 10.3390/nu11061275.

Lv, H., Gao, Z., Wang, Y., Xie, Y., Guan, M., Liao, H., & Xu, Y. (2023). Global characteristics and trends of presbycusis research from 2002 to 2021: A bibliometric study. *The American Journal Translational Research, 15*(4), 2407–2425.

Lyubomirsky, S. (2008). *The How of Happiness: A Scientific Approach to Getting the Life You Want*. Penguin.

Lyubomirsky, S., Sheldon, K. M., & Schkade, D. (2005). Pursuing happiness: The architecture of sustainable change. *Review of General Psychology, 9*(2), 111–131.

Lyyra, T. M., Törmäkangas, T. M., Read, S., Rantanen, T., & Berg, S. (2006). Satisfaction with present life predicts survival in octogenarians. *Journals of Gerontology Series B: Psychological Sciences and Social Sciences, 61*(6), 319–326.

Maccora, J., Peters, R., & Anstey, K. J. (2021). Gender differences in superior-memory SuperAgers and associated factors in an Australian cohort. *Journal of Applied Gerontology, 40*(4), 433–442.

Magai, C., Consedine, N. S., Krivoshekova, Y. S., Kudadjie-Gyamfi, E., & McPherson, R. (2006). Emotion experience and expression across the adult life span: Insights from a multimodal assessment study. *Psychology and Aging, 21*(2), 303.

Makarem, S. C., Hunt, J. M., Mudambi, S., & Aaronson, W. E. (2010). *Emotions and cognitions in consumer health behaviors: A model of hope and control applied to chronic illnesses*. [Ph.D. dissertation, Temple University]. http://digital.library.temple.edu/u?/p245801coll10,96030.

Malek, M. H., Hüttemann, M., & Lee, I. (2018). Mitochondrial structure, function, and dynamics: The common thread across organs, disease, and aging. *Oxidative Medicine and Cellular Longevity*, 1863414. doi: 10.1155/2018/1863414.

Malouff, J. M., Thorsteinsson, E. B., Schutte, N. S., Bhullar, N., & Rooke, S. E. (2010). The five-factor model of personality and relationship satisfaction of intimate partners: A meta-analysis. *Journal of Research in Personality*, *44*(1), 124–127.

Malvea, A., Babaei, F., Boulay, C., Sachs, A., & Park, J. (2022). Deep brain stimulation for Parkinson's disease: A review and future outlook. *Biomedical Engineering Letters*, *12*(3), 303–316. doi: 10.1007/s13534-022-00226-y.

Mansfield, P., & Grannell, P. (1975). Diffraction and microscopy in solids and liquids by NMR. *Physical Review B, 12(9)*, 3618–3634.

Marchiondo, L. A., Gonzales, E., & Williams, L. J. (2019). Trajectories of perceived workplace age discrimination and long-term associations with mental, self-rated, and occupational health. *The Journals of Gerontology Series B: Psychological Sciences and Social Sciences*, *74*(4), 655–663.

Markus, H. R., & Kitayama, S. (1991). *Cultural variation in the self-concept*. In J. Strauss & G. R. Goethals (Eds.), *The Self: Interdisciplinary Approaches* (pp. 18–48). Springer New York.

Markus, H., & Nurius, P. (1986). Possible selves. *American Psychologist*, *41*(9), 954.

Marlowe, F. (2007). Hunting and gathering: The human sexual division of foraging labor. *Cross-Cultural Research*, *41*(2), 170–195. doi: 10.1177/1069397106297529.

Maroso, M. (2023). A quest into the human brain. *Science*, *382*(6667). doi: 10.1126/science.adl0913.

Martial, C., Fritz, P., Gosseries, O., Bonhomme, V., Kondziella, D., Nelson, K., & Lejeune, N. (2025). A neuroscientific model of near-death experiences. *Nature Reviews Neurology*, *21*, 297–311 doi: 10.1038/s41582-025-01072-z.

Martin, S. S., Aday, A. W., Almarzooq, Z. I., Anderson, C. A. M., Arora, P., Avery, C. L., Baker-Smith, C. M., Gibbs, B. B., Beaton, A. Z., Boehme, A. K., Commodore-Mensah, Y., Currie, M. E., Elkind, M. S. V., Evenson, K. R., Generoso, G., Heard, D. G., Hiremath, S., Johansen, M. C., Kalani, R., Kazi, D. S., Ko, D., Liu, J., Magnani, J. W., Michos, E. D., Mussolino, M. E., Navaneethan, S. D., Parikh, N. I., Perman, S. M., Poudel, R., Rezk-Hanna, M., Roth, G. A., Shah, N. S., St-Onge, M.-P., Thacker, E. L., Tsao, C. W., Urbut, S. M., Van Spall, H. G. C., Voeks, J. H., Wang, N.-Y., Wong, N. D., Wong, S. S., Yaffe, K., Palaniappan, L. P., & American Heart Association Council on Epidemiology and Prevention Statistics Committee and Stroke Statistics Subcommittee (2024). 2024 heart disease and stroke statistics: A report of US and global data from the American Heart Association. *Circulation*, *149*(8), e347–e913. doi: 10.1161/CIR.0000000000001209.

Martini, E., Stirparo, G. G., & Kallikourdis, M. (2018). Immunotherapy for cardiovascular disease. *Journal of Leukocyte Biology*, *103*, 493–500.

Martinez, G. M., & Daniels, K. (2023). Fertility of men and women aged 15–49 in the United States: National Survey of Family Growth, 2015–2019. *National Health Statistics Reports*, (179). doi: 10.15620/cdc:122080.

Maslach, C., & Leiter, M. P. (2016). Understanding the burnout experience: Recent research and its implications for psychiatry. *World Psychiatry*, *15*(2), 103–111.

Masten, A. S. (2001). Ordinary magic: Resilience processes in development. *American Psychologist*, *56*(3), 227–238.

Mather, J. A., Anderson, R. C., & Wood, J. B. (2010). *Octopus: The Ocean's Intelligent Invertebrate*. Timber Press.

Mathot, E., Liberman, K., Cao Dinh, H., Njemini, R., & Bautmans, I. (2021). Systematic review on the effects of physical exercise on cellular immunosenescence-related markers – An update. *Experimental Gerontology*, *149*, 111318. doi: 10.1016/j.exger.2021.111318.

Mayo Clinic (2023a). Cardiac catherization. www.mayoclinic.org/tests-procedures/cardiac-catheterization/about/pac-20384695. Accessed July 26, 2025.

Mayo Clinic (2023b). Respiratory syncytial virus (RSV). www.mayoclinic.org/diseases-conditions/respiratory-syncytial-virus/symptoms-causes/syc20353098. Accessed July 26, 2025.
Mayo Clinic (2024a). Alzheimer's disease. www.mayoclinic.org/diseases-conditions/alzheimers-disease/symptoms-causes/syc-20350447. Accessed November 13, 2025.
Mayo Clinic (2024b). Parkinson's disease. www.mayoclinic.org/diseases-conditions/parkinsons-disease/symptoms-causes/syc-20376055. Accessed November 13, 2025.
Mayo Clinic (2024c). Young-onset Alzheimer's: When symptoms begin before age 65. www.mayoclinic.org/diseases-conditions/alzheimers-disease/in-depth/alzheimers/art-20048356. Accessed November 13, 2025.
Mayo Clinic (2025a). Implantable cardioverter defibrillators (ICDs). www.mayoclinic.org/tests-procedures/implantable-cardioverter-defibrillators/about/pac-20384692. Accessed July 26, 2025.
Mayo Clinic (2025b). Osteoporosis. www.mayoclinic.org/diseases-conditions/osteoporosis/symptoms-causes/syc-20351968. Accessed November 18, 2025 November.
Maymone, M. B. C., Laughter, M., Pollock, S., Khan, I., Marques, T., Abdat, R., Goldberg, L. J., & Vashi, N. A. (2021). Hair aging in different races and ethnicities. *Journal of Clinical and Aesthetic Dermatology, 14*(1), 38–44. https://pmc.ncbi.nlm.nih.gov/articles/PMC7869811/pdf/jcad_14_1_38.pdf.
McAuley, W. J., & Blieszner, R. (1985). Selection of long-term care arrangements by older community residents. *The Gerontologist, 25*(2), 188–193.
McDermott, L., Hameed, I., & Lau-Zhu, A. (2024). Cultural adaptations, efficacy, and acceptability of psychological interventions for mental health in adults with refugees and asylum-seeker status: A systematic review. *Trauma, Violence, & Abuse, 25*(5), 3758–3776. doi: 10.1177/15248380241262262.
McEwen, B. S., & Stellar, E. (1993). Stress and the individual. Mechanisms leading to disease. *Archives of Internal Medicine, 153*(18), 2093–2101.
McHale, S. M., Updegraff, K. A., & Whiteman, S. D. (2012). Sibling relationships and influences in childhood and adolescence. *Journal of Marriage and the Family, 74*(5), 913–930.
McLellan, A. T. (2017). Substance misusue and substance use disorders: Why do they matter in healthcare? *Transactions of the Americal Clinical and Climatological Association, 128*, 112–130.
McNamara, N. B., Munro, D. A. D., Bestard-Cuche, N., Uyeda, A., Bogie, J. F. J., Hoffmann, A., Holloway, R. K., Molina-Gonzalez, I., Askew, K. E., Mitchell, S., Mungall, W., Dodds, M., Dittmayer, C., Moss, J., Rose, J., Szymkowiak, S., Amann, L., McColl, B. W., Prinz, M., Spires-Jones, T. L., Stenzel, W., Horsburgh, K., Hendriks, J. J. A., Pridans, C., Muramatsu, R., Williams, A., Priller, J., & Miron, V. E. (2023). Microglia regulate central nervous system myelin growth and integrity. *Nature, 613*, 120–129. doi: 10.1038/s41586-022-05534-y.
McRae, K., & Gross, J. J. (2020). Emotion regulation. *Emotion*, 20(1), 1–9. doi: 10.1037/emo0000703.
Meade, R. D., Akerman, A. P., Notley, S. R., Kirby, N. V., Sigal, R. J., Kenny, G. P. (2024). Effects of daylong exposure to indoor overheating on thermal and cardiovascular strain in older adults: A randomized crossover trial. *Environmental Health Perspectives, 132*(2), 27003.
Medawar, P. (1952). *An Unsolved Problem of Biology*. H. K. Lewis & Co.
Medina, M., & Castillo-Pino, E. (2019). An introduction to the epidemiology and burden of urinary tract infections. *Therapeutic Advances in Urology, 11*. doi: 10.1177/1756287219832172.
Medvedev, Z. A. (1990). An attempt at a rational classification of theories of ageing. *Biological Reviews of the Cambridge Philosophical Society, 65*(3), 375–398. doi: 10.1111/j.1469-185x.1990.tb01428.x.

Mehta, C. M., Arnett, J. J., Palmer, C. G., & Nelson, L. J. (2020). Established adulthood: A new conception of ages 30 to 45. *American Psychologist, 75*(4), 431.
Mehta, K. M., & Yeo, G. W. (2017). Systematic review of dementia prevalence and incidence in United States race/ethnic populations. *Alzheimer's & Dementia, 13*(1), 72–83.
Mehta, N. K., Lee, H., & Ylitalo, K. R. (2013). Child health in the United States: Recent trends in racial/ethnic disparities. *Social Science & Medicine, 95*, 6–15.
Melkonian, S. C., Jim, M. A., Reilley, B., Erdrich, J., Berkowitz, Z., Wiggins, C. L., Haverkamp, D., & White, M. C. (2018). Incidence of primary liver cancer in American Indians and Alaska Natives, US, 1999–2009. *Cancer Causes & Control*, 29(9), 833–844. doi: 10.1007/s10552-018-1059-3.
Menardi, A., Dotti, L., Ambrosini, E., & Vallesi, A. (2022). Transcranial magnetic stimulation treatment in Alzheimer's disease: A meta-analysis of its efficacy as a function of protocol characteristics and degree of personalization. *Journal of Neurology, 269*(10), 5283–5301. doi: 10.1007/s00415-022-11236-2.
Mendez, M. F. (2019). Early-onset Alzheimer disease and its variants. *Continuum (Minneapolis Minnesota), 25*(1), 34–51. doi: 10.1212/CON.0000000000000687.
Menec, V. H., & Chipperfield, J. G. (1997). Remaining active in later life: The role of locus of control in seniors' leisure activity participation, health, and life satisfaction. *Journal of Aging and Health*, 9(1), 105–125.
Mercurio, M., de Filippis, R., Spina, G., De Fazio, P., Segura-Garcia, C., Galasso, O., Gasparini, G. (2022). The use of antidepressants is linked to bone loss: A systematic review and metanalysis. *Orthopedic Reviews, 14*(6), 38564. doi: 10.52965/001c.38564.
Merhav, M., & Wolbers, T. (2019). Aging and spatial cues influence the updating of navigational memories. *Scientific Reports, 9*, 11469.
Merians, A. N., Gross, G., Spoont, M. R., Bellamy, C. D., Harpaz-Rotem, I., & Pietrzak, R. H. (2023). Racial and ethnic mental health disparities in U.S. Military Veterans: Results from the National Health and Resilience in Veterans Study. *Journal of Psychiatric Research, 161*, 71–76. doi: 10.1016/j.jpsychires.2023.03.005.
Meyer, I. H. (1995). Minority stress and mental health in gay men. *Journal of Health and Social Behavior*, 38–56.
Meyer, I. H. (2003). Prejudice, social stress, and mental health in lesbian, gay, and bisexual populations: Conceptual issues and research evidence. *Psychological Bulletin, 129*(5), 674.
Michaels, R. (2024). What explains the great resignation? *Economic Insights, 9*(2), 10–18.
Milkie, M. A., Sayer, L. C., Nomaguchi, K., & Yan, H. X. (2025). Who's doing the housework and childcare in America now? Differential convergence in twenty-first-century gender gaps in home tasks. *Socius, 11*, doi: 10.1177/23780231251314667.
Miller, G. A. (1956). The magical number seven, plus or minus two: Some limits on our capacity for processing information. *Psychological Review, 63*, 81–97.
Miller, S. M. (1987). Monitoring and blunting: Validation of a questionnaire to assess styles of information seeking under threat. *Journal of Personality and Social Psychology, 52*, 345–353. doi: 10.1037//0022-3514.52.2.345.
Miloyan, B., Byrne, G. J., & Pachana, N. A. (2014). Age-related changes in generalized anxiety disorder symptoms. *International Psychogeriatrics, 26*(4), 565–572.
Mitchell, B. A. (2022). Empty nest. In D. Gu & M. E. Dupre (Eds.), *Encyclopedia of Gerontology and Population Aging* (pp. 1637–1642). Springer International Publishing.
Mitchell, B. A., Wister, A. V., & Zdaniuk, B. (2019). Are the parents all right? Parental stress, ethnic culture and intergenerational relations in aging families. *Journal of Comparative Family Studies, 50*(1), 51–74.
Mitchell, S. L., Teno, J. M., Kiely, D. K., Shaffer, M. L., Jones, R. N., Prigerson, H. G., Volicer, L., Givens, J. L., & Hamel, M. B. (2009). The clinical course of advanced

dementia. *The New England Journal of Medicine, 361*(16), 1529–1538. doi: 10.1056/NEJMoa0902234.

Miwa, S., Kashyap, S., Chini, E., & von Zglinicki, T. (2022). Mitochondrial dysfunction in cell senescence and aging. *Journal of Clinical Investigation, 132,* e158447. doi: 10.1172/JCI158447.

Moen, P. (1996). A life course perspective on retirement, gender, and well-being. *Journal of Occupational Health Psychology, 1*(2), 131.

Mohammadi, A., Behboodi Moghadam, Z., Ghelichkhani, F., Alidost, F., Naghizadeh, S., Haghparast, Z., & Azizi, M. (2022). Prevention of osteoporosis in menopausal women: A systematic review of nonpharmacological clinical trials. *Journal of Education and Health Promotion, 11,* 287. doi: 10.4103/jehp.jehp_1253_21.

Mohseny, M., Amanpour, F., Mosavi-Jarrahi, A., Jafari, H., Moradi-Joo, M., & Davoudi Monfared, E. (2016). Application of Cox and parametric survival models to assess social determinants of health affecting three-year survival of breast cancer patients. *Asian Pacific Journal of Cancer Prevention, 17*(S3), 311–316.

Möllborn, S., Kolk, M., & Evertsson, M. (2025). Recent trends in parenthood in Swedish same- and different-sex marriages: Emerging gender and socioeconomic differences. *Genus, 81*(20). doi: 10.1186/s41118-025-00256-1.

Mollon, J., Knowles, E. E. M., Mathias, S. R., Gur, R., Peralta, J. M., Weiner, D. J., Robinson, E. B., Gur, R. E., Blangero, J., Almasy, L., & Glahn, D. C. (2021). Genetic influence on cognitive development between childhood and adulthood. *Molecular Psychiatry, 26*(2), 656–665. doi: 10.1038/s41380-018-0277-0.

Montano, V., & Mercado, J. L. (2025). Career exploration stage and employment outcome of marketing management graduates: An exploratory factor analysis. *American Journal of Multidisciplinary Research & Developmen*t (AJMRD), *7*(1), 19–33.

Monto, M. A., & Carey, A. G. (2014). A new standard of sexual behavior? Are claims associated with the "hookup culture" supported by General Social Survey data? *The Journal of Sex Research,* 51(6), 605–615. doi: 10.1080/00224499.2014.906031.

Moreland, B., Kakara, R., & Henry, A. (2020) Trends in nonfatal falls and fall-related injuries among adults aged ≥ 65 Years – United States, 2012–2018. *MMWR Morbidity Mortality Weekly Report, 69,* 875–881.

Morley, J. E., Morris, J. C., Berg-Weger, M., Borson, S., Carpenter, B. D., Del Campo, N., Dubois, B., Fargo, K., Fitten, L. J., Flaherty, J. H., Ganguli, M., Grossberg, G. T., Malmstrom, T. K., Petersen, R. D., Rodriguez, C., Saykin, A. J., Scheltens, P., Tangalos, E. G., Verghese, J., Wilcock, G., Winblad, B., Woo, J., & Vellas, B. (2015). Brain health: The importance of recognizing cognitive impairment, an IAGG consensus conference. *Journal of the American Medical Directors Association, 16*(9), 731–739. doi: 10.1016/j.jamda.2015.06.017.

Moore, S. E., Jones-Eversley, S. D., Tolliver, W. F., Wilson, B., & Harmon, D. K. (2022). Cultural responses to loss and grief among Black Americans: Theory and practice implications for clinicians. *Death Studies, 46*(1), 189–199. doi: 10.1080/07481187.2020.1725930.

Moreno-Agostino, D., Stone, A. A., Schneider, S., Koskinen, S., Leonardi, M., Naidoo, N., Tobiasz-Adamczyk, B., Haro, J. M., Miret, M., Kowal, P., Ayuso-Mateos, J. L., & Chatterji, S. (2020). Are retired people higher in experiential wellbeing than working older adults? A time use approach. *Emotion, 20*(8), 1411–1422. doi: 10.1037/emo0000637.

Morreall, J. (1991). Humor and work. *Humor: International Journal of Humor Research, 4*(3–4), 359–374.

Morrison, J. H. & Baxter, M. G. (2012). The ageing cortical synapse: Hallmarks and implications for cognitive decline. *Nature Reviews Neuroscience, 13*(4), 240–250. doi: 10.1038/nrn3200.

Most, J., & Redman, L. M. (2017). Aging and cardiovascular disease: Lessons from calorie restriction. In N. Bergeron, P. W. Siri-Tarino, G. A. Bray, & R. M. Krauss (Eds.), *Nutrition and Cardiometabolic Health* (pp. 191–208). CRC.

Motoki, K., Spence, C., & Velasco, C. (2023). When visual cues influence taste/flavour perception: A systematic review. *Food Quality and Preference*, 111, 104996. doi: 10.1016/j.foodqual.2023.104996.

Mott, M. C., Gordon, J. A., & Koroshetz, W. J. (2018). The NIH BRAIN Initiative: Advancing neurotechnologies, integrating disciplines. *PLoS Biology, 16*(11), e3000066. doi: 10.1371/journal.pbio.3000066.

Mroczek, D. K., & Kolarz, C. M. (1998). The effect of age on positive and negative affect: A developmental perspective on happiness. *Journal of Personality and Social Psychology, 75*(5), 1333.

Mudrik, L., Boly, M., Dehaene, S., Fleming, S. M., Lamme, V., Seth, A., & Melloni, L. (2025). Unpacking the complexities of consciousness: Theories and reflections. *Neuroscience & Biobehavioral Reviews, 170*, 106053. doi: 10.1016/j.neubiorev.2025.106053.

Muller, H. J. (1938). The remaking of chromosomes. *The Collecting Net, 13*, 181–198.

Multi-Society Task Force on PVS (1994). Medical aspects of the persistent vegetative state (1). *The New England Journal of Medicine, 330*, 1499–1508.

Murata, S., Ebeling, M., Meyer, A. C., Schmidt-Mende, K., Hammar, N., & Modig, K. (2024). Blood biomarker profiles and exceptional longevity: Comparison of centenarians and non-centenarians in a 35-year follow-up of the Swedish AMORIS cohort. *GeroScience, 46*, 1693–1702. doi: 10.1007/s11357-023-00936-w.

Murphy, S. L., Kochanek, K. D., Xu, J., & Arias, E. (2024). Mortality in the United States, 2023. *NCHS Data Brief, 521*, CS356116. doi: 10.15620/cdc/170564.

Murty, V. P., & Dickerson, K. C. (2016). Motivational influences on memory. In S. Kim, J. Reeve, & M. Bong (Eds.), *Recent Developments in Neuroscience Research on Human Motivation (Advances in Motivation and Achievement. Vol. 19.)* (pp. 203–227). Emerald Group Publishing Limited. doi: 10.1108/S0749-742320160000019019.

Naik, N. S. (2024). Uplifting and uncanny conversations around death and dying: Qualitative study among Indian adolescents and emerging adults. *SAGE Open, 14*(2), 1–10. doi: 10.1177/21582440241242204.

Nakamura, K., & Ogata, T. (2016). Locomotive syndrome: Definition and management. *Clinical Reviews in Bone and Mineral Metabolism, 14*, 56–67. doi: 10.1007/s12018-016-9208-2.

Nakamura, K. A. (2008). "Super-aged" society and the "locomotive syndrome". *Journal of Orthopaedic Science, 13*(1), 1–2. doi: 10.1007/s00776-007-1202-6.

Nanayakkara, N., Curtis, A. J., Heritier, S., Gadowski, A. M., Pavkov, M. E., Kenealy, T., Owens, D. R., Thomas, R. L., Song, S., Wong, J., Chan, J. C.-N., Luk, A. O.-Y., Penno, G., Ji, L., Mohan, V., Amutha, A., Romero-Aroca, P., Gasevic, D., Magliano, D. J., Teede, H. J., Chalmers, J., & Zoungas, S. (2021). Impact of age at type 2 diabetes mellitus diagnosis on mortality and vascular complications: Systematic review and meta-analyses. *Diabetologia, 64*(2), 275–287. doi: 10.1007/s00125-020-05319-w.

Narayanan, D., Chandrasekaran, A. S., Raj S, E. A., & Vyas, N. (2025). Gender disparities in end-of-life care: A scoping review of patient, caregiver and care provider perspectives in low-and middle-income countries. *BMC Palliative Care, 24*(62), 1–9. doi: 10.1186/s12904-025-01702-9.

Narr, R. K., Allen, J. P., Tan, J. S., & Loeb, E. L. (2019). Close friendship strength and broader peer group desirability as differential predictors of adult mental health. *Child Development, 90*(1), 298–313. doi: 10.1111/cdev.12905.

Narvaez, D., Moore, D. S., Witherington, D. C., Vandiver, T. I., & Lickliter, R. (2022). Evolving evolutionary psychology. *American Psychologist*, 77(3), 424.

National Academies of Sciences, Engineering, and Medicine (2016). *Families Caring for an Aging America*. National Academies Press.

National Academies of Sciences, Engineering, and Medicine, Division of Behavioral and Social Sciences and Education, Health and Medicine Division, Board on Behavioral, Cognitive, and Sensory Sciences, Board on Health Sciences Policy, Committee on the Health and Medical Dimensions of Social Isolation and Loneliness in Older Adults (2020). *Social Isolation and Loneliness in Older Adults: Opportunities for the Health Care System*. National Academies Press.

National Alliance for Caregiving, & AARP (2020). Caregiving in the U.S. www.caregiving.org/wp-content/uploads/2021/01/full-report-caregiving-inthe-united-states-01-21.pdf.

National Alliance on Mental Illness (2025, February 18). The 2024 NAMI Workplace Mental Health Poll. www.nami.org/support-education/publications-reports/survey-reports/the-2024-nami-workplace-mental-health-poll/.

National Center for Health Statistics (2010, March 3). New marriage and cohabitation data available. *Centers for Disease Control and Prevention*. https://blogs.cdc.gov/nchs/2010/03/03/964/.

National Center for Health Statistics (2014). Long term care services in the United States: 2013 overview. Government Printing Office.

National Collaborating Centre for Mental Health (UK) (2010). *Depression: The Treatment and Management of Depression in Adults (Updated Edition)*. British Psychological Society.

National Funeral Directors Association (2024). Statistics. https://nfda.org/news/statistics. Retrieved April 17, 2025.

National Human Genome Research Institute (2018). Genetics vs. genomics fact sheet. www.genome.gov/about-genomics/fact-sheets/Genetics-vs-Genomics.

National Institute on Aging (n.d.) How smell and taste change as you age. www.nia.nih.gov/health/teeth-and-mouth/how-smell-and-taste-change-you-age. Accessed November 13, 2025.

National Institute on Aging (2021). What are palliative care and hospice care? www.nia.nih.gov/health/hospice-and-palliative-care/what-are-palliative-care-and-hospice-care. Retrieved April 24, 2025.

National Institute on Aging (2022) What are the signs of Alzheimer's disease? www.nia.nih.gov/health/alzheimers-symptoms-and-diagnosis/what-are-signs-alzheimers-disease. Accessed November 13, 2025.

National Institute on Aging (2024). Heart health and aging. www.nia.nih.gov/health/heart-health/heart-health-and-aging. Accessed July 25, 2025.

National Institute on Aging (2025). Exercise and physical activity. www.nia.nih.gov/health/exercise-and-physical-activity. Retrieved April 13, 2025.

National Poll on Healthy Aging (2022, April). Older adults' preparedness to aging in place. Institute for Healthcare Policy and Innovation.

Nauta, M. M. (2010). The development, evolution, and status of Holland's theory of vocational personalities: Reflections and future directions for counseling psychology. *Journal of Counseling Psychology, 57*(1), 11.

Nazar, G., Cabezas, M. F., Alcover, C. M., Soto-Contreras, E., Reyes-Molina, D., Bustos, C., & Leiva, A. M. (2025). How does retirement really affect physical health? A systematic review of longitudinal studies. *Ageing & Society*, 1–18.

Nebli, A., & Rekik, I. (2021). Adversarial brain multiplex prediction from a single brain network with application to gender fingerprinting. *Medical Image Analysis, 67*, 101843. doi: 10.1016/j.media.2020.101843.

Needham, B. L., Ali, T., Allgood, K. L., Ro, A., Hirschtick, J. L., & Fleischer, N. L. (2023). Institutional racism and health: A framework for conceptualization, measurement, and analysis. *Journal of Racial and Ethnic Health Disparities, 10*(4), 1997–2019. doi: 10.1007/s40615-022-01381-9.

Nekolaichuk, C. L. (2015). Hope in end-of-life care. In E. Bruera, I. Higginson, C. F. von Gunten, & T. Morita (Eds.), *Textbook of Palliative Medicine and Supportive Care* (2nd ed.) (pp. 743–749). CRC Press, Taylor & Francis.

Nelson, T. D. (2005). Ageism: Prejudice against our feared future self. *Journal of Social Issues, 61*(2), 207–221.

Newman, D. B., Tay, L., & Diener, E. (2014). Leisure and subjective well-being: A model of psychological mechanisms as mediating factors. *Journal of Happiness Studies, 15*, 555–578.

Ng, A. E., Adjaye-Gbewonyo, D., & Vahratian, A. (May 5, 2023). Health conditions and health care use among American Indian and Alaska Native adults by tribal land residential status: United States, 2019–2021. *National Health Statistics Report*. Number 185. U.S. Department of Health and Human Services. Centers for Disease Control and Prevention. www.cdc.gov/nchs/data/nhsr/nhsr185.pdf. Accessed June 5, 2025

Niethammer, M., Tang, C. C., Ma, Y., Mattis, P. J., Ko, J. H., Dhawan, V., & Eidelberg, D. (2013). Parkinson's disease cognitive network correlates with caudate dopamine. *NeuroImage, 78*, 204–209. doi: 10.1016/j.neuroimage.2013.03.070.

Nietzel, M. (2024). Percentage of adults with college degree edges higher, finds new Lumina Report. Forbes. www.forbes.com/sites/michaeltnietzel/2024/02/01/percentage-of-us-adults-with-college-degrees-edges-higher-finds-lumina-report/.

Nisar, M., Tasleem, Z., Muhammad, S. A., Javid, A., Rasool, M. F., Karuniawati, H., Al-Tamimi, S. K., & Rehman, A. U. (2024). The direct cost of chronic kidney disease (CKD) reported in Asian countries: A systematic literature review. *Cost Effectiveness and Resource Allocation, 22*, 65. doi: 10.1186/s12962-024-00566-9.

Noble, K., Brown, L. S., Elvis, P., & Lang, H. (2022). Cochlear immune response in Presbyacusis: A focus on dysregulation of macrophage activity. *Journal of the Association for Research in Otolaryngoly, 23*, 1–16. doi: 10.1007/s10162-021-00819-x.

Officer, A., Pautex, S., Badache, A., Broers, B., & Prina, M. (2024a). Systematic review on attitudes towards death and dying in adults 50 years and older living in countries with community transmission of COVID–19. *Archives of Gerontology and Geriatrics, 127*, 1–11. doi: 10.1016/j.archger.2024.105573.

Officer, A., Prina, M., Badache, A., Broers, B., Gnanapragasam, S., & Pautex, S. (2024b). Factors associated with attitudes toward death and dying in the second half of life: A scoping review. *Death Studies*, 1–14. doi: 10.1080/07481187.2024.2414248.

Noel, S. E., Santos, M. P., & Wright, N. C. (2021). Racial and ethnic disparities in bone health and outcomes in the United States. *Journal of Bone and Mineral Research, 36*(10), 1881–1905. doi: 10.1002/jbmr.4417.

Noetel, M., Sanders, T., Gallardo-Gómez, D., Taylor, P., del Pozo, B. Cruz, van den Hoek, D., Smith, J. J., Mahoney, J., Spathis, J., Moresi, M., Pagano, R., Pagano, L., Vasconcellos, R., Arnott, H., Varley, B., Parker, P., Biddle, S., & Lonsdale, C. (2024). Effect of exercise for depression: Systematic review and network meta-analysis of randomised controlled trials. *BMJ, 384*, e075847. doi: 10.1136/bmj-2023-075847.

Nolen-Hoeksema, S., & Davis, C. G. (2004). Theoretical and methodological issues in the assessment and interpretation of posttraumatic growth. *Psychological Inquiry, 15*(1), 60–64.

Noonan, K., Horsfall, D., Leonard, R., & Rosenberg, J. (2016). Developing death literacy. *Progress in Palliative Care, 24*(1), 31–35.

Nguyen, L., Murphy, K., & Andrews, G. (2022). A game a day keeps cognitive decline away? A systematic review and meta-analysis of commercially-available brain training programs in healthy and cognitively impaired older adults. *Neuropsycholy Review, 32*(3), 601–630. doi: 10.1007/s11065-021-09515-2.

Nyanamba, J. M., Hanebutt, R., Goodwin, A., Gonzalez-Detrés, C., Kapatamoyo, K., Bamwine, P., Okonkwo, M. N., Kodiamplakkal, H., Narisetti, L., Murry, V. M., & Walker, P. (2024). African descent populations in the United States are not monolithic: A scoping review of African immigrants mental health and coping strategies. *Cultural Diversity and Ethnic Minority Psychology, 30*(4), 713–739. doi: 10.1037/cdp0000688.

Odhiambo, L. A., Anaba, E., Stephens, P. C., Cheruvu, V. K., & Zullo, M. D. (2023). Community-based approach to assess obstructive respiratory diseases and risk in urban African American churches. *Journal of Immigrant and Minority Health, 25*(2), 389–397. doi: 10.1007/s10903-022-01405-w.

Ogawa, T., Annear, M. J., Ikebe, K., & Maeda, Y. (2017). Taste-related sensations in old age. *Journal of Oral Rehabilitation, 44*, 626–635. https://doi-org.proxy-tu.researchport.umd.edu/10.1111/joor.12502.

Ogolsky, B. G., Dobson, K., Rivas-Koehl, M., Kawas, G., & Hardesty, J. L. (2025). The progression of college student romantic relationship development: Stability and change over 10 years. *Personal Relationships, 32*(1), e12590.

Oliveira, A., Fidalgo, A., Farinatti, P., & Monteiro, W. (2024). Effects of high-intensity interval and continuous moderate aerobic training on fitness and health markers of older adults: A systematic review and meta-analysis. *Arch Gerontology Geriatrics, 124*, 105451. doi: 10.1016/j.archger.2024.105451.

Oliver-Blackburn, B. (2024, June 18). Half sibling relationships and family communication. *Oxford Research Encyclopedia of Communication*. https://oxfordre.com/communication/view/10.1093/acrefore/9780190228613.001.0001/acrefore-9780190228613-e-1458. Retrieved May 30, 2025.

Olmstead, S. B., Conrad, K. A., & Anders, K. M. (2018). First semester college students' definitions of and expectations for engaging in hookups. *Journal of Adolescent Research, 33*(3), 275–305. doi: 10.1177/0743558417698571.

Olofsson, J. K., Ekström, I., Larsson, M., & Nordin, S. (2021). Olfaction and aging: A review of the current state of research and future directions. *i-perception, 12*(3), doi: 10.1177/20416695211020331.

Olson, J. R., Goddard, H. W., & Marshall, J. P. (2013). Relations among risk, religiosity, and marital commitment. *Journal of Couple and Relationship Therapy, 12*, 235–254.

Oluwoye, O., & Weeks, D. L. (2024). Ethnoracial differences in family members' early contact with formal and informal resources on the pathway to care during the early stages of psychosis. *Community Mental Health Journal, 60*(2), 244–250. doi: 10.1007/s10597-023-01163-5.

Ormel, J. (1980). Do neuroticism inventories measure personality traits or psychosocial stress? *Acta Psychiatrica Scandinavica, 62*(S285), 196–203.

Ortiz-Ospina, E. (2017). "Life Expectancy" – What does this actually mean? *OurWorldInData.org*. https://ourworldindata.org/life-expectancy-how-is-it-calculated-and-how-should-it-be-interpreted.

O'Shea, A., Cohen, R. A., Porges, E. C., Nissim, N. R., & Woods, A. J. (2016). Cognitive aging and the hippocampus in older adults. *Frontiers in Aging Neuroscience, 8*, 298. doi: 10.3389/fnagi.2016.00298.

Osso, L. A., & Hughes, E. G. (2024). Dynamics of mature myelin. *Nature Neuroscience, 27*, 1449–1461. doi: 10.1038/s41593-024-01642-2.

Oswald, A. J., & Powdthavee, N. (2008). Does happiness adapt? A longitudinal study of disability with implications for economists and judges. *Journal of Public Economics, 92*(5–6), 1061–1077.

Owen, C. M., Pal, L., Mumford, S. L., Freeman, R., Isaac, B., McDonald, L., Santoro, N., Taylor, H. S., & Wolff, E. F. (2016). Effects of hormones on skin wrinkles and rigidity vary by race/ethnicity: Four-year follow-up from the ancillary skin study of the Kronos Early Estrogen Prevention Study. *Fertility and Sterility, 106*(5), 1170–1175.e3. doi: 10.1016/j.fertnstert.2016.06.023.

Owen, J., & Fincham, F. D. (2011). Young adults' emotional reactions after hooking up encounters. *Archives of Sexual Behavior, 40*, 321–330. doi: 10.1007/s10508-010-9652-x.

Owji, S., & Shoja, M. M. (2020). The history of discovery of adult neurogenesis. *Clinical Anatomy, 33*(1), 41–55. doi: 10.1002/ca.23447.

Pace, J. E., & Grenier, A. (2017). Expanding the circle of knowledge: Reconceptualizing successful aging among North American older Indigenous peoples. *The Journals of Gerontology Series B: Psychological Sciences and Social Sciences, 72*(2), 248–258. doi: 10.1093/geronb/gbw128.

Pachana, N. A. (2024). Anxiety in later life and across the lifespan: Progress and future directions. *GeroPsych: The Journal of Gerontopsychology and Geriatric Psychiatry, 37*(2), 63–69. doi: 10.1024/1662-9647/a000315.

Paggi, M. E., Jopp, D., & Hertzog, C. (2016). The importance of leisure activities in the relationship between physical health and well-being in a life span sample. *Gerontology*, 62(4), 450–458.

Pakenham, K. I., & Cox, S. (2009). The dimensional structure of benefit finding in multiple sclerosis and relations with positive and negative adjustment: A longitudinal study. *Psychology and Health, 24*(4), 373–393.

Palmore, E. (2001). The ageism survey: First findings. *The Gerontologist, 41*(5), 572–575.

Pamplona, R., Jové, M., Gómez, J., & Barja, G. (2023). Programmed versus non-programmed evolution of aging. What is the evidence? *Experimental Gerontology, 175*, 112162. doi: 10.1016/j.exger.2023.112162.

Pan, S., Mayoral, S. R., Choi, H. S., Chan, J. R., & Kheirbek, M. A. (2020). Preservation of a remote fear memory requires new myelin formation. *Nature Neuroscience, 23*(4), 487–499. doi: 10.1038/s41593-019-0582-1.

Panzeri, S., Janotte, E., Peque´no-Zurro, A., Bonato, J., & Bartolozzi, C. (2023). Constraints on the design of neuromorphic circuits set by the properties of neural population codes. *Neuromorphic Computing and Engineering, 3*, 012001. doi: 10.1088/2634-4386/acaf9c.

Park, C. H., Kim, B. R., Park, H. K., Lim, S. M., Kim, E., Jeong, J. H., & Kim, G. H. (2022). Predicting superagers by machine learning classification based on the functional brain connectome using resting-state functional magnetic resonance imaging. *Cerebral Cortex, 32*(19), 4183–4190.

Park, C. L., Chmielewski, J., & Blank, T. O. (2010). Post-traumatic growth: Finding positive meaning in cancer survivorship moderates the impact of intrusive thoughts on adjustment in younger adults. *Psycho-oncology, 19*(11), 1139–1147.

Park, D., Lee, E., Yang, S., & Ware, O. D. (2024). Patterns of familial and racial trauma and their associations with substance use disorders among racial/ethnic minority adults. *Journal of Racial and Ethnic Health Disparities, 11*(6), 3606–3617. doi: 10.1007/s40615-023-01812-1.

Park, D. C., & Festini, S. B. (2017). Theories of memory and aging: A look at the past and a glimpse of the future. *The Journals of Gerontology Series B: Psychological Sciences and Social Sciences, 72*, 82–90.

Park, S. Y., Setiawan, V. W., Crimmins, E. M., White, L. R., Wu, A. H., Cheng, I., Darst, B. F., Haiman, C. A., Wilkens, L. R., Marchand, L., & Lim, U. (2024). Racial and ethnic differences in the population-attributable fractions of Alzheimer disease and related dementias. *Neurology, 102*(3), e208116. doi: 10.1212/WNL.0000000000208116.

Parker, J. S., Haskins, N., Clemons, A., McClure, E., & Washington, J. (2022). Early career Black women in school-based mental health fields: Understanding their experiences of workplace discrimination. *Journal of School Psychology, 92*, 49–65.

Parker, K., & Minkin, R. (2023, September 14). Public has mixed views on the modern American family. *Pew Research Center*. www.pewresearch.org/social-trends/2023/09/14/public-has-mixed-views-on-the-modern-american-family/.

Parkinson's Europe (n.d.). Parkinson's statistics. https://parkinsonseurope.org/facts-and-figures/statistics/. Accessed November 13, 2025.

Parkinson's Foundation (n.d.). What is Parkinson's? www.parkinson.org/understanding-parkinsons/what-is-parkinsons. Accessed November 13, 2025.

Parnia, S., Post, S. G., Lee, M. T., Lyubomirsky, S., Aufderheide, T. P., Deakin, C. D., Greyson, B., Long, J., Gonzales, A. M., Huppert, E. L., Dickinson, A., Mayer, S., Locicero, B., Levin, J., Bossis, A., Worthington, E., Fenwick, P., & Shirazi, T. K. (2022). Guidelines and standards for the study of death and recalled experiences of death–a multidisciplinary consensus statement and proposed future directions. *Annals of the New York Academy of Sciences, 1511*(1), 5–21. doi: 10.1111/nyas.14740.

Patterson, P., & Gong, G. (2009). Addressing health disparities in immigrant populations in the United States. In S. Kosoko-Lasaki & C. T. Cook, *Cultural Proficiency in Addressing Health Disparities*. Jones and Bartlett.

Pei, R., & Zaki, J. (2025). Connecting with others: How social connections improve the happiness of young adults. *World Happiness Report*.

Pengpid, S., & Peltzer, K. (2021). Depression and generalised anxiety and associated factors among adults in Bhutan: Results of national cross-sectional survey in 2019. *Asian Journal Of Psychiatry, 67*, 102959. doi: 10.1016/j.ajp.2021.102959.

Perlstadt, H. (2024a). The US public health Tuskegee syphilis study: A sociological perspective. In *Assessing Social Science Research Ethics and Integrity: Case Studies and Essays* (pp. 71–106). Springer International Publishing.

Perlstadt, H. (2024b). A history of social science ethics and regulations in the United States. In *Assessing Social Science Research Ethics and Integrity: Case Studies and Essays* (pp. 17–39). Springer International Publishing.

Perrin, A., & Atske, S. (2021). About three-in-ten U.S. adults say they are 'almost constantly' online. *Pew Research Center*. www.pewresearch.org/short-reads/2021/03/26/about-three-inten-u-s-adults-say-they-are-almost-constantly-online/.

Pes, G. M., Dore, M. P., Tsofliou, F., & Poulain, M. (2022). Diet and longevity in the blue zones: A set-and-forget issue? *Maturitas*, 164, 31–37. doi: 10.1016/j.maturitas.2022.06.004.

Peterson, C. (2006). *A Primer in Positive Psychology*. Oxford University Press.

Peterson, C., Park, N., & Sweeney, P. J. (2008). Group well-being: Morale from a positive psychology perspective. *Applied Psychology, 57*(s1), 19–36.

Pham, S., Porta, G., Biernesser, C., Walker Payne, M., Iyengar, S., Melhem, N., & Brent, D. A. (2018). The burden of bereavement: Early-onset depression and impairment in youths bereaved by sudden parental death in a 7-year prospective study. *The American Journal of Psychiatry, 175*(9), 887–896. doi: 10.1176/appi.ajp.2018.17070792.

Phillips, S. P., Auais, M., Belanger, E., Alvarado, B., & Zunzunegui, M. V. (2016). Life-course social and economic circumstances, gender, and resilience in older adults: The longitudinal International Mobility in Aging Study (IMIAS). *SSM – Population Health, 2*, 708–717. doi: 10.1016/j.ssmph.2016.09.007.

Pierewan, A. C., & Tampubolon, G. (2015). Happiness and health in Europe: A multivariate multilevel model. *Applied Research in Quality of Life, 10*, 237–252.

Piette, J. D., Hampstead, B. M., Marinec, N., Chen, J., & Roberts, J. S. (2023). A pilot randomized trial of a purposeful and stimulating volunteer opportunity: Program satisfaction and potential impacts on perceived cognitive change in a neurologically mixed sample of older adults. *Alzheimer Disease & Associated Disorders, 37*(3), 237–242.

Pinheiro, P. S., Medina, H., Callahan, K. E., Kwon, D., Ragin, C., Sherman, R., Kobetz, E. N., & Jemal, A. (2020). Cancer mortality among US Blacks: Variability between African Americans, Afro-Caribbeans, and Africans. *Cancer Epidemiology, 66*, 101709. doi: 10.1016/j.canep.2020.101709.

Pitkälä, K. H., Pöysti, M. M., Laakkonen, M. L., Tilvis, R. S., Savikko, N., Kautiainen, H., & Strandberg, T. E. (2013). Effects of the Finnish Alzheimer disease exercise trial (FINALEX): A randomized controlled trial. *JAMA Internal Medicine, 173*(10), 894–901. doi: 10.1001/jamainternmed.2013.359.

Polidori, M. C., & Mecocci, P. (2022). Modeling the dynamics of energy imbalance: The free radical theory of aging and frailty revisited. *Free Radical Biology andl Medicine, 181*, 235–240. doi: 10.1016/j.freeradbiomed.2022.02.009.

Ponzo, V., Bo, M., Favaro, E., Merlo, F., Isaia, G., Presta, R., Collo, A., Riso, S., & Bo, S. (2024). Does presbygeusia really exist? An updated narrative review. *Aging Clinical and Experimental Research, 36*, 84. https://doi.org/10.1007/s40520-024-02739-1.

Popescu, I., Duffy, E., Mendelsohn, J., & Escarce, J. J. (2018). Racial residential segregation, socioeconomic disparities, and the White-Black survival gap. *PLoS One, 13*(2), e0193222.

Pouillot, R., Santillana Farakos, S., & Van Doren, J. M. (2022). Modeling the risk of low bone mass and osteoporosis as a function of urinary cadmium in U.S adults aged 5079 years. *Environmental Research, 212*(Pt B), 113315. doi: 10.1016/j.envres.2022.113315.

Poulain, M., & Herm, A. (2024). Exceptional longevity in Okinawa: Demographic trends since 1975. *Journal of Internal Medicine*, 387–99.

Poulain, M., Herm, A., & Pes, G. M. (2013). The blue zones: Areas of exceptional longevity around the world. *Vienna Yearbook of Population Research*, 11, 87–108. www.jstor.org/stable/43050798.

Poulain, M., Pes, G. M., Carru, C., Ferruci, L., Baggio, G., Franceschi, C., & Deiana, L. (2006). The validation of exceptional male longevity in Sardinia. In J.-M, Robine, E. M. Crimmins, S. Horiuchi, & Z. Yi (Eds.), *Human Longevity, Individual Life Duration, and the Growth of the Oldest-old Population* (pp.147–166). Springer. doi: 10.1007/978-1-4020-4848-7_7.

Poulain, M., Pes, G. M., Grasland, C., Carru, C., Ferrucci, L., Baggio, G., Franceschi, C., & Deiana, L. (2004). Identification of a geographic area characterized by extremelongevity in the Sardinia island: The AKEA study. *Experimental Gerontology, 39*, 1423–1429. doi: 10.1016/j.exger.2004.06.016.

Prajjwal, P., Inban, P., Sai, V. P., Shiny, K. S., Lam, J. R., John, J., Sulaimanov, M., Tekuru, Y., Wasi, U. I., Haq, M., Marsool, M. D. M., Sivarajan, V. V., & Amir Hussin, O. (2024). The effects of the interplay between vitamins, antibiotics, and gut microbiota on the pathogenesis and progression of dementia: A systematic review and meta-analysis. *Health Science Reports, 7*(1), e1808. doi: 10.1002/hsr2.1808.

Pressman, S. D., & Cohen, S. (2005). Does positive affect influence health? *Psychological Bulletin, 131*(6), 925.

Prigerson, H. G., Boelen, P. A., Xu, J., Smith, K. V., & Maciejewski, P. K. (2021). Validation of the new DSM-5-TR criteria for prolonged grief disorder and the PG-13 Revised (PG-13-R) scale. *World Psychiatry*, 20(1), 96–106. doi: 10.1002/wps.20823.

Prigerson, H. G., Horowitz, M. J., Jacobs, S. C., Parkes, C. M., Aslan, M., Goodkin, K., Raphael, B., Marwit, S. J., Wortman, C., Neimeyer, R. A., Bonanno, G., Block, S. D., Kissane, D., Boelen, P., Maercker, A., Litz, B. T., Johnson, J. G., First, M. B., & Maciejewski, P. K. (2009). Prolonged grief disorder: Psychometric validation of criteria proposed for DSM-V and ICD-11. *PLoS Medicine*, 6(8), e1000121.

Proyer, R. T., Gander, F., Bertenshaw, E. J., & Brauer, K. (2018). The positive relationships of playfulness with indicators of health, activity, and physical fitness. *Frontiers in Psychology, 9*, 1440.

Pruitt, S. L., Lee, S. J. C., Tiro, J. A., Xuan, L., Ruiz, J. M., & Inrig, S. (2015). Residential racial segregation and mortality among Black, White, and Hispanic urban breast cancer patients in Texas, 1995 to 2009. *Cancer, 121*(11), 1845–1855.

Psarra, E., & Kleftaras, G. (2013). Adaptation to physical disabilities: The role of meaning in life and depression. *European Journal of Counselling Psychology, 2*(1), 79–99.

Pyrkov, T. V., Aychaciov, K., Tarkhov, A. E., Menshikov, L. I., Gudkov, A. V., & Fedichev, P. O. (2021). Longitudinal analysis of blood markers reveals progressive loss of resilience and predicts human lifespan limit. *Nature Communications*, 12, 2765. doi: 10.1038/s41467-021-23014-1.

Qin, S., & Xia, Y. (2015). Grieving rituals and beliefs of Chinese families. In J. Cacciatore & J. DeFraine (Eds.), *The World of Bereavement* (1st ed.) (pp. 69–80). Springer.

Quashie, N. T., & Andrade, F. C. (2018). Family status and later-life depression among older adults in urban Latin America and the Caribbean. *Ageing and Society, 40,* 233–261. doi: 10.1017/S0144686X18000879.

Qureshi, A. A., Mohammad, J., Mohammed Elkandow, A. E., Hanumanthappa, J., Ariboyina, A. K., & Türkmen, S. (2022). The end-of-life care in the emergency department setting with respect to the Middle East countries and comparison with the Western countries. *Turkish Journal of Emergency Medicine, 22*(1), 1–7.

Rachoin, J. S., Debski, N., Hunter, K., & Cerceo, E. (2024). Factors associated with Do Not Resuscitate status and palliative care in hospitalized patients: A national inpatient sample analysis. *Palliative Medicine Reports, 5*(1), 331–339. doi: 10.1089/pmr.2024.0030.

Radbruch, L., De Lima, L., Knaul, F., Wenk, R., Ali, Z., Bhatnaghar, S., Blanchard, C., Bruera, E., Buitrago, R., Burla, C., Callaway, M., Munyoro, E. C., Centeno, C., Cleary, J., Connor, S., Davaasuren, O., Downing, J., Foley, K., Goh, C., Gomez-Garcia, W., Harding, R., Khan, Q. T., Larkin, P., Leng, M., Luyirika, E., Marston, J., Moine, S., Osman, H., Pettus, K., Puchalski, C., Rajagopal, M. R., Spence, D., Spruijt, O., Venkateswaran, C., Wee, B., Woodruff, R., Yong, J., & Pastrana, T. (2020). Redefining palliative care—A new consensus-based definition. *Journal of Pain and Symptom Management, 60,* 754–764. doi: 10.1016/j.jpainsymman.2020.04.027.

Rainer, M., Xie, B., Schmidt-Vaivao, D., Soakai, L., Jablonski, G., Delgado, C., DeHart, J., & Palmer, P. (2024). Resilience and adversity among Older Pacific Islanders in Southern California. *Asian American Journal of Psychology, 15,* 275–285. 10.1037/aap0000341.

Rajan, K. B., Weuve, J., Barnes, L. L., McAninch, E. A., Wilson, R. S., & Evans, D. A. (2021). Population estimate of people with clinical AD and mild cognitive impairment in the United States (2020–2060). *Alzheimer's & Dementia, 17*(12), 1966–1975.

Rakowska, M., Bagrowska, P., Lazari, A., Navarrete, M., Abdellahi, M. E., Johansen-Berg, H., & Lewis, P. A. (2022). Cueing motor memory reactivation during NREM sleep engenders learning-related changes in precuneus and sensorimotor structures. *bioRxiv*, 477838. doi: 10.1101/2022.01.27.477838.

Ramírez García, J. I. (2019). Integrating Latina/o ethnic determinants of health in research to promote population health and reduce health disparities. *Cultural Diversity & Ethnic Minority Psychology, 25*(1), 21.

Ranu, J., Kalebic, N., Melendez-Torres, G. J., & Taylor, P. J. (2023). Association between adverse childhood experiences and a combination of psychosis and violence among adults: A systematic review and meta-analysis. *Trauma Violence Abuse, 24*(5), 2997–3013. doi: 10.1177/15248380221122818.

Raup, J. L., & Myers, J. E. (1989). The empty nest syndrome: Myth or reality. *Journal of Counseling & Development, 68*(2), 180–183. doi: 10.1002/j.1556-6676.1989.tb01353.x.

Rawal, S., Duffy, V. B., Berube, L., Hayes, J. E., Kant, A. K., Li, C. M., Graubard, B. I. & Hoffman, H. J. (2021). Self-reported olfactory dysfunction and diet quality: Findings from the 2011–2014 National Health and Nutrition Examination Survey (NHANES). *Nutrients, 13*(12), 4561. doi: 10.3390/nu13124561.

Rawal, S., Hoffman, H. J., Bainbridge, K. E., Huedo-Medina, T. B. & Duffy, V. B. (2016). Prevalence and risk factors of self-reported smell and taste alterations: Results from the 2011-2012 US National Health and Nutrition Examination Survey (NHANES). *Chemical Senses*, 41(1), 69–76. doi: 10.1093/chemse/bjv057.

Regnoli, G. M., Rosa, B. D., & Palombo, P. (2022). "Voice to the youth": An interpretative phenomenological analysis of how Italian young adults experienced the pandemic. *Mediterranean Journal of Clinical Psychology, 10*, 1–30.

Rein, D. B., Wittenborn, J. S., Burke-Conte, Z., Gulia, R., Robalik, T., Ehrlich, J. R., Lundeen, E. A., & Flaxman, A. D. (2022). Prevalence of age-related Macular Degeneration in the US in 2019. *JAMA Ophthalmoly, 140*(12), 1202–1208. doi: 10.1001/jamaophthalmol.2022.4401.

Rhee, M. K., Mor Barak, M. E., & Gallo, W. T. (2016). Mechanisms of the effect of involuntary retirement on older adults' self-rated health and mental health. *Journal of Gerontological Social Work, 59*(1), 35–55.

Ribeiro, F. S., Teixeira-Santos, A. C., & Leist, A. K. (2022). The prevalence of mild cognitive impairment in Latin America and the Caribbean: A systematic review and meta-analysis. *Aging Mental Health, 26*(9), 1710–1720. doi: 10.1080/13607863.2021.2003297.

Ricci, F., Torales, J., Bener, A. B., Castaldelli-Maia, J. M., Chumakov, E., Bellomo, A., & Ventriglio, A. (2023). Mental health of ethnic minorities: The role of racism. *International Review of Psychiatry, 35*, 258–267. doi: 10.1080/09540261.2023.2189951.

Riegel, K. F. (1973). Dialectic operations: The final period of cognitive development. *Human Development, 16*(5), 346–370. doi: 10.1159/000271287.

Rholes, W. S., Simpson, J. A., & Friedman, M. (2006). Avoidant attachment and the experience of parenting. *Personality and Social Psychology Bulletin, 32*(3), 275–285.

Richman, J. (1995). The lifesaving function of humor with the depressed and suicidal elderly. *Gerontologist, 35*(2), 271–273.

Rietdijk, C. D., Perez-Pardo, P., Garssen, J., van Wezel, R. J., & Kraneveld, A. D. (2017). Exploring Braak's hypothesis of Parkinson's disease. *Frontiers in Neurology, 8*, 1–9. doi: 10.3389/fneur.2017.00037.

Ristow, M., & Schmeisser, K. (2014). Mitohormesis: Promoting health and lifespan by increased levels of reactive oxygen species (ROS). *Dose-Response, 12*, 288–341.

Roberto, K. A., & Stroes, J. (2019). Grandchildren and grandparents: Roles, influences, and relationships. In J. Hendricks, *The Ties of Later Life* (pp. 141–153). Routledge.

Robinson, M. N., Erving, C. L., & Thomas Tobin, C. S. (2023). Are distressed Black women also depressed? Implications for a mental health paradox. *Journal of Racial and Ethnic Health Disparities, 10*(3), 1280–1292.

Rogalski, E., Huentelman, M., Roberts, A., Maher, A., McIlroy, B., Van Ooteghem, K., Finger, E., Lim, A., Okonkwo, O., Goldstein, F., Parrish, T., Scholtens, D., Weintraub, S., Geula, C., & Mesulam, M.-M. (2022). The SuperAging Research Initiative: A multisite consortium focused to identify factors promoting extraordinary cognitive aging. *Alzheimer's & Dementia, 18*, S11. doi: 10.1002/alz.066407.

Rogers, C. R. (1961). *On Becoming a Person: A Therapist's View of Psychotherapy*. Houghton Mifflin.

Rogers, F., & Metzler-Baddeley, C. (2024). The effects of musical instrument training on fluid intelligence and executive functions in healthy older adults: A systematic review and meta-analysis. *Brain and Cognition, 175*, 106137. doi: 10.1016/j.bandc.2024.106137.

Rolland, Y., Pillard, F., Klapouszczak, A., Reynish, E., Thomas, D., Andrieu, S., Rivière, D., & Vellas, B. (2007). Exercise program for nursing home residents with Alzheimer's disease: A 1-year randomized, controlled trial. *Journal of the American Geriatrics Society, 55*(2), 158–165. doi: 10.1111/j.1532-5415.2007.01035.x.

Rolls, E. T., Feng, R., & Feng, J. (2023). Lifestyle risks associated with brain functional connectivity and structure. *Human Brain Mapping, 44*(6), 2479–2492. doi: 10.1002/hbm.26225.

Rosenfeld, M. J., Thomas, R. J., & Hausen, S. (2019). Disintermediating your friends: How online dating in the United States displaces other ways of meeting. *Proceedings of the National Academy of Sciences of the United States of America, 116*(36), 17753–17758. doi: 10.1073/pnas.1908630116.

Rosenthal, T., Touyz, R. M., & Oparil, S. (2022). Migrating populations and health: Risk factors for cardiovascular disease and metabolic syndrome. *Current Hypertension Reports, 24*(9), 325–340.

Ross Rothweiler, B., & Ross, K. (2019). Fifty years later: Reflections on the work of Elisabeth Kübler-Ross M.D. *The American Journal of Bioethics, 19*(12), 3–4. doi: 10.1080/15265161.2019.1674551.

Rossouw, J. E., Anderson, G. L, Prentice, R. L., LaCroix, A. Z., Kooperberg, C., Stefanick, M. L., Jackson, R. D., Beresford, S. A. A., Howard, B. V., Johnson, K. C., Kotchen, J. M., Ockene, J., & Writing Group for the Women's Health Initiative Investigators (2002). Risks and benefits of estrogen plus progestin in healthy postmenopausal women: Principal results from the Women's Health Initiative randomized controlled trial. *JAMA, 288*(3), 321–333.

Roth, G. A., Mensah, G. A., Johnson, C.O., Addolorato, G., Ammirati, E., Baddour, L. M., Barengo, N. C., Beaton, A. Z., Benjamin, E. J., Benzinger, C, P., Bonny, A., Brauer, M., Brodmann, M., Cahill, T. J., Carapetis, J., Catapano, A. L., Chugh, S. S., Cooper, L. T., Coresh, J., Criqui, M., DeCleene, N., Eagle, K. A., Emmons-Bell, S., Fegin, V. L., Fernández Solà, J., Fowkes, G., Gakidou, E, Grundy, S. M., He, F. J., Howard, G., Hu, F., Inker, L., Karthikeyan, G., Kassebaum, N., Koroshetz, W., Lavie, C., Lloyd-Jones, D., Lu, H. S., Mirijello, A,. Temesgen, A. M., Mokdad, A., Moran, A. E., Muntner, P., Narula, J., Neal, B., Ntsekhe, M., de Oliveira, G. M., Otto, C., Owolabi, M., Pratt, M., Rajagopalan, S., Reitsma, M., Ribeiro, A. L. P., Rigotti, N., Rodgers, A., Sable, C., Shakil, S., Sliwa-Hahnle, K., Stark, B., Sundström, J., Timpel, P., Tleyjeh, I. M., Valgimigli, M., Vos, T., Whelton, P. K., Yacoub, M., Zuhlke, L., Murray, C., Fuster, V., & GBD-NHLBI-JACC Global Burden of Cardiovascular Diseases Writing Group (2020). Global burden of cardiovascular diseases and risk factors, 1990–2019. *Journal of the American College of Cardiology, 76*, 2982–3021.

Rouxel, P., Chandola, T., Kumari, M., Seeman, T., & Benzeval, M. (2022). Biological costs and benefits of social relationships for men and women in adulthood: The role of partner, family and friends. *Sociology of Health & Illness, 44*(1), 5–24.

Rowe, J. W., & Kahn, R. L. (1997). Successful aging. *The Gerontologist, 37*(4), 433–440.

Roy, C., & Andrews, H. A. (1999). *The Roy Adaptation Model* (2nd ed.). Appleton & Lange.

Rudnicka, E., Napierała, P., Podfigurna, A., Męczekalski, B., Smolarczyk, R., & Grymowicz M. (2020). The World Health Organization (WHO) approach to healthy ageing. *Maturitas, 139*, 6–11. doi: 10.1016/j.maturitas.2020.05.018.

Rue, P. (2018). Make way, Millennials, here comes Gen Z. *About Campus, 23*(3), 5–12. doi: 10.1177/1086482218804251.

Rumelhart, D. E., McClelland, J. L., & PDP Research Group (1986). *Parallel Distributed Processing (Vol. 1): Explorations in the Microstructure of Cognition: Foundations*. MIT PRESS. doi: 10.7551/mitpress/5236.001.0001.

Rusbult, C. E., & Van Lange, P. A. (2003). Interdependence, interaction, and relationships. *Annual Review of Psychology*, 54(1), 351–375.

Ryff, C. D. (1989). Beyond Ponce de Leon and life satisfaction: New directions in quest of successful ageing. *International Journal of Behavioral Development, 12*(1), 35–55. doi: 10.1177/016502548901200102.

Ryff, C. D. (2014). Psychological well-being revisited: Advances in the science and practice of eudaimonia. *Psychotherapy and Psychosomatics, 83*(1), 10–28.

Sachdev, P. S., Lipnicki, D. M., Kochan, N. A., Crawford, J. D., Thalamuthu, A., Andrews, G., Brayne, C., Matthews, F. E., Stephan, B. C. M., Lipton, R. B., Katz, M. J., Ritchie, K., Carrière, I., Ancelin, M.-L., Lam, L. C. W., Wong, C. H. Y, Fung, A. W. T., Guaita, A., Vaccaro, R., Davin, A., Ganguli, M., Dodge, H., Hughes, T., Anstey, K. J., Cherbuin, N., Butterworth, P., & Ng, T. P. (2015). The prevalence of mild cognitive impairment in diverse geographical and ethnocultural regions: The cosmic collaboration. *PLoS One, 10*(11), e0142388. doi: 10.1371/journal.pone.0142388.

Sadighi Akha, A. A. (2018). Aging and the immune system: An overview. *Journal of Immunological Methods, 463*, 21–26. doi: 10.1016/j.jim.2018.08.005.

Safiri, S., Mahmoodpoor, A., Kolahi, A. A., Nejadghaderi, S. A., Sullman, M. J. M., Mansournia, M. A., Ansarin, K., Collins, G. S., Kaufman, J. S., & Abdollahi, M. (2023a). Global burden of lower respiratory infections during the last three decades. *Front Public Health, 10*, 1028525. doi: 10.3389/fpubh.2022.1028525.

Safiri, S., Noori, M., Nejadghaderi, S. A., Mousavi, S. E., Sullman, M. J. M., Araj-Khodaei, M., Singh, K., Kolahi, A. A., & Gharagozli, K. (2023b). The burden of Parkinson's disease in the Middle East and North Africa region, 1990–2019: Results from the global burden of disease study 2019. *BMC Public Health, 23*(1), 107. doi: 10.1186/s12889-023-15018-x.

Saidi, A., Neha & Sharma, O. P. (2024). The mediating role of rumination on stress and adaptive coping strategies among working adults. *Indian Journal of Positive Psychology, 15*(4), 483–486. https://iahrw.org/our-services/journals/indian-journal-of-positive-psychology/.

Sala, G., & Gobet, F. (2019). Cognitive training does not enhance general cognition. *Trends in Cognitive Sciences, 23*, 9–20. doi/l 10.1016/j.tics.2018.10.004.

Salari, N., Ghasemi, H., Mohammadi, L., Behzadi, M. H., Rabieenia, E., Shohaimi, S., & Mohammadi, M. (2021). The global prevalence of osteoporosis in the world: A comprehensive systematic review and meta-analysis. *J Orthop Surg Res, 16*, 609. doi: 10.1186/s13018-021-02772-0.

Salari, N., Karami, M. M., Bokaee, S., Chaleshgar, M., Shohaimi, S., Akbari, H., & Mohammadi, M. (2022). The prevalence of urinary tract infections in type 2 diabetic patients: A systematic review and meta-analysis. *European Journal of Medical Research, 27*(1), 20. doi: 10.1186/s40001-022-00644-9.

Salas-Wright, C. P., & Schwartz, S. J. (2019). The study and prevention of alcohol and other drug misuse among migrants: Toward a transnational theory of cultural stress. *International Journal of Mental Health and Addiction, 17*(2), 346–369. doi: 10.1007/s11469-018-0023-5.

Sales, A. F. S., Pandolfo, I. L., de Almeida, C. M., Parisi, J. R., Garcia, L. A., Martignago, C. C. S., Renno, A. C. M., & Vassão, P. G. (2022). Intense Pulsed Light on skin rejuvenation: A systematic review. *Archives of Dermatological Research, 314*(9), 823–838.

Sandor, C. M. (2025). Gay and lesbian parenting: Choices, choices and more choices. In K. Thompson & D. McCann (Eds.), *Couples as Parents* (pp. 50–63). Routledge.

Santomauro, D. F., Melen, S., Mitchison, D., Vos, T., Whiteford, H., & Ferrari, A. J. (2021). The hidden burden of eating disorders: An extension of estimates from the global burden of disease study 2019. *The Lancet Psychiatry, 8*, 320–328. doi: 10.1016/S2215-0366(21)00040-7.

Sattin, D., Magnani, F. G., Bartesaghi, L., Caputo, M., Fittipaldo, A. V., Cacciatore, M., Picozzi, M., & Leonardi, M. (2021). Theoretical models of consciousness: A scoping review. *Brain Science, 11*(5), 535. doi: 10.3390/brainsci11050535.

Saxena, S., Orley, J., & Whoqol Group (1997). Quality of life assessment: The World Health Organization perspective. *European Psychiatry*, *12*, 263s–266s.
Schaeffer, K. (2024). U.S. centenarian population is projected to quadruple over the next 30 years. *Pew Research Center*. www.pewresearch.org/short-reads/2024/01/09/us-centenarian-population-is-projected-to-quadruple-over-the-next-30-years/.
Schaie, K. W., & Willis, S. L. (2010). The Seattle Longitudinal Study of Adult Cognitive Development. *Bulletin of the International Society for the Study of Human Development*, *37*, 24–29.
Schaie, K. W., Willis, S. L., & Caskie, G. I. (2004). The Seattle Longitudinal Study: Relationship between personality and cognition. *Neuropsycholy, Development, and Cognition, Section B: Aging, Neuropsychology and Cognition*, *11*(2–3), 304–24. doi: 10.1080/13825580490511134.
Scharf, M. (2016). Maturing and aging together: Emerging adult grandchildren-grandparents relationships. In J. J. Arnett (Ed.), *The Oxford Handbook of Emerging Adulthood* (pp. 203–212). Oxford University Press.
Scheibe, S., & Carstensen, L. L. (2010). Emotional aging: Recent findings and future trends. *The Journals of Gerontology Series B: Psychological Sciences and Social Sciences*, 65(2), 135–144.
Schetter, C. D., Feinstein, L. G., Taylor, S. E., & Falke, R. L. (1992). Patterns of coping with cancer. *Health Psychology*, *11*(2), 79–87.
Schindler, I., Berg, C. A., Butler, J. M., Fortenberry, K. T., & Wiebe, D. J. (2010). Late-midlife and older couples' shared possible selves and psychological well-being during times of illness: The role of collaborative problem solving. *The Journals of Gerontology Series B: Psychological Sciences and Social Sciences*, *65*(4), 416–424. doi: 10.1093/geronb/gbq030.
Schmiemann, G., Kniehl, E., Gebhardt, K., Matejczyk, M. M., & Hummers-Pradier, E. (2010). The diagnosis of urinary tract infection: A systematic review. *Deutsches Ärzteblatt International*, *107*, 361–367. doi: 10.3238/arztebl.2010.0361.
Schmitz, A., & Trübner, M. (2025). Division of labour in families: An integrative dyadic classification approach. *Families, Relationships and Societies*, *14*(2), 268–286. doi: 10.1332/20467435Y2023D000000011.
Schneider, J. L., Rowe, J. H., Garcia-de-Alba, C., Kim, C. F., Sharpe, A. H., & Haigis, M. C. (2021). The aging lung: Physiology, disease, and immunity. *Cell*, *184*(8), 1990–2019. doi: 10.1016/j.cell.2021.03.005.
Schouler-Ocak, M., & Moran, J. K. (2022). Racial discrimination and its impact on mental health. *International Review of Psychiatry*, *35*(3–4), 268–276.
Schulz, R., & Decker, S. (1985). Long-term adjustment to physical disability: The role of social support, perceived control, and self-blame. *Journal of Personality and Social Psychology*, *48*(5), 1162–1172.
Seblova, D., Berggren, R., & Lövdén, M. (2020). Education and age-related decline in cognitive performance: Systematic review and meta-analysis of longitudinal cohort studies. *Ageing Research Reviews*, *58*, 101005. doi: 10.1016/j.arr.2019.101005.
Seguin, M., & Roberts, B. (2017). Coping strategies among conflict-affected adults in low- and middle-income countries: A systematic literature review. *Global Public Health: An International Journal for Research, Policy and Practice*, *12*(7), 811–829. doi: 10.1080/17441692.2015.1107117.
Seifert, A., & Schlomann, A. (2021). The use of virtual and augmented reality by older adults: Potentials and challenges. *Frontiers in Virtual Reality*, *2*, 639718.
Seiffge-Krenke, I., & Gelhaar, T. (2008). Does successful attainment of developmental tasks lead to happiness and success in later developmental tasks? A test of Havighurst's (1948) theses. *Journal of Adolescence*, *31*(1), 33–52.
Seligman, M. E., & Csikszentmihalyi, M. (2000). Positive psychology: An introduction. *American Psychologist*, *55*(1), 5–14.

Sematlane, N., Knight, L., Dube, T. L., Delport, A., Campbell, L., Masquillier, C., & Wouters, E. (2024). Adapting to, integrating and self-managing HIV as a chronic illness: A scoping review. *Discover Public Health, 21*, 163. doi: 10.1186/s12982-024-00272-0.

Sematlane, N. P., Knight, L., Masquillier, C., & Wouters, E. (2021). Adapting to, integrating and self-managing HIV as a chronic illness: A scoping review protocol. *BMJ Open, 11*(6), e047870. doi: 10.1136/bmjopen-2020-047870.

Serido, J., LeBaron, A. B., Li, L., Parrott, E., & Shim, S. (2020). The lengthening transition to adulthood: Financial parenting and recentering during the college-to-career transition. *Journal of Family Issues, 41*(9), 1626–1648.

Serpico, D. (2021). The cyclical return of the IQ controversy: Revisiting the lessons of the resolution on genetics, race and intelligence. *Journal of the History of Biology, 54*(2), 199–228. doi: 10.1007/s10739-021-09637-6.

Shaffer, C. (2019, June 14). What is neuroanatomy? *News-Medical*. www.news-medical.net/health/What-is-Neuroanatomy.aspx. Retrieved June 6, 2024.

Shakeel, M. K., & Goghari, V. M. (2017). Measuring fluid intelligence in healthy older adults. *Journal of Aging Research*, 8514582. doi: 10.1155/2017/8514582.

Settersten Jr., R. A., & Ray, B. (2010). What's going on with young people today? The long and twisting path to adulthood. *The Future of Children, 20*(1), 19–41.

Shanahan, M. J. (2000). Pathways to adulthood in changing societies: Variability and mechanisms in life course perspective. *Annual Review of Sociology, 26*(1), 667–692.

Shonkoff, J. P., Phillips, D. A., & National Research Council (2000). The developing brain. In J. P. Shonkoff & D. A. Phillips (Eds.), *From Neurons to Neighborhoods: The Science of Early Childhood Development*. National Academies Press (US).

Sharabi, L. L. (2024). The enduring effect of internet dating: Meeting online and the road to marriage. *Communication Research, 51*(3), 259–284. doi: 10.1177/00936502221127498.

Sharetts, R., Moein, S. T., Khan, R., & Doty, R. L. (2024). Long-term taste and smell outcomes after COVID-19. *JAMA Network Open, 7*(4), e247818. doi: 10.1001/jamanetworkopen.2024.7818.

Sharifi, M., Nodehi, D., & Bazgir, B. (2023). Physical activity and psychological adjustment among retirees: A systematic review. *BMC Public Health, 23*(1), 194.

Sharpe, T. L., Edwards, T., Mann, N., Lee, Y., Bonomo, A., & Donkin, V. (2025). Exploring research on the coping strategies of Black survivors of homicide victims: A scoping review. *Homicide Studies, 29*(1), 6–44. doi: 10.1177/10887679241277126. (Original work published online 2024.)

Shaw, A. R., Perales-Puchalt, J., Valdivieso-Mora, E., McGee, J. L., Vaduvathiriyan, P., & Vidoni, E. D. (2022). Effectiveness of non-pharmaceutical interventions on cognitive function among non-demented African American and Latino older adults in the USA: A scoping review. *Ethnicity & Health, 27*(4), 929–945. doi: 10.1080/13557858.2020.1828292.

Shea, J. L. (2020). Menopause and midlife aging in cross-cultural perspective: Findings from ethnographic research in China. *Journal of Cross-Cultural Gerontology, 35*(4), 367–388. doi: 10.1007/s10823-020-09408-6.

Sheffield, A. M., & Smith R. J. H. (2019). The epidemiology of deafness. *Cold Spring Harbor Perspectives in Medicine, 9*, a033258. doi: 10.1101/cshperspect.a033258.

Shehadeh, F., Zacharioudakis, I. M., Kalligeros, M., Mylona, E. K., Karki, T., van Aalst, R., Chit, A., & Mylonakis, E. (2020). Varying vaccination rates among patients seeking care for acute respiratory illness: A systematic review and meta-analysis. *Open Forum Infectious Diseases, 7*(7), ofaa234. doi: 10.1093/ofid/ofaa234.

Shen, X. (2020). Constructing an interactionist framework for playfulness research: Adding psychological situations and playful states. *Journal of Leisure Research, 51*(5), 536–558.

Sheppes, G., & Gross, J. J. (2011). Is timing everything? Temporal considerations in emotion regulation. *Personality and Social Psychology Review, 15*(4), 319–331.

Shifren, K. (1996). Individual differences in the perception of optimism and disease severity: A study among individuals with Parkinson's disease. *Journal of Behavioral Medicine, 19*, 241–271.

Shifren, K. (2009). *How Caregiving Affects Development*. American Psychological Association.

Shimada, H., Doi, T., Tsutsumimoto, K., Makino, K., Harada, K., Tomida, K., Morikawa, M., & Arai, H. (2025). Combined effects of social isolation and loneliness on disability incidence in older adults. *Archives of Gerontology and Geriatrics, 131*, 105749–105749. doi: 10.1016/j.archger.2025.105749.

Shippee, T. P., Wilkinson, L. R., Schafer, M. H., & Shippee, N. D. (2019). Long-term effects of age discrimination on mental health: The role of perceived financial strain. *The Journals of Gerontology Series B: Psychological Sciences and Social Sciences, 74*(4), 664–674.

Shohayeb, B., Diab, M., Ahmed, M., & Ng, D. C. H. (2018). Factors that influence adult neurogenesis as potential therapy. *Transl Neurodegener, 7*, 4. doi: 10.1186/s40035-018-0109-9.

Shrout, P. E., & Rodgers, J. L. (2018). Psychology, science, and knowledge construction: Broadening perspectives from the replication crisis. *Annual Review of Psychology, 69*(1), 487–510.

Shultz, K. S., & Wang, M. (2011). Psychological perspectives on the changing nature of retirement. *American Psychologist, 66*(3), 170.

Siahpush, M., Spittal, M., & Singh, G. K. (2008). Happiness and life satisfaction prospectively predict self-rated health, physical health, and the presence of limiting, long-term health conditions. *American Journal of Health Promotion, 23*(1), 18–26.

Siegler, R. S., Duncan, G. J., Davis-Kean, P. E., Duckworth, K., Claessens, A., Engel, M., Susperreguy, M. I., & Chen, M. (2012). Early predictors of high school mathematics achievement. *Psychological Science, 23*(7), 691–697. doi: 10.1177/0956797612440101.

Sies, H. (2020). Oxidative stress: Concept and some practical aspects. *Antioxidants* (Basel), *9*(9), 852. doi: 10.3390/antiox9090852.

Silberman, S. (2022, April). Chronic inequities: Measuring disease cost burden among older adults in the U.S. A health and retirement study analysis. *National Council on Aging*. https://ncoa.org/article/the-inequities-in-the-cost-of-chronic-disease-why-it-matters-for-older-adults.

Simpson, J. A., & Rholes, W. S. (2019). Adult attachment orientations and well-being during the transition to parenthood. *Current Opinion in Psychology, 25*, 47–52.

Sinclair, C., Joffe, T., Ginnivan, N., Parker, S. K., & Anstey, K. J. (2024). A scoping review of workplace interventions to promote positive attitudes toward older workers and reduce age-based discrimination. *Work, Aging and Retirement, 10*(2), 61–76.

Singh, D., Monga, A., de Moura, H. L., Zhang, X., Zibetti, M. V. W., & Regatte, R. R. (2023). Emerging trends in fast MRI using deep-learning reconstruction on undersampled k-space data: A systematic review. *Bioengineering, 10*, 1012. doi: 10.3390/bioengineering10091012.

Singh, K., Sharma, D., Kaur, M., Gauba, K., Thakur, J. S., & Kumar, R. (2017). Effect of health education on awareness about oral cancer and oral self-examination. *Journal of Education and Health Promotion*, *6*(1), 27.

Sinnott, J. D. (1984). Postformal reasoning: The relativistic stage. In M. Commons, F. Richards, & C. Armon (Eds.), *Beyond Formal Operations* (pp. 298–325). Praeger.

Sinnott, J. D. (1998). *The Development of Logic in Adulthood: Postformal Thought and its Applications*. Plenum Press.

Sinnott, J. D., Hilton, S., Wood, M., & Douglas, D. (2020). Relating flow, mindfulness, cognitive flexibility, and postformal thought: Two studies. *Journal of Adult Development, 27*(1), 1–11. doi: 10.1007/s10804-018-9320-2.

Siskowski, C. (2006). Young caregivers: Effect of family health situations on school performance. *The Journal of School Nursing, 22*(3), 163–169.

Skoblow, H. F., & Gilligan, M. (2025). Stressors and resources among adult child caregivers in the presence or absence of siblings. *The Gerontologist, 65*(3), gnaf006.

Smith, B. W., deCruz-Dixon, N., Erickson, K., Guzman, A., Phan, A., & Schodt, K. (2023). The effects of an online positive psychology course on happiness, health, and well-being. *Journal of Happiness Studies, 24*(3), 1145–1167.

Smith, J. (2024). Respiratory health and aging: Understanding age-related changes, common conditions, and effective strategies for maintaining optimal lung function in older adults. *Journal of Clinical Respiratory Medicine, 8*(4), 222. www.alliedacademies.org/journal-clinical-respiratory-medicine/.

Smith, M. D., Kromash, R., Siebert, S., Gratz, K. L., Moore, K. E., & Tull, M. T. (2025). The relation of health anxiety to treatment utilization among patients with substance use disorders: The moderating role of racial/ethnic background. *Substance Use & Misuse, 60*(1), 28–38. doi: 10.1080/10826084.2024.2403122.

Snyder, C. R. (2002). Hope theory: Rainbows in the mind. *Psychological Inquiry, 13*(4), 249–275.

Snyder, C. R., Rand, K. L., & Sigmon, D. R. (2002). Hope theory: A member of the positive psychology family. In C. R. Snyder & S. J. Lopez (Eds.), *Handbook of Positive Psychology* (pp. 257–276). Oxford University Press.

Snyder, C. R., Sympson, S. C., Ybasco, F. C., Borders, T. F., Babyak, M. A., & Higgins, R. L. (1996). Development and validation of the State Hope Scale. *Journal of Personality and Social Psychology, 70*(2), 321.

Sobhan., N. (2024). An overview of the anatomy and physiology of respiration. *Eurasian Journal of Chemical, Medical & Petroleum Research (EJCMPR), 3*(2), 499–514.

Social Security Administration (2023). *Annual Statistical Supplement to the Social Security Bulletin.* www.ssa.gov/policy/docs/statcomps/supplement/2023/supplement23.pdf. Accessed November 13, 2025.

Solberg, B., Glavin, K., Berg, R. C., & Olsvold, N. (2023). "Opening up a well of emotions": A qualitative study of men's emotional experiences in the transition to fatherhood. *Nursing Open, 10*, 13. doi: 10.1002/nop2.1482.

Solomon, J. C. (1996). Humor and aging well. *American Behavioral Scientist, 39*(3), 249–271.

Soma, T., & Nagata, M. (2022). Immunosenescence, inflammaging, and lung senescence in asthma in the elderly. *Biomolecules, 12*(10), 1456. doi: 10.3390/biom12101456.

Son, J. M., & Lee, C. (2021). Aging: All roads lead to mitochondria. *Seminars in Cell & Developmental Biology, 116*, 160–168. doi: 10.1016/j.semcdb.2021.02.006.

Song, C., Buysse, A., Zhang, W. H., & Dewaele, A. (2024). Minority stress and relationship satisfaction in same-sex couples: A meta-analysis. *Family Relations, 73*(5), 2996–3014.

Sörensen, J., Rzeszutek, M., & Gasik, R. (2021). Social support and post-traumatic growth among a sample of arthritis patients: Analysis in light of conservation of resources theory. *Current Psychology, 40*, 2017–2025.

Southerland, J. L., Slawson, D. L., Pack, R., Sörensen, S., Lyness, J. M., & Hirsch, J. K. (2016). Trait hope and preparation for future care needs among older adult primary care patients. *Clinical Gerontologist, 39*(2), 117–126.

Spearman, C. (1904). "General intelligence," objectively determined and measured. *The American Journal of Psychology, 15*(2), 201–293. doi: 10.2307/1412107.

Spencer, S. A., Rylance, J., Quint, J. K., Gordon, S. B., Dark, P., & Morton, B. (2023). Use of hospital services by patients with chronic conditions in sub-Saharan Africa: A systematic review and meta-analysis. *Bulletin of the World Health Organization, 101*(9), 558–570G. doi: 10.2471/BLT.22.289597.

Spies, G., Ahmed-Leitao, F., Hoddinott, G., & Seedat, S. (2022). Effects of unhealthy alcohol use on brain morphometry and neurocognitive function among people with HIV. *Journal of NeuroVirology, 28*, 35–45. doi: 10.1007/s13365-021-01027-2.

Sridhar, S., Khamaj, A., & Asthana, M. K. (2023). Cognitive neuroscience perspective on memory: Overview and summary. *Frontiers in Human Neuroscience, 17*, 1217093. doi: 10.3389/fnhum.2023.1217093.

Stabellini, N., Cullen, J., Bittencourt, M. S., Moore, J. X., Sutton, A., Nain, P., Hamerschlak, N., Weintraub, N. L., Dent, S., Tsai, M. H., Banerjee, A., Ghosh, A. K., Sadler, D., Coughlin, S., Barac, A., Shanahan, J., Montero, A. J., & Guha, A. (2024). Allostatic load/chronic stress and cardiovascular outcomes in patients diagnosed with breast, lung, or colorectal cancer. *Journal of the Americal Heart Association, 13*(14), e033295. doi: 10.1161/JAHA.123.033295.

Stanton, A. L., & Revenson, T. A. (2013). Adjustment to chronic disease: Progress and promise in research. In H. S. Friedman (Ed.), *The Oxford Handbook of Health Psychology* (pp. 242–268). Oxford University Press.

Stanton, A. L., Revenson, T. A., & Tennen, H. (2007). Health psychology: Psychological adjustment to chronic disease. *Annual Review of Psychology, 58*(1), 565–592.

Starr, R., Tadi, P., & Pfleghaar, N. (2024). Brain Death. *StatPearls*. www.ncbi.nlm.nih.gov/books/NBK538159/.

Statista (2023). LGBT identification in the U.S. www.statista.com/statistics/719674/american-adults-who-identify-as-homosexual-bisexual-or-transgender/#:~:text=In%202023%2C%207.6%20percent%20of,surveyed%20adults%20identified%20as%20LGBT.

Staudinger, U. M., & Greve, W. (2015). Resilience and aging. In N. A. Pachana (Ed.), *Encyclopedia of Geropsychology*, (pp. 1–9). Springer.

Steenland, K., Karnes, C., Seals, R., Carnevale, C., Hermida, A., & Levey, A. (2012). Late-life depression as a risk factor for mild cognitive impairment or Alzheimer's disease in 30 US Alzheimer's disease centers. *Journal of Alzheimer's Disease*, 31, 265–275. doi: 10.3233/JAD-2012-111922.

Stein, J. D., Khawaja, A. P., & Weizer, J. S. (2021). Glaucoma in adults-screening, diagnosis, and management: A review. *JAMA*, 325, 164–174. doi: 10.1001/jama.2020.21899.

Steptoe, A. (2019). Happiness and health. *Annual Review of Public Health, 40*, 339–359.

Steptoe, A., & Wardle, J. (2011). Positive affect measured using ecological momentary assessment and survival in older men and women. *Proceedings of the National Academy of Sciences, 108*(45), 18244–18248.

Sternberg, R. (1988). *The Triarchic Mind: A New Theory of Intelligence*. Viking Press.

Sternberg, R. J. (1997). Construct validation of a triangular love scale. *European Journal of Social Psychology, 27*(3), 313–335.

Sternberg, R. J. (2020). Rethinking what we mean by intelligence. *Phi Delta Kappan, 102*(3), 36–41. doi: 10.1177/0031721720970700.

Sternberg, R. J. (2022). The search for the elusive basic processes underlying human intelligence: Historical and contemporary perspectives. *Journal of Intelligence, 10*(2), 1–21. doi: 10.3390/jintelligence10020028.

Sternberg, R. J., Preiss, D. D., & Karami, S. (2023). An historical causal-chain theory of conceptions of intelligence. *Review of General Psychology, 27*(3), 320–335. doi: 10.1177/10892680231158790.

Stevenson, A., Misra, S., Girma, E., Isvoranu, A. M., Akena, D., Alemayehu, M., Atwoli, L., Gelaye, B., Gichuru, S, Kariuki, S. M., Kwobah, E. K., Kyebuzibwa, J., Mwema, R. M., Newman, C. P., Newton, C. R. J. C., Ongeri, L., Stroud 2nd, R. E., Teferra, S., Koenen,K. C., & Seedat, S. (2024). Relationships between trauma types and psychotic symptoms: A network analysis of patients with psychotic disorders in a large, multi-country study in East Africa. *Comprehensive Psychiatry, 133*, 152504. doi: 10.1016/j.comppsych.2024.152504.

Stewart, A. L., Hays, R. D., & Ware Jr., J. E. (1988). The MOS short-form general health survey: Reliability and validity in a patient population. *Medical Care, 26*(7), 724–735. doi: 10.1097/00005650-198807000-00007.

Stocker, C. M., Gilligan, M., Klopack, E. T., Conger, K. J., Lanthier, R. P., Neppl, T. K., O'Neal, C. W., & Wickrama, K. A. S. (2020). Sibling relationships in older adulthood: Links with loneliness and well-being. *Journal of Family Psychology, 34*(2), 175–185. doi: 10.1037/fam0000586.

Stone, A. A., Schwartz, J. E., Broderick, J. E., & Deaton, A. (2010). A snapshot of the age distribution of psychological well-being in the United States. *Proceedings of the National Academy of Sciences, 107*(22), 9985–9990.

Stone, J. B. (1998). Traditional and contemporary Lakota death, dying, grief, and bereavement beliefs and practices: A qualitative study. *All Graduate Theses and Dissertations, Spring 1920 to Summer 2023, 4055*. https://digitalcommons.usu.edu/etd/4055.

Storeng, S. H., Sund, E. R., & Krokstad, S. (2020). Prevalence, clustering and combined effects of lifestyle behaviours and their association with health after retirement age in a prospective cohort study, the Nord-Trøndelag Health Study, Norway. *BMC Public Health*, 20, 1–10.

Strelow, B., O'Laughlin, D., Anderson, T., Cyriac, J., Buzzard, J., & Klindworth, A. (2024). Menopause decoded: What's happening and how to manage it. *Journal of Primary Care and Community Health, 15*. doi: 10.1177/21501319241307460.

Striedter, G. F., Srinivasan, S., & Monuki, E. S. (2015). Cortical folding: When, where, how, and why? *Annual Review of Neuroscience, 38*(1), 291–307. doi: 10.1146/annurev-neuro-071714-034128.

Stroebe, M., & Schut, H. (1999) The Dual Process Model of coping with bereavement: Rationale and description, *Death Studies, 23*(3), 197–224. doi: 10.1080/074811899201046.

Stroebe, M., & Schut, H. (2010). The Dual Process Model of coping with bereavement: A decade on. *OMEGA – Journal of Death and Dying, 61*(4), 273–289. doi: 10.2190/OM.61.4.b.

Stroebe, M., Schut, H., & Boerner, K. (2017). Cautioning health-care professionals: Bereaved persons are misguided through the stages of grief. *OMEGA – Journal of Death & Dying, 74*, 455–473. doi: 10.1177/0030222817691870.

Stumme, J., Krämer, C., Miller, T., Schreiber, J., Caspers, S., & Jockwitz, C. (2022). Interrelating differences in structural and functional connectivity in the older adult's brain. *Human Brain Mapping, 43*(18), 5543–5561. doi: 10.1002/hbm.26030.

Su, J., Jogamoto, A., Yoshimura, H., & Yang, L. J. (2021). Menopausal symptoms among Chinese and Japanese women: Differences and similarities. *Menopause, 29*(1), 73–81. doi: 10.1097/GME.0000000000001874.

Sun, F., Norman, I. J., & While, A. E. (2013). Physical activity in older people: A systematic review. *BMC Public Health, 13*, 1–17. doi: 10.1186/1471-2458-13-449.

Sun, F. W., Stepanovic, M. R., Andreano, J., Barrett, L. F., Touroutoglou, A., & Dickerson, B. C. (2016). Youthful brains in older adults: Preserved neuroanatomy in the default mode and salience networks contributes to youthful memory in superaging. *J Neurosci, 36*, 9659–9668. doi: 10.1523/JNEUROSCI.1492-16.2016 pmid:27629716.

Sun, H., Saeedi, P., Karuranga, S., Pinkepank, M., Ogurtsova, K., Duncan, B. B., Stein, C,. Basit, A., Chan, J. C. N., Mbanya, J. C., Pavkov, M. E., Ramachandaran, A., Wild, S. H., James, S., Herman, W. H., Zhang, P., Bommer, C., Kuo, S., Boyko, E. J., & Magliano, D. J. (2022). IDF Diabetes Atlas: Global, regional and country-level diabetes prevalence estimates for 2021 and projections for 2045. *Diabetes Res Clin Pract, 183*, 109119. doi: 10.1016/j.diabres.2021.109119.

Super, D. E. (1980). A life-span, life-space approach to career development. *Journal of Vocational Behavior, 16*(3), 282–298.

Swanson, H. L. (2017). Verbal and visual-spatial working memory: What develops over a life span? *Developmental Psychology, 53*(5), 971–995. doi: 10.1037/dev0000291.

Sweeney, T. J., & Witmer, J. M. (1991). Beyond social interest: Striving toward optimum health and wellness. *Individual Psychology: Journal of Adlerian Theory, Research and Practice, 47*(4), 527–540.

Sze, J. A., Gyurak, A., Goodkind, M. S., & Levenson, R. W. (2012). Greater emotional empathy and prosocial behavior in late life. *Emotion, 12*(5), 1129.

Takiguchi, Y., Kikutani, M., & Matsui, M. (2023). Evaluating positive effects of leisure from a life-course perspective: A literature review. *Psychologia, 65*(1), 35–57.

Tanaka, T., Narazaki, M., & Kishimoto, T. (2014). IL-6 in inflammation, immunity, and disease. *Cold Spring Harbor Perspectives in Biology*, 6(10), a016295. doi: 10.1101/cshperspect.a016295.

Tandler, N., & Proyer, R. T. (2022). Deriving information on play and playfulness of 3–5-year-olds from short written descriptions: Analyzing the frequency of usage of indicators of playfulness and their associations with maternal playfulness. *Behavioral Sciences, 12*(10), 385.

Tandler, N., Schilling-Friedemann, S., Frazier, L. D., Sendatzki, R., & Proyer, R. T. (2024). New insights into the contributions of playfulness to dealing with stress at work: Correlates of self-and peer-rated playfulness and coping strategies. *New Ideas in Psychology, 75*, 101109.

Tanner, J. L. (2006). Recentering during emerging adulthood: A critical turning point in life span human development. In J. J. Arnett & J. L. Tanner (Eds.), *Emerging Adults in America: Coming of Age in the 21st Century* (pp. 21–55). APA Books.

Tavares, J., Cohen, M. A., Silberman, S., & Popham, L. (2023). Medicaid utilization among middle-age and older adults: A health and retirement study longitudinal analysis (1998 to 2014). *Journal of Aging & Social Policy, 35*(3), 343–359.

Taylor, E. H., Hofmeyr, R. H., Torborg, A., Tonder, C. V., Boden, R., Earle, E., Nejthardt, M. B., Kabambi, K. F., Isaacs, M. A., Usenbo, A., Gerber, C., Spuy, K. V., Mrara, B., Ndhlovu, T., Chen, A., Swanevelder, J., Coetzee, J., & Biccard, B. M. (2020). Risk factors and interventions associated with mortality or survival in adult COVID-19 patients admitted to critical care: A systematic review and meta-analysis. *South African Journal of Anaesthesia and Analgesia, 26*(3), 116–127. doi: 10.36303/SAJAA.2020.26.3.2428.

Taylor, E. J. (1993). Factors associated with meaning in life among people with recurrent cancer. *Oncology Nursing Forum, 20*(9) 1399–1405, discussion, 1406–1407.

Taylor, M. J. (2023, February 13). Have more sex, please! *The New York Times*. www.nytimes.com/2023/02/13/opinion/have-more-sex-please.html.

Taylor, P. (2009). Growing old in America: Expectations vs. reality. *Pew Research Center*. www.pewsocialtrends.org/2009/06/29/growing-old-in-america-expectations-vs-reality/.

Taylor-Piliae, R. E., Newell, K. A., Cherin, R., Lee, M. J., King, A. C., & Haskell, W. L. (2010). Effects of Tai Chi and Western exercise on physical and cognitive functioning in healthy community-dwelling older adults. *Journal of Aging and Physical Activity, 18*(3), 261–279.

Teo, Z. L., Tham, Y. C., Yu, M., Chee, M. L., Rim, T. H., ...*et al*. (2021). Global prevalence of Diabetic Retinopathy and projection of burden through 2045: Systematic review and meta-analysis. *Ophthalmology, 128*(11), 1580–1591. doi: 10.1016/j.ophtha.2021.04.027.

Ter-Pogossian, M. M., Phelps, M. E., Hoffman, E. J., & Mullani, N. A. (1975). A positron-emission transaxial tomograph for nuclear imaging (PETT). *Radiology, 114* (1), 89–98. doi: 10.1148/114.1.89.

Tesfaye, A. H., Sendekie, A. K., Kabito, G. G., Engdaw, G. T., Argaw, G. S., Desye, B., Angelo, A. A., Aragaw, F. M., & Abere, G. (2024). Post-traumatic stress disorder and associated factors among internally displaced persons in Africa: A systematic review and meta-analysis. *PLoS One, 19(4)*, e0300894. doi: 10.1371/journal.pone.0300894.

Theeke, L., Carpenter, R. D., Mallow, J., & Theeke, E. (2019). Gender differences in loneliness, anger, depression, self-management ability and biomarkers of chronic illness in chronically ill mid-life adults in Appalachia. *Applied Nursing Research, 45*, 55–62.

Thoits, P. A. (2010). Stress and health: Major findings and policy implications. *Journal of Health and Social Behavior, 51*(Suppl.), S41–S53.

Thomas, T. K., Ritter, T., Bruden, D., Bruce, M., Byrd, K., Goldberger, R. Dobson, J., Hickel, K., Smith, J., & Hennessy, T. (2016). Impact of providing in-home water service on the rates of infectious diseases: Results from four communities in Western Alaska. *Journal of Water and Health, 14*(1), 132–141.

Thomas Tobin, C. S., Gutiérrez, Á., Farmer, H. R., Erving, C. L., & Hargrove, T. W. (2023). Intersectional approaches to minority aging research. *Current Epidemiology Reports, 10*(1), 33–43.

Thompson, A., Smith, M. A., McNeill, A., & Pollet, T. V. (2024). Friendships, loneliness and psychological wellbeing in older adults: A limit to the benefit of the number of friends. *Ageing & Society, 44*(5), 1090–1115.

Thurstone, L. L., & Thurstone, T. G. (1949). *Examiner Manual for the SRA Primary Mental Abilities Test (Form 10-14)*. Science Research Associates.

Togonu-Bickersteth, F., Akinyemi, A. I., Aransiola, J. O., Adegoke, A. A., & Popoola, B. I. (2023). Subjective wellbeing of community dwelling older adults in Nigeria. *Journal of Cross-Cultural Gerontology, 38*(3), 285–306. doi: 10.1007/s10823-023-09483-5.

Tong, L., Miguel, C., Panagiotopoulou, O.-M., Karyotaki, E., & Cuijpers, P. (2023). Psychotherapy for adult depression in low- and middle-income countries: An updated systematic review and meta-analysis. *Psychological Medicine, 53*(16), 7473–7483. doi: 10.1017/S0033291723002246.

Trammell, A. R., Goldstein, F. C., Parker, M. W., & Hajjar, I. M. (2024). Characterization of African-American super-agers in the National Alzheimer's Coordinating Center cohort. *Journal of the American Geriatrics Society, 72*, 1995–2005.

Tran Van Hoi, E., De Glas, N. A., Portielje, J. E. A., Van Heemst, D., Van Den Bos, F., Jochems, S. P., & Mooijaart, S. P. (2023). Biomarkers of the ageing immune system and their association with frailty – A systematic review. *Experimental Gerontology, 176*, 112163. doi: 10.1016/j.exger.2023.112163.

Troll, L. E., & Fingerman, K. L. (1996). Connections between parents and their adult children. In C. Magai & S. H. Mcfadden (Eds.), *Handbook of Emotion, Adult Development, and Aging* (pp. 185–205). Academic Press.

Trubitsyn, A. G. (2020). The mechanism of programmed aging: The way to create a real remedyor senescence. *Current Aging Science, 13*(1), 31–41.doi: 10.2174/1874609812666191014111422.

Tulving, E. (1972). Episodic and semantic memory. *Organization of Memory, 1*, 381–403.

Turkson-Ocran, R. N., Nmezi, N. A., Botchway, M. O., Szanton, S. L., Golden, S. H., Cooper, L. A., & Commodore-Mensah, Y. (2020). Comparison of cardiovascular disease risk factors among African immigrants and African Americans: An analysis of the 2010 to 2016 National Health Interview Surveys. *Journal of the American Heart Association, 9*(5), e013220. doi: 10.1161/JAHA.119.013220.

Turvey, C. L., & Klein, D. M. (2008). Remission from depression comorbid with chronic illness and physical impairment. *American Journal of Psychiatry, 165*(5), 569–574.

Twenge, J. M. (2017). *iGen: Why Today's Super-connected Kids are Growing Up Less Rebellious, More Tolerant, Less Happy—and Completely Unprepared for Adulthood—and What That Means for the Rest of Us*. Simon and Schuster.

Twenge, J. M., & Campbell, W. K. (2018). Cultural individualism is linked to later onset of adult-role responsibilities across time and regions. *Journal of Cross-Cultural Psychology, 49*(4), 673–682. doi: 10.1177/0022022118764838.

Twycross, R. (2024). Assisted dying: Principles, possibilities, and practicalities. An English physician's perspective. *BMC Palliative Care, 23*, 99. doi: 10.1186/s12904-024-01422-6.

Ubel, P. A., Loewenstein, G., & Jepson, C. (2005). Disability and sunshine: Can hedonic predictions be improved by drawing attention to focusing illusions or emotional adaptation? *Journal of Experimental Psychology: Applied, 11*(2), 111.

Uhlenbusch, N., Löwe, B., Härter, M., Schramm, C., Weiler-Normann, C., & Depping, M. K. (2019). Depression and anxiety in patients with different rare chronic diseases: A cross-sectional study. *PloS One, 14*(2), e0211343.

Umucu, E., Chan, F., Phillips, B., Tansey, T., Berven, N., & Hoyt, W. (2024). Evaluating optimism, hope, resilience, coping flexibility, secure attachment, and PERMA as a well-being model for college life adjustment of student veterans: A hierarchical regression analysis. *Rehabilitation Counseling Bulletin, 67*(2), 94–110.

UNAIDS (2025). Fact sheet 2025. www.unaids.org/sites/default/files/2025-07/2025_Global_HIV_Factsheet_en.pdf. Accessed July 26, 2025.

United Nations, Department of Economic and Social Affairs, Population Division (2017). World population ageing 2017—highlights. (ST/ESA/SER.A/397).

United Nations Office on Drugs and Crime (2024). UNODC World Drug Report 2024: Harms of world drug problem continue to mount amid expansions in drug use and markets. www.unodc.org/unodc/en/press/releases/2024/June/unodc-world-drug-report-2024_-harms-of-world-drug-problem-continue-to-mount-amid-expansions-in-drug-use-and-markets.html. Accessed January 8, 2025.

Uppal, S. (2006). Impact of the timing, type and severity of disability on the subjective well-being of individuals with disabilities. *Social Science & Medicine, 63*(2), 525–539.

U.S. Department of Health and Human Services (2000). Effects on well-being and quality of life. In *Oral Health in America: A Report of the Surgeon General*. National Institute of Dental and Craniofacial Research. http://www.nidcr.nih.gov/DataStatistics/SurgeonGeneral/sgr/chap6.htm.

U.S. Fish & Wildlife Service (2015, June 12). U.S. fish and wildlife service finalizes rule listing all chimpanzees as endangered under the endangered species act [Press Release]. www.fws.gov/press-release/2015-06/us-fish-and-wildlife-service-finalizes-rule-listing-all-chimpanzees.

Vaish, K., Patra, S., & Chhabra, P. (2020). Functional disability among elderly: A community-based cross-sectional study. *Journal of Family Medicine and Primary Care, 9*, 253.

Valenza, M., Facchinetti, R., Menegoni, G., Steardo, L., & Scuderi, C. (2021). Alternative targets to fight Alzheimer's disease: Focus on astrocytes. *Biomolecules, 11*(4), 600. doi: 10.3390/biom11040600.

Van Acker, I., Song, C., Elaut, E., & Dewaele, A. (2025). LGBTQ+ partnerships. In D. Mortelmans, L. Bernardi, & B. Perelli-Harris (Eds.), *Research Handbook on Partnering across the Life Course* (pp. 89–101). Edward Elgar Publishing.

van Heemst, D. (2010). Insulin, IGF-1 and longevity. *Aging and Disease, 1*, 147–157.

van Zyl, L. E., Gaffaney, J., van der Vaart, L., Dik, B. J., & Donaldson, S. I. (2024). The critiques and criticisms of positive psychology: A systematic review. *The Journal of Positive Psychology, 19*(2), 206–235.

Vanhaelen, Q. (2019). Non-programmed (nonadaptive) aging theories. In D. Gu & M. Dupre, M. (Eds.), *Encyclopedia of Gerontology and Population Aging*. Springer, Cham. doi: 10.1007/978-3-319-69892-2_50-1.

Vargo, D., Zhu, L., Benwell, B., & Yan, Z. (2021). Digital technology use during COVID-19 pandemic: A rapid review. *Human Behavior and Emerging Technologies, 3*(1), 13–24.

Vaquero, J. J. & Kinahan, P. (2015). Positron Emission Tomography: Current challenges and opportunities for technological advances in clinical and preclinical imaging systems. *Annual Review of Biomedical Engineering, 17*, 385–414. doi: 10.1146/annurev-bioeng-071114-040723.

Vauclair, C. M., Hanke, K., Huang, L. L., & Abrams, D. (2017). Are Asian cultures really less ageist than Western ones? It depends on the questions asked. *International Journal of Psychology, 52*(2), 136–144.

Veenhoven, R. (2008). Healthy happiness: Effects of happiness on physical health and the consequences for preventive health care. *Journal of Happiness Studies, 9*(3), 449–469.

Veenhoven, R., & Hagerty, M. (2006). Rising happiness in nations 1946–2004: A reply to Easterlin. *Social Indicators Research, 79*(3), 421–436.

Vehkalahti, K., Armila, P., & Sivenius, A. (2021). Emerging adulthood in the time of pandemic: The COVID-19 crisis in the lives of rural young adults in Finland. *YOUNG, 29*(4), 399–416.

Venkatapuram, S., & Thiyagarajan, J. A. (2023). The capability approach and the WHO healthy ageing framework (for the UN Decade of Healthy Ageing). *Age & Ageing, 52*, iv6–iv9.

Verbrugge, L. M., & Yang, L.-S. (2002). Aging with disability and disability with aging. *Journal of Disability Policy Studies, 12*(4), 253–267.

Vidaurreta, M., Lopez-Dicastillo, O., Serrano-Monzo, I., Belintxon, M., Bermejo-Martins, E., & Mujika, A. (2022). Placing myself in a new normalized life: The process of becoming a first-time father. A grounded theory study. *Nursing & Health Sciences, 24*(1), 11. doi: 10.1111/nhs.12906.

Vigezzi, G. P., Gaetti, G., Gianfredi, V., Frascella, B., Gentile, L., d'Errico, A., Stuckler, D., Ricceri, F., Costa, G., Odone, A., Amerio, A., Ardito, C., Carioli, G., Costa, G., d'Errico, A., Fontana, D., Frascella, B., Gaetti, G., Gentile, L., & Gianfredi, V. (2021). Transition to retirement impact on health and lifestyle habits: Analysis from a nationwide Italian cohort. *BMC Public Health, 21*(1). doi: 10.1186/s12889-021-11670-3.

Villani, A., Ferrillo, M., Fabbrocini, G., Ocampo-Garza, S. S., Scalvenzi, M., & Ruggiero, A. (2023). Hair aging and hair disorders in elderly patients. *International Journal of Trichology, 14*(6), 191–196. doi: 10.4103/ijt.ijt_90_21.

Vinodh Kumar, G., Lacey, S., & Sathian, K. (2023). Physical activity is associated with behavioral and neural changes across the lifespan. *Neuroscience Letters, 810*, Article 137355. doi: 10.1016/j.neulet.2023.137355.

Vints, W. A. J., Ahwaz, F. G., Westhof-Jacobs, C., Drozdova-Statkevičienė, M., Česnaitienė, V. J., Ziv, G., Pauwels, L., Levin, O., Verbunt, J., & Masiulis, N. (2024) The effects of a single bout of high-intense strength exercise on cognitive function and postural dual-task control in older adults. *International Journal of Sport and Exercise Psychology, 22*(8), 2064–2084, doi: 10.1080/1612197X.2023.2255604.

Viola, E., Martorana, M., Airoldi, C., Meini, C., Ceriotti, D., De Vito, M., De Ambrosi, D., & Faggiano, F. (2023). The role of music in promoting health and wellbeing:

A systematic review and meta-analysis. *European Journal of Public Health, 33*(4), 738–745. doi: 10.1093/eurpub/ckad063.

Vogels, E. A., & McClain, C. (2023). Key findings about online dating in the U.S. *Pew Research Center*. www.pewresearch.org/short-reads/2023/02/02/key-findings-about-online-datingin-the-u-s/.

Vohs, K. D., & Baumeister, R. F. (Eds.) (2011). *Handbook of Selfregulation: Research, Theory, and Applications* (2nd ed.). Guilford Press.

Vondracek, F. W., & Porfeli, E. J. (2011). Fostering self-concept and identity constructs in developmental career psychology. In P. J. Hartung & L. M. Subich (Eds.), *Developing Self in Work and Career: Concepts, Cases, and Contexts* (pp. 53–70). American Psychological Association. doi: 10.1037/12348-004.

Vyas, L. (2022). "New normal" at work in a post-COVID world: Work–life balance and labor markets. *Policy and Society, 41*(1), 155–167.

Vyawahare, H., & Shinde, P. (2022). Age-related Macular Degeneration: Epidemiology, pathophysiology, diagnosis, and treatment. *Cureus, 14*(9), e29583. doi: 10.7759/cureus.29583.

Wagner, A. R., Kobel, M. J. & Merfeld, D. M. (2023). Increased roll tilt thresholds are associated with subclinical postural instability in asymptomatic adults aged 21 to 84 years. *Frontiers in Aging Neuroscience*, 15, 1207711. doi: 10.3389/fnagi.2023.1207711.

Waldinger, R. J., & Schulz, M. S. (2010). What's love got to do with it? Social functioning, perceived health, and daily happiness in married octogenarians. *Psychology and Aging, 25*(2), 422–431.

Walker, J. G., Jackson, H. J., & Littlejohn, G. O. (2004). Models of adjustment to chronic illness: Using the example of rheumatoid arthritis. *Clinical Psychology Review, 24*(4), 461–488.

Wallerstein, J. (2019). *The Good Marriage: How and Why Love Lasts*. Plunkett Lake Press.

Walsh, K., Gilmore, A. K., Barr, S. C., Frazier, P., Ledray, L. E., Acierno, R., Ruggiero, K. J., Kilpatrick, D. G., & Resnick, H. S. (2022). The role of discrimination experiences in postrape adjustment among racial and ethnic minority women. *Journal of Interpersonal Violence, 37*(19–20), NP17325–NP17343. doi: 10.1177/08862605211028006.

Wanberg, C. R., Ali, A. A., & Csillag, B. (2020). Job seeking: The process and experience of looking for a job. *Annual Review of Organizational Psychology and Organizational Behavior, 7*(1), 315–337.

Wanberg, C. R., Kanfer, R., Hamann, D. J., & Zhang, Z. (2016). Age and reemployment success after job loss: An integrative model and meta-analysis. *Psychological Bulletin, 142*(4), 400.

Wang, C. L., Liu, Y., Gao, Y. L., Li, Q. S., Liu, Y. C., & Chai, Y. F. (2023). Factors affecting do-not-attempt-resuscitation (DNAR) decisions among adult patients in the emergency department of a general tertiary teaching hospital in China: A retrospective observational study. *BMJ Open, 13*(10), e075714. doi: 10.1136/bmjopen-2023-075714.

Wang, F., Ren, S. Y., Chen, J. F., Liu, K., Li, R. X., Li, Z. F., Hu, B., Niu, J. Q., Xiao, L., Chan, J. R., Mei, F. (2020). Myelin degeneration and diminished myelin renewal contribute to age-related deficits in memory. *Nature Neuroscience, 23*(4), 481–486. doi: 10.1038/s41593-020-0588-8.

Wang, J. R., Li, R. Q., & Huang, X. F. (2024). Research progress in functional regeneration methods and mechanisms of taste buds. *Chinese Journal of Stomatology, 59*, 389–393.

Wang, M., & Shultz, K. S. (2010). Employee retirement: A review and recommendations for future investigation. *Journal of Management, 36*(1), 172–206.

Wang, N., Yan, X., Imm, K., Xu, T., Li, S., Gawronska, J., Wang, R., Smith, L., Yang, L., & Cao, C. (2024). Racial and ethnic disparities in prevalence and correlates of depressive symptoms and suicidal ideation among adults in the United States, 2017–2020 pre-pandemic. *J Affect Disord, 345,* 272–283. doi: 10.1016/j.jad.2023.10.138.

Wang, Q., Chair, S. Y., Wong, E. M. L., & Li, X. (2016). The effects of music intervention on sleep quality in community-dwelling elderly. *Journal of Alternative and Complementary Medicine, 22,* 576–584.

Watson, K. B., Wiltz, J. L., Nhim, K., Kaufmann, R. B., Thomas, C. W., & Greenlund. K. J. (2025). Trends in multiple chronic conditions among US adults, by life stage, Behavioral Risk Factor Surveillance System, 2013–2023. *Preventing Chronic Disease, 22,* 240539. doi: 10.5888/pcd22.240539.

Watson-Jones, R. E., Busch, J. T. A., Harris, P. L., & Legare, C. H. (2017). Does the body survive death? Cultural variation in beliefs about life everlasting. *Cognitive Science, 41* (Suppl 3), 455–476. doi: 10.1111/cogs.12430.

Watters, A. M., Pearce, C., Backman, C. L., & Suto, M. J. (2013). Occupational engagement and meaning: The experience of ikebana practice. *Journal of Occupational Science, 20*(3), 262–277.

Ward, H., Whitaker, M., Flower, B., Tang, S. N., Atchison, C., Darzi, A., Donnelly, C. A., Cann, A., Diggle, P. J., Ashby, D., Riley, S., Barclay, W. S., Elliott, P., & Cooke, G. S. (2022). Population antibody responses following COVID-19 vaccination in 212,102 individuals. *Nature Communications, 13,* 907, 1–6. doi: 10.1038/s41467-022-28527-x.

Ward, R. A. (2010). How old am I? Perceived age in middle and later life. *The International Journal of Aging and Human Development, 71*(3), 167–184.

Ware Jr., J. E. (2000). SF-36 health survey update. *Spine, 25*(24), 3130–3139.

Watson, K. B., Wiltz, J. L., Nhim, K., Kaufmann, R. B., Thomas, C. W., & Greenlund, K. J. (2025). Trends in multiple chronic conditions among US adults, by life stage, Behavioral Risk Factor Surveillance System, 2013–2023. *Preventing Chronic Disease, 22,* 240539. doi: 10.5888/pcd22.240539.

Weeks, L. E., Keefe, J., & Macdonald, D. J. (2012). Factors predicting relocation among older adults. *Journal of Housing for the Elderly, 26*(4), 355–371.

Wei, W., Zhang, K., Chang, J., Zhang, S., Ma, L., Wang, H., Zhang, M., Zu, Z., Yang, L., Chen, F., Fan, C., & Li, X. (2024). Analyzing 20 years of resting-state fMRI research: Trends and collaborative networks revealed. *Brain Research, 1822,* 148634. doi: 10.1016/j.brainres.2023.148634.

Weinert, C., Cudney, S., & Spring, A. (2008). Evolution of a conceptual model for adaptation to chronic illness. *Journal of Nursing Scholarship, 40*(4), 364–372.

Weissman, C. (2010). "The Origins of Species: The debate between August Weismann and Moritz Wagner." *Journal of the History of Biology, 43,* 727–66.

Wells, Y. D., & Kendig, H. L. (1997). Health and well-being of spouse caregivers and the widowed. *The Gerontologist, 37*(5), 666–674.

West, L. J., Dember, W. N., & Epstein, W. (2024). Perception. *Encyclopedia Britannica.* www.britannica.com/topic/perception. Accessed June 26, 2024.

Wettstein, M., & Wahl, H. W. (2017). Plasticity of aging. In N. A. Pachana (Ed.), *Encyclopedia of Geropsychology* (pp. 1823–1831). Springer.

Wetzel, M., & Hank, K. (2020). Grandparents' relationship to grandchildren in the transition to adulthood. *Journal of Family Issues, 41*(10), 1885–1904.

Whitbourne, S. K., & Ebmeyer, J. B. (2013). *Identity and Intimacy in Marriage: A Study of Couples.* Springer Science & Business Media.

Whitfield, T., Barnhofer, T., Acabchuk, R., Cohen, A., Lee, M., Schlosser, M., Arenaza-Urquijo, E. M., Böttcher, A., Britton, W., Coll-Padros, N., Collette, F., Chételat, G., Dautricourt, S., Demnitz-King, H., Dumais, T., Klimecki, O., Meiberth, D., Moulinet, I., Müller, T., Parsons, E., Sager, L., Sannemann, L., Scharf, J., Schild, A. K., Touron, E., Wirth, M., Walker, Z., Moitra, E., Lutz, A., Lazar, S. W., Vago, D., Marchant, N. L. (2022). The effect of mindfulness-based programs on cognitive function in adults: A systematic review and meta-analysis. *Neuropsychology Review, 32*(3), 677–702. doi: 10.1007/s11065-021-09519-y.

Whitten, L. A. (2012). *Functional Magnetic Resonance Imaging (fMRI): An Invaluable Tool in Translational Neuroscience*. RTI Press. doi: 10.3768/rtipress.2012.op.0010.1212.

Wijeyaratne, L., Spruijt, O., Jayasinghe, S., Kane, S., Ramadasa, U., & Philip, J. (2025). What is a good death in South Asia? A systematic review and narrative synthesis. *Journal of Nursing Scholarship, 57*(4), 653–677. doi: 10.1111/jnu.70002.

Williams, D. R., Lawrence, J. A., & Davis, B. A. (2019). Racism and health: Evidence and needed research. *Annual Review of Public Health, 40*(1), 105–125. doi: 10.1146/annurev-publhealth-040218-043750.

Williams, D. R., & Mohammed, S. A. (2013). Racism and health I: Pathways and scientific evidence. *American Behavioral Scientist, 57*(8), 1152–1173. doi: 10.1177/0002764213487340.

Williams, G. C. (1957). Pleiotropy, natural selection and the evolution of senescence. *Evolution* (N.Y). *11*, 398–411.

Willis, A. W., Roberts, E., Beck, J. C., Fiske, B., Ross, W., Savica, R., Van Den Eeden, S. K., Tanner, C. M., Marras, C., & Parkinson's Foundation P4 Group (2022). Incidence of Parkinson disease in North America. *NPJ Parkinsons Disease, 8*, 170. doi: 10.1038/s41531-022-00410-y.

Wilson, K. A., Bar, S., Dammer, E. B., Carrera, E. M., Hodge, B. A., Hilsabeck, T. A. U., Bons, J., Brownridge III, G. W., Beck, J. N., Rose, J., Granath-Panelo, M., Nelson, C. S., Qi, Grace, Gerencser, A. A., Lan, Jianfeng, Afenjar, A., Chawla, G., Brem, R. B., Campeau, P. M., Bellen, H. J., Schilling, B., Seyfried, N. T., Ellerby, L. M., & Kapahi, P. (2024). OXR1 maintains the retromer to delay brain aging under dietary restriction. *Nature Communications, 15*, 467 (2024). doi: 10.1038/s41467-023-44343-3.

Winterhalter, P. R., & Simm, A. (2022). How justified is the assumption of programmed aging in reminiscence of Weismann's theories? *Biochemistry (Moscow), 87*(1), 35–53. doi: 10.1134/S0006297922010047.

Witmer, J. M., & Sweeney, T. J. (1992). A holistic model for wellness and prevention over the life span. *Journal of Counseling and Development, 71*(2), 140–148.

Witmer, J. M., Sweeney, T. J., & Myers, J. E. (1998). *The Wheel of Wellness*. Authors.

World Health Organization (1997) Quality of Life Assessment (WHOQOL): Development and general psychometric properties. *Social Science Medicine, 46*(12), 1569–1585. doi: 10.1016/s0277-9536(98)00009-4.

World Health Organization (2001). IFC: International classification of functioning, disability and health. WHO: Geneva, Switzerland.

World Health Organization (2015). World report on ageing and health. *World Population Review*. https://worldpopulationreview.com/country-rankings/life-expectancy-by-country#10-countries-with-the-shortest-life-expectancies-united-nations-2023.

World Health Organization (2017). Clinical criteria for the determination of death. WHO: Geneva: Switzerland. Licence: CC BY-NC-SA 3.0 IGO.

World Health Organization (2019). 2019 STEPS country report Bhutan. www.who.int/publications/m/item/2019-steps-country-report-bhutan. Accessed on July 29, 2025.

World Health Organization (2022a). Mental health. www.who.int/news-room/fact-sheets/detail/mental-health-strengthening-our-response. Accessed January 3, 2025.

World Health Organization (2022b). Mental disorders. www.who.int/news-room/fact-sheets/detail/mental-disorders. Accessed January 5, 2025.

World Health Organization (2022c). Refugee and immigrant health. www.who.int/news-room/fact-sheets/detail/refugee-and-migrant-health. Accessed January 5, 2025.

World Health Organization (2023a). Achieving well-being: A global framework for integrating well-being into public health utilizing a health promotion approach. www.who.int/publications/m/item/wha-76—achieving-well-being–a-global-framework-for-integrating-well-being-into-public-health-utilizing-a-health-promotion-approach. Accessed January 5, 2025.

World Health Organization (2023b). Burden of disease attributable to unsafe drinking-water, sanitation and hygiene, 2019 update. WHO: Geneva: Switzerland. Licence: CC BY-NC-SA 3.0 IGO. https://iris.who.int/handle/10665/370026. Retrieved April 13, 2025.

World Health Organization (2023c). Dementia. www.who.int/news-room/fact-sheets/detail/dementia. Accessed February 9, 2025.

World Health Organization (2024a). COVID-19 epidemiological update. WHO: Geneva, Switzerland. www.who.int/publications/m/item/covid-19-epidemiological-update-edition-173. Retrieved March 16, 2025.

World Health Organization (2024b). Health and well-being. www.who.int/Data/Gho/Data/Major-Themes/Health-and-Well-Being. Accessed January 3, 2025.

World Health Organization (2024c). Post-traumatic stress disorder. www.who.int/news-room/fact-sheets/detail/post-traumatic-stress-disorder. Accessed January 8, 2025.

World Health Organization (2024d). Top 10 leading causes of death. www.who.int/news-room/fact-sheets/detail/the-top-10-causes-of-death. Accessed November 23, 2025.

World Health Organization (2024e). World Health Organization-Five Well-Being Index (WHO-5). www.who.int/publications/m/item/WHO-UCN-MSD-MHE-2024.01. Accessed January 3, 2025.

World Health Organization (2025a). Deafness and hearing loss. www.who.int/news-room/fact-sheets/detail/deafness-and-hearing-loss. Accessed November 13, 2025.

World Health Organization (2025b). Global AGEing and adult health study. www.who.int/data/data-collection-tools/study-on-global-ageing-and-adult-health/sage-waves. Accessed January 20, 2025.

World Health Organization (2025c). Global health estimates 2021. Geneva: Switzerland. www.who.int/data/global-health-estimates. Retrieved April 13, 2025.

World Population Review (2023). Explore the world population through data. https://worldpopulationreview.com/. Accessed November 23, 2025.

World Population Review (2025a). Countries where euthanasia is legal 2025. https://worldpopulationreview.com/country-rankings/where-is-euthanasia-legal#title. Retrieved March 20, 2025.

World Population Review (2025b). In what states is euthanasia legal in the United States? https://worldpopulationreview.com/state-rankings/euthanasia-legal-in-what-states#in-what-states-is-euthanasia-legal-in-the-united-states. Retrieved March 20, 2025.

Wright, M., Oxley, F., & von Stumm, S. (2025). Measuring adulthood–A meta-analysis of the markers of adulthood scale. *European Journal of Psychological Assessment*. *40*(6), 515–528. doi: 10.1027/1015-5759/a000873.

Wright-Berryman, J., & Huber, K. (2024). Barriers and solutions to equitable funeral care in the U.S. for the LGBTQIA+ community. *Death Studies*, 1–12. doi: 10.1080/07481187.2024.2433100.

Wu, J. R., Iwanaga, K., Chan, F., Hu, W., Zhou, K., Chen, X., Chan, C. C. H., & Tansey, T. N. (2023). The constructs of the Lazarus and Folkman's stress-appraisal-coping theory as predictors of subjective well-being in college students during the ongoing COVID-19 pandemic. *Journal of Asia Pacific Counseling, 13*(2), 41–65. doi: 10.18401/2023.13.2.3.

Wurm, S., Warner, L. M., Ziegelmann, J. P., Wolff, J. K., & Schüz, B. (2013). How do negative self-perceptions of aging become a self-fulfilling prophecy? *Psychology and Aging, 28*(4), 1088.

Wurm, S., Wiest, M., Wolff, J. K., Beyer, A. K., & Spuling, S. M. (2019). Changes in views on aging in later adulthood: The role of cardiovascular events. *European Journal of Ageing, 17*(4), 457–467. doi: 10.1007/s10433-019-00547-5.

Xu, J., & Roberts, R. E. (2010). The power of positive emotions: It's a matter of life or death—Subjective well-being and longevity over 28 years in a general population. *Health Psychology, 29*(1), 9–19.

Yaden, D. B., Claydon, J., Bathgate, M., Platt, B., Santos, L. R. (2021). Teaching well-being at scale: An intervention study. *PLoS One, 16*(4), e0249193.

Yaffe, K., Vittinghoff, E., Hoang, T., Matthews, K., Golden, S. H., & Zeki Al Hazzouri, A. (2021). Cardiovascular risk factors across the life course and cognitive decline: A pooled cohort study. *Neurology, 96*(17), e2212–e2219. doi: 10.1212/WNL.0000000000011747.

Yajima, K., Seya, T., Iwayama, K., Hibi, M., Hari, S., Nakashima, Y., Ogata, H., Omi, N., Satoh, M., & Tokuyama, K. (2014). Effects of nutrient composition of dinner on sleep architecture and energy metabolism during sleep. *Journal of Nutritional Science and Vitaminology, 60*, 114–121. doi: 10.3177/jnsv.60.114.

Yan, G., Zhang, Y., Wang, S., Yan, Y., Liu, M., Tian, M., & Tian, W. (2024). Global, regional, and national temporal trend in burden of major depressive disorder from 1990 to 2019: An analysis of the global burden of disease study. *Psychiatry Research, 337*, 115958. doi: 10.1016/j.psychres.2024.115958.

Yang, W., Zhao, X., Chai, R., & Fan, J. (2023). Progress on mechanisms of age-related hearing loss. *Front Neurosci, 17*, 1253574. doi: 10.3389/fnins.2023.1253574.

Yang, Y. (2012). Is adjustment to retirement an individual responsibility? Socio-contextual conditions and options available to retired persons: The Korean perspective. *Ageing & Society, 32*(2), 177–195.

Yang, Y., Tang, S., Wang, X., Zhen, Y., Zheng, Y., Zheng, H., Liu, L., & Zheng, Z. (2023). Eigenmode-based approach reveals a decline in brain structure–function liberality across the human lifespan. *Communications Biology, 6*, 1128. doi: 10.1038/s42003-023-05497-4.

Yang, Y., Yang, B., Wang, B., Zhou, H., Yang, M., & Liu, B. (2024). Prediction factors and models for chronic kidney disease in type 2 diabetes mellitus: A review of the literature. *Clinical and Translational Discovery, 4*(5), e355. doi: 10.1002/ctd2.355.

Yarnal, C. M., Chick, G., & Kerstetter, D. L. (2008). "I did not have time to play growing up… so this is my play time. It's the best thing I have ever done for myself": What is play to older women? *Leisure Sciences, 30*(3), 235–252.

Yavas, E., Gonzalez, S., & Fanselow, M. S. (2019). Interactions between the hippocampus, prefrontal cortex, and amygdala support complex learning and memory. *F1000Res, 31*(8), F1000 Faculty Rev-1292. doi: 10.12688/f1000research.19317.1.

Yawn, B. P., Mintz, M. L., & Doherty, D. E. (2021). GOLD in practice: Chronic obstructive pulmonary disease treatment and management in the primary care setting. *International Journal of Chronic Obstructive Pulmonary Disease, 16*, 289–299. doi: 10.2147/COPD.S222664.

Yong, J., Johnson, J. D., Arvan, P., Han, J., & Kaufman, R. J. (2021). Therapeutic opportunities for pancreatic β-cell ER stress in diabetes mellitus. *Nature Reviews Endocrinology, 17*(8), 455–467. doi: 10.1038/s41574-021-00510-4.

Younger-Coleman, N., Cumberbatch, C., Campbell J., Ebanks, C., Williams, D., & O'Meally V. (2017) *Jamaica National Drug Use Prevalence Survey 2016 – Technical Report for the OAS/CICAD & NCDA*. Kingston, Jamaica.

Yu, R., Han, B., Wu, X., Wei, G., Zhang, J., Ding, M., & Wen, X. (2023). Dual-functional network regulation underlies the Central Executive System in working memory. *Neuroscience, 524*, 158–180. doi: 10.1016/j.neuroscience.2023.05.025.

Yu, Y., Xiao, L., & Chamberlain, D.J. (2021). Perceptions of care in patients from culturally and linguistically diverse background during acute and critical illness: A integrative literature review. *Australian Critical Care, 34*(5), 486–495. doi: 10.1016/j.aucc.2020.11.004.

Yuan, P., Voelkle, M. C., & Raz, N. (2018). Fluid intelligence and gross structural properties of the cerebral cortex in middle-aged and older adults: A multi-occasion longitudinal study. *NeuroImage, 172*, 21–30. doi: 10.1016/j.neuroimage.2018.01.032.

Yusoff, S., Hassan, S. A., & Othman, W. N. (2019). Traditional and complementary treatments among Malay, Chinese and Indian chronic diseases: A systematic review. *Malaysian Journal of Medicine and Health Sciences, 15*(SUPP1), 178–183.

Zakeri, M. A., Rahiminezhad, E., Salehi, F., Ganjeh, H., & Dehghan, M. (2021). Burnout, anxiety, stress, and depression among Iranian nurses: Before and during the first wave of the COVID-19 Pandemic. *Frontiers in Psychology, 12*, 789737. doi: 10.3389/fpsyg.2021.789737.

Zapletal, A., Wells, T., Russell, E., & Skinner, M. W. (2023). On the triple exclusion of older adults during COVID-19: Technology, digital literacy and social isolation. *Social Sciences & Humanities Open, 8*(1), 100511.

Zatz, M., Silva, M. V. R., de Castro, M. V., & Naslavsky, M. S. (2022). The 90 plus: Longevity and COVID-19 survival. *Molecular Psychiatry*, 27, 1936–1944. doi: 10.1038/s41380-022-01461-6.

Zautra, A. J. (2003). *Emotions, Stress, and Health*. Oxford University Press.

Zautra, A. J., Arewasikporn, A., & Davis, M. C. (2010a). Resilience: Promoting well-being through recovery, sustainability, and growth. *Research in Human Development, 7*(3), 221–238.

Zautra, A. J., Hall, J. S., & Murray, K. E. (2010b). Resilience: A new definition of health for people and communities. In J. R. Reich, A. J. Zautra, & J. S. Hall (Eds.), *Handbook of Adult Resilience* (pp. 3–29). Guilford Press.

Zemla, J. C., Gooding, D. C., & Austerweil, J. L. (2023). Evidence for optimal semantic search throughout adulthood. *Scientific Reports, 13*, 22528. doi: 10.1038/s41598-023-49858-9.

Zeng, L., Perry, L., & Xu, X. (2023a). Self-care behaviours and related cultural factors among Chinese immigrants with cardiovascular disease in western countries: An integrative review. *Journal of Clinical Nursing, 32*(9–10), 1599–1614. doi: 10.1111/jocn.16120.

Zeng, L., Zhao, X., Yu, Y., Hu, T., Li, C., Wu, M., & Yang, F. (2023b). Effects of Tai Chi on depression of middle-aged and older adults: An updated systematic review and meta- analysis. *BMC Complementary Medicine and Therapies, 23*(1), 382. doi: 10.1186/s12906-023-04207-1.

Zhang, C., Chen, G., & Tang, G., Xu, X., Feng, Z., Lu, Yuanjun, Chan, Y.-T,. Wu, J., Chen, Y., Xu, L., Ren, Q., Yuan, H., Yang, D.-H., Chen, Z.-S., Wang, N., & Feng, Y. (2023). Multi-component Chinese medicine formulas for drug discovery: State of the art and future perspectives. *Acta Materia Medic, 2*(1), 106–125. doi: 10.15212/AMM-2022-0049.

Zhang, X., Liu, Y., Li, S., Lichtenstein, A. H., Chen, S., Na, M., Veldheer, S., Xing, A., Wang, Y., Wu, S., & Gao, X. (2021). Alcohol consumption and risk of cardiovascular disease, cancer and mortality: A prospective cohort study. *Nutrition Journal, 20*(1), 1–10. doi: 10.1186/s12937-021-00671-y.

Zhang, Y., & Harris, P. L. (2022). Talking about people who are not there: Children's early references to absent caregivers and absent friends. *First Language, 42*(3), 405–425. doi: 10.1177/01427237221074141.

Zhang, Y.-P., Zhang, W.-H., Zhang, P., Li, Q., Sun, Y., Wang, J.-W., Zhang, S. O., Cai, T., Zhan, C. & Dong, M.-Q. (2022). Intestine-specific removal of DAF-2 nearly doubles lifespan in Caenorhabditis elegans with little fitness cost. *Nature Communications, 13*, 6339. doi: 10.1038/s41467-022-33850-4.

Zhang, Z., Liu, H., & Cho, S. W. (2020). Early-life socioeconomic status, adolescent cognitive ability, and cognition in late midlife: Evidence from the Wisconsin Longitudinal Study. *Soc Sci Med, 244*, 112575. doi: 10.1016/j.socscimed.2019.112575.

Zhou, E., Kyeong, Y., Cheung, C. S., & Michalska, K. J. (2022). Shared cultural values influence mental health help-seeking behaviors in Asian and Latinx college students. *Journal of Racial and Ethnic Health Disparities, 9*, 1325–1334. doi: 10.1007/s40615-021-01073-w.

Zhou, R., Belge, T., & Wolbers, T. (2023). Reaching the goal: Superior navigators in late adulthood provide a novel perspective into successful cognitive aging. *Topics in Cognitive Science, 15,* 15–45. doi: 10.1111/tops.12608.

Zhu, J., Cui, Y., Zhang, J., Yan, R., Su, D., Zhao, D., Wang, A., & Feng, T. (2024). Temporal trends in the prevalence of Parkinson's disease from 1980 to 2023: A systematic review and meta-analysis. *The Lancet, 5,* e464–e479. doi: 10.1016/S2666-7568(24)00094-1.

Ziada, A. S., Smith, M. R., & Côté, H. C. F. (2020). Updating the free radical theory of aging. *Frontiers in Cell Development Biology, 8,* 1–5. doi: 10.3389/fcell.2020.575645.

Zimmerman, J. E., Theine, P., & Harding, J. T. (1970). Design and operation of stable rf-biased superconducting point-contact quantum devices, etc. *Journal of Applied Physics, 41*(4), 1572–1580. doi: 10.1063/1.1659074.

Zirra, A., Rao, S. C., Bestwick, J., Rajalingam, R., Marras, C., Blauwendraat, C., Mata, I. F., & Noyce, A. J. (2023). Gender differences in the prevalence of Parkinson's Disease. *Movement Disorders Clinical Practice, 10*(1), 86–93. doi: 10.1002/mdc3.13584.

Zouhal, H., Jayavel, A., Parasuraman, K., Hayes, L. D., Tourny, C., Rhibi, F., Laher, I., Abderrahman, A. B., Hackney, A. C. (2022). Effects of exercise training on anabolic and catabolic hormones with advanced age: A systematic review. *Sports Medicine, 52*(6), 1353–1368. doi: 10.1007/s40279-021-01612-9.

Zunzunegui, M. V., Alvarado, B. E., Guerra, R., Gomez, J. F., Ylli, A., & Guralnik, J.M. (2015). The mobility gap between older men and women: The embodiment of gender. *Archives of Gerontology and Geriatrics, 61,* 140–148.

Index

Note: Locators in *italic* indicate figure, in **bold** indicate tables and in ***bold-italic*** indicate boxes

For Product Safety Concerns and Information please contact our EU
representative GPSR@taylorandfrancis.com
Taylor & Francis Verlag GmbH, Kaufingerstraße 24, 80331 München, Germany

www.ingramcontent.com/pod-product-compliance
Ingram Content Group UK Ltd.
Pitfield, Milton Keynes, MK11 3LW, UK
UKHW020156200926
475702UK00016B/2727

* 9 7 8 1 0 3 2 7 7 4 8 2 4 *